INDEX OF
DEDICATIONS AND
COMMENDATORY
VERSES

INDEX OF DEDICATIONS AND COMMENDATORY VERSES

IN ENGLISH BOOKS

BEFORE 1641

BY

FRANKLIN B. WILLIAMS, Jr.

LONDON
THE BIBLIOGRAPHICAL SOCIETY
1962

BIBLIOGRAPHICAL SOCIETY PUBLICATION
FOR THE YEAR 1960
PUBLISHED 1962

4599

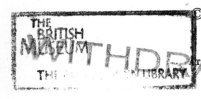

PRINTED IN GREAT BRITAIN
AT THE UNIVERSITY PRESS, OXFORD
BY VIVIAN RIDLER
PRINTER TO THE UNIVERSITY

TO THE

FELLOWSHIP OF LIBRARIANS

WHOSE LEARNING, PATIENCE AND KINDNESS

MADE THE BOOK POSSIBLE

WHOSE RARE LAPSES

MADE THE PURSUIT EXCITING

CONTENTS

INTRODUCTION

CONCEIVED as an aid to biographical research in the form of a key to the contributors of commendatory verses and the recipients of dedications in British books before 1641, this index has been expanded to cover the other material found in preliminary leaves, such as epistles by editor, printer, or bookseller. The volume should be of use to students of patronage, publishing conditions, bibliography, and literary, social, and political history. As the scope of the index grew, the plan for a comprehensive introduction withered; the following remarks are limited to (i) the historical setting, (ii) the scope and method of the book, (iii) the degree of coverage achieved within this plan, and (iv) acknowledgement of the generous aid that made the work possible.

In short, readers must look elsewhere for a comprehensive survey of Renaissance literary patronage, including such aspects as motives for dedicating books, the grounds for choosing patrons, and the rewards sought or received. The editor refrains without reluctance from discussing the conventions of dedicatory epistles and their contents, all too often hackneyed and monotonous. Nor is there space to treat plagiarism of dedication texts or the instances (noted in the index) of usurpation of epistles by later editors or booksellers. Since this index will necessarily be the basis for future studies of literary patronage, students are cautioned that some instances of patronage—even important ones—are not reflected in it for technical reasons. Thus John Donne's relations with the Drury family are unmentioned for the simple reason that no formal dedication is involved.[1] Other types of material ignored through editorial policy are listed in the second section of this introduction.

I. HISTORICAL SETTING

Since the dedication of Renaissance printed books merely extended the custom of medieval manuscripts, remoter origins may be ignored and attention may focus on evolutionary developments. With the models of the classics before them, the humanists unquestionably stimulated the quantity, if not the quality, of literary patronage. In medieval works the dedication is often embedded in the text or incorporated in a brief foreword or explicit. In the evolution of the formal dedicatory epistle in early printing, an intermediate phase is recognizable in which the epistle is distinct from the text, yet still serves as the critical and editorial preface.[2]

---

[1] Similarly the absence from this book of the name of William Shakespeare is to be attributed to editorial rules rather than anti-Stratfordian views.

[2] A collection of model examples by Aldus Manutius was available to the Elizabethan reader in *STC* 17286.

However, before the death of Henry VIII the customary order of title-page, dedication, and epistle to the reader is established in more pretentious books. A proliferation of dedications accompanies the increasing urge to publish in the reign of Elizabeth and continues unabated through the *STC* period. One may safely generalize that from Caxton to 1640 there is a steady increase in book dedications—not merely in absolute numbers but, more importantly, proportionately in the increasing volume of publication.

This spread of dedications can be roughly charted. Works of scholarship and formal *belles-lettres*, especially in Latin but also in English, were dedicated from the incunabula period. The custom applied to both original works and translations, so that dedications appear in most English bibles. In the reign of Henry VIII the weightier works of religious and political controversy sought patrons for obvious reasons, although surreptitious pamphlets did not. The more pretentious works of instruction and devotion were showing dedications by mid-century, yet such an influential book as Tottell's *Miscellany* appeared without a dedication in 1557. Under Elizabeth, perhaps Thomas Churchyard was as responsible as anyone for the extension of the practice to slighter 'literary' works of all varieties, whether prose or verse, and by the end of the reign it was general among popular pamphlet-writers like Greene and Nashe, followed in turn by Breton, Dekker, Rowlands, and John Taylor. It is customarily assumed that these Grub Street writers relied upon their modest dedication fees as much as they did upon the pittances they received from the booksellers.

It is notorious that, apart from closet-drama and translations of the classics, plays were not regarded as literature until after 1600. Jonson, Marston, and Chapman were the pioneers who judged plays worthy of patrons, so that by the death of James the custom was general if a play was actually published by its author. Similarly sermons, except when organized into treatises or commentaries, were usually not dedicated during the Tudor period. This was particularly true of the pamphlet issues of popular puritan preachers like Dent, Dering, and Henry Smith, which for the most part were committed to the press by reporters and booksellers rather than by their authors. Lancelot Andrewes and other conservative preachers continued the tradition in the next century, and the puritan Thomas Hooker's sermons appeared without dedications as late as the 1630's. But although Robert Abbot apologized in 1610 for dedicating *The Old Waye* to Archbishop Bancroft because it was 'somewhat beside custom to make Dedications of printed Sermons', his attitude was already obsolete. On the contrary, with the works of Perkins, Adams, and Hieron, sermons become one of the most prolific sources of dedications. Sermon collections are among the illustrations of the curious principle that the sum is greater than its parts, for a collection of which every part has its individual dedication (including even the appendix in 25682) may still have a fresh general dedication—presumably inscribing the title-page and the table of contents to the favoured worthy. For number and variety of dedications, the curious may be referred to the folio *Works* of Joseph Hall or John Taylor.

The classes of publications quite immune to dedications are mostly ephemeral or austere. They include news pamphlets, corantos, chap-books, and broadside ballads. Of broadsides other than ballads, only a tiny fraction are dedicated (e.g. 25943), and dedications are scarce in almanacs (the exceptional epistles always appearing in the prognostication half). Also without dedication are official publications, whether political or ecclesiastical, such as proclamations, documents, propaganda pamphlets, service books (from missals and primers to Common Prayer), general and diocesan visitation articles, &c. Many law books of quasi-official character are undedicated, as well as the serial statutes and year-books. In Stuart times nearly all other varieties of books were, if not regularly at least frequently, dedicated.

Unlike dedications, commendatory verses were mainly a Renaissance innova-tion, spread among circles of humanist scholars. In a process roughly comparable to the spread of dedications, these metrical puffs began in works of scholarship and *belles-lettres* and then under Elizabeth intruded into vernacular literature. In Stuart times they were extended to plays, and even occasionally to volumes of sermons (where the Scots may have led the way). Thomas Newton seems to have been the first to collect his scattered Latin commendations of his friends into his own published poetry. Later Ben Jonson, James Shirley, and others accepted their English contributions into their official works, but in general such exercises in flattery were—very properly—regarded as ephemeral. Their primary interest is biographical: they rarely achieve the intrinsic interest, let alone the literary merit, of Jonson's tribute to Shakespeare. Scattered evidence exists of how writers and booksellers solicited commendatory poems from acquaintances and incor-porated them in the manuscript before it went to the printer (a fact independently confirmed by the survival of unpublished manuscripts with such apparatus). I know of no evidence that anyone was ever paid for a commendatory poem, and in general I would suggest that the phenomenon deserves study for its social, as much as its literary, interest. Suspicious circumstances occasionally suggest that some of these tributes were in fact perpetrated by the subject himself, but proof is wanting. The possibility of ghost-writing is even more plausible, but has seldom been argued.[1] The vogue of commendatory verses was sufficiently established by Stuart times for the appearance of a minor tradition of burlesque or mock-commendatory verse.

The fact that Caxton was the most consistent practitioner illustrates the truth that in England the printer's or bookseller's epistle was congenial with the art of printing. Such epistles continued throughout our period, but rarely do they show the verve or interest of Caxton's essays. Licences, privileges, and imprimaturs,

---

[1] The argument of George B. Parks that George Peele ghost-wrote the verses signed by Drake, Hawkins, &c., in *STC* 19523 has not won general approval. See *JEGP* xli (1942), 527-36.

reflecting successive stages of encouragement and control of the press, are surveyed in Section III of the text but need not be summarized here.

II. INTENTION, SCOPE, AND METHOD

The aim of this work is to index the preliminaries of British books before 1641 (regardless of whether they were actually listed in the 1926 *Short-Title Catalogue*) on the basis of a fresh personal examination of the original editions or of photographic copies (such as microfilm). The hope is to achieve a complete survey that will limit errors to the editor's own fallibility. Because of the prevalence of imperfect copies and of bibliographical variants, many books had to be inspected in several exemplars. As the project proceeded and editorial standards clarified, it became advisable to repeat most of the work of the first few years, as well as to verify later results by spot-check. Thus a constant improvement in technique and a corresponding increase in humility jointly spurred the editor's addiction to the pleasant vice of visiting libraries.

The term *preliminary* has not been construed narrowly; relevant material is recorded whether printed at the front, middle, or end of books. Rigour has been relaxed to incorporate the addressees of individual emblems in books by Geoffrey Whitney and Andrew Willet, and of the individual pieces in epistolary collections by Joseph Hall Robert Markham, Augustine Taylor, and Diggory Whear. The editor's will was too weak to exclude two catalogues that fascinated him: Mary Fage's excruciating anagrams serve as a Caroline social register (including some mythical people!), and the list of purchasers issued with Minsheu's dictionary is a census of the Jacobean literary world.

The reader may be warned that some works important in British literary history —for instance, the early editions of *Utopia*—do not qualify for inclusion in the *Short-Title Catalogue*. Even within the scope of *STC*, certain classes of material have been arbitrarily ignored by the editor. These various categories may be briefly listed:

   (a) This index ignores all *manuscript* material, both literary codices and holograph inscriptions within printed books.

   (b) Following *STC* policy, this index ignores books of British writers that were printed abroad, unless they are in English, Welsh, or Gaelic.

   (c) Routine commercial reprints of foreign books in Latin are entirely ignored except in the rare instances when a British name is involved. This class mainly comprises cheap schoolbooks (rhetorics, texts of Aesop, Cicero, Mantuan, &c.), and totals about 440 editions, many of them unrecorded.[1]

   (d) Original foreign preliminaries of books published in English translation are ignored unless Englishmen are involved. Of course, the preliminaries written for the translation are scrupulously indexed.

---

[1] These British reprints remind one that Continental books in the learned languages were a major staple of the Elizabethan book trade. This neglected fact has little bearing, however, on the subject of this monograph.

(*e*) Since English translators are thus treated as authors, their names are not indexed. Editors, however, are indexed.

(*f*) Since this is an index of preliminaries rather than contents, it does not list the contributors to poetical miscellanies, collections of complimentary verses, or other anthologies.

(*g*) Routine imprimaturs are not individually listed but are comprehensively surveyed in Section III.

(*h*) On the other hand, although *STC* excludes independent engraved prints, I have included those that came to my attention. Many others, however, are described by Arthur M. Hind in *Engraving in England*.

A survey of the first two categories above would be of high value to students of literary patronage. Will some bibliographer prepare the way by check-listing the Latin works published abroad by British writers?

The organization of the index into personal, non-personal, and bibliographical sections will be clear from inspection or from a glance at the table of contents. Personal names, which constitute by far the largest section, are spelt and alphabetized according to principles stated in the Memoranda before the text. Whenever the individuals are identifiable, dedications to *unnamed* office-holders are indexed only in the personal section—indeed, alternate entries are made for a few doubtful bishops. The result is that in the institutional section individual offices seldom appear, except for mayors and other municipal worthies; here the complexity of overlapping municipal, calendar, legal, and imprint years appeared unmanageable. As far as feasible, each name is identified with a known historical individual and supplied with an abbreviated reference to the most accessible biographical source. Unsparing effort has been devoted to this pursuit, in which the works of other scholars have been—depending on one's viewpoint—conscientiously searched or unconscionably plundered. Little time could be spared for search in unpublished records, but a few identifications were gleaned at Somerset House. Of the unidentified names, some will doubtless be solved by other specialists. A few may be fictions, as probably are some of the unsolved initials.

Pseudonyms and latinized names, as well as initials, provide fascinating puzzles, many of which remain to be solved. The problems and the techniques that have been applied cannot be summarized here, but reference may be made to the editor's discussions elsewhere:

'An Initiation into Initials', *Studies in Bibliography*, ix (1957), 163–78.
'Renaissance Names in Masquerade', *PMLA*, lxix (1954), 314–23.

New methods and new insights continued to develop. Thus the linguistic preciosity of Renaissance scholars is further illustrated in an instance clarified for me by Lawrence Marwick and Myron Weinstein of the Library of Congress: the Hebrew signature of Cornelius Bertram is not merely an adequate transliteration of his name, but is translatable as 'Bertram, God's trumpet'. And a method of concealment quite new to me is disclosed in Professor Elkin C. Wilson's edition of *The Lamentation of Troy*, 1594: the brief motto on the title-page provides in verbal, rather than the usual linear, acrostic the solution Ogle to the author's initials, I. O.

The editorial problems in the non-personal sections are sometimes matters of obsolete or obscure facts, but more often difficulties in semantics. If it is awkward to cope with the careless Renaissance use of the term 'printer', what can be said of verbal precision in religious controversy? 'True lovers of the Gospel', one surmises, may have little meaning beyond 'people favouring my side'. To the extent of his ability, the editor has cleansed such phrases of the *odium theologicum* and has classified them by the inferred sense rather than by the literal appearance.

Part III of the index contains bibliographical details—un- rather than full-dress—on variant dedications of all varieties, a subject that fascinates the editor but cannot here be discussed at length.[1] Besides individual printed presentation epistles only recently recognized as a distinct category, these include cancelled, split, and anomalous dedications, as well as the better-known change of patron in successive editions. An analysis of changes for which plausible reasons may be found indicates that death of the patron led to change four times as often as any other cause. These other causes include succession in office, preference for a more powerful patron, and substitution of a new patron by editor or bookseller in a late reprint. Changes resulting from disgrace or retirement of a patron are very few. It is in Part III that one must look for evidence of the abuse of literary patronage mentioned by satirical writers during the Jacobean period and, on the basis of these allusions, often affirmed by modern writers on patronage. As described by the satirists, this abuse consisted of collecting repeated dedication fees by presenting to the more naïve gentry copies of books for which individual dedications had been printed, under the false pretence that each represented the normal form of the edition. Now it may be conceded that much evidence may have been lost, for the stray books of gulls would have been more subject to disappearance than the libraries of the knowing. Yet a dispassionate search of Part III leads to the conclusion that extremely little evidence survives of sharp practice in dedicating, apart from the transparent devices of an Abraham Darcie. It behoves literary historians to be more sceptical when quoting Jacobean pamphleteers.

Scattered through the index is information on minor matters that might interest if collected, such as dedications to patrons who died just after or even before publication, blunders in the names of patrons,[2] and other misadventures or mental lapses. The brevity of the editorial form, however, forces omission of many piquant details, such as the fatuous text of a dedication to Lady Alice Dudley that deliberately calls attention to her husband, who had run off to Italy with another woman.

[1] The reader is referred to *The Library*, 5th ser., x (1957), 11–22.
[2] See 'Those Careless Elizabethans: Names Bewitched', PBSA, liv (1960), 115–19.

III. DEGREE OF COVERAGE

Compiling this book has been the editor's avocation since 1936 and, indeed, except for four war years, his chief concern during many weeks of each year. Over these decades he has worked in 130 libraries, which, leaving aside those in Dublin and Paris, are about evenly divided between Britain and the United States. The time spent in individual libraries varied from an hour to years; although many are not even mentioned in this volume, all these libraries were essential in its compilation.

As an aid to future workers, some idea may be given of the cut-off date of research in various libraries. In so far as information was obtainable, this index represents the holdings of the chief British libraries in 1956. Included are *STC* addenda that had been acquired or had come to light at, among others, the British Museum, Lambeth, Rylands, the national libraries of Scotland and Wales, and the university libraries of Oxford, Cambridge, London, Durham, Edinburgh, Glasgow, and Aberdeen. The cut-off date is 1959 for the Folger Shakespeare Library, 1958 for the Library of Congress and the Pierpont Morgan Library, 1957 for Harvard and Yale, and varying dates in the 1950's for the other chief United States libraries except the Huntington (1938). It may be assumed that the index incorporates all *STC* addenda of any consequence recorded in the *Huntington Library Supplement to the Short-Title Catalogue* or in the second (1950) edition of William W. Bishop's *Checklist of American Copies*. David Ramage's British *Finding-List* (1958) appeared too late for use, but this editor was kindly permitted to skim through the manuscript files while it was in preparation, and it may be added that Dr. Ramage's indirect contribution was great, for it was at his appeal that various libraries had freshly canvassed their holdings shortly before my visits. A hasty check indicates that Ramage's appendix lists about fifteen unrecorded titles that have escaped this index; these are chiefly found at libraries unvisited by this editor—St. Andrews and some English provincial universities. It may further be confessed that the editor worked in only fifteen of the college libraries at Oxford and Cambridge, and that—not to mention lesser book centres—he did not find opportunity to visit Eton, Shrewsbury, Winchester, or Chatsworth.[1]

The original manuscript—more properly, filing case of slips—for the *Short-Title Catalogue*, preserved at the British Museum, often proved a helpful source of information. Ironically, it is most useful in confirming ghosts, but it also helps one to locate single sheets and books that present cataloguing problems. *A Catalogue of Catholic Books, 1558–1640*, published in 1956 by A. F. Allison and D. M. Rogers, seemed at the time a mixed blessing, for it greatly increased the labours of this indexer and yet came too late to permit full coverage. Messrs. Allison and Rogers not only made the second half of their work available in manuscript before

---

[1] As far as *unique* items are concerned, data have been incorporated on Chatsworth books acquired by the British Museum in 1958. Some inquiries were also made about the Chatsworth books sold at auction in 1958.

publication, but both then and since have provided much bibliographical information. Their fruitful work has greatly increased the value of this index.[1]

To summarize, this index is based on notes made by the editor while personally examining more than 37,000 copies of 29,800 items of early British printing, including 4,400 *STC* addenda (1,500 of them fresh titles). In addition, the editor has accepted into his files reliable reports on 150 others books and has, by correspondence, verified points on hundreds of additional copies. He has checked his findings against Madan, Greg, and other modern full-dress bibliographies, but has seldom consulted W. C. Hazlitt and earlier bibliographers. His thought has been that this is a fresh survey of the evidence and that all the errors should be new ones.

The result of this industry is that although hundreds of additional editions and issues of *STC* books have probably escaped the net, and an uncertain number of unrecorded titles (such as the unique corantos at Belvoir Castle now fully described by Folke Dahl), the residue of items that are actually listed in the 1926 *STC* is astonishingly small. It is true that the editor tired of proclamations. After finding that 923 of them uniformly lacked dedications, he felt safe in neglecting the rest. It also proved inconvenient to see *every* edition of those standard items, bibles and liturgies.[2] But apart from these special categories (proclamations, bibles, and liturgies), the editor finds that after making allowance for ghosts,[3] the number of *STC* books not seen is less than sixty, nearly all of them untraceable. The missing books are listed below in the hope that this notice may bring copies to light in time for inclusion in the revised *STC*.

Books not Inspected

Two items the editor found it inconvenient to inspect or have examined for him: a ballad and a Stanbridge grammar.

7280   23181

Dispersed and Untraced

The supposedly unique copies of the following are untraced since sale. Some were perhaps ghosts, especially those from the Jaggard collection.[4]

263	4319	10988	13715	19443	23613
1061	4320	10989	17521	19715	24244
3063	6715	11092a	18928a	22465	25526
3620	10836	11556	19003	23388	25792

[1] The residue of Allison and Rogers finds are supposed to contain little indexable material. The new titles unaccounted for here are, by A. and R. numbers, 74, 85, 140, 224, 228, 237, 266, 301, 432, 537, 700, 757, 831, 880.

[2] Similarly there is an innocuous deficit of fourteen diocesan visitation articles.

[3] My own computation indicates that—quite apart from duplicate entries and independent listing of items that are properly parts of other books—*STC* erroneously includes about 400 items, a quarter of them either post-1640 or printed abroad, the remainder ghosts or errors of various types. As other scholars are aware, establishing a ghost requires more work than indexing a dozen books.

[4] Thus 13715 is presumably a copy of 13716 lacking its main title-page. Others have been silently eliminated, e.g. 24057.

Destroyed

The British Museum reports the loss of these unique items in the blitz. Possibly some listed in the next group were similar casualties at Lambeth, the Guildhall, and Sion College.

3302	3354	4451	9501	15182	24898

Not Found

Although in other instances it was possible to find substitute copies, no exemplars were found of the following items. In particular, they could not be located at the libraries cited in *STC*. The possible explanations include ghosts, erroneous accrediting, faulty cataloguing, failure of charge records, misshelving, war loss, and theft; it would be folly for the editor to attempt an accounting.

873	13005	16725	18706a	21309
2737	13410	17267	19290	24731
3691	14868	17283	19519	24894
4052	14869	17383	20173	25098
5321	15103	18469	20429	25513

Lost Editions and Imperfect Copies

The brevity of the preceding lists leaves a misleading impression for several reasons. Some books are not known to have survived. In addition, the original editions have not yet come to light for such titles as 3473, 4244, 12216 and other titles by Robert Greene, 13167, 15230, 23447, and 25096. Numerous intermediate editions of frequently printed works are missing, but these losses seldom affect the contents to be indexed.[1] Unhappily a number of books survive only in imperfect copies or fragments. Some of these certainly had, and others may have had, dedications and commendatory verses. The following are samples rather than a census of this group:

23	5312	13513	17500	20366	24629
541	5456	13594	Aberdeen *Theses, 1637*-E².		
The Arte of Angling, 1577-PN.			R. Hoper, *Of a vertuous life*, [*1580*]-F.		

IV. ACKNOWLEDGEMENTS

Whatever my ability at digging, it is manifest that to beg I am unashamed. That this book is an individual undertaking rather than a collaboration is only technically true, for without the interest and assistance of scores of people it would not have been completed. Even were it possible, it is impracticable to list

---

[1] Those sceptical of lost editions are invited to consider two books unknown to *STC*. Of Henry Valentine's *Private Devotions*, Folger has the seventh edition, 1635, and Bodley the eleventh, 1640; and of R. I., *Dives and Lazarus*, the National Library of Wales has the fourth edition, 1623, and the British Museum the twenty-first, 1677!

all to whom I am indebted. Although a full accounting is impossible, some of the major creditors must be named. While the encouragement of Ronald B. McKerrow helped the duckling from the egg, any swan-like features in the final product derive from Dr. F. S. Ferguson and Professor William A. Jackson, whose matchless knowledge of the bibliography and whereabouts of *STC* books made a comprehensive survey feasible. Professor Jackson has been tireless in drawing attention to unrecorded variants. Decisive field-work at the final stage was made possible by a 1955-6 fellowship from the John Simon Guggenheim Memorial Foundation, supplemented by a sabbatical grant from Georgetown University.

The guardian repositories of the books themselves, libraries of every variety, must next be mentioned. Two in particular have borne the brunt. Since the autumn of 1939 the Folger Shakespeare Library has been my base of operation; its book resources are equalled only by the helpfulness of the staff under, successively, Joseph Q. Adams and Louis B. Wright. Substantial progress had already been made by 1939 at my previous base, Harvard University Library; although by then I had surveyed its holdings, extensive acquisitions since 1939 have been the pleasant occasion for frequent revisits. Besides these two, libraries that have been hosts for months on end and have provided books by the thousand include the British Museum, the Bodleian, C.U.L., and the Huntington. Steady work for weeks at a time has proceeded at Lambeth, the Boston and New York Public Libraries, Union Theological Seminary, and the Library of Congress (microfilm holdings as well as books). The foundations and privately endowed libraries have been a mainstay in my search, ranging from the venerable names of Chetham, Pepys, and Marsh down to Rylands, Dr. Williams, and Wellcome; or, in the United States, from Carter Brown, Newberry, and Pierpont Morgan to the most recent, the Rosenbach Foundation in Philadelphia and the Carl H. Pforzheimer Library (the Carl and Lily Pforzheimer Foundation) in New York.

The university libraries, from Aberdeen, Edinburgh, and Glasgow to Wisconsin, Chicago, and Illinois—urban like Columbia and London, or rural like Virginia and Williams—generously assisted the project. Many that I was unable to visit supplied information, from St. Andrews to Texas, or on the Continent (Hamburg, Jena, Munich). Although the time available for the college libraries at Cambridge was brief, maximum benefits accrued through the aid of H. M. Adams, H. S. Bennett, A. N. L. Munby, R. W. Ladborough, and others. At Oxford the unpublished intercollegiate catalogue directed my limited time to best advantage. I acknowledge the kindness of the President and Fellows of Corpus Christi College, as well as of the Librarians of Christ Church, Worcester, Queen's, and others, not forgetting Professor F. P. Wilson. Schools included Downside, Dulwich, and Stonyhurst. Theological seminaries, as far apart dogmatically as geographically, were most helpful, whether Ware, Ushaw, and Blairs, Princeton and Union, General Theological in New York, or Lutheran at Philadelphia. It was a joy to work in some of the venerable cathedral libraries, such as Durham, York, Lincoln, Peterborough, and St. Paul's. Other libraries may be barely mentioned by type, such as municipal public libraries and those of medical societies, historical societies (both general and denominational), religious communities, and museums.

This litany of the libraries, it is clear by now, may more aptly be termed a hymn of thanksgiving for the librarians. But with 130 libraries involved, some of them (like Harvard) being in fact groups of libraries, it is out of the question to print a roll of the hundreds of chiefs and staff members who earned campaign ribbons. But for aid and encouragement beyond the call of duty, mention must be made of William Beattie, I. A. Doyle, Sir Frank Francis, L. W. Hanson, J. G. McManaway, J. C. T. Oates, and W. S. Wright. It would strain credulity to recount the inconveniences that British librarians incurred to enable me to complete my work within time limitations—not merely relaxing posted library hours, but even deferring or interrupting their personal holidays. As an American who had been told that it was difficult to gain entrance to some libraries, I marvelled at the liberty of operation allowed when entry was granted. Sometimes one was merely locked in with the books (though being locked in at Trinity College, Dublin, was accidental when I fell asleep after tea). It was a completely atypical English library that asked me to fee a guard, who slept for me while I inspected books!

My mind goes back to the late summer of 1939. While the treasures of the British Museum were being crated and trucked away, Dr. Ferguson—lest my final days in England be wasted—put me to work in his own library (much of it subsequently given to the National Library of Scotland). This incident is symbolic of the interest and friendliness that book collectors have shown to this project. Those who have gone to some trouble to assist me include, alphabetically, Thomas W. Baldwin, Apsley Cherry-Garrard, the Viscount Cobham, the Earl of Crawford and Balcarres, Harrison D. Horblitt, Arthur A. Houghton, Jr., Sir Arthur P. Howard, Wilmarth S. Lewis, the late C. K. Ogden, Lessing J. Rosenwald, Louis Silver, and Robert H. Taylor. One more witness joins the roll of students acknowledging the assistance of the antiquarian booksellers. The privilege of viewing books, the tracing of copies, and other helpful information have been repeatedly accorded by such firms as Dobell, Edwards, Fleming, Hodgson, Alan Keen, Quaritch, Rosenbach, Seven Gables, Sotheby, and Thorpe. Those who have lent microfilm or aided in other ways include G. Blakemore Evans, William E. Miller, Charles Mish, William Nelson, and Lawrence V. Ryan.

Quite apart from those who did their best without avail, the roll of scholars who have made definite contributions is unmanageable. Some have drawn attention to, searched out, or examined books, such as John Alden, Arthur T. Austing, J. M. G. Blakiston, Arthur Brown, Canon W. K. Lowther Clarke, Dr. W. M. Dickie, David F. Foxon, John Hayward, Virgil B. Heltzel, Miss Carolyn Merion, F. N. L. Poynter, Dennis E. Rhodes, Dr. Eleanor Rosenberg,

Dorothy M. Schullian, Chester L. Shaver, Ernest A. Strathmann, Dick Taylor, Jr., Bernard M. Wagner, and Dr. Fritz Woelcken of Munich.

In 1958 a number of Scottish scholars formed a benevolent conspiracy to identify several of their obscurer Renaissance compatriots. The group performing this service for the *Index* included J. R. Seaton and Alexander Rodger of the National Library, Robert Donaldson of Edinburgh University Library, and John Durkan of Glasgow. As individuals, many others have aided in the identification of patrons and versifiers, and a few have solved initials or pseudonyms. In these fields helpers include R. C. Bald, Cyprian Blagden, W. H. Challen, Martin Cleary of Cardiff, Claire Cross, John Crow, Mark Eccles, Rudolf Gottfried, Mrs. Diana P. Hobby, Francis R. Johnson, Harold W. Jones of Wallasey, Miss M. E. Kronenberg, William H. McCarthy, Jr., George B. Parks, William Ringler, and Dr. Eleanor Withington. Those who have clarified linguistic problems include Daniel A. Fineman of the Hebrew University and my old friend T. Rowland Powel of the Library Association. Nor should I forget the Marquis of Salisbury, Robert Ayers, Giles E. Dawson, Richard M. Hosley, J. B. Oldham, or Professor K. F. Russell of Melbourne.

Unfortunately, there are dozens of other names that should have been fitted in somewhere, such as, to list a few, R. O. Dougan, Mrs. Sue M. Foster, the late Sir Walter Greg, Martin R. Holmes, the Rev. Nicholas J. Kelly, Miss Dorothy Mason, Miss F. E. Ratchford, and Gilbert M. Troxell of the Yale Elizabethan Club. The town clerks of Newcastle and Shrewsbury and the clerk of the Haberdashers' Company may stand as representatives of officers who have given courteous assistance, and Syon Abbey at South Brent as a type of the groups that provided information. Indeed, suspicion grows that the number of readers of this volume may scarcely equal the number of people who will welcome its publication merely as a relief from annoying queries. The standard of scholarship that I sought, but have doubtless failed, to attain was set by a teacher who did not live to see the book, Professor Hyder E. Rollins; with some justice, he thought me a slow worker.

F. B. W.

Washington
  April, 1962

MEMORANDA

THIS index of dedications and other preliminary material in British books before 1641 is designed to convey the maximum information with the greatest precision in the minimum space. Books are accordingly cited only by the serial numbers in Pollard and Redgrave's *Short-Title Catalogue*, without access to which this book is useless. In the main index each condensed entry consists of two parts: (*a*) the name and identification of the person, and (*b*) the list of dedications and other items. For the benefit of hasty or casual users, the method of entry is here explained in reverse order. Little information can be extracted from this index unless at least the first half of these memoranda are digested.

MATERIAL INDEXED

Method and sigla. In the index half of each entry, all *italicized* figures are *dates* while all normal figures are *STC* serial numbers except in obvious bibliographical citations. The material is classified in the following order of priority:

oooo   An unqualified *STC* number indicates a dedication *to* the individual.

The following sigla may be prefixed:

★   The dedication is shared with others.

†   His wife is mentioned with the patron. The wife is not separately indexed unless there is an independent epistle.

¶   The dedication applies to only part of the book.

Epistle   Either prose or verse addressed *to* the individual, supplementing a dedication to someone else. Classification as an epistle rather than as a second dedication may at times be arbitrary.

Presentation   A printed presentation epistle in a unique copy more fully described in section III. B. 5.

Edits   The book is edited *by* the individual, with or without epistles. This normally implies evidence within the book itself.

Verse   Commendatory verses *by* the individual.

Prose   Preliminary prose *by* the individual, including printer's epistles and dedications not by the author.

See   Relevant material not qualifying in the previous categories.

Minsheu List   Appearance on the list of purchasers often bound with Minsheu's *Ductor in linguas* [on the variant states, see *J. Q. Adams Memorial Studies* (1948), p. 766].

Entries are in numerical order within each sequence, followed by titles not recorded in *STC*. The edition cited is always the *earliest* known that contains the item in question. Preliminary material was usually retained in reprints, but the fate of items in subsequent editions is formally ignored in this index unless it involves a significant change (as a shift in patron), or unless it qualifies under the next symbol:

(0000)   A number in parentheses identifies a *collection* which incorporates the *preceding* item. These are listed because they are often more accessible than the rare original editions.

[see changes]   and entries like 'superseding' indicate that another edition was dedicated otherwise. Details are found in section III. B. 4.

=   The equation sign, as in 1186 = 14347, shows that *STC* has listed the same edition in two places. This may locate additional copies.

¶   An equation like 1189 = ¶3243 implies that the first is properly *part* of the latter, or at least was also issued in that form.

Ghost   The edition as described in *STC* is mythical.

All dedications are by the author or translator unless the contrary is specified. A person is indexed no more than twice for one book—for material addressed to him and for material written by him; readers should be alert for multiple occurrences.

   STC Addenda. Eligible books omitted from *STC* have been cited when known to the editor and when necessary to perfect entries under his editorial principles. Unrecorded works are cited by author (ignoring translator), highly abbreviated title, date, and location of copy. Additional editions or issues of recorded titles are cited by date and location, linked to the pertinent *STC* number, as '*1562*-WIS. of 1210'. While the more sensational addenda have been incorporated, it would be foolhardy to regard this index as an interim substitute for the revised *STC*. There has been occasion to mention only a fraction of the 4,400 addenda the editor has seen, and he has seen only a part of those known to the *STC* revisers. Furthermore, no effort has been made to anticipate the decimal system of the revised *STC*, since (*a*) such numbers are meaningless until the revision appears, and (*b*) the current numeration is subject to change up to time of publication. The method employed in this index should be convenient with either the original or the revised *STC*.

   Library Locations. Location of a copy is specified only under these circumstances: (*a*) when the title or edition does not appear in *STC*; (*b*) when the book has changed hands; (*c*) when *STC* cites only an imperfect or inaccessible copy; or (*d*) when the existence of variant or imperfect copies makes it mandatory to cite a type-copy. The *STC* location symbol is hyphenated to the number, e.g. '7571-LC.'; it should not be construed to affirm uniqueness. The copy is usually the first one the editor examined; another may be more conveniently located in an American or British library.

CHANGED OR DISCONTINUED SYMBOLS

BAMB. Now deposited at DUR.[5]

CH. Correct address is: Williamstown, Mass.

E.[3] *STC* books were mostly sold in 1960.

FOLG. Now F. (see below).

HH. Except bibles, now at F.

PFOR. Now Pforzheimer Foundation, New York.

SB. Now at Heythrop College, Chipping Norton.

WASH. Redesignated LC.

WASH.[2] Now AML. (see below).

WS. Now at L.

Among other libraries that have been dispersed are: CL., COWAN (much now at E.), DUR.[4], J., WH. The following symbols used in this index are a few from the large number the revised *STC* will add to the list appearing at page xvi of the original *STC*:

ADDITIONAL LIBRARIES

AML. National Library of Medicine, Bethesda, Maryland* [formerly WASH.[2] and other incarnations].

BO.[4] Boston Medical Library.

BO.[5] Massachusetts Historical Soc.

BRISTOL Bristol Reference Library.

C.[17] Sidney Sussex College.

C.[19] Peterhouse.

CHATS. Chatsworth (Duke of Devonshire).

CHI. University of Chicago.

CLARK W. A. Clark Libr., Los Angeles.

CU. Columbia Univ., New York.

D.[6] National Library of Ireland.

DE. Downside Abbey, Bath.

F. Folger Shakespeare Library, Washington [inc. former FOLG., HH.].

HAT. Hatfield House (Marquis of Salisbury).

ILL. University of Illinois, Urbana.

L.[26] Brompton Oratory.

L.[30] University of London.

L.[38] University College, London.

L.[43] London Library.

LC. Library of Congress, Washington [formerly WASH.].

MICH. University of Michigan, Ann Arbor.

MIN. University of Minnesota, Minneapolis.

NY.[4] New York Academy of Medicine.

NY.[11] General Theological Seminary.

PN.[2] Princeton Theological Seminary.

ROS. Rosenbach Foundation, Philadelphia.

STOCKHOLM Royal Library, Stockholm.

TEX. University of Texas, Austin.

U. Union Theological Seminary, New York.

USHAW St. Cuthbert's Coll., Ushaw.

V. Univ. of Virginia, Charlottesville.

WIS. Univ. of Wisconsin, Madison.

A few other libraries, dealers, and collectors are sometimes cited in a form that should be transparent to bookmen.

Additional Locations: Most students are aware that many additional copies of

---

* The rare books section, previously housed in Cleveland, Ohio, was moved this spring (1962) to its permanent home in the Washington suburbs.

STC books are located by Allison and Rogers (see below) and in the following catalogues:

> William W. Bishop, *A Checklist of American Copies of STC Books*, 2nd ed. (1950).
> David Ramage, *A Finding-List . . . in the British Isles* (Durham, 1958).

NAME AND IDENTIFICATION

Historical Basis. The first part of each index entry consists of an alphabetized name, precise identification, and usually a bibliographical citation (which, as noted below, may be implied rather than printed). The aim was to identify each name with a known individual traceable in documents other than the book in question. *The user may assume that this goal was achieved whenever an unqualified identification is supplied.* An identification within inverted commas conveys information—very probably true—that is derived exclusively from the book in question.[1] Information in brackets has been deduced from the book, and if it is *queried*, is merely a conjecture. A name without identification is unknown— that is, either quite elusive or possessed by multiple candidates without decisive links.

Spelling of Names. The names of unidentified persons retain the original spelling. The spelling of known persons is normalized according to modern usage, follow- ing authorities like *DNB* even when they are irrational. However, the original spelling is noted *within* the entry if it is eccentric or interesting, and it is cross- referenced if likely to give trouble. Continental scholars are usually indexed by the latinized forms appearing in the original books, like Ramus, rather than by the vernacular form often used in *STC*. If a *man's* family name is followed by a form in parentheses, like (La Ramée), this is—as the case may be—the vernacular or learned equivalent.

Women's Names. The form for indexing women was devised for brevity and precision rather than elegance. To borrow E. C. Bentley's phrase of Henry VIII, the Tudor age was one of 'monogamy, recurrent'. Regardless of the style in the dedication, women are accordingly indexed under the married family name of their highest social status, with cross-reference from any other style to which books were dedicated. In the typical entry

BACON (Butts), Anne = Sir Nicholas I Bt.,

we have the married name, the maiden name, and the Christian name linked to the name of the husband (who in turn may be distinctly identified). In brief, while parentheses supply vernacular equivalents in names of men, in names of women they are equivalent to *née*. Except for *suo jure* peeresses, the proper style of a woman in this index can only be surmised from the style of her husband— assuming that she survived long enough to enjoy it. Scottish books often provide a further complication by addressing married women by their maiden names.

---

[1] The fact that courtesy titles also appear in inverted commas can hardly cause confusion.

Alphabetizing. This index may be used equally by scholars pursuing specific persons and by students anxious to identify the people they encounter in books. Renaissance spelling was unstandardized for proper names as well as other words. Father and son might come as far apart as Fenn and Venn.[1] Whatever the spelling, this index alphabetizes according to an imaginary norm that groups Smiths of all varieties in a single sequence, and integrates related names like Carew–Carey–Cary. Cross-references will familiarize readers with the system and moderate the shock of finding Ben Jonson among the Johnsons. Up to the limit of three letters, abbreviated names are alphabetized as simple initials; for example, Ed. Ats. is listed as if it were E. A. The purpose is to prevent them from becoming lost. At *Pseudonyms* there is a cumulative cross-reference to all *unsolved* pseudonyms, unsolved signature mottoes, and fictitious names. May one add a caution that the hundreds of initials are Pandora's box? Yet what researcher seeking John Smith will be able to resist the entries under 'J. S.'?

Method of Identification. The content of the identification may be chosen for precision rather than major significance, and may be primarily concerned with distinguishing between men of the same name. Its brevity is excused by the fact that it is usually followed by reference to a work giving fuller biographical details. No citation was deemed necessary for some categories, notably sovereigns, peers, baronets, and bishops: if not in *DNB*, they are easily found in other reference works. In British titles, *Lord* indicates either a Scottish peer or a Scottish lord of session, unless, of course, it is a courtesy title within inverted commas.

Implied Citations. Though omitted for brevity, citations may be uniformly assumed for the following categories:

Actor	Sir Edmund Chambers, *The Elizabethan Stage*, or its sequel by Gerald E. Bentley.
Alderman [of London]	Alfred B. Beaven, *The Aldermen of London*.
Bookseller	The Bibliographical Society dictionaries of booksellers and printers, edited in series by E. Gordon Duff, Ronald B. McKerrow, and Henry R. Plomer.
Gray's Inn, etc.	Members of the Inns of Court are traceable in the published registers unless exception is noted.
Lord Mayor [of London]	See *Alderman*.
Marian exile	Christina H. Garrett, *The Marian Exiles*.
Minister	The term is *arbitrarily* restricted to ministers of the Church of Scotland[2] whose biographies appear under the specified parishes in Hew Scott, *Fasti Ecclesiae Scoticanae*.
Printer	See *Bookseller*.

[1] The researcher faces other difficulties, such as the chronic confusion of Edward and Edmund, or of Anne and Agnes.

[2] The few exceptions are easily recognized as continental Calvinists.

Reference Works Cited. The following key lists works cited frequently in this index. There is no effort to trace the most authoritative source on each person; the intent is to indicate a convenient starting-point for study. Some citations automatically extend the identification; for instance, 'Foster' or 'Venn' indicates the man's university, while 'Keeler' asserts his membership in the Long Parliament. Other books and periodicals are sparingly cited in forms that should be easily comprehended.

ADB	*Allgemeine Deutsche Biographie.*
Allison	A. F. Allison and D. M. Rogers, *A Catalogue of Catholic Books in English 1558–1640.*
BM, BN	The printed general catalogues of the British Museum and the Bibliothèque Nationale.
Brown	The biographical appendix to Alexander Brown, *The Genesis of the United States* [persons concerned with the Virginia Company].
Burrage	Champlin Burrage, *The Early English Dissenters.*
CSPD, etc.	*Calendar of State Papers, Domestic* [or *Irish, Venetian*].
DAB	*Dictionary of American Biography.*
Dahl	Folke Dahl, *A Bibliography of English Corantos 1620–1642.* Items not in *STC* are cited by Dahl serial number.
DNB	*Dictionary of National Biography.* [Candidly, the editor often relied on the *Concise DNB* because of its convenience.]
DWB	*The Dictionary of Welsh Biography.*
Foster	Joseph Foster, *Alumni Oxonienses: 1500–1714.* The citation adds date of matriculation to distinguish between men of the same name.
Gillow	Joseph Gillow, *A Biographical Dictionary of the English Catholics.*
Greg	Sir Walter Greg, *A Bibliography of the English Printed Drama to the Restoration.* Plays are cited by Greg serial numbers.
Grove	*Grove's Dictionary of Music and Musicians.*
Hind	Arthur M. Hind, *Engraving in England in the Sixteenth and Seventeenth Centuries.*
Jöcher	C. G. Jöcher, *Allgemeines Gelehrten-lexicon.* Used for obscure continental scholars.
Keeler	Mary F. Keeler, *The Long Parliament: A Biographical Study.*
NBG	*Nouvelle Biographie Générale*, ed. J. C. F. Hoefer. Most citations are also valid for *Biographie Universelle*, ed. Joseph and Louis Michaud.
PCC	Will in the Prerogative Court of Canterbury, with year of probate, which normally is year of death.
Schickler	Fernand de Schickler, *Les Églises du Refuge en Angleterre.*
Schotel	G. D. J. Schotel, *Biographisch Woordenboek der Nederlanden.*

STC   A. W. Pollard and G. R. Redgrave, *A Short-Title Catalogue of English Books 1475–1640.*

Taylor   E. G. R. Taylor, *The Mathematical Practitioners of Tudor and Stuart England.*

Venn   John and J. A. Venn, *Alumni Cantabrigienses.* Date of matriculation is added to distinguish men of the same name.

Vis. Hants, &c. The printed heraldic visitations of the county named, usually among the publications of the Harleian Society.

Waters   Henry F. Waters, *Genealogical Gleanings in England.*

Wing   Donald Wing, *Short-Title Catalogue 1641–1700.*

Possibilities of Error. In a work of this character and magnitude, errors will inevitably occur. Since they vitiate the whole scheme, it is hoped that misprints in *STC* numbers are indeed few. The following potentialities are perhaps not mortal offences:

(1) Unintended omission of material as a result of (*a*) unsuspecting use of imperfect copies, (*b*) existence of unknown variant states, (*c*) sheer oversight in examining books, or (*d*) accidental misplacing of index cards.

(2) Errors in identifying persons. While the great majority of identifications are certain beyond question, many rest on probability. Any regular user should, as a matter of course, scrutinize each item with the suspicion that the patron may have been misidentified, that two persons of the same name may be merged, or that a single man may be treated as two.

I. PERSONAL INDEX

AR., *Lord* (18182). *See* T. ARUNDELL, *I Baron.*

A., *Lady* B. [? Blanche Arundell]. 743.

A., B. T., *Bend.* [? Bro. T. Anderton]. Edits 17278.

A., C. Verse 3705 [anon. in 3706]; prose 12476 signed 'Concussus, surgo. C.A. xHxSx'.

A., D., *Gentlewoman* [? Dorothy Arundell]. 22950 (22963).

A., D. Verse 3905.

A., E. (12141). *See* EDWARD ALLISTON.

ATS., Ed. (7498). *See* EDWARD ATSLOWE.

A., E., *Layman. See* 12662 (12706, 12635).

A., F. [? Francis Appleby]. Verse 14665.

A., F. Verse 6014.

A., G. Verse 18478 (18773), 22621, Seneca, *Shortnesse of life, 1636*-HD.

AL., G. Verse 18809.

A., H., *at London.* 17151.

A., H. ★19806; verse 2765 = 16696.

A., I. (15716). *See* JAMES ARTHUR.

A., I. [? John Adamson]. Verse 135, 22566.

A., I., *Kt.* 7285.

A., I., *Oxon.* Verse 21752.

A., I., *Minister.* Edits 6 [cf. 5265].

A., I. 982; edits 974 [? Austin], 14493; verse 1695, 2774, 12100, 17115, 17922; prose 3929; *see also* 3544.

A., Jo. [? the author]. Verse 644.

A., L. Verse Plutarch, *President for parentes, 1571*-HN.

A., Le. Verse 19970.

A., M., *Perugino.* Prose 11636 (11638).

A., M. [? for A. M(unday)]. Prose 19447-F.

ARD., Ma[ster?]. Verse 3074.

A., *Lady* M. C. 18326.

A., M. D. (19171). *See* HENRY AIRAY.

A., MI. (3544). *See* MIA.

A., N., *Philomathes.* Verse 13988.

A., N. P. Verse 3108.

AD., Pa. (14373). *See* PATRICK ADAMSON.

A., R., *M.D. See* RICHARD ANDREWS.

A., R. [? R. Allott]. Verse 15685 [misprinted A. R. in 15688].

A., R. [? Roger Ashton]. 370-0.¹⁷ [but N. R. in later-0.⁵].

A., R., *Oxon.* Verse 12216 [earlier ed. lost].

A., R. Verse 11688, 22567, 24096.

A., S. [*Recusant*]. 11490.

A., S. 15351.

A., T., *of Inner Temple.* ¶11988–9, first part of 17127-0.

A., T. Verse 778, 15267, 15268, *Tarletons treatises, 1578*-F.

A., Th. Epistle 133 only.

A., V. Verse 24523.

A., W., *Editor. See* HENRY CHARTERIS *Jr.*

A., W. [? Sir W. Alexander]. Verse 15710.

A., W. Edits 22449 [? Aylesbury]; verse 12210, 23123.

ABARROW (Foster), Andrea = *Sir* William (*Vis. Hants*). 24371 as Barrow.

ABBAS. *See* ABBOT.

ABBAY, R. Verse 688.

ABBAY, Thomas, *Colonist* (Brown). Edits 22791.

ABBOTT, Ed. Verse 15078.

ABBOT, George, *Archbishop of Canterbury.* Chronologically:
To 1610: 1867, 7354; epistle 24939 by Dorset; verse 4756, prose 12894.
1611: ★1364, ¶3459, 4645 superseding Bancroft, 11577, 11580, 14462, 21711, 22182, ★¶25690.
1612: 5127, 5563, 12056, ★18147, 19484, 24026.
1613: ¶3462 (3452), 4631, 7140 = ¶7136 (7137), 17597, 20505, 25281, ★¶25699 superseding Whitgift.
1614: 3618 by editor, 20344, 20913.
1615: ★17622, ★17698 [only fragment known of *1614*-HD.].
1616: ¶686, 4960, 6887, 12100, ★12972, 13006, 18579, 23031, ¶23582 (23575, 21653).
1617: 6884, Delaune, *Christians tryumph*-U.; Minsheu List.

ABBOT, George, *Archbishop* (*cont.*)
1618: 245 by editor, ¶11216, *11496, 13931–32, 19933; *see* 3534.
1619: 47 by editor, 3951; epistle *19813.
1620: 4959, 6424, 12674 (12708, 12635), 17681; epistle 21761.
1621: 18316, *25923, R. Johnson, *Way to glory*-O.; epistle 22634.
1622–3: 7143, 7316 later to Eliz. of Bohemia; *see* 25373.
1624: 1498, 10738, *11701, *12648c (12635), 17610.
1625: ¶20509, 24512, *25919; presentation 583; *see* 17331.
1626–7: 5395, 20471, 21477; prose 9247.
1628, *etc.*: *4126, 4600, 7121, *14555 [*1632* lost], *16825, 21176, *22787; *see* 10863 *under* ANOMALOUS DEDICATIONS.

ABBOT, John, *Poet* (*DNB*). *See* 24924.

ABBOT, Sir Maurice, *Lord Mayor* (*DNB*). *150, *1504, *4661, *6531, *¶11346, 13359, *16825, *21094, 22493 by editor, *25663, *25952, Freake, *Priuiledges of vpright*, [*1639*]-F.; epistle *25963.

ABBOT, Robert, *Bishop of Salisbury*. *6420; *see* 19813.

ABBOT, Thomas [? *Son of Robert*]. Edits 47.

ABDY, Anthony, *Alderman*. Epistle *25963.

ABELL, Laurence, *of Broadgates Hall* (Foster). *See* 736.

ABELL, William, *Alderman* (*DNB*). *11347, *22532.

ABERNETHY, Alexander, *IX Lord Saltoun*. *See* 10667.

ABERNETHY, John, *Bishop of Caithness*. Verse 19781; *see* 10667.

ABGAR, *King of Edessa* [Eusebius I. xiii], GA-MALIEL [Acts v. 34], *and* JAIRUS [Mark v. 22] *as types of goodwill*. 6581 *spelt* Agbarus.

ABNEY, George, *of Inner Temple* (? Venn 1584). *24596.

ACHELLEY, John, *Merchant Taylor, d. 1586*. Verse 19523 issue at L.

ACHELEY, Thomas, *Poet* (*STC*). Verse 25118a.

ACHESON, Gilbert, *Bailie of Edinburgh*. *138 only, W. M., *Edinburghs alphabet*, n.d.-E.

ACHESON, Robert, *Bailie of Edinburgh*. *13173, *Edinburghs alphabet*, n.d.-E.

ACOURT, William, *Warden of Haberdashers*. *13514 [13513 imperfect].

ACTON, John, *Canonist* (*DNB*). *See* 17108.

ACTON, Sir William, *I Bt.* *6493.

ACUÑA, Diego Sarmiento de, *Conde de Gon-domar*. 7376; epistle 22094 (22064).

ADAMIDES. *See* ADAMSON.

ADAMS, John, *of Lincoln's Inn* (Foster 1571). Prose 6823.

ADAMS, Richard, *Rector of Yeovilton* (Foster 1604). Epistle *1941.

ADAMS, Thomas, *Bookseller*. Prose 24472 un-signed.

ADAMS, Thomas, *of Trinity College* (Venn 1594). *18206.

ADAMSON, John, *Principal at Edinburgh* (*DNB*). Verse 2363 = 3989, 5931 (5909), 7486, 7487, 18063, 19781, 21101, 22565, 22566, P. Anderson, *Grana angelica*, 1635-F.; prose 18290; *see also* I.A.

ADAMSON, Patrick, *Archbishop of St. Andrews*. Verse 14373, Cicero, *Opera*, 1585-F.; *see* 22028.

ADERB, F. Verse 4503 (4509).

ADOLPH, *Prince of Veere*. 10467.

ADRIANUS, 'Lord of Hoyncop'. *See* WINSSEN.

AEDIE, Andrew, *Principal of Marischal College*. Verse 11149.

AEGIDIUS, Petrus. *See* GILES.

AETON. *See* AYTON.

AGBARUS (6581). Variant form of ABGAR.

AGGEUS (Agge), Augustinus, *Haius* (BM). Edits 4115.

AGLAIA, 'Shepherdess' [*fiction*]. 3682.

AIKENHEAD, David, *Lord Provost of Edinburgh*. *88, *138, *5927 (5909), *13258, *20696, *23262; epistle *18360.

AIKEROD *or* ACRED, Ambrose, *LL.D.* (Venn). *18206.

AINSLIE, Andrew, *Bailie of Edinburgh*. *139; epistle *18360.

AINSWORTH, Henry, *Separatist* (*DNB*). *See* 19098.

AIRAY, Adam, *of St. Edmund Hall* (Foster 1605). Prose 14896.

AIRAY, Henry, *Provost of Queen's* (*DNB*). *6420, *19171 as M. D. A., 20609 by editor, 20619 by editor, 23500 (23502); epistle *25787 only.

AISGILL, Henry, *Preacher* (Foster). *25150.

AISGILL, Joshua, *Fellow of Corpus* (Foster). Verse 13620.

AIWOOD, Richard, *Vicar of Great Milton* (Foster as Wood 1598). Minsheu List.

AKOKAKOS. Verse 6385.

ALABASTER, William, *Poet* (*DNB*). Epistle 10799.

ALCOCK, Anth. *See* 25438.

ALDERSEY, Thomas, *Haberdasher and M.P.* (PCC 1598). 19860 and *1596*-F.

ALDERSEY, Thomas, '*Merchant Adventurer, London*'. Epistle *25847 only.

ALDERSEY, William, *Mayor of Chester d. 1625.* *¶23720.

ALDRICH, George, *of Trinity College* (Venn). Verse 20051.

ALDRICH, Jo. [*presumably one in* Venn]. Approbation 737.

ALDRICH (Aldrisius), Robert, *Scholar* (*DNB*). Verse 13807, 13811.

ALDRISIUS. *See* ALDRICH.

ALDWORTH, ——, '*Captain in Bristol trained bands*'. Epistle *19155.

ALDWORTH, Thomas, *Bristol merchant* (Brown). 1049 and *1589*-O.[8]

ALEPH, Johan. Prose 2370 [name dropped 2371].

ALEXANDER [*pseudonym*]. 3556.

ALEXANDER, *Bishop of Lincoln, d. 1148* (*DNB*). 21783.

ALEXANDER, Francis, *Prebendary of Winchester* (Foster). Minsheu List.

ALEXANDER, John, '*Scholar*'. Verse 7363.

ALEXANDER, Sir Robert, *Groom of the stable. See* 18105.

ALEXANDER, William, *Earl of Stirling.* *1404 by editor, *12069, ¶15366, ¶21096, ¶25215 (25207); epistle J. Cockburne, *Iudas kisse*, *1605*-E.; verse 73, 7196 (7189, 7216, etc.), 7247, 7253 signed Alexis and Parthenius, 7257 (7255), 20566, Cockburne, *Gabriels salutation, 1605*-E., *see* W. A.; *see* 10667.

ALEXIS (7253). *See preceding entry.*

ALFRED, *King.* 863.

ALINGTON, George, *Secondary of Pipe Office* (*Vis. Lincs.*). *24132 superseding Mountjoy; Minsheu List.

ALINGTON, Sir Giles, *of Horseheath, d. 1522.* 17242 (3546).

ALINGTON, Sir Giles, *Father of I Baron.* *6213.

ALLDE, Edward, *Printer* (*DNB*). Epistle 6341; prose 3492, 16913.

ALLDE, John, *Printer* (*DNB*). Prose 13912, 24062.

ALLEN, Abraham, *Warden of Barber Surgeons.* *24578.

ALEYN, Charles, *Poet* (*DNB*). Verse 22444.

ALLEN, Edmund, *Ambassador* (*DNB*). Prose 17330.

ALLEYN, Edward [? *the actor, DNB*]. *See* 12662 (12706, 12635).

ALLEN, Edward, *Alderman.* *17886.

ALLEN (Westby), Elizabeth = George *Brother of Cardinal. See* LADY I. D.

ALLEYN, George. Verse 408 for *1607*.

ALLEN, Henry, *Vicar of Brent* (Venn 1610). Epistle *1941.

ALLEN, Henry, *of Corpus Christi* (Foster 1634). Verse 91.

ALLEN, John, *of Corpus Christi* (Foster 1569). Verse 6787.

ALLEYNE, John. ¶126 (110).

ALLEN, Matthew, '*Minister at Horsham*'. *See* 13923.

ALLEINE, Richard, *Rector of Dicheat, father o, Richard-DNB.* Epistle *1941.

ALLEN, Robert, *Clergyman* (Venn 1570). Edits 20337, 20338.

ALANE *or* ALLEN, Robert. Verse 12748, 15710.

ALLEN, Thomas, *of Gloucester Hall d. 1632* (*DNB*). *See* 12612, 18087.

ALLEN, Thomas, *Fellow of Eton* (Foster 1589). Helps edit 14629.

ALLEN, Thomas, *Vicar of Elham* (Foster 1601). *See* 25327.

ALENUS, Gualterus [? Venn 1560]. Verse 3437.

ALLEN, William, *Cardinal* (*DNB*). *See* 3799, 11458.

ALLEN, Sir William, *Lord Mayor.* 19475.

ALLEN, William, *Son of preceding.* 22927.

ALLEN, Zouch, *Exchequer agent* (PCC 1621). Minsheu List.

ALLENSON, John, *Puritan divine* (DNB). Edits 25367, 25368, 25370.

ALLEY, Peter, *Captain with Raleigh 1618*. Verse 5808, 5810 [cf. 23769].

ALLEY, William, *Bishop of Exeter*. *1710.

ALLISTON, Edward, *of Emmanuel* (Venn). Edits 18948, verse 12141 as E. A.

ALLISON, Richard, *Composer* (Grove). Verse 10700.

ALLISON, William, '*Norwich minister*'. Verse 11574.

ALLOTT, Robert, *Editor* (DNB). Verse 17868, 19793; *see* R. A.

L'ALMA MIA PACE. Prose 14467.

ALOYSIA, *Madonna* (24730). See CARVAJAL.

ALPORT, Edward, *Preacher* (STC). Friends of: 537.

ALSINOIS, *Comte d'*. Pseudonym of N. Denisot.

ALSOP, Bernard, *Printer*. Prose 18097 rewritten 18098, unsigned 1705 and 4281, initials 11175 usurping old dedication.

ALSOP, John, *Chaplain to Laud* (Venn 1617). Book licenser *1639*; typical licence in 25955.

ALTHAM, James, *of Mark Hall, father of next*. †5116.

ALTHAM, Sir James, *Judge* (DNB). *23830, W. Leigh, *Dreadfull day*, *1610*-F.; prose 20138.

ALTHAM (Leventhorpe), Joan = Sir Edward *of Mark Hall*. 12182.

ALTHUSIUS, Joannes, *Professor of Law* (ADB). *14047.

AMERY, Robert, *Sheriff of Chester*. See 5118.

AMES, William, *Puritan divine* (DNB). Prose 1640, 3532 [both anon. but revealed in later editions]; *see* 11650.

AMHERST, Arthur, *of St. John's* (Foster). Verse 22888.

AMINTAS [*pseudonym*]. 18371.

AMMONIO, Andrea, *Latin secretary* (DNB). Verse 25585.

AMOURS, Guillelmus. See 20417.

ANDERSON, Anthony, Jr. [*presumably son of author*]. Verse 566.

ANDERSON, Sir Edmund, *Judge* (DNB). *570, 4719, 5330, *6439, 7268 by editor, 18634, 23450, 23451, 23708, *1603* version of 24600-CHI., 25267, W. Clever, *Foure bookes*, *1597*-F., A. Gregory, *De legibus*, *1583*-HD.; epistle 16696.

ANDERSON, Sir Henry, *Alderman of London*. 18487.

ANDERSON, Sir Henry, *Alderman of Newcastle* (Keeler). *14491.

ANDERSON (Essex), Joan = William, *Mother of Edmund I Bt*. ¶21649.

ANDERSON (Smyth), Magdalen = Sir Edmund. ¶5220.

ANDERSON, Patrick, *Physician* (DNB). Edits 4366.

ANDERSON, Sir Richard, *of Penley, father of Henry I Bt*. 14319; *see* 25327.

ANDERTON, Lawrence, *Controversialist* (DNB). See 18176 as BRERELEY.

ANDERTON, Margaret, *Niece of preceding*. See TURVILE.

ANDERTON, Thomas, *O.S.B. See* B. T. A.

ANDREA, Ab. *See* ANDREWS.

ANDREAS, Bernard, *Poet* (DNB). Verse 13809.

ANDREWES, ——, *Preacher* [? Bartimaeus STC]. See 25438.

ANDREWES, Henry, *Alderman*. *13347.

ANDREWS, John, *Poet* (DNB). Minsheu List.

ANDREWES, Lancelot, *Bishop of Winchester*. 413, ¶1124 (1109), 3581, *11496, 11761 superseding Nowell, ¶12485, *17698 [*1614* known only by tp.-HD.], 18011, *¶25690; epistle 5338, 16696; presentation Maier; Minsheu List.

ANDREWE, Laurence, *Printer* (DNB). Prose 6904.

ANDREWS, Michael, *Master of Barber Surgeons*. Epistle *25963.

ANDREWS, Richard, *College of Physicians*. Signed verse 1311, 4496, 10701 [and see plate], 22219; initialed verse 12550, 16883, 20187.

ANDREW, Richard, '*Merchant*'. Minsheu List.

ANDREWE, Thomas, *Poet* (DNB). Verse 7209 (7210), 21408.

ANDREWES, Sir Thomas, *Lord Mayor*. *¶21202.

ARMIN, Robert, *Actor* (*DNB*). Prose 7293, 21482.

ARMINE, Sir William, *Father of next*. Perkins, *Arte of prophecying, 1607*-HD. (19649).

ARMINE, Sir William, *I Bt.* 25957.

ARMOURER, Hugh, *of Amsterdam congregation* (Burrage). *5345.

ARMSTRONG, Archibald, *Court jester* (*DNB*). 1372, 23780 (23725), 23786, ¶23725 [earlier edition lost, *Honour conceal'd*].

ARMSTRONG, Gabriel, *Esq.* [? *of Notts.*]. †24313 [wife named Margaret].

ARMESTRONG, W. Verse T. Wye, *Briefe discourse, 1580*-C.[6]

ARNOLD, Elizabeth. *See* 24316.

ARNOLD (Horsey), Grace = William, *Daughter of Sir Ralph*. Epistle 5582.

ARNOT, James *and* John. *See* SIR ROBERT.

ARNOT, Sir John, *Lord Provost of Edinburgh.* *17700.

ARNOT, Sir Robert, *of Fernie.* Epistle R. Williamson, *Paedagogia, 1635*-E. with brothers James, John, and William [Robert and James also in earlier edition C.[3]].

ARNOT, William. *See* ROBERT.

ARRIS, Jasper, *Warden of Barber Surgeons.* Epistle *25962.

ARSCOTT, Edmund, *of Tetcott, Devon* (Foster). R. Pecke, ¶*Two sermons, 1632*-F.

ARSCOTT (Walrond), Mary = Edmund. R. Pecke, ¶*Two sermons, 1632*-F.

ARTEF, Io. *See* 24306 [unsigned in 24305].

ARTHUR, *Prince of Wales.* 24796; Linacre trans. Proclus, *Sphaera*, [? *1522*]-L. [from *1499* foreign ed.].

ARTHUR, James. Verse 15716 initialed, 15717 signed.

ARTHUR, William, *Minister of St. Cuthbert's, Edinburgh.* Verse 21101; *see* HENRY CHARTERIS Jr. for joint editing.

ARUNDELL (Jerningham), Anne = John of Chideock (*Vis. Dorset*). Trithemius, *Threefold mirror, 1633*-F.

ARUNDELL (Philipson), Anne = Thomas I Baron. 4552.

ARUNDELL, Daniel, '*Physician*' (? Foster). Verse 13260.

ARUNDELL, Dorothy, *O.S.B., daughter of Sir John of Lanherne. See* D. A.

ARUNDEL, Thomas, *Archbishop of Canterbury. See* 3260 [3259 all imperfect].

ARUNDELL, Sir Thomas, *of Lanherne* (*DNB*). Epistle 19166.

ARUNDELL, Thomas, *I Baron Arundell.* 18182; see 6270-L., 10667, 17332.

ASCHAM, Antony, *Ambassador* (*DNB*). Verse 3.

ASCHAM (Howe), Margaret = Roger. Prose 832.

ASCHAM, Roger, *Author* (*DNB*). Verse 20064 and *1561*-HN.

ASCHAM, William. 3578; see 3588.

ASHFIELD, Sir Edmund, *of Inner Temple* (Foster 1584). 19507 (19504); see 19511.

ASHFIELD, Robert, *of Stowlangtoft, Suff., d. 1613.* J. More, *¶Three sermons, 1594*-PN.[2]

ASTLEY or ASHLEY, Sir Andrew, *of Writtle* (*Vis. Essex*). See 12662 (12706, 12635).

ASHLEY, Sir Anthony, *Clerk of Privy Council* (*DNB*). G. Phillips, †*Aprill of the Church, 1596*-D.

ASTLEY, John, *Master of the Jewel House* (*DNB*). 830, *¶22064 and *1561*-HN.; prose 830.

ASHLEY or ASTLEY, Sir John, *Master of the Revels.* Verse 5642.

ASTLEY (Grey), Margaret = John-*DNB*. 22942.

ASHLEY (Weston), Phillipa = Anthony I Bt. 22394.

ASTLEY, Richard, *Warden of All Souls* (Foster 1593). *21731; see 25327.

ASHTON, Abdias, *Fellow of St. John's* (Venn). See 25368.

ASHTON, Anne. ¶25096.

ASHTON, Peter, *of Trinity College* (Venn 1605). *18206.

ASSHETON, Ralph, *Father of Ralph I Bt.* 1882.

ASHTON, Roger, *d. at Tyburn 1592.* See R. A.

ASHWELL, William, *Alderman.* Epistle *25963.

ASHWOOD, Henry, *M.A.* (Foster). Verse 21660.

ASHWORTH, John, *of Lincoln's Inn.* Minsheu List.

ASKE, Robert, *Goldsmith and bridgemaster.* 21685.

ASKWITH, Robert, *Mayor of York.* ★20493.

ASPINWALL, Edw. [*Lancs.*]. Verse 12866 [earlier lost].

ASSHAW, Leonard, *of Lancashire* (Foster). Verse 25394 (25389).

ASTLEY. *See* ASHLEY.

ASTON (Willoughby), Anne = Thomas *I Bt.* 21688.

ASTON (Sadleir), Gertrude = Walter *I Baron.* 14483.

ASTON, Jayes (20977). *See* JOYCE COLEPEPER.

ASTON, Sir Thomas, *of Aston* (Foster 1599). ★7293.

ASTON, Walter, *I Baron Aston.* 3198, 7189 (7216, 7222), ¶7197 (7189, 7216, etc.), 7204, 7209, 7211 (7222), 7217, 7222, ★11068 only, ¶17334, †22427; *see* 10667.

ATEIUS. *See* ATYE.

ATEN AIDE EN LA FOI. Anagram; *see* A. FAYUS.

ATHOW *or* OTHOW, John, *of Gray's Inn* (*1608*). ¶13320.

ATKINS (Hawkins), Annabella = Sir Henry *of Clapham. S. R., Ruth reuiued, 1639-0.*[5]

ATKINS, Hugo. Verse 11464.

ATKIN, John, *Mayor of King's Lynn.* ★21075.

ATKYNS, Richard, *of Tuffley, Gloucs., bencher of Lincoln's Inn.* ¶13821; *see* 13825.

ATKINS, William. Verse 19300.

ATKINS, William, *of Gray's Inn* (*1631*). Verse 22458.

ATKINSON, Christopher, *M.D.* (Foster). Verse 22929.

ATLEE, Richard, *of East Dereham, Norf.* A. Gurney, †*Doleful discourse, 1581*-HN.

ATSLOWE, Edward, *Physician* (*DNB*). Verse 7498 signed D. Ed. Ats.

ATLOW *or* ATELOW, Henry, *Esq.* Minsheu List.

ATOCHA, IOHANNES de, '*Student of J. Gower M.A.*' Verse 12141.

ATTERSOLL, William, *Puritan, d. 1640* (*DNB*). Verse 23278, 24127.

ATWATER, William, *Bishop of Lincoln.* 13811.

ATYE, Sir Arthur, *D.C.L.* (Foster). ¶11739.

AUCHER, Sir Anthony, *of Bishopsbourne, Master of Jewel House.* 9968.

AUCHER, Sir Anthony, *of Bourne* (Brown). Presentation 23350 *misprinted* Anger.

AUCHINLECK, Patrick, *Minister at Alves.* Verse 10820.

AUDELY, Amy. 21348.

AUDELEY (Packington), Anne = Sir Henry *of Berechurch.* 21628.

AWDELAY, John, *Printer* (*DNB*). Verse 21855, prose 24999.

AUDELAY, *Lady* Lucia. *See* TUCHET.

AUDLEY, Thomas, *I Baron Audley.* 20062, 20116.

AUDLEY, Thomas, *Esq.* [? *of Beds.*]. 24594.

AUDOENUS *and* AUGER. *See* OWEN *and* AUCHER.

AUERSPERG, Weickard von. *See* WEICKARDUS.

AUGUR, Nicolaus, *M.A.* (Venn). Verse 15078.

AUNGIER, Gerald, *II Baron Aungier.* 11763; *see* 10667.

AURELIUS, Abraham, *Pastor* (*DNB*). ★7358 by editor; Minsheu List; *see* 23920, 23923.

AURELIUS, Jean Baptiste, *Father of preceding. See* JOAN. BER., *Aurel.* (? misprint).

AUSTIN (? Brigham), Anne = William-*DNB.* Edits 972.

AUSTIN, Robert, *Chaplain to Abp. Abbot* (Venn 1612). Book licenser *1633-4.*

AUSTIN, William, *Writer, d. 1634* (*DNB*). Verse 5808, 5810 [cf. 23769], 20756.

AVENET. *See* AVENON.

AVENON (Sampto), Agnes = Sir Alexander *Lord Mayor. See* 19868.

AWBREY, John [*London merchant*]. ★5533.

AWBREY, Robert, *Draper.* ★18280.

AWDELAY. *See* AUDLEY.

AWEN. *See* OWEN.

AXTELL, Stephen, *M.B.* (Foster). Verse 6044a.

AYLESBURY, Thomas, *M.A.* (*DNB*). *See* 10738.

AYLESBURY, William, *Translator* (*DNB*). *See* W. A.

AYLETT, Robert, *Master in Chancery* (*DNB*). 21195 (21196).

AYLMER, John, *Bishop of London.* 572, 4301 by editor, 4401 serving also for 14610 (14579), 4420 [Bunny abridgement], 7432, 11693, ¶11758, ★11804, 12910, ★14608, 14920,

AYLMER, John, *Bishop (cont.)*
  *18728 [freak substitution for Sandys], 19497
  later to Puckering, 19520, *21748 (21751),
  23869, Beza, *Euident display, 1578*-F., F. Kett,
  Epistle to papists, 1585-L.², Wittewronghelus,
  De vera fide, 1581-HATF. by editor [cf. 4301];
  epistle *3871; *see* 18773, 25695.

AYLMER, Theophilus, *Archdeacon* (Venn 1583).
  23115; *see* 24099.

AYLOFFE, *Sir* William, *I Bt.* 26081.

AYLOFFE, William, *'J.P. in Herts.'* *¶25677
  superseding Heton in 25673.

AYLVA, Hobbe van, *of Franeker* (Schotel).
  *¶550 [from earlier foreign].

AYLWORTH, Anthony, *M.D.* (Foster). Verse
  4759; Minsheu List.

AYLEWORTH, Aishton, *Esq.* P. Galloway,
  Cathechisme, 1588-E.² by bookseller.

AISCOUGH, ——, *'Counsellor at law'* [? *Edward
  of Lincoln's Inn*]. Minsheu List.

AYSCOUGH *or* ASKEW, *Sir* Edward, *of South
  Kelsey* (Keeler). †5357.

AYSCOUGH, James, *of Gray's Inn (1633).* See
  15466.

AYTON, *Sir* Robert, *Poet* (*DNB*). *1404 by
  editor, 7479, 10695, 19089 by editor, *¶19850,
  22561 by bookseller; verse 343 (347), 5956,
  5958, 10885; Minsheu List.

B

B., *'of Northants, at Stoke Lodge'.* 24904.

B., A. *Caution: These initials are normally a
  mask; most of these entries are fictions.* Cf.
  'Cousins A.B.C.D.' in 24567.

B., A. [*supposedly Earl of Essex*]. Prose 23642
  (23645).

B., A., *Clergyman.* Edits 23302 (23306), 23304
  (23306), 23307 (23313), 23308, 23309
  (23313).

B., A., *of C.C.C.* [*Cambridge*]. Verse 24928.

B., A., *of Franciscan Third Order.* *23212.

B., A. 3271 by editor [replaced in 3272];
  edits 3191, 24142, 24188; verse 3189, 11419,
  13582, 13964, 18133; prose 10734 only,
  17323, 18305; *see* 7578.

B., *Sir* B., *Kt.* 17181.

B., B. [? *Barnabe Barnes*]. Verse 11098 only.

B., C. (11643), *see* CHRISTOPHER BARKER;
  (24046), *see* CLEMENT BARKSDALE.

B., C. [? Christopher Brooke]. Verse 18909.

B., C. Edits 1029; verse 23377; prose 11321.

B., D. (14335). See D[R. RICHARD] BANCROFT.

B., E. (3242). See EDWARD BAGSHAW.

B., E., *'Servant to Countess Culemburg* [*Netherlands*]'. Epistle 15527.

B., E. [? *Edmund Bolton*]. Verse 584, 7207,
  13592.

B., E. [*Friend of dramatists*]. Verse 4946, 18346
  (18337), 20770.

B., E., *'Scholar'.* See 12662 (12706, 12635).

B., E. Epistle 16683; verse 288 [? Blount or
  Burton], 3272, 6446, 13941; prose 22999.

B., Ev. Verse 14782.

B., F. (3848). See FRANCIS BLACKWELL.

B., F. [? *Francis Beaumont*]. Verse 1695.

B., *Mrs.* F. 4282.

B., F. Edits 3922 and variant-HD., 11189.

B., Favour. Verse 23058.

B., G., *de med. Tem.* (18909). *See* B. G.

B., G., *Cantab.* [? William Boston]. Verse
  12216 [earlier lost], 12224, 12270.

B., G., *Cantabrigiensis.* Verse 23689.

B., G., *Sr.,* and G. B., *Jr.* See 25438.

B., G. Edits 18767-8; verse 3053, 20825,
  24928, 26005; prose 1377.

B., H. (3566), *see* SIR I. B. DE L.; (6364), *see*
  HUGH BROUGHTON; (10935), *see* HENRY
  BEESLEY.

B., H. Verse 407 for *1631*, etc., 5077, 23080
  (23084).

B., S[*ir*] I., B. [*presumably* John Beaumont,
  II Bt.]. Verse 12205.

B., *Sir* I., *de* L., and son H. B. [*presumably Sir*
  James Bellingham *of Levens and* Henry].
  ¶3566.

B., I. [*perhaps bookseller* Bellamy]. Edits
  20286.

B., J. [? John Beaumont]. Verse 1666 =
  18972 (1665).

B., J. Edits 10617, 19204; verse 3635, 10784,
  11636 (11638), 14788, 19337, 25227; prose
  22487, 25786; *see* 12662 (12706, 12635).

B., I., Brother of. 1047.

Bo., Io., *Miles.* Verse 21649.

B., Io. *or* John. Verse 5567, 11096.

BER., Ioan., *Aurel.* Verse 1491 [? AURELIUS].

B., *Mrs.* K. 632.

B., L., *S.T.L. See* 22091 [different book from 22090].

B., L., *in Italy* [? *fiction*]. *See* 12629.

B., L. *See* 21131.

B., M., *Wife to D. B., Esq.* 21137.

B., *L*[*ady*] M. 24259.

B., Mary [*Recusant*]. *24141 and Allison 825.

B., M., *his mother.* 20286 by editor I. B., *q.v.*

B., M., *Oxoniensis.* Verse 17784.

B., M. Verse 15078 [initials later vanish], 25317.

B., M. D. M, S.M.S.M.G.I.MIM.H.M.B.M. S.R.B.M, R.M. KN.B.M.B.I.M, NP.W.C. PA. my brethren M. I.C.W.B.A.P.M. MM. E, C .CD. G.M.A. [see *Studies in Bibliog.* ix. 178]. *¶19608.

B., N. Verse 13247, 18611, 24908, 25090, 25741.

BR., Ni. *See* NICHOLAS BRETON.

B., P., *of Middle Temple* [? Peter Bevis]. Verse 686, 18911.

B., P. Verse 11636 (11638).

B., R. [? Richard Bullein]. Verse 4040.

B., Ri., *Cantabr.* Verse 164.

B., R., *Cantabrigiae, also S. Hosp., and S.S.M.* Verse 17824.

B., R., *'Londinas'.* Verse 21752.

B., *M. R., Preacher.* Prose 17857.

B., R., *Worshipful M.* 17998.

B., R. Edits 1065, 19819 only, *Mirrour to warres, 1589*-L.; verse 383, 3635, 3894 [? author], 7045 [? Busby], 12750, 21361, 25336; prose 9554, 24097; *see* 12662 (12706, 12635).

BR., R. Verse 6364, others signed R. B.

B., S., *Sch. M. Rector* (25327). *See* SAMUEL BERNARD.

B., S. Edits 1067, 3810.

B., T. (10668). *See* THOMAS BERNHERE.

B., T., *Esq.* Verse 6190.

B., T. Verse 10667, 11636 (11638), 15559,

18904 [anon. in prior edition-c.²], 22222, 25224; prose 22164; *see* 16590.

B., Tho. Verse 23752.

BIR., Tho. Verse 25440.

B., V. D. Verse 1851.

B., W., *Int. Temp.* (18909). *See* WILLIAM BROWNE.

B., W., *S.J.* (24542). *See* WILLIAM MALONE.

BAR., W. (11596). *See* WILLIAM BARCLAY.

B., W., *Esq.* [? William Basse; *cf.* 1547]. Edits 22062; verse 3914.

B., W., *Affinis-domesticus.* Verse 2774.

B., W. Edits 4313 [cf. 5186]; verse 111, 1666 (1665), 1695, 6984, 11688, 11803, 17632, 17634, 21094, b.s. print of Overbury-L.; *see* 6216.

BR., Wi., *of Gray's Inn.* Verse 3074.

BABINGTON, Gervase, *Bishop of Worcester.* 51, 14058, 21781, 22807 by editor; epistle *1352a; *see also* HENRY PARRY (12662).

BABINGTON, William, *Son of next* (Foster 1600). Verse 18926.

BABINGTON, Zachary, *LL.D.* (Foster). Edits 18926.

BACCHUS. *See* BACKHOUSE.

BACHELOR (Bachalaureus), James, *Brechin scholar at Paris* (*Reg. Sec. Sig.*). Epistle Vaus, *Rudimenta, 1531*-A.

BACKHOUSE (Borlase), Elizabeth = Samuel (*Vis. Berks.*). *¶23854.

BACKHOUSE (Henshaw), Florence = *Sir* John (*Vis. Berks.*). *¶23854.

BACKHOUSE, Nicholas, *'Merchant adventurer'.* ¶16684.

BACCHUS, Ro. [? *the next*]. Verse 13510.

BACKHOUSE, Rowland, *Alderman.* *6493.

BACON (Cooke), Ann = *Sir* Nicholas (*DNB*). 2004 by author, *13805 some copies, 14591 only by editor, 24995, 25627 (25620); *see* 25695.

BACON (Butts), Anne = *Sir* Nicholas *I Bt.* 2004 by translator, *4207.

BACON, Anthony, *Diplomatist* (*DNB*). 1137 later to Constable, etc., 6227 by author, 6788, 21658, 21661 and further fragment-F. (21649), Du Nesme, *Miracle of peace, 1599*-HN. (21649).

BACON, *Sir* Edmund, *II Bt.* ★364, ¶12680 (12706, 12635), 20894; *see* 12662 (12706, 12635).

BACON, Edward, *of Shrubland Hall* (*DNB*). ★364, ★†3088, ★11743 ? by editor.

BACON, Francis, *Viscount St. Albans.* Chronologically:
  1606–14: ★364, ★1663, 17625; *see* 19511.
  1615–16: 3635, 3927, 11803 and *1616*-L., ¶17509, 25995.
  1617: 10805 by editor, 21622, 24311, 24315, 24616 only, 25985; Minsheu List.
  1618: 7139 = ¶7136 only, 10598, ¶11216, ★11496, ¶11597, 13249, 25046 by editor (25031 and *1623*-F.), 25731 by editor.
  1619: 7370, ¶10926, 11192, 11828, 19568, 24016 by printer superseding Montagu; epistle ★19813.
  1620: 3370, 12184, ★19824, 21325 (21326, etc.), 24643 later to Charles, 25441, 25615.
  1621–5: 590 [see changes], ★20163, 20767 (*1627* nonce collection-NY.[11]); *see* 17331.

BACON (Littel), Helen = Edward. ★4695, ★21187 and *1627*-HD.

BACON (Meautys), Jane = *Sir* Nathaniel, *K.B., and previously* Cornwallis. 19312, 19314 shared in 19315, ★19320 and *1618*-F. (19311 as general ded.), 19321.

BACON, Lionel, *Son of Edward.* ★26105.

BACON, *Sir* Nathaniel, *d. 1622* (*DNB*). ★364.

BACON, *Sir* Nathaniel, *K.B., painter* (*DNB*). †19315, †19320 and *1618*-F. (19311 as general ded.), †19321.

BACON, Nathaniel, *Puritan, d. 1660* (*DNB*). ★26105; Minsheu List.

BACON, *Sir* Nicholas, *Lord Keeper* (*DNB*). 6858 by editor, ★¶10674, 23213, †24408, 24686, 24800 by editor [see changes].

BACON, *Sir* Nicolas, *I Bt.* ★†364, †366, 11821.

BACON, Nicholas, *Son of preceding.* 15036.

BACON, Nicholas, *Son of Edward.* ★26105.

BACON, Philip, *Son of Edward.* ★26105; Minsheu List.

BADCLYF (21362). Misprint for RADCLYF.

BADDELEY, Richard, *Secretary to Bishop Morton* (*STC*). Edits 4528; verse 5808, 5810 [cf. 23769].

BADEN, Giles, *D.D., Dean* (Venn). Verse 24316.

BADGER, Thomas, *Printer.* Epistle 12854 (12816).

BADIUS, Jodocus (Josse), *Ascensius, printer.* Edits 16116, 17107, 17108.

BAGULEY, Henry, *of Emmanuel* (Venn). Edits 12714 (12635).

BAGNAL, *Sir* Nicholas, *Marshal* (*DNB*). Pico, *Twelve rules, 1589*-HN.

BAGNALL, William, *Friend of theatre people* (*N & Q, 1957,* p. 55). Verse 1429; consider W. B.

BAGSHAW, Christopher, *Controversialist* (*DNB*). See 7268.

BAGSHAW, Edward, *the elder, Royalist* (*DNB*). Edits 3226, 3242 (3224), 3244, 3249, 3256 (3224).

BAÏF, Jean-Antoine de (*NBG*). Verse 3166.

BAYLEY, Edward, *Surgeon at Bart's.* Edits ★24713 whence 24706.

BAILEY, John, *Mayor of Marlborough.* 19945a.

BAYLY, Lewis, *Bishop of Bangor.* ¶1601.

BAYLIE, Richard, *President of St. John's* (Foster 1601). 11570, ★25328; edits 19037; *see* 5138.

BAILLIE, Robert, *of Edinburgh Town Council.* W. M., ★*Edinburghs alphabet*-E.

BAYLY, Thomas, *Royalist divine* (*DNB*). Edits 23948.

BAYLY, Thomas, *M.A.* [*probably the preceding*]. Verse 21620.

BAYLEY, Walter, *Physician* (*DNB*). ★1970.

BAINARD. *See* BAYNARD.

BAINBRIDGE, John, *Astronomer* (*DNB*). Edits 20398; verse 13620; prose 12612, 19302.

BAINBRIGG, Thomas, *Master of Christ's* (*DNB*). See 13518.

BAINRAFE. Anagram of Farnaby.

BAKER, Arthur, *of Inner Temple* (Foster). *See* 15466.

BAKER, George, *Surgeon* (*DNB*). ★18281, ★24577 [date problem]; verse 1360 only, 16870 and *1597*-HN.; prose 11750, 12469, 14917, 24723; *see* 5442.

BAKER, George, *Bookseller.* Prose 22561.

BAKER, *Sir* Henry, *I Bt.* †¶59, 1641 by editor, 12711 (12708, 12635), 13538, ¶23582a [sometimes ¶23582] (23575, 21653).

BAKER, *Sir* John, *Lawyer* (*DNB*). 19493.

BAKER, *Sir* John, *II Bt.* R. Abbot, *Holinesse of churches, 1638*-F.

BAKER, John, *of Mayfield, Sussex, d. 1668.* 19579 by editor (19570).

BAKER, *Sir* Richard, *of Sissinghurst, son of Sir John*-DNB. 22241, 22242.

BAKER, SAMUEL, *Divine* (*DNB*). Book licenser, *1634–40*.

BAKER, Thomas, '*Mertonensis*'. Verse 24042.

BAKER, *Sir* Thomas, *Brother of John I Bt.* †24415a.

BAKER, William (5097). *See* BARKER.

BAKER, William. Edits 14010.

BAKER, William, *of Middle Temple* (Foster 1604). Edits 3613 [signed in 3614]; verse 5808, 5810 [cf. 23769], 22174.

BALCANQUHALL, Robert, *Minister of Tranent.* Verse 14906.

BALCANQUHALL, Walter [*probably Jr., possibly Sr., both DNB*]. Verse 7487.

BALDUINUS (Boeidens), Joannes, *Bookseller.* Verse 16116 [later usurped by Worde].

BALDWIN, Justinian, *M.A.* (Foster). Verse 21239.

BALDWIN, William, *Author* (*DNB*). Verse 15205.

BALE, John, *Bishop of Ossory.* Edits 848, 850, 15180, 15445, 17320.

BALE, John *and* Paul, *Sons of preceding.* 1290.

BALES, Peter, *Calligraphist* (*DNB*). Verse 21057.

BALFOUR, *Sir* James, *Lord Pittendreich* (*DNB*). *See* 21875.

BALFOUR, James, *II Baron Balfour. See* 10667.

BALFOUR, *formerly* Arnot, Robert, *II Lord B. of Burleigh. See* 10667.

BALGAY, Nicholas, *D.D.* (Foster). Verse 4759.

BALL, *Sir* Peter, *Father of William.* ¶4945, 7165.

BALL, Thomas, *Divine* (*DNB*). With T. Goodwin edits 20218, 20226, 20231, 20270, perhaps 20239.

BALL, William, *Astronomer* (*DNB*). ¶4945, one issue 18343; *see also* next.

BALL *alias* BENNET, William, *Esq.* Verse 13316.

BALLANUS, Pet. Verse 17409.

BALLENDINUS *or* BALLENTINUS. *See* BELLENDEN.

BALLIOLUS, Jacobus. Verse 1404.

BALLOWE, William, *D.D.* (Foster). Epistle *20147; verse 11516.

BALMFORD, James, *Divine* (*DNB*). Epistle 11666.

BAMPFIELD, Hugh, *of North Cadbury.* 22990.

BANCROFT, John, *Bishop of Oxford.* *6420, 11567; epistle *25787 only, *25796; *see* 25327.

BANCROFT, Richard, *Archbishop of Canterbury.* Chronologically:
1591–8: 4167 later to Worcester, 12099, *23363.
1599: 1423, 3841, 23449; edits 14335 [cf. 14658].
1600–2: 1449, ¶25698 [see changes]; epistle 13597.
1603–4: ¶1822, 5222, 5882, *20574.
1605: 11575, 14023, ¶18174, *¶25682 (25685); epistle 20147, *1352a.
1606: 1827 (1826), 4644 later to Abbot, 10857 [the earlier edition], ¶13887, 14036 = 16449a, 16897, 23470.
1607: 5564, 5900, 14611 by editor, 15535, 17595, 19295, 21228, 25693.
1608: ¶5334 superseding Topcliffe, ¶7125, 11206, 15536, 20298, ¶25686 (25685).
1609: 3455 (3452), 7124, 18115, 24064, J. Freeman, *Apologie for ministers*-L.²; epistle 3858.
1610: 53, 4091, 4637, 12346 by editor, 14622 by editor.

BAND *alias* BROWNE, R. Edits 16759 as Band, later Browne.

BANDUS, Erricus. *See* HENRY BOND.

BANISTER, John, *Surgeon* (*DNB*). *723, 2779, 12499, *1594* protestant version of 16645-HD., ¶16909 by editor [see changes]; verse 1209; prose 5444; *see* 5447.

BANKES, *Sir* John, *Judge* (*DNB*). ¶13384 by bookseller superseding Yelverton, 20160, *22508.

BANKES, Richard, *Printer.* Privilege to, 2967.

BARBAROSSA, Richardus. *See* LICHFIELD.

BARBER, Barnarde, '*in Banbury*' [*? fiction*]. 1465.

BARBIER, John, *Parisiensis.* Edits 14467 only, 21773.

BARCLAY. *See also* BERKELEY.

BARCLAY, Alexander, *Poet* (*DNB*). Prose *1526* ed. 23182–DUL. [23181 not seen].

BARCLAY, David. Verse 4745, 14786, 21101.

BARCLAY, George. Verse 148.

BARCLAY, John, *Author* (*DNB*). Edits 1408; *see* 5097; *see* EUPHORMIO.

BARCLAY, Patrick, *of Towie, nephew of the author.* 1406.

BARCLAY, William, *Jurist, d. 1608* (*DNB*). See 1402 (1387).

BARCLAY, William, *Author* (*DNB*). Verse 11596 signed W. Bar.

BARD, George, *Vicar of Staines* (Venn 1584). Prose 19853.

BARFIELD, Lewis, *M.A.* (Foster). Verse 21029 (21032).

BARFORDE, William. Prose 18073.

BARGRAVE, Isaac, *Dean of Canterbury* (*DNB*). ★5410 by editor.

BARKER, Bestney, *of St. Giles* (*Vis. Essex*). 15249.

BARKER, Christopher, *Printer* (*DNB*). Signed prose 11643a [the earlier issue], 20203, 24328; unsigned 2878 (2146), 19341, 24050.

BARKER, John, *Mayor of Bristol.* ★18347.

BARKER, John. Verse 16944.

BARKER, Robert, *Printer* (*DNB*). Unsigned prose 11618, 14392, 14395.

BARKER, Robert, *Serjeant-at-law, Inner Temple.* 13506.

BARKER, Thomas, *Merchant adventurer* (PCC 1628). ¶16684.

BARKER, Sir Thomas, *Brother of John I Bt.* 1786.

BARKER, Walter, *Fellow of St. John's* (Venn). Verse 12188.

BARKER or BAKER, William, *of New College* (Foster 1622). Verse 5097.

BARKHAM, ——, 'Secretary to Hamburg merchants'. Minsheu List.

BARKHAM, Sir Edward, *Lord Mayor.* ★¶11346, ★14669, ★17744, ★17886, 17895, ★23345 superseding Bolles.

BARKHAM, George, *of St. John's* (Foster). Verse 6233.

BARKHAM, John, *Dean of Bocking* (*DNB*). 6233, 11633; edits 5975.

BARKHAM, Thomas. Verse 23041 and 23044.

BARKSDALE, Clement, *Author* (*DNB*). Edits 24046 initialed.

BARLAEUS, Casparus, *Poet* (*NBG*). Verse 22064, sometimes 22102, etc.

BARLAEUS (van Baerle), Melchior, *Author* (*NBG*). Verse 18601, 18602, 18603 as Rabilae (anagram).

BARLEY, ——, 'of Petworth'. 4910 by printer.

BARLEY, William, *Printer.* Prose 4910, 5876, 12925, 18418, ? 20867, 25409.

BARLOW (Lovell), Dorothy = John *of Slebech d. 1671.* 21102.

BARLOW, Francis. Epistle 4036–L. [earlier O. imperf.].

BARLOW, George, *Brother of Thomas* (Foster). Verse 1441a.

BARLOW, Ralph, *Archdeacon of Winchester* (Foster). Minsheu List.

BARLOW, Randolph, *Schoolmaster* (Venn). ★19293a; verse 3944, 13480.

BARLOW, R[ichard?], *Brother of next.* See 1441a.

BARLOW, Thomas, *Bishop of Lincoln.* Edits 21812.

BARLOW, Timothy, *Bookseller.* Minsheu List.

BARLOW, William, *Bishop of Chichester.* ★1710, ¶1710.

BARLOW, William, *Bookseller.* Same as Barley the printer.

BARLOW, William, *Bishop of Lincoln.* ¶3458, 4014, ¶6890, 14694.

BARLOW, William, *of Amsterdam.* Edits 3215.

BARNABY, Richard, *of Hill, Worcs., d. 1597.* See 3757.

BARNABY or BURNABY, Thomas, *of Watford, Northants.* 12253-L., 12300; verse 12224; *see also* BRABINE.

BARNARD. *See* BERNARD.

BARNARDISTON (Soame), Jane = *Sir* Nathaniel ★¶1477.

BARNARDISTON, Sir Nathaniel, *Puritan* (*DNB*). ★¶1477.

BARNES, Barnabe, *Poet* (*DNB*). ★12903; verse 12903 [cf. 18369], 11158; *see also* B. B.

BARNES, Bartholomew, *Alderman.* *1092 by editor.

BARNES (Manwood), Dorothy = *Sir* William (*Vis. Kent*). Epistle *3917 (25890).

BARNES, Edward, *Alderman.* *20756.

BARNE, *Sir* George, *the younger, Lord Mayor.* *11255, 14925, *15595, *20852 later to Buckle, *23326 [see changes].

BARNSUS, Ioannes [*one of those in* Venn]. Prose 23874.

BARNE, John, *Esq.* 15233 (15241).

BARNES, John, *Bookseller.* Prose 1196 (24617), 5857, 7319, 19201.

BARNES, Joseph, *Printer.* Prose 4759, 7600, 19019 issue-L., 19340, 21084; his press corrector, prose 5789.

BARNES, Richard. Verse 12895.

BARNES, Robert, *Son of Joseph* (Foster 1590). Edits 19046.

BARNES, William. Verse 23704.

BARNHAM, Benedict, *Alderman* (*DNB*). Plato, *Axiochus*, 1592-PFOR. by bookseller.

BARNHAM, *Sir* Francis, *Father of Robert I Bt.* *¶3463.

BARNAM, Tho. (? Venn 1564). Verse 25584, Medius part.

BARNEWALL (Talbot), Genet = Robert *VII* Baron Trimleston. 18745.

BARNWELL, Henry, '*of Terrington, Norf.*' 19517.

BARNEWALL, Robert, *VII Baron Trimleston.* See 10667.

BARRETT, Edward, *Grandfather of next.* 4036-L. [only part in impf. earlier O.].

BARRETT, Edward, *I Lord B. of Newburgh.* 5980, 5983 by editor, †7108, †7149, 12454, T. Tuke, *Treasure of true-loue, 1608*-F.; see 10667.

BARRETT (Lytton), Elizabeth = Edward. 17302.

BARRETT, William, *Bookseller.* Prose 13046, 22965, perhaps 13541; see 5811.

BARINGTON, Elizabeth. *See* Cato, *Precepts, 1638*-HN.

BARRINGTON, *Sir* Francis, *I Bt.* *¶1477, 7415 (7427), 13393 and *1607*-U. (13378), †26077 by editor; epistle *†25848 only.

BERINGTON, Humphrey, *Merchant, Aldermanbury.* *23307 by editor (23313).

BARRINGTON (Cromwell), Joan = *Sir* Francis *Bt.* *¶1477, *12873, 21169 (21173).

BARRINGTON, *Sir* Thomas, *Father of Sir Francis.* 25014.

BARRINGTON, *Sir* Thomas, *II Bt.* †14963; epistle *†25848 only.

BARROW, *Lady* (24371). *See* ABARROW.

BARROW, Henry, *Brownist* (*DNB*). Edits 5555; epistle *11868.

BARROW, Isaac (see *Vis. Camb.*). Verse 6206.

BARROW, Maurice, *of Barningham* (Venn). ¶17730.

BARROWES, William. *See* BURGH.

BARRY, David, *I Earl of Barrymore.* 1528, 7545; see 10667.

BARSTERDUS (21029). *See* BASTARD.

BARTIM, Joh., '*Theol.*' Verse 13939.

BARTLET, John, *Sr., Bookseller.* Prose 23836; epistle 12853 (12816).

BARTON, Edward, *Ambassador* (*DNB*). Prose 3846.

BARWELL, Edmund, *Master of Christ's* (Venn 1564). *19749 (19649); see 25695.

BARWICKE, Thomas, '*servant to Grindal*'. Verse 11224 only.

BARWOOD, W., *Gent.* Verse Patridophilus, *Preservative poem, 1636*-BO.[4]

BASFORD, George, *Master of Leathersellers.* 24687.

BASH, *Sir* Edward, *Chamberlain of Exchequer* (Venn 1608). 18947.

BASILLE, Theodore. Pseudonym of Thomas Becon.

BASKERVILLE, Hannibal, *Antiquary* (*DNB*). *See* 19511.

BASKERVILLE, *Sir* Humfrey, *of Eardisley* (Foster). Epistle †6332.

BASKERVILLE, *Sir* Simon, *Physician* (*DNB*). Prose 19302; see 14791.

BASKERVILLE, *Sir* Thomas, *General* (*DNB*). Prose 6551.

BASSETT, *Sir* Arthur, *Captain in Ireland.* *See* 23779.

BASSET (Peryam), Elizabeth = *Sir* Robert *of Umberleigh.* 22878 and *1610*-F.

BASSET, William, '*J.P. in Derby and Staffs.*' †10684.

BASSON, Thomas, *Leyden bookseller*. Verse 25340.

BASTARD, Thomas, *Satirist (DNB)*. Verse 5808, 5810 [cf. 23769], 21029 (21032).

BASTIAN, William, '*Studious in mathematics*'. Verse 17217.

BATE, John, *Mechanician (STC)*. Verse 1099.

BATE, Robert [*? of Derbys.*]. *21523.

BATES, Roger, *D.D.* (Foster). Minsheu List.

BATEMAN, Richard, *Fellow of Eton* (Venn 1598). *25129.

BATEMAN, Richard, *Alderman*. Epistle *25963.

BATEMAN, Robert, *Alderman and chamberlain of London*. Epistle 25182, *25963.

BATEMAN, Walter, *Mayor of Reading*. *23840.

BATHURST, Stephen, *Preacher* (Venn). *See* 13923.

BATMAN, Stephen, *Author (DNB)*. Prose 1538, 21181.

BATT, Anthony, *O.S.B. (DNB)*. *See* B. E. T.

BAUDIUS, Dominicus, *Poet (NBG)*. Verse 16650.

BAWTRY, Leonard, *Serjeant-at-law, Lincoln's Inn*. *11670.

BAYLEY, *etc. See* BAILEY.

BAINARD, George [*? of Wilts.*]. †¶25164.

BAYNARD (Stapleton), Ursula = *Sir Robert of Lackham*. *¶5769.

BAYNES, Roger, *Author (DNB)*. Epistle 24330; verse 24324, 24330.

BAYNHAM, Daniel. Verse 13260.

BAYNHAM, Joseph, *of Westbury* (Vis. Gloucs.). †11871 by bookseller.

BAYNAM, Thomas. 19424.

BAYNING (Glenham), Anne = Paul *I Viscount*. 25670.

BAYNING, Paul, *Alderman*. *20854 superseding Barne.

BAYNING, Paul, *II Viscount*. *See* 10667.

BAYNING (Naunton), Penelope = Paul *II Viscount*. 1652 = 19042.

BAYNTON, *Sir* Andrew, *Scholar (DNB)*. Prose 19166.

BAYNTON, *Sir* Henry, *of Bromham, Wilts*. †¶25164.

BEACON. *See* BECON *or* BACON.

BEALE, Bartholomew, *the elder, of Walton and Gray's Inn*. †¶13384 and *1634*-MICH. by bookseller superseding Lady Yelverton.

BEALE (St. Barbe), Edith = Robert. 19583 (19570) by editor.

BEALE, Francis [*allegedly Francis–DNB*]. *See* 14747.

BEALE, Jerome, *Vice-Chancellor of Cambridge* (Venn). Edits 4487.

BEALE, John, *Printer*. Prose 3588, 12126 (*Works, 1639*-N.), 13423 (13379, redirected 13384 and *1634*-MICH.), ¶13379 (as before), 23068–8a.

BEALE, Nicholas, *City captain*. *21095; epistle *1507.

BEALE, Robert, *Diplomatist (DNB)*. 18114, 25185.

BEALE, Robert, *Royalist divine (DNB)*. Verse 14269.

BEARD, Thomas, *Puritan divine (DNB)*. Prose 19129, 19130.

BEATON, James, *Archbishop of St. Andrews* (DNB). 3166, 3168.

BEAUCHAMP (Berkeley), Elizabeth = Richard *XII Earl of Warwick*. 3200.

BEAUFORT, Margaret, *Countess of Richmond* (DNB). 3124, 3547 by printer, 10902, 15793 by printer; *see* 10900, 14042, 15806a, 20195, 23955; *Lyf of saynt Ursula*-L.

BEAULIEU, James [*? alias John*], *French Secretary (CSPD)*. Minsheu List.

BEAUMONT, Francis, *Schoolmaster* (Venn 1565). Prose 5077.

BEAUMONT, Francis, *Dramatist (DNB)*. Verse 11068, 14751 from lost ed. of 14763, 14759 (14751), 14783 (14751); *see* F. B.

BEAUMONT, Francis, *S.J., son of John I Bt.* Verse 1694.

BEAUMONT, John, *B.D.* (Venn 1570). Verse 14608.

BEAUMONT, *Sir* John, *I Bt*. Verse 7189 (7216, 7218), 7209 (7210), 13800 [conceivably II Bt.]; prose 3220; *see* I. B.

BEAUMONT, *Sir* John, *II Bt*. Edits 1694; *see* I. B.

BEAUMONT, Joseph, *Poet* (DNB). Verse 12964.

BEAUMONT, Sapcote, *II Viscount*. *See* 10667.

BEAUMONT, Thomas, *I Viscount*, 19790.

BEAW, William, *Bishop of Llandaff*. Verse 3.

BECANUS, Martinus, *S.J.* (*NBG*). Epistle 24119; *see* 19205.

BECK, Abraham, *Dutch merchant in London*. Minsheu List.

BECKET, Leonard, *Bookseller*. Verse 1547.

BECON, Basil, Rachel *and* Theodore, *Children of next* (Venn). ¶1710.

BECON, Thomas, *Divine* (*DNB*). 4325; edits 1723 [cf. 4047 and see 1710] as Basille; verse 24368.

BEDLES, Francis *and* William, *Gent*. 86.

BEDELL, William, *Treasurer to Margaret Beaufort*. *See* 22608.

BEDELL, William, *Bishop of Kilmore* (*DNB*). Epistle *18805; *see* 12662 (12706, 12635).

BEDINGFIELD, Sir Henry, *Father of Henry I Bt.* †¶21869, 25768.

BEDINGFIELD, Thomas, *Gentleman pensioner* (*DNB*). *¶6402-F. only; prose 3220.

BEDWELL, William, *Arabic scholar* (*DNB*). Edits 19925; *see* 17944.

BEECHER (St. John), Elizabeth = *Sir* William (*Vis. Beds.*). *¶6890.

BEECHING, John, *M.A.* (Venn). *See* 13923.

BEEDOME, Thomas, *Poet* (*DNB*). Verse 10694, 21094.

BEESLEY, Henry, *D.D.* (Foster). Verse 10935.

BEESTON, Christopher, *Actor*. Verse 13309; *see* 13327.

BEESTON, Sir Hugh *or* Hukin, *of Ches*. *7293.

BEESTON, William, 'Brewer', *alias* 'Apis Lapis'. 1584, 18377.

BEESTON, William, *Actor*. *See* 13327.

BEKE *or* BEAKE, Robert. Verse 25090.

BELLASIS, Sir Henry, *I Bt.* 15329 (17396 and *1625*-N.).

BELASYSE, Thomas, *I Viscount Fauconberg*. ¶3586; *see* 10667.

BELLASSES, William. 17874.

BELASYSE, Sir William, *of Morton House, d. 1641*. 4646 (4647).

BELBI, Francesco. Verse 3074 [not in Venice ed.].

BELCHIER, William, *Father of Daubridgcourt-DNB*. Verse 12500.

BELL, David. Verse 19150 only.

BELL, Francis, *O.F.M.* (*DNB*). Edits 1802, 19167.

BELL, John, *Dean of Ely* (Venn 1548). *See* 25695.

BELL, John, 'Master of Ratcliff School [Stepney]' (? Venn 1564). Verse 164.

BELL, John, Sr., *Rector of Glasgow University*. Verse 3447; *see* 3449.

BELL, Sir Robert, *of Norf.* (Venn 1606). Epistle 15037.

BELL, Robert, *of Wimbledon, merchant* (Brown). *11651 (11679, 11652).

BELL, Thomas, *Controversialist* (*DNB*). *See* 19403.

BELLAMY, John, *Bookseller*. *See* I. B. (20286).

BELLAND, Edmund, *Prior of Austin Friars, London* (Venn). Prose G. Petrus, *Opus sane*, 1524-O.⁹

BELLARMINE, Robert, *Saint*. Epistle 12055, 12060.

BELLASIS, Belosses, Belussis. *See* BELASYSE.

BELLEFOREST, François de, *Author* (*NBG*). Verse 3166.

BELLENDEN, Adam, *Bishop of Aberdeen*. 15359-A.; *see* 10667.

BELLENDEN (Ker), Elizabeth = *Sir* James, *Mother of I Lord B.* ¶5943 (5909).

BELLENDEN, Thomas [*probably* Bannatyne, *Minister of Douglas*]. Verse 21101.

BELLENDEN, Walter. Verse 14929, 15312, 19781, 23070.

BELLINGHAM (Backhouse), Elizabeth = Richard (*Vis. Berks.*). *¶23854.

BELLINGHAM, Sir Henry, *I Bt. See* I. B. *de L.*

BELLINGHAM, Sir James, *Father of preceding*. *15342; *see* I. B. *de L.*

BELLINGHAM, Thomas, *of Newtimber, d. 1649*. *17642.

BELLINGS, Richard, *Historian* (*DNB*). Verse 22454.

BELLOMAYUS, Joannes, *Valesius, Grammarian*. Edits 10082, 23148a, 23160 and *1526*-M., 25469, 25564 [all for Worde].

BELLOT, Jacques, *of Caen, resident in London* (STC). Verse 6735, *1596*-Y. only of 6749.

BELUSSIS. *See* BELASYSE.

BELWOOD, Mark, *Physician* (CSPD). Verse 13191.

BENEDETTI, Pietro, *Italian at Antwerp* (BM). Verse Vaenius, *Emblemata, 1608*-F.

BENEDICTUS, Samuel, *of Sidney Sussex* (Venn). Verse 7294.

BENEFIELD, Richard, *of Gray's Inn.* Verse 20692.

BENEFIELD, Sebastian, *Divine* (DNB). *1938; see 25327.

BENEVOLUS. Anagram of Benlowes.

BENLOIS, Ed., '*of London*' [? Benleys PCC 1590]. T. Wilcox, *Christian exposition, 1587*-F (25620).

BENLOWES, Edward, *Poet* (DNB). 7235, ¶11082 [and plates in some copies], 11084 (11054), 20540; verse 11082, 11769 and 11782, 20540, 20548 (20542), 22509, 22533, 25025.

BENLOWES, William, *Brother of Edward.* Verse 11082.

BENN, *Sir* Anthony, *Recorder of London* (Foster). *23332 superseding Montagu, *23344 later to Littleton.

BENNET, ——, '*Captain, Yarmouth militia*'. *21093.

BENNETT, [David, *Under-*]keeper, St. James's Palace* (CSPD 1625). Minsheu List.

BENNET (Crofts), Dorothea = *Sir* John *the younger.* Epistle 19909.

BENNETT, Edward, *Merchant and shipowner* (STC). *11131, *25843.

BENNET, Henry, *of Calais* (DNB). Verse 11420.

BENNET, Henry, *I Earl of Arlington.* Verse 14959.

BENNET, *Sir* John, *Civilian* (DNB). ¶1822, *5977, *19699 (19649) by editor; Minsheu List.

BENNET (Vierendeels), Leonora = *Sir* John. *20675 (20668) by editor.

BENNET, Matthew, *Clergyman* (Foster 1599). Verse 11544.

BENNET, Robert, *Bishop of Hereford.* ¶13841,

15136; prose 14608; possibly the bishop in Minsheu List.

BENNETT, *Sir* Thomas, *Lord Mayor.* *5062, *12750, *12863, 13703, 17257, *17886, *20756, *23329 superseding Saltonstall.

BENNETT, Thomas, *Alderman, nephew to preceding.* *20756.

BENNET, W., '*Anglo-Britan.*' Verse 12488.

BENSON, John, *Bookseller.* Prose 13798, 14771, 22344.

BENTHAM, Thomas, *Bishop of Lichfield.* *1710, 4066.

BERAUD, P., R. [? Pierre, BM]. Verse 21139.

BERCULA *and* BERINGTON. *See* BERTHELET *and* BARRINGTON.

BERKELEY. *See also* BARCLAY.

BERKELEY Family. *See* 6270.

BERKELEY, Elizabeth (3200). *See* BEAUCHAMP.

BARKLEI, Elisabetta. Epistle 92.

BERKELEY (Killigrew), Elizabeth = *Sir* Maurice (*Vis. Soms.*). *1616*-O. of *1965 only [earlier lost].

BERKELEY (Nevill), Elizabeth = *Sir* Henry (*Vis. Soms.*). *1965 and *1616*-O.

BERKELEY (Carey), Elizabeth = *Sir* Thomas, *later* Chamberlain. *4497, 10513, 18379; see 4510.

BERKELEY (Stanhope), Elizabeth = George *VIII Baron.* 24988; Minsheu List.

BERKELEY, Frances (15469). *See* SHIRLEY.

BERKELEY, George, *VIII Baron.* 4159, *¶4497, ¶7373 and 7375, 17641, 22463, 23124, *†24928, 24987, 25176; see 10667, 17332; Minsheu List.

BERKELEY, Gilbert, *Bishop of Bath and Wells.* *1710, 15256, 18663, 21064, B. Traheron, *Aunswere to papiste, 1558*-L.[2]

BERKELEY, *Sir* Henry, *Bt.* Minsheu List.

BERKELEY (Stanhope), Jane = Henry *VII Baron.* 11576, 11581, 11582.

BERKELEY, Joan, *O.S.B., abbess.* ¶*1611*-HD. of 3369 only by editor, 6802 = 19815, 19940.

BERKELEY, Mary (15469). *See* ZOUCH.

BERKELEY, Maurice, *of Christ Church* (Foster 1632). Verse 5097.

BERKELEY, *Sir* Robert, *Judge* (DNB). *24297; see 10667.

BERKELEY, Thomas, *V Baron. See* 1536, 13438.

BERLICOMIUS, Balduinus, *Dutch poet* (Jöcher). Verse 21657.

BERMINGHAM, Richard, *XI Baron Athenry. See* 10667.

BARNARD, Edward, *of Downside* (*Vis. Soms.*). R. Bernard, *Staffe of comfort, 1616*-F.

BERNARDUS, Jacobus, *Londoniensis* [*see* BAR-NARDE, PCC 1540]. 699 by editor.

BERNARD, James, *of Trinity College* (Venn 1625). Verse 25436.

BARNARD, John, *Brother of Edward*. R. Bernard, *Staffe of comfort, 1616*-F.

BERNARD, Jos. Verse 1578.

BERNARD, Richard, *Puritan divine* (*DNB*). *See* 21109, 22877.

BERNARD, Samuel, *Master of Magdalen School* (Foster 1607). *See* 25327.

BERNARD, Thomas, *Divine* (*DNB*). Edits 1924.

BARNARD, William, *Warden of Drapers. See* 18600.

BERNEY, Thomas, *of Gray's Inn* [*more than one*]. 20491.

BERNHER, Augustine, *Minister* (*DNB*). Edits 15284 (15276, 15277).

BERNHERE, Thomas, *Separatist preacher* (Venn). Epistle 10668.

BERRIDGE, John, *Precentor of Lincoln* (Venn 1586). *¶5359.

BERRIER, Stephen, *Prebendary of Wells* (Venn). Verse 24604, 24609.

BERRY, Dorothy. Verse 20388.

BERRY (Jacobs), Mary = George *of Cranfield, sister of John I Bt.* *15333.

BERRY, Robert, *Alderman of Chester*. *¶23720.

BERTHELET, Thomas, *Printer*. Verse 5718, 10464, 11005; signed prose 5639, 11008 [initialed 11014], 25570, G. Petrus, *Opus sane, 1524*-O.9; unsigned prose 4690 (14876), 4891, 7713 (14873), 9271, 9301, 9562, 12143, 12436, 15217, 26069; *see* 5734.

BERTIE Family. *17361.

BERTIE, Catharine, *Duchess* (*DNB*). *See* BRANDON.

BERTIE, *Lady* Elizabeth. *See* STAPLETON.

BERTUS, Franciscus. Verse 13472.

BERTIE, Francis, *Son of Robert I Earl.* *5363 (5355).

BERTIE, Montagu, *II Earl of Lindsey. See* 10667.

BERTIE, Peregrine, *XI Baron Willoughby.* 3845 (3887), 10547, 18755, 22855; epistle 16696; *see* R. B., *Mirrour to warres, 1589*-L.

BERTIE, *Sir* Peregrine, *Son of Robert I Earl.* *5363 (5355).

BERTIE, Richard, *Marian exile* (*DNB*). 19809.

BERTIE, Robert, *I Earl of Lindsey.* *¶4497, 6103 by editor, 7329, 10549, 11690, ¶16887 cancelled, *22796, 23592; *see* 10667, 17332.

BERTIE, Robert *and* Vere, *Sons of preceding.* *5363 (5355).

BERTRAM, Bonaventure-Corneille, *Hebraist* (*NBG*). Hebrew verse 2032 = 2357 [from foreign ed.].

BERTUS. *See* BERTIE.

BEST, ——, 'Schoolmaster in London'. Minsheu List.

BEST, Arthur, *M.A.* (Venn), *signed* ΑΡΚΤΟΥΡ. ὁ ΛΩΣΤΟΣ. Verse 22174, 22177.

BEST, Charles, *Poet* (*DNB*). Verse 15434, 20339.

BEST, George, *Grocer* (*Vis. London*). Minsheu List (spelt Besse).

BEST, John, *Bishop of Carlisle.* *1710.

BETON, William, *Surgeon at Bart's.* Edits *24713 (24706).

BETTES, John, *Gent.* Verse 20998.

BETTS, Richard, *D.D.* (Venn). Verse 19299.

BEVERLEY, Peter, *of Staple Inn* (*STC*, ? Venn). Verse 10791.

BEVERLEY, William, *of Willingham Cherry* (Venn). Epistle 5355; verse 5355.

BEVILL, *Sir* Robert, *the elder, of Chesterton* *Fens map in 17827.

BEVIS, Peter, *of Middle Temple* (Foster). Verse 17526, 17530; *see* P. B.

BEWE, William (3). *See* BEAW.

BEWLEY, Thomas, *Alderman.* W. Freake, *Priuiledges of vpright, 1639*-F.

BEZA, Theodorus, *Reformer* (*NBG*). Verse 3990, 4414, 18776, 21656 (21649), Gregory XIII, *Oration, 1585*-HN.; prose 21285

BLAGGE (North), Mary = Thomas, *Sister of Henry I Bt.* *5657.

BLAIKLOCK, Lawrence, *Bookseller.* Prose 1665.

BLAKE, Edward. Verse 21640.

BLAN., G. [*presumably* W. Blandie]. Verse 25671.

BLANCHARD, M., '*Médecin*'. Verse 21139.

BLAND, *Sir* Thomas, *Father of Thomas I Bt.* *17638.

BLANDIE, William, *Author* (*DNB*). See BLAN.

BLANKE, *Sir* Thomas, *Lord Mayor.* *10607; verse 1573 ed. 19426-HN.

BLANCKS, William, *of Caius College* (Venn). Verse 7365.

BLAXTON, Henry, *of Clare Hall* (Venn 1561). See 13923.

BLAYNEY, Edward, *I Baron Blayney.* See 23779.

BLAYNEY, Henry, *II Baron Blayney.* See 10667.

BLECHINDEN, Thomas, *Fellow of St. John's* (Venn 1609). *5410 by editor; prose 22230.

BLENCOWE, Anthony, *Provost of Oriel* (Foster). *6420, *6422, *6426.

BLENCOWE, John, *of Gray's Inn* (Foster 1607). See 23779.

BLENCOW (Walleston), Mary = John (Foster 1591). *13471.

BLENNERHAISET, Jane. See 22610 (22608).

BLENERHASSET (——), Mabel = Thomas *of Cumberland.* *14896.

BLEVERHASSET, Ralph [*of Norf.*]. Epistle 15037.

BLENERHAISET, William, *Esq.* 25010 by editor.

BLEVERHASSET. See BLENERHASSET.

BLOMER, *Sir* Henry, *of Hatherop* (Foster). 22638.

BLOMFIELD, Simon, *of Emmanuel College* (Venn). Verse 7294.

BLOOTHER. See BLUDDER.

BLOUNT (Boteler), Anne = Mountjoy *I Earl.* Epistle *15465.

BLOUNT, Charles, *V Baron Mountjoy.* Epistle *19166 by A. Baynton.

BLOUNT, Charles, *Earl of Devonshire.* 1111, 1559, 3081, 3660-HOUGHTON, 6261 only, 7276, 7374, 10650, 12216 [earlier lost], 12414 by editor, 13695, 17385, 18364, 18895, 19974,

*20339, 21031, 21311, ¶21661 and further fragment-F. (21649), 24131 later to Montagu, 25610, *¶25682 only; epistle *6165, 6333, 16696; see 24638.

BLOUNT, *Sir* Charles, *of Mapledurham.* *23099.

BLOUNT, Edward, *Bookseller* (*DNB*). 17415 only by editor; signed prose 288, 3957, 4917, 6200, 7274, 7439, 11634, 14831, 17088, 17413; unsigned and uncertain 13541; see 5811.

BLOUNT, *Sir* Henry, *of Gray's Inn* (*DNB*). *11163; verse 352, 6307.

BLOUNT, James, *VI Baron Mountjoy.* ¶1881, 10880 by editor, 24685.

BLOUNT, *Sir* Michael, *of Mapledurham, Lieutenant of Tower.* ¶5220.

BLOUNT, Mountjoy, *I Earl of Newport.* ¶1099, *¶4497, *¶6072, *¶13264, *21092 and 1637-O.[11], *24928; see 10667; Minsheu List.

BLOUNT (Devereux), Penelope. See RICH.

BLOUNT, Pope. See THOMAS POPE BLOUNT.

BLOUNT, Richard, *Esq.* N. Breton, *Historie of Frederigo,* 1590-O.[5]

BLUNT, Richard, *Esq.,* 'of Dedsham, Sussex'. Epistle *24125.

BLOUNT, *Sir* Richard, *of Mapledurham.* 1474; see 4588, J. Bowle, *Sermon at Mapple-Durham,* 1616-O.

BLOUNT, *Sir* Thomas Pope (Foster 1574). 3666, *25282.

BLOUNT, William, *IV Baron Mountjoy.* 193 (24849).

BLOWER, Ralph, *Printer.* Signed prose 11040, 23606; unsigned 17844.

BLUDDER, *Sir* Thomas, *the elder, of Reigate.* *¶12317; see 23725 [not 23779].

BLUDWORTH, John, *Vintner* (*Vis. London*). *5533.

BLUETT, William, *of University College* (Foster). Verse 18777.

BLUNDEN, Humphrey, *Bookseller.* Unsigned prose 6315, 25870 [and signed ded. in some copies].

BLUNDESTON, Laurence, *of Gray's Inn* (? Venn as Blunston). Verse 12048.

BOARDMAN, Andrew, *Divine* (*DNB*). Verse 6843.

BODENHAM, John, *Anthology publisher* (*DNB*). 381, 3189, 3191, 15685, all by editors.

BODENHAM, *Sir* Thomas (*1608* of 15687-BRISTOL). Error for John.

BODENHAM, Thomas, *Son of Sir Roger.* Epistle 6332.

BODINUS, Tho. Verse 12488.

BODLEY, Christopher, *Clergyman* (*Vis. Devon*). Verse 374.

BODLEY, Laurence, *Canon of Exeter* (*DNB*). 20352 (20351, 20345).

BODLEY, Miles, *Brother of Sir Thomas.* Verse 4427.

BODLEY, *Sir* Thomas, *Diplomatist* (*DNB*). 959 by editor, 16698, 19048; epistle 736.

BODVEL, *Sir* John, *of Bodvel, Carnarvon.* *25716 (25718).

BOINE, *Laird of* (1406). *See* JAMES OGILVY.

BOIS. *See* BOYS.

BOISCOT, Ferdinand de, *Ambassador from Austria.* *4494.

BOLD, William, *Porter of Tower and of 'Academ Roial'.* Verse 688.

BOLEYN, Thomas, *Earl of Wiltshire.* 10504 (10505), 24943.

BOLIUS, Io., '*V.D. Administrer*' [? Boyle, *q.v.*]. Verse 25737.

BOLLES, *Sir* George, *Lord Mayor.* *17886, 17899, *23332 [see changes], *23344 [see changes].

BOLTON, Edmund, *Poet* (*DNB*). Edits *Tricorones, 1607*-F.; verse 4507 (4509), 14783 (14751); *see* E. B.

BOLTON, *Sir* Richard, *Lawyer* (*DNB*). Edits 14130.

BOMELIUS, Eliseus, *Physician* (*DNB*). Verse 1710.

BOMELIUS, Henricus, *German preacher* (*see* preceding). Verse 1295.

BONDE, *Sir* George, *Lord Mayor.* 981.

BOND, Henry, *of Cornwall* (Foster 1595). *See* 10934.

BOND, John, *Physician* (*DNB*). Edits 13790a.

BOND, John, *Secretary to Ellesmere. See* 5811.

BOND, Martin, *Merchant* (*DNB*). *1636* iss. *14538-C.², superseding Campbell [in 11346], *21095, W. Freake, *Esras pulpit, 1639*-F.; epistle *1507.

BOND, Nicholas, *President of Magdalen* (*DNB*). *4012, 21733, 21736.

BONHAM, Edward, *Son of William.* Verse 11772.

BONHAM, John [*Kin of preceding*]. Verse 11772.

BONHAM, Thomas, *Physician* (*DNB*). *21594; epistle *24124; verse 5446, *1622* ed. 11122-C.⁶

BONHAM, Thomas, *Fellow of King's* (Venn 1622). Verse 11772, 11780 (11773).

BONHAM, William, *London vintner* (*Vis. Essex*). *†11772.

BONIAN, Richard, *Bookseller.* Unsigned prose 22332.

BONNER, Edmund, *Bishop of London.* 19786, 21678, Ambrose, *Prayer, 1555*-F.; supervises 5990, 12795; prose 11585, 21678, Boxall, *Oratio, 1555*-C.⁷; see 11593.

BONNER, Henry, '*London schoolmaster*'. *See* 25737.

BONNER, Humphrey, *Alderman of Nottingham.* *24596.

BONTIUS (Bondt), Gulielmus, *Leyden lawyer* (Schotel). *See* 22176.

BOOKER, John, *Astrologer* (*DNB*). Edits 20743.

BOOTH, *Sir* George, *I Bt.* *7293.

BOOTH, John, *of Corpus Christi* (Venn 1621). Verse 7365, 11464.

BOOTH, Richard, '*Citizen of London*'. Edits 10882; Minsheu List.

BOOTH, Robert, *of St. John's* (Venn 1565). Presentation 6843; verse 6839, 6843.

BOOTH (Egerton), Vere = William. Epistle 6332.

BOOTH, William, *Son of Sir George.* 20862.

BOOTHBY, Thomas, *of St. Antholin, London.* Epistle *12203.

BORASTON, William, *Shropshire physician* (*STC*). Edits 24712.

BORBONIUS, Nicolas, *Poet* (*NBG*). Verse 3045.

BORGARUCCI, Giulio, *Physician* (*DNB*). Verse 4782; prose 1359.

BURLACY, Alexander, *Esq.* Verse 13509.

BORLACE (Litton), Anne = John, *Mother of next.* *4692.

BORLACE, *Sir* William, *the elder* (Foster 1581). *†4692, *4695.

BOROUGH. *See* BURGH.

BORRON, Ro., '*Nephew of author*'. *See* 25438.

BORROWELL. *See* BURRELL.

BORTHWICK, John, *X Lord Borthwick*. *See* 10667.

BOSTOCKE, ——, '*Lecturer*'. Minsheu List.

BOSTOCK, Richard, *of Inner Temple* (Venn). *See* 4997.

BOSTON, William, *M.A.* (Venn 1569). Verse 1846; *see* G. B.

BOSVILE, *Sir* Ralph, *of Bradbourne, Kent, militia officer*. T. Morley, *First book of ayres, 1600*-F.; epistle 1506; verse 1507 early state.

BOSWELL, William, *Vicar* (Foster 1597). *See* 23920, 23923.

BOSWELL, *Sir* William, *Diplomatist* (DNB). Verse 21069.

BOTELER. *See* BUTLER.

BOTHWELL, John, *II Lord Holyroodhouse*. *See* 10667.

BOTREVICUS. *See* BUTTERWIKE.

BOUDOWINS, ——, *D.C.L.*, '*Dutchman*'. Minsheu List.

BOULENGIER, Giles, *Huguenot bookseller* (Alien Returns). Prose J. de Beauchesne, *Clef de l'escriture*-N.

BOUMAN, Maximiliane, '*Dordrecht surgeon*'. Prose 12498.

BOUND. *See* BOWNDE.

BOURCHIER, Arthur, *Ballad writer* (STC as Bour). Verse 25438.

BOURCHIER (St. John), Dorothy = Edward *IV Earl*. *★¶*4497.

BOURCHIER, Edward, *IV Earl of Bath*. *See* 10667, 17331; Minsheu List.

BOURCHIER, William, '*Lord Bourchier*', *d. 1483*. 4853.

BOURCHIER, William, *III Earl of Bath*. 563, ¶10535, ¶10539, 23471.

BOURKE, Edmund, *IV Baron B. of Castle Connell*. *See* 10667.

BOURKE (Walsingham), Frances, *Countess*. *See* DEVEREUX.

BOURKE, Miles, *II Viscount Mayo*. *See* 10667.

BOURKE, Richard, *IV Earl of Clanricarde*. 11524, *★*17699; epistle 6333; *see* 10667.

BOURKE, Theobald, *I Baron B. of Brittas*. *See* 10667.

BOURKE, Thomas, *II Viscount B. of Clanmories*. *See* 10667.

BOURNE, Francis, *of Doddington* (*Vis. Kent*). *★*11127.

BOURNE, *Sir* John, *Secretary of State*. 5581.

BOURNE, Nicholas, *Bookseller*. Perhaps unsigned prose 11783, 13528, 18883, 23009.

BOURN, Reuben, '*olim Cantab.*' Verse 13554, 13555.

BOVEY, BOWY. *See* BUY.

BOWDLER, Tamberlaine, *of Gray's Inn* (Foster). Verse 3.

BOWEN, John, *Bookseller*. Prose P. Galloway, *Catechisme, 1588*-E.[2]

BOWES (Musgrave), Eleanor = Robert. *★*14320; epistle 16696.

BOWES (Aske), Elizabeth = Richard *of Norham Castle*. 15072 and earlier-G.

BOWES, *Lady* Isabel. *See* DARCY.

BOWES, *Sir* Jerome, *Ambassador* (DNB). 6758, 11579.

BOWES, *Sir* Martin, *Lord Mayor*. 20970 by bookseller.

BOWES, Robert, *Ambassador* (DNB). Epistle 16696.

BOWES, *Sir* Thomas, *of Much Bromley* (*Vis. Essex*). Epistle, *see* next.

BOWES, Thomas, *the younger* (Venn 1646). Cato, *Precepts, 1638*-HN.

BOWES, *Sir* William, *Ambassador, d. 1611*. 19736 and *1597*-F. (19646).

BOWLES, Anne, *Gentlewoman*. *★¶*12315 by editor.

BOWLES (Wentworth), Diana = Lewis *of Herts*. *★¶*110.

BOWLE, John, *Bishop of Rochester*. *★*11772; *see* 10667.

BOWMAN, Francis, *Oxford bookseller*. Prose 12455.

BOWMAN, John, *Chancellor of St. Paul's* (Foster). Verse 4012, 18985 and *1606*-HD.

BOWMAN, Nathaniel, *of Suff.* (Venn). *★*3926 misprinted Bownannus.

BOWNDE, Alexander, *Brother of next*. Verse 3437.

BOWNDE, Nicholas, *Divine* (*DNB*). Edits 18074 and *Three sermons, 1594*-PN.[2]; verse 1492.

BOWNDE, Richard, *Brother* (Venn). Prose 3439 [date problem].

BOWNELL, Thomas. See 1655.

BOWYER, *Sir* Edmund, *the elder, of Camberwell* (*Vis. Surrey*). *12916 reissued *Three sermons, 1599*-LINC., †¶12917, 24913.

BOYER, Edmund, *Esq.* Verse 13988.

BOWYER, *Sir* Henry, *of Cuckfield* (*Vis. Sussex*). *11367.

BOWYER, John, *Brother of Sir Edmund.* *12916 as above.

BOWYER, Michael, *Actor.* *6314.

BOWYER, Nicholas. Verse 11645 (11638), 25348.

BOWYER, Robert, *Uncle of William I Bt.* *23099.

BOWYER, *Sir* William, *of Staffs.* (Keeler). *†21437.

BOWYER, William, '*Soldier*'. Prose 24910.

BOYD, Alexander [see *Delit. poetarum Scot.*]. Verse 15713.

BOYD, Andrew, *Bishop of Argyle.* 3444; see 10667.

BOYD (Fleming), Anne, *Lady. See* RAMSAY.

BOYD (Hamilton), Christian = Robert *VII* Lord. See 3446a.

BOYD, Robert, *VIII Lord Boyd.* See 10667.

BOYLE (Feilding), Elizabeth, *Countess of Guildford.* Epistle *15465.

BOYLE, John, *Minister of Eckford.* See BOLIUS.

BOYLE, Lewis, *I Viscount Boyle.* See 10667.

BOYLE, Richard, *I Earl of Cork.* 5461, *7114, 7265, 14510; see 10667.

BOYLE, Richard, *I Earl of Burlington.* †20501.

BOYLE, Roger, *I Earl of Orrery.* See 10667.

BOYNTON, *Sir* Matthew, *I Bt.* 6196.

BOYS, *Lady* [*probably* Jane *below*]. 20682 by editor.

BOYS, *Sir* Edward, *the elder, of Nonington* (*Vis. Kent*). *†24966.

BOYS, *Sir* Edward, *the younger.* *†24966.

BOYS (Walker), Jane = *Sir* John *Recorder.*

DuMoulin, *Preparation vnto fasting, 1620*-F.; see LADY BOYS.

BOYSE, John, *Esq.* [*? the next*]. 7296 = 2990.

BOYS, *Sir* John, *Recorder of Canterbury.* ¶3458 (3452), *†24966.

BOYS, John, *Dean of Canterbury* (*DNB*). *22398, 25109.

BOIS, John, *Bible translator* (*DNB*). ¶6192; helps edit 14629; verse 6839; prose 11326.

BRABAZON, William, *I Earl of Meath.* See 10667.

BRABINE, Thomas, *Gent.* [*sometimes thought anagram of* Barnaby]. Verse 12272.

BRACEGIRDLE, John, *Poet* (*DNB*). Verse 24127.

BRACKLEY, Thomas, *M.A.* (Venn). Verse 13247.

BRADBRIDGE, William, *Bishop of Exeter.* 4074, 18665 and *1571*-F., Bullinger, *Exhortation to ministers, 1575*-D.

BRADDYLL, Ralph, *Principal of St. Mary Hall* (Foster). *6420.

BRADLEY, Alex. Verse 14321.

BRADLEY, George, *Warden of Louth, d. 1663.* Verse 3997.

BRADLEY, John, *City captain.* *21095; epistle *1507.

BRADSHAW, Alexander, *Brother of Thomas-DNB.* Edits 3508.

BRADSHAIGH (Norris), Anne = James *of Haigh.* *19168 by bookseller.

BRADSHAW, Francis, *Fellow o, Magdalen* (Foster 1579). Minsheu List.

BRADSHAW, John, *Windsor Herald.* Verse 13260, 24756.

BRADSHAW, John, *Son of William-DNB.* Edits W. Bradshaw, *Discourse of Sinne, 1640*-U.

BRADWELL or BREDWELL, Stephen, *Clerkenwell physician* (*STC*, Munk). Verse 13316, 17921, 21011; prose 11750.

BRADWOOD, Melchisidec, *Printer.* Unsigned prose 6164.

BRAHAM, Robert, *Editor* (*DNB*). Edits 5580.

BRAHE, Steen, *Politician, brother of Tycho.* *¶6217.

BRAMSTON, Edmund, '*Pupil of J. Gower M.A.*' Verse 12141.

BRAMSTON, *Sir* John, *the elder*, *Judge* (*DNB*). ★10667, ★24297.

BRAMSTON, William (Venn 1639). Verse 12141.

BRANCH (Nicolson), Helen = *Sir* John. *See* 23579 (21654) and two pamphlets-HN.

BRANDON (Willoughby), Catharine = Charles *Duke*, later Bertie. 2045, 4450, 5276, 10429, 15271 and earlier-L. (15276) by editor, 15284 (15276, 15277) by editor, 19870; epistle 25816; arms in 2791a, 2853, 15291, 24441a, 24784; *see* 4827.

BRANDON, Charles, *Duke of Suffolk*. Epistle Whittinton, *Epigrammata, 1519*-HN.

BRANTHWAITE. *See* BRATHWAITE.

BRANTINGHAM, Elias, *of Gray's Inn*. Verse 841.

BRASEBRIDGE, Rowland, *of Chepping Wycombe* (PCC 1585). 11990.

BRASBRIDGE, Thomas, *Divine* (*DNB*). ★16860.

BRATHWAITE (Lawson), Frances = Richard. 3553; *see* 3554, 3567.

BRATHWAITE, Richard, *Poet* (*DNB*). 18346 (18337); verse 22796, 23205, 24756, 26103.

BRATHWAITE, Richard, *five sisters of*. ¶3586; epistle Brathwaite, *Good wife, 1618*-O. (12747.)

BRANTHWAITE, Robert, 'Gaoler at the Tower'. 23752; verse 23779 (23725), 23791 (23725), 23806 (23725).

BRATHWAITE, Thomas, *Brother of Richard*. ¶3568.

BRANTHWAITE, William, *Master of Caius* (*DNB*). ★13877; *see* 635; Minsheu List.

BRANTHWAITE, William, *Cant*. Verse 23806 (23725).

BRAYTHWAYT, William, *London clergyman* (Venn 1595). Edits 24715.

BRAY, Edmund, *the elder*, *of Barrington, Gloucs*. 4699.

BRAY, William, *Divine* (*DNB*). *See* 23066; book licenser, *1632–40*.

BRECKMAN, Abraham, 'Middelburg merchant'. ¶5346.

BREDWELL. *See* BRADWELL.

BREET, Mercy. ★¶25795.

BREIFILDE, Io. Verse 936.

BREMER, William, 'Physician'. Edits 24707.

BRENT, *Sir* Nathaniel, *Warden of Merton* (*DNB*). †5454, 7072, 21350; edits 17598, 19048; *see* 25327; Minsheu List.

BRENT, William. 18924.

BRERELEY, John. Pseudonym of Lawrence Anderton.

BRERETON, John, *Mayor of Chester*. ★¶23720.

BRERETON, Richard, *of Wettenhall* (*Vis. Ches.*). ★7293.

BRERETON, William, *II Baron B*. *See* 10667.

BREREWOOD, Edward, *Antiquary* (*DNB*). *See* 4238.

BREREWOOD, *Sir* Robert, *Judge* (*DNB*). Edits 3612, 3618.

BRETNOR, Thomas, *Physician* (*DNB*). Verse 20187, 23779; *see* 5584.

BRETON (Legh), Anne = Nicholas *of Little Catthorpe, Leics*. 3673.

BRETTON, Clement, *D.D.* (Venn 1619). Verse 11464.

BRETON, Nicholas, *Poet* (*DNB*). Verse 10513, 10596, 23791 (23725), engr. portrait Countess of Bedford-L.

BRETTON, William, *Bookseller*. 4115.

BRETT, *Sir* John, *of Edmonton* (*Vis. Mdsx.*). 23434 by stationer.

BRETTARGH, William, *Husband of Katharine*-DNB. Prose 12866 [earlier lost].

BREWER, Thomas, *Author* (*DNB*). Verse 1547, 13316, 17921, 23806 (23725), 25227.

BREWS (Scrope), Jane = Thomas. *See* 22594 (22608).

BREWSTER, John, *Esq*. ¶1029 by editor.

BREWSTER, John, *Mayor of Gloucester 1632*. ★12171.

BREWSTER, William, *Colonist* (*DNB*). Unsigned prose 4709.

BRIAN. *See* BRYAN.

BRICKET, John, *Master Cook at Eltham* (Hasted). 12631, 12634.

BRIDEOAKE, Ralph, *Bishop of Chichester*. Verse 20694.

BRIDGEMAN, John, *Bishop of Chester*. ¶13380 by bookseller, 14038, ¶23720; *see* 10667.

BRIDGEMAN, *Sir* Orlando, *Lord Keeper* (*DNB*). I. Ambrose, ¶*Prima & ultima, 1640*-F.

BRIDGES. *See* BRYDGES.

BRIGGS, Henry, *Mathematician* (*DNB*). Edits 18351; prose 12613; *see* 5584, 25327; Minsheu List.

BRIGGS, Sampson, *M.A.* (Venn). Verse 3.

BRIGHTWELL, Richard. Pseudonym of John Frith.

BRINSLEY (Hall), Barbara = John *the elder*. *See* 12662 (12706, 12635).

BRINSLEY, John, *the elder, Schoolmaster* (*DNB*). Epistle Cato, *Precepts, 1638*-HN.; edits 23191, G. Webbe, *Confabulatiunculae, 1627*-HN.

BRIONAEUS, Martinus, *Writer* (BN). Verse 1849.

BRISCOUS, Reginaldus [*cf.* PCC 1604]. Verse 3944.

BRISTOW, Richard, *Controversialist* (*DNB*). Epistle 4697.

BRIXIUS (DeBrie), Germanus, *Writer* (NBG). 18088.

BROAD, William, *London apothecary.* Verse 19300.

BROCKET (Moore), Elizabeth = *Sir* John. ¶5220.

BROCKET, *Sir* John, *of Brocket Hall, Herts.* *¶4432, 12803, *25622 (25620), M. A., *Catechisme, 1592*-F.

BRODIE, Alexander, *Lawyer* (*DNB*). 15358-A.

BRODREPP, Richard, *of Middle Temple* (*1596*). Verse 24607.

BRODUS. *See* BROAD.

BROELMANUS, Stephanus, *Cologne poet* (BM). Verse 22929.

BROG. *See* BURGH.

BROGDON, William, *of Trinity College* (Venn). Verse Staveley, *Breef discourse*-HN.

BROGRAVE, *Sir* John, *Lawyer* (*DNB*). 12981 by bookseller [see changes].

BROGRAVE, John, *Father of Thomas I Bt.* Verse 11157.

BROKE. *See* BROOKE.

BROOME (——), Joan = William, *Bookseller.* Unsigned prose 17050.

BROME, Richard, *Dramatist* (*DNB*). Edits 11071; verse 14788, 17444, 17921, 18342 (18337), 23704.

BR[OME], St., *'Brother of preceding'.* Verse 3819.

BROMFIELD (? Faucett), Anne = Robert. *15334.

BROMFIELD, *Sir* Edward, *Lord Mayor.* *11347, *22532, 23119, ¶23120, *23509.

BROMLEY (Beswick), Anne = *Sir* Henry. *21242 and *1627*-PN.[2]

BROMLEY, *Sir* Edward, *Baron of Exchequer.* *4329 later to Williams; prose 20138.

BROMLEY, *Sir* Henry, *Son of next.* 13203 with unnamed brothers and sisters, 14057, *19620 by editor superseding Essex, 20587.

BROMLEY, *Sir* Thomas, *Lord Chancellor* (*DNB*). 1582, 2761, 4442, 4950, 5250, 7388 by editor, 10566, 10978 by editor, 11034, *12745, *12746, 14275, 14635 by editor, 15163, 16634, 16978, *18270, *18272, 22272, 23934, 23973, 25345, Lloyd's *Almanack, 1582*-L., T. Rogers, *General session,* 1581-F., A. Gregory, *De legibus, 1583*-HD.

BROMLEY, Thomas, *'of Dorfold, Cheshire'.* Epistle 25225.

BROMLEY, *Sir* Thomas, *Son of Sir Henry.* 17360; Minsheu List.

BROMLEY, William, *'Secretary to Sir Thomas'.* *¶6230; *see* 15447.

BROMWELL, James, *Rector of Polstead* (Venn 1603). *3926.

BROOKE, ——, *M.A., Magdalen College* [? William, 1610]. Minsheu List.

BROOKE, *Sir* Calisthenes, *Brother of John* (Brown). *24096.

BROOKE, Christopher, *Poet* (*DNB*). Epistle 3917 (25890); verse 3914, 5807 as Richer for Bookes, 5808, 5810 [*cf.* 23769], 7204 and 7201, 15588; *see* 5811; Minsheu List.

BROOKE (Colepeper), Elizabeth = *Sir* Robert *of Cockfield Hall.* 22494 by editor.

BROOKE, George, *IX Baron Cobham.* 1717 (1710).

BROOKE, George, *Conspirator* (*DNB*). ¶25206; *see* 25438.

BROOKE *alias* Cobham, *Sir* Henry (*DNB,* but *d. 1592*). 12461 by bookseller.

BROOKE, John, *Baron Cobham 1645.* *24096; Minsheu List.

BROOKE, *Lady* Nevill [? Katherine Neville = *Sir* Richard]. 11032.

BROWNLOW, Richard, *Lawyer* (*DNB*). *1909 and *1613*-F. [cf. 6025].

BRUCE (Cecil), Diana. *See* VERE.

BRUCE, Edward, *I Lord B. of Kinloss.* Epistle 6333.

BRUCE, Edward, *II Lord Bruce.* 6906.

BRUCE, George, *Lord* (1203). Error for Thomas, *I Earl.*

BRUCE, George *and* John, 'Sons of Laird of *Earlshall*'. Epistle R. Williamson, *Elementa, 1624*-E.

BRUCE (Clerk), Magdalen = Edward *I Lord B.*, *later* Fullerton. 7414 by editor, *12117 only, 21331.

BRUCE, Peter, *Regent of St. Leonard's.* See 21553.

BRUCE, Robert, *Presbyterian* (*DNB*). 1857; *see* 20633.

BRUCE, Thomas, *I Earl of Elgin.* *1203 as George, 15270, 21151; *see* 10667.

BRUDENELL, Thomas, *I Earl of Cardigan.* 6544, ¶17936; *see* 10667.

BRUEN, John, *Puritan* (*DNB*). *2731, *23545.

BRUNIUS. *See* BROWNE.

BRUYN, Ambrosius de (*STC*). Verse 712.

BRIAN, Edward. Verse 23759.

BRYAN, *Sir* Francis, *Courtier* (*DNB*). 17502; *see* 12436.

BRIAN, Thomas, *Physician* (Venn 1622), Patients of. 3723.

BRYCE, *Sir* Hugh, *Lord Mayor.* See 24762.

BRYDGES (Stanley), Anne = Grey *V Baron Chandos, later* Touchet. *6330, ¶11521; epistle 18511.

BRYDGES, Elizabeth, *Maid of Honour, daughter of next.* Verse 16696, 20170.

BRYDGES (Clinton), Frances = Giles *III Baron Chandos.* *1609* ed. of 20826-C.² by editor.

BRYDGES, George, *VI Baron Chandos.* See 10667, 17332.

BRIDGES, John, *Bishop of Oxford.* See 10771, 17453, etc.

BRYDGES (Hopton), Mary = William *IV Baron.* Epistle 7293 by editor.

BUBB, William, *Gent.* [? *the next*]. Verse 12216; prose 12295.

BUBB, William, *Confidence man* (*TLS 1928*, p. 28). 21027; verse 23779 only; prose 21027; *see* Ramage, p. 99.

BUCHANAN, George, *Historian* (*DNB*). Epistle 12913; *see* 1404.

BUCHANAN, Thomas, *Minister of Ceres.* ¶21279.

BUCHANAN, William, *Minister of Methven.* Verse 5933, W. Cowper, *Jacobs wrestling, 1607*-LINC.

BUCHINSKI, Stanislaus, 'Secretary to the false *Demetrius*'. See 12662 (12706, 12635).

BUC, *Sir* George, *Poet* (*DNB*). Verse 4508 (4509), 25118a.

BUCK, George, *Great-nephew of preceding.* Edits 3997; verse 22794, 26103.

BUCK, John. 19334.

BUCKE, Paul, *Actor.* See 25784.

BUCK, *Sir* Peter, *of Rochester* (*Vis. Kent*). †19683 (19649).

BUCK, Thomas, *Cambridge printer.* Unsigned prose 13183.

BUCKLE, —— [*Somerset preacher*]. Epistle *1941.

BUCKELL, *Sir* Cuthbert, *Lord Mayor.* *20854 superseding Barne, 23397.

BUCKERIDGE, John, *Bishop of Ely.* *17698 [*1614* known only by tp.-HD.]; edits 602, 606; *see* 17944; Minsheu List.

BUCKLAND (——), B. = Edmund, *Mother of Ralph-DNB.* 4008.

BUCKMINSTER *or* BUCKMASTER, Thomas, *Almanac-maker* (*DNB*). Verse 23361, 25295.

BUCKWORTH, Theophilus, *Bishop of Dromore.* 14715.

BUDDEN, John, *Professor of Law* (*DNB*). *6420; verse 1653, 21033, 24610.

BUDGE, Bridget. 6410.

BUDGE, John, *Bookseller.* Prose 12775, 12776 (748).

BUDGEN, William, *of Brasenose* (Foster). Verse 23278.

BUGGANS, *Dominus.* Verse 13941.

BUGS *or* BUGGE, Edward, *Sergeant-at-arms* (*Vis. Essex*). See 10738.

BULKLEY. Acrostic verse 3506.

BULKELEY, Arthur, *Bishop of Bangor.* *2983 = 21617.

BULKELEY, Edward, *Controversialist* (Venn 1555). Edits 5397; prose 11227.

BULKELEY, Lancelot, *Archbishop of Dublin.* 14073 by editor.

BULKELEY, Richard, *of St. John's* (Venn 1624). Verse 7365, 21460.

BULL, Henry, *Theologian* (*DNB*). Edits 13742 (13752).

BULL, John, *Goldsmith, d. 1589. See 6219.*

BULL, Stephen, *of All Souls* (Foster). *See* 25438.

BULL, William, *Mayor of Wells.* 1046.

BULLEIN, Richard, *Brother of next. See* R. B.

BULLEIN, William, *Physician* (*DNB*). Verse 18060 and *1564*-HN., 24631.

BULLINGER, Heinrich, *Reformer* (*NBG*). 1304 by author; *see* 25427.

BULLINGHAM, Edward. Verse 26103.

BULLINGHAM, John, *Bishop of Gloucester.* 14728; verse 374.

BULLINGHAM, Nicholas, *Bishop of Lincoln.* *1710; *see* 10026.

BULLOCK, John, *of Inner Temple* (*1590*). 1919.

BULTEEL, James *and* Peter, *Merchants* (*Vis. London*). 20390.

BUNBURY, *Sir* Henry, *of Stanney, Ches., d. 1634.* *7293.

BUNCE, *Sir* James, *I Bt.* *21095.

BUNNY, Edmund, *Writer* (*DNB*). Edits 4414; revises 19355; *see* 19362.

BURBY, Cuthbert, *Bookseller.* Signed prose 12306, 18868; unsigned Plato, *Axiochus, 1592*-PFOR.; *see* 17834 cancelled.

BURBY, Edward, *Archdeacon* (Foster 1616). 14748.

BURCH, John van der (Schotel). 16817.

BURGAINE. *See* BURGOYNE.

BURGIS, James, '*Geometry teacher, London*'. Verse Penkethman, *Pinnace, 1629* (Bagford, Harl. 5949).

BURGESS, John, *Puritan* (*DNB*). Epistle 20484; edits 5364, 25620; prose 20096; Minsheu List.

BURGES, John, *Clerk of Exchequer. See* 23779 only.

BURGES (——), Margaret = John *of Kingswood, Wilts.* [*untraced*]. *See* 4184.

BURGH, *often spelt* Borrow(es). *See also* BOURKE.

BURGH, George, *Cantabrig.* (Venn 1582). Verse 21661 (21649).

BOROUGH, Jane. *See* WENTWORTH.

BURGH, *Sir* John, *Commander* (*DNB*). 13696 (3427).

BURGH, Thomas, *V Baron Burgh.* *3508, 12190 by editor, 13562, 15698 (15699); epistle 16696.

BOROUGH, Walter, *Son of next.* 542 later to Montgomery.

BOROUGH, William, *Navigator* (*DNB*). 18647, 21078.

BURROWES, William, *Alderman of Bristol.* *24027 as Barrowes.

BROG, *Sir* William, *Colonel in Scots Brigade.* Epistle 25939.

BURGOYNE, George [? *of Herts.*], *nine sons of.* *See* 25438.

BURGOYNE (Kempe), Jane = John *I Bt.* 12333 (12330).

BURGOYNE, Robert, *of Wroxall, d. 1613.* *†5382.

BURHILL, Robert, *Divine* (*DNB*). Edits 22807; verse 4012, 6333.

BURLACY. *See* BORLACE.

BURLAMACHI, Philip, *Italian merchant in London.* Minsheu List.

BURLEY, Nicholas. Verse 22794.

BURLZ, Thomas [? *of Depden, Suff.*]. *See* 12662 (12706, 12635).

BURNABY. *See* BARNABY.

BURNELL, Edward [? Venn 1565]. Verse 374.

BURNET, Robert, *of Barns, advocate, d. 1633* (*Edinb. M.A., 1609*). Verse Primrose, *Apologie, 1628*-ROSEBERY.

BURNET, *Sir* Thomas, *I Bt.* †12491.

BURNOPPE, Richard, '*Vicar of East Grinstead, Sussex*'. *See* 13923.

BURRANT, Robert, *Editor* (*DNB*). Edits 15683.

BURRE, Walter, *Bookseller.* Prose 1674 only, 7456 = 17869, presentation 11319.

BURRELL, Andrewes, *of Wisbech* (Wing). *Fens map in 17827.

BURROWES. *See* BURGH.

BURT, Thomas, *London preacher* (*STC*). Verse 15434 and 15433-L. [inserted?].

BURTON, *Sir* Edward *of Gray's Inn* (Foster 1581). *11380.

BURTON, Edward, *D.D.* (Foster 1616). Verse 288.

BURTON, Francis, *Bookseller*. Prose 605, 24063, 26014.

BURTON, Gregory, *Almanac-maker*. *See* 5584.

BURTON, Henry, *Independent* (*DNB*). Epistle 4205, 5144.

BURTON, Robert, *Author* (*DNB*). Verse 21033.

BURTON, Samuel, *Archdeacon* (Foster 1586). ¶12671 (12707, 12635); epistle 23108; *see* 12662 (12706, 12635).

BURTON, Stephen, *Warden of Drapers*. W. Freake, *Priuiledges of vpright*, 1639-F.

BURTON, William, *Regius professor* (Venn 1578). Verse 6206.

BURTON, William, *Antiquary* (*DNB*). Presentation 716.

BURTON, William, *Schoolmaster* (Foster 1625). Verse 13554.

BUSBY, John, *the elder, Bookseller*. Prose 16654, 22954.

BUSBY, Richard, *Headmaster* (*DNB*). Verse 21351; *see* R. B.

BUSH, Abraham, *M.A.* (Foster). Verse 5533.

BUSHELL, *Sir* Edmund. Error for Edward.

BUSHELL, *Sir* Edward, *Equerry*. 22462; Minsheu List.

BUSHELL, Edward, *Brother of Thomas-DNB*. *See* 4187.

BUSHEL, Thomas, *Bookseller*. Prose 20053.

BUSHER, William, 'Nephew of author'. 7622.

BUSLEYDEN, Jerome, *Diplomatist* (*NBG*). Epistle 18095.

BUSSIE, *Sir* Raleigh, *of Glamorgan* (Foster). Verse 23352.

BUSSY, Marke de, 'Lord of Berville'. 1851.

BUST, Henry, *M.D.* (Foster 1560). Verse 4756, 11516.

BUSTE, John, *of Christ Church* (Foster 1561). Verse 1924.

BUST, Matthew, *the younger, of King's College* (Venn 1593). Edits 14622.

BUTLER, Charles, *Author* (*DNB*). Edits Ramus, *Rhetorica*, 1597-L.

BUTLER, Edmund, *III Baron Dunboyne*. *See* 10667 as Edward.

BOTELER (Drury), Frances = *Sir* Robert *of Woodhall, Herts*. 13873; Minsheu List.

BUTLER, Fra. Verse 22454.

BUTLER, George, *of Ellerton, Council of North*. ¶21638.

BUTLER, James, *I Duke of Ormond*. *See* 10667.

BUTLER, John, 'Captain'. Verse 18673.

BOTELER, John, *I Baron B. of Brantfield*. *See* 10667.

BUTLER (Gedge), Mary = John *of Tobie Priory, Essex*. ¶22848 [earlier lost].

BOTELER, Nathaniel, *Navy captain* (*DNB*). Minsheu List as *Sir*.

BOTELER, Oliver, *of Wooton Bourne End* (*Vis. Beds.*). 6031.

BUTLER, Pierce, *I Viscount Ikerrin*. *See* 10667.

BUTLER, Richard, *III Viscount Mountgarret*. *See* 10667.

BUTLER, Sylvester. *See* SYLVESTER.

BUTLER, Thomas, *X Earl of Ormonde*. 13797, 17761, Falckenburgius, *Goliath*, 1579-BO.[5]; epistle 23080 (23084).

BUTLER, Thomas, *III Baron Caher*. *See* 10667.

BUTLER, Walter, *IV Earl of Ormonde*. 17761.

BUTLER, William, *Physician* (*DNB*). ¶18809.

BUTT, Giles de, *London merchant*. *20678 (20668) by editor as But.

BUTTER, Nathaniel, *Printer* (*DNB*). Epistle 23806; signed prose 6427, 11189, 12690; unsigned 11783, 11790, 11796, 13528, 18750, 23009, Dahl 48-HD.

BUTTERFIELD, Robert, *Controversialist* (*DNB*). Epistle 4136.

BUTTERWIKE *or* BOTREVICUS, John. Verse 18886, 25337, 25341.

BUTTON, *Sir* Thomas, *Admiral* (*DNB*). *14623, *17388 (17390), engr. print, *Council of War*-L.[5]

BUTTS, Henry, *Master of Corpus* (Venn). Edits 4486.

BUTTES, Thomas, *of Ryburgh* (Venn). 6199.

BUY (Bowy, Bovey), James, *Equerry*. Epistle some copies *4747-0.

BYDDELL *alias* SALISBURY, John, *Printer*. Verse 10479 unsigned.

BYFIELD, Adoniram, *Puritan* (*DNB*). Edits 4221, 4233.

BYFIELD (——), Elizabeth = Nicholas. Edits 4211 (4212).

BYFIELD, Nicholas, *Puritan* (*DNB*). *See* 3622; Minsheu List.

BYNG, Andrew, *Regius professor* (*DNB*). Minsheu List.

BYNG, Robert, *of Gray's Inn. See* 5811.

BYNG, Thomas, *Civilian* (*DNB*). Epistle 12905; verse 4782, 6578; prose 6577.

BYNNEMAN, Henry, *Printer* (*DNB*). Signed prose 713, 18309, 20089 disavowed by author 20090; unsigned 1972, 3169, 11635, 12629, 18773; *see* 12899.

BYRD. *See* BIRD.

BYRES, John, *Dean of Gild, Edinburgh.* *13258.

BYRON, John, *Esq.* [? *Grandfather of next*]. 5787.

BYRON, John, *I Baron Byron.* 20051.

BYRON, Nicholas [? Venn 1612]. Verse 20051.

BYRON, Richard, *II Baron Byron.* Verse 20051.

C

C., Sr. [*probably* Cary *the translator*]. Verse 20490.

C., A. Edits 5587; verse 11082, 12208, 20502 [? Cook].

C., A. S. F. [? A. S., *filius* C.] Verse 22624.

C., Barth. [? Clerke]. Verse 20309.

C., B. Verse 11636 (11638), 11643.

C., C., *Gent.* Verse 15318.

C., C. Edits 3248 (3255); verse 688; prose 15409, 18156.

C., D. Edits 20005 (20003).

C., E. (1635), *see* CHARKE; (6968), *see* ED. CH.

C., Edm. (10779). *See* CALAMY.

CH., Ed. M. (11944). *See* MAHONIDES.

C., Elizabeth, *Daughter of Robert, Esq.* 18336.

C., *Signora* E. [*presumably* Caryll]. Epistle 24097.

C., E., '*Brother of the translator*'. 4302 [post-STC].

C., E. Verse 3053, 6839, 11636 (11638); prose 6067, 13423 (13379), 22490 [? Culverwell.]

CH., Ed. Verse 6968.

CH., Ez. *See* CHARKE.

C., F., *Esq.* Verse 18202.

C., F. Edits 3272; verse 23248; prose 17663.

C., G. (14783). *See* CHAPMAN.

C., M. G., '*Minister at Edinburgh*' [*untraced*]. *See* 13217.

C., G. [*probably* William Camden]. Verse 12188.

C., G. Verse 5355, 13516, 14947, 15457, Faureau, *Briefe direction, 1618*-0.[5]

CH., G. Verse 19485.

Co., G. Edits 6281 = 22917.

C., H. (20366a). *See* CHETTLE.

C., H. [Crooke *according to* 12312]. Edits 12322 (12312).

C., H., '*near Bishopsgate*'. 3215 by editor.

C., H., *M.A.* [*Cambridge*]. Verse 12964.

C., M. H., *Esq.* 19067.

C., H. Verse 3220, 17745 [? Crowch], 22222; *see* 25499.

CR., H. Verse 6818.

C., I., *Philomath.* Verse 13988.

C., I. Edits 4283, 13542, 18518; verse 688, 5950, 10667, 11464, 11515, 12482, 12796, 13798, 14008, 14783, 15540, 17816, 18532, earlier 18904-C.[2], 22796; prose 13461.

CL., Ia. [? Clayton]. Verse 1694.

C., I. M., '*V. Med. Doctor*'. Verse 16870 and *1597*-HN. [? I. M., *Chirurgeon*].

C., I. M. Verse 12748.

C., L., *S.T.D. See* 25597.

C., M. (14591), *see* MATTHEW PARKER; (23992), *see* THOMAS CARRE.

C., La[dy], M. Alonso de Madrid, *Briefe methode*-0., Allison 269.

C., M., *Esq. See* 25438.

C., M. Edits 25591 [? Coverdale]; verse 2765 = 16696 [? Cosworth], 11636 (11638), 12100, 15515, Faureau, *Briefe direction, 1618*-O.[5]

C., N. Verse 1392.

C., P., '*Surgeon*'. Verse 24578.

C., P., '*Praeli corrector*'. Verse 4489; *see also* R. WINTERTON.

C., P. Prose 3108.

C., P. D. Verse 24579.

C., R. (3818). *See* ROBERT CHAMBERLAIN.

C., *Sir* R. [? Carey]. Edits ¶1805 and verses.

C., *Sir* R. 24145.

C., R., *Esq.* 1048.

C., R., *D.D.* Prose 25786.

C., R., '*Trinity, Cambridge*' [? Chapman]. Verse 1167 from 1177.

C., R., *Cant.* Verse A. S., *Booke of bulls, 1636*-HD.

C., R., *Gent.* Verse 15318.

C., R. [*Friend of author*]. Verse 1002, 1003, 1004, and 1001 unsigned.

C., R. Verse 4199, 7487, 11205, 13203, 15078, 18909, 25348, Seneca, *Shortnesse of life, 1636*-HD; *see* 20808.

CA., R. Verse 18910.

CA., Si. (21649). *See* SIMON CARRILL.

CAL., Sa. (23779). *See* SAMUEL CALVERT.

C., S. Verse 5471-HD.

CR., S. Verse 24137.

CR., Sa. Verse 23520.

C., Th. (25891). *See* THOMAS CRANLEY.

C., T., *I.C., Cantabr. Eborac.* Verse 6014.

C., T., *Au. Glo., Oxon.* Verse 1311.

C., D[r]. T., M[*edicus*]. *See* 25438.

C., T., *M.D.* *¶3585.

C(H)., T. [*presumably* Churchyard]. Verse 11636 (11638), 25334.

C., T. [*presumably* Cartwright]. *20881.

C., T. Epistle *13579; verse 91, 135, 501 for *1609*, 1311, 11096, 13069, 22678, 24523.

Co., Ty. Verse 10944.

C., S[ir]. W. ¶3571.

C., W., *Aulae Glo., Oxon.* Verse 1311.

C., W., *Doctor.* Verse 12345-HD.

C., W. Edits 4232 [? Crashaw], 14817 [? Crashaw], 14034; verse 12489, 13247; prose 15040, *1629* ed. of 25769-PN.[2]

CADENET, Honoré d'Albert, *Marquis, French envoy.* Gul. Gohaeus, *Panegyrikon, 1621*-F.

CADMAN, Thomas, *Bookseller.* Prose 25349.

CADEMAN, *Sir* Thomas, *Physician (DNB).* See 16777.

CAESAR (Woodhouse), Anne = *Sir* Julius. 12989, *20538.

CAESAR, Augustus, *of Inner Temple* (Foster). Verse 3914.

CAESAR, *Sir* Charles, *Son of Julius.* *20538; Minsheu List.

CAESAR, *Sir* John, *Son oj next.* *20538.

CAESAR, *Sir* Julius, *Judge (DNB).* 650 by editor [see changes], 847, *6204a, 6626, 11279, †¶12312 by editor, 15467, 15691 by printer, *1596* ed. ¶16909-HD. by editor [see changes], †17231 by bookseller, 18612, 18854 by bookseller 18996, 19659 (19648) later to Bridgewater, 21017, 21666, 21778, ¶24024, *25241, *¶25699 superseding Salisbury, Churchyard, *Wonders of ayre, 1602*-L.[2], E. Sadler, *Organon, 1605*-BO.[5]; epistle *6165, 12607; see Brathwait, *Querela*-HN., 19511; Minsheu List.

CAESAR, Robert, *Son of preceding.* ¶20535, *20538.

CAIUS, John, *the elder (DNB).* Verse 13809.

CAIUS, John, *Physician (DNB).* Prose 4782.

CAIUS, Thomas, *Author (DNB).* Verse 23229.

CALAMY, Edmund, *the elder, Puritan (DNB).* Edits 10779 [name in 10780].

CALANDRINUS, Caesar, *Minister of Dutch Church.* Verse 961.

CALDWELL, Edward, *Barber surgeon.* Edits 18204.

CALDWELL, William, '*Sergeant of Bakehouse*'. Minsheu List.

CALFHILL, James, *Divine (DNB).* Epistle 17497; edits C. Vermigli, *Carmina, 1561*-HN.; verse 1710, 5686.

CALL, Giles, *Bailiff of Yarmouth.* *21093.

CALLIOPE. 1666 = 18972 (1665).

CALMELIE. Misprint for Calveley.

CALOPHYSUS. Verse 24624.

CALTHORPE, Barthram, *Esq.* [see *Vis. Norf.*]. See 25438.

CALTHROPE, *Sir* Charles, *Lawyer* (*DNB*). See 25438.

CALTHORPE, James [*of Norf.*]. Epistle 15037.

CALTHORPE (Lewkenor), Katherine. *See* LEWKENOR.

CALVE., Io., '*Ex inter: Temp:*' [*untraced*]. Verse 14008.

CALVELEY, *Sir* George, *of Lea* (*Vis. Ches.*). 14010 by editor.

CALVELEY, Hugh, *of Lea, Ches., d. 1607.* *7293 misprinted Calmelie.

CALVERLEY, *Sir* William, *of Calverley* (*Vis. Yorks.*). See 10910.

CALVERT (Mynne), Anne = George *I Baron.* 21103 and *1620-0.*

CALVERT (Arundell), Anne = Cecil *II Baron.* 17746.

CALVERT, Cecil, *II Baron Baltimore. See* 10667.

CALVERT, George, *I Baron Baltimore.* ¶7471, ¶13799; epistle 24604; *see* 23779 only, 25854; Minsheu List.

CALVERT, Robert, *of Mount Calvert, Ulster planter. See* 23779 only.

CALVERT, Samuel, *Clerk in foreign service, d. 1621.* Verse 23779 only.

CALVIN, Jean, *Reformer.* 1304 from Latin edition; prose 12365, 15259.

CALY, Robert, *Printer.* Signed prose 25114; unsigned 25388.

CAMBELL. *See* CAMPBELL.

CAMDEN, William, *Historian* (*DNB*). ¶14751, 25325 later to Pembroke; epistle 3834, 13592, 22177; presentation 14773; verse 826, 7491 [7492 earlier], 12188 and doubtless those by G. C., 12625, 20966, 21239, 22929, 23895; prose 3220; see 17944, 25327; Minsheu List.

CAME, Thomas, *M.A.* (Foster). Verse 24610.

CAMEL, Thomas, *Ballad writer. See* 5225.

CAMERON, John, *Theologian, d. 1625* (*DNB*). Epistle 25939.

CAMPBELL (Douglas), Agnes = Archibald *VII Earl.* 337; *see* 14849 as Anne.

CAMPBELL, Anne, *Daughter of Margaret below.* ¶3446.

CAMPBELL, Archibald, *V Earl of Argyll.* 16604, 18688.

CAMPBELL, Archibald, *VII Earl of Argyll.* 19461; *see* 10667.

CAMPBELL, *Sir* Colin, *II Bt.* *21267 as Dominus Glenurquhae.

CAMPBELL, Elizabeth, *of Kinyeancleugh, friend of Knox.* 6324.

CAMBELL, *Sir* James, *Lord Mayor.* 6509, *¶11346 [see changes], *14489, *17886, *23345 [see changes]; epistle *25963.

CAMPBELL, James, *Earl of Irvine. See* 10667.

CAMPBELL, John, *I Earl of Loudoun.* 14997; *see* 10667.

CAMPBELL (Douglas), Margaret = Archibald *Marquis of Argyll.* ¶3446.

CAMPBELL, Neil, *Bishop of the Isles. See* 10667.

CAMPBELL, Patrick. Verse 4533.

CAMBELL, *Sir* Thomas, *Lord Mayor.* *13159, 13564, *23864, J. Bentley, *Harmonie of scriptures, 1600-L.*

CAMPION, Edmund, *S.J.* (*DNB*). Epistle 12745; verse 23229; *see* 5005.

CAMPION, Henry, *Mercer, d. 1588.* 980.

CAMPION, Thomas, *Poet* (*DNB*). Verse 1468, 5808 and 5810, 7091, 10827, 20756.

CANAYE, Philippe, *Seigneur de Fresne* (*NBG*). See FRESNE.

CANCELLAR, James, *Theologian* (*DNB*). Edits 17321 = 17322 [earlier-L. impf.].

CANDIDO. *See* MATTHEW GWINNE.

CANDIDO, Il [*perhaps same as preceding*]. Verse 736.

CANDISH *and* CANDLER. *See* CAVENDISH *and* CHANDLER.

CANFIELD, Benedict, *Capuchin* (*DNB*). *See* 3902.

CANIN, Isaac, *Printer at Dort.* Prose 11513.

CANN, William, *Mayor of Bristol.* Epistle *19155.

CANON, John [? *name cropt*]. Verse 13595.

CANNON, *Sir* Thomas, *of Haverford West* (Foster). Verse some copies 6347-F.

CAPPEL, Aaron, *Pastor of French Church. See* 17944; Minsheu List.

CAPELL, *Sir* Arthur, *of Hadham, Herts.* *¶4497,

6066, *¶25677 superseding Heton; sons of, *¶4497.

CAPELL, Christopher, *Mayor of Gloucester.* *12172 [see changes].

CAPELL (Aldersey), Dorothy = *Sir* Henry *of Rayne Hall* (*Vis. Surrey*). R. Lovell, *High way to honor, 1627*-F.

CAPEL, Richard, *Puritan* (*DNB*). Edits (all 19570) 19572, 19578, 19579, 19582, 19583, 19586, 19588, 19589, 19591.

CAPEL (Montagu), Theodosia = *Sir* Henry. *19731 (19648 appendix) by editor.

CAPELIN, John, *Burgess of Southampton.* 25403 by editor.

CAPLIN, John, *of Southampton* (*Inner Temple*). *21669 (21672-O).

CAPELIN, Nicholas, '*Father of the translator*', 16814 by editor.

CARCELLIUS, Ioannes (18089). A fiction.

CARDINAL, William, *of Council of the North.* *1823.

CAREW, CAREY, CARY, *etc.*

CAREY Family (Hunsdon). *See* 6270-HN.

CAROW, Anne. 11901 and 11902.

CARY, Anne Clementina, *O.S.B.* (Gillow). 12350 by editor.

CARY, Christopher, *Sheriff of Bristol.* *18347.

CAREY, *Sir* Edmund. Error for Edward.

CAREW, Edmund, *of Inner Temple* (Foster 1624). *See* 15466.

CARY, *Sir* Edward, *Master of Jewel House, father of Henry I Viscount.* 11564 as Edmond, 25666.

CAREY, Elizabeth (18379). *See* BERKELEY.

CAREW (Bryan), Elizabeth = *Sir* Nicholas-*DNB*. 21741 [earliest ed.].

CAREY (Spenser), Elizabeth = George *II Baron Hunsdon.* ¶5220, 18366, 20015 (20003), ¶23078 (23084); epistle 16696, some copies 23080.

CAREY (Trevannion), Elizabeth = Robert *I Earl of Monmouth.* 18199, ¶20303 (20304).

CAREW (Bland), Elizabeth = *Sir* Philip. 4613 usually cancelled.

CAREY (Tanfield), Elizabeth = Henry *I Viscount Falkland.* 1805, 3192 by bookseller

superseding Bodenham, *6338, ¶7193 (7189, 7216, etc.), 17471 only by bookseller.

CAREW, *Sir* Francis, *K.B.* *¶19850; epistle some copies *4747-O.

CAREW, *Sir* Gawen, *Brother of Sir Peter.* 5001.

CAREY, George, *II Baron Hunsdon.* 1311, 2014, 5249, 7091, †11041 [title is *Diamond of devotion*], †11048, 13253 by editor, 13255, 15318, 16649, 18126, 18858, 20020 (20018, 20003), 24335, ¶25082, 25086, R. W., †*Order of Matrimonie, 1580*-D.; epistle *6165, 16696.

CARIE, George. ¶24151.

CAREW, George, *I Earl of Totnes.* 4617, ¶5220, *11496, *17388 (17390), 17819, ¶20910, *21003, engr. print *Council of war*-L.[5]; presentation 17944; *see* 17332; Minsheu List.

CAREY, Henry, *I Baron Hunsdon.* 1538 by editor, 1542, 1583, 4033, 4256, ¶5376, *¶10674, 13050, 16664, 25079, ¶25080 only; epistle some copies 23080 (23084).

CAREY, Henry, *I Earl of Dover.* 129 (115), *¶4497, *†5538, second issue 7020-L., 13313, 13358, 13936, 19462 by bookseller, 19518, *22796, 24308, *25386; epistle *4747; *see* 10667, 17332; Family of: *see* 6270.

CAREY, Henry, *II Earl of Monmouth.* 13038, *¶20910.

CARY, Henry, *I Viscount Falkland.* 583, 4311 [date is *1623*], 15502, 22524, 23604, *23803, 25375; epistle 24604; *see* 668; Minsheu List; Family of: *see* 6270.

CAREY, John, *II Earl of Dover.* 21011; *see* 10667.

CAREY (Knyvett), Katherine = *Sir* Edward. Epistle 16696.

CARY, *Sir* Lorenzo, *Son of Henry I Viscount.* 24161.

CARY, Lucius, *II Viscount Falkland.* Verse 7045, 10645, second issue 12397, 21724 (21725), 21725; *see* 10667.

CAREY (Hyde), Mary = John *III Baron Hunsdon.* *25386.

CAREW, *Sir* Matthew, *Son of Sir Matthew-DNB*. ¶4187.

CAREW, *Sir* Peter, *Soldier* (*DNB*). 18575.

CAREW, *Sir* Peter, *d. 1581* (Foster 1572). *See* 5235.

CARY, *Sir* Philip, *Son of Sir Edward*. Epistle 6332.

CAREW, Richard, *Antiquary (DNB)*. Epistle 16696.

CAREY, Robert, *I Earl of Monmouth*. 7275, 12241, 12260; epistle some copies ★4747-O., 23581 (23575, 21653); *see* 10667.

CAREW, Thomas, *of Crowcombe, Soms., d. 1604*. ★4616.

CAREW, Thomas, *Poet (DNB)*. Epistle some copies ★4747-O.; verse 6303, 6304, 6309 spelt Crew in some copies, 7045, 17220, 17713, 21725.

CARY, Thomas, *Translator* (Venn 1623 and *MLN* 1941). Verse Payne's engraving *Soveraigne of seas*, 1637-L.

CAREY, Thomas, *Son of Robert I Earl*. ★4628, ★¶20910.

CARY, Valentine, *Bishop of Exeter*. Prose 4481.

CARY, Victoria (15465). *See* UDALL (UVEDALE).

CARY, William, *Mayor of Bristol*. ★24027.

CAREW, Wymond, *Son of Richard* (Venn). Verse 13519.

CARGILL, Thomas, *Rector of Aberdeen School*. Verse 14786, 14787.

CARGILL, William, *of Marischal College*. Verse 16694 as Cargillus.

CARLEILL, Carlell. *See* CARLILE.

CARLESSE, Henry, '*of Southwark Martial Garden*'. Epistle ★14922.

CARLETON (Killegrew), Anne = George *Bishop*. ★14896.

CARLETON (Houghton), Anne = *Sir* John *I Bt.* Epistle ★23580 by editor.

CARLETON, Dudley, *Viscount Dorchester*. 14832a by bookseller superseding Carlisle; *see* 23803.

CARLETON, George, *Bishop of Chichester*. †¶7471, ¶21842, 24702, 24705; verse 4503 (4509).

CARLTON, Nicholas, *Composer* (Grove). *See* 24099.

CARLETON, Samuel, *City captain*. ★16942, ★21095, †22149; epistle ★1507; verse 1507 [two in one issue].

CARLETON, *Sir* Thomas, *of Carleton Hall*. 4630 by editor.

CARLTON, Thomas, '*Ensign under Smith in Transylvania*'. Verse 22788 (22790).

CARLEILL, CARLELL, CARLEY, CARLILE, etc.

CARLILE, Christopher, *Divine (DNB)*. Verse 374 as Carley, 1582, 4938, 7168, 14725, 16624, 19150 only, 24631.

CARLEILL, Christopher, *Commander (DNB)*. 19183 by bookseller.

CARLELL, Lodowick, *Dramatist (DNB)*. 6529.

CARMELIANUS, Peter, *Poet (DNB)*. Edits 22588; verse *1508* ed. 696-DUR.⁵, 17242 (3546) and earlier Latin-O., 19827.

CARMICHAEL, James, *Minister at Haddington* (DNB). Verse 22626.

CARMICHAEL, James, *Jr., Son of preceding*. Verse 22626.

CARMICHAEL, John, *Minister at Kilconquhar*. ★18171-A.

CARNEGIE, David, *I Earl of Southesk*. 10671, ¶15684, ¶20656; *see* 10667.

CARNEGIE, William, *Deacon 'conveener', Edinburgh*. W. M., ★*Edinburghs alphabet*-E.

CARPENTER, Anthony. R. Joyner, *Itis*, *1598*-PFOR.

CARPENTER, Nathanael, *Author (DNB)*. *See* 21323, 25327.

CARPENTER, Richard, *Divine, d. 1627 (DNB)*. *See* 25327.

CARR(E). *See* KER.

CARYLL, *Signora* E. *See* E. C.

CARYLL, *Sir* Edward, *of Harting, Sussex, d. 1610*. 22171.

CARRILL, Simon, *of Inner Temple* (Foster). Verse further piece 21661-F. (21649).

CARYLL, Thomas, *of Exeter College* (Foster 1604). Verse 20362-S.

CARTER, George, *of Clare Hall* (Venn 1621). Verse 12964.

CARTER, John, *Bailiff of Yarmouth*. ★21093.

CARTER, Nicholas, '*Physician*'. ★21594.

CARTER, Peter, *Logician (DNB)*. Edits 22251 and *1568*-DUL.

CARTER, Richard, *of Amsterdam congregation* (Burrage). Epistle ★5345.

CARTER, William, *D.D.* (Venn 1528). Verse 22250.

CARTNER, M. Verse 22796.

CECIL, William, *Baron Burghley* (*cont.*)
1584-5: 3119, *13962, 17785, 24775, 25364b
[earliest ed.], *25888.
1586-9: ¶4503 later to Elizabeth, 5486, 20519
by bookseller, 24008 revised by bookseller
*1589-*ILL. [see changes], 25334, 25366.
1590: *1662, 11862, 11869, *21746 and 21749,
25675; epistle 23080 (23084).
1591: 1523, 3890 (3887), 6220 and 6221,
22685 (22718).
1592-3: 3593 by editor [3592 ghost], 12463,
*18635, 19767 [? foreign], 22717 by book-
seller replaced in 22718 by ded. from 22685.
1596, etc.: 5602, 11748 later to Raleigh, 11750,
18638; epistle 16696; *see* 4496, 23318.

CECIL, WILLIAM, *II Earl of Salisbury.* *3961,
*¶4497, 7156, *12376 superseding father,
13968 superseding father, ¶17661 only and
¶17661 (23582, 21653), 17666, †20335, 21127,
21786, 22629, 24116, De la Faye, *Larmes
funebres-*HAT.; epistle *11087, 13634 some
copies; presentation 13222; *see* 10667, 17331.

CECIL, William, *II Earl of Exeter.* *¶4497,
5830, ¶12657 (12708, 12635), 13202 by
reviser superseding FitzWilliams; *see* 10667,
17331.

CECIL, William, *XVII Baron Ros.* Minsheu
List.

CEOLWULF, *Saint.* 1778.

CHADERTON, LAURENCE, *Theologian* (*DNB*).
13406 (13380), 22392; epistle *18805; verse
1492; *see* 25695; Minsheu List.

CHADERTON, William, *Bishop of Lincoln.* 5880;
epistle *1352a; verse 19149 as Chathertonus;
see 25438.

CHAFIN, Thomas, *D.D.* (Foster 1609). Minsheu List.

CHALKE or CHOCK, Sir Alexander, *of Wiltshire*
(*Vis. Soms.*). †25155.

CHALONER, Edward, *D.D.* (Foster). Minsheu
List.

CHALONER, Sir Thomas, *the elder, Diplomatist*
(*DNB*). 25874 [see changes].

CHALONER, Sir Thomas, *the younger,
Naturalist* (*DNB*). Epistle 21660; prose
4938; *see* 12662 (12706, 12635), 19511.

CHALONER, Timothy. 13521.

CHAMBERLAIN (Carey), Elizabeth. *See* BER-
KELEY.

CHAMBERLAIN, Richard, *Clerk of Court of
Wards* (*Inner Temple*). *See* 10738.

CHAMBERLAIN, Robert, *Alderman.* *†7133
(7137).

CHAMBERLAIN, Robert, *Poet* (*DNB*). Verse
3818 [only initials some copies], 17921,
18343 (18337), 20770, 23704.

CHAMBERLAIN, Sir Thomas, *Judge* (*DNB*).
13823.

CHAMBERLAIN, Thomas, *City sergeant-major.*
Epistle 5668.

CHAMBERS, James, *Physician to Charles I.*
15510.

CHAMBERS, Nathaniel, *of Gray's Inn.* Verse
13247, 24698.

CHAMBERS, Richard, *D.D.* (Venn 1595).
4205, *20678 (20668).

CHAMBERS, Sabine, *S.J.* (*DNB*). Verse 4759.

CHAMPAIGNE, Piers, *Esquire for body, d. 1511.*
See 12512.

CHAMPERNOWNE (Creukerne), Amy = *Sir*
Arthur. ¶13378 as Anne.

CHAMPERNOWNE, Sir Arthur, *of Dartington,
d. 1578.* 17980.

CHAMPERNOWNE (Popham), Elizabeth = *Sir*
Richard. 13429 (13378).

CHAMPERNOWNE, Henry, *of Modbury, d. 1649.*
13394 (13380).

CHAMPERNOWNE, Philip, *of Middle Temple*
(Foster). Verse 17921.

CHAMPERNOWNE, Sir Richard, *of Modbury,
Devon.* 13422 (13378), 13563, Anon., *Mans
arraignment, 1607-*F. by bookseller.

CHANDLER or CANDLER, Richard, *Teller of
Exchequer.* 20032 by bookseller.

CHANDLER, Richard, *Incumbent of Stoke
Trister, Soms.* Epistle *1941.

CHAPMAN, George, *Poet* (*DNB*). Edits 17414;
verse 3830, 4252 = 11827, 5473, 10854,
11068, 14782 (partly 14751), 14783 only,
18428; *see Library, 1941-2,* p. 169.

CHAPMAN (   ), Grace = William *Citizen.*
*4769.

CHAPMAN, Henry, *Mayor of Newcastle.* *14491.

CHAPMAN, John. Verse 5808, 5810 [cf.
23769].

CHAPMAN, Laurence, *Bookseller.* Prose 13903.

CHAPMAN, Thomas, *Son of Thomas scrivener
d. 1620.* 11648 (11652).

CHAPMAN, Thomas, *Recorder of Leicester.* *19788.

CHAPPERLINE, John [*of the 'Academ Roial'*]. Verse 13800; *see* 6341.

CHAPPUYS, Joannes, *Paris editor* (BM). Edits 17108.

CHARD, Thomas, *Bookseller.* Prose 1077.

CHARKE, Ezechiel, *Puritan* (Venn 1603). Edits [often only initials] 1628, 1629, 1635, 1642, 1649; prose 20283; *search* E. C.

CHARKE, William, *Puritan* (*DNB*). 19401; verse 6577, 24631; prose 4882 from a lost book; *see* 4534, 4709, 18744, 19393.

CHARLES V, *Emperor.* *13080, *13081.

CHARLES I, *King.* Chronologically:
To 1611: 4542, 5393, *12488; epistle 6162; *see* 5568, 5807.
1612: *3768, *5128, *17701, ¶18987; *see* 19511, 23760.
1613: 1602 and *1612*-L.² (1624), 4117, *5107, 6197, 11309, 12614, 12754, 13000, 13952, 15433, 17870, 20291, 20294, ¶20304, 20563 and undated Quin, *Votum*-E., some copies 20994, 25143, ¶25699 superseding Essex; epistle 384, 25891 (25911); *see* 4546.
1614: 12627, 12652 (12706, 12635), 14859, 14990, 17837, 18349 (18351), 20300, ¶23581 (23575, 21653), 24994, 25661 (25664); *see* 23811 *under 1616*; epistle 11370; *see* 23779 (23725).
1615: 1387, 4632, ¶16829 (23582, 21653), 21726, 23338 [see changes]; epistle 14665.
1616: 161, ¶686, 7174, ¶7346, 13545, 14344 by editor (14346), 20159, 20748, 22788, 22933 superseding sister, ¶23582 (23575, 21653), ¶23811 [unique 23810 impf.] re-written *1627*-L. (23725), E. W[eston], *Triple cure*-HD.; epistle 20835.
1617: 14467 only by editor, ¶17335 [see changes], 17872, 20187, ¶21328, 23543, *Dolphins danger*-PENROSE by editor; epistle 17199; Minsheu List.
1618: 46, *¶1412, 3062, ¶11216, *11496, ¶24025, S. Stock, *Practice to finde ease*-USHAW [earlier lost]; epistle 7547, 14844, 15715.
1619: ¶148 by editor, 766 by editor, 4541, 6326, 12749 (12748), 17123, *17699, 17873, 18993, 20486 [diff. trans. from 20485], 20494, 20566, 22636, 25914; epistle 19813, 21858, 23511 (sometimes 4523).
1620: 3607, 7313, 11253 (21653, sometimes

23575), 14383 (14346), 14382 (14412, 14345), *14450 superseding Henry, 15366, 18178, *19824, 23103; epistle 3370.
1621: 12616, 13276, 14969, 21860, 24871; epistle 22634; *see* J. Murton, *Humble supplication*-BO.
1622: 1155 (1109), 1159 (1109), 6359 superseding Martin [perhaps intended for Henry], 7229, ¶7367, 12962, 17332, 17986, 18483, *20166, 22793 [see changes], 24644 superseding Bacon; epistle 10689.
1623: *42, 160 (15705) by editor, 759, 794 by bookseller, *4487, 6238 by editor superseding Elizabeth, ¶11180, 12604, 17221, *17956, *19027, 19480, 24648, 25939; epistle *7376.
1624: 341, 3739, 4139, 4640, 4747, 4750–52, 7033, 13003, 14693, *15432, *17260, 18610, 20550, 21479, 22092 (22064), 23699 by printer superseding Elizabeth, 24925, 25090a superseding Lennox; epistle 5961.
1625: 4477, †4484, *¶4497, 10862 and added epistle -C.², 12887a, *13240, *17308, 17331, 18030, 18359, 18416, 19030, 19031, 20293, 20356, ¶20509, †20565, 20774, *21492, 21663 and 21655, 23353, 23599 by editor, 23772 (23725), 24604, 25646, Du Moulin Jr., *Carmen*-O.; epistle 13550; *see* 904, 6045.
1626: 1168 by editor, 3185, 4153, 4527 by printer, 4633, 5020, 7050 (7041), 10911 second state, 12659 (12636), 12755, ¶13579, 13766, 18186, 18544 by editor, 18964, 19529, 20508, 21767, 24609, 25171, 26083; epistle J. Leech, *Strenae*-E.²; *see* 7548.
1627: 354, †1052, 1571, *4137, 6608, 12971, 14971, 15110, 15537, 17213, 17731 (17730), 22526, Sictor, *Panegyricon*-F.; epistle 3926.
1628: 1393, *4146, 4155, 5028, 5369, 10863, 11946 (11947), 12974, 14965, 18673, 20462, 23070, 25899, J. P[yne], *Heart of king*-HD.; epistle 5370, 7477; *see* 10051, 20648.
1629: 602 by editor, 606 by editor, 1126 (1124), 1694, 1926, 2415, †¶3447, 4498, 7478, 7480, 10731, ¶11691, ¶15312, *19069, 21474; epistle 1624 and *1629*-N., 22529.
1630: 6542, 7476, 17711, 18360, 20385, 20533; epistle 19032, 22633, ¶23725 [earlier lost]; *see* 23868.
1631: 4113, 4151, †4486, 6063, 6301, 12509, †13047, *13272, 13992, 20829, 25223; endorses 2732 = 14389.
1632: 3473 [earlier lost], 4475, 11877, 23369, 25737, 26068 by editor, J. Bill, *Accompts cast up*-L.³⁸ ; epistle 11876, 18966.

CHARLES I (*cont.*)

1633: 555 [epistle adapted from 15259!],
¶2767, 2798 by bookseller, 2947 by editor,
3443, 4480, 4491, 5398 by editor, 7076
(7486), 11916, 12702 = 12664, 14269,
14444, 15716, 17715, 19033, †19034, †19035,
19173, 20135, ¶20656, 20659 [and see tp.
20658], 21475, 21552 (19173), 23132, 23371,
25194, Z. Boyd, *Rex Pater*-E., W. Forbes,
Panegyrick-HN.; epistle 26010; *see* 1237.

1634: 1878 (20540), 14313, 17333, 22396,
23597, 24826 later to son, 25778; *see* 739,
17829a [post-*STC*], 22628.

1635: 4479, 10637, 11221, 14712, 17719,
20522, 20944, 22175, 23781, *25900.

1636: 1223, 4134, 4141, ¶5021 = 19036,
10730, 13274, 16769, 17827, 18034, †21724
(21725), 25718.

1637: 1568, 4492, *†10667, 13267, 13367,
15306, 17219, †19037, 20454, 20474, *21092
and *1637*-O.[11], 21540, 25028 (25030).

1638: 5138, 14317, 14501, †19038, 20784
superseding Surgeons, 21725 afresh, 25775 =
5149; *see* 24715.

1639: 6390, 12205, 12646b, 15298, †20488,
†20490 by author, 23066, 24548a, 25025,
25963 superseding Smith.

1640: *1167, 4154 = 10913, †4495, 7038 by
editor, 12397, 12586, 12661, *†13872,
*17178, 18197, 19039, 19112, 19302, 21476,
26084, 26103; *see* 5771.

His Household as Prince: Epistle 12616, some
copies 4747-O.; his Commissioners of
revenue, 18606; courtiers accompanying
him to Spain, epistle 4747.

CHARLES II, *King*. ¶347 superseding Henry,
1109 by editor, *1167, 1186 by editor, 1432
by bookseller, 1543, 3904, 4191, 4196, 6232,
6347, 7295, *10667, 12145, 12529, 13621 and
1639-HD. by editor [see changes], *13872,
14307, 15078, 19032, *20529, 20652 by editor,
21637, 24827, superseding father, *25900,
26010.

Epistle: 4486, 7476, 12509, 20522, 21641
(15080), 21725.

Presentation: 22918 [in *1660*!].

CHARLES IX, *King of France*. Epistle 1463 =
10577.

CHARLES EMANUEL I, *Duke of Savoy*. ¶1397
from earlier foreign including 'London'
1624-PARIS.

CHARLES FREDERICK, *of Gulick. See* KARL.

CHARLES LOUIS, *Elector*. 4525 by editor super-

seding Cotton, *7317 superseding Abbot,
*10667, 11404 and 11406, 12860, *¶13264,
17444, 18022.

CHARLET, Francis, *M.A.* (Foster). Verse 4194.

CHARLEY, Edward, *Barber surgeon*. Epistle
*11203.

CHARLTON, Geoffrey, *Bookseller*. Prose 11600
[? erroneous, for author].

CHARNOCK (Crispe), Elizabeth = Roger.
23717 with husband.

CHARNOCK, Roger, *of Gray's Inn. See preceding.*

CHARTERIS, Henry, *the elder, Printer* (*DNB*).
Signed prose 13150, 15658; unsigned impf.
early ed. 1378-PML., 7074, 16585.

CHARTERIS, Henry, *the younger, Divine* (*DNB*).
Edits 21269, 21270, 21274; jointly with
W. A[rthur]. edits 21272, 21277, 21281,
21283; verse 2363 = 3989, 21101.

CHARTERIS, Robert, *Printer. See* 19528.

CHARTERIS, Thomas, *Bailie of Edinburgh.*
*13173, W. M., *Edinburghs alphabet*-E.

CHATHERTONUS. *See* CHADERTON.

CHAUCER, Lewis, *Son of Geoffrey*. ¶5068.

CHAWORTH, George, *I Viscount Chaworth.*
See 10667.

CHEKE, Sir John, *Scholar* (*DNB*). 857a, 11802,
24056; edits 14634; verse 4654, 22250; prose
4778.

CHEKE, Sir Thomas, *of Pirgo, son of Sir Henry.*
131.

CHESHIRE, Richard, *Vicar of Heston* (Foster).
Minsheu List.

CHESTER, John, *Captain, son of Sir William*-
DNB. Verse 19523.

CHESTER, Sir Robert, *of Royston* (Venn 1585).
*11367, ¶13586, *¶25677 superseding Heton.

CHESTER, Sir William, *Lord Mayor* (*DNB*).
3114, 3168, 14276 [including 4855].

CHETTLE, Henry, *Dramatist* (*DNB*). Prose
17206 signed T. N. [*see* 5123]; verse and
prose 20366a-L. [unique 20366 impf.].

CHETWOOD, Sir Richard, *of Odell, Beds*. 5397
by editor.

CHETWODE, Robert [? *Son of preceding*]. *See*
24099.

CHETWYND, Edward, *Dean of Bristol* (*DNB*).
Epistle *1941; Minsheu List.

CHEUS. *See* CHEW.

CHEVREUSE, Claude de Lorraine, *Duc de*, K.G. *10667.

CHEW, Thomas, *M.A.* (Foster 1559). Verse 23229.

CHEYNEY, *Sir* Francis, *of Chesham Bois* (Venn). *23101, L'Espine, *Comfort for conscience, 1591*-C.[4]

CHEYNEY, Henry, *Baron Cheyney.* 18441.

CHEYNEY (Wentworth), Joan = Henry Baron. 15222, 15588, 18419.

CHENEY (Powle), Mary = *Sir* Francis [*as having married a Rev. Mr. Marston*]. *19168 by bookseller.

CHEYNEY, Richard, *Bishop of Gloucester.* *1710.

CHIBBORNE, *Sir* Charles, *Sergeant-at-law, Lincoln's Inn.* *11670; Minsheu List.

CHIBBORNE, Hanameell, *Son of preceding.* ¶21202.

CHIBBORNE (Young), Margaret = *Sir* Charles. 21194.

CHICHELE, Henry, *Archbishop of Canterbury.* 17102.

CHICHESTER, Arthur, *I Baron Chichester.* 1587, *7336, 16433, *17388 (17390), *21003, ¶23723, C. Hampton, *An inquisition, 1622*-HD., engr. print *Council of war*-L.[5]; *see* 443 for *1612*-D.[6]

CHICHESTER, Edward, *I Viscount Chichester. See* 10667.

CHICHESTER (Harington), Frances = *Sir* Robert. *23273.

CHICHESTER (Perrot), Lettice = Arthur *I* Baron. 24615 and *1611*-HD. [see changes].

CHICHESTER, *Sir* Robert, K.B., *of Devon.* 4683 (*Three sermons, 1617*-LINC.).

CHIDLEY, Robert, *Recorder of London.* Edits 18389.

CHILLINGWORTH, William, *Theologian* (DNB). *See* 11110 = 25776, 25780.

CHITHAM, Thomas, '*London schoolmaster*'. Verse 13506.

CHITTING, Henry, *Chester Herald* (DNB). Verse 24756.

CHOCK. *See* CHALKE.

CHOLMLEY, Henry [? *son of Sir Henry of Burton Coggles*]. 13815.

CHOLMONDELEY, *Sir* Hugh, *Soldier, d. 1596* (DNB). *See* 25438.

CHOLMONDELEY, *Sir* Hugh, *the younger, d. 1601. See* 25438.

CHOLMLEY, Hugh, *Controversialist* (DNB). Epistle 4136, 12709 (12636); *see* 12662 (12706, 12635).

CHOLMONDELEY (Holford), Mary = *Sir* Hugh-DNB. *7293.

CHOLMONDELEY, Robert, *Earl of Leinster.* *7293.

CHOLMONDELEY, Robert, *I Viscount Cholmondeley. See* 10667.

CHRISPYN. *See* CRISPIN.

CHRISTIAN IV, *King of Denmark.* 1402 [and see 1387], *10667, *17699, 20630, E. Bolton, *Tricorones, 1607*-F.; epistle 16618, 16631, *23511 (sometimes 4523).

CHRISTIE, Thomas, *M.A., schoolmaster of Burntisland* (*Reg. Gt. Seal*). *See* 25737.

CHRISTINA, *Queen of Sweden.* Presentation collected 23521, etc.

CHRISTISON, William, *Minister at Dundee. See* 10820.

CHRISTMAS, John *and* Matthew, *Artists. See* 13327.

CHRISTMAS, William, *Alderman.* ¶16684.

CHRISTOPHER. *See* Mahonides.

CHUBB, Matthew, *of Dorchester* (*Vis. Dorset*). *14745.

CHUDLEIGH, *Sir* George, *I Bt.* 13391 (13378), *13396 (13379).

CHUDLEIGH, I. Verse 7046.

CHURCHEY, George, '*of Lyon's Inn*' (? Foster). Prose 7268.

CHURCHOUSE, George, *Mayor of Salisbury.* *19169.

CHURCHYARD, Thomas, *Writer* (DNB). Edits 12190, 18977a; verse 800, 4607, 13941, 14725 pt. iv, 16624, 16870 and *1597*-HN., 20978, 22608, T. Wye, *Briefe discourse, 1580*-C.[6]; Opponent of, *see* 5236, 22644.

CHUTE, Anthony, *Poet* (DNB). *12903; verse 12903 [see 18369].

CHUTE, *Sir* George, *of Sussex* (Foster). Minsheu List.

CHYTRAEUS, Nathan, *Poet* (NBG). Edits 3988 from earlier foreign ed.

CIDUS, Roderius (1808?–DUR.⁵). A fiction.

CIRENBERG, Johann, *Donor to Bodleian.* 21351.

CITOLINI, Alessandro, *of Serravalle* (*Ency. Ital.*). Verse 4738.

CLAPHAM, Henoch, *Theologian* (*DNB*). Verse 24121, W. Perkins, *Reformation of covetousnesse, 1603-*F.

CLAPHAM, John, *One of six clerks, Chancery.* 10594; Minsheu List.

CLAPHAM, Luke, *Father of author* (Venn). 20059.

CLARA MARIANA, *Abbess. See* TYLDESLEY.

CLARE, *Saint.* 5350.

CLARE, *Sir* Ralph, *Royalist* (*DNB*). Epistle some copies *4747-0.

CLARKE, —— [*of some London parish*]. *5700.

CLARKE, ——, '*Ensign, Middlesex militia*'. Epistle *5668.

CLERK, *Sir* Alexander, *Lord Provost of Edinburgh.* *13173, *14995, W. M., *Edinburghs alphabet-E.

CLERKE, Bartholomew, *Civilian* (*DNB*). Epistle 12904; prose 4938, 12904; *see* 18773; *see* BARTH. C.

CLARKE, *Sir* Edward, *Steward of Reading.* *23840, †23849 by editor.

CLERK, John, *Bishop of Bath and Wells.* Verse 13083 unsigned.

CLARKE, John, *Steward of Charterhouse.* ¶5667.

CLARKE, John, *Bookseller.* Unsigned prose 22232.

CLARKE, John, *Lincoln schoolmaster* (*STC*). Edits 10452; *see next.*

CLERKE, John [? *the preceding*]. Edits 15251.

CLARKE, Josias [? *Foster; also one Gray's Inn*]. Verse 5808, 5810.

CLARKE, Nathaniel, *M.A.* (Venn 1631). Verse 5363 (5355).

CLARKE, Nowell (23725). Error for Nowell Warner.

CLARKE, Richard, *of Gray's Inn.* Verse 841.

CLERKE, Richard, *Divine* (*DNB*). *5453.

CLERKE, Richard, *of Lincoln's Inn.* Verse 6307.

CLARKE, *Sir* Robert, *Judge* (*DNB*). 11850.

CLARKE, Robert, *Warden of Watermen.* *¶23725 superseding Warner in 23779, *23817 superseding Cordwainers.

CLARKE, *Sir* Simon, *I Bt.* Minsheu List.

CLERKE, William, *of King's College* (Venn 1467). Edits 16230, 17724.

CLERK, William. Edits 25884.

CLAUDUS, David, *Translator* (BM). Verse 2032 = 2357.

CLAVEL (Willoughby), Frances = John, *Author's mother.* Epistle *5370.

CLAVEL, John, *Highwayman* (*DNB*). Verse 17636; his friends at court, epistle 5369.

CLAVELL, *Sir* William, *of Dorset* (Foster). Epistle 5369; verse 5808, 5810 [cf. 23769].

CLAVERING, *Sir* James, *I Bt.* *3.

CLAVERING, Robert, *Town Clerk of Newcastle.* 1628 by editor.

CLAY, Matthew [*presumably* Venn]. Book licenser *1638–40*, obscure but busy.

CLAYTON, Thomas, *Regius professor* (Foster 1591). *14457, 20382; epistle 6420; verse 13620; prose 12612, 19302; *see* 25327.

CLEAVER, John, *Fellow of Eton* (Foster 1618). *25129.

CLEBURNE, Edmund, *of Cliburne, Westm.* *14297a.

CLEBURNE, Thomas, *of Queen's College* (Foster). Verse 1441a.

CLEMENT VIII, *Pope.* 1408 and 1409 (22393); epistle 4832 = 19392; *see* 3102.

CLEMENT, Dorothy, *Poor Clare, daughter of John-DNB.* *19784.

CLEMENT, Richard, *of the Artillery Company.* Verse 1506.

CLEMENT, William, *Physician* (Venn 1590). Approves 12888, 25355.

CLEERE, *Lady* Anne [? *for Agnes Crane = Sir Edward of Ormesby*]. *¶4220 and *1619-*HD.

CLERE (Wroth), Elizabeth = *Sir* Francis *of Norfolk.* ¶13446; epistle 18521.

CLERK, Clerke. *See* CLARK.

CLES, Bernard, *Cardinal* (*ADB*). 10656.

CLEYBROOKE (Knatchbull), Mary = Paul *of Nash Court* (*Vis. Kent*). 23288.

CLEIBROOKE, William, '*Mercer and merchant*'. *6437.

CLEYPOLE, Sir John, *of Norborough, Northants.* 114.

CLIFFORD (*later* Sackville *and* Herbert), Anne, Countess (DNB). ¶6241, 19499; epistle 6258 (6263, 6238), 15227, *23581 (23575, 21653).

CLIFFORD, Sir Conyers, *Commander* (DNB). 24540.

CLIFFORD (Cecil), Frances = Henry *V Earl.* ¶13142.

CLIFFORD, Francis, *IV Earl of Cumberland.* 4255, ¶4547, ¶23720; *see* 10667, 17331.

CLIFFORD, George, *III Earl of Cumberland.* †796, 3427 by editor superseding Lincoln, 5738, 11275, 12252 [12251 impf.], 12285, 12343, *12923, 13601, 15215, 22265, 22468, 26019 later to Henry; epistle 6333, 16696, 23080 later state (23084); *see* 7099.

CLIFFORD, Henry, *II Earl of Cumberland.* *24361.

CLIFFORD, Henry, *V Earl of Cumberland.* ¶4547 and earlier state-F., *10667, ¶23720.

CLIFFORD (Russell), Margaret = George *III Earl.* 1339, ¶6261 (6236, 6239), 12170, *12293, *¶12312 by editor, *16662a, *18247, 19725 and *1597*-F. (19646), *21787, 22470, *23086 (23084), Hieron, *Certaine meditations, 1615*-E.² (13379), H. Peacham, *Sermon vpon Job, 1591*-O.⁹; epistle 6258 (6263, 6238), 15227, 16696; *see* 24638.

CLIFFORD, Thomas, *of Ugbrooke, Devon, d. 1634.* 25942.

CLIFTON, Sir Gervase, *of Clifton, d. 1588.* 24583.

CLIFTON, Gervase, *I Baron Clifton.* 12295, 17355 later to Lennox, 17376 later to Carnarvon, 17868, 18129.

CLIFTON, Sir Gervase, *I Bt.* 11468.

CLINTON *alias* FIENNES, spelt Fine, *etc.*

CLINTON (Fiennes), Bridget = Theophilus *IV Earl.* 5432.

CLINTON, Edward, *I Earl of Lincoln.* 418-O.⁵, 3422 later to Cumberland, 4470, 6860 afresh 6864, *¶10674, *12745, *12746, 21500; *see* 18773.

CLINTON (Fitzgerald), Elizabeth = Edward *I Earl.* ¶10572 later to Leicester, 24778.

CLINTON (Morrison), Elizabeth = Henry *II Earl.* ¶649.

CLINTON (Knevitt), Elizabeth = Thomas *III Earl.* 5389, N. Larke, *Practice of thankefulnesse, 1622*-O., *21013.

CLINTON, Henry, *II Earl of Lincoln.* 24328 by printer, 13838.

CLINTON, Theophilus, *IV Earl of Lincoln.* *¶4497, ¶16887 cancelled, *20241 by editor; *see* 10667, 10738, 17331.

CLINTON, Thomas, *III Earl of Lincoln.* 21018.

CLITHEROW, Anne, *Augustinian, daughter of Margaret*–DNB. Allison 551.

CLITHEROW, Sir Christopher, *Merchant* (DNB). *150, *3536, *7164, 12074 (sometimes 12071), 13348a, *16825; epistle *25963.

CLYVE, St. Verse 24756.

CLORUS. Verse 7253.

CLOUT, Colin. *See* EDMUND SPENSER.

CLOWES, William, *the elder, Surgeon* (DNB). *723; edits *24713 (24706); verse 1209, 1359, 1360, 6984; prose 1358 (1357), 16870 and *1597*-HN.

CLOWES, William, *the younger, Surgeon* (DNB). Epistle *11203, *25963.

CLUSIUS (L'Ecluse), Carolus, *Botanist* (NBG). ¶16650 superseding Hunsdon.

CLUTTERBOOK, William, *M.A.* (Venn). Verse 7365.

COATES, Roger, *Mayor of Leicester.* *19788.

COB *or* COBBE, Peter, *Writing master in Milk Street.* Verse Penkethman, *Pinnace, 1629*-L. (Harl. 5949); *see* Ames title-pages, ii. 951.

COBHAM, Sir Henry (DNB). *See* BROOKE.

COBUURNE. *See* COCKBURN.

COCHRAN, James, *Dean of Gild, Edinburgh.* *139; epistle *18360.

COCK, COCKE. *See also* COKE.

COCK, George, *Mayor of Norwich.* *¶18493.

COCK, Sir Henry, *of Broxbourne, royal cofferer.* *¶4432, *6468; presentation 6498.

COCKE, I. Verse 23250.

COCKBURN (Sandilands), Alison = John *of Ormiston.* 1340 by printer.

COCKBURN (Douglas), Elizabeth = Samuel *of Temple Hall. See* W. Fowler, *Funeral sonet*-E.²

COCKBURNE (Hamilton), Jean = William *Laird of Skirling.* J. Cockburne, *Gabriels salutation and Iudas kisse, 1605*-E.

COLEMAN, Edmund. Verse 10693, 10694, 18947.

COLEMAN, Thomas, *Divine (DNB)*. Epistle 1576.

COLEPEPER, Edmund, *B.D.* (Foster 1573). Verse 24042.

COLEPEPER, John, *Esq.*, '*J.P. in Sussex*' [*? brother Wm. I Bt.*]. *11380.

CULPEPER (Aston), Joyce = *Sir* Martin. 20977 as Jayes Aston.

COLEPEPER, Martin, *Warden of New College* (Foster). Verse 4759, 24042.

CULPEPER, Mary. 16924.

COLEPEPER, *Sir* Thomas, *of Hollingbourne* (Foster 1591). *¶3463.

COLET. See COLLETT.

COLFE, Abraham, *Divine (DNB)*. *25790, H. Robrough, *Balme from Gilead, 1626*-F.

COLFE, Isaac (Foster 1605). *25790.

COLFE, ——, *Six brothers of two preceding*. *25790.

COLLARD, Christopher, *of St. Martin-in-the-Fields*. See 19511.

COLLARD, Ja. Verse 19777.

COLLES, Edmond. Verse 22460.

COLLES, George, *Son of next*. ¶21846 by editor.

COLLES, John, *the elder, of Barton, Soms., d. 1607*. G. Macey, *Sermon at Charde, 1601*-F.

COLLES, John, *d. 1627, son of preceding*. 21843, 21847.

COLET, John, *Dean of St. Paul's (DNB)*. 10472 and *1556*-F. [from earlier foreign ed.]; prose 5544 = 10497; see 17806.

COLLETT, Thomas, *of Middle Temple*. Verse 17921, 17922.

COLLEY (Whitney), Dorothy = ——. See 25438.

COLLEY, *Sir* Henry, *of Castle Carbery, d. 1637*. See 23779.

COLYNGBORNE, Richard [see PCC 1571]. 21614.

COLLINGWOOD, Francis, *of Trinity College* (Venn). Verse J. Bellot, *Pronostication, 1590*-O.[5]

COLLINS, Daniel, *Vice-provost of Eton* (Venn). *25129.

COLLINES, Ri. [*probably the teacher at Christ's Hospital*]. Verse 11096.

COLLINS, Samuel, *Divine (DNB)*. *18206; verse 11081; see 635, 636, 11020; Minsheu List.

COLINSON, Gilbert, *Bailie of Aberdeen*. W. Mercer, *Bon-acords decorement, 1633*-E.

COLINSON, Thomas, *Bailie of Aberdeen*. *22471.

COLOMA, Don Carlos, *Spanish ambassador*. *4494.

COLQUHOUN, Ge. Verse 7075-E.[2]

COLT, Oliver, *Minister at Foulden*. Verse 10696.

COLVILE (Spencer), Alice = *Sir* Thomas *of Marshe's Manor*. 24393.

COLVILLE (Melville), Elizabeth, *Poet (DNB)*. 13942.

COLVILLE, James, *II Lord Colville*. See 10667.

COLVIUS, Peter, *of Bruges, classicist, d. 1594*. Verse 25438.

COMBES, Thomas. Verse 21011.

COMBE, William, *Sheriff of Warwick, d. 1610*. ¶7183.

COMBER, Thomas, *Dean of Carlisle (DNB)*. 5905, 20692; edits 4492; see 13518.

COMPTON, *Lady* Anne. See SACKVILLE.

COMPTON (Sackville), Cecily = *Sir* Henry K.B. *¶4497, *22971 (22965) by editor, *Psalter of Virgin, 1624*-L.

COMPTON (Spencer), Elizabeth = William *I Earl*. 12565.

COMPTON, Henry, *I Baron Compton*. 7516 by bookseller, 10579, *11708, 12403 by editor.

COMPTON, Spencer, *II Earl of Northampton*. Some copies *¶4497; epistle *4747 [2 in some copies]; see 10667.

COMPTON, *Sir* Thomas, *Brother of next*. Minsheu List.

COMPTON, William, *I Earl of Northampton*. *4023, *¶4497, 6327, 11123, 19546, ¶23720 T. Middleton, *Ghost of Lucrece, 1600*-F.; epistle 24604; see 17331; Minsheu List.

CONANT, John, *B.D.* (Foster 1605). Epistle *1941.

CONDELL, Henry, *Actor (DNB)*. 24562; edits *22273.

CONHAM. *See* CONNAM.

CONINGSBY (Nevill), Cicely = Fitzwilliam *of Hampton Court, Heref.* Epistle 23582a (23575, 21653).

CONINGSBY, Francis, *Captain, surveyor of ordnance.* Epistle *10598.

CONINGSBY, Fitzwilliam, *of Hampton Court* (Foster). 6292 for *1615.*

CONISBY, Humphrey [? *Brother of preceding*]. 1980.

CONINGSBY (North), Mary = Sir Francis *of South Mimms.* *¶4497.

CONINGSBY, Sir Ralph, *of St. Albans* (Foster). *25282.

CONNAM *or* CONHAM, Abraham, *B.D.* (Venn). Verse 1492; prose 1095 (1077).

CONQUEST, Edward [? *Sir Edmund*-Venn]. 3677.

CONRADUS, Sigismundus. Verse 15078.

CONSCIENCE, William. Epistle 4036-L. [earlier-O. impf.].

CONSTABLE (Roper), Anne = Philip *I Bt.* 11317 and earlier-O.

CONSTABLE, Francis, *Bookseller.* Prose 4682 (*Three sermons, 1617*-LINC.).

CONSTABLE, Henry, *Poet* (*DNB*). Verse 14379, 22534.

CONSTABLE, Henry, *Viscount Dunbar. See* 10667.

CONSTABLE, Sir John, *of Yks.* 1141 [see changes]; Minsheu List.

COUNSTABLE, Thomas, *Esq.* 13490 and un-dated-G. [see changes].

CONSTANS (Constant), Leonard, *Huguenot pastor* (BN). Verse 21649.

CONSTANTER (24033). Presumably Huygens.

CONTRARIA contrarijs: Vigilantius: Dormi-tanus. *See* DORMITANUS.

CONWAY, Edward, *I Viscount Conway.* *¶4497, *¶6072, 11768 [see changes], *14440, *17388 (17390), 21426, 23113, 23920 and 23923, 24299, engr. print *Council of war*-L.[5]; Minsheu List.

CONWAY, Edward, *II Viscount Conway.* 5570, 11882; *see* 10667.

CONWAY, Sir John, *Governor of Ostend* (*DNB*). Verse 10791.

CONWAY (Hueriblock), Katherine = Edward *I Viscount.* ¶24175.

CONY-CATCHER, Cuthbert [*fiction*]. Prose 5656-HN. [alias 5655].

CONNIERS, Fr. [*probably* Francis Conyers *o, Ragley*]. Verse 23779.

COOGENES, Jacobus, *Bredanus.* Verse 12890.

COOK, COOKE(s). *See* COKE.

COOLLE *and* COOLEY. *See* COLE *and* COLLEY.

COOPER, Drury, *of Gray's Inn* (Venn 1618). Verse 22454.

COWPER, John. 19808.

COOPER (Coperario, Coprario), John, *Musician* (*DNB*). *See* 24099.

COOPER (Hicks), Mary = *Sir* John *I Bt.* *11688.

COOPER, Thomas, *Bishop of Winchester.* 567, 20368, *21748 (21751); edits 7661, more in 7662; *see* 17456.

COOPER, Thomas, *Divine* (*DNB*). Prose 6690.

COORTESSE. *See* CURTIS.

COOTE, Sir Charles, *I Bt.* Epistle 18811.

COOTH, John, *M.A.* (Foster 1612). Edits *15134.

COPE (Paston), Anne = *Sir* Anthony *I Bt.* *6945 and *1609*-U. by editor, 12848 (12816).

COPE, Sir Anthony, *I Bt.* †3552 supersed-ing Ramsey, 6954, 6968, 17040.

COPE, Sir Edward, *of Eydon* (Venn 1566). ¶11872.

COPE (Chaworth), Elizabeth = *Sir* William *II Bt.* *6945 and *1609*-U. by editor.

COPE, Isabel *alias* Elizabeth. *See* RICH.

COPE, Sir Walter, *Politician* (*DNB*). 12135.

COPE, Sir William, *II Bt.* *6957.

COPLAND, Patrick, *Aberdeen benefactor and Bermuda minister.* *1494 erroneously as Peter.

COPLAND, Robert, *Printer* (*DNB*). Edits Bruni, Guystarde a. Sygysmende, *1532*-L.; Verse 965, 1386, 5092, 5733-PML., 6933, 14558 [? earlier lost], 14559, 15050, 17545, 18475, 23707, 25008.

COPLAND, William, *Printer* (*DNB*). Un-signed prose 260.

COPLANUS, Petrus. *See* PATRICK COPLAND.

COPLEY, Anthony, *Poet* (*DNB*). 1060 by editor; 'Jesuited cousin' of, see 5735, 'dis-Jesuited' in 5736.

COPPEN (Norton), Anne = *Sir* George *Clerk of Crown.* *11772.

COPPEN, Elizabeth [? = *George*], Robert, *and* Thomas (Foster and Venn), *Daughter-in-law and sons of preceding.* *11772.

COPPINGER, Francis, *Nephew of Lord Cobham.* 18582.

COPPOCK, Richard, *of Hart Hall* (Foster). Verse 11475.

COPRARIO. *See* COOPER.

CORBETT, *Sir* Andrew, *of Morton* (*Vis. Shrops.*). *†21437.

CORBET (Barret), Anne = *Sir* Thomas. 21527.

CORBET, Clement, *Civilian* (*DNB*). *¶4338.

CORBET, John, *Divine* (*DNB*). *See* 18062.

CORBET, *Sir* John, *II Bt.* Verse 5097.

CORBET, *Sir* Miles, *of Sprowston, Norf.* *11572; see 25438.

CORBET, Richard, *Bishop of Oxford.* 13619; verse 7045 as Dr. C. B. of O., 5808, 5810 [cf. 23769].

CORBET, Robert. Verse 24603.

CORBET, *Sir* Thomas, *of Sprowston.* †¶18493.

CORBETT, *Sir* Vincent, *of Morton* (*Vis. Shrops.*). *†21437.

CORDELL, Edward, *One of six clerks* (PCC 1590). 18866 by printer.

CORDELL, *Sir* John, *Alderman.* *22531; epistle *25963.

CORDELL, *Sir* William, *Master of the Rolls* (*DNB*). 9527 by editor, 11037, 11049, 15142, 18413, 25976.

CORDIN, Thomas. Verse 13799.

CORICAEUS *alias* C. A. R. Verse 21137.

CORHAM, William, *Esq.* Minsheu List.

CORNISH, Thomas, *Bishop of Tyne* (*Ath. Oxon.*). 3545.

CORNYSSHE, William, *Musician* (*DNB*). Verse 22608.

CORNUAPES (13815). Mask of author Hornby.

CORNWALLIS, *Sir* Charles, *Diplomatist* (*DNB*). 4961.

CORNWALLIS, Frederick, *I Baron Cornwallis.* 11910.

CORNWALLIS, *Lady* Jane. *See* BACON.

CORNWALLIS, *Sir* William, *Essayist* (*DNB*). *¶5583 [1613 lost].

CORROZET, Gilles, *Writer* (*NBG*). Verse 3045.

CORSELIS, Lucas, *Merchant, of Dutch Church.* Minsheu List.

CORY, Edward, *M.A.* (Venn). Verse 13580 (13579).

CORYATE (? Williams), Gertrude = George-*DNB*. *See* 5809 (23725), 5811.

CORYATE, Thomas, *Traveller* (*DNB*). 23807 (23725); epistle 23791 (23725); see 23769 (23725).

COSIN, John, *Bishop of Durham.* Edits 4495.

COSENS, Samuel, *of Exeter College* (Foster). Prose 24702.

COSSAEUS (de Cossé), Charles I, *Comte de Brissac* (*NBG*). ¶3983 (3990) from earlier foreign ed.

COTTERELL (Allen), Anne = *Sir* Clement. ¶16913 by printer [see changes].

COTTERELL, *Sir* Clement, *Groom Porter* (*Vis. Lincs.*). *†1956, ¶16913 by printer [see changes].

COTTIGNOLE (16899). *See* GRATIANUS.

COTTINGTON (Meredith), Anne = Francis *I Baron.* ¶13167 [earlier lost].

COTTINGTON, Francis, *I Baron Cottington.* 14791; epistle *4747 [two in some copies]; see 10667.

COTTON, *Sir* Allen, *Lord Mayor.* *3837, 5852 [earlier lost], *11467, *17886, H. Robrough, *Balme from Gilead, 1626-*F.

COTTON, Bartholomew, *of Starston* (*Vis. Camb.*). Epistle 15037.

COTTON, Charles, *the elder, father of Charles-DNB.* 11071 by editor.

COTTON, Clement, *Religious writer* (*STC*). As patentee, privilege in 1630-F. of 7126.

COTTON (Brocas), Elizabeth = *Sir* Robert *I Bt.* 17953.

COTTON, Henry, *Bishop of Salisbury.* ¶23913.

COTTON (Walshe), Joyce = *Sir* Rowland. Epistle 5870.

COTTON (Harvey), Lucy = Thomas *of Connington.* ★15319.

COTTON (Hulme), Mary = William *Bishop.* 26058.

COTTON, Richard, *of Combermere* (*Vis. Ches.*). See 25438.

COTTON, *Sir* Robert, *I Bt.* 4300, 4521 [see changes], ¶14443, 19500 [see changes], 22172; epistle 13592; *see* 5811, 18087, 25327.

COTTON, *Sir* Rowland, *of Bellaport* (Venn 1596). 15593; verse 5808, 5810 [cf. 23769]; *see* 23779.

COTTON, William, *Bishop of Exeter.* 4663, ¶4682 (*Three sermons, 1617*–LINC.) by bookseller, 10536, 14035 = 16449, 20299; epistle ★1352a.

COTTON, William, *Bookseller.* Prose 23434.

COURT, Thomas, *of University College* (Foster 1598). Verse 19777.

COURTEN, *Sir* William, *Merchant* (*DNB*). 13511, 14933.

COURTENAY, Edward, *XI Earl of Devon.* 191.

COURTHOPE, Peter, *of Cranbrook, Kent.* †¶59.

COVELL, Thomas, *City captain.* ★21095; epistle ★1507.

COVELL, William, *Sub-dean* (*DNB*). 25226; prose 4644.

COVENTRY (Aldersey), Elizabeth = Thomas *I Baron.* 21117.

COVENTRY, John. 18153.

COVENTRY, John, *Son of I Baron* (Keeler). 11052, ¶23573, H. Bennet, *Pastors plea, 1640*–D.

COVENTRY, *Sir* Thomas, *Judge, d. 1606* (*DNB*). J. Frewen, ★†*Certaine instructions, 1587*–FLEMING.

COVENTRY, Thomas, *I Baron Coventry.* ★548, 1229, 1600, ¶3567 superseding Yelverton, 4114 (4113), 4195, 5844 [see changes], 6154 by editor, ★6213 [diff. book from 6212], 10740, 10757, †11379, 12109, ¶12116, 12368, 13171, 13990, 17179, 17613 (17606, 17612), 18382, 19092 by editor, ¶19879, 20332, 20927, 21766, †22400, †22798 by editor, 23015, *1631* of 24017–E. by printer [see changes], ¶24513, 24699, 25212 (25207), 25617, T. Bedingfield, *Cura pastoralis, 1629*–F., H. Valentine, *Private devotions, 1635*–F. [earlier lost]; epistle 20166; *see* 10667.

COVENTRY, Thomas, *II Baron Coventry.* 10597; epistle ★11379.

COVENTRY, Thomas, *Esq.* [? *the preceding*]. 24157.

COVENTRY, Walter, *Warden of Drapers.* ★18280.

COVERDALE, Miles, *Bible translator* (*DNB*). ★6810 = 11888 (10400) [? earlier lost]; edits 5886, 10808; prose anon. in 1280 is signed 1286; *see* M. C. (25591).

COVERT (Shirley), Jane = *Sir* Walter. 11466.

COVERT, Thomas. Verse 25584.

COVERT, *Sir* Walter, *of Sussex* (Brown). †893.

COWLAND, John. Verse 11096.

COWPER. *See* COOPER.

COX, Leonard, *Schoolmaster* (*DNB*). Edits 15604; verse 19166.

COX, Richard, *Bishop of Ely.* ★1710, ★4043 (4044), 25665; epistle 25427; prose 25665; *see* 10026, 24673.

COXE, *Sir* Richard, *Clerk of the Green Cloth, son of preceding.* Minsheu List.

COX, Ro., '*Student*'. Verse 6332.

COXE, William, *Canon of Chichester* (Foster 1596). Epistle 24704 and answer.

COYSH, John, *of Inner Temple* (Foster). Verse 15463 and 15464, 15466.

CRADOCK, Edward, *Alchemist* (*DNB*). Verse 4738, 4761.

CRADOCKE, John, *Cutler without Temple Bar* (*CSPD*). 3714.

CRADOCK, Matthew, *Merchant* (*DNB*). ★5676; epistle ★25963.

CRAFORDIUS. *See* CRAWFORD.

CRAFFT, Henricus, '*Jurisperitus acad. Nassau*'. ★14047.

CRAIG, Alexander, *Poet* (*DNB*). Epistle 1406; verse 12066.

CRAIG, John, *the elder, Physician* (*DNB*). Verse 12550, 12555; Minsheu List.

CRAIG, *Sir* Thomas, *Feudalist* (*DNB*). Verse 14293, 21101, 21875, 21877, 22624.

CRAIG, William, *Regent of philosophy, Edinburgh.* Verse 21101.

CRAKANTHORPE, George, *Brother of next* (Foster). Edits 5983.

CRAKANTHORPE, Richard, *Divine* (*DNB*). R. Aylett, ¶*Brides ornaments, 1625*-F. [posthumously].

CRANE (Hobart), Dorothy = *Sir* Robert. 10755, *11764 [see changes].

CRANE, Nicholas, *Presbyterian* (*DNB*). *See* 4709.

CRANE, Ralph, *Poet* (*DNB*). *16674.

CRANE, Robert, *Principal of New Inn Hall* (Foster). Verse 4759, 21029 (21032).

CRANE, *Sir* Robert, *Bt.* *†26087.

CRANFIELD (Brett), Anne = Lionel *I Earl.* ¶24175.

CRANFIELD, Lionel, *I Earl of Middlesex.* 4992, 5709, ¶11988 and 11989, 17852 superseding Vere, 17985, 23773 (23725); verse 5808, 5810 [cf. 23769]; *see* 10667, 17331.

CRANFIELD, Thomas, *Mercer, father of preceding.* *1092 by editor.

CRANLEY, Thomas, *Poet* (*DNB*). Epistle 25891 (25911); verses in same signed Th. C.

CRANMER, Samuel, *Alderman.* *13351.

CRANMER, Thomas, *Archbishop of Canterbury.* 1722 (1710), 3287, 14019, 20843, 21041, ¶24673; prose 2070 and many later Bibles like 2099, 3962 = 10387; *see* 2068 tp., 5163, 11233, 22819.

CRANSTOUN, John, *II Lord Cranstoun. See* 10667.

CRANSTOUN, William, *Minister of Kettle.* *18171.

CRASHAW, Raleigh, *Colonist* (Brown). Verse 22788 (22790).

CRASHAW, Richard, *Poet* (*DNB*). Signed verse 15520; 22400; unsigned verse 608, 14269.

CRASHAW, William, *Puritan divine* (*DNB*). *128 (107); edits 917, 3218, 4610, 5841, *19678 (19649), 19699 (19649), ¶19649 [earlier lost], 19707 and *1605*-M. (19649), 19733 (19648), 25354, *1609* of 20826-C.²; prose T. Tuke, *Christian directions, 1610*-HAT.; *see* 23920, 23923; Minsheu List; *also search* W.C.

CRAVEN, Jo. Verse 11468.

CRAVEN, *Sir* William, *Lord Mayor* (*DNB*). 1638 by bookseller, 12203, *¶13247, *17700, *18263, *20756, *23331 [see changes], *23864, W. Dorke, *Tipe of friendship, 1589*-HN.

CRAVEN, William, *I Earl of Craven.* 1557, 11156, 12452, 18845 and 18845a by editor,

20098, 21460, 24794 by editor Farnaby, R. Baker, *Meditations upon consolatorie psalmes, 1640*-F., Gaultier, *Miles gloriosus, 1630*-L.; epistle 13620 only; *see* 10667.

CRAFORDUS *alias* LUNNAEUS, Robertus. Verse 18166, 18167.

CRAWFURD, Thomas, *Professor* (*DNB*). Verse 135, 3904, 6032, 18290, 19781, P. Anderson, *Grana angelica, 1635*-F.; *see* 25737.

CRAFORD, Tho. Verse 22444.

CRAWLEY, *Sir* Francis, *Judge* (*DNB*). ¶110; *see* 10667.

CRAWLEY, John, *of Gray's Inn* (Venn 1625). *See* 15466.

CREEDE, Thomas, *Printer* (*DNB*). Signed prose 18053; unsigned 1667, 15379, 20002.

CREED, William, *Divine* (*DNB*). Verse 3, 22888.

CREIGHTON. *See* CRICHTON.

CRESSEWELL, Richard. 421 for *1624*.

CREW, John, *I Baron Crew of Stene.* 3248 (3255) by editor, *†5379.

CREW, *Sir* Ranulphe, *Judge* (*DNB*). 4766, *11670, 11675 (11652).

CREW, T. (some copies 6309). *See* CAREW.

CREW (Bray), Temperance = *Sir* Thomas. *13471.

CREW, *Sir* Thomas, *Speaker of the House* (*DNB*). 5378, 12852, 12853 (12816 and *Six sermons, 1628*-O.), 22121.

CRICH, Edmund, *Master of Merchant Taylors.* Minsheu List.

CRICH, John, *Son of preceding.* Minsheu List.

CREIGHTON *or* CRICHTON, Robert, *Bishop of Bath and Wells.* *18206; verse 7365; prose 11326.

CRICHTON, William, *S.J.* (*DNB*). 4894.

CRICHTON, William, *I Earl of Dumfries.* *1203, 5932 (5909); *see* 10667; Minsheu List.

CRIPS. *See* CRISP.

CRISP (Prescott), Anne = *Sir* Nicholas *I Bt.* Epistle 25182.

CRISP, Ellis, *Alderman, brother of next.* *11654 (11652).

CRISP, Nicholas, *Merchant.* *11654 (11652), *¶11672 (11679, 11652).

CRISP, Sir Nicholas, *I Bt.* †11663 (11652),
*16942, *†22151, *†23717, 25182; epistle
*1507, 25184, *25963.

CRISP, Samuel, *Brother of preceding.* *†22151,
*†23717; epistle 25182.

CRISP, Tobias, *Antinomian* (*DNB*). *23717.

CRISPIN, Richard, *Canon of Exeter* (Foster).
See 18575.

CRITON *and* CRITTONUS. *See* CRICHTON.

CRITOPYLUS, Metrophanes, *Greek at Oxford*
(*Ath. Oxon.*). Verse 12791, 22390.

CROCKET, Tho. Verse 17201.

CROFTS, Anthony, *of Gray's Inn.* Verse 14008,
23249.

CROFTS, Sir Henry, *of Saxham, Suff.* Epistle
19909.

CROFT, Sir James, *the elder, Lord Deputy*
(*DNB*). *¶10674; *see* 18773.

CROFTS, Sir John, *of Saxham* (Venn 1581).
7460, †¶21869, ¶26081.

CROFTS (Shirley), Mary = Sir John. 19909,
¶20552, 25392 (25389).

CROFT, Sir William, *Gentleman to Prince*
(Foster 1609). Epistle some copies *4747-O.

CROOKE, Andrew, *Bookseller.* Prose 11072.

CROKE, Charles, *Professor* (*DNB*). Verse 3914.

CROKE, Sir George, *Judge* (*DNB*). *6025 and
*1613-F., 7311, *24297; *see* 10667.

CROOKE, H., *Dr.* [*unidentified*]. *See* H. C.

CROKE, Sir John, *Judge* (*DNB*). 5301 by
editor Cogan; edits 14901.

CROOKE, John, *Esq.* [? Croke, *I Bt.*]. 3708 and
*1607-L.

CROKE (Bennett), Mary = Sir George. 7337
[date is *1630*].

CROOKE, Samuel, *Divine* (*DNB*). Epistle
*1941.

CROOKE, Thomas, *Divine* (*DNB*). See 4709.

CROKE, Unton, *the elder, d. 1671* (*DNB*).
Verse 3914.

CROKER (Riddall), Joan = John *of Batsford,
Gloucs.* *¶25971.

CROMER, William, *of Tunstall, d. 1598* (*Vis.
Kent*). *11127; epistle 19148 only.

CROMPTON (Crofts), Frances = Sir John.
Epistle 19909.

CROMPTON, Sir John, *of Skerne, Yks.* †3830.

CROMPTON, John. Verse 5569.

CROMPTON, Richard, *Lawyer* (*DNB*). Edits
10978.

CROMPTON, Sir Thomas, *Civilian* (Foster).
Edits 5824.

CROMWELL, Gregory, *I Baron Cromwell.* 201,
5323a, 24847, and *1539-O*.

CROMWELL, Henry, *Son of next.* 21081.

CROMWELL, Sir Oliver, *K.B., of Hinching-
brooke.* 1658, 13929; *see* 7095.

CROMWELL, Thomas, *Earl of Essex.* 908, 2817
only, 7643 later dropped, 10492, 11393
[11392 impf.], 15604 by editor, 16009, 18109,
20521; *see* tp. 2068 [excised 2072].

CROMWELL, Thomas, *I Earl of Ardglass.* 4318;
see 10667, 17332.

CROOKE. *See* CROKE.

CROPLEY, John, *D.D.* (Venn 1596). Minsheu
List.

CROSHAW. *See* CRASHAW.

CROSLEY, Alexander, *M.A.* (Foster). Verse
4192 only.

CROSSE, Henry, '*Barnstaple merchant*'. Prose
6058.

CROSSE, Richard, *Clergyman* (Foster 1597).
Edits 24536.

CROSSE, William, *Poet* (*DNB*). Continues
12376; *see* 24099.

CROSSING, Francis, *of Exeter* (Foster). 23559
(23563).

CROTTENDINE, Abraham, *of Amsterdam congregation* (Burrage). *5345.

CROUCH *or* CROWCH, Humphrey, *Ballad-
writer* (*DNB*). Verse 17745.

CROUCH, Thomas, *Fellow of King's* (Venn
1626). Verse 13519.

CROWE, William, *Master of Barber Surgeons.*
Verse 5447.

CROWLEY, Robert, *Author and printer* (*DNB*).
*6810 = 11888 (10400), *16860; edits 22136;
prose 16860, 20973, 24468a, 25588; unsigned
prose 19906; *see* 15218, 15221, 25295.

CROWTHER, Joseph, *M.A.* (Foster). Verse
5097.

CROXTON, John, *of Ravenscroft, d. 1599* (*Vis.
Ches.*). See 25438.

CROY, Iohannes de la, '*Leyden printer*' (11735). Mystification of J. Wolfe.

CRUGGE, John. Verse 5461.

CRUSO, John, *Civilian* (*DNB*). Epistle 15037.

CRUXONIUS, Richardus, '*Theologus*'. Verse 21752.

CRYCH *and* CRYMES. *See* CRICH *and* GRYMES.

CUDNER, Robert, *Merchant* (*Vis. London*). Epistle 23779 only; verse 23779 (23725).

CUDWORTH, Ralph, *D.D.* (Venn 1589). Epistle *1941; edits 19680 (19649).

CUFAUDE, Will. Verse 18342 (18337).

CUFF, Henry, *Author* (*DNB*). Verse 4503 (4509).

CUFF, William, *of Lincoln's Inn* (Foster). Verse 19777.

CULLEN, Gilbert, *Bailie of Aberdeen*. *22471.

CULME, William, *M.A.* (Foster). Verse 6787.

CULPEPER. *See* COLEPEPER.

CULVERWEL, Ezechiel, *Vicar* (Foster). Edits 6640; prose 21215; *search* E. C.

CUNNINGHAM, Alexander, *V Earl of Glencairn*. 6320.

CUNINGHAM, William, *Physician* (*DNB*). Verse 11529 (24723); prose 15192.

CUNNINGHAM, William, *IX Earl of Glencairn*. *See* 10667 as Alexander.

CURLL, Walter, *Bishop of Winchester*. 58, 60, *1928, 20161, 23993. *See* 10667; Minsheu List.

COORTESSE, John, '*Minister of Yapton, Sussex*'. *See* 13923.

CURTEYSE, Thomas, *Gent*. Verse *1573* of 19426-HN.

CURWEN, Sir Patrick, *Bt*. †6044a.

CURSON, Sir John, *of Waterperry* (*Vis. Oxfs.*). Minsheu List.

CURZON, Sir John, *I Bt*. *†5379.

CUSACK, Christopher, *Founder of Irish College, Douay*. *11026.

CUSHMAN, Robert (*STC*). *See* R. G. [*sic*].

CUTTS, Sir John, *the elder, of Essex* (Venn 1561). *25622 (25620); *see* 25695.

CYGNUS (14782). *See* HUGH HOLLAND.

CYPRIAN, Charles. *See* 3388.

D

D., *Countess of*. T. Riley, *Triall of conscience*, 1639-F.

D., *Lady*. Epistle 16696.

D., *Lady* Alicia (19511). *See* DUDLEY.

D., A. B. C., '*Cousins*' [*mask*]. 24567.

D., A., *Gentlewoman*. Verse 7160.

D., A. Verse 23376; prose 4940 as '*printer*' [*editor*]; *see* 11872 [? Danvers].

D., Car. Verse 19337.

D., D. Verse 14783 [? Digges]; prose 18758 [? fiction]; caution: in inscriptions *D.D.* means *dedicates*.

D., D. R. (23462). *See* R. D.

DuTR., D., '*Paris physician*'. Verse *1606* of 18985-HD, 18985, 18986.

D., E. [*traditionally* Dyer]. 23937.

D., M. E. Verse 12972.

D., F., *Kt*. Verse 21624.

D., Sir G. *See* 3589.

D., G., *Cantab*. Verse 73.

D., G. Verse 501 for *1630*, 11419, 13800, Plutarch, *President for parentes, 1571*-HN.; prose W. Pelham, *Meditations, 1625*-F.

D., H. (6175). *See* HENRY H[OLLAN]D.

D., H. Prose 25663; *see* 14555 ['*at H.*'].

D., I. (14783), *see* JOHN DONNE; *of Hereford* (19343), *see* J. DAVIES; I. D., *Tam arte quam Marte* (21057), *see* DAVIES *of Hereford*.

D., I., *of Middle Temple* [*presumably Sir J. Davies*]. Verse 4985.

D., I., *of Caius College*. Verse 24928.

D., I., *Scoto-Britannus*. Verse 6014, 13582.

D., I., '*Divine*'. Peruses 12891.

D., J. 10910; edits 12734; verse 686, 11636 (11638), 14275, 15434, 17816 as M. I. D., 19529; *see* 12456, 24434.

DA., Io. [*supposedly* Davies of Hereford]. Verse 6485.

DEB., I. Verse 11636.

D., I. B., *Nobilis Flor*. Verse 7376.

D., Sir K. [*unquestionably* Digby]. Prose 12613.

D., K. Verse 11636.

D., L. Edits 6029.

D., M. (15686, etc.). All accepted as by Drayton.

DR., PR. *See* 25438.

D., R., *Esq.* Verse 19615.

D., R. [*presumably* Daniel *the bookseller*]. Prose 794.

D., R. 23462 as D. R. D.; prose 1718 [? Day]; verse 17816 as M. R. D., Faureau, *Briefe direction, 1618*-O.[5]

D., R. Y. S. M. L. A., *Mother of.* 24714.

D., S. (10513). *See* THOMAS S[OROCOL]D.

D., S. Verse 5582.

D., T. (26041). *See* THOMAS DEW.

D., T., *of St. John's, Oxford.* Verse 4762.

D., T., *Cantabr.* Verse 164.

D., T., *B.D., Minister.* Verse 13582.

D., T. Verse 12915; prose 15640.

D., Sir W. [? *fiction*]. *See* 7434.

D., W., *Exoniae.* Verse 17824.

D., W. [*ascribed to* Drummond]. Verse 22566, 22570.

D., W. Verse 3635; *see* 12696 (12706, 12635) as '*revolted [to Rome]*'.

D., Z. Verse 1695.

DABBE. *See* TAB.

DABITOT, Giles [? *fiction*]. Verse 13540.

DABORNE, Robert, *Dramatist* (*DNB*). Verse 3830, 23779 only.

DACCOMB, James, *of Stepleton, Dorset.* 3659.

DACCOMBE, Sir John, *Chancellor of the Duchy of Lancaster.* 7472, 18628 [see changes]; Minsheu List.

DACKHAM, DACKOMBE. *See* DACCOMB.

DAYSIE, The. Verse 6735.

DALBY, Dorothy, '*Widowed mother of author*'. 25387.

DALE, Henry, *Merchant* (*Vis. London*). 16989.

DALE, Valentine, *Civilian* (*DNB*). 14860.

DALGLEISH, Nicol, *Minister of Pittenweem.* Epistle *148 posthumously.

DALLINGTON, Sir Robert, *Master of Charterhouse* (*DNB*). Verse 15139 as Dillington.

DALLISON, Sir Maximilian, *of Halling, Kent.* 3685.

DALTON, Richard, *of Pilling* (Venn 1595). Epistle 25226.

DALTON, Robert, *Brother of preceding.* ¶25224.

DALZELL, Robert, *1 Earl of Carnwath.* *See* 10667.

DAMMAN, Sir Adrian, *Diplomat and professor at Edinburgh.* Verse 14293, 14379, 14786, 14787, 21101.

DAMMAN, Theophilus, *Son of preceding.* Verse 21657.

DAMPORT. *See* DAVENPORT.

DANBY (Eure), Margaret = Thomas. 3931.

DANETT (Bellamy), Agnes = John *of Westhope* (PCC 1626). 13820.

DANET, Tho. Verse 23248.

DANIEL (Vinor), Anne = Sir William *Judge.* Epistle 1598.

DANIEL, John, *of Clement's Inn, Translator.* Verse 19832.

DANIEL, John, *Musician* (*DNB*). Edits 6238; *see* 24099.

DANIEL, Roger, *Cambridge printer.* Unsigned prose 13183; *see* R.D.

DANIEL, Samuel, *Poet* (*DNB*). Verse 7492 [earlier than 7491], 11099, 12415, 18041, 18428, 21649; *see* 16658, 19480, 23779 only; for S. D. (10513) *see* SOROCOLD.

DANIEL, William, *of Gray's Inn* [? *1608: more than one*]. Minsheu List.

DANSELL, Sir William, *Receiver, Court of Wards.* 1585, *19547.

DANSKIN (Dantiscanus), Henry, *St. Andrews poet.* Verse 74, 1496, 14786.

DANTER, John, *Printer.* Prose 1487, 17866, 19775 in Welsh, 22666.

DANVERS, Daniel, Dorothy, *and* Samuel. Epistle 11872.

DANVERS, Henry, *1 Earl of Danby.* 11624, ¶12654 (12707, 12635), 14316, *22808 by editor, 23563, J. Baker, *Prayers*-O.[6]; *see* 10667, 17332, 25327.

DARCY, Sir Arthur, *Son of Thomas-DNB.* 15204, 26141.

DARCY, Brian, *of Tiptree, Essex.* *1591.

DARCY, Sir Edward, *Groom of Privy Chamber.* 25203.

DARCY, Sir Francis, *of Mdsx.* (Foster). *¶4220 and *1619*-F.

Davies, Richard, *Brother of John of Hereford.* Verse 6333.

Davies, Ri. Edits 5118.

Davis, Robert, *City captain.* ⋆21095; epistle ⋆1507.

Davies, Silvanus, *Son of John of Hereford.* Verse 24603.

Davye, Will., '*Bencher, Lincoln's Inn*' [*? error for* Henry]. Minsheu List.

Davison. *See* Davidson.

Davy du Perron, Jacques, *Cardinal* (*NBG*). Some copies 4570-L.; *see* 4740 (14346) *and* 4741.

Dawes, *Sir* Abraham, *Farmer of Customs.* †4177 by bookseller, ⋆15115, ⋆24660 [24659 a ghost].

Dawes, Lancelot, *Divine* (*DNB*). Verse 1441a.

Dawson, Thomas, *Printer.* Unsigned prose 3132.

Day, Angell, *Writer* (*DNB*). Verse 18428.

Day, John, *Printer* (*DNB*). Epistle 11223; signed prose 11800, 24670; unsigned prose 375, 2087, 2853, 14018 (14021), 17628 (1492), 18685 (18677); patent to 4812.

Day, John, *Dramatist* (*DNB*). Verse 5461 only.

Day, Martin, *D.D.* (Venn). Minsheu List.

Day, Richard, *Printer* (*DNB*). Edits 11224; signed prose 1574 of 19466-F. [signature later sporadic]; unsigned prose 1489; *see* R. D.

Day, Richard, *Gent.* Verse 24096.

Day, Richard, *D.D.* (Venn 1622). Verse 13519.

Day, Thomas, *Gentleman of the Chapel. See* 24099.

Day, William, *Divine, fl. 1666* (*DNB*). Verse 13519.

Deane, *Sir* John, *of Essex* (Foster 1595). ⋆19601.

Deane, *Sir* Richard, *Lord Mayor.* ⋆6493, ⋆17886, ⋆23345 [see changes]; *see* 22532.

Death, Anthony, *Schoolmaster* (Venn 1617). Verse 10667.

Debney, Robert, *Mayor of Norwich.* ⋆7323.

De Brie, Dirk *or* Theodore, *Engraver* (*DNB*). Edits 12786.

De Burgh. *See* Bourke.

De Courcy, Gerald, *XIV Baron Kingsale. See* 10667.

Dee, Francis, *Bishop of Peterborough. See* 10667.

Dee, John, *Mathematician* (*DNB*). Verse 19775, 20800 initialed, 20801 *and* 1570-O.[12]; prose 10560, 10749; friend of: edits 6459.

Deeble, Nicholas, *M.A.* (Foster 1604). Verse 6330, 6333.

De Eugain, ——, '*Captain, Yarmouth militia*'. ⋆21093.

De Grey. *See* Grey.

De Heere, Lucas, *Painter* (*DNB*). Verse 18601, 18603.

De Insula. *See* Lisle.

Deios, Laurence, *Divine* (*DNB*). Verse 23278.

Dekker, Thomas, *Dramatist* (*DNB*). Verse 3819, 5326, 12863, 19165, 23806 (23725).

Delabere, John, *M.D.* (Foster). Verse 4759.

De Laine, Walter, *Minister of Dutch Church and 'Biblioscopus'.* Edits 2799.

Delapeend. *See* Peend.

Delaune, H. [*see* Venn *and* Wing]. Verse 1805.

Delaune, Isaac, *Son of next.* Verse 4427.

Delaune, William, *Divine* (*DNB*). Verse 11750.

Delbridge, John, '*of Barnstaple*' [*cf.* PCC 1622]. ⋆¶4682.

De l'Ecluse, Jean, *Separatist elder at Amsterdam* (Burrage). ⋆18789.

Deloenus. *See* Delaine.

Dempster, Thomas, *Writer* (*DNB*). Verse 7547.

Denham, Henry, *Printer* (*DNB*). Verse 22136; unsigned prose 21865.

Denham, *Sir* John, *the elder, Judge* (*DNB*). ⋆1943, ⋆11202, ⋆11670; *see* 10667.

Dynham, William, *of Middle Temple* (*1521*). Verse early ed. of 10478-HN., 20140; prose 9516.

Denniston *or* Danielstoun, James, *of Edinburgh Town Council.* ⋆5927 (5909).

Denison, John, *Divine* (*DNB*). Epistle ⋆23840.

DENISON, Stephen, *of Cree Church* (Venn). Verse 22389; prose 5842.

DENISOT, Nicolas, *French poet* (NBG). Verse 3166 as Comte d'Alsinois [anagram].

DENNETIÈRES, Pierre, 'Gentilhomme Tournisien'. Verse 18603; *see* NOOT, *Het bosken*, [1568]-F.

DENNY, Sir Anthony, *Courtier* (DNB). 6156, 14637, 24654.

DENNY, Sir Edward, *Soldier, uncle of next.* 19877.

DENNY, Edward, *I Earl of Norwich.* ¶12635, 12647, *12648, ¶12650, ¶12652, ¶12658, ¶12671, 12677, 12705, 12709, 12712—mostly all (12706, 12635, etc.); *see* 12662 (12706, etc.).
16874, *18523, 18963, 19668 and 19669 (19649) by editor, 19750 (19647), 19757 (19647), 20027 (20011, 20003), 21203, *22808 by editor, *†¶23582 (23575, 21653), 25202, 25656, 26002, 26005; *see* 10667, 17332.

DENNY (Champernon), Joan = *Sir Anthony.* ¶13910.

DENNY (Cecil), Mary = *Edward I Earl. See* 12662 (12706, 12635).

DENNY, Sir William, *Serjeant-at-law, father of next.* *22508.

DENNY, Sir William, *Bt.* Verse 15036.

DENNY, William, *Esq.*, 'Sergeant major'. Verse 7366.

DENSELL. *See* DANSELL.

DENT, Daniel, *Fellow of King's* (Venn). Verse 13519.

DEPUP, John, *Schoolmaster* (Venn). Verse 1410.

DE QUESTER. *See* QUESTER.

DERING (Vaughan), Anne = *Edward. See* PROUSE.

DERING, Edward, *Puritan divine* (DNB). Verse 19149; prose 4794 [really by Dering]; *see* 13774.

DEARING, John, *Gent.* [of Kent]. *11127.

DESAINLIENS or HOLYBAND, Claude, *Language teacher* (STC). Verse 18276.

DES MONS, Engelbert, 'Secretary to Count Mansfield'. Verse 21139.

DETHICK, Henry, *Archdeacon* (Foster). Edits 13485; verse 4783, 23229.

DETHICK, Humphrey, *Gentleman usher to Charles I.* Epistle some copies *4747-O.

DETHICK, Sir William, *Garter King of arms* (DNB). ¶16910 by editor [see changes].

DE TILIA NEMORE. *See* LYNDWOOD.

DEVEREUX Family. *17361.

DEVEREUX (Walsingham), Frances = Robert II Earl, previously Sidney. 5228, ¶11171, 15459, *18103, ¶23077 (23084), 25121; epistle 6333, 16696.

DEVEREUX (Scudamore), Jane = *Sir William of Merevale.* 7199 only.

DEVEREUX (Knollys), Lettice, *Countess. See* DUDLEY.

DEVEREUX, Robert, *II Earl of Essex.* Chronologically:
To 1587: 6364 by editor, 12239, 12912, 15096, 15454, 19871, 24060.
1588–9: 3056 by editor, 5541, 11735, 13143 by editor, ¶15097, 19534, 19872.
1590: 7277, 11734, 12915, 13590, 15638 only, 25119, 25732, J. Bellot, *Pronostication*-O.⁵; epistle 23080 (23084).
1591: *3508, 11625 by editor, 16810, 19619 [see changes]; Essex supposedly did prose signed A. B. in 23642 (23645).
1592: 3873, 5577, 11515, ¶17648 [see changes], 23455, 25695, ¶25696 [see changes], A. Pérez, *Pedaços de historia*-HD.
1593: 12913, 13948, 14917, 17121, 23468; epistle 1469-L.
1594: 756 = 20157, 1054, 3834, 4174 [see changes], 11870, 18284, 19398, 19991.
1595: 3436 [see changes], 5245, 5883, 13898, ¶17669, 18428, 21788; epistle 4544.
1596: 11866, 16872, 18192, 18540, 20606 (20613 and 1613-C. as letter to Elizabeth!), J. Perrott, *Discovery of discontented mindes*-O.; *see* 9203–8.
1597: 1445, 15111, 17906 [17905 ghost], 18614, 23281; epistle 16696.
1598: 11854, 13632 later to Henry, 13635 only, 20158, 20601, ¶21661 and further piece-F. (21649), 23644, 24620.
1599: 6054, 7303, 11834, 12995, 18146, 22554, 25368 by editor; *also see* 7099, 19511.

DEVEREUX, Robert, *III Earl of Essex.* ¶686, *3961, ¶5393, *¶6072, 7463, *11496, ¶12712 (12706, 12635), ¶16887 cancelled, 17921, ¶21869 only, ¶23582 (23575, 21653); epistle 6333, *11087; *see* 10667, 12662 (12706, 12635), 17331; Minsheu List.

DEVEREUX, Walter, *I Earl of Essex.* 10867 [earlier lost], 15541.

DEVIL, Adherents of. Epistle 6794.

DEVRIEND, Petrus. Verse 21657.

DEW, Thomas, *Bookseller*. Prose 26041 signed, some copies initialed.

D'EWES, Gerrard, *Printer* (*DNB*). Consider A. D. (4940).

DEWHURST, Bernard, *Surveyor and mathematician*. *13070.

DEWHURST, Robert, *M.A.* (Foster 1559). Verse 23229.

DICAEOPHILE, Eusebius. *See* FOGNY.

DICK, Jo. [*? Minister of Inch*]. Verse 3904.

DICK, *Sir* William, *Lord Provost of Edinburgh* (*DNB*). *13173, *13258, W. M., *Edinburghs alphabet*-E.

DICONSON, Abraham, *D.D.* (Venn). Verse 13936.

DICKSON, Alexander, *Scottish mnemonist, d. Winchester* (*STC*). ¶19065 as Disconus; *see* 19064.

DICKSON, David, *Scottish divine* (*DNB*). Epistle 71 (70); verse 22186.

DICKINSON, Io. [*? John, STC*]. 23248.

DICUS, Hugh, *Reading preacher* (Foster). Epistle *23840.

DIETRICHSTEIN, Erasmus, *Styrian noble*. Sözinger, *Disputatio, 1610*-O.⁵

DIGBY [*cryptically*, 'To Digbies noble worth']. *11125.

DIGBY (Walcot), Beatrice = John *I Earl*, *previously* Dyve. *6880 (6886).

DIGBY, E. [*supposedly the next*]. Epistle 16658.

DIGBY, Everard, *Author* (*DNB*). *See* 23872.

DIGBY, George, *II Earl of Bristol*. 19942 by editor.

DIGBY, John, *I Earl of Bristol*. 20121; *see* 10667, 17331, 17332; Minsheu List.

DIGBY, Kellam *or* Kenelm, [*? Venn 1552*]. Presentation 6843.

DIGBY, *Sir* Kenelm, *Author* (*DNB*). 688, 4165, 5904, 14439, 16828, 17717 [serving also for 17718], 18087 by editor, 18899, 18979, 21470, 22435 by editor; epistle 20692; from external evidence edits 14754, prose 911; *see* K. D.

DIGBY, Robert, *I Baron D. of Geashill*. Epistle some copies *4747-O.; *see* 10667.

DIGBY, Simon, *Secretary to John I Earl*. Minsheu List.

DIGGES, *Sir* Dudley, *Diplomatist* (*DNB*). 1442, ¶3452, 7343, 14305a, *21175, *22508; verse 5808 and 5810 [cf. 23769]; *see* 10667.

DIGGES, Dudley, *Son of preceding* (*DNB*). Edits 6874; verse 5097, 21725.

DIGGES, Edward, *Governor of Virginia, brother of preceding*. Verse 24137.

DIGGES, Leonard, *Poet* (*DNB*). Verse 288, 22273, 22344, 24137 posthumously.

DIGGES, Thomas, *Mathematician* (*DNB*). Edits 6848, 6858, 6864; prose 5486, 6462.

DIGGES, Thomas, *Esq.* 6368.

DIGGES, Thomas Posthumous, *of Barham, Kent, b. 1590*. *¶3588; birth an issue in 5493.

DILKE (Bonham), Elizabeth = Thomas *of Maxstoke* (*Vis. Warw.*). *¶11773 [*see* changes].

DILLINGTON. *See* DALLINGTON.

DILLON, James, *I Earl of Roscommon*. *See* 10667.

DILLON, Thomas, *IV Viscount Dillon*. *See* 10667.

DIOTORUS, Zacharias, *Phrysius, Erasmus' protégé in Warham's service*. Verse 13811.

DISCONUS (19065). *See* DICKSON.

DISLE, Henry, *Printer*. Prose 7516.

DITCHFIELD *or* DICHFIELD, Edward, *City captain*. *21095; epistle *1506, *1507.

DIVE. *See* DYVE.

DIXIE, Thomas, *of Gray's Inn* (Venn 1624). Verse 1353.

DIXIE, *Sir* Wolstan, *Lord Mayor* (*DNB*). 23283, *25335 [*see* changes], *Jehovah*, [1576]-L.² by J. Daniel trans.

DIXIE, *Sir* Wolstan, *I Bt.* 1353.

DIXON, William, *M.A.* (Foster 1575). Verse 23278.

DOBS, Tho. Verse 13260.

DOCHEN, Thomas, *M.D.* (Foster 1564). Verse 4756, 4759, 21029 (21032).

DOCWRA, Edmund, *of Chamberhouse, Berks*. 15242 and *1574*-F. by editor.

DOCWRA, Henry, *I Baron Docwra*. 11400 by editor.

DOCWRA, Theodore, *II Baron Docwra*. *See* 10667.

DODDE, John, '*Sussex preacher*'. See 13923.

DOD, John, *Puritan divine* (*DNB*). Edits 5386, 6935; prose 22476.

DOD, John, *of Tushingham, brother of author*. *2731.

DOD, John, *of Broxton, Ches., nephew of author*. *2731.

DODDRIDGE, Sir John, *Judge* (*DNB*). T. S., *Christus redivivus, 1624*-F.; Minsheu List.

DODDRIDGE, Richard, *of Exeter College* (Foster). Verse 12757.

DODGE, Edward, *Esq.* 6275.

DODINGTON, Bartholomew, *Greek scholar* (*DNB*). Greek verse 1492, 4503 (4509), 6037, 6843, 12188, 14608; prose 6577.

DORINGTON, Francis, *of St. Antholin's, London*. Epistle *12203.

DODINGTON or DORINGTON, Sir William, *of Breamore, Hants, d. 1638*. 19348, ¶25096; presentation 716.

DODSWORTH, John, *of Thornton Watlass* (Venn 1613). *14297a.

DOESBORCH, Jan van, *Antwerp printer*. See 22367 [good copy at L.¹⁶].

DOGGETT, John, *Merchant Adventurer*. 25842.

DOILY. See DOYLY.

DOLMAN. See PARSONS.

DOMINIS, Marco Antonio de, *Divine* (*DNB*). B. Robertson, *Sapientia, 1618*-CHATS.; edits 21760.

DONATI, Edouardo [? *fiction*]. See 11636 only.

DONE, Donne, Dones, Dunn(e), Dunche, Duns.

DUNS (Dunche), ——, *Esq.*, '*of Berks*'. Minsheu List.

DUNN, Charles, *of Christ Church* (Foster). Verse 24042.

DONNE, Sir Daniel, *Civilian* (*DNB*). Minsheu List.

DUNN, George, *Warden of Barber Surgeons*. Epistle *25963; verse 25963.

DONNE, George, *Son of poet John*. Verse 11157, 11163, 13356, 17637.

DONE, Jane, *Daughter of Sir John of Utkinton* (*Vis. Ches.*). ¶21196, 21197.

DUN, Io. [? Foster 1523]. Verse 1242.

DONNE, John, *Poet and Dean of St. Paul's* (*DNB*). *106 (115), *7021, 19801, 24090; verse 5808 and 5810 [cf. 23769], 14783 (14751); see 5811; Minsheu List.

DONNE, John, *the younger, Writer* (*DNB*). Edits 7038.

DONE, John [*perhaps the preceding*]. Verse 22790.

DONES, John [*supposedly* Dunche]. Verse 5808, 5810 [cf. 23769].

DUNCHE, William, *of Avebury and Gray's Inn* (*1611*). 1392.

DONNING, John, *Customer of Rye* (*Vis. Sussex*). 709.

DORINGTON. See DODINGTON.

DORMAN, Thomas, *Catholic divine* (*DNB*). See 18740.

DORMER (Herbert), Anna Sophia = Robert *I Earl*. *6271, *25719 (25718); epistle *15465.

DORMER (Browne), Elizabeth = Robert *I Baron*. 11323; see 23776.

DORMER, Jane, *Duchess of Feria* (*DNB*). 11181 [? earlier lost], 18083 by printer.

DORMER, Robert, *I Baron D. of Wyng*. 13224.

DORMER, Robert, *Earl of Carnarvon*. *10530, 11203, †11204, 17378 [see changes], 17639, 20347; see 10667, 17332.

DORMITANUS. Verse 25755 signed 'Contraria Contrarijs: Vigilantius: Dormitanus'. Solution dubious; Hotson proposed collaboration of R. Wakeman and E. Napper.

DORNAVIUS (Dornau), Caspar, *Philologist* (*NBG*). Verse 4508 (4509).

DORRELL. See DARRELL.

DORVILLE, Frederick, *B.D.* (Foster). Minsheu List.

DOUBLEDAY, Edward, *Warden of the Mint*. Minsheu List.

DOUCE. See DOWSE.

DOUGALL, Robert, *Bailie of Edinburgh*. *13258.

DOUGHTON. See DOWTON.

DOUGLAS, Alexander, *Bishop of Moray*. Epistle 1406.

DOUGLAS (Keith), Anne = William *VII Earl of Morton*. 22565.

DOWGLAS, Anthony, '*Parson at Southwick, Sussex*'. See 13923.

Douglas, Archibald, *VIII Earl of Angus.* Epistle 4660.

Douglas (Duglassius), G[eorge, *one of two given Edinb. M.A. in 1599*]. Verse 21101.

Douglas, James, *IV Earl of Morton.* Epistle 22207.

Douglas, James, '*Courtier*' [*? Dep. Secretary for Scotland*]. *12178.

Douglas, John, *Archbishop of St. Andrews.* See 10820.

Douglas, John, *Chaplain at Utrecht and minister at Crail.* See 25939.

Douglas, *Lady* Margaret, *Countess of Lennox* (*DNB*). 777.

Douglas, Robert, *Viscount Belhaven.* 23760; see 10667.

Douglas, William, *VII Earl of Morton.* *1203, 7075-E.², *12066, †22568 [see changes]; see 10667.

Douglas, William, *I Marquis of Douglas.* *12066; see 10667.

Douglas, William, *I Earl of Queensberry.* See 10667.

Dousa (Van der Does), Jan, *the elder, Dutch poet* (Schotel). Verse 14787, 24931 from foreign ed., 25340.

Dousa, Jan, *the younger, Son of preceding.* Verse 25340, 25438; see 25438.

Dove, John, *Divine* (*DNB*). Verse 21029 (21032), 21032.

Dove, Thomas, *Bishop of Peterborough.* *¶1412; epistle *1352a.

Dove, Thomas, *Archdeacon, son of preceding.* 23801 (23725).

Dover, Robert, *Lawyer and sportsman* (*DNB*). 24954.

Dowland, John, *Composer* (*DNB*). Verse 2497, 10700, 20756; see 19511, 24099.

Dowle, John, *of Bristol* (Foster 1615). Verse 6072.

Downes, Andrew, *Greek professor* (*DNB*). Epistle 13592; edits 14629, 17121; Greek verse 6843, 12312, 18473; see 635, 636, 17944, Cangiser, *Davidis votum*-C.⁵

Downe, John [*? Surgeon*]. Verse 5412.

Downe, John, *Divine* (*DNB*). Verse 12612.

Downe, Nicholas, '*of Barnstaple*'. *¶4682.

Downey, Nicholas, *M.A.* (Foster 1635). Verse 12757.

Downhall, C. [*supposedly the next*]. Verse 22929, 25118a.

Downhall, Gregory, *Civilian* (Foster). *See preceding.*

Downham, George, *Bishop of Derry.* 7137; Minsheu List.

Downham, John, *Puritan divine* (*DNB*). 1045; edits 7117, 23507.

Downham, William, *Bishop of Chester.* *1710.

Downing, Edmund, *M.A.* (Venn). Verse 5363 (5355).

Downing, Josua, *of Rotherhithe, naval officer.* *11651 (11679, 11652).

Dowse, *Sir* Francis, *of Broughton, Hants.* 26116.

Dowse, *Sir* Gabriel, *of Hampshire* (Foster). †25156.

Dowse, George, *Gent.* [*? of Hants*]. 15190.

Douce, Stephen, *Master of Whittington College.* *21800.

Dowton, Arthur. Verse 24316.

Dowton, Arthur, *Warden of Barber Surgeons.* Epistle 19191.

Doily, Edward [*of Norf.*]. Verse 15037.

D'Oyly, *Sir* Henry, *of Shottisham, Norf.* ¶21869.

D'Oyly, John, '*of Aldbourn, Wilts.*' Prose 25930.

D'Oylie, Thomas, *M.D. and Spanish scholar* (*DNB*). Verse 19619.

Drake (Sydenham), Elizabeth = *Sir* Francis. 10943.

Drake, *Sir* Francis, *Admiral* (*DNB*). 4700 by editor, 5869, 13193, 16806, 17784, 18064, *19537, 21084, La Ramée, *Art of arithmeticke*, 1592-L.; verse 19523; prose 18544; see 12556.

Drake, *Sir* Francis, *I Bt.* 1436, *†12891; edits 18544.

Drake, *Sir* John, *of Ashe, Devon.* *†1954 superseding Pakenham.

Drake, Richard, *Equerry to Elizabeth.* See 25438.

Drake, Richard, *of Pembroke College* (Venn 1625). Verse 22400.

Drakes. *See* Draxe.

DRANT, Nevill. Prose 12185.

DRANT, Thomas, *Divine and poet (DNB)*. Verse 4738, 11223, 16624, 18478 (18773), 22251 and *1568*-DUL., 24631.

DRANT, Thomas, 'M.A., Cant.' [presumably of Shaston-STC]. Verse 24809.

DRAPER, Thomas, 'B.D.' See 10738.

DRAPER, Thomas, 'M.A., Oxon.' [presumably Foster 1627]. Verse 13555.

DRAXE, Thomas, *Divine (DNB)*. See 10567 as Drakes.

DRAYTON, Christopher, *Nephew of Michael* (Foster). Verse 10694.

DRAYTON (Grey), Mary = William. Verse 4746 (17509).

DRAYTON, Michael, *Poet (DNB)*. 1695; epistle *971, 16658; signed verse 1694, 3914, 5808 and 5810 [cf. 23769], 6330, 13249, 13580 (13579), 14896, 17868, 18296, 20825, 22249, 22634; initialed verse accepted in canon 15686, 18116, 20366a (20367), 25225.

DRAYTON, Thomas, *Clergyman* (Venn). Verse 24316.

DREW, Robert, *of Poulshot, Wilts*. R. Dyer, †*Christian's theorico-practicon, 1633*-F.

DRINKWATER, Peter, *Mayor of Chester*. *¶23720.

DROPE, Thomas, *M.A.* (Foster 1571). Verse 4759.

DRUMMOND, James, *I Earl of Perth*. †6580.

DRUMMOND, John, *II Earl of Perth*. See 10667.

DRUMMOND, John, *II Lord Maderty*. See 10667.

DRUMMOND, William, *Poet (DNB)*. Signed verse 338 (347), 5931 (5909), 12067, 14906, 18063, 19781; *see* 135 and see W. D.

DRUMMOND (later Ker), William, *II Earl of Roxburghe*. Epistle 25939.

DRURY (Bacon), Anne = *Sir* Robert. 10545, ¶12679 (12706, 12635).

DRURY, *Sir* Dru, *Courtier (DNB)*. 5244, *11127, 12321 by bookseller, 12322 by editor (*12312 by another editor).

DRURY, *Sir* Dru, *I Bt.* 19515; epistle 15037; Minsheu List.

DRURY, *Sir* Dru, *of Rollesby, Norf.* 4168.

DRURY, *Sir* Robert, *of Hawsted, Suff., d. 1615.*

Most copies ¶7488 only, ¶12679 (12706, 12635); see †12662 (12706, 12635).

DRURY, *Sir* William, *Marshal of Berwick (DNB)*. 5201.

DRURY, William, *of Watergate, Sussex, d. 1646.* 1323, 17830.

DRYDEN, *Sir* Erasmus, *I Bt.* 6950 (6944) by editor, 6963.

DRYDEN, John, *Father of preceding.* 25956.

DUCAEUS (Duc), Fronton, *S.J. (NBG)*. See 4742.

DUCIE, *Sir* Robert, *I Bt., Lord Mayor.* 15568, *17886, *23345 by editor [see changes], *23505 by printer; see 22531.

DUCIE, Robert, *of Aston, son of preceding.* 1665 by bookseller, 20770.

DUCK, *Sir* Arthur, *Civilian (DNB)*. *1943, 12078 (12071), 21198.

DUCKET, *Sir* Francis, *of Grayrigg* (Venn 1580). 3574.

DUCKET, Gregory, *D.D.* (Venn). Minsheu List.

DUCKET, *Sir* Lionel, *Lord Mayor.* *23323 [see changes].

DUDLEY. *Also see* SUTTON *alias* DUDLEY.

DUDLEY (Leigh), Alice, *Duchess Dudley (DNB)*. 21036 [perhaps cancelled; see changes], 24304, 24312; see 19511.

DUDLEY, Ambrose, *Earl of Warwick.* 1358, 3420, †4393, 5002, 5003, 6168, 6893, *¶10674, Latin version *10773-L.², †10846 [earlier lost], 11443, 11450 and *1570*-F., 11621, 11845, 14943, 15040, *18778, 18807, 19121, 20998, 22243, 23358, 24324, †24507 (24491), 24911, 25349, 25401; epistle 25438; see 18773, 19731.

DUDLEY (Russell), Anne = Ambrose *Earl of Warwick* [she is sometimes called Mary]. ¶649, 2497, 4999, 5642, *11276, 11853, *12293, ¶12315 by editor, 12608, 15042, 15139, 16995, 17244, 18013, *18247, 18627 [see changes], *23086 (23084), 23652, 24326, Mornay, *Christian meditations*, [1587]-BUTE, Peacham, *Sermon upon Job, 1591*-O.⁹; epistle 16696; see 24638; see *Library*, 1943-4, p. 177.

DUDLEY, Anne, *Daughter of Alice, later =* Sir Rich. Holbourne. See 19511.

DUDLEY (Southwell), Elizabeth = *Sir* Robert. See SOUTHWELL.

DUDLEY, Henry, *Son of the next.* See Leland, *Naenia, 1545*-G.

DUDLEY (Guilford), Jane = John *Duke.* First state only of 14652a [earliest ed.].

DUDLEY, John, *Duke of Northumberland.* 1294, 1849, 4813, 6142, 18244, 24018.

DUDLEY, John, *Earl of Warwick, d. 1554.* 12595 by editor, *24361, 25799.

DUDLEY (Knollys), Lettice = Robert *Earl, previously* Devereux, *later* Blount. ¶7183, 7510, 23843 (23855), *24596, 25769, 25796, Gerardus, *True tryall, 1586*-L. [see changes], engr. port. Leicester-F.

DUDLEY (Russell), Mary, *Countess.* See ANNE.

DUDLEY, Robert, *Earl of Leicester.* Chronologically:
To *1561*: *1005, 3158 = 12387 (3152), 6119, 24684.
1562: 6214 by bookseller, 11725, 12148 [epistle later revised], 12191.
1563-4: 10868, 11435, 11529 (24723), 15542 by bookseller, 20604, 24670 by printer.
1565: 3152, 4558, 5686, 18955 [fresh epistle 18956], 23319 [see changes], 24777.
1566: 1534, 14726, 22229.
1568-71: 3053, 11488, ¶25067; see *Joshua* in 2099 [cf. 2105, 2108].
1572-3: 4044, 5952, 11442, 12464 later to Hatton, 17520, 25807.
1574-5: 3161, 4444, 5786, 11190, 25879 [see changes].
1576-7: 825 by editor, 1532, 4738, ¶13568, 14927, 18886, 20870 by bookseller [earlier lost].
1578: *¶10674, 11096, 11444 and earlier-HD., ¶12901, 13974.
1579: 4452, 6848 by editor, 12606 [earlier lost], 18158 [see changes].
1580-1: 6037 by editor, 5103 and 5102, 10844, *12745, *12746, 23333 [see changes].
1582: 3810, 11736, 13961, 18250, *18270, *18272, 22906; see 18773.
1583: 6823, 10764, *¶14596 by editor, 18101 by editor, 23945.
1584: 2964 (2962), 4461 by editor, 4762, *13962, 20626, 21809.
1585: 4759, 10573 [see changes], Latin version *10773-L.², 12299; see 7286 = 19045, 7287.
1586: 6052 and 6053, 22589, 24110, 25438; see 25340.
1587: 2025, 4473, 5377 film-CU., 18149, 22551 by editor, *23107.
1588 and belated: 13966, ¶23078 (23084),

23689 by bookseller, *24480; *see* 5444 tp. of pt. ii, 5602, 11097, 11515, 21516.

DUDLEY, Sir Robert, *Imperial duke* (DNB). 7202 [see changes], 7574.

DUFFLAEUS. See KILIANUS.

DUGARD, Thomas, *M.A.* (Venn). Verse 24175.

DUKE, Gilbert, *of Christ's College* (Venn 1553). Verse 19148, 19150.

DUN, Laird of (22011). *See* JOHN ERSKINE.

DUNBAR, John, *Epigrammatist* (STC). Verse 12748.

DUNBAR, Thomas, *Minister of St. Andrews* [*Elgin presbytery*]. Verse 698a.

DUNCHE. *See* DONNE.

DUNCOMB (Poynes), Elizabeth = William. *906.

DUNCOMBE, John, *of Gray's Inn* (Foster 1610). Verse 23100a.

DUNDAS, George, *Son of next.* St. Andrews (Leonard) *Theses, 1612*-O.⁶

DUNDAS, Sir Walter, *of Dundas.* St. Andrews (Leonard) *Theses, 1612*-O.⁶

DUNLOP, Ge. Verse 7075-E².

DUNN. *See* DONNE.

DUNSTER, John, *M.A.* (Foster 1595). Verse 21660.

DU PERRON. *See* DAVY DU PERRON.

DUPORT, James, *Master of Magdalene* (DNB). Verse 11464, 20692.

DUPORT, John, *Biblical scholar* (DNB). *25680.

DUPPA, Brian, *Bishop of Winchester.* 11569, 16893 by editor; presentation 716; edits 19033, 19034, 19035, and on external evidence 14784.

DURDANT, William. *25263.

DURIE, John, *S.J.* (DNB). Epistle 25362 [25361 a ghost].

DURIE, John, *Divine, d. 1680* (DNB). Epistle 6293; verse 24523, broadside *Gustavus triumphans*-L.

DURIE, Robert, *Minister* (DNB). *18171-A.

DURWARD, Jo. [*Schoolmaster*]. See 25737.

DUTTON (Egerton), Elizabeth = John *of Ches.* Epistle *6332 [6331 a ghost].

DUTTON, John, *Royalist* (Keeler). *See* 25327.

DUTTON, Sir Ralph, *Father of Ralph I Bt.* 17442.

DUTTON (Anderton), Thomasin = Thomas *of Dutton.* ★7468.

DUTTON, William, *Father of John above* (Foster 1572). ★25150.

DUYTS, Johannes. ★557 and *1629*-HD. from earlier foreign.

DWABENE. *See* DAUBENEY.

DYAT, Dyet. *See* DYOTT.

DYER, Sir Edward, *Courtier and poet* (DNB). 1651, 6817, 10529, ¶11739, 17771, 18005 and added ¶18006, 20092, two *1579* pamphlets by T. N.-HN.; epistle 6333, 16696, 20170; *see* 25438; *see* E. D.

DYER, James, *of Middle Temple* (*1571*). Edits ★7388.

DYER (Fitzwilliams), Mary = Sir Richard. ★5775 by editor and author.

DYER, Sir William, *of Staughton, Hunts.* T. Cooper, ★†*Converts first love, 1610*-ILL.

DYKE, Daniel, *Baptist, d. 1688* (DNB). Edits 7414.

DYKE, Jeremiah, *Puritan divine* (DNB but *d. 1639*). Edits 7398 and new tables *1617*-F., 7407, 7408, 7410—all (7394); prose 3733.

DYMOKE, Charles, *Champion, son of next.* 12416 by bookseller superseding next.

DYMOKE, Sir Edward, *Royal champion, d. 1625.* ¶5220, ¶5769, 11900, 12415 by bookseller [see above], 24593.

DYNAMIUS *and* DYNHAM. *See* DENHAM.

DYNNE, Francis, *of Inner Temple.* Verse 3830, 3914.

DYOTT, Anthony, *Recorder of Tamworth* (*Inner Temple*). Verse 15433.

DYSON, Humphrey, *Book collector.* Edits 7758a, ★23345 [most copies without initials].

DIVE, *Lady* Beatrice. *See* DIGBY.

DIVE, *Lady* Elizabeth. ★6888.

DIVE, John, *of Ridlington Park* (Venn). ★†5382.

DYVE, Sir Lewis, *of Bromham, Beds., d. 1592.* 11640.

DYVE, Sir Lewis, *Royalist* (DNB). ★†11126.

E

E., C.D. *of* [*presumably* Frances Cecil, *Countess Dowager of Exeter*]. Presentation 11027.

E., C. (12674). *See* EDWARD COFFIN.

E., D. Verse 13358; *see* 25438.

E., E. *See* H. H. (14589).

E., G., *Surgeon.* Edits 24710.

E., G. Edits 23938.

E., H. Verse 13801 only.

E., J. (1641, 1646), *see* JOHN ELMSTONE; (12613), *see* J. [HALL, *Bishop of*] *Exeter.*

E., I. Verse 17403; *see* 25438.

E., M. Verse 21094.

E., M. C. M. (18066). M. Cresacre More, Esq. [the author].

E., R., '*Medicus*'. *See* 25438.

EL., R. Verse 24137.

E., S. (24930). *See* EDMUND LECHMERE [*alias* STRATFORD].

E., S., *Gent.* ¶13454.

E., T., *Esq.* Verse 1067.

E., T. Perhaps merely edits 7437; verse 3480.

EARLE, Erasmus, *Serjeant-at-law* (DNB). Minsheu List.

EARLE, John, *Bishop of Salisbury.* Verse 21351.

ERLE *or* EARLE, Sir Walter, *of Dorset* (Keeler). ★†1956.

EAST, Thomas, *Printer* (DNB). Edits 2482 and 2488; prose 10540, 18862, 18864, 18866; unsigned verse 6787.

EASTLAND, George, *Musician.* Edits 7095.

ECHLIN, John, *Professor at St. Andrews* (STC). Verse 7351, 14786, 14787.

EDEN (Darcy), Mary = Sir Thomas *the younger* (*Vis. Essex*). ★12873, ★21242 and *1627*-PN.[2]

EDES, Richard, *Dean* (DNB). Verse 4759, 11515, 11516, 11737, 11739, 23701.

EDGAR, Edward, *Bailie of Edinburgh.* Epistle ★18360.

EDGAR, Ezechiel, *Rector of Hawstead* (Venn 1594). Epistle ★18805.

EDGCUMBE, Piers, *Son of Sir Richard d. 1562.* 7159.

EDGWORTH, Thomas, '*Under-treasurer of Windsor*'. 18514.

EDMONDES, Sir Clement, *Clerk to the Council* (*DNB*). 14466 [see changes]; Minsheu List.

EDMONDES (Lydcott), Dorothy = Sir Christopher (*Vis. Surrey*). 7 by bookseller.

EDMONDES, Henry, *Fellow of King's* (Venn). Verse 13519.

EDMONDS, Mich. Verse 23818.

EDMONDES, Sir Thomas, *Diplomatist* (*DNB*). 4740 and 4741, 5857 by bookseller, *10667, ¶12656 (12708, 12635), *23803; Minsheu List.

EDMOND, Thomas, '*in Low Countries*'. Epistle 15715.

EDMOND, Sir William, *Colonel in Dutch service*. Epistle 25939.

EDMONSTONE, James, *Minister of St. Ninians*. Verse P. Anderson, *Grana angelica*, 1635-F.

EDOLPH, Sir Robert, *of Kent* (Brown). *¶25795.

EDRICHUS. *See* ETHEREGE.

EDWARD IV, *King*. 4594, 5293, 13175, 21057; *see* 13438, 24189.

EDWARD V, *King*. 15383; *see* 11193 (11194).

EDWARD VI, *King*. Chronologically:
To 1547: 2419, 10460, 11797, 14918; prose 13639.
1548: 1295, ¶¶2854, 3196, 5993, 12721, *17115; *see* Hind, i. 55, plates.
1549: 166 and 1548-L.[13], 2077, 2768, 4079, 15445 by editor, 18770.
1550: 2080 superseding father, 4076 (4056), 4626, *13763, 15188, 17300.
1551: 1271, *13757, 15263, 16566, 20812, 25809.
1552: 2867 by printer [cf. 2872], 7662 by editor superseding father, ¶15259 [cf. 555]; epistle 12595.
1553: 2984, 6004 by author, 11716 [see changes]; injunction to schoolmasters 4807, 4812, 4813.
Belated: 1275, 4396 from early foreign ed., *1558* of 20799-CU. [earlier lost; see changes]; epistle 20309.

EDWARDS, David, *Warden of Drapers*. W. Freake, *Priuiledges of vpright*-F.

EDWARDS, John, *Deputy Constable of Chirk Castle*. 20399 and dated ed.-G.

EDWARDS, John [*of Kent*]. *11127.

EDWARDS, Richard, *Master of Apothecaries*. *¶11751.

EDWARDS, Robert, *Merchant of Aldermanbury*. *23307 (23313) by editor; epistle *25847.

EDWARDS, Thomas, *D.C.L.* (Foster 1581). Minsheu List.

EGENOLF, Christian, *German poet* (*NBG*). Verse 3988 from early foreign ed.

EGERTON (Spencer), Alice. *See* STANLEY.

EGERTON (More), Elizabeth = Thomas I Viscount. Epistle 16696.

EGERTON (Stanley), Frances = John I Earl. *6330, ¶11521, ¶13474; epistle 18511.

EGERTON, Sir John, *of Egerton, d. 1614*. *7293.

EGERTON, John, *I Earl of Bridgewater*. †901, ¶3589, *¶4497, 4754, one issue *†7326 [Darcie trans.], *11119, 12516 (12523), 12519, 12520, *12551, 19664 superseding Caesar, 20772, 20775, 20776, 20785 (20784), 23061 (23060), †¶23720, 23921, I. M[abb?], *Adams tragedie*, 1608-HD., J. Mabb, *Afflicted mans vow*, 1609-HD.; epistle 4198 only; presentation 5986, 12030, 22792; *see* 10667, 17331; Minsheu List.

EGERTON, John, *II Earl of Bridgewater*. 6273, 17937 by Lawes.

EGERTON, Ralph, *of Ridley, Ches., d. 1619*. *7293.

EGERTON, Sir Richard, *of Ridley*. *7293.

EGERTON, Stephen, *Puritan divine* (*DNB*). Edits 12317, 21214; prose 6125 [signed in 1603-F.], 18420, 20337, 21215, 24768 [earlier lost]; *see* 21221.

EGERTON, Thomas, *Viscount Brackley, Lord Chancellor*. Chronologically:
To 1596: 1828, *1829, 1853, 5238, 14015, 14017, 18513, 23362.
1597: 196, 7087, 14976; epistle 16696.
1598: 3928, 4197, 14960, 16918, 24890.
1599: 4756, *6282 by editor, 25703 (25699) [see changes], R. Vaughan, *Baites of fishing*-L.
1600: 7147 and 7150 (7141), *11119, 11578, 20150, 21089, 24002, 24581, ¶25698 [see changes].
1601–2: 4025, 4941, *6439, 17226a, 22401, 24727.
1603–5: 1833, 10801, *12554, 23456; epistle 6258 (6263, 6238); *see* 6165.
1606–7: 3405, †6337, 13473 and 1607-F. [see

ELIZABETH I—*cont.*

1600: 4507 [see changes], 4954, 15437, 16613, 16628, 23698, Boazio map of Ireland-L.; *see* 3518 = 6873.

1601: 6236 [see changes], 13597, 21358, 24637 [see changes], 25220 [see changes]; *see* 18432.

1602: 16616, 18835, 20071 (20068), 22164.

Belated: 1134, 18544, ¶20613 and *1613*-c.; epistle 20613 and *1613*-c. [usurped from Essex ded. 20606]; *see* 15113, 23776.

Court of: Maids of honour, 5638, epistle 11831, 25764; ladies of privy chamber, 11276; ladies at court, epistle 16696, 23080 only.

Gentlemen pensioners: epistle 5797; pages, epistle 18380; courtiers, epistle 16696.

All that loved Elizabeth: 5121.

ELIZABETH, *Queen of Bohemia.* Chronologically. *See also joint †dedications with* FREDERICK.

Early: 5694 [see changes], 5704, *12488; *see* 5568.

1610–11: 5653 by bookseller [usurped from Elizabeth I], ¶7182, 13246 by author; epistle 15227; *see* 5807.

1612: 15426, *17701, *17705, 22932 [earlier lost; see changes], 25901 (25890, 25911); *see* 19511.

1613: 5848 [see changes], 20982, 22125 [? from foreign]; epistle 384, 11309, 25891 (25911); *see* 736, 4546.

1614–16: 7395 [earlier lost] (7394), 15402, 19514, ¶23581 (23575, 21653), 25186; epistle 11370.

1618–19: 1130, *17699, 20664; *see* 15715, 23511 (sometimes 4523).

1620's: ¶3447, 11983, 25847, J. Elborough, *Churches glory*, n.d.-F.; epistle 18610.

1630–5: 2735, 12007, 12581, 18780, E. Audeley, *All the kings*, *1633*-L.[11]

Later: *7317 [see changes], 14500, 19099 by widow, A. Rivat, *Six meditations*, *1639*-A. by author; presentation 21725.

ELIZABETH, *Princess, daughter of Charles I.* *10667.

ELIZABETH, *Princess Palatine, Abbess of Herford.* 20938.

ELIZABETH, *Duchess of Brunswick-Wolfenbüttel, sister of Queen Anne.* *17699.

ELLENBERGER, Heinrich, *Marburg dissertationist* (BM). Verse 16650.

ELLIOTT. *All spellings.*

ELLIOT, Edward, *of Newland, father of Sir Thomas.* 12605.

ELIOT, James, *Groom of Privy Chamber.* Epistle some copies *4747-O.

ELIOT (Gedge), Jane = Edward *of Newland.* ¶22848 [earlier lost].

ELIOT, John, *Linguist (STC).* Verse 12295, 15097.

ELIOT, John, *Esq.*, *'friend of Bacon'* [*presumably of Gray's Inn*]. See 4187.

ELLIOT, M., *Gent. 1582* of 15533-L. only.

ELLIOT (Towse), Mary = Sir Thomas. *¶1477.

ELYOTT, Orlando, *M.A.* (Venn). Verse 26103.

ELLIOT, Sir Thomas, *of Newland Hall* (Venn 1589). *¶1477, 17834-ROS. cancelled.

ELIOT, Thomas, *Esq., of Balreske, Meath.* L. R., *Genealogie of protestants, 1621*-E.[2]

ELLIS, James, *Mayor of Leicester.* *19788; prose 19788.

ELLICE, Robert, *of Gray's Inn.* 11163; verse 6307.

ELLICE, Thomas, *of Gray's Inn, brother of Robert.* Verse 6307, 11165 2nd issue.

ELLIS, Walter, *Merchant adventurer of Bristol.* Epistle *19155.

ELLISON, Edmond, *'Commander of the George & Eliz.'* 23735.

ELMER. *See* AYLMER.

ELMES. *See* HELMES.

ELMSTONE, John, *Master of Cranbrook School* (? Foster). As I. E. edits 1641, 1646.

ELPHINSTONE, Alexander, *IV Lord Elphinstone.* See 10667.

ELPHINSTONE (Ker), Anne = John *II Lord Balmerino.* 15654 (15684).

ELPHINSTONE, James, *I Lord Balmerino.* St. Andrews (Salvator) *Theses, 1608*-E.[2]; epistle 6162.

ELPHINSTONE, James, *Lord Coupar.* St. Andrews (Salvator) *Positiones, 1617*-O.[6]; *see* 10667.

ELPHINSTONE, John, *II Lord Balmerino.* See 10667.

ELPHINSTONE, William, *Bishop of Aberdeen, Shades of.* 11152.

ELPHINSTONE *or* ELVESTON, *Sir* William, *Cupbearer to Charles I.* Verse 24604.

ELST, Guilielmus vander. *557 and *1629*-HD. from earlier foreign.

ELTOFTES, John, '*of Skipton school*' [? *Inner Temple*, PCC 1559]. Verse 857a.

ELTON, Edward, *B.D.* (Venn). Prose 1336 [title is *Modest reply*], 3786.

ELVESTON. *See* ELPHINSTONE.

ELWOOD, William, *Mayor of Sandwich.* *23317.

EMERSON, William. Verse 15607.

EMET, Abell [? *fiction*]. Verse 25755.

EMLEY, Lawrence, '*Magd. Col., Oxf.*' [? *error for* Theophilus]. Verse 5808 and 5810 [cf. 23769].

EMLEY, Theophilus, *of Magdalen College* (Foster). *See preceding.*

ENDERBY, Percy, *Writer* (BM). Verse 26103.

ENGENTINUS, Philippus, *Writer* (NBG). Verse 10472 and *1556*-F.

ENGLEBERT, William, *Military engineer* (CSPD). 19998, 20000.

ENGLEFIELD (Browne), Jane = *Sir* Francis *I Bt.* 17663 by editor.

ENGLEFIELD (Brooksby), Winifred = *Sir* Francis *II Bt.* 3272 by editor [see changes].

ENGLYSSHE, Michael, *Alderman. See* *864.

ENSLEY. *See* AINSLIE.

EPSELEY, William [? *fiction*]. Verse 13540.

ERASMUS, Desiderius, *Scholar.* Revises 5544 = 10497; *see* 15602 and *1531*-M. Editorial material by Erasmus in foreign books is often used in British editions like 4843, 4854, 14809.

ERBURY, Antony, *Somerset clergyman* (Foster 1589). Epistle *1941.

ERNEST CASIMIR, *Count of Nassau-Dietz, d. 1632* (NBG). ¶550 from earlier foreign.

ERONDELLE, Pierre, *French teacher* (STC). Edits 6750.

ERRA PATER, *Memory of.* 24693 [alias 24692].

ERSKINE, Alexander, '*Viscount Fenton*', *d. 1633.* *¶22567 misnamed John.

ERSKINE (Murray), Anabel = John *I Earl of Mar. See* 14850 and *1603*-L.

ERSKINE (Pierrepont), Elizabeth = Thomas *I Earl.* Epistle 23581 (23575, 21653).

ERSKINE, James, *VI Earl of Buchan. See* 10667.

ERSKINE, John, *Reformer, d. 1591* (DNB). 22011 as Laird of Dun.

ERSKINE, John, *I Earl of Mar and Regent.* 10820.

ERSKINE, John, *II Earl of Mar.* 573, 18210, 20386, *¶25682 (25685); epistle 6333, 15715, 20567.

ERSKINE, John, *III Earl of Mar.* P. Anderson, *Grana angelica, 1635*-F., St. Andrews (Salvator) *Theses*, *1631*-E.; *see* 10667.

ERSKINE, John, *IV Earl of Mar. See* 10667 misnamed James.

ERSKINE, John, *Minister of Dun.* James Anderson, *Winter night*-E.

ERSKINE, John (22567). Error for Alexander.

ERSKINE (Stuart), Mary = John *II Earl.* 4366 by editor, 5937 and *1607*-LINC. (5909), ¶5943 (5909), *¶12478, 12569 = 14560, 23601 rewritten 23598, A. Symson, *Godly exposition, 1622*-F. [see changes].

ERSKINE, Thomas, *I Earl of Kellie.* 385, *1203, ¶4578, 6583 (6587), ¶12652 (12706, 12635); epistle 6333, 20567; *see* 10667; Minsheu List.

ERSKINE, *Sir* Thomas, *Gentleman to Prince Henry.* 384.

ESMOND, Laurence, *Baron E. of Limerick. See* 10667.

ESSEX (Harcourt), Jane = William *Bt.* ¶21649.

ESSEX, Joan. *See* ANDERSON.

ESSEX, *Sir* William, *Bt.* 12367.

ESSINGTON, William, *Merchant* (Brown). *5676.

ESTIENNE. *See* STEPHANUS.

ESTMOND, John, *Principal of New Inn Hall* (Foster 1568). ¶18777; verse 21029 (21032).

ESTOUTEVILE. *See* STUTVILLE.

ETHEREGE (Edrichus), George, *Scholar* (DNB). Edits 22405.

ETHEREGE, George, *Master of Vintners.* *18901.

ETHERIDGE, John, *Vicar of Halstead* (Venn). 18948 by editor.

EDRICHUS, T. [*presumably kin of George*]. Verse 7498.

EUPHORMIO [*presumably* John Barclay]. Edits 4744.

F

F., W., *'Challenged to a duel'* [*but* W. E. *in table contents*]. *See* 12662 (12706, 12635).

F., W. Edits 1648 (1633); verse 12866, 17570, 22224.

FABRICIUS, George, *German scholar* (NBG). Prose 3990 and 3988 from foreign ed.

FAGG, Edward, *Gent.* [*of Kent*]. *11127.

FAIRCLOUGH. *See* FEATLEY.

FAIRFAX, ——, *'Ensign in Dutch service'* [*several of name*]. Epistle 25939.

FAIRFAX (Howard), Alethea = Thomas *II* Viscount. *Mistical crowne of Mary, 1638-*L.

FAIRFAX (Sheffield), Mary = *Sir* Ferdinand. *1934.

FAIRFAX, Thomas, *I Lord F. of Cameron.* Verse 13191; *see* 10667.

FAIRFAX, Thomas, *I* [*or possibly* Thomas *II*] *Viscount Fairfax*. *See* 10667.

FAIRLAEUS. *See* FARLEY.

FAIRUT, *Sir* William. Misprint for Faunt.

FAIS, Michael. *557 and *1629*-HD. from earlier foreign.

FALCKENIER, Johan., *Colon.* Hebrew prose 4260.

FANE *or* VANE.

FANE (——), Elizabeth = *Sir* Ralph-DNB. 6090.

FANE, Francis, *I Earl of Westmorland.* *¶1412; *see* 17331.

FANE, *Sir* George. *Brother of preceding.* *¶1412 spelt Fayen.

VANE *or* FANE, Henry, *of Hadlow, father of next.* [*1603*]-C. of 14376 by editor [*1589* issue lost], *22247.

VANE, *Sir* Henry, *the elder, Statesman* (DNB). 7357, 17451; *see* 10667.

FANE (Neville), Mary, *Baroness Despenser* [*conjectural; an earlier ed. would indicate Elizabeth above*]. 937 and *1581*-L. as Lady Fane.

FANE (Mildmay), Mary = Francis *I Earl.* 1636 by editor.

FANE (Vere), Mary = Mildmay *II Earl, previously* Townshend. ¶11081.

B 8564

FANE, Mildmay, *II Earl of Westmorland.* *See* 10667.

FANE *or* VANE, *Sir* Thomas, *of Burston, Kent, d. 1606.* *22247, W. Perneby, *Direction to death, 1599-*PN.²

FANSHAWE, *Sir* Henry, *Remembrancer of Exchequer* (DNB). 894, 20815 by bookseller [*see changes*], 25023.

FANSHAWE, Thomas, *Remembrancer of Exchequer* (DNB). *570, *¶12312 by editor; *see* 18773.

FANSHAWE, *Sir* Thomas, *Master of Crown Office, uncle of next.* 4881, 20672 (20668) by editor, 20828, *24132 [*see changes*], 24576.

FANSHAWE, Thomas, *I Viscount Fanshawe.* 13468.

FARBRACE (Faerbraceus), Edward, *M.A.* (Foster). *See* 25327.

FARWELL, John, *of Inner Temple* (1631). *See* 15466.

FAREWELL, Richard, *of Middle Temple.* Edits *7388.

FARGANUS, Martinus. Prose 19783.

FARINGDON, Hugh, *Abbot of Reading* (DNB). 5946.

FARLEY, Henry, *Freeman of London* (STC). Verse 13581 [Hen. Far. some copies].

FARLEY (Fairlaeus), Robert, *Poet* (STC). Verse 14929, 19781, R. Williamson, *Paedagogia, 1635-*E.

FARMER. *See* FERMOR.

FARNABY, Thomas, *Schoolmaster* (DNB). Edits 14889, 16883, 17492, 22218, 24794; verse 250, 5808 and 5810 [cf. 23769], 12509, 12791, 15078, 24316, 26068; prose 4496; *see* 25327, 25737.

FARQUHAR, Edward, *Bailie of Edinburgh.* *88 as Forker, *23262 as Ferquard.

FARRAT, Thomas, *Schismatic separatist at Amsterdam* (Burrage). *5345.

FARRER. Listed with Ferrar(s).

FASTOLF, *Sir* John, *Warrior* (DNB). *See* 5293.

FAUNT, *Sir* William, *of Foston, Leics.* T. Cooper, *†*Converts first love, 1610-*ILL. misprinted Fairut.

FAVOUR, John, *Divine* (DNB). ¶1940.

K

FAUCET, George, *of York, d. 1620.* Epistle 3191.

FAWCETT, Thomas, *Bookseller.* Usurps earlier prose 11174, 15382.

FAWKENER, Everard, *Warden of Haberdashers.* 10718, 10719, *13514 [13513 impf.].

FAUKENER, Ihon. Edits 13910.

FAWKENER, Thomas, *Bailiff of Shrewsbury.* *24043.

FAYUS (LaFaye), Antonius, *Huguenot minister (NBG).* Verse 2032 = 2357, 21649, French version of 5154-STE-GENEVIÈVE-Paris under anagram *Aten aide en la foy.*

FEATHERSTONE. *See* FETHERSTONE.

FEATLEY *or* FAIRCLOUGH, Daniel, *Controversialist (DNB).* *5453, 11673; edits 17101, supposedly 14579; verse 17610, 22390; prose 5130, 5844, 5983, 11082, 11666, 12980, 23923; *see* 3767, 5131, 23920; Minsheu List.

FECKENHAM, John, *Abbot (DNB). See* 12131.

FEILDE *and* FEILDING. *See* FIELD *and* FIELDING.

FELIPPE, Bartolomeo, *Professor of law at Lisbon.* Epistle in his *Tractado, 1589-L.*

FELIS, Colonus [*facetious version of untraced George Gale or ? Ailour*]. Verse 12141.

FELL, Samuel, *Dean of Christ Church (DNB).* *4259, 12515; prose 12612; *see* 5138, 25327; Minsheu List.

FELLTHAM, Owen, *Author (DNB).* Verse 1392 as Ow. Fell., 20694.

FELTON, John, *the elder, Bailiff of Yarmouth.* *26097.

FELTON, Nicholas, *Bishop of Ely.* 3950 as Dr. N. F., 25741 only.

FELTON, Robert, *Fellow of Pembroke* (Venn). Verse 24316.

FENN *and* VENN.

VENN, John, *Regicide and city captain (DNB).* *1505, *21095; epistle *1507.

FENN *or* VENN, Sir Richard, *Lord Mayor.* 13349, *1626* of *13515-O.², *¶19303, *19598, *22533; epistle *12203.

FENN, Robert, *M.A.* (Venn). Verse 11087.

FENNER, ——, *Widow of William, d. 1640-DNB.* Does presentation of 10779.

FENNER, Edward, *Judge (DNB).* 25019 and earlier *1593-O.*

FENNOR, William, *Courtier (STC).* 23741 (23725), 23804 (23725).

FENTON, Ed. *See* 1599.

FENTON, John, *Master of Barber Surgeons.* Epistle *25962.

FENTON, Joseph, *Master of Barber Surgeons.* 21603 only by editor, *24577; epistle *11203.

FENTON, Roger, *Divine (DNB).* Prose 25786.

FENTON, Sir William, *Son of Sir Geoffrey-DNB.* Verse 5808 and 5810.

FENYS. *See* FIENNES.

FERBRAND, William, *Bookseller.* Epistle R. Armin, *Foole upon foole, 1600-*F. but not named.

FERDINAND, *King of the Romans, d. 1654.* T. Stapleton, *Catechismus, 1639-*N.

FEREBY, Anthony, *Purveyor to Ordnance Office (CSPD).* Verse 22796 misprinted Ffreby.

FERM, Charles, *Principal of Fraserburgh (DNB).* Verse 21267.

FERMOR *or* FARMER, Henry, *Clerk of Peace, Mdsx.* 6522, 19628-ZÜRICH.

FERMOR, Thomas [*one of those of Barsham, Norf.*]. 4649.

FERNE, Henry, *Bishop of Chester (DNB).* Verse 7365.

FERNE, Sir John, *Writer, of Council in the North (DNB).* *1823, *19699 (19649) by editor.

FERNE, Sir John, *Naval officer (CSPD).* 23726 (23725) spelt Fearne.

FERRERS, Henry, *of Baddesley Clinton* (Foster). Verse 18886 as Ferrarius.

FERRERS, Sir Henry, *I Bt.* *†24928 spelt Pherres.

FARRER, John, *Gent.* [*reading uncertain*]. *5829.

FERRERS (Topsfield), Katherine = Edward. *15334.

FERRAR, Nicholas, *Theologian (DNB).* From external evidence edits 13183.

FERRAR, Robert, *Bishop of St. David's.* *2983 = 21617.

FERRERS (Muschamp), Susan = William, *previously* Topsfield. *15334.

FERRERS, William, *the elder, Alderman.* *20756.

FERRERS, William, *Son of preceding (Vis. Mdsx.).* 5535.

FERRAR, William, *Brother of Nicholas-DNB.* Verse 3914.

FERRERIUS, Joannes, *Italian scholar in Scotland.* Verse 24623a.

FERRIÈRES, Jean de, *Vidame of Chartres.* 17409 by editor.

FERRIS, Richard, *Serjeant-surgeon to Elizabeth.* Prose 11529 (24723).

FETHERSTONE *or* FEATHERSTONE, Henry, *Bookseller.* 10838; Minsheu List.

F[ETHERSTONE], I. ['*Brother of author*']. Prose 5154 [possibly J. FIELD].

FETTIPLACE (Ayleford), Anne = *Sir* Edmund *of Childrey.* *14896.

FETIPLACE, Charles. Verse 21094.

PHETIPLACIUS, Joannes, '*filiolus Richardi*' [*presumably one of Foster's*]. Epistle 4758.

PHETTIPLACE, Michael, *Colonist* (Brown). Verse 22788 (22790).

PHETIPLACIUS, Richardus, *Armiger.* 4758.

PHETTIPLACE, William, *Brother of Michael.* Verse 22788 (22790).

FEUGERAY, Guillaume de, *Huguenot minister* (Schickler). Edits 17409.

FFREBY (22796). Misprint for Fereby.

FIAMMETA, G., '*Nobilis Mediolanensis*'. Verse 7376.

FEILD, Francis, *M.A.* (Foster 1583). Verse 4012.

FIELD, James. Verse 5808 and 5810 [cf. 23769].

FIELD, John, *Master of Barber Surgeons.* Verse 11529 (24723).

FEILDE *or* FIELD, John, *Puritan divine* (DNB). As I. F. [proof in 15068] edits 6701 and [? earlier] undated-F., HN., 6732 and probably 6726—all (6676).
Edits: 15068; prose 18744, 24780, untraced epistle in F. copy 19915; *see* 4709; *see* I. F.

FIELD, John, '*of London*' [*probably preceding despite date difficulty*]. *25624.

FIELD, Nathan, *Actor* (DNB). Verse 11068 [fully signed 11069], 14759, some copies 14783-L. as N. F.

FIELD, Nathaniel, *M.A.* (Foster). Edits 10858 [by his father].

FIELD, Richard, *Printer* (DNB). Epistle (unnamed) A. Pérez, *Pedaços de historia*, [1592]-FSF.; signed prose 10653.

FIELD, Theophilus, *Bishop of Hereford.* Edits

19154 and related pamphlet-L.²; verse exchange 23352, 23353; prose 1571; Minsheu List.

FILDUS, Gulielmus. Verse 13482 = 17787.

FIELDING (Felding), Basil, *Ancestor of next.* 1757 and earlier-PML. (1710).

FEILDING, Basil, *II Earl of Denbigh. See* 10667.

FEILDING, Elizabeth (15465). *See* BOYLE.

FYLDINGE, Ferdinand, *of Lincoln's Inn* (Venn). Verse 21315.

FEILDING, George, *I Earl of Desmond. See* 10667.

FEILDING (Villiers), Susan = William *I Earl.* ¶10725 [alone 10729], *23447, G. Jay, *Sermon, 1632-*F.; *see also* D., *Countess of.*

FEILDING, William, *I Earl of Denbigh.* Epistle *4747; *see* 10667, 17331.

FIENNES (*numerous spellings*). *Also see* CLINTON *alias* FIENNES.

FIENNES (Bourchier), Anne = Thomas *VIII Baron Dacre. See* 22610 (22608).

FIENNES (Sackville), Anne = Gregory *X Baron Dacre.* 5647 = 6121.

FIENNES (Cecil), Frances = James *II Viscount Saye.* 17654.

FIENNES, William, *I Viscount Saye and Sele.* †6935 by editor, *6957, 20231 by editor, *20241 by editor; *see* 10667, 17332.

FILDUS. *See* FIELD.

FILMER, *Sir* Edward, *Father of next.* *¶25795.

FILMER, *Sir* Robert, *Writer* (DNB). 10885 by editor.

FINCH Family. *17402.

FINCH (Heydon), Anne *or* Agnes = Theophilus *II Bt.* *¶4220 and *1619*-HD.

FINCH (Heneage), Elizabeth, *Countess of Winchilsea.* 7407 (7394) by editor, 7419 (7427), 14300.

FINCH, *Sir* Heneage, *Speaker of the House* (DNB). *14489, *17886.

FYNCHE, Henry, '*Merchant*'. 13484.

FINCH, *Sir* Henry, *Serjeant-at-law* (DNB). *11127; Minsheu List.

FINCH, John, *Baron Finch of Fordwich.* 3997 by editor, 21253; *see* 10667.

FINCH, *Sir* Moyle, *I Bt.* †¶25795.

FINCH, *Sir* Nathaniel, *of Gray's Inn, son of Sir Henry.* ★11163; Minsheu List.

FINCH, Thomas, *II Earl of Winchilsea.* †7429, ★17402, 17922, 22635, 25173; *see* 10667.

FYNDFAULT, Oliver [*fiction*]. Epistle C. Thimmelthorpe, *Short inventory, 1581*-HN.

FINET, *Sir* John, *Courtier* (*DNB*). Minsheu List.

FINLASON, Thomas, *Edinburgh printer.* Epistle 15373; unsigned prose 3444.

FISH, Cornelius, *Chamberlain of London.* ★20756.

FISH, John. Verse 688.

FISHBORNE, Richard, *Mercer and merchant* (Brown). ★3001 only by editor.

FISHER, Ambrose, *M.A.* (Venn). Verse 6062, 24313.

FISHER, Benjamin, *Bookseller.* Signed prose 6789 [some copies unsigned], 20642 [signed in 20643], 22786; unsigned prose 6983, 20652.

FISHER, Jasper, *Divine* (*DNB*). Verse 25103.

FISHER, John, *Saint* (*DNB*). 10496 by printer; epistle 24943; *see* 11387 (24436); his sister Elizabeth: *see* WRIGHT.

FISHER, John, *S.J.* (*DNB*). Epistle (unnamed) 25395 (25389).

FISHER, Robert, *Churchman* (Foster 1507). 10496.

FISHER, Thomas [? *Sir* Thomas, *I Bt.*]. ¶18521.

FISHER, *Sir* Thomas, *II Bt.* 11909.

FISHER, Thomas, *Mathematician* (*STC*). Edits 25932.

FISTIE CANKIE, John de [*fiction; cf.* 12686, *sig.* L8]. Verse J. Taylor, *Most horrible satyre*-HN.

FITTON, Anne, 'Maid of honour' [*error for either* Mary Fitton *or* Anne Fitton Newdegate, *q.v.*]. 14923.

FITTON, Charles, *Mayor of Chester.* ★¶23720.

FITTON, *Sir* Edward, *I Bt.* ★4268.

FITTON, Mary, *Maid of honour* (*DNB*). Epistle 11831; *see* ANNE FITTON.

FITZALAN, Henry, *XII Earl of Arundel.* 3197, ★3480, 6446 by printer [*1570*-CU. impf.], ★¶10674, 15266-F. by printer, ★24361.

FITZALAN, Henry, 'Lord Mautravers', *d. 1556.* 19811.

FITZALAN, William, *IX Earl of Arundel.* 24873.

FITZGEFFREY, Charles, *Poet* (*DNB*). Verse 6333, 18114, 21649, 23294, 24610; *see* 25327.

FITZJEFFREY, *Sir* George, *of Barford, Beds.* ¶110.

FITZGERALD (Kildare) Family. *See* 6270-L.

FITZGERALD, Edward, *Lieut. of Gentlemen Pensioners.* 17209.

FITZGERALD (Howard), Frances = Henry *XII Earl of Kildare, later* Brooke. ★6270, 20167.

FITZGERALD, George, *XVI Earl of Kildare.* 22454; *see* 10667.

FITZGERALD, Gerald, *XV Earl of Kildare.* ★¶12738.

FITZGERALD, Thomas, *X Earl of Kildare.* Epistle ★19166.

FITZHERBERT, Edward, *Son of Thomas.* 11017.

FITZHERBERT, Richard, *Somerset clergyman* (Foster 1591). Epistle ★1941.

FITZHERBERT, Thomas, *S.J.* (*DNB*). *See* 5561.

FITZHERBERT, William, *Sheriff of Bristol.* ★20513.

FITZJAMES, *Sir* John, *of Dorset* (Brown). 14816.

FITZJAMES, Richard, *Bishop of London. See* 22557.

FITZMAURICE, Patrick, *XVIII Baron Kerry. See* 10667.

FITZPATRICK, Barnabas, *V Baron of Upper Ossory. See* 10667 *as* MacGilpatrick.

FITZROY, Henry, *Duke of Richmond.* ¶7483.

FITZROY (Howard), Mary = Henry *Duke of Richmond.* 84, 1712 (1710).

FITZWILLIAMS, John, *Governor of Merchant Adventurers.* ★1210 and 1562-L.[38] [*see* changes].

FITZWILLIAM, Thomas, *I Viscount Fitzwilliam. See* 10667.

FITZWILLIAM, Walter, *Brother of William I Baron* (Venn). *See* 12662 (12706, 12635).

FITZWILLIAM, *Sir* William, *Lord Deputy of Ireland* (*DNB*). ★568, 13196 [*see* changes], †¶13478, W. H., *Misterie of Megiddo, 1589*-C.[2]

FITZWILLIAMS, William, *Gentleman pensioner* [? *same as next*]. ★884; prose 884.

FITZWILLIAM, *Sir* William, *Father of next.* ★24963.

FITZWILLIAM, William, *I Baron Fitzwilliam*. See 10667.

FLASKET, John, *Bookseller*. Prose *Mans arraignment*, *1607*-F.

FLEET, Thomas, *Alderman of Worcester*. 14086 as Flit.

FLEETWOOD (Luke), Anne = *Sir* Miles. *6880 (6886), *6885, *6888.

FLEETWOOD, *Sir* George, *of the Vache, Bucks*. L'Espine, *Comfort for conscience*, *1591*-C.⁴; see 12662 (12706, 12635).

FLEETWOOD, *Sir* Miles, *Receiver, Court of Wards*. *6882, 23821 by editor.

FLEETWOOD, Thomas, *of the Vache, Master of the Mint*. 4069.

FLEETWOOD, William, *Recorder of London* (DNB). 886, *10607, *10845, *25341 [cf. 25335], 25347, J. Danyel, *Jehovah, [1576]*-L.²; epistle 20109 by editor; verse 4938, 15175; indexes 20041, 20042; see 18773.

FLEETWOOD, *Sir* William, *of Cranford, Mdsx*. 4131.

FLEMING, Abraham, *Poet* (DNB). Edits or indexes 1411, 4301 and Latin original-HAT. [by Wittewronghelus], 4442, 4562, 5685 [unsigned in some copies], 5723, 11237, 13569, 14860 [with verse in some states], 17446, 25881 and *1584*-F.; verse 7607, 14927, 18101, 19151, 22265, 25348; prose 15072.

FLEMING, John, *II Earl of Wigtown*. ¶23367; see 10667.

FLEMING (Livingston), Margaret = John *II Earl*. See 3446a.

FLEMING, Samuel, *of King's College* (Venn). Verse 12188; prose 11224 only.

FLEMING, *Sir* Thomas, *Judge* (DNB). 6638 and *1609*-F. by editor, 15140, 23464, 25589 by editor.

FLEMING, *Sir* Thomas, *of Stoneham, son of preceding*. Minsheu List.

FLEMING, Thomas, *of Stoneham, son of preceding*. W. Jones, *Exposition of catechisme*, *1633*-U.

FLEMING, William, *XIV Baron Slane*. See 10667.

FLESHER, Miles. See FLETCHER.

FLETCHER, Giles, *the elder, Civilian* (DNB). Verse 1492, 11224, 12597.

FLETCHER, Giles, *the younger, Poet* (DNB). Edits 20174.

FLETCHER, Henry. Verse 24603.

FLETCHER, John, *Dramatist* (DNB). Verse 14759; see I. F.

FLETCHER *or* FLESHER, Miles, *Printer*. Epistle T. Field, *Earths encrease*, *1624*-C.²; unsigned prose 7045, 9329 rewritten 9330.

FLETCHER, Phineas, *Poet* (DNB). Edits 11054; verse 11058 [cf. *MLR* xlvi. 437], 11060; see 24099.

FLETCHER, Richard, *Bishop of London*. *52, *21748 (21751); see 13923.

FLETCHER, Thomas, *of Lincoln's Inn*. Epistle 10945 (7567).

FLETCHER, William. Verse 21033.

FLINT, Robert, '*Maior of Queenborough*' [fiction]. Verse 13540.

FLIT, Thomas (14086). See FLEET.

FLOOD. See LLOYD.

FLORENATIS, Remaclus. See ARDENNE.

FLORIO, John, *Author* (DNB). 3667 only, 10424 by bookseller [see changes], G. Markham, *Most exact discourse*, *1605*-DUKE OF GLOUCESTER.

FLOWER, Francis, *of Magdalen College* (Foster). Verse 13874.

FLOWER, Francis, *Gentleman pensioner and textbook monopolist*. 21482 by bookseller, 22536 by bookseller.

FLOWERDEW, Edward, *Judge* (DNB). See 25438.

FLOWERDEWE, Edward. Verse 21640.

FLOYD, Flud, Flood. See LLOYD.

FOGNY, Jean de, *Rheims printer*. Unsigned prose 15505.

FOLJAMBE, *Sir* Francis, *Bt*. *17638.

FOLJAMBE, *Sir* Thomas, *Brother of preceding*. T. Cooper, *†Converts first love*, *1610*-ILL. as Fulgean [date problem].

FOLKES, Thomas, *of Lincoln's Inn* (Venn 1561). Verse 5446.

FOLLIOTT, Henry, *I Baron Folliott*. See 23779.

FOLLIOTT, Thomas, *II Baron Folliott*. See 10667.

FONTANUS. See FOUNTAIN.

FOOTE, Philip. See FOTE.

FORBES, Alexander, *XI Lord Forbes.* 15508.

FORBES, Alexander, *I Lord F. of Pitsligo.* ¶11144, Aberdeen *Theses, 1626-*A.; *see* 10667.

FORBES, Arthur. Verse 11150.

FORBES, Arthur, *X Lord Forbes. See* 10667.

FORBES (Keith), Jean = Alexander *I Lord.* 6124, *¶12478.

FORBES, John, *Professor of divinity (DNB).* 11151; verse 11149; *see* 11143.

FORBES, Patrick, *Bishop of Aberdeen.* 1493, 11139, 15509, 16929, *18790, 22474, 23347, 23349; *see* 10667, 14709.

FORBES, Walter, *Poet* [*cf.* 5023]. Verse 3445, 12489, 12492, 14906, 18063.

FORBES, William, *Bishop of Edinburgh.* *22472.

FORBES, William, *of Tolquhon.* 5957 by editor.

FORCET *or* FORSET, Edward, *Writer* (Venn). Prose 14608.

FORD, Edward, *Merchant adventurer of Aldermanbury.* *23307 (23313) by editor; epistle *25847.

FOORD (Popham), Elizabeth = Thomas *of Ilsington, Devon.* 17683a.

FORD, John, *of Gray's Inn.* *11163, 11164, 14788; verse 11157.

FORD, John, *Dramatist (DNB).* Verse 1468, 3819, 5461, 13356, 17637, 17642, 22460, 25176.

FORD, Joseph, *Rector of Mixbury* (Foster). Verse 91.

FOORTH *or* FORD, Robert, *of Butley, Suff.* 11454.

FORTH, Robert, *Master in Chancery* (Venn 1552). 20802 by editor.

FOORD, Robert. Verse 17752.

FORD, William, *Divine (DNB). See* 5811.

FORGIUS (Des Forges), Yvo, *French author* (BM). Verse 1849.

FORKER. *See* FARQUHAR.

FORREST, Edward, *Oxford Bookseller.* Unsigned prose 19571 (19570).

FORESTUS, I. Verse 21819 [? from foreign ed.].

FORESTER, FORSTER. *See* FOSTER.

FORSET. *See* FORCET.

FORTESCUE (Smyth), Alice = *Sir* John. ¶5220.

FORTESCUE (Stanley), Frances = *Sir* John *I Bt.* *906.

FORTESCUE, George, *Essayist (DNB).* Verse 1694, 13800.

FORTESCUE, Henry, *Esq.* ¶107.

FORTESCUE, *Sir* John, *Chancellor of Exchequer (DNB).* *3944 by editor, 10753, 16655, 17849; epistle 6165, 16696.

FORTESCUE, *Sir* William, *Son of preceding* (Foster 1578). *19620 by editor [see changes]; Minsheu List.

FORTH, FOORTH. *See* FORD.

FORTNAIUS, N. M. Verse 19511.

FORTUNE, Moore, *of Jesus College* (Foster). Verse 11544.

FOST., I. Verse 21356.

FOST., Rich. [*doubtless* Forster *below*]. Verse 7498.

FORSTER, Edmund, *City captain.* *21095; epistle *1507.

FORRESTER, George, *I Lord Forrester. See* 10667 misnamed John.

FORESTER, James, *Medical writer (DNB).* Edits 13253 as Fourestier.

FOSTER, John, *M.A.* (Venn 1576). Verse 164.

FORSTER, *Sir* John, *Warden of Marches (DNB).* 428, *¶4102.

FORSTER, John, *the younger, 'Dublin merchant'. See* 7098.

FOSTER, John, *Draper* [*several of name*]. *18280.

FOSTER, John, *of Mdsx. militia.* Epistle *5668; presentation 5670.

FORSTER, Matthew, *City captain.* *21095; epistle *1507.

FOSTER, Reginald, *of the Inner Temple. See* 15466.

FORSTER, Richard, *Physician (DNB).* Verse 12550; prose Morus, *Tabulae, 1584-*O.[14]; *see* FOST.

FOSTER, Thomas, *of the Inner Temple, brother of Sir Robert.* Epistle 5538.

FOSTER, William [? Venn 1567]. Verse 18886.

FOTE *or* FOOTE, Philip [*cf. CSPD 1618*]. Prose 22791 presentation.

FOTHERBY, Charles, *of Gray's Inn* (Venn 1627). Verse 20692.

FOTHERBY, Martin, *Bishop of Salisbury.* Minsheu List.

FOTHERBY, Robert, *Kin of preceding.* Verse 11205.

FOULIS, Sir David, *I Bt.* 25217 (25207); epistle 23581 (23575, 21653); *see* 19511.

FOULIS, Edward, *Fellow of All Souls* (Foster). Verse 5097.

FOULIS, Sir James, *Clerk of registry council.* See 21875 and *Actis, 1540-*E.

FOUNTAIN (Fontanus), Robert, *French teacher in London.* Prose 6748; *see* R. F.

FOWBERIE, Catherine, *Widow* [*? of Newbold, Yks.*]. 6990.

FOWLER, Abraham, *Versifier* (*DNB*). Verse 21239.

FOWLER, John, *Antwerp printer* (*DNB*). Signed verse 18083; unsigned prose 14506 (14565), 18083.

FOWLER, Thomas, *Esq.* 17848.

FOWLER, William, *Poet* (*DNB*). Verse 14373 as M. W. F., 14379; *consider* M. V. F.

FOX, Daniel, *of Gray's Inn.* Verse 17921.

FOXE, John, *Martyrologist* (*DNB*). Edits 2961, 6006, 12593, 19929, 24436 and *1572-*HN.; prose 16975, 16993, 20850, 21051; *see* 12343, 25295.

FOX, John. Verse 22444.

FOXE, Richard, *Bishop of Winchester.* 5643; edits 16233.

FOXE, Roger, *Gent.* Verse 7304.

FOXE, Samuel, *Diarist* (*DNB*). Edits 11237.

FOXE, Simeon, *Physician* (*DNB*). Epistle P. Bowne, *Pseudo-medicorum anatomia, 1624-*L.; *see* 20384.

FOY, John, *M.A.* (Venn). Verse 14269.

FOYLE, James. Verse 860.

FRANCIS, *of Assisi, Saint.* *Rule of thirde order, 1624-*L.

FRANCIS I, *King of France.* 4414 (4415, 4426) from foreign eds.

FRANCIS II, *King of France.* See 5041 = 9183 and French version-HN.

FRANCIS, *Duke of Anjou.* 1855.

FRAUNCES, Edward, *Schoolmaster* (Venn 1624). Verse 20692.

FRANCIS, Elizabeth, '*of Brumsted, Norf.*' Presentation 7031 by bookseller.

FRANCKTON, John, *Dublin printer.* Prose *1612* Farmer almanac-D.[6]

FRANKLIN, Edward, *Rector of Kelshall* (Venn 1566). See 25695.

FRANKLIN, George, *Alderman.* ¶16684; epistle *25963; *see* G. F.

FRANKLIN, Sir John, *of Willesden* (*Vis. Mdsx.*). Minsheu List.

FRASER, Andrew, *I Lord Fraser.* See 10667.

FRASER, Simon, *VI Lord Lovat.* St. Andrews (Leonard) *Theses, 1631-*E.; *see* 10667.

FRASER, Thomas, *Laird of Strichen, d. 1656.* 22259.

FREAKE, Edmund, *Bishop of Norwich.* 11759, *14608.

FREAKE, Edmund, *Son of preceding.* See 25438.

FREAKE (Clavel), Elizabeth = Robert (*Vis. Dorset*). Epistle *5370.

FRECKLETON, Ferdinando [*see MLN* lviii. 542]. Verse *Tarletons treatises, 1578-*F.

FREDERICK I, *King of Bohemia.* Chronologically:
    1612: †Early state-HN. of 4252 = 11827, *†5128, †25705 and 25707; *see* 23760 only.
    1613: 736, †960, 4546, *5107, †11308, †13355 [blank in L.], † 19022, †25157; epistle 384.
    1614–19: 539 [from foreign ed.], 1152, *12858; epistle †11370, †20835, †23581 (23575, 21653).
    Later: *†15432, *†21492, *22103 (22064), *22529; epistle †22634, 25939.

FREDERICK HENRY, *Son of preceding.* *12858; *see* 17331.

FREDERICK HENRY, *Prince of Orange.* *10667, *†20489.

FREDERICK ULRIC, *Duke of Brunswick.* See 19050.

FREDERICK, Christopher, *Master of Barber Surgeons.* *24577; epistle *25962.

FRIDERICUS, Ioh., '*à Metzenhausen Lutzenburgius*'. Verse 21657.

FREEMAN, M. Verse 14008.

FREEMAN, Ralph, *Lord Mayor*. 13348, *16686, *18901, *19566, 20405, *23345 by editor [see changes]; *see* 22530, 22531.

FREEMAN, *Sir* Ralph, *Civilian (DNB)*. 250.

FREEMAN, William, *Warden of Haberdashers and merchant. 1626–0.*[2] of *13515, *16686.

FRÉGEVILLE, Jean de, *Writer* (BM). Verse 13903 [cf. 18369].

FRELLON, François, *Lyons printer*. Prose 3045.

FRENCH (Godfrie), Mary = John *of Inner Temple*. Prose 13905.

FRENCH, Peter, *Cantabr*. (Venn 1578). Verse 23278.

FRENCH, Thomas, *Mayor of Cambridge*. *23820.

FRENCHHAM, Thomas, '*Sussex preacher*'. See 13923.

FRERE. *See* FRYER.

FRESNE, *Seigneur de* [*presumably* Philippe Canaye]. Verse 24871.

FREWEN, Accepted, *Archbishop of York*. *5410 by editor, 19572 (19570) by editor; edits 19032, 19038, 19039; *see* 25327.

FROBISHER, *Sir* Martin, *Navigator (DNB)*. Verse 19523.

FRODRINGHAM, Tho. Prose 3215.

FRYE (Frius), Peter, *M.A.* (Foster). Verse 6787.

FRERE, Daniel, *Bookseller*. Prose 20647.

FRYER *or* FRERE, John, *Physician, fl. 1571 (DNB)*. Verse 374, 6577, 12596, 12597.

FRYER, John, *Physician, d. 1672 (DNB)*. See 3931.

FRYER, Thomas, *Physician* (Venn 1553). Verse 12550, 12555; *see* 17944.

FRERE, Tobias, '*Attorney*' [? *Gray's Inn*]. Minsheu List.

FULFORD, Thomas, *of Fulford, Devon, d. 1610*. 5000.

FULFORD (Bamfield), Ursula = Thomas. J. G., *Steps of ascension, 1625-L.*; epistle 5000.

FULGEAN. *See* FOLJAMBE.

FULKE, Samuel, *Brother of next*. Verse 11419.

FULKE, William, *Puritan divine (DNB)*.

Epistle 11420; prose 22247; *see* 3802, 4709, 18744.

FULLWAR, Francis, *Esq*. 5318.

FULLERTON, *Sir* James, *Gentleman of Bedchamber*. *1203, *1404 by editor, †12117, *12178, 18608, 20392, 20549, 21098; epistle 23581 (23575, 21653); Minsheu List.

FULLERTON, John, *of Edinburgh Town Council*. W. M., *Edinburghs alphabet*-E.

FULLERTON, *Lady* Magdalen. *See* BRUCE.

FULLWOOD, William, *Author (DNB)*. Edits 15542.

G

G., A., '*B.D., of Gloucester Hall*' [? *fiction*]. Verse 1311.

G., A., '*Sister of author*'. ¶19068.

G., A. Verse 2947, 11084 (11054), 19548.

G., B., *Medij Temp*. [G. B. *in* F. *copy*]. Verse 18909.

G., B. Verse 4325, 6436, 20097 [? Garter].

GAR., Ber. *See* BERNARD GARTER.

G., C., *ex Oxon*. [*doubtless* Christopher Goodfellow]. Verse 3818, 3820, 4943, first issue 4946, 17921, 18343 (18337), 18346 (18337), 20770, 23704.

G., C., *M.A*. Verse 12174.

G., C. [*a preacher*]. Prose 15049.

G., D. G., *See* GOOSSEN.

G., E. [*presumably* Edward Grimston]. Edits 7742.

G., E. ¶17486 [? Guilpin]; verse 6485, 14927, 18910, 21649.

G., F. [*probably of Oxford*]. Verse 18114.

G., G. (12613). *See* GODFREY GOODMAN.

G., G., *a divine*. Prose 12796.

G., G. Verse 3202, 3894, 7274 [? Gaywood], 18862.

GA., G. [*perhaps* George Gaywood]. Verse 4243 (4245), 4508 (4509).

G., H. G. (18534). *See* HUMPHREY GIFFORD, *Gent*.

G., H., *Esq*. [? Goodere]. Verse 7205 (7232).

G., H. Verse 6410.

GR., Hen., *Grayanus* [*presumably* Grimston, *1597*]. Verse 841.

G., I., P[*rocancellarius*] (4489). *See* GOSTLIN.

G., I. (21055). *See* JOHN GREGORY.

G., I., *M.A.*, *Cambridge, student of physic.* Prose 5444.

G., I., *of Inner Temple* [*cf.* R. G.]. *11928.

G., I., '*Avocat*'. Verse 21139.

G., I., *Esq.* Verse 3075.

G., I. Edits 22493; verse 17824, 20596 as M. I. G., 21408, 24928.

GA., Io. Verse 14321.

GR., Io. [*probably* John Graile]. Verse 12171 [I. G. in 12172].

G., L., *Cantabrigiensis.* Verse 1534.

G., M. (4758). *See* GWINNE.

G., M. Verse 1695, 12100.

G., M. D. V. N. [*probably* M. D. V., N(*obilis*) G (?)]. Verse 7376.

G., N. Verse 15078.

G., P. [*probably* Patrick Gordon]. Verse 11596.

G., P. M. Verse 19074.

G., R., *of Plymouth, New England.* Prose 20074 [? misprint for R. C(ushman)].

G., R., *of Inner Temple* [*cf.* I. G.]. *11928.

G., R., *C.C.C.* [*Cambridge*]. Verse 24928.

G., R., *Armiger.* Verse 17509.

G., R., *Translator of earlier version of* 7298-BO. Epistle 7298.

G., R. Verse 19299; brother-in-law of, *see* 11504.

G., S. Verse 7192.

G., T., *and* P. N. *See* THOMAS GOODWIN.

G., T., *of Leics.* [? Gilbert]. *19788.

G., Tho. [? Goffe]. Verse 17642.

G., T. [*supposedly* Thomas Gokin]. Claims only to edit 6579.

G., T. Verse 1016, 1532, 12750, 19778 [? Goffe], 23725, 25109; prose 24436.

Go., Tho. (25026). *See* GOAD.

G., W. (3242). *See* WILLIAM GOUGE.

G., W., *Esq.* [? Goodyer]. Verse 7205.

G., W., *Gent., of London.* 17156.

B 8564

G., W. Verse 17922; prose T. Shepheard, *Sincere convert, 1640-*V. [? Gouge].

GR., W. (4127). *See* GREENHILL.

GAGER, William, *Latin dramatist* (*DNB*). Edits 22551; verse 3683, 4761, 11739.

GAINSFORD, *Sir* Thomas, *of Crowhurst, Surrey.* 3577 (3589), *¶3588.

GAINSFORD, Thomas, *Author and journalist* (*DNB*). Verse 18909.

GAINSFORD, W. Verse J. Taylor, *Most horrible satyre-*HN.

GALE, George. *See* COLONUS FELIS.

GALE, Henry, *M.A.* [*untraced*]. Verse 12299.

GALE, Thomas, *Surgeon* (*DNB*). Epistle 4036-L. [earlier-O. impf.]; prose 15192.

GALLARD, Robert, *Norwich clergyman* (Venn 1602). Edits 18493.

GALLOWAY, Patrick, *Scottish divine* (*DNB*). *5302 and *1618-*E.[2] by editor; edits 14376, 14380.

GAMALIEL (6581). *See* ABGAR.

GAMON, Hannibal, *Puritan divine* (*DNB*). *See* 25327.

GAMULL *or* GAMWELL (Bavand), Alice = Thomas *Recorder of Chester.* Presentation *11319 by bookseller.

GAMULL, Andrew, *Alderman of Chester* (PCC 1627). *¶23720.

GAMULL, William, *Mayor of Chester.* *¶23720.

GARBRAND, John, *Divine* (*DNB*). Edits 14596, 14603 and table 14604, 14614 (14579); verse 25807 partly reprinted 3129.

GARBRAUDUS (some copies 3129). Misprint for Garbrandus.

GARDINER, *Sir* Christopher, *Colonist* (*DAB*). Verse 18202.

GARDINER, Christopher, *of Haling, Surrey, d. 1661.* Verse 24823.

GARDNER, Daniel, *M.A.* (Venn 1561). *See* 13923.

GARDINER, Daniel. Verse 13480.

GARDINER, John, *Mercer* (PCC 1618). *20756.

GARDINER, John, *Bailiff of Shrewsbury* (*Vis. Shrops.*). *24043.

GARDINER, Richard, *Puritan* (Venn 1564). Verse 1410; *see* 4709.

GARDINER, Richard, *Divine* (*DNB*). *4259.

L

GARDINER, *Sir* Robert, *Chief Justice of Ireland.* 1479 (9697), †3442 and *1608*-HD., ¶21869.

GARDINER, Stephen, *Bishop of Winchester.* 13741, 22250; *see* 1291, 5991, 11593, 14827, *Copie of a letter,* [*1554*]-PML.

GARDNER, Thomas, '*of Boreham, Essex*' [? *Sir* Thomas *of Tollesbury*]. 3651 [earlier lost].

GARDINER, *Sir* Thomas, *of Basing, Surrey,* d. *1632.* 22395.

GARDINER, *Sir* Thomas, *Recorder of London* (*DNB*). *22532 [diff. work from 22531]; verse 3914.

GARDINER, *Sir* William, *of Lagham, Surrey,* d. *1622.* 7610.

GARDYNE, Alexander, *Scots poet* (*DNB*). Verse 12067.

GARGRAVE, *Sir* Richard, *of Yks.* (Venn). 18857 [diff. trans. from 18856], ¶23580 by editor; Minsheu List.

GARNONS, John, *D.D.* (Venn 1608). Verse 18806.

GARRARD, Garrarde, Garrett. *See* GERARD.

GARRAWAY, *Sir* Henry, *Lord Mayor* (*DNB*). *6531, *¶11346, 13350, *13467, 17941, *21094, 25972 = ¶25971; epistle *25963.

GARRAWAY (Clitherow), Margaret = *Sir* Henry. Presentation 25971.

GARRAWAY, William, *the elder, Merchant, brother of Sir Henry.* Epistle *25963.

GARRET, Garrett. *See* GERARD.

GARSET, Robert, *Esq., of the Virginia Company.* 18590.

GARTER, Bernard, *Poet* (*DNB*). Verse 6130; *see* 4555; *consider* B. G.

GARTH, Richard, *Clerk of the Petty Bag.* 10879.

GARTHWAITE, Henry, *Clergyman* (Venn, *STC*). Verse 21094.

GASCOIGNE, George, *Poet* (*DNB*). Edits 11881; verse 4608, 6738, 24328 including T. M. Q. [Gascoigne now believed the translator of book]; *consider* G. G. (18862).

GASGOIGNE, *Sir* William, *of Sedbury* (Foster 1581). 21333.

GASNALL, Thomas. Verse 4497.

GASTON-JEAN-BAPTISTE, *Duke of Orleans.* 25851 and *1626*-F. [but French version of *1635*-L. impf. and earlier lost].

GATAKER, Thomas, *Puritan divine* (*DNB*).

Edits 3521, 3523; prose 7619, 11530, 23860, 25035 (25031 and *1623*-F.) [25034 a ghost]; *see* 1336, 10738.

GATES, *Sir* John, *Statesman* (*DNB*). 4068.

GATES, Mary, *Daughter of Sir Henry of Seamer, Yks.* 3703.

GATHOUSE, —— [*Somerset preacher*]. Epistle *1941.

GAWDY, *Sir* Bassingbourne, *of West Harling, Norf.* ¶19680 (19649).

GAWDY, *Sir* Clipsby, *of Gawdy Hall, son of Sir Thomas.* *4616.

GAWDY, Framlingham, *of West Harling.* Epistle 15037.

GAWDY, *Sir* Francis, *Judge* (*DNB*). *1592*-F. of *¶6402 only.

GAWDY, *Sir* Henry, *K.B., son of Sir Thomas.* 2784-L., *11572.

GAWDY, *Sir* Robert, *of Claxton* (*Vis. Norf.*). Epistle 15037.

GAWDY, Thomas, *Serjeant-at-law, d. 1556. See* 20040.

GAWDY, *Sir* Thomas, *Judge* (*DNB*). 20097.

GAWEN, Frances, *O.S.B., abbess at Cambrai.* 1923.

GAWEN, Thomas, *Roman Catholic writer* (*DNB*). Verse 5097 as Gowen, 21351.

GAYER, *Sir* John, *Lord Mayor* (*DNB*). *3536; epistle *25963.

GAYTON, Edmund, *Author* (*DNB*). Verse 20694.

GAYWOOD, George, *Revenue collector.* 21407; verse 21661 (21649); *see* G. G. *and* G. GA.

GEE, George *and* John, *Brothers of the author.* Edit 11700.

GEE, John, *Anti-Catholic writer* (*DNB*). Prose 25161.

GEE, *Sir* William, *of the Council in the North.* By editor †19707 and *1605*-M. (19649, cf. 19648).

GEERE, John, *M.A.* (Foster). Edits *Tropo-schematologia, 1602*-O.[3] [? author].

GEERE, William, *City captain.* *21095; epistle 1507.

GELDENHAUR, Gerhard, *Noviomagus* (*NBG*). Verse 18095 [from earlier foreign ed.].

GELLIBRAND, Henry, *Mathematician* (*DNB*). Prose 25234; *see* 14444.

GELLIE *or* JOLLIE, John, *Scottish physician (STC)*. Verse 18063.

GEMINUS, Papyrius, *Eliates* [*? pseudonym*] *(STC)*. Prose 20140.

GENINGES, John, *Franciscan Provincial (DNB)*. 11728 by editor; *see* 19794.

GENT, Tho. Verse 23779 (23725).

GENTILI, Alberico, *Civilian (DNB)*. Epistle 11730; verse 4012, 11099, 11515, 11516; prose 13887.

GENTILI, Robert, *Infant prodigy (DNB)*. Prose 11741.

GENTILI, Scipione, *Brother of Alberico*. Epistle 11730; verse 11737.

GEOFFREY, Geofridus. *See* JEFFERY.

GEORGE, *Saint: Lovers of*. 25409.

GEORGE. *All British men named*. 25409.

GEORGE, *Duke of Clarence, d. 1478*. 4920.

GEORGE, *Duke of Saxony, d. 1539*. 292.

GERANIUS, Cephas. Prose 17314.

GERARD, GARRARD(E), GARRETT, etc.

GERARDE, ——, '*at Bononie, Italie*'. *See* 4834 = 19406.

GERARD (Ratcliffe), Dorothy = William *of Harrow*. *18156.

GERARD, Dutton, *III Baron Gerard*. *See* 10667.

GERARD (Dutton), Eleanor = Gilbert *II Baron, later* Needham. ¶23720.

GARRARD, George, *Master of Charterhouse* (Foster). *See* 5811.

GERARD, *Sir* Gilbert, *Master of the Rolls (DNB)*. 5226 [misprinted William Jarret in first issue], 11128, 25343.

GERARD, Gilbert, *II Baron Gerard*. †7468; *see* 17332.

GARRARD, *Sir* Jacob, *I Bt.* *11347 as James, *22532 [diff. book from 22531].

GARRARD, James. *See preceding*.

GERARD, John, *Herbalist and surgeon (DNB)*. *24577; verse 5448.

GARRARDE, *Sir* John, *Lord Mayor*. *7146, *11653 (11652) by editor, *17886, *20756, *23864.

GARRARD, *Sir* John, *I Bt.* 1418.

GERARD, Thomas, *I Baron Gerard*. *¶11600, ¶25224; edits 11625.

GERARD, *Sir* Thomas, *I Bt.* 7461, 23722.

GARRARDE, *Sir* William, *Lord Mayor*. *5798 [see changes], 18489 by bookseller.

GARRETT, William, *Bookseller*. Prose 16843.

GEREE, John, *Puritan divine (DNB)*. Edits 19589 (19570).

GERMAN *and* GERVOYSE. *See* JERMYN *and* JERVOISE.

GESNER, Conrad, *Naturalist (NBG)*. ¶4346 and 4347.

GETHING, Richard, *Writing-master (DNB)*. *See* 13327 plate ix.

GEVEREN, Sheltco à, *Obscure author*. Prose to translator 11805.

GIBBONS, Orlando, *Composer (DNB)*. *See* 24099.

GIBB, *Sir* Henry, *I Bt., of the Bedchamber*. *12178.

GYBBES, Elizabeth, *Abbess of Syon*. 25414 (25413 probably the earlier).

GIBBES, Henry, *Mayor of Bristol*. *24027.

GIBBS, Thomas, *of Virginia Company* (Brown). *17362.

GYBBES, William [*? of Elmstone, Kent*]. ¶1710 [earlier lost].

GIBSON, *Sir* Alexander, *Lord Durie, d. 1644 (DNB)*. 10669.

GIBSON, Anthony, *Groom of the Chamber (STC)*. 16857 by bookseller; verse 12500, 19165; claims only to edit 11831.

GIBSON, George, *Merchant Taylor*. 5650.

GIBSON, *Sir* John, *Master in chancery* (Venn 1558). Presentation 379.

GIBSON, Thomas, *Printer (DNB)*. Unsigned prose 13178, *Annotations in Josue*-NY.

GIFFORD, Emanuel, *of the Privy Chamber* (Venn). 5583 [*1613* lost], *12178.

GIFF[ORD], G., *Gent*. Verse 13776.

GIFFORD, 'Gabriel'. Name in religion of William below.

GIFFORD, *Sir* George, *Gentleman pensioner, brother of William*. Perhaps 17124 only, †18268.

GIFFORD, George, *Divine (DNB)*. *See* 1523, 12339; review preceding entry.

GIFFORD, Humphrey, *Poet (DNB)*. As H. G. G. verse 18534 [reprinted from 11872].

GIFFARD, James, '*Professor of French*'. Edits 6754 and *1628*-L.

GIFFORD, John, *Physician* (Foster 1584). Verse 24042; *see* 14791.

GYFFORD, John. Verse 5808 and 5810 [cf. 23769].

GIFFARD, John, *of Landcross, Devon.* ¶12657a (12635), miscalled Sir John in late edition.

GIFFORD, Sir Richard, *of King's Somborne, Hants.* †12973, *20914a.

GIFFARD, Roger, *Physician* (*DNB*). 14814.

GIFFORD, William, *Archbishop of Rheims* (*DNB*). 934 and *1621*-F. as Gabriel.

GILBERT (Campe), Jane = William *D.D.*, *friends of.* Epistle 11882.

GILBERT, Sir Humphrey, *Navigator* (*DNB*). 4015 = 19308, 10823.

GILBERT, Sir John, *Brother of preceding.* 11881, 25978 as Jylbert.

GILBERT, Nicholas, *of Bowringsleigh (Vis. Devon).* ¶13378 as Gilberd.

GILBERT, Raleigh, *Son of Sir Humphrey.* 21087 [see changes].

GILBERT, William, *Scientist* (*DNB*). Prose 1442.

GILBOURNE, Thomas, *Esq.* [? *of Kent*]. 5988.

GILBY, Anthony, *Puritan divine* (*DNB*). Prose 4697.

GILES, Sir Edward, *of Bowden (Vis. Devon).* †20133, ¶25941.

GILES, Nathaniel, *Composer* (*DNB*). Verse 20756; *see* 24099.

GILES (Aegidius), Peter, *Town clerk of Antwerp.* 18094, Erasmus, *Parabolae*-F.; prose 18095—all from early foreign editions.

GILL, Alexander, *the elder, Master of Paul's School* (*DNB*). Verse 841 as Guil, 23041 and 23044; prose 667; Minsheu List.

GILL, Alexander, *the younger, Master of Paul's* (*DNB*). Verse 11912, 12791, 12967 (12964), 13555.

GILL, Sir George, *of Wyddial* (Venn 1582). *¶25677 [see changes] as Ghill.

GILL, George, *Son of Alexander the elder.* Verse 11877.

GILL, John [*probably kin of Sir George*]. Verse 6969 and *1605*-C. as Gyll; *see* 25695.

GILL, Nathaniel, *Son of Alexander the elder* (Foster). Verse 11877.

GILLAM *or* GILHAM, Thomas, *Barber surgeon.* 6520.

GILLIE, William. *5533 by editor.

GILLINGHAM, Thomas, *M.A.* (Foster, 1560). *See* 13923.

GILPIN, Bernard (*DNB*), *Unnamed kinsman of.* Verse 4647.

GUILPIN, Edward, *Poet* (*STC*). Verse 19793; *see* E. G.

GINCHI, Gasparo. Verse 6735.

GIPPES, Thomas, *Clothworker* (Brown). H. Robrough, *Balme from Gilead, 1626*-F.

GITTINS, Ralph, *Schoolmaster* (Venn). Verse 14890.

GITTYNS, Thomas, *of the Inner Temple.* Verse 17921.

GLEDSTANES *or* GLADSTONE, Alexander, *Minister at St. Andrews.* ¶1496.

GLADSTANES, George, *Archbishop of St. Andrews.* 21555, H. Danskin, *De remoris*-E.[2]; unique imprimatur in 12066.

GLANVILLE, John, *B.D.* (Foster 1611). Verse 21033, 23135.

GLANVILLE, Sir John, *the younger, Serjeant-at-law* (*DNB*). Verse 3914.

GLAREANUS VADIANUS. *See* VADIANUS.

GLASEOR, William, *Vice-chamberlain of Chester.* 488 [and lost earlier eds.].

GLEANE, Sir Peter, *Mayor of Norwich.* *7323; epistle †11574.

GLEDSTANES. *See* GLADSTANES.

GLEG, James, *Schoolmaster of Dundee.* Verse 1496.

GLEMHAM (Sackville), Anne = Sir Henry. 17091 by bookseller, 18518 by editor.

GLEMHAM, Sir Charles, *Master of Household* (Foster). Epistle some copies *4747-O.

GLEMHAM, Sir Thomas, *Royalist* (*DNB*). ¶4338 as Glenham; Minsheu List as Glemend.

GLOVER, ——, 'Clerk to Lord Justice Hobart'. Minsheu List.

GLOVER, Alexander, *Exchequer clerk.* *See* 23779.

GLOVER, George, *Engraver* (*DNB*). *See* 13327 plate vii.

GLOVER, Josse, *Preacher who died taking first press to New England* (Waters). Prose S. Egerton, *Comforts to strengthen, 1630*-PN.[2]

GLOVER, Richard, 'Common councilman, of St. Swithin's'. ★5676.

GLOVER, Robert. Verse 1429.

GLOVER, Sir Thomas, of Willesden, ambassador. 6508.

GLYNN, Thomas, of Glynnllivon (Foster). ¶14704 [1641].

GOAD, Christopher [? Venn 1569]. See 25695.

GOAD, George, Master at Eton (DNB). ★21848 by editor; verse 12964.

GOAD, John, Headmaster (DNB). Verse 22888.

GOAD, Roger, Provost of King's (DNB). 13398; see 4709, 18744, 25695.

GOAD, Thomas, Divine, d. 1638 (DNB). Verse 1880 [1879 a ghost] under anagram "Οδ' ὠμὸς ἀγαθός, 4749, 12648c (12635), 17610, 22390, 25026 (7068) as Tho. Go.; prose 14624 signed in later ed.; see 10738; Minsheu List.

GOD. This list of formal dedications and related material ignores ejaculations like 'Soli Deo gloria' and routine invocations. As might be expected, the material is all Christian. The propriety of such dedications is discussed in the 'dedication' of 18198.
GOD: 10583, 12898, 13183, 19069, 19420; see 1064, 1730 (1710), 2734, 16160, 20529, 22234, 25939.
THE TRINITY: 17780, 21764, ¶23367, ★Rule of thirde order, 1624-L.; see 1333, 2811 = 3735, 18050, ¶23725 [earlier lost].
JESUS CHRIST: 4156 [cf. 4140], 6879 by author, 9229 and 9232 and 9233 (14344, 14346), 12694 (12706, 12635), 14955, 15047, 21676, 24970, 25033a (25031 and 1623-F.) [25033 a ghost], 25688 with Bishop of Lincoln by editor; see 589, 7171, 10008, 11222, 25699.
JESUS CHRIST in the Eucharist: 21694; see 11026.
KING OF KINGS: 1630-L. of 590 [see changes].
GOD and the Church: 972, 12100, 12660 = ¶12636, 23067 [see changes]; see 364.
DEO, Ecclesiae, Tibi: 20600.
GOD, Church, Republic of Letters: 23065.
DEO, Patriae et Posteris: 4496 (4497, 4502).
DEO, Patriae, Tibi: 5488, 5511 and later parts, 15167, 15784.
DEO et Anglorum laribus: 24153.
TRINITY and James I: 2348.
JEHOVAH and [separately] Privy Council: 24622.

GOD, Those that love, etc.: See religious section under ENGLAND.

GODFREY, Edward, 'Merchant'. ¶12609.

GODFREY, Thomas, Keeper of the game for bears. 23739.

GODLEY, Henry, Vicar of Onehouse (Venn). See 12527.

GODLYF, Thomas, 'Minister at Garneley, Sussex [? Goringlee]'. See 13923.

GODOLPHIN, Sir Francis, Grandfather of Sidney. 13890.

GODOLPHIN, Francis, of Treveneage (Keeler). 23568 (23563).

GODOLPHIN, John, Civilian (DNB). Verse 3.

GODOLPHIN, Sidney, Poet (DNB). Verse 7046, 21725.

GODWIN. Listed with GOODWIN.

GOEDDAEUS, Johannes, Professor of law at Herborn (ADB). ★14047.

GOFFE. See GOUGH.

GOLD. Listed with GOULD.

GOLDING, Arthur, Translator (DNB). Verse 1410; consider A. G. (19548).

GOLDING, Sir Edward, I Bt. 22439.

GOLDING (Roydon), Elizabeth = Sir Thomas (PCC 1596). 4882 by editor [see changes].

GOLDING, Percival, Son of Arthur. Edits 11400, erroneously called the translator.

GOLDING, Ursula (24291). Error for Arthur [although both his mother and wife were so named].

GOLDINGHAM, William, M.A. (Venn 1565). Verse 11627, 23095.

GOLDINGHAM, William, of Gray's Inn (Venn 1602). Minsheu List.

GOLDSMITH, John, Vicar of Henfield (Foster 1611). Prose exchange 24704.

GOLDWELL, John, Father of the author. ★11988 and 11989.

GOLDWELL, Thomas, Bishop of St. Asaph. Possevino, Treatise of masse, 1570-ST.

GOLDWIER, William, Gent. [of Christchurch, Hants]. One issue of ★13507.

GOLLOP, [Gibbes, Rector of Odcombe] (Foster). See 5809.

GOMERSALL, Robert, Dramatist (DNB). Verse 11464.

GOMMARIS, Antonius. ★557 and *1629*-HD. from earlier foreign.

GONDI, Henri de, *Cardinal de Retz*. Epistle 17598.

GONDOMAR. *See* ACUÑA.

GONELL, William, *Friend of Erasmus* (DNB). Verse G. Petrus, *Opus sane, 1524*-O.⁹

GOOCH *or* GOCH(E). *See also* GOOGE.

GOOCH, Henry, *D.D.* (Venn). ★18206; *see* 13518.

GOODALL, Baptist, *Merchant and poet* (STC). Verse 860.

GOODERUS, William, *Master of Barber Surgeons*. ★24578; verse 5442, 5448 (5442); prose 1358 (1357).

GOODFELLOW, Christopher, *of the Inner Temple* (Foster 1635). *See* C. G.

GOODFELLOW, Robin. 'Publishes' 23685; prose 4579.

GOODLER, William, *Captain for Muscovy Company*. ★19566.

GOODMAN, Gabriel, *Dean of Westminster* (DNB). 164, 4374, 20844, 21797 = 14504.

GOODMAN, Gabriel [? *the preceding*]. Verse 7388.

GOODMAN, Godfrey, *Bishop of Gloucester*. ¶548, 1986; prose 12612, more 12613 as G. G. with answer; prose to his editor 12026; *see* 10667.

GOODMAN, Grace, '*Niece of author*'. ¶5853 and earlier *1637*-PN.²

GOODMAN, John, '*Minister of Ferring, Sussex*'. *See* 13923.

GOODRICH, Thomas, *Bishop of Ely*. French version 6000-PFOR., 13940 [see changes], 16430, T. Ruddoke, *Remembraunce for ministers, 1551*-L.²

GOODRICK, *Sir* Henry, *of Ribston, Yks*. 15360-A.

GOODRIDGE, Richard, *of Christ Church* (Foster 1635). Verse 10829.

GOODWIN, *Sir* Francis, *of Upper Winchendon* (Vis. Bucks.). L'Espine, ★*Comfort for conscience, 1591*-C.⁴

GODWIN, Francis, *Bishop of Hereford*. Prose 12612; Minsheu List; *see* MAHONIDES.

GOODWIN, John, *Republican divine* (DNB). Prose 20660.

GOODWYN, John, *Arithmetic teacher in London* (Venn, *which uncertain*). Verse 13988.

GOODWIN, Robert. Verse 22249.

GOODWIN, Thomas, *the elder, Divine* (DNB). Edits with Thomas Ball, *q.v.*; with P. Nye edits 22476, 22486, 22488, 22492, 22494, 22512a, 22515, 22521.

GODWIN, Thomas, *Master of Abingdon School* (DNB). *See* 25327; Minsheu List.

GOODWIN, William, *Dean of Christ Church* (DNB). ★1938, ★6420, 7372, 20119, ★23108, R. Faureau, ★*Briefe direction to French, 1618*-O.⁵; epistle 17245; edits 19023, 19024; Minsheu List.

GOODERE, GOODYER, GOODYEAR, etc.

GOODYER (Goodyer), Frances = *Sir* Henry. ¶7193 (7189, 7216, etc.).

GOODYER, *Sir* Henry, *Literary patron, d. 1627* (DNB). ¶7193 (7189, 7216, etc.), ¶7222; verse 5808 and 5810 [cf. 23769]; *see* H. G. *Esq.*

GOODYEAR, Samuel, *of St. John's* (Venn). Verse 6839.

GOODYEAR, Thomas, *Warden of the Drapers*. W. Freake, ★*Priuiledges of vpright, 1639*-F.

GOODERE, Thomas, '*Curiae Wardorum*' [? *Gray's Inn*]. Verse 17921.

GOOGE, Barnabe, *Poet* (DNB). Prose 20978.

GOOSSEN, Gerard, *Physician and almanacmaker, of Dutch Church*. Verse 18601, 18602, Noot, *Het bosken,* [*1568*]-F. as D. G. G.; *see* 165.

GORBO IL FIDELE. Verse 7203.

GORDON, *Sir* Alexander, *I Bt*. 11595, 12489, 16694; epistle 11596.

GORDON, Alexander, *Son of preceding*. 11145.

GORDON (Campbell), Anne = George *II Marquis of Huntly*. 11147, 12479, 20596; epistle 12067.

GORDON, Arthur. Verse 5956, 12066, 21317.

GORDON, *Sir* Francis, *Agent in Poland and donor to King's College, Aberdeen*. W. Guild, *Christian passover, 1639*-E.²

GORDON, George, *I Marquis of Huntly*. ¶15715; *see* 10667.

GORDON, George, *II Marquis of Huntly*. ¶5393, 5960 [see changes], 11142, 12067, 13579 **by** editor, 13580, †14847, 15356, *¶15684, 21141, 23348, 25866; see 10667.

GORDON, George, 'Lord Gordon', d. 1645. See 10667.

GORDON (Stuart), Henrietta = George I Marquis. *17699.

GORDON, John, XIII Earl of Sutherland. See 10667.

GORDON, John, I [or perhaps II] Viscount Kenmure. See 10667.

GORDON (Sedley), Muriel = Brampton of Assington, Suff. *21187 and 1627-HD.

GORDON, Patrick, Poet (DNB). See P. G.

GORDON, Robert, of Straloch, antiquary. Verse 12067, 12482.

GORDON, Sir Robert, I Bt. 21327.

GORDON, William, Mediciner of King's College, Aberdeen. 12065.

GOWER, Ewers, of Jesus College (Venn). Verse 22400.

GOWER, John, Poet (DNB). *5094 (5068).

GORE, Sir John, Lord Mayor. *11467, *16753, *17886, *23345 by editor [see changes], *23930 [see changes], 25175; see 22532 [diff. work from 22531].

GORE, Richard, Merchant, brother of preceding. *25846.

GORE, Thomas, of King's College (Venn). Verse 11772.

GOWRE, William, Esq., 'Critic and poet' [untraced]. 22460 [conceivably error for John Gower, M.A.-STC].

GORE, William, the elder, Alderman, brother of Sir John. *17886.

GORGES, Agneta. See PHELIPS.

GORGES, Sir Arthur, Poet (DNB). Prose 9226.

GORGES, Carew, Son of preceding. Edits 16884.

GORGES, Edward, I Baron Gorges. *Fens map in 17827, 18609; see 10667.

GORGES, Sir Ferdinando, Commander (DNB). *13396 (13379).

GORGES, Francis, Brother of Edward. 7086.

GORGES, Sir Robert, of Wraxhall, Soms. *†1928.

GORGES, Sir Thomas, of Privy Chamber and Langford, Wilts. 1611-E.² of 22107 [see changes].

GORING, George, Father of next. *11367.

GORING, George, I Earl of Norwich. *11367, 16944; epistle *4747; see 10667, 12662 (12706, 12635).

GORING, George, 'Lord Goring', d. 1657 (DNB). ¶13264.

GORSAN, Nicholas, 'of Trowell, Notts., Irish planter'. *19490.

GOSSON, Stephen, Author (DNB). Verse 6787, 11096, 14092, 16807.

GOSTELOW or GORSTELOW, Richard, M.A. (Foster 1631). Verse 20694.

GOSTLIN, John, Master of Caius College (DNB). *636; prose 4489; see 25438.

GOSTOCK, ——, Captain, 'Mustermaster of Middlesex'. Epistle *5668.

GOSTWICK (Wentworth), Anne = Sir Edward II Bt. *¶110.

GOSTWICK (Owen), Jane = Sir William I Bt. ¶110.

GOSTWICK, Roger, B.D. (Venn). Verse 12613.

GOSTWICK, Sir William, I Bt. †117, *6882.

GOSYNHYLL, Edward, Poet (DNB). Epistle 18067 unnamed.

GOTSLEBIUS (Gottsleben), Joannes, Professor at Herborn (ADB). *14047.

GOUDGE, Mary, Abbess. See GOUGH.

GOUGE, Thomas, Nonconformist, d. 1681 (DNB). Verse 7235, 13519.

GOUGE, William, Puritan divine (DNB). Edits 4235 (4212), 10873, 12113; prose 3226, 3242 (3224) as W. G., 4211 (4212), 5844, 6114 and earlier 1623-U., 12980, 21221, 22392, 23584, 25971.

GOUGENOT, N. Verse 21139.

GOUGH, GOFFE, etc.

GOUGH, John, Printer (DNB). Prose 3033 [also royal privilege].

GOUGH, John, Dramatist (STC). Verse 20770.

GOUGH or GOUDGE, Mary, Abbess at Gravelines. 1611-HD. of ¶3369 by editor.

GOUGH, Richard, 'of Hereford, uncle of author'. 17939.

GOFFE, Thomas, Poet (DNB). Verse 19778; see T. G. and THO. G.

GOULART, Simon, Geneva pastor (NBG). Prose 21274.

GREENWAY, *Sir* Anthony, *of Leckhampstead* (*Vis. Bucks.*). *23101.

GRENEWAY, Antony, *S.J.* (Foster). Verse 7211 (7222), 21361.

GREENWELL, John, *Merchant adventurer.* ¶16684.

GREENWOOD, John, *Divine, d. 1593* (DNB). Epistle *11868.

GREENEWOOD, Robert, 'of Westerton [? Yks.]'. 13626.

GREGORY XIII, *Pope.* *11629.

GREGORY XV, *Pope. See* Widdrington, *Supplicatio, 1621-L.*²

GREGORY, John, *Orientalist* (DNB). Edits 21055 as I. G.

GREIRIUS. *See* GRIER.

GRENT, William, *Explorer* (Foster). Verse 22790.

GRENVILLE, *Sir* Barnard, *of Cornwall, father of next.* ¶10535 as Graynvill, 10537, 19947.

GRENVILLE, *Sir* Bevil, *Royalist* (DNB). 21490.

GRENVILLE (Bevile), Elizabeth = *Sir* Barnard. 10538 spelt Greynvile.

GRENVILLE, R. [*probably* Richard (Foster 1638)]. *3.

GRESHAM, *Sir* Thomas, *Financial agent* (DNB). 87, 545 by bookseller, 11746, 15336, 21360, often spelt Gressam.

GRESHAM, *Sir* William, *Brother of preceding.* 19070.

GRESSAM. *See* GRESHAM.

GRESSHOPE or GRASHOP, Thomas, *of All Souls* (Foster). Reading guide 2125 and most later Geneva Bibles (21494 and earlier-O.). [In 2126-9 forms inserted s. sh. with own imprint.] *See* ANON. VERSE, 'Here is . . .'.

GREVILLE, Charles, *of Milcote* (*Vis. Warw.*). Minsheu List.

GREVILLE, *Sir* Edward, *of Milcote.* *19620 [see changes].

GREVILLE, Fulke, *I Baron Brooke.* Some copies *¶4497, ¶6261 (6236, alternative epistle 6241), ¶12654 (12707, 12635), 13099, *17388 (17390), ¶18057a, 19838 by bookseller, engr. print *Councell of war-L.⁵; epistle 16696; believed editor 22539; *see* 12662 (12706, 12635), 17332.

GREVILLE, Peter, *Brother of Charles* (? Foster). Minsheu List.

GREVILLE, Robert, *II Baron Brooke.* 3733, 12037, 19552, 23507 by editor, 25410 and earlier 1634-F.; *see* 10667.

GREY *and* GRAY.

GRAY, Andrew, *VII Lord Gray.* 7353; *see* 10667.

GRAY, *Sir* Andrew, *Colonel in service of Frederick.* ¶12748, 23751 (23725); *see* Ramage, p. 99.

GREY, *Lady* Anne [*probably* (Jernegan) = *Lord* Edward, *later* Walsingham]. 1734 and 1756 (1710).

GREY (Windsor), Anne = Henry *I Baron Grey of Groby.* *25764.

GREY, Anne (4746). *See* MASTERS.

GREYS, Anth. [*perhaps* Foster *as* Gray]. Verse 6332.

GREY, Arthur, *XIV Baron Grey of Wilton.* ¶11636 only, 11645 (11638), 13030, *15441, 23019, 23022; epistle 23080 (23084); *see* 3958.

GREY, Charles, *VII Earl of Kent.* 14948 [date is *1616*].

GREY (Talbot), Elizabeth = Henry *VIII Earl.* 11538, *18041 [see changes], ¶24137, 24138 [see changes], De Beau Chesne, *Clef de l'escriture-N.

GREY (Brandon), Frances = Henry *Duke of Suffolk.* Epistle 25816.

GRAIUS, H. Verse 24308.

GREY, Henry, *Duke of Suffolk.* ¶4076 from early foreign, 21065, *24361 posthumously, 25816.

GREY, Henry, *VI Earl of Kent.* 122, ¶19764 (19647).

GREY, Henry, *VIII Earl of Kent.* Some copies †¶4497; *see* 10667, 17331.

GREY, Henry, *I Earl of Stamford. See* 10667, 17332.

GREY (Morrison), Jane Sibella = Arthur *XIV Baron.* 19046, *23024, ¶25348.

GREY, John, '*M.A., Medicinae licentiatus*'. Verse 12964.

GREY (Dade), Mary = Richard *of Inner Temple.* ¶4746 (17509).

GREY, Mary, *Daughter of preceding. See* DRAYTON.

GREY, Nicholas, *Headmaster of Eton* (*DNB*). Edits 21035; Minsheu List.

GRAY, Patrick, *VI Lord Gray.* Verse 4473.

GREY, Penelope, *Daughter of Mary above.* Verse 4746 (17509).

GREY, Richard, *III Earl of Kent. See* 7271, 17242.

GREY, Robert, '*Groom of bedchamber to Charles*' (Venn 1612). 17911.

GREY (Bertie), Susan = Reginald *V Earl of Kent.* Epistle 15227.

GREY, Thomas, *XV Baron Grey of Wilton.* *23024.

GREY, Thomas, '*Lord Grey*', *d. 1657* (*DNB*). *12417 by bookseller.

GRAY, Thomas, *Bailie of Aberdeen.* W. Mercer, *Bon-acords decorement, 1633*-E.

GRAY, Walter, *Almanac maker* (? Venn 1577). Verse 12896.

GREY, William, *Son of Arthur.* 21737.

GREY, William, *I Baron Grey of Werke. See* 10667.

GREY, Sir William de, *of Merton, Norf.* Epistle 15037.

GRAY, Sir William, *Treasurer of Edinburgh.* *13173, W. M., *Edinburghs alphabet*-E.

GREYNVILE, GRAYNVILE. *See* GRENVILLE.

GRIER, George, *Minister at Haddington.* Verse 21101.

GRIFFIN *and* GRIFFITH. *All spellings.*

GRIFFITH, Edmund, *Bishop of Bangor. See* 10667.

GRIFFIN, Edward, *the elder, Printer.* Epistle 23806 unnamed; unsigned prose 3585.

GRYPHITH, Elliseus. *See* 25438.

GRIFFIN, George. Verse 5808 and 5810.

GRIFFITH, George, *Bishop of St. Asaph.* Verse some copies 6347.

GRIFFITH, Sir Henry, *of Agnes Burton and the Council in the North.* *6020 [earlier lost].

GRYFFYTH, Hugh, *Gent.* Verse 19338.

GRIFFIN, John, *Barber surgeon.* Verse 1360.

GRIFFITH, Mary. 974 by editor.

GRUFFITH, William, '*of Coredaney, Angles[ey]*'. *See* '*Library*', *1959*, p. 90.

GRIFFITH, William, *D.C.L.* (Foster 1615). Verse some copies 6347.

GRIMALD, Nicholas, *Poet* (*DNB*). Verse 7662, 24368.

GRIMSTON, Bernye, *Son of Elizabeth-DNB.* 12407.

GRIMSTON, Edward, *Comptroller of Calais* (*DNB*). 26136.

GRIMSTON, Sir Harbottle, *I Bt.* 1593.

GRIMSTON, Sir Harbottle, *II Bt. See* 13327 plate viii.

GRIMSTON, Sir Henry, *of Gray's Inn* (Venn 1599). *See* HEN. GR.

GRIMSTON, Thomas, *M.D.* (Venn 1573). Epistle 17913.

GRINDAL, Edmund, *Archbishop of Canterbury.* 1492 by editor, ¶1710 and *1710, *4043 (4044), *4063 (4058), 4096, 4400, 4448, 4870 by printer, Latin version 6775-O., 7169, 10588, 11419, *11804, 12345-HD., *14608, 15653, 17174 by editor, 18478 only [supplementing Parker deceased], *18701, *18708, *18711, *18712, *18726, *18730, 18769, 19626, 24776, *1568*-F. of 25877 [see changes], Vermigli, *De exhumatione carmina, 1561*-HN. by editor; epistle 7168, *17497; *see* 10026.

GRINNELL, Thomas, *Mayor of King's Lynn.* T. Purchas, *Communicants duty, 1639*-PN.[2]

GRIPHUS. *See* GRYPHUS.

GROOS, Thomas, *Esq.* Verse 3508.

GROOT, Laurentius de. *557 and *1629*-HD. from earlier foreign.

GROSVENOR, Richard, *Father of Richard I Bt.* *7293 misprinted Granesnor.

GROTIUS, Hugo, *Writer* (*NBG*). Verse 4745, Vaenius, *Emblemata, 1608*-F.

GROVE, Francis, *Captain, Southwark martial garden.* *14922.

GROVE, Henry, '*Steward of Southwark martial garden*'. Epistle *14922.

GROVE, John, *Bookseller.* Prose 11541.

GROVE, Robert. R. Bernard, *Staffe of comfort, 1616*-F.

GRUTER, Jan, *Scholar* (*NBG*). Verse 4505 (4509), 13582.

GRYMES *or* CRYMES, Sir George, *of Surrey* (Foster). Verse 11157.

GRYMES, Sir Thomas, *of Peckham.* 7621.

GRYNAEUS (Gryner), Simon, *Scholar* (*NBG*). Prose 15288, 24293, both from early foreign eds.

GRYPHUS or GRIPHUS, Petrus, *Pisanus*, papal nuncio (*STC*). R. Ardenne, *Palamedes, 1512-*HN.; prose Seyssell, *Oratio*-F.

GRYSE and GUADUS. *See* LE GRIS and WADE.

GUALTER, Gualterus. *Listed with* WALTER.

GUARDA. *See* MIRA GUARDA.

GUARINUS, O.S.B., *Prior of Worcester, d. 1140.* 21102.

GUEST, Edmund, *Bishop of Salisbury.* ★1710; *see* 10026.

GUIL and GUILPIN. *See* GILL and GILPIN.

GUILD, William, *Scottish divine* (*DNB*). 1536I-A., ★22472.

GUILDENSTERN, Nicholas. *See* GYLLENSTIERNA.

GUILDFORD (Somerset), Elizabeth = *Sir* Henry. Minsheu List.

GUILDFORD, Sir Henry, *of Hemstead, Kent.* 19807; *see* 23088 (23084).

GUILLIM, GUILLIAMS, etc. *Listed with* WILLIAMS.

GUISE. *See* GYSE.

GUNNELL, Richard, *Actor.* Verse 22788 (22790).

GUNNING, Peter, *Bishop of Ely.* Verse 7294, 15520.

GUNSON, Richard [*presumably* Foster *as* Gunston]. Verse 5542 (25944).

GUNSON, Tho. Verse 10784.

GUNTER, H. Prose 23843 (23855).

GUNTER, Nicholas, *Mayor of Reading.* ★23840.

GURDON. *Listed with* GORDON.

GURLIN or GIRLING, *alias* GWYN, Nathaniel, *of Lincoln's Inn* (Venn). 24825; verse 10945 (7567) with answer, 22634 as Gwin.

GURLIN, Thomas, *Mayor of King's Lynn.* ★21123.

GURNEY, Edmund, *Divine* (*DNB*). Verse 25224.

GURNEY (Lewkenor), Martha = Thomas *of West Barsham.* Epistle ★4693.

GOURNEY, Richard, *Alderman, d. 1597.* ★12307.

GOURNEY, Thomas, *of Denham, West Suff.* ★20337 by editor.

GUSTAVUS ADOLPHUS, *King of Sweden, Memory of.* 20573.

GUTHRIE, Alexander, *Town Clerk of Edinburgh.* W. M., ★*Edinburghs alphabet*-E.

GUTHRIE, John, *Bishop of Moray. See* 10667.

GUY, John, *Colonizer* (*DNB*). Verse 24604, 24609; Minsheu List.

GUIN, Lo. [*presumably* Lewis (Venn 1555)]. Verse 6364.

GWINNE, Matthew, *Physician* (*DNB*). Epistle P. Bowne, *Pseudo-medicorum anatomia, 1624-*L.; signed verse 4756, 4761, 11516, 24610; initialed verse 4758; verse as 'Il Candido' 11098, 11099, 18041 only, 18042.

GWIN, Morgan. *See* WYNNE.

GWIN, N. (22634). *See* NATHANIEL GURLIN.

GWYN, Owen, *Master of St. John's* (Venn 1584). Minsheu List.

GWYNN, Rowland, *City lieutenant.* Verse 1506, 1507.

GYLLENSTIERNA, Nils, *Swedish ambassador.* Presentation 18662 as Nicholas Guildenstern.

GYLLYVER, I., 'of Egginton, Derby'. ★20207.

GYSE or GUISE, Sir William, *of Brockworth, Gloucs.* 4595.

H

H., A., *Ex Temp: Med:* [? Antony Hawkins]. Verse 14008.

H., A. Verse 91, 12885, 25185 (1357).

H., B. Verse 1695; *see also* D. B. H.

HE., Ba. Verse L. Staveley, *Breef discourse*-HN. headed Ba. He. but signed T. F.

H., C., *M.A., Magdalen College, Oxford.* Verse 1311.

H., C. Verse 13190 [? Herbert]; prose 24526 [? the translator].

H., D. B., *Captain.* 11527 supposedly (12221) but no such copy found.

H., E. (3271). *See* EDWARD HUGHES.

H., E. Verse 5569, 11636 (11638), 13801.

H., F. Verse 3894, 18910, 21094.

H., G. (13470). *See* R. H.

H., G. Edits 22478; verse 6316, 11636 (11638), 13245; *see* 23970 only.

changes], 20361 (20345); edits 7152; *see* 25327; Minsheu List.

HAKEWILL, William, *Antiquary* (*DNB*). †6061, 7331; *see* 5811; Minsheu List.

HAKLUYT, Richard, *Geographer* (*DNB*). Prose 15481.

HALES (Kemp), Alice = Sir James, *later* Lee. 12272 only.

HALES, Sir Charles, *of the Council in the North.* *1832, *19699 (19649) by editor, *¶25795.

HALES, Sir Edward, *1 Bt.* 20168.

HALES, H. Verse 4654.

HALES, John, *Author, d. 1571* (*DNB*). ¶2854.

HALES, John, *Fellow of Eton* (*DNB*). *25129; *see* 25327.

HALES (Wood), Margaret = Sir James-*DNB*. 19148 [see changes].

HALKERSTON, James, *Scottish colonel in foreign service.* Verse 4473.

HALL, ——, '*Herefordshire ox-leech and taborer*'. 12032.

HALL, Edward, *Son of Joseph* (Foster 1635). Verse 12757.

HALL, George, *Fellow of King's* (Venn 1625). Verse 13519.

HAULE *or* HALL, Henry, *of Maidstone* (*Vis. Kent*). †3410.

HALL, Henry, *Treasurer of Middle Temple.* *6014.

HALL, John, *Surgeon and poet, d. 1566?* (*DNB*). Verse 11529 (24723).

HALL, John, *Father of Joseph.* See 12662 (12706, 12635).

HALL, John, *Minister of St. Giles, Edinburgh.* *5302 and *1618-E.²* by editor.

HALL, John, F[*ilius, presumably son of preceding*]. Verse 13258.

HALL, John, *Schoolmaster* (Venn 1618). Verse 351, 22444.

HALL, John, *of Gray's Inn.* Verse 26068.

HALL, John, *Son of Joseph* (Foster 1635). Verse 12757.

HALL, Joseph, *Bishop of Exeter.* 1789, 4180, 4859, 5144, 6427 by bookseller, *7152 by editor, 12136, 21844 by editor, ¶25993, 25994, 26111; epistle 4136, 23581 (23575, 21653), 23582 (23575, 21653); verse 12312, 21650, 23578, 25368, and probably anon.

verse 7022, 7023 (both 7045); prose 3768, 7152, 12613 as J. E[xon].; *see* 10667; Minsheu List.

HALL, Nathaniel, *Gent.* Verse 18993.

HALL, Richard, *Grocer* (Brown). *24596.

HALL, Robert, *of Gray's Inn* (Venn 1584). Verse 24316.

HALL, Robert, *Archdeacon* (Foster 1622). Edits 12687 (12636).

HALL, Rowland, *Printer.* Signed prose 4438; unsigned 2007 and *1563-O.*, 4458.

HALL, Samuel, *Brother of Joseph* (Venn 1597). See 12662 (12706, 12635).

HALL, Samuel, *Son of Joseph* (Foster). Verse 12757.

HALL, Thomas, *Brother of John* (*first above*). Verse 15192.

HALL, Thomas, *Vicar of Wells* (Foster 1581). Epistle *1941.

HALL, Thomas, *Rector of Pylle, Soms.* Epistle *1941.

HALL, William, *Printer.* Verse 18276; perhaps unsigned prose 24472.

HALL, William [*presumably son of John of Edinburgh*]. Verse 13258.

HALLELUIAH (5885). *See* HENRY HOLLAND.

HALLIDAY. See HOLLIDAY.

HALSEY, Sir Cuthbert. *See* HALSALL *in next series.*

HALSWELL, HALSALL, HASSALL, etc.

HALSEWELL (Wallop), Bridget = Sir Nicholas *of Somerset.* 13392 (13378).

HALSALL, Sir Cuthbert, *of Lancashire* (Foster). ¶25224 as Halsey.

HALSWELL, Hugh, *D.D.* (Foster 1612). *14457.

HASILL *or* HASSALL, Robert, *Ballad-writer.* Verse 1468; *cf. next.*

HALSWELL, Robert, *of Lincoln's Inn* (Foster 1602). Verse 5808 and 5810 [cf. 23769].

HASSALL, Thomas, *Gent.* [*believed* Venn]. Verse 7194 (7189, 7216).

HAM, Reuben, [*of Christchurch, Hants*]. One issue *13507.

HAMBIE, R. Verse 13260.

HAMDEN. See HAMPDEN.

HAMILTON Family. See 23373.

HAMILTON, Charles, *Bailie of Edinburgh.*
*139.

HAMILTON, James, *II Earl of Arran.* See 15672
(15658).

HAMILTON, James [? *Minister of Kirknewton*].
Edits 21282.

HAMILTON, James, *II Marquis of Hamilton.*
3089, *7336, *17260, *17699, 20391, 21862
misnamed John; *see* 15715; *see next.*

HAMILTON, James [*either preceding or next*].
2776 = 20554.

HAMILTON, James, *I Duke of Hamilton.* *1203,
¶3448, 4678, *12726, *¶15684, 18690, 20359
and *1624*-NY.¹¹ (20345), ¶21624, *23725,
24910 by editor; epistle *4747, 12205; prose
67 [earliest ed.]; *see* 10667, 17331, 22048,
22058.

HAMILTON, James, *I Earl of Abercorn.* 14293,
16870 [see changes].

HAMILTON, James, *II Earl of Abercorn.* *17699;
see 10667.

HAMILTON, James, *I Viscount Clandeboye.* See
10667.

HAMILTON, Jean, *Lady Skirling.* See COCK-
BURNE.

HAMILTON, John, *Archbishop of St. Andrews.*
See 15672 (15658).

HAMILTON, John, *fl. 1568–1609* (DNB).
Epistle 13945; *see* 11213.

HAMILTON, John, *Marquis* (21862). Error for
James, *II Marquis.*

HAMILTON, John, *of Broomhills and Edinburgh
Town Council.* W. M., *Edinburghs alphabet*-E.

HAMILTON, Robert, *Son of next.* *20697.

HAMILTON, Thomas, *I Earl of Haddington.* 137,
5931 (5909 with more), ¶15366, ¶19781,
20856–20860 inclusive, 21856, ¶22567, 25210
(25207); epistle *15715; *see* 10667.

HAMILTON, Thomas, *II Earl of Haddington.*
¶19781.

HAMLINUS, Aegidius. See 15246.

HAMMERSLEY, *Sir* Hugh, *Lord Mayor.* *162,
*6313, *6531, *11653 (11652) by editor,
¶11691, *12111 (12116), *17649 by editor
[see changes], *17886, *19566, 19803, 20766,
*23345 by editor [see changes], *24697,
*26064; epistle *15364; *see* 22532 [diff. work
from 22531].

HAMMOND, Anthony, *of St. Alban's Court,
Kent.* *Fens map in 17827.

HAMMOND, John [*probably Venn* 1570]. Verse
14608.

HAMMOND, John, *Physician* (DNB). Verse
12550.

HAMMOND, John. Verse 4194.

HAMOND, Thomas [*cf. next*]. Edits 25232.

HAMMOND, Thomas, *of Gray's Inn* (Venn
1608). ¶13320, ¶13340, 17412 by editor;
see 13327 plate ix.

HAMPDEN Family (Bucks.). 25965.

HAMPDEN, *Sir* Alexander, *of Hartwell* (PCC
1618). *25965.

HAMPTON, Christopher, *Archbishop of Armagh.*
15501.

HAMPDEN, Griffith, *of Hampden, Bucks.* 11920
as Gryffyn.

HAMDEN, *Sir* John. Presentation 6514.

HANBURY, Edm. [*probably Edward of Middle
Temple*]. Minsheu List.

HANBURY, Edward, *Son of next.* *11769 and
11782.

HANBURY, *Sir* John, *of Kelmarsh, Alderman of
London.* *11769 and 11782, *11772, 23586,
23587.

HANCOCKE, John, *of Brasenose College* (Foster
1617). Verse 17804.

HANCOCK, William, *Mayor of Coventry.*
*13770.

HAND, Francis, *M.A.* (Venn). ¶12299.

HANDSON. See HANSON.

HANFORD, *Sir* Humphrey, *Alderman.* *18321.

HANFORD, William. Verse 3944.

HANHAM, Thomas, *of Dean's Court* (Brown).
*†1929.

HANIA, Suffridus *or* Sjoerd, *of Franeker* (Schotel). *550 from earlier foreign.

HANKINSON, Hu., 'Officer under Viscount
Wimbledon'. See 22106.

HANLEY, Robert, 'Merchant'. Verse 13480.

HANMER, *Sir* John, *I Bt.* ¶23720.

HANMER, John, *Bishop of St. Asaph.* *25719
(25718).

HANMER, Meredith, *Historian* (DNB). See
4534 = 19393.

HANNAY, Patrick, *Poet* (*DNB*). Verse 15712.

HANNAY, Robert, '*Kinsman of preceding*'. Verse 12748.

HANNIBAL—*Ghosts of Hannibal and Scipio.* 18341 (18337).

HANSLEY, John, *Archdeacon of Colchester* (Venn). Book licenser *1639-40*.

HANDSON, John, [? Hanson-*DNB*]. Verse 23779 only.

HANSON or HANDSON, Ralph, *Accountant, Chancery auditor.* Verse 21094; prose 17224.

HARBORNE, John, *of Tackley* (*Vis. Oxfs.*). 6611 by bookseller, 13547.

HARBORNE, William, *Ambassador* (*DNB*). See 25438.

HARC., Ed., '*London merchant*'. A. Gurth, *Most true newes, 1597-*L.[2]

HARDBERDE. *See* HERBERT.

HARDING, George. Variant designation of George Berkeley, *q.v.*

HARDING, HARDEN, or HAWARDEN, John, *Principal of Brasenose* (Foster *as* Hawarden). 11249 as Harding.

HARDING, John. Verse 6984 with motto *Fato prudentia maior.*

HARDING, Thomas, *Divine* (*DNB*). 7062; epistle 14600 (14579); *see* 14606 (14579).

HARDING, Thomas, *Historian* (*DNB*). Verse 19511; Minsheu List.

HARDWICK, John, '*Steward of Southwark martial garden*'. Epistle *14922.

HARDY, '*Sir*' William. *5768.

HARE (Coventry), Elizabeth = *Sir John of Stow.* 912.

HARE, Hugh, *Bencher of Inner Temple.* *1909 and *1613*-F., *16677.

HARE, Hugh, *I Baron Coleraine.* 352 [see changes], 1795 = ¶19925; *see* 10667.

HARE, John, *Treasurer of Inner Temple, father of preceding.* *6014, *16677.

HARE, Sir John, *of Stow Bardolf, Norf.* Epistle †11379, 15037.

HARE, Margaret (7104). *See* MONTAGU.

HARE, Nicholas, *of Stow, Recorder of Lynn.* *16677.

HARES, Thomas (Venn). Prose 13877.

HAREBROWNE. *See* HARBORNE.

HARFLEET, *Sir* Christopher, *of East Kent.* 12771, *21175.

HARGREVE, Ambrose. Epistle 13626.

HARGRAVE, Henry, *Rector of Stretton-in-street, Rutl.* Prose 11838.

HARINGTON (Kelway), Anne = John *I Baron.* 4213 (4220 and *1619*-F.), *4466, *5849 [see changes], 6098, 6761, 6762, ¶7193 (7189, 7216), 7408 (7394) by editor, *11765 [see changes], 12180, *14296, *18041 [see changes], *23273, 23422, 24396; epistle 7232 only but reprinted in text 7195.

HARINGTON, *Sir* Edward, *II Bt.* 10923, T. Cooper, *Converts first love, 1610-*ILL.

HARINGTON (Markham), Isabella = John *the elder.* 19136.

HARINGTON, *Sir* James, *of Exton, father of next.* *568.

HARINGTON, *Sir* James, *I Bt.* *4887, T. Cooper, *Converts first love, 1610-*ILL.

HARRINGTON, James, *Political theorist* (*DNB*). Verse 5363 (5355).

HARRINGTON, John, *Bookseller.* Prose 2726.

HARINGTON, John, *the elder, Poet* (*DNB*). *¶20064 and *1561*-HN.

HARINGTON, *Sir* John, *Wit and author* (*DNB*). 6496; verse 5642, 5808 and 5810 [cf. 23769 misattributed, right in 23725]; *see* 12662 as S. H. I., corrected (12706, 12635).

HARINGTON, John, *I Baron H. of Exton.* *568, *4887, †6960 and *1608*-ILL., †7141 and *1608*-DUL., †¶7182, †11842, ¶13245, †17702, *24963, *†25621; epistle †5694 [see changes], †5704; *see* 19511.

HARINGTON, John, *II Baron Harington.* ¶5393, 7176 [see changes], 11841, 24031; verse 18985 [see also text].

HARRINGTON, Joseph, *of Emmanuel College* (Venn). Verse 12141.

HARINGTON, Thomas, *of Boothby Pagnell* (*Vis. Lincs.*). 21709 (21706).

HARRINGTON, Villiers, *of Clare Hall* (Venn). Verse 18948 (some copies signed, others initialed).

HARLACKINDEN, Martin, *of Woodchurch* (*Vis. Kent*). See 25626 misprinted Walter, corrected in errata and (25620).

HARLACKINDEN, Roger, *of Warehorne* (*Vis. Kent*). *25625 (25620).

HARLACKENDEN, Thomas, *of Gray's Inn* (Venn 1585). 25738.

HARLACKINDEN, Walter (25626). Error for Martin.

HARLACKINDEN, Walter, *Kin of next.* *25625 only [unless a confusion like preceding entry].

HARLACKINDEN, William, *Brother of Roger.* *25625 (25620).

HARLESTON, Thomas, *of Pembroke College* (Venn 1630). Verse 23516.

HARLEY (Conway), Brilliana = *Sir* Robert. 13822, *15567.

HARLOWE, John. ¶12609.

HARLEY, Richard, *of New College* (Foster). Verse 4759, 21029 (21032).

HARLEY, *Sir* Robert, *Master of the mint* (*DNB*). †¶11659 (11652), 19910 by editor, *23850.

HARLOWE. *Listed with* HARLEY.

HARMAN, James. Verse T. Powell, *Loves leprosie, 1598-*L. SILVER.

HARMAR, John, *the elder, d. 1613* (*DNB*). Edits 14635, 14636.

HARMAR, John [? *the next*]. Verse 12748.

HARMAR, John, *the younger, d. 1670* (*DNB*). Edits 14469–71; verse 19302; search I. H.

HARPUR, *Sir* Henry, I Bt. Verse 19924.

HARPER, John, '*of London*'. *25624.

HARPER, *Sir* John, *of Derbyshire, father of Henry* 188 and *1617*-HN., *24596.

HARPER, Thomas, *Printer.* Signed prose 23293 (1357), 24323; unsigned 7210, *Luciani libri duo, 1636-*F. [? from foreign ed.].

HARRINGTON. *See* HARINGTON.

HARRIOT, Thomas, *Mathematician* (*DNB*). Epistle 13635 only, 14947.

HARRIS, *Sir* Christopher, *of Devon* (Brown). *13396 (13379).

HARRIS, H. Verse 4946.

HARRIS, John, *Regius professor* (*DNB*). Verse 13018, 26130; Minsheu List.

HARRIS, John, *of Christ Church* (Foster 1621). Verse 10885.

HARRYS, Mary, '*Widow*'. 11422 by editor.

HARRIES, Richard, *Cousin of Davies of Hereford* [? *Gentleman usher-CSPD*]. Verse 24603; *see* 6341.

HARRIS, Richard, *D.D.* (*DNB*). Verse 20187.

HARRIS, Robert, *D.D.* (*DNB*). Verse 11544.

HARRIS, Thomas, *Bencher of Lincoln's Inn.* *11670.

HARRISON, Gilbert, *Alderman.* *23307 (23313) by editor.

HARRISON, John, *Master of Paul's School* (Venn 1570). Verse 14608.

HARRISON, John, *the elder, Bookseller.* Signed prose 23689; unsigned 22630.

HARRISON, John, *Envoy to Barbary* (*DNB*). Prose 3212; presumably the I. H. editing 1377, 21515.

HARRISON, John, *Headmaster of Eton.* *25129.

HARRISON, Lucas *or* Luke, *Printer.* Unsigned prose 2017, 3811.

HARRISON, Philip, '*Iuris utriusque licent.*' (? Venn 1568). Verse 22929.

HARRISON, Richard, *Printer.* Unsigned prose 4415.

HARRISON, Robert, *Cursitor, Court of Chancery* (*Vis. London*). *6582.

HARRISON, T. [? Thomas, Venn 1579]. Verse 889 only.

HARRISON, Thomas, *Biblical scholar* (*DNB*). *18206.

HARRISON, William, *Treasurer of East India company* (Brown). *25952.

HARRY the Porter [*a fiction*]. Verse 13540.

HARSNETT, Samuel, *Archbishop of York.* *22787.

HART, Andrew, *Edinburgh printer* (*DNB*). Epistle 1405, 1406; signed prose 3980 [usurped from Waldegrave]; unsigned prose 1378, 15666, 16592.

HART, John, *S.J.* (*DNB*). Prose 20626 (20630).

HART, *Sir* John, *Lord Mayor.* *12307, *15250, 16654 by bookseller, *23327 [see changes], 23633a, J. Stockwood editions of 6712, *1582*-L., etc.

HART, John, *Religious writer* (Wing). Edits 22798, 25236.

HART, *Sir* Percival, *of Lullingstone, d. 1580.* 11266.

HART, *Sir* Percival, *of Lullingstone* (Foster). Some copies *¶4497.

HART, Sara (19553). *See* ZOUCHE (Hart).

HARTLIB, Samuel, *Educator* (DNB). Edits 23305; prose 15077 and 15802, *15078a signed rarely-HD. [? possibly some copies 15078].

HARTWELL, Abraham, *the elder* (DNB). Verse 11223, 12596.

HARTWELL, Robert, *Mathematics teacher in Fetter Lane.* Edits 3151, 20807.

HARVET. See HERVET.

HARVEY, Christopher, *Poet* (DNB). Edits 19910, Harvey Sr., *Conditions of christianity, 1636*-L.[4]

HARVEY, Daniel, *Merchant, brother of William.* Epistle *21094.

HARVEY, Eliab, *Alderman.* Epistle *21094.

HARVEY (Ratcliffe), Elizabeth = James (*Vis. Mdsx.*). *18156.

HARVEY, Gabriel, *Poet* (DNB). Epistle 12913, 23089 (23084); verse 23080; *see* 12907, 12910.

HARVEY, *Sir* Gawin, *of Romford* (*Vis. Essex*). Minsheu List.

HARVEY, James, *Surgeon to Queen Anne.* Epistle and verse 16870.

HARVEY, John *and* John, *Brother and nephew of William.* Epistle *21094.

HARVEY, Martin, *of Middle Temple* (Venn). See 15466.

HARVEY, Matthew *and* Michael, *Brothers of William.* Epistle *21094.

HARVEY, Richard, *Astrologer* (DNB). Verse 12901; *see* 12905.

HARVEY, Robert. Verse 17642, 22460.

HARVEY, *Sir* Sebastian, *Lord Mayor.* 6607 (6605), *12123 [see changes].

HARVEY, William, *Physician* (DNB). Epistle 20385, *21094.

HERVEY, William, *Baron Hervey of Kidbrooke.* *¶4497; *see* 10667.

HERVEY, *Sir* William *of Ickworth, d. 1660.* *5129.

HARWARD, Andrew, *B.D.* (Venn). Verse 13519.

HARWOOD, William. See 19922.

HASELWOOD, Edmund, *of 'Ringstone'* (PCC 1587). 929.

HASSALL, HASILL, etc. *Listed with* HALSWELL.

HASTINGS (Dudley), Catherine = Henry

III Earl. 2033, 4098, 5566, *¶12312 by editor, *21787, 22891; epistle 1598.

HASTINGS (Stanley), Elizabeth = Henry V Earl. 3776, *6330, ¶11521; epistle 18511.

HASTINGS, Ferdinando, *VI Earl of Huntingdon.* 3774, ¶19303.

HASTINGS, Francis, *II Earl of Huntingdon.* *24361.

HASTINGS, Francis, 'Lord Hastings', *d. 1595.* *11743 from foreign original.

HASTINGS, *Sir* Francis, *Puritan politician* (DNB). *2878, 21682, *21787, 25583-L.; *see* 19418.

HASTINGS, George, *I Earl of Huntingdon.* 13999 [from *c. 1534* but unique HAIGH impf.].

HASTINGS, George, *IV Earl of Huntingdon.* *1603-CHI. of 24600 [see changes].

HASTINGS, *Sir* George, *Brother of Henry V Earl.* 24818; presentation J. Taylor, *Court of guard, 1626*-F.

HASTINGS, Henry, *III Earl of Huntingdon.* 585, 1257 by editor [see changes], 2007 and 1563-O., 2032 = 2357, 2037, 2802 (2057) by editor [see changes], 3548, 3885, 4055, 4090, 4101, 4398, 4439, 4654, 4778 (4781), †6227, 17122, 17299, *18778, 23285, 24492, Falckenburgius, David, 1579-BO.[5]; *see* 2108 Proverbs, 4397 tp., 12929.

HASTINGS, Henry, *V Earl of Huntingdon.* 3775, ¶12652 (12706, 12635), 12666 (12706, 12635), 12685, 13461, ¶19303, *24596, 25987 [earlier lost]; *see* 10667, 17331.

HASTINGS, *Sir* Henry, *of Gray's Inn* (Venn 1592). See 10738.

HASTINGS, Henry, *Son of George IV Earl.* 17756.

HASTINGS, Sarah. See ZOUCHE.

HASTINGS, Walter, *Brother of Henry III Earl.* See 668.

HASTINGS, William, *I Baron Hastings.* 24762.

HATCH, William, *Headmaster of Tonbridge* (Venn). Verse 23278.

HATCHER, Thomas, *Antiquary* (DNB). Edits 4686, 12596, 12597; verse 374, 6577, 13520; *see* 4346.

HATCLIFFE, [William], *Avenor royal, d. 1620.* Minsheu List..

HATHWAY, Richard, *Dramatist* (DNB). Verse 3189.

HATLEY, John, *M.A.* (Venn 1591). Verse 13936, 13939.

HATTON, *Sir* Christopher, *Lord Chancellor* (*DNB*). Chronologically:
1572–3: 16624, 18977a; *see* G. T., *Table gathered*-L.[2]
1575–7: 5232, 6459, 12465 [see changes], 19832, 21239.
1578: 713 by printer, 1972, 4342, *¶10674, *¶12901, 18309 by printer [see changes], 20089 by printer, 20978, 22215.
1579–80: 5235, 6841, 6843, 16951.
1581–4: 10552, 17295, 21002, 21002a, 25337 only; *see* 18773.
1587–9: 4253, 4761, 12908, 20698, 21227, 21237, 22912, *24480, 24931; *see* Agas map of Oxford-O.
1590: 1181 by editor, 1312, *1662, 6842, 14464, 14636 by editor, 16621, *21746 and 21749, 22163 by bookseller, 25841; epistle 23080.
1591 and belated: 17162, 23359; *see* 5602.

HATTON, *Sir* Christopher, *K.B., father of next.* 11826, ¶13957-M.[3], 23602; Minsheu List.

HATTON, Christopher, *I Baron Hatton.* *¶4497, 7467, 12937; epistle 20692.

HATTON (Gawdy), Elizabeth = *Sir* William. 12271.

HATTON, George, *Brother of Richard* (Venn). *23728, *23812 (both 23725); verse 23728 (23725).

HATTON (Leigh), Mary = *Sir* Robert. 18973.

HATTON, Richard, *Son of next* (Venn 1623). *23728, *23812 (both 23725); verse 23728 (23725).

HATTON, *Sir* Robert, *of Bishopsbourne* (Keeler). Minsheu List.

HATTON, *Sir* Thomas, *I Bt.* *¶4497.

HATTON, *alias* NEWPORT, *Sir* William, *d. 1597.* 842 = 13102, 3179 by bookseller, *4755, ¶5220, 6400, *¶1592-F. of 6402 only, 19876.

HAVILAND, John, *Printer.* Signed prose 4196; unsigned 24703; *see* M. FLESHER.

HAWARDEN. See HARDING.

HAWES, HAWGH, etc. *See also* HAGHE.

HAWES, *Sir* James, *Lord Mayor.* 6092, 7241.

HAWES, John, *Goldsmith, treasurer of Christ's Hospital* (*Vis. London*). *7164, *17649 by editor.

HAWES, John, *Warden of Haberdashers.* *13514 [13513 impf.].

HAWGHE, Walter, *of Norwich* (Venn). Verse 3146, 19299.

HAWKINS, Antony, *of Middle Temple.* See A. H.

HAWKINS, Arthur. Verse second state 19523-L.

HAWKINS, Francis, *S.J.* (*DNB*). Verse 12205.

HAWKINS, Henry, *of Peterhouse* (Venn). Verse 1492.

HAWKINS, *Sir* John, *Naval commander* (*DNB*). Verse 19523.

HAWKINS, John, *M.D., translator* (*DNB*). Verse 12205 as I. H. M. D.

HAWKINS, Judith, [? *of Kent*]. Epistle 584.

HAWKINS, Ma. [? *Mark, shipowner*]. Verse 22796.

HAWKINS, Richard, *Bookseller.* Unsigned verse 1672, 1679; unsigned prose 1683.

HAWKINS, *Sir* Thomas, *Translator* (*DNB*). Verse 1694, 12205 as S. T. H.

HAWKINS, William, *Mayor of Plymouth, d. 1589* (*DNB*). *14926.

HAWKINS, William, *Poet* (*DNB*). Verse 11877.

HAWLEY, *Sir* Henry, *Father of Francis I Baron.* *21838.

HAWLEY, John, *Principal of Gloucester Hall* (Foster). *6420.

HAXBY, Stephen, *B.D.* (Venn). Verse 10936.

HAY, Alexander, *Lord Easter Kennet* (*DNB*). Certifies 21884-5, 21887.

HAY (Douglas), Elizabeth = Francis *IX Earl.* Epistle 12168.

HAY, Francis, *IX Earl of Erroll.* See 10667, 12972.

HAY, Francis, *Son of preceding.* Epistle 1493.

HAY, George, *I Earl of Kinnoull.* *12726, 13993, 14711, 14996, ¶15684, *17207, *17208; edits 21900; *see* 10667 [perhaps intended for his son].

HAY (Denny), Honoria = James *I Earl of Carlisle.* ¶18521, 18525, ¶23581 (23575, 21653); *see* 12662 (12706, 12635).

HAY, James, *I Earl of Carlisle*. *1203, ¶5393, ¶5958, *6329, *7336, 10743, *11496, 12645, *12648 (12706, 12635), ¶12650 (12706, 12635), ¶12656 (12708, 12635), ¶12658 (12635), 14713, 14831 and variant-L. by stationer [see changes], ¶15366, 15367, 15494, *18523, 20028, ¶21328, *¶23582 (23575, 21653), 24293, ¶25215 (25207), †25657, ¶25939 only, R. Ayton, *Basia, 1605*-E.², T. Dempster, ¶*Strena, 1616*-L., T. Rhaedus, *Memoriae*-A., B. Robertson, *Blow for pope, 1615*-L. [cf. 20110 without ded.], Weckherlin, *Panegyricke, 1619*-HN.
Epistle: 1402, †4538, *4747, 20166, 24604. *See* 12662 (12706, 12635), 17331; Minsheu List.

HAY, James, *II Earl of Carlisle*. 12687 (12636) by editor, 15248; *see* 10667.

HAY, John, '*of Ranasse*'. Epistle 1406.

HAY, Sir John, *Lord Barra* (*DNB*). 136, W. M., *Edinburghs alphabet*-E.; certifies 21902.

HAY, John, *I Earl of Tweeddale. See* 10667.

HAY (Percy), Lucy = James *I Earl of Carlisle*. *4226 (excluded from 4221, etc., by copyright trouble), *¶6332 [6331 a ghost].

HAY, Robert, *Master of Robes, brother of James I Earl*. ¶12652 (12706, 12635); epistle T. Dempster, *Strena, 1616*-L.; *see* 12662 (12706, 12635), 23779 only.

HAYDOCK, Richard, *Physician* (*DNB*). Verse 4756.

HAYDOCK, William, *Son of preceding* (Foster). Verse 25096 [earlier lost].

HAYES, Martha, *Daughter of next*. ¶18303 and *1631*-NY.

HAYES, Sir Thomas, *Lord Mayor*. *5693, *20756.

HEYMAN, Sir Peter, *Politician* (*DNB*). *21175.

HAYMAN, Ralph, *of Selling* (*Vis. Kent*). Epistle *19148 only as Heimund.

HAYMAN, Robert, *Epigrammatist* (*DNB*). 22380.

HAYNE *or* HAYNES. *All spellings*.

HAINES, John, '*of Oldholt, Essex*'. ¶21202.

HEYNES, Simon, *Dean of Exeter* (*DNB*). Epistle *24673.

HEINES, Tho. *See next*.

HAYNE, Thomas, *Schoolmaster* (*DNB*). Verse 13259, 13260 as Heines; Minsheu List.

HAYNE, William, *Schoolmaster* (*DNB*). Edits 3491 as Haine; Minsheu List as Haynes.

HEYWARD, Edward, *of Inner Temple* (Venn 1600). 22177 rewritten 22178; verse 3914, 7219 [7220 earlier?], 14751, 22174.

HAYWARD, Sir George, *Son of Sir Rowland*. ¶6499.

HAYWARD, James, *of Gray's Inn*. Verse 1506.

HAYWARD, John, *Mayor of Faversham*. Epistle *19683 only.

HAYWARD, Sir John, *Historian* (*DNB*). Edits 25731; Minsheu List.

HAYWARD (Smith), *Lady* Katherine. *See* SCOTT.

HAYWARD, Sir Rowland, *Lord Mayor*. †11039 [see changes], *11255, *19875, *24713 (24706) by editor, 25943.

HAYWOOD. *See* HEYWOOD.

HEABURN. *See* HEYBOURNE.

HEALEY *or* HEYLEY, John, *Rector of Rushbrooke* (Venn 1586). Epistle *18805 as Heylei.

HEATH, John, *of St. John's* (Foster 1600). Verse 13018.

HEATH, Nicholas, *Archbishop of York*. *20796; oversees 2072.

HEATH, Richard, *Treasurer of Christ's Hospital*. *¶13247.

HEATH, Sir Robert, *Judge* (*DNB*). 3395, *Fens map in 17827, 23718, H. Goodcole, *Prodigals teares, 1620*-O.; epistle in variant only 5369-HD.; presentation 22784; verse 23278.

HEATH, Robert, *Poet* (*DNB*). Verse 7294.

HEATHER, William, *Musician* (*DNB*). 13508; *see* 24099.

HEIGHAM, Edward, *M.A.* (Foster). Prose 5870.

HEIGHAM, Sir John, *Son of Sir Clement*-DNB. 11818, *19915, ¶24786.

HEIGHAM, John, *earlier* Roger, *Catholic publisher* (*DNB*). Edits 3369 as R. H. [John in *1611*-HD.], 4830, 14569, 17276 and earlier eds. unsigned, *1620*-F. of 24627a, 24731b; probably unsigned prose 21697.

HEIGHAM, Roger. *See preceding*.

HIGHAM, William, '*J.P. in Essex*'. ¶6230.

HEIMUND. *See* HAYMAN.

HEINSIUS, Daniel, *Scholar* (*NBG*). Verse 14787, 22219, 23917, O. Vaenius, *Emblemata, 1608*-F.

HELE (Bray), Alice = Ellis *of Bovey Tracey*. J. G., *Steps of ascension, 1625*-L.

HELE, *Sir* Francis, *of Devon, brother of Sir Warwick*. *24642.

HELE, *Sir* John, *of Wembury, son of preceding*. 23571 (23572).

HELE (Courtenay), Margaret = *Sir* Warwick. 1438 (1435), 13417 (13378), 13428 (13379); *see* LADY M. H.

HELE, Sampson, *of Gnaton* (Foster 1597). ¶13378 [? earlier lost].

HELE, *Sir* Warwick, *of Wembury, Devon, d. 1625*. *13396 (13379).

HELING, ——. *128 (107).

HELMES, *Sir* Henry, *of Gray's Inn*. Verse 5642 as Elmes; Minsheu List.

HELME, John, *Bookseller*. Perhaps prose 21605.

HELME, William, *B.D.* (Foster 1584). Verse 20362-O.

HEM, John de, *London merchant* (PCC 1626). 20115.

HEMER, ——, 'Somerset preacher'. Epistle *1941.

HEMING, John, *Actor* (*DNB*). Edits 22273.

HEN. *See* HENN.

HENDERSON, Alexander, *Presbyterian divine* (*DNB*). Epistle 71 (70).

HENDERSON, *Sir* Robert, *Colonel in Dutch service*. Epistle 25939.

HENDLEY, *Sir* Thomas, *of Kent* (Foster 1576). †¶59.

HENDRED, William, 'Prior of Leominster'. 19918 and frag. *1508* = 19623.

HENEAGE (Poyntz), Anne = *Sir* Thomas. 6077.

HENEAGE, *Sir* Thomas, *Vice-chamberlain* (*DNB*). 355, *3944 by editor, 6155 by editor, 7168, 7171 (7170), 10834, ¶11739, 13973 and *1588*-G., 15447 by editor, 16993, 19380 rewritten 19382, 22221.

HEN[N], Tho., 'Groom of great chamber to Prince'. Epistle some copies *4747-O.

HENNINGHAM. *See* HEVENINGHAM.

HENOLENA, Pedro. Verse 24137.

HENRIETTA MARIA, *Queen consort*. *See also* joint dedications with Charles I.
Recusant books: 1922, 3898, 4872, 5569, 6385, 17129, 18066, 18331, 21023, 24924 by convent.
Of French interest: 4549, 7475, 7477, 10869, *20490, A. Darcie, *Theatre de la gloire, 1625*-L., *Grammaire angloise, 1625*-O.
General dedications: 4194, ¶5021 = 19036, 5026, 13327, *13872, 15464 [see changes], 15465, 19300, 21542, ¶1627-L. of 23811 (23725) [see changes], 24641 (24645), *25900.
Epistles: 4480, 5369, 7476, 12509, 18966, 19033, 19039, 20522, 21725; *see* 16548, etc., 24604.
Ladies of her court: Epistle 5369.
Physicians at her confinement: Epistle 12509.

HENRY IV, *King of England*. 12142.

HENRY V, *King of England*. 5579 (13346a), 17023, 25005.

HENRY VI, *King of England*. 17015 unnamed.

HENRY VII, *King of England*. 7269, 12943, 12945, 12949 [12948 impf.], 14557, 19325, 19326 frag., Seyssel, *Oratio*-HN.; *see* 13439, 16179, 16182a, 16257.

HENRY VIII, *King of England*. Chronologically:
1509–19: ¶1497, 12140 = 14999a = 17017, 12953, 15121; *see* 5579, Whittinton, *Epigrammata, 1519*-HN.
1520–9: 11396, 11397, 24944, 25481; *see* 770, 10082, 10656, 10883 (10884).
1530–2: 5068 by editor, 7635, 12143 by printer, 16797, 19166.
1534–5: 1470 (24436), 2063 [see changes], 4240, 4370, 5278, 5292.
1536–8: 2066, 2816 and 2818 [disavowed by author], 5163, 7659, 21753; official prose 10033.
1539: 2067, 2748 = 23710, 7630 (24849), 11402, 19211, 21679; *see* 2068.
1540–1: 2799, 10751, 11470, 23236, 24164.
1543–4: 5718, 14634, 15440, 15443, 24165, 24353; prose 5168; *see* 1291.
1545: 837, 14630, 15444, 24355, Leland, *Bononia*-G.; prose 16040.
1546: 1801 and issue-HN., 22815, 22820; *see* 10884.
Belated: 916 from early foreign, ¶2854 from early foreign, 15180, 21616, *¶22608, 23689 from early foreign; *see* 15445 [cf. 3834 appendix], 15447, 17789.

HERBERT, Frances, '*Gentlewoman*'. 18299.

HERBERT, George, *Poet* (*DNB*). 1174; verse 1167 from 23917; prose 24571.

HERBERT, Henry, *II Earl of Pembroke*. 1090 (1077), 1095 (1077), *1500, 11343, *11708, ¶14725, *19605, *21132, 21611, 22552 by editor, 24532; *see* 11515.

HERBERT, *Sir* Henry, *Master of the Revels* (*DNB*). Does imprimaturs *1632–40*.

HERBERT, James, *Son of Philip IV Earl*. *25719 (25718).

HERBERT, *Sir* John, *Secretary of State, d. 1614.* ¶4578 [? earlier lost], J. Lawrence, *Politica, 1590–L.²* by publisher, G. Wintter, *Disputatio, 1610–C.¹⁷*

HERBERT (Sidney), Mary = Henry *II Earl of Pembroke*. 1081, 1598, 3632, 3648, 3683, 6245 (6238 some copies), 6253 rewritten 6254, ¶6254 (6261, 6236), *6338, 11338–41 inclusive, 13875, 17994, 18121, *18509, 22539, ¶23078 (23084), 23692, 25117 by editor.
Epistle: 1469–L., 6333, 15227, 16696, 23080 late state (23084).
Presentation: 11516.
Helps edit 22540: *see* 23527, 23776.

HERBERT (Talbot), Mary = William *III Earl*. *11160, De Beau Chesne, *La Clef de l'escriture-N*.; epistle 1598.

HERBERT (Villiers), *Lady* Mary. *See* STUART.

HERBERT (Naunton), Penelope = Philip *IV Earl*. *See* BAYNING.

HERBERT, Philip, *IV Earl of Pembroke*. *For joint dedications with his brother, see* WILLIAM, *III Earl, below.*
As I Earl of Montgomery: 543, 544 [see changes], *917 by editor [see changes], 3172, ¶4676, *6329, ¶11160, *11496, ¶12657 (12708, 12635), 12752, 13509, 15495, ¶17334, 17632, †¶17936, *†18509, 18594, 21378, *23725, ¶23725 [23732 dated *1617* impf.], †24525 by bookseller, †25717 (25718), *†25719 (25718).
As Pembroke: 4931, 6779, 10875, 13190, 14480, 19155, 20262 by editor, 20786, ¶20944, 21775, *25900.
Epistle: 6333, 12555, 23447; *see* 10667, 17331; Minsheu List.

HERBERT, Philip, *V Earl of Pembroke*. *24160, *25719 (25718); *see* 10667.

HERBERT (Vere), Susan = Philip *IV Earl*. (*All as Countess of Montgomery.*) *6271-L., *11160, ¶23720; epistle 1598, 13634 [rarely 13633] (13624), 23581 (23575, 21653).

HERBERT, William, *I Earl of Pembroke*. *3480, 4343, 13221, 20309, 21076, 22223, *24361, 26066.

HERBERT, William, *III Earl of Pembroke*. Chronologically except first group:
Jointly with brother Philip: 1077 by bookseller, 4919, 7274, ¶10553, 11207, 17676, 18615, 22273 by editors, 23526, 25721, Vaenius, *Emblemata, 1608-F.*; epistle 13633 (13624), 24604.
To 1602: *1500, *6336, 6373, 14695, 19336 (19335), 24042 [date is *1592*].
1603–9: ¶6259 (6263), ¶11160, 12686, 13848 by bookseller, 13958, ¶21650; epistle 6333.
1610–12: 916 by bookseller [see changes], *1234 [see changes], 14759 (14751), 24603; *see* 19511.
1613–15: 10840, 11076, 12775 by bookseller [see changes]; epistle 25891 (25911); *see* 23779 (23725).
1616: 111, 686, ¶3914, 6342, 10426 by bookseller [see changes], 10784, ¶14751, 19344, 22399; epistle 23582 (23575, 21653).
1617: 13394a (13380), 13530, 18205, ¶23732 (23725) [note date]; Minsheu List.
1618–19: 6821, *11496; epistle *3832, *19813.
1620–2: ¶15366, *†18509, 19025, 20398 by editor, 24099, R. BRUEN, *Pilgrimes practice, 1621-O.*
1623: 4936, *7336, 12646 (12635), 22097 only, ¶23720.
1624: 12030, 19769, 20111, 20553 = 2782, ¶20942.
1625: 130 (115), 4111, ¶4676, 4934, 11951, 23863-HD. cancelled, 25326 [see changes], 25935 by editor; *see* 12930, 17331.
1626–7: 14497, ¶16887 cancelled, 20358, 21091, 24617 [see changes]; epistle 3926.
1628–9: *104, 4937 by editor, 14318, ¶24513, 24926, 24965, 26131 = 26131a [see changes]; *see* 25327.
1630: 7101, 10733, 19772, *22796, *23725, 24037.

HERBERT, *Sir* William, *of St. Julians, d. 1593* (*DNB*). Epistle 5232; *see* 5156 = 15526.

HERBERT, *Sir* William, *of Swansea, d. 1609.* 6743 [see changes]; epistle *1095 (1077).

HERBERT, William, *Poet, fl. 1604* (*DNB*). Verse 3914, 10513.

HERBERT, William, *I Baron Powis.* *1466 more 1466a, 3713; *see* 10667.

HERBERT, William, *Son of Philip IV Earl.* *25719 (25718).

HERDSON, John, *Skinner, d. 1622.* 25931; presentation 19447-HN.

HERGEST, William (*STC*), *Unnamed cousins of.* Epistle 13203.

HERIOT, Alexander, *Bailie of Edinburgh.* *88, *23262.

HERLACKINDEN. *See* HARLACKINDEN.

HERNE, HERON, HIERON, HIREN, HYRNE.

HERON (Brooke), Anne = *Sir* Edward (*Vis. Lincs.*). 18053, *24096.

HYRNE, Clement, *of Norfolk* (Venn). Epistle 15037.

HERNE, Edward, *of Lincoln's Inn, son of Lady Anne.* See 15466.

HERON, John, *Headmaster, Rochester School* (Foster 1538). Verse 7662, 10555.

HERON, John, '*Courtier*' [? *Lincoln's Inn*]. *12178.

HIERON, Jo. Verse 24137.

HERNE, Richard, *Alderman.* *17886.

HYRNE, *Sir* Thomas, *Mayor of Norwich.* *7323, *18480 as Hiren, *26085 as Hieron, 26096.

HERICKE (May), Joan = *Sir* William-*DNB.* *¶4220 and *1619*-HD., 25307 = *¶25229.

HERRIES, *Sir* Hugh, *Physician to James VI.* Epistle 20567.

HERRING, Francis, *Physician* (*DNB*). Verse 4396, 7304, 11750, 12312, 16649, different 16650, 21032, 23723.

HERVET, Gentian, *Humanist churchman* (*Ath. Oxon.*). Edits 699; *see* 17445 as Harvet.

HERVEY. *Listed with* HARVEY.

HESKETH, *Sir* Thomas, *of the Council in the North.* *19699 (19649) by editor, *¶19733 (19649, cf. 19648) by editor, J. Clapham, *Ordines militum,* [*1603*]-HD.

HESKYNS, Thomas, *Divine* (*DNB*). *See* 11433.

HESTER, John, *Distiller* (*DNB*). Edits 10880.

HETON, Martin, *Bishop of Ely.* *4837, 25673 [see changes], *¶25682 (25685); verse 4761.

HEVENINGHAM, *Sir* Arthur, *of East Anglia, d. 1630.* 14633, †¶21869, 24519.

HEVENINGHAM, *Sir* John, *of Inner Temple* (Venn 1592). †¶21869; epistle 15037.

HEWES. *See* HUGHES.

HUETUS, Robertus. Verse 13435.

HEWETT, *Sir* Thomas, *Clothworker* (Brown). ¶3571 as Sir T. H. the elder [Huet in L.], 6536, *23788 (23725) as Howet.

HEYBOURNE *alias* RICHARDSON, *Sir* Ferdinando, *Musician and of Privy Chamber* (Grove). 10700 as Heaburn; verse 23666 as Richardson.

HEYDON, *Sir* Christopher, *of Baconsthorpe* (PCC 1580). 12939.

HEYDON, *Sir* Christopher, *Writer* (*DNB*). 24152.

HEYDON, *Sir* John, *Brother of preceding.* *¶21869.

HEYDON, *Sir* John, *Lieutenant of the ordnance* (*DNB*). 1100 = ¶1099.

HEYGATE, Thomas, *of the Inner Temple.* Verse 3914.

HEYLET, Daniel, *M.A.* (Venn 1606). Verse 18493.

HEYLEY. *See* HEALEY.

HEYLYN, Edward, *of Inner Temple, brother of Peter-DNB.* Verse 13276.

HEYLYN, Rowland, *Sheriff of London* (*DNB*). *16753.

HEYMAN, HEYNES, HEYWARD. *See* HAYMAN, HAYNES, HAYWARD.

HEYTON, Francis, *of Greenwich* (PCC 1623). Gerardus, *True tryall, 1602*-F. [see changes].

HEYWOOD, Peter, *of Westminster, d. 1642.* Verse 23447.

HEYWOOD, Thomas, *Dramatist* (*DNB*). Edits 1383 [signed in some copies, others as H. T.], 17412; verse 10667, 14788, 17201, 17444, 17745, 17921, 19511, 25227, 26068, 26103; prose 5673.

HAYWOOD, William, *Divine* (*DNB*). 26017; book licenser *1631–7.*

HICKS, Baptist, *I Viscount Campden.* 5339, 11689, 12831 (12816), *20756, *†23056, 23473; Minsheu List.

HICKES, *Sir* Elias *or* Ellis, *Naval officer* (*CSPD*). 19501.

HICKES *alias* BRIDGEHAMPTON, John, *Master gunner* (*CSPD*). Verse 1099.

HICKS, Richard, *of Trinity College* (Venn). See 13923.

HICKES, Thomas, *Chaplain of Christ Church, Oxford* (*DNB*). Edits 16893.

HICKMOTE, ——. Minsheu List.

HICSON. *See* HIGSON.

HIERON *or* HIREN. *See* HERNE.

HIGGINS, Anthony, *Dean of Ripon* (Venn). Verse 6843.

HIGGINS, John, *Poet* (*DNB*). Edits 13941; verse 24631; prose J. Lawrence, *Politica, 1590*-L.[2]

HIGGONS, Robert, *Father of next.* Prose 13541.

HIGGONS, Theophilus, *Divine* (*DNB*). *See* 13541.

HIGGONS, Thomas, *D.D.* (Foster 1582). 3372.

HIGHAM. *See* HEIGHAM.

HIGHLORD, John, *Alderman.* *22531; epistle *25963.

HIGSON *or* HICSON, Samuel, *of Trinity College* (Venn). *18206.

HILDERSHAM, Richard [cf. *Vis. Camb.*]. 19804 [19805 earlier but impf.].

HILDERSAM, Samuel, *Divine* (*DNB*). Edits 13459, 13463.

HILERMIUS, Robertus. Verse 25799.

HILL, ——, 'B.D., *Hart Hall*,' [? Joseph (Foster 1593)]. Minsheu List.

HILL, Adam, *Divine* (*DNB*). Epistle and prose 13948.

HILLS, John, *Master of St. Catharine's* (Venn 1579). *12178, *25680.

HILL, John, '*Bermondsey preacher*'. Edits 7619.

HILL, Nicholas, *Philosopher* (*DNB*). Epistle 13592.

HILL, Otwell *or* Ottho, *of St. John's* (Venn). Verse 6839.

HILL, R. Verse 21094.

HILL, Robert, *Divine* (*DNB*). Epistle 23581 (23575, 21653); edits 12318, 18494, 19731 and 19748 (19649, cf. 19648; earlier of 19748 lost); verse 21069; prose 73, 13380, 22182.

HILL, William, *of Poundsford* (*Vis. Soms.*). 21833.

HILL, William. *Consider* Montanus.

HILLIARD, Nicholas, *Miniature-painter* (*DNB*). One issue 13507-L., F.

HILSEY, John, *Bishop of Rochester.* Edits 16009; licenses 3943.

HILTON, Andrew, '*Host of Horseshoe, Daventry*'. *23767 as George, changed to Andrew and alone 23768 (23725).

HILTON, George. *See preceding.*

HILTON, Thomas, *X Baron Hilton.* 4039.

HYND (Wentworth), Elizabeth = *Sir* William (*Vis. Camb.*). ¶6890.

HYNDE, *Sir* Francis, *of Cambridgeshire* (Venn). *15516.

HINDE, William, *Puritan divine* (*DNB*). Edits 6935, 20609, 20619.

HINSON, William, *of Lincoln's Inn* (Venn 1594). ¶10539.

HINTON *or* HENTON, William, *Archdeacon of Coventry* (Venn). Epistle 7185; verse 14608.

HIRTIUS. *See* HYRDE.

HITCHCOCK, Francis, *Brother of next.* Verse 13531.

HITCHCOCK, Robert, *Military writer* (*DNB*). Edits 11625.

HITCHCOCK, Thomas *the elder, of Lincoln's Inn.* Minsheu List.

HITCHCOCKES, William, *Gent.* Verse 19832.

HORE, Bartho. Verse 5461 only.

HOARE, John, *M.A.* (Venn 1640). Verse 6044a.

HOBART, HUBBARD, HUBBERT, HUBERT.

HOBART *or* HUBBERT, Anthony, *of Hales* (*Vis. Norf.*). 20584; epistle 15037.

HOBART (Bell), Dorothy = *Sir* Henry *I Bt.* 11678 (11652), *11764 [see changes].

HOBART, *Sir* Henry, *I Bt., Lord Chief Justice.* *4329 [see changes], *6204a, *7021, one issue *†7326-L. [tr. A. Darcie], *11496, 11658 (11652), *11670, *18606, *19349, 19791, 23412, 25165, J. Bury or Bery, *Schole of godly feare, 1615*-L.; Minsheu List.

HOBART, *Sir* John, *II Bt.* *¶4338, one issue *†7326-L., ¶11681 (11652), 18896 by editor, 25231; epistle 15037.

HOBART, Miles, *Esq.* (? Venn 1566). *See* 25438.

HOBART, *Sir* Miles, *K.B., of Plumstead, Norf.* Epistle 15037.

HOBART, Nicholas, *M.A.* (Venn). Verse 12964.

HUBERT, *Sir* Richard, *Groom porter, brother of Sir Francis.* 4979, 10686, 13901.

HOBBES, Thomas, *Actor.* 21424.

HOBMAN, Francis, *B.D.* (Venn). Verse 11326.

HOBSON, Anthony, '*Minister of Lyminster, Sussex*'. *See* 13923.

HOBSON, Henry, *Mayor of Bristol.* *20513.

HOBSON, William, *Sheriff of Bristol.* Epistle *19155.

HOBY, *Sir* Edward, *Controversialist* (*DNB*). ¶4503 [see changes], 11114, *11127, ¶19622.

HOBY, *Lady* Elizabeth. *See* RUSSELL.

HOBY (Carey), Mary = *Sir* Edward. Epistle 16696.

HOBY, Peregrine, *Son of Sir Edward* (*DNB*). Verse 13540.

HOBY, *Sir* Philip, *Diplomatist* (*DNB*). 3963.

HOBY, *Sir* Thomas Posthumus, *Son of Sir Thomas-DNB.* †4233 by editor, †5847, *†14320.

HOBYNOLL (23080). Assumed to be Gabriel Harvey.

HOCKIN, George, *B.D.* (Foster). *See* 25327.

HOCKENHULL, Ralph, *of London* (PCC 1603). *20155, L'Espine, *Comfort for conscience, 1591-C.⁴

HODGES, John, *Alderman.* *18321.

HODGSON, John (Venn 1509). *See* 16896.

HODGSON, John, *Hatter in Paul's Churchyard.* 11634 by bookseller, as Hodgson *alias* John Hatter or John of Paul's Churchyard.

HODGSON, Samuel, *M.A.* (Venn 1571). Verse 6843.

HODGSON *or* HODSON, William, *Author* (*DNB*). Verse 14753 [one plagiarized from 686].

HOGHERDE. *See* HUGGARDE.

HOLBEACH, Henry, *Bishop of Lincoln.* *See* 24673.

HOLBEIN, Hans, *Painter* (*DNB*). Woodcut 25968.

HOLBOURNE (Dudley), Anne. *See* DUDLEY.

HOLBOURNE, Anthony, *Composer* (*DNB*). Verse 10700, 18133; *see* 7095.

HOLBROOKE, William, *Preacher* (STC). Edits 20669, 20672, 20675, 20678 (20668), 20683.

HOLCROFT (Aungier), Lettice = *Sir* Henry (*Vis. Surrey*). Epistle *11763.

HOLCROFT, *Sir* Thomas, *of Vale Royal* (Brown). *7293, †19751 (19649) by editor; Minsheu List.

HOLDER, Andrew, '*of Southwark martial garden*'. Epistle *14922.

HOLDER, Clement, *M.A.* (Venn). *See* 19922.

HOLDER, Mary, *Sister of William-DNB.* *19553.

HOLE, William, *Engraver* (*DNB*). Dedicates first issue-HN. of 4252 = 11827.

HOLFORD, Richard, *of Gray's Inn* (*Vis. London*). 3819.

HOLL, Augustine, *of Heigham, Norf.* Epistle 15037 as Austine.

HOLL[AND], Ab[raham], *Poet* (*DNB*). Verse 14771 and 14753.

HOLLAND (——), Elizabeth = Henry *d. 1604.* Prose 12317.

HOLLAND, Henry, *Divine, d. 1604* (*DNB*). Edits 12312, 12315, 21282; verse 19775.

HOLLAND, Henry, *Bookseller* (*DNB*). Edits or prose 1592, 5885 signed HalleluiaH [? author], 6175 signed H[ollan]D, 12539, 13579, 26068 [with verses to him]; verse 13580 only; *see* 4510 at Vvvv3ᵛ.

HOLLAND, Hugh, *Poet* (*DNB*). Verse 250, 3220, 4252 = 11827 and earlier-HN., some copies 4974, rarely 5807-L., 5808 and 5810 [cf. 23769], 10700, 13800, 14782 (14751), 14782 only signed Cygnus, 22219, 22273; *see* 5811, 7095.

HOLLAND, *Sir* John. *I Bt.* *¶4338; epistle 15037.

HOLLAND, Philemon, *Translator* (*DNB*). Edits 12539, 24015 and prose in *1631-E.*; verse 10596.

HOLLAND, Robert, *Welsh poet* (*DNB*). *See* 12872.

HOLLAND, Thomas, *Regius professor, d. 1612* (*DNB*). ¶20362-O.; verse 4756, 4758, 4765, 11516, 21029 (21032).

HOLLAND, *Sir* Thomas, *Father of John* **above.** †11598, †11599.

HOLLAWAY. *See* HOLLOWAY.

HOLLES, *Sir* George, *Sergeant-major, brother of next.* Epistle 22090 (22102, 22064).

HOLLES, John, *I Earl of Clare.* ★1963, 25293; see 10667.

HOLYDAY, Barten, *Poet* (*DNB*). 11992 (11993); verse 13798; Minsheu List.

HOLLIDAY, Sir Leonard, *Lord Mayor.* ★21296.

HOLLIDAY, William, *Alderman.* ★861, 1644 [earlier lost] (1629) by bookseller, 1645 by bookseller, ★5707 [see changes], ★17886.

HOLLINGUS *or* HOLLINS, Edmund, *of York* (Foster). Verse 1777 from foreign ed.

HOLLOWAY, John, *East India committee-man.* Epistle ★25963.

HOLLOWAY, Wil. [? *Merchant at Ragusa*]. Prose 26122.

HOLWAY *or* HOLLOWAY, William, *of Christ Church* (Foster 1632). Verse 10829.

HOLME, John, *M.A.* (Venn 1584). Verse 21032.

HOLMES, Leonard, *Bailiff of Yarmouth.* ★20832a as Hoames.

HOLMES, Nathaniel, *Divine* (*DNB*). See N. H.

HOWLTE, M., '*Preacher*'. See 25438.

HOLT, Thomas, *B.D.* (Foster 1603). Verse 19041.

HOLT, Sir Thomas, *I Bt.* 12360.

HOLWORTHY, Richard, *Mayor of Bristol.* Epistle ★19155.

HOLYBAND *and* HOLYDAY. See DESAINLIENS *and* HOLLIDAY.

HOLYOAKE, Francis, *Lexicographer* (*DNB*). Edits 21032, 21033.

HOLYOAKE, Thomas, *Divine* (*DNB*). Edits 13621 and *1639*-HD.

HOME *and* HUME. See *also* HOLME, HULME.

HUME, Alexander, *Poet, d. 1609* (*DNB*). Verse 14786, 21101.

HUME, Alexander, *Schoolmaster* (*STC*). Verse 22567.

HOME, Alexander, *I Earl of Home.* Epistle 6333, 15715.

HOME (Ruthven), Beatrix = *Sir* John *of Cowdenknowes.* 17120.

HUME, David [*presumably the 1588 Edinburgh M.A.*]. Verse 21101.

HUME, David, *Historian* (*DNB*). See 5915.

HOME, George, *I Earl of Dunbar.* ★5912 only, ¶5956, 5959 [see changes], 17942 by editor,

21785, W. Guild, *Only way to salvation, 1608-*PN.[2]

HOME, James, *III Earl of Home.* See 10667.

HUME, Sir John, *of North Berwick.* ¶15715.

HUME, Sir John, *of Renton.* St. Andrews (Salvator) *Theses, 1621-*E.

HOME, *Lady* Margaret. *See* STEWART.

HOME (Sutton), Mary = Alexander *I Earl of Home.* ¶15715.

HUME, Sir Patrick, *Master of the hawks.* ¶15268.

HOMMIUS, Festus, *Dutch theologian* (*ADB*). Verse 553 from foreign ed.

HONDIUS (Hondt), Hendrick, *Printer.* Prose 17827.

HONNYWOOD, Robert, *Esq.,* '*of Hoxton*'. †14299.

HONYWOOD, Thomas, *of Sene, Kent, d. 1580.* Epistle ★19148 only.

HOOD, Paul, *Rector of Lincoln College* (Foster). See 25327.

HOOD, Thomas, *Mathematician* (*DNB*). ★13070; edits 3427.

HOOKER, John, *Antiquary* (*DNB*). Edits 13569, 14129.

HOOKER, Peter, *of Corpus Christi* (Foster). Verse 19041.

HOOKER, Richard, *Theologian* (*DNB*). 4707 = 13721.

HOOKER, Thomas, *Divine* (*DNB*). Prose 21187 [not in *1627*-F.].

HOOPER, John, *Bishop of Gloucester.* Prose 3962 = 10387.

HOOPER, John. Verse 10694.

HOPUS, Cuthbertus. Verse 164.

HOPE, Richard, '*Soldier*'. Verse 22855.

HOPE, Sir Thomas, *I Bt., Lord Advocate.* 10696, 15369, 17139, 22260, 23261, 26109.

HOPKINS, Henry, *Warden of the Fleet.* ★15597.

HOPKINS, John, *Psalm-translator* (*DNB*). Verse 23229.

HOPKINS, Jo. Verse 11226.

HOPKINS, Sampson, *Mayor of Coventry.* ★17311 [not named].

HOPKINS, William, *of the Middle Temple.* Verse 6303.

HUNT, ——, *D.D.*, '*Royal chaplain*'. Minsheu List.

HUNT, Anthony, *of Lincoln's Inn*. Minsheu List.

HUNT, Christopher, *Exeter bookseller*. Prose 23697.

HUNT, George, *Rector of Collingborne Ducis* (Foster 1571). 25297.

HUNT, Matthew, *Oxford bookseller*. Prose 10013.

HUNT, Robert, *Vicar of Heathfield, Sussex* (PCC 1608). Verse 584.

HUNT, Sir Thomas, *of Lambeth, Fishmonger.* 4705.

HUNT, Thomas, *Esq.* Minsheu List.

HUNTLEY, George, *M.A.* (Foster). See 25327.

HUNTON, ——, '*Physician*' [*presumably the next*]. 5288.

HUNTON, Anthony, *Physician* (Venn). Verse 11750.

HURLSTON, Hugh, *Clerk of alienations* (PCC 1606). *20155.

HURLESTON, Randall, *Puritan* (STC) [? *the later M.P., Inner Temple*]. Verse 24368.

HURLESTONE, Richard, *Esq.* [? *of Picton, Cheshire*]. See 10910.

HURRIE, Stephen, *M.A.* (Venn). Verse 12967 as St. Hu. (12964 as Hurius), 12964.

HURST, Denis, '*Minister at Alfriston, Sussex*'. See 13923.

HUSSEY, Sir James, *Civilian* (Foster 1583). Verse 4756.

HUSSEY, John, *I Baron Hussey*. 14553.

HUSSEY, Margaret. See 22610 (22608).

HUSSEY, Sir Richard, *of Adbrighton* (*Vis. Shrops.*). *†21437.

HUSSEY, Sampson, *Fellow of New College* (Foster 1584). Verse 24042.

HUSSEY, Thomas, *Esq.*, '*Cousin*'. 3598, 3599.

HUSSEY, Thomas, '*J.P. in Dorset*'. 14745.

HUTCHINSON, Ralph, *President of St. John's* (DNB). Verse 4756.

HUTCHINSON, Sir Thomas, *of Notts.* (Venn 1606). *19488.

HUTTON, Henry, *of Jesus College* (Venn 1625). Verse 7365, 11464.

HUTTON, John, *Esq.* [? *of Camb.*]. 11863 (*Certaine sermons*, 1597-F.).

HUTTON, John, *Son of Sir Timothy* (? Venn 1624). *14297a.

HUTTON, Joshua, *Clergyman* (Venn). Verse 21239.

HUTTEN, Leonard, *Divine* (DNB). See 17944; Minsheu List.

HUTTON, Matthew, *Archbishop of York.* *1829.

HUTTON, Matthew *and* Philip, *Sons of Sir Timothy* (Venn 1615, 1618). *14297a.

HUTTON, Richard, *Armourer and creditor of Bynneman*. Prose 18101.

HUTTON, Sir Richard, *Judge* (DNB). 3579, *3906, ¶13799, Brathwait, ¶*Querela clientis*-HN., R. Oxley, *Sermon, 1622*-HD.; *see* 10667.

HUTTON, Sir Richard, *Son of preceding.* 3584 (3572).

HUTTON, Thomas, *Son of next.* *14297a.

HUTTON, Sir Timothy, *of Marske* (Venn 1588). *1816, 14028, *†14320; Posterity of, 14297a.

HUTTON, Timothy, *Son of preceding.* *14297a.

HUYGENS (Hugenius), Sir Constantyn, *Statesman* (NBG). Epistle 24033 from foreign ed.; verse 13040 [? from foreign ed.], 24033 signed Constanter.

HYDE, Edward, *Divine, d. 1659* (DNB). Verse 7365, and perhaps 7031 anon. (7045 signed) by some thought next man.

HYDE, Edward, *I Earl of Clarendon.* Verse 6307, 20692; *see* preceding.

HYDE, Francis, *Ambassador* (Foster). 11995 (11993), *14457.

HYDE, Sir Laurence, *Queen's attorney* (Foster 1579). *24027.

HYDE, Sir Leonard, *of Throcking, Herts.* *¶25677 [see changes].

HYDE, Thomas, *Somerset clergyman* (Venn 1596). Epistle *1941.

HYDE, '*Sir*' William [*apparently error for Esq.; several of name*]. 15706.

HYNDE. *See* HINDE.

HYRDE, Richard, *Translator and physician* (Foster). Edits 10477; verse 15636 as Hirtius.

HYRNE. *See* HERNE.

HYTHER, R. Verse in sequel to 21661-F. (21649 as R. H.).

I

I *or* J *initials all listed here.*

J., D[*ominus*]. Epistle 1576 as 'viro D. J. S. P. D.'

I., A. Verse 16884.

I., B. *See* BEN JOHNSON.

I., B. Edits Allison 228.

I., C. Prose 23345.

I., *Lady* D., 'recusant at Louvain' [? *mask for Elizabeth Allen, q.v.*]. 4830 by printer.

I., D. Verse 3272, 4325; *see head of this series.*

I., D. D. F. Verse 7376.

I., G., *Philomus.* Verse 13548.

I., G. Prose 15233 (15241), 15516.

I., S[*ir*] H. (12662). Misprint for S. I. H[arington].

I., *Sir* H., 'Recusant'. *1611*-HD. of ¶3369 by printer.

I., H. Edits 599, 22477; verse 4655 anon. [signed in 4656], 21501, 21510.

I., I., *Cantab.* Verse 5529.

I., I. Verse 12184 [? Jones], 17816 [? Johnston] as M. I. I., 22960 only; *see* 25438 [*Esq.*].

JON., J. [*probably* Johnston]. Verse 21274.

I., M., *Philomathematic.* Verse 13548 [cf. G. I.].

I., M. 18974; epistle 19068.

I., N. (14297). *See* NATHANIEL JACKSON.

I., *Mrs.* P. [? *of Totnes*]. 13542 by editor.

I., R. Verse 3894, 5869, 13799, 18611; prose 4177, 13381 [physician].

Jo., *Mrs.* R. (14720). *See* JONES.

J., S., 'of St. John's [*Cambridge*]'. Verse 1880 [1879 a ghost].

I., S. [*presumably of Cambridge*]. Verse 7235, 15520.

I., S. Epistle 15268 [a divine]; verse 24296.

I., S*r*. T. Verse 25896.

I., T. [*Friend of dramatists, perhaps Sir Thomas Jay*]. Verse 17642, 22454.

I., T. 1417; verse 6410.

I., W. (23530). Reversed initials of John Wilson.

I., W. Edits 6980; verse 20996 [Gent.]; *see* 12662 (12706, 12635) as condemned for murder.

I., Z. [*probably* Zachary Jenkinson]. Prose 11838.

IGNOTO. Verse 15715, 23080, 24096.

ILES, Thomas, *D.D.* (Foster 1604). *4259.

INCE, Nicholas, *Mayor of Chester.* *¶23720, J. Barlow, *Seasonable discourse, 1627*-F. (1435).

INCE, Randulphus, *of Trinity College, Dublin.* Edits 14073.

INCERTO. Verse 18127 only.

INCOGNITO, *Il.* Verse 24593.

INGHAM, Edw. Verse 22790 (22796), 22794.

INGLIS, Thomas, *Dean of gild, Edinburgh.* *5927 (5909).

INGMETHORPE, Thomas, *Schoolmaster* (DNB). Verse 22390.

INGOLDSBY, Sir Richard, *the elder, of Lenborough, Bucks.* *23101.

INGRAM, Sir Arthur, *Courtier* (DNB). Minsheu List.

INGRAM, Sir Arthur, *Son of preceding.* *21639.

INGRAM, James, *Deputy warden of the Fleet.* *12332 (12331), *15597.

INSULA, *De. See* LISLE.

IRBY, Anthony, *Bencher of Lincoln's Inn* (Venn 1559). Minsheu List.

IRBY, Sir Anthony, *the younger* (Venn 1620). ¶11082.

IRELAND, *Sir* Thomas, *of Gray's Inn and Bewsy Hall.* *6024.

IRETON, John, *Puritan* (Venn). Verse (part Hebrew) 1492; *see* 4709.

IRVINE, *Sir* Alexander, *of Drum* (DNB). Aberdeen *Positiones, 1626*-A.

IRVINE (Douglas), Marion = Alexander, *Mother of preceding.* ¶12478.

ISAACSON, William, *D.D.* (Venn 1613). Verse 14269.

ISKOMBERGIUS, Christophorus. Verse 11739.

ISLIP, Adam, *Printer.* Initialed prose *Fift booke of Amadis, 1598*-CHERRY-GARRARD, A. C[hute], *Tabaco, 1595*-HN.; unsigned prose 15228.

P

JAMES VI *and* I—*cont.*
   3452, 3905, 12602-HN. [both HN. and L.
   impf.], *14428, 17175, 17222, 17226, 18029,
   18227, 18982, *20166, 22522, 24756; *see*
   12482.
   1623: 1108 (1109) and 1167 [cf. 1164], *4487,
   7376 by editor, 14520, 19026, *19027, 22077
   (22064), 23352, 23511 (4523 often missing),
   25909, *Ruine of Calvinisme*-W., J. Walker,
   Glasse for papists-O.; epistle 24091, 25939.
   1624: 4502 (4497), 4751 and 4752, 5961,
   11189, 12524, 24509, 24542, 25054 (25031),
   25382, T. Field, *Earths encrease*-C.²; *see* 22092
   (22064).
   1625: 3095, 5975 by editor, 17598, 17729,
   early state of 10911-DE. [normally *1626*
   with added ded. to Charles]; *see* 14425,
   18359.
   Belated: ¶1124, ¶1397 from early foreign inc.
   'London *1624*'-PARIS., 3222, 5864, 6982,
   ¶14754, Linlithgow map in 17827 from
   earlier foreign, 18033, 20648, ¶22550;
   epistle 21654, 22633; prose 24555 (24544).
   Peers supporting him in infancy: 3967.
   Court or courtiers: *6519, ¶14751, ¶21872 and
   1616 in some copies 21870; epistle *10688,
   25916 (25890, 25911).
   English knights with James at Aberdeen:
   Epistle 25191.
   Unnamed knight attending: 3847.
JAMES II, *King.* *10667, *25900; epistle 4480,
   19035, 20522, 21641 (15080).
JAMES *or* JOCKEY, '*Keeper of Falcon at Castle
   Hedingham*'. 12141 [facetious].
JAMES, Francis, *Civilian* (Foster 1581). 11956
   [see changes]; epistle 21660.
JAMES, Francis, *of New College* (Foster 1627).
   Verse 91, 5097.
JAMES, James, *Mythical Edinburgh printer.* Un-
   signed prose 1463 = 10577 and 1464.
JAMES, John, *M.D.* (Venn 1564). *See* 25438.
JAMES, John. Verse 6333.
JAMES, Richard, *Scholar* (DNB). Edits 18087;
   verse 22796.
JAMES, Thomas, *Bodley's librarian* (DNB).
   *12348 by editor; edits 959, 25589, 25935;
   verse 4756, 21033, 24610; *see* 12662 (12706,
   12635); Minsheu List.
JAMES, William, *M.A.* (Venn 1562). Verse
   24631.
JAMES, William, '*Theol*[*ogus*]'. Verse 18986
   and *1606*-HD. [18985-L. impf.].

JAMES, William, *Bishop of Durham.* 4099,
   *4837, 5469, 14315, 24275.
JANSSON. *See* JOHNSON.
JARRET, William (5226). Error for Gilbert
   Gerard.
JAY, JAYE, JAEY, JEAY, JEYE.
JAEY, Henry, *Mechlin bookseller.* Prose 4125.
JAYE *or* JEYE, Henry, *Alderman.* ¶13247;
   epistle *12203.
JEAY, Stephen, *of Lincoln's Inn* (Foster). *See*
   15466.
JEAY *or* JAY, Sir Thomas, *of Netheravon, Wilts.*
   (? Foster 1613). *17642; verse 17639, 17640,
   probably 17642 as T.I. [*N & Q 1960*, p. 30].
JAYRUS (6581). *See* ABGAR.
JEFFERIE, John. Verse 24316.
JEFFERY, John, *D.D.* (Venn 1610). *5410 by
   editor.
JEFFERIES, Leonard, *of Earls Croome* (*Vis.
   Worcs.*). J. Frewen, **†*Certaine instructions,
   1587*-FLEMING.
GEOFREDUS, Tho., *Britanno-Brigas.* Verse
   24702.
JEFFES, Abel, *Printer.* Epistle 18372 unnamed;
   signed prose *Mirrour of friendship, 1584*-HN.
JEGON, John, *Bishop of Norwich.* ¶3437 [see
   changes], 3438, *21069, 23289.
JEMMAT, William, *Puritan divine* (DNB).
   Edits 23821, 23823, 23837 (23842), 23849.
JENKINSON, Zacharias, *Rutland preacher* (Foster).
   See Z. I.
JENNINGS, William, *Dean of Gloucester.* *13756
   as Jenyns.
JERMYN, Anne *and* Frances. *See* POLEY *and*
   WOODHOUSE.
JERMYN, Henry, *I Earl of St. Albans.* *6304,
   6305.
JERMYN, *Sir* Robert, *of Rushbrooke* (Venn
   1550). †4460, *11820, *19915, J. More,
   ¶Three godly sermons, 1594-PN.²; *see* 25438.
JERMYN, Robert, *Son of preceding* (Venn 1597).
   See 12662 (12706, 12635).
JERMYN, *Sir* Thomas, *Vice-chamberlain, father of
   Henry.* ¶14743, 21873, 24032, 24633; *see*
   10667.
JERMYN, Thomas, *Courtier, son of preceding*
   (Keeler). Epistle some copies *4747-O.

JERNINGHAM, *Sir* Henry, *I Bt.* R. Webb, *†Key of knowledge, 1622*-PN.[2] as Jernegan.

JERVOISE, *Sir* Thomas, *of Shropshire* (Keeler). †1069 as Gervoyse.

JESUS CHRIST. *See under* GOD.

JEWEL, John, *Bishop of Salisbury.* *1710, *4043 (4044), 5317, 7063, 12758, 12760, 12761, 13250 = 13842, 23234, 24668 (24669) [? from earlier foreign]; epistle 4074 [? from foreign], 7167 = 22271; prose 25807; *see* 12762, 20726, 20729.

JEWEL, William, *M.A.* (Foster 1603 as Juell). Verse 12747 (12748); *see* 7098.

JOACHIMI, Albert, *Dutch diplomatist* (Schotel). 961.

JOBSON, *Sir* Francis, *Lieutenant of the Tower* (DNB). *24113.

JOCELIN, Turrell, *of Turrell, Essex, husband of author.* 14624.

JOHN, *King of England.* ¶13569.

JOHN, *of Paul's Churchyard. See* HODGSON.

JOHN CASIMIR, *Count Palatine and Elector.* Prose 11348.

JOHN., D. C. (7498). *See* CHRISTOPHER JOHNSON.

JOHNSON, JOHNSTON, JONSON, etc.

JOHNSON, Abraham, *of Lincoln's Inn.* 3771 and *1612*-CU.

JOHNSON, Abraham, *M.A.* (Venn). Minsheu List.

JOHNSTON, Archibald, *Lord Warriston* (DNB). Officially subscribes, partly edits 1205, 21905, 21907, 22048, 22050, 22060.

JOHNSTON, Arthur, *Poet and physician* (DNB). Verse 1493, 3809, 5097, 11151, 12491, 13191, 19781, 25189.

JONSON, Benjamin, *Dramatist* (DNB). 17479; epistle 23791 (23725); *see* 5811.
Signed verse: 288, 1694, 3666, 3819, 3830, 3914, 5807, 5808 and 5810 and allegedly editor [cf. 23769], 7190, 7491 [and 7492 earlier] (14751), 10827 (14751), 10828 (14751), 10869, 11068, 13249, 13592, 14008, 14889 including B. I., 16887, 21470, 21649 (14751), 22177 (14754), 22273 including B.I., 23447.
Initialed verse: Canonical 22218, 23248, 26040; dubious 23123, 25090a; *see also* I. B. (14788).
Anonymous verse: 20637 (14754).
Initialed prose: 10733.

JOHNSON *or* JONSON, Christopher, *Poet and physician* (DNB). Edits 25403; verse 6787, 7498 as D. C. Iohn., Dethick, *Oratio*-L.[13]; *see* 25671.

JOHNSON, Edmund, *Schoolmaster* (Venn). Verse 23899.

JOHNSON, Edm. [*Pupil of John Gower M.A.*]. Verse 12141.

JOHNSON, Edward, *of the Inner Temple.* Verse 3917 (25890).

JOHNSON, Francis, *Separatist* (DNB). 14664; epistle *19608; *see* 236, 14335.

JONSON, James. *See* 25438.

JOHNSTON, James, *Portioner of Ballencreiff.* Verse 11750.

JOHNSTONE, James, *I Earl of Hartfell. See* 10667.

JOHNSTON, John, *Scottish poet* (DNB). T. Mierbekius, *Theses*-E.[2]; epistle 21285 (21286); verse 3985 = 2362 only, 7351, 21657.

JOHNSON, John, *Almanac-maker.* Verse 20187.

JANSSON, Jan, II, *alias* John Johnson, *Printer.* Prose 17827.

JOHNSON, Levinus. Verse 374.

JOHNSON, Paul, *of Fordwich* (*Vis. Kent*). ¶1710.

JOHNSON, R., '*of Egginton, Derby*'. *20207.

JOHNSON, Robert, *the elder, Alderman.* 1042, *17886.

JOHNSTON, Robert, *Provost of Aberdeen.* *22471.

JOHNSON, Thomas, *Botanist* (DNB). Edits ¶1592, 11751; verse 19300.

JOHNSTON, William, *M.D., Professor at Aberdeen.* Verse 1493, 1494.

JOHNSON, William, *of Queens' College* (Venn 1627). Verse 11464.

JOLLES, *Sir* John, *Lord Mayor.* 5876 by bookseller, *12122 [see changes], *17886, *18522, *19513, 21079, *26024.

JONES, *Sir* Francis, *Lord Mayor.* *5708 [see changes], *6017, *7146, *17886, 23117, 23118.

JONES, Henry, *Son of Alderman Sir Roger.* 4974.

JONES, Inigo, *Architect* (DNB). 18304; verse 5808 and 5810 [cf. 23769]; *see* 5811.

JONES, James. Verse 23704.

JONES, John [*probably the DNB physician*]. Verse 16653.

JONES, John, *alias* Leander à Sancto Martino, O.S.B. (*DNB*). Edits 6385.

JONES, John, *Son of the printer William* (Venn 1615). Verse 12184.

JONES, John, *Fellow of King's* (Venn 1627). Verse 13519.

JONES, John, *Dramatist: friends of.* 14721.

JONES, Luke. Verse 15433.

JONES, Philip, *Cirencester preacher* (Foster 1581). Verse 12625.

JO[NES], Mrs. R. *14720.

JONES, Richard, *Printer* (*DNB*). Signed prose 3631, 3633, 5615 = 10925, 15589, 17425 [first edition], 18371, 18489, 19430 as R. I. [presumably from lost earlier ed.; later usurped by J. Wright], 19880, 21135 and 1577-HD., 25347; unsigned verse 19426 [superseded 19430 by prose as above], 21105, 24411, 25439; *see* 3683 *and* GREG no. 90.

JONES, Richard, *'Courtier'* [*? of Gray's Inn*]. *12178.

JONES, Robert, *'of London'*. *25624.

JONES, Roger, *I Viscount Ranelagh. See* 10667.

JONES, Sa. [*perhaps* Samuel, *customs searcher*]. Verse 23779 only.

JONES (Bavand), Sara = Thomas (*Vis. Ches.*). Presentation 11319.

JONES, Stephen, *of St. John's* (Venn). Verse 7294, 21460, 21638.

JONES, Thomas, *Bookseller, son of Richard.* Epistle 19333 unnamed; signed prose 1060, 4899.

JONES, Thomas, *Common serjeant of London, of Gray's Inn.* H. Goodcole, **Prodigals teares,* 1620-O.

JONES, William, *Bookseller, d. 1618.* Prose 12321 only, 18073.

JONES, William, *Printer, d. after 1631.* Signed prose 14722, 15515, 23505 as W. I. P[rinter].

JONES, William, *'of Uske, Gent.' See* 10011 [? author].

JONES, William, *Commentator, d. 1636* (*DNB*). Prose 3437.

JONES, *Sir* William, *Judge* (*DNB*). *24297; *see* 10667.

JONSON. *See* JOHNSON.

JOOPE, John, *of the Amsterdam congregation* (Burrage). *5345; edits 5337.

JORDAN, Agnes, *Abbess of Syon.* *17542.

JORDEN, Edward, *Physician* (*DNB*). Minsheu List.

JORDEN, Edw. Verse 22794, 22796.

JORDAN, John, *'Servant to Lieut. of Ordnance'.* Edits 21483.

JORDAN, Nicholas, *of Chichester and Inner Temple.* 1626 by bookseller, 1644 [earlier lost] (1629).

JORDAN, Thomas, *Poet* (*DNB*). Verse 20770, 21011.

JOSCELYN, John, *Scholar* (*DNB*). Edits 11893 as Josselinus.

JOSUA, Richard, *Senior.* Prose 11858.

JOSUA, Richard, *Junior.* Prose 11858 [probably shorthand reporter].

JOYE, George, *Controversialist* (*DNB*). *See* 11588.

JOYEUSE, François de, *Cardinal* (*NBG*). 3094.

JUBIN, Jean, *'Senonois'.* Verse 24871.

JUEL *and* JUELL. *See* JULIUS *and* JEWEL.

JUGGE, Richard, *Printer* (*DNB*). Prose 2867 and 2872; unsigned prose 19476; *see* 14795 [named in later edition].

JULIUS II, *Pope. See* 25585.

JULIUS, Alexander, *Poet* (*STC*). Edits 3989 = 2363.

JULIUS (Juel), Christian, Eric, *and* Gregory, *Danes at Oxford* (*Ath. Oxon.*). ¶20362-S.

JUNIUS. *See* YOUNG (and elsewhere DU JON).

JUXON, John, *Citizen, d. 1626* (*Vis. London*). 6604 and first ed.-O. with his children Elizabeth, John, Mary, Sarah, and Thomas.

JUXON, William, *Archbishop of Canterbury.* 11121 by editor, *14457, 17609, 25218 (25209, sometimes 25208); *see* 10667.

JYLBERT. *See* GILBERT.

K

K., Sir E. [? *fiction*]. Prose 21057.

K., E. [*Often thought mask of Spenser*]. Prose and gloss 23089 (23084).

K., E. Verse 6839 [also of Cambridge origin].

K., F. Verse 6044a.

K., G., *M.A.* Verse 21455.

K., *Lady* G. O. C. 7240.

K., H. (7045). *See* HENRY KING.

K., I. (22435). *See* JOHN KIRKE.

K., I., *D.D.* [*Recusant*]. ¶1611-HD. of 3369 by editor.

K., I., *M.A.* Verse 25224.

K., I. Edits 14611.

K., L. *19806.

K., P. Verse 5869.

K., Ph., *M.A.* Verse 21687.

KIN., Ph. (1694). *See* PHILIP KYNDER.

K., R., of L[*incoln*] Col. [*Doubtless Richard Kilbye*]. Prose 23474 (23488).

K., R. Verse 11167, 15540.

K., T. Edits 24664; verse 1245 [1244 impf.].

KAINZAEUS, David, 'N. *Abredoniensis*'. Verse 21657.

KARL FRIEDRICH, *Son of Wilhelm V Duke of Gulich*. One issue Noot, *Het bosken, 1568-* HAARLEM.

KAUNICZ, Charles, *Baron de*. Verse 5591 [presumably from foreign].

KAY, Edward [*Merchant*; ? Edmond, PCC 1618]. *11131.

KAY, John, *the younger, Gent*. 13228.

KEABLE, George, *Esq*. [? *of Northants*.]. 458 = 13500, 5468, 13498 [earlier lost except *1571-* HN. tp.].

KEARNEY, William, *Printer*. Prose 19183.

KEATE, Edmund. *See* 10697.

[KEDERMYSTER], Richard, *Abbot* (*DNB*). ¶16790 [conceivably for Richard Mounslow].

KEDGEWIN, Thomas, *of Emmanuel College* (Venn). Verse 25224.

KEEPER. *See* KEPER.

KEILLO, Charles, *Treasurer of Aberdeen*. W. Mercer, *Bon-acords decorement, 1633*-E.

KEITH, George, *V* [*alias IV*] *Earl Marischal*. 25188, G. Gray, *Oratio funebris, 1614*-A.; *see* 17329.

KEITH, Sir George, *Recruiter for Danish service*. Verse 14906.

KEITH, *Lady* Jean. *See* FORBES.

KEITH (Ogilvy), Margaret = George *V* Earl. Epistle 12067.

KEITH (Erskine), Mary = William *VI* Earl. 2366, *¶12478, 18290, 22570.

KEITH, Sir Robert, *of Benholm*. 1403.

KEITH, William, *VI Earl Marischal*. †12492, †14852, *18790, G. Gray, *Oratio funebris, 1614*-A.; *see* Marischal Academy, *Lachrymae, 1635*-E.[3]

KEITH, William, *VII Earl Marischal*. 22262, 22473; *see* 10667.

KELLAM, Laurence, *Douay printer*. Unsigned prose 26000; his press corrector: prose 11017.

KELLETT, Edward, *Divine* (*DNB*). *21848 by editor.

KELLISON, Matthew (*DNB*). Friend of. Did table 14912.

KELLY, John, *of Trinity College, Dublin*. Verse 17762.

KELLIE, Sir Thomas, *Courtier and advocate* (*STC*). St. Andrews (Salvator) *Theses, 1627*-E.[2]

KEMP (Herris), Dorothy = Robert, *Mother of Sir Robert*. 15555 by editor.

KEMP, Edward, *of Queens' College* (Venn). Verse 12935, 12936, 14269.

KEMPE, John, *Citizen* [? *and Draper*]. ¶1710.

KEMP, Sir Robert, *I Bt*. *¶4338.

KEMP, Sir Thomas, *of Wye, Kent*. 17820.

KEMP, William, *Actor* (*DNB*). 534.

KEMPTHORNE, John, *Esq*. 14631 and *1588*-HD.

KENDALL, Thomas. First issue 4946 [then cancelled].

KENDRICK, John, 'Merchant in Nürnberg' [? *the Lord Mayor*]. 10933.

KENESTON. *See* KYNASTON.

KENNE, Christopher [*probably of Kenn, PCC 1592*]. ¶10572 [see changes].

KILLIGREW, Sir William, *Courtier, d. 1622* (*DNB*). *†3807, 11231, †22907.

KILLINGBECKE, Margaret. Epistle *1610*-F. of 6990.

KILVERT, Richard, *Lawyer* (*DNB*). 5125 by bookseller.

KING, ——, *D.D.* [*of Soms.*]. Epistle *1941.

KING, Adam, *Scottish poet, sometime of Paris University* (*STC*). *14993; verse 7487; *see* 4568.

KING, Alexander, *Advocate and assessor of Edinburgh.* *14993.

KING, Edward, *Friend of Milton* (*DNB*). Verse 12936.

KING, Henry, *Bishop of Chichester and poet.* ¶2774, *4259, 17602; signed verse 21725; unsigned verse 7031 (7045 initialed).

KING, Humphrey, *Wit* (*DNB*). 3678, 18370, A. C[hute], *Tabaco, 1595*-HN. by printer.

KING, John, *Bishop of London.* 1594, 1861, 1863 (1866), 1870 [1871 a reissue], ¶2774 post-humously, 4116, 6591 (6587), *11496, 11907, ¶13841, 13930, 13938, 14321, *17698 [*1614*-HD. only frag.], *18147, 19088 = ¶*1616*-HD. of 19093, 20174 by editor, 20333, 20503, 20514 by editor Purset, *20916, 22574, 22880 [should be shifted after 22847], 23096 by editor, *¶25699 [see changes].
Epistle: 23344 only, 23582 [see also *Dd4] (23575, 21653), 24992.
Edits: 19043; *see* 17944, 19511, 20507; Minsheu List.

KING or REGIUS, John, *Preacher at Dutch Church. See* 5533, 23920 and 23923; Minsheu List.

KING, John, *Canon of Westminster* (Foster 1589). Minsheu List.

KING, John, *Divine, d. 1639* (*DNB*). *4259, 17608 (17603).

KING, Philip, *Archdeacon, brother of preceding.* ¶2774.

KING, Samuel, *of St. James, Clerkenwell.* Verse 13370, 23779 only.

KINGSLEY, William, *Archdeacon of Canterbury* (Foster 1597). 57, *5410 by editor, *22398.

KINGSMILL, Andrew (*DNB*), *Sister of.* 15000; *also see* 15003.

KINGSMILL, Richard, *of Highclere, brother of Andrew.* 6494 [earlier lost; author is Deloney].

KINGSMILL, William, *of New College* (Foster 1602). Edits 25021 = 15009.

KINGSTON, Felix, *Printer.* Unsigned prose 5361, 13541.

KINGSTON, John, *Printer.* Unsigned prose 10663.

KINGSTON (Fetiplace), Susan = John. 6157 (16932).

KINLOCH (Kinalochus), Patrick, *of Alderston, advocate, d. 1639.* Verse D. Primrose, *Apologie for advocates, 1628*-ROSEBERY; *see also* 17142.

KINNERSLEY or KINARDSLEY, Anthony, *of Loxley* (*Vis. Staffs.*). *†21437.

KINSCHOT, Louis van, *Father of the poet Caspar.* Edits 24033 [from Leyden *1625*].

KIRKBY, Thomas, *of Brasenose* (Foster 1566). *See* 13923 misprinted Kickebye.

KIRKE, George, *Courtier* (*DNB*). *1203, *¶19850; epistle some copies *4747-0.

KIRKE, John, *Dramatist* (*DNB*). Edits 22435 [one issue signed, other initialed].

KIRKHAM, John. Verse 7607.

KIRKHAM, Robert, *Clerk of the Signet.* Minsheu List.

KYRTON, Dorothy, '*of Thrup, Northants.*' 13928.

KIRTON, Thomas, *Common serjeant of London* [? *Inner Temple*]. *Mirrour of friendship, 1584*-HN. by printer.

KITCHIN, Abell, *Mayor of Bristol.* *18347.

KITCHIN, Anthony, *Bishop of Llandaff.* *1710, *2983 = 21617.

KITCHIN, Thomas, *Fellow of Trinity* (Venn 1591). Minsheu List.

KIDSON, Robert [? Venn]. Verse 11326.

KITSON, Sir Thomas, *the younger, of Hengrave Hall, d. 1603.* †10596.

KNAP, Joseph, '*of Southwark martial garden*'. Epistle *14922.

L

LAWNE, Christopher, *Controversialist (STC)*. See 5449.

LAWRENCE, Adam, '*Uncle*'. 778.

LAWRENCE, Giles, *Regius professor (DNB)*. Verse 1924, 6578, 12188.

LAWRENCE, Henry, *Puritan statesman (DNB)*. 20218 by editors.

LAWRENCE, J., '*Brother of author*'. Verse 778.

LAWRENCE, Sir John, *I Bt.* Minsheu List.

LAWSON, James, *Reformer (DNB)*. Verse 144 (148) as Lausonius.

LAWSON (——), Mary = John '*of Milton*'. With unnamed children 22836 (*Three treatises, 1634*-F.).

LAWSON, William, *Writer (DNB)*. Edits 6612 and earlier-HD. as Lauson.

LAYBOURNE [? Roger], '*Barber surgeon near Billingsgate*'. See 5446.

LAYER, Thomas, *Mayor of Norwich*. 18494 by editor.

LAYER, Thomas, *of Booton* (Venn 1602). Epistle 15037.

LAYFIELD, John, *Divine (DNB)*. Verse 15433; see 17944, 19511.

LAYTON. See LEIGHTON.

LEANDER de sancto Ioanne, *M.B.* [*untraced*]. Verse 20124.

LEANDER à Sancto Martino. See JOHN JONES, *O.S.B.*

LEARMONTH, Sir John, *of Balcomie*. St. Andrews (Salvator) *Theses, 1614-*O.[6]

LE BON, Sir John [*fiction*]. 21314.

LECEY. See LACEY.

LECHMERE *alias* STRATFORD, Edmund, *Divine (DNB)*. Epistle 24930 as S. E.

LECTIUS (Lect), Jacobus, *Professor at Geneva (NBG)*. Verse 21649 only.

LEE, LEA, LEGH, LEIGH, LEY.

LEE, Edward, *Archbishop of York*. See 5163, map in 12624.

LEIGH, Edward, *of Gray's Inn*. 1482.

LEIGH, Edward, *Writer (DNB)*. Edits 25317.

LEIGH (Harington), Frances = *Sir* William. ★4884.

LEIGH, Sir Francis, *Father of next*. ★12551; Minsheu List.

LEIGH, Francis, *I Earl of Chichester*. Epistle 13621 and *1639*-HD.; see 10667.

LEE, George. 21386 [cf. Hugh Lee].

LEIGH, George, John, *and* William, *Sons of author*. Epistle 15402.

LEE, Sir Henry, *Master of the Ordnance (DNB)*. 12432 [rewritten in 12433]. 21469 by editor; see 7099.

LEY, Henry, *II Earl of Marlborough*. 421 for 1627; see 10667.

LEIGH, Henry, *of Rushall, father of author*. 15410.

LEE, Hugh, *Esq*. Presentation 21393 [cf. George Lee].

LEE, Isaac, *Alderman and merchant*. ¶16684 = 16690.

LEA, James, *Translator of 17132*. Verse 19619.

LEY, James, *I Earl of Marlborough*. ★5837, ★11670, ¶11681 (11652), 13204, †25162; epistle ★6205, 20166; see 17331; Minsheu List.

LEIGH, John, *B.D.* (Foster 1591). Verse 18114 as Leeus.

LEY, John, *Divine (DNB)*. Prose 19778; see 25327.

LEE, Joyce, *Poor Clare, sister of Archbishop Edward*. 19898 (18076) as Leygh.

LEY (Pettie), Mary = James *I Earl*. ¶25164.

LEIGH (Egerton), Mary = Thomas *I Baron*. Epistle ★6332 [6331 a ghost].

LEIGH, Nicholas, *Translator of 10499*. Verse 1410, 13482 = 17787.

LEIGH, Sir Peter or Piers, *of Cheshire* (Venn 1580). ★¶11600, 15424, 19924, ¶25224.

LEE, Sir Richard, *Ambassador, brother of Sir Henry*. 12642 (12706, 12635); see 12662 (12706, 12635).

LEIGH, Richard. Verse 23760, 23779 only, 23806 (23725).

LEE, Sir Richard, *of Inner Temple and Lee, Ches., d. 1627*. ★†21437.

LEE, Richard, *Preacher* (Venn 1606). Edits 25315.

LEE, Robert, *Esq.* [*perhaps brother of Sir Henry*]. ★¶12270.

LEE, Sir Robert, *Lord Mayor*. ★6070, ★13589 [see changes], ★14671, ★23343 [see changes], ★23929 [see changes

LEIGH (Hampden), Ruth = Henry. *See* SCUDAMORE.

LEE, Tho. Verse 936 [diff. trans. from 935].

LEE, Thomas, *Captain (DNB)*. 21086.

LEIGH, *Sir* Thomas, *I Bt., grandfather of next.* *4023.

LEIGH, Thomas, *I Baron Leigh.* †4532, 7178 [and 7177 probably later; see changes].

LEIGH, *Sir* Urian, *of Adlington, d. 1627.* *7293, 15422.

LEIGH, Walter, *Swordbearer to the Lord Mayor.* 3722.

LEA, William, *'Vicar of Christchurch, Hants'.* One issue *13507.

LEE, William *the elder, Bookseller.* Probably prose 20944 as 'Printer'.

LEECH, ——, *of Virginia Company, secretary to Pembroke* [? John *DNB*]. Minsheu List.

LEECH (Loechius), Andrew, *of St. Andrews (STC).* Verse T. Mierbekius, *Theses*-E.[2]

LEECH, David, *Poet (DNB).* Verse 15373, 16930, Aberdeen *Positiones,* 1627-A. as D. L.

LEECH, Humphrey, *S.J. (DNB).* ¶1867.

LEECH, John [*perhaps father of John-DNB*]. Verse 1410.

LEET, I. D., *'of Leyden'* [? J. de Laet, *historian*]. Verse 19302.

LEEVING, Timothy, *Recorder of Derby* (Foster). Epistle 23099.

LEGATE, John, *the elder, Printer (DNB).* Signed prose 24009 and *1589-*ILL. [see changes for alterations]; unsigned prose 19647, afresh 19649.

LEGATE, John, *the younger, Printer (DNB).* Unsigned prose 5837.

LEGGE, Cantrell, *Cambridge printer.* Epistle 14950 unnamed; unsigned verse 4487.

LEGGE, Martha, *'Laundress for Middle Temple'.* 23787 (23725).

LE GRIS or GRYCE, Anthony, *of Brockdish (Vis. Norf.).* 1723 by editor Becon [cf. 4047].

LE GROS, *Sir* Charles, *of Crostwight* (Keeler). *¶4338; epistle 15037.

LEICESTER, *Sir* George, *of Toft, Ches., d. 1612.* *7293 as Leister.

LEIGH, LEGH. *See* LEE.

LEIGHTON (Knollys), Cecilia = *Sir* Thomas. 3132; epistle 16696.

LEIGHTON, *Sir* Thomas, *Captain of Guernsey.* P. Merlin, *Christians combat,* 1591-L. [by both author and trans.].

LEIGHTON, Thomas. Verse 13988.

LEIGHTON, *Sir* William, *Poet (DNB).* Verse 2497.

LEKE or LEEKE, Francis, *I Earl of Scarsdale. See* 10667.

LEKE, James, *of Peterhouse* (Venn). Verse 7365.

LEKPREVICK, Robert, *Edinburgh printer (DNB).* Unsigned prose 10819, 12968, 22028.

LELAND, John, *Antiquary (DNB).* Verse 23899.

LELLO, *Sir* Henry, *of Ashdon, warden of the Fleet.* *12332 (12331).

LE MAÇON (Massonius), Robert, *Sieur de la Fontaine, minister of French Church (STC).* Epistle 4882 [from lost catechism]; edits 24667, more prose 24668; *see also* R. L. M.

LE MAÇON (Massonius), Timothy [? Venn 1581 as Mason]. Verse 4427.

LE MAIRE, Jacques, *Explorer (NBG).* Verse 4869 and *1611-*E.

LEMAN, *Sir* John, *Lord Mayor.* *¶13247, *17886, *21015; epistle 24698.

LE METAIR, George, *of First Fruits office* (Foster as Limiter). Minsheu List.

LE MOYNE (Monachus), Guy, *Tutor to Charles I.* Verse 15078.

LENNARD (Slany), Elizabeth = *Sir* Samuel *of Wickham.* *1629 by editor.

LENNARD, Henry, *XII Baron Dacre.* 14733, 26095.

LENNARD (Fiennes), Margaret, *Baroness Dacre.* 4997, 15460, 24127.

LENNARD, Richard, *XIII Baron Dacre.* 25094; *see* 17332, posthumously 10667 [error for Francis, XIV Baron].

LENNARD, Sampson, *Father of Henry XII Baron.* 4103, 5052 [see changes]; epistle *24125.

LENNARD, Samson, *Herald (DNB).* Verse 24756; Minsheu List.

LENTON, Francis, *Poet (DNB).* Verse 23447.

LEO X, *Pope.* 11536, 13078 (13083).

LEPTON, John, *Groom of Privy Chamber, Overbury witness.* Verse 15433.

LEPUS (LeLièvre), Constantinus, *Editor* (BN). Prose 15818, etc.

LERKYN, John, '*Pastor of Itchingfield, Sussex*'. See 13923.

LE SAUX du Saussé, Marin, *Huguenot minister* (Schickler). Verse 18157 and 1578-F. as M. L. S.

LESK, William, *M.A., King's College, Aberdeen*. Verse 12488.

LESLIE, Alexander, *I Earl of Leven*. Promulgates 21914.

LESLIE, Andrew, *V Earl of Rothes*. 7352.

LESLIE, George, *of Edinburgh Town Council*. W. M., *Edinburghs alphabet-E.

LESL[IE], I. Verse 11596.

LESLIE, John, *VI Earl of Rothes*. 14906, 21554; see 10667.

LESLIE, John, *Bishop of Clogher*. ¶2767.

LESLIE, Patrick, *II Lord Lindores*. See 10667.

LESLIE, Patrick, *Provost of Aberdeen*. W. Mercer, *Bon-acords decorement, 1633-E.

LESLIE, William, *Principal* (DNB). See next.

LESSIUS, Guil. [*believed the preceding*]. ¶1407.

LESTRANGE (Stubbe), Alice = *Sir* Hamon. *22133; see 12527.

LESTRANGE (Lewkenor), Anne = *Sir* Nicholas *I Bt*. *18806.

LESTRANGE, *Sir* Hamon, *Father-in-law of preceding*. *¶4338, *11572, ¶21869; epistle 15037.

LEUCUS, I., '*Schoolmaster*' [? Lewis]. Verse 12967 (12964).

LEVENTHORPE, Charles, *V Bt*. 12176.

LEVENTHORPE, Edward [? *the next*]. Verse 12747 (12748), 12748.

LEVENTHORPE, Edward, *Son of Sir John below*. 12177.

LEVENTHORPE (Brograve), Joan = *Sir* John. 12175, 24314.

LEVENTHORPE, *Sir* John, *I Bt*. 12183, †12185, 14734, †24307, †24753, Tuke, †*Christian directions, 1610-*HAT.

LEVENTHORPE, John, *Son of preceding*. 12179.

LEVER, Ri. Verse 18351.

LEVER, Thomas, *Divine* (DNB). *6810 = 11888 (10400); prose 3485 only.

LEVESON (Mildmay), Christiana = *Sir* John *the elder*. 15197, 24317.

LEVESON, *Sir* John, *the elder* (Foster 1575). 5982.

LEVESON, *Sir* John, *the younger* (Foster 1598). 24309.

LEVESON, *Sir* Richard, *of Kent* (Keeler). 5978.

LEVETT, John, *the younger, Son of author*. Edits 15555.

LEVET, Thomas, *of Tixover, Rutland*. 957 = 13268 by bookseller.

LEVINUS (17944a). See MONCK.

LEVISTON. See LIVINGSTON.

LEWIN, *Sir* Justinian, *Gentleman of Privy Chamber, son of next*. 24967.

LEWIN, William, *Civilian* (DNB). 10835, 23280; epistle 12899 with reply; see 18773.

LEWIS, David, *Judge* (DNB). 5615 = 10925 by printer, Hemmingsen, *Godlie exposition, 1580-*PN.²; see 18773.

LEWIS, Hugh, *Poet, translator of 25260* (DWB). Verse 19775.

LEWIS, John, *M.A., writer* (Venn 1614). Verse 351.

LEWIS, Thomas, *of the Van* (PCC 1595). Epistle *1095 (1077).

LEWIS, W. [cf. *Vis. London*]. Verse 21094.

LEWES, William, '*of London*'. 11903.

LEWIS, William, *Provost of Oriel* (DNB). Minsheu List.

LEWKNOR, *Sir* Christopher, *of Middle Temple* (Keeler). See C. L.

LEWKENOR, Edmund, *M.A.* (Venn 1559). Verse 10423, 23229.

LEWKENOR, *Sir* Edward, *of Suffolk* (Venn 1559). †11859; children of, 20338; memory of, †15561.

LEWKENOR, *Sir* Edward, *the younger, d. 1618* (Venn 1599). 377, *20337 by editor.

LEWKENOR, Edward, *Son of preceding* (Venn 1629). 18805.

LEWKENOR (Russell), Elizabeth = Edward. *18806.

LEWKENOR, Katherine, *Daughter of Sir Edward the younger, later* Calthorpe. *18806.

LEWKENOR, *Sir* Lewis, *Courtier* (Venn and STC). Epistle 24124, 24135; verse 5808 and 5810 [cf. 23769]; see 668.

LEWKENOR (Neville), Mary = *Sir* Edward *the younger*. 4693, *18806.

LEWKENOR, Mary, *Daughter of Sir Edward the younger.* ★18806.

LEWKENOR, Sir Richard, *Judge, of the Middle Temple.* 15566, 24261.

LEWKENOR, Richard, *of Sussex* (Foster 1604). 383.

LEWKENOR, Sir Robert, *of Acrise* (Venn 1604). ★20337, epistle ★4693.

LEWKENOR, Thomas, *Physician, brother of Sir Lewis. See* 668.

LEY *and* LHUYD. *See* LEE *and* LLOYD.

LICHFIELD, John, *Oxford printer.* Epistle 23754 (23725) unnamed; signed verse 19027, 19033; unsigned prose 11514, perhaps 19571 (19570).

LICHFIELD, Leonard, *Printer* (DNB). Signed verse 5021 = 19036, 19037, 19038, 19039; unsigned prose 4119, perhaps 17750.

LICHFIELD, Richard, *Barber for Trinity, Cambridge.* 18369 as Richardo Barbarossa [cf. 12906].

LIDDELL (Woodward), Bridget = Sir Thomas *d. 1627.* 16652.

LYDALL, Richard. Verse 21640.

LILY (Goddard), Dorothy = Peter-*DNB.* Edits 15600, 15601.

LILLY, Edmund, *Master of Balliol* (Foster). Verse 4756, 4759, 4761.

LYLY, John, *Dramatist* (DNB). Verse 4761, 16696, 25118a.

LILY, Maria, *Daughter of Dorothy above.* Verse 15600.

LILY, William, *Grammarian* (DNB). 13807; epistle 5542 (25944) [earlier lost], 5544 = 10497; verse 5542 [signed in 5543], 13811, 15635, 15636; *see Antilycon . . . R. Whitintoni, 1521-*CHATS.

LIMBERT, Stephen, *Schoolmaster* (Venn). Verse 19299, 25438 [also see text].

LINACRE, Thomas, *Physician* (DNB). Prose 11532.

LINDSAY, Alexander, *Bishop of Dunkeld. See* 10667.

LINDSAY, Alexander, *II Lord Spynie. See* 10667.

LINDSAY, David, *Bishop of Edinburgh.* Verse 7351, 19781; *see* 10667.

LINDSAY, David, *I Lord Lindsay of Balcarres. See* 10667.

LINDSAY, David, *Minister of Belhelvie.* Verse 11151.

LYND[SAY], G., '*Andreapol.*' Verse 74.

LINDSEY, G. Verse 189.

LINDSAY, George, *XIV Earl of Crawford. See* 10667.

LINDSAY, James, *VII Lord L. of the Byres.* 10769 by printer.

LINDESIUS, Joannes [*probably the next*]. Verse 3991.

LINDSAY, John, *Lord Menmuir* (DNB). ¶6217; *see preceding.*

LINDSAY, John, *VIII Lord L. of the Byres.* 16931.

LINDSAY, John, *XVII Earl of Crawford.* St. Andrews (Leonard) *Theses, 1632-*E.; *see* 10667 misnamed James.

LINDSAY, Patrick, *VI Lord L. of the Byres.* Epistle 4660.

LINDSAY, Patrick, *Archbishop of Glasgow.* ★12480, ¶19781; *see* 10667.

LYNDESAY, Walter. Verse 15713.

LINDSELL, Augustine, *Bishop of Hereford.* Edits 23948; Minsheu List as Lindsey.

LINDSELL, William, *Rector of Marham* (Venn 1573). *See* 7529 [also sig. D5].

LINEWRAY, Sir John, *Surveyor of ordnance.* 3646, 3674, 3702.

LING, Nicholas, *Bookseller.* Edits 15685; probably prose 3191 only as L. N.

LING, W. Verse 23704.

LINGHAM, William, *Warden of Barber Surgeons.* Epistle ★25963.

LIPSIUS, Justus, *Belgian author* (NBG). Epistle 12551, 24031; *see* 22213, 25438.

LISLE, Laurence, *Bookseller.* Prose 6515; unsigned prose 18904, afresh 18908 signed, enlarged 18909.

LISLE (De Insula), William, *Scholar* (DNB). Verse 6206.

LISTER, Sir Matthew, *Physician* (DNB). ★¶14704; verse 19302.

LITHGOW, William, *Traveller* (DNB). Verse 12748.

LITHODIUS, Joannes. Verse 1295.

LITTLE, Francis, *of Christ Church* (Foster). Edits 23504.

LITTLE, T. Verse 22631.

LITTILL, William, *Lord provost of Edinburgh.* 21284.

LITTLETON, Edmund, *Puritan preacher (CSPD* 1591). Prose 1086.

LITTLETON, Edward, *I Baron Littleton.* ★23345 by editor.

LITTLETON, Richard, *Son of the author.* 15719 (18394) and 15760.

LITTLETON, T., *Gent.* Verse 13783.

LITTON. *See* LYTTON.

LIVELY, Edward, *Professor (DNB).* Hebrew verse 1492.

LIVINGSTONE, Alexander, *II Earl of Linlithgow.* See 10667.

LEVISTON *or* LIVINGSTON, James, *Groom of the Bedchamber, uncle of Newburgh.* ★1203, ★10530 only; epistle some copies ★4747-0.

LIVINGSTON, James, *I Earl of Callendar.* See 10667.

LIVINGSTONE (Howard), Katherine = James *I Earl of Newburgh.* Epistle ★15465.

LEVYSTONE, Robert, *Gentleman of Bedchamber* (*CSPD*). 12334.

LHUYD, LLOYD, LOYD, LLWYD, FLOYD, FLUDD, FLOOD.

LLOYD, David, *D.C.L.* (Foster 1612). *See* D. LL.

LLOYD, George, *Bishop of Chester.* 12870 [and disguised *1625-*F.], ★25394 (25389).

LLOYD, Griffith, *Regius professor* (Foster 1564). 11740.

LLOYD *or* FLOYD, Hugh, *of Jesus College* (Venn 1628 as Floyd). Verse some copies 6347.

LLWYD, Humphrey, *Physician (DNB).* Prose 18855, 20309.

LLOYD, Humphrey, *Alderman of Chester.* ★¶23720.

FLUDD, James, *D.D.* (Venn 1603). Minsheu List.

LLOYD (Luidus), John, *Scholar (DNB).* Edits 1430, 14814, 22552.

LLOYD, *Sir* John, *Serjeant-at-law, Inner Temple.* ★18995, 18998.

FLOYD, John, *S.J. (DNB).* Epistle 17101 as J. R.

LLOYD *or* FLOOD, Ludovic, *Poet (DNB).* Verse 3128, 16636, 19775, 20978.

LLOYD (Lloyd), Margaret = John *of Rhiwaedog.* 1624 and *1629-*N.

LLOYD, *Sir* Marmaduke, *Magistrate* (Foster). ★13514 [13513 impf.], ★¶23720.

LLOYD, R., *M.A., of Oriel* (*presumably* Richard, Foster 1592). Verse 1311.

LLOYD, R. Prose 24007a.

LLOYD *or* FLOYD, *Sir* Robert, *Admiral* (*CSPD*). ¶21869; Minsheu List.

FLOYD, Thomas, *Author (DNB).* See T. FL.

LLOID, Th. Verse 23895.

LLOYD, Thomas, *B.C.L.* (Foster 1623). Verse 5097.

FLUDE, Walter, *Gent.* 1053 by printer.

LLUELYN, Martin, *Poet (DNB).* Verse 10829.

LLYN. *Listed with* LYNNE.

L'OBEL, Matthias de, *Botanist (NBG).* Prose 11748, 11750.

LOCKEY, William, *of the Inner Temple.* Minsheu List.

LOCKSMITH, William, *'Almoner Bart's Hosp., Gloucester'.* ★12171 only.

LODGE (Laxton), Anne = *Sir* Thomas. 21634 by bookseller.

LODGE, *Sir* Thomas, *Lord Mayor (DNB).* ★5798 [see changes].

LODGE, Thomas, *Author (DNB).* Verse 1312 (1311), 5432, 12309, 21002.

LOE. *Listed with* LOWE.

LOECHIUS. *See* LEECH.

LOFTUS, Adam, *Archbishop of Dublin.* 17650.

LOFTUS, Adam, *I Viscount Loftus.* ★7114, 18811; see 10667.

L'OISEAU DE TOURVAL, John, *Denizened physician from Paris* (*CSPD*). Verse 5808 and 5810; prose 5830.

LOISELEUR, Pierre, *de Villiers, Minister of the French Church.* Edits 2802; verse 17409, 24667.

LOK, Henry, *Poet (DNB).* Verse 14379.

LOK, Michael, *Traveller (DNB).* See map 12624.

LOND, Tho. Verse 1360 only.

LONDON, Richard, *of Caius College* (Venn). Verse 22400.

LONG (Warre), Amie = Gifford (*Vis. Wilts.*). ¶25164.

LONG, John, '*London minister*' [cf. Venn 1562]. Verse 12606.

LONG, Richard, *Mayor of Bristol* (Keeler). Epistle *19155.

LORISECA, Wolfgang, '*Cassel professor*'. Verse 5591 [? from foreign ed.].

LORTE, Sir Roger, *I Bt., Poet*. Verse 6307.

LORTE, William [*apparently editor for L.Becket*]. Verse 1547, 1550 and *1623*-F., 6019 (6025), 13051 and *1620*-HD., 18515.

Λῶστος. *See* BEST.

LOUIS XIII, *King of France*. 1390 [from foreign ed.], 1398 (1397), 1501; *see* 19511.

LOUIS V, *Landgrave of Hesse-Darmstadt*. ¶21812 [from foreign ed.].

LEWIS, *Count Palatine. See* CHARLES LOUIS.

LOUNFORD. *See* LUNSFORD.

LOVE, Nicholas, *Warden of Winchester College* (Foster 1588). Minsheu List.

LOVE, Richard, *Dean of Ely* (*DNB*). Verse 20540.

LOVELACE, John, *II Baron Lovelace*. 22448 misnamed Richard, 25436.

LOVELACE, Leonard. Verse 18886.

LOVELACE (Dodsworth), Margaret = Richard *I Baron*. ¶4577-LINC. [F. impf.].

LOVELACE, Richard, *I Baron Lovelace*. 22448; *see* 10667—both errors for John above.

LOVELACE, Sir Richard, *Poet* (*DNB*). Verse 3, 91.

LOVELACE, William, *the elder, Serjeant-at-law, Gray's Inn*. †6901, 12048, 21865.

LOVELL (Carey), Anne = Sir Francis *of Harling, Norf.* *5538.

LOVELL (Roper), Jane = Sir Robert, *Daughter of John I Baron*. 1341.

LOVERING, Thomas, *Schoolmaster* (Venn 1612). Verse 12967 (12964), 12964.

LOVET, Sir Robert, *of Liscombe* (Foster). *Fens map in 17827.

LOWE, John, *Jr., Esq.* 12720.

LOWE, Sir Thomas, *Lord Mayor*. *7146, *13515, *16688, *17886, *20756, *21296.

LOE, William, *the elder, Divine* (*DNB*). Epistle 23582a (23575, 21653); Minsheu List.

LOE, William, *the younger, Compiler* (*DNB*). Verse 22631.

LOWER, Pe. Verse 18496.

LOWER, Thomas, *M.A.* (Keeler). 16873.

LOWNES, Humphrey, *the elder, Printer*. Initialed prose 16857, 21650 [later usurped by Young], 23578; unsigned 21653.

LOWNES, Matthew, *Bookseller*. Prose 4918; *see* 5811.

LOWSON, Vedast, *Bailie of Aberdeen*. W. Mercer, *Bon-acords decorement, 1633*-E.

LOWTH (Ludus), John, *Archdeacon of Nottingham* (Venn 1545). Verse 14725.

LOWTHER, Richard, *of Gray's Inn* (Foster 1602). Presentation 3573.

LOZEL[ERIUS]. *See* LOISELEUR.

LUCADELPHIUS, Theotimus, *alias* T. W. L. Verse 3218.

LUCAS, Henry, *of the Middle Temple* (*DNB*). ¶7194 (7189, 7216); verse 7204 and 7201.

LUCAS, John, *Junior* (Venn 1554). Verse 11419.

LUCAS, John. 24477.

LUCAS, Peter, '*Gunner*'. Verse 22855.

LUCELLUS, Franciscus (issue 18089-DUR.⁵). Fiction.

LUCKYN, Sir William, *I Bt.* ¶20535.

LUCY (Spencer), Alice = Sir Thomas *of Charlecote d. 1640*. *15567.

LUCY, Sir Edmund, *of Broxbourne and Inner Temple*. *See* 12662 (12706, 12635).

LUCY, George, *of Gray's Inn* (Foster). Verse 14755 (14753).

LUCY, Sir Thomas, *of Charlecote, d. 1640* (*DNB*). 24111; epistle 21660.

LUDUS *and* LUIDUS. *See* LOWTH *and* LLOYD.

LUKE (Knightley), Elizabeth = Sir Oliver, *Mother of Samuel-DNB*. *6885, *6888.

LUKE, Joachim van der, '*of Mecklenberg*'. ¶3988 by editor [from foreign ed.].

LUKE, Sir Oliver, *Father of Sir Samuel* (Keeler). *6882, ¶6886.

LUMISDEN. *See* LUMSDEN.

LUMLEY, John, *I Baron Lumley, d. 1609.* 415, 4248, 10787, 13697 [inc. engr. charts reissued *1622-*O.], ¶13699.

LUMLEY, *Sir* Martin, *Lord Mayor.* *¶11346, *15325, *17649 by editor [see changes], *17886, 17901, *22150, *23345 by editor [see changes]; *see* 22531.

LUMLEY, Richard, *I Viscount Lumley.* 17088 by bookseller; *see* 10667.

LUMSDEN, James, *Laird of Airdrie, near Glasgow.* 17138 as Lummisden.

LUMISDEN, Matthew, *Dean of Gild, Aberdeen.* W. Mercer, *Bon-acords decorement, 1633-*E.

LUNAN, Alexander, *Regent of King's College, Aberdeen.* Prose 25190.

LUNDIE, John, *Poet (DNB).* Verse 11151.

LUNDORPIUS, Joh. Verse 3988 and 3990 [from foreign eds.].

LUNSFORD, *Sir* John, *of Wilegh, Sussex.* *11380 misprinted Lounford.

LUPO, Joseph, *Court musician, father of Thomas Sr.-DNB.* Verse 18284.

LUPTON, Thomas, *Writer (DNB).* Verse 14725 [twice], 20978.

LUTTRELL, Thomas, *of Gray's Inn.* Verse 841.

LYDALL *or* LYDDELL. *See* LIDDELL.

LYDIA, *of Acts* xvi. 14. *See* THEOPHILUS.

LYDUS. *See* LLOYD.

LYFORD, William, *Divine (DNB).* Edits 19942.

LYLY. *See* LILY.

LYNCH, John, *M.A.* (Venn 1608). Minsheu List.

LYNDE, Enoch, *Ordinary post to Holland* (CSPD 1632–34 and Waters). Verse 23779 (23725).

LYND., G. (74). *See* LINDSAY.

LYNDE, *Sir* Humphrey, *Controversialist (DNB).* 11112, 13037, 23528 [all as opponent]; edits 20752; *see* 10738.

LYNN, Geo. Verse 23704.

LLYN, H. Welsh verse 6364.

LYNNE, Walter, *Printer (DNB).* Prose 3015 = 17117, 12104, 14576.

LYNOLD, Edmund, *of Healing, Lincs.* [suspended vicar, CSPD 1635]. *See* 10453.

LYON, Frederick, *Brother of next.* St. Andrews (Leonard) *Theses, 1618-*O.[6]

LYON, James, *Brother of John II Earl.* 18065, St. Andrews (Leonard) *Theses, 1618-*O.[6]

LYON, John, *Louvain printer.* Prose 3802.

LYON, John, *II Earl of Kinghorne.* *20658, St. Andrews (Leonard) *Theses, 1617-*O.; *see* 10667.

LYON, William, *Bishop of Cork.* 24122.

LYTTON *or* LITTON, *Sir* Rowland, *of Knebworth* (Venn 1576). *¶25677 [see changes], M. A., *Short catechisme, 1592-*F.

M

M. ¶13491 [*Gent.*]; epistle 3747 [*melancholicke friend*].

MIA [? *Master I. A.*]. Verse 3544.

M., A. (14373) *see* ALEX. MONTGOMERIE; (21274) *see* ANDREW MELVILLE.

M., A. [*perhaps* Andrew Melville]. Verse 17138, 17816, Hume frag.-F. akin to 13949.

M., A. [*believed* Anthony Munday]. Edits 3189; prose 19447 [M. A. in variant issue; probably translator].

M., A., '*Sister of author*'. 17136.

M., A. 25779-C. by editor; edits 12430.

MAR., Anth. Verse 24593.

M., B. R. (*1621* of 10442). *See* BART. ROBERTSON.

M., C. [*probably* Christopher Marlowe]. Edits 25117.

M., C. Verse 18948; *see* 19511.

MA., Cl., *Med.* Verse 13144.

M., Da. 1439 (1435).

M., D. T. C. (25483). *See* T. C.

M., E. (2418 = 16599) *see* MILLAR; (11943) *see* MAHONIDES.

M., *Lady* E. F. de La Croix, *Little garden, 1626-*M. by editor.

M., E. Verse 21029 [? Michelborne], 21620; *see* 20040.

M., F. Epistle 16658.

M., F. L. D. S. *See* JOHN JONES, *d. 1636.*

M., G. (20980). *See* MARCELLINE.

M., G., *Esq.* [*probably* George Mainwaring]. *See* 25438.

M., M[*aster*] G., *in Gratious street* [*fiction*]. 19399 [cf. M. N. in 22994].

M., G. Verse 3978, *1622*-C.[6] of 11122; sisters of, *see* GREGORY MARTIN.

M., H. Verse 10693, 11081, 11636, 13170.

M., J. [*portrait versifier*]. Verse or inscription 13624, 20652, 25896.

M., I. [*believed* James Mabbe]. Verse 22273.

M., I., *Gentlewoman* [? Mordaunt]. *See* GREENWOOD, *Ioyfull tractate, 1616*-L. (12327).

M., I., *Londinensis.* Verse 6578.

M., I., *Esq.* Verse (with answer) 3508.

M., I., *Gent.* Verse 13776, 24096.

M., I. [*Scottish*]. Verse 5956, 14786.

M., I. Edits 15056 [*probably* Markham]; verse 1999, 12171, 14608 [of Cambridge?], 15466, 18911; prose 3637, 4199.

I★M
F } Cipher [? of author] in 716.
A★M

M., Io. Verse 20309.

M., I., S. (22274). *See* I. M. S.

M., L. A. B. V. *See* ANTHONY BROWNE, *II Viscount.*

M., L., *vtcumque* P. Verse 15555.

M., L[*ady*] M. 1839 and *1621*-ST.

M., M., *C.P.M.D.E.E.P.C.* (667). *See* MICHAEL MAIER.

M., M. [?*Clergyman*]. Edits 18925.

M., P. Verse 21029 (21032) [of Oxford?], 23970 only.

M., R. Edits 6103, 10094; verse 778, 6364, 15192, 17997 with reply; prose 17303 [? Marbeck]; wife of, presentation 18633 by R. M.

M., Rodolphus. Verse 12632-F.

M., R. A. D. (20187). *See* R. A.

M., R. L. [*presumably* Robert Le Maçon]. Verse 18157 and *1578*-F.

M., S. Verse 22631, 22790.

M., T., *Anabaptist* (19489). *See* THOMAS MANNERING.

M., T. (24926a, 24928). *See* THOMAS MOTTERSHED.

M., T. Becon, *Cristian praiers, 1569*-L.[2] [? earlier lost]; verse 15685, 17201, 23123; *see* 13918.

M., Tho. Verse 1411.

M., W. [*probably* William Malim]. *See* 25438.

M., W., *Coelum non Solum.* Verse 24062.

M., W., *Esq.* [*perhaps* William Mathew]. Verse 19338.

M., W. Verse 778, 12885, 13988, 17203, 25786 [initials later dropped].

MAB *or* MABBE, James, *Scholar* (*DNB*). Verse 11099, probably 22273 as I. M.

MABB, Ralph, *Bookseller.* Signed prose 631, 974, 12502; unsigned perhaps 21094.

MACALPINE *or* MACHABAEUS, Christian, *Son of next.* Edits 17174; verse 16827.

MACALPINE *or* MACHABAEUS, John, *Reformer* (*DNB*). *See* 15672 only.

MACARNESSE, Thomas. Verse 22790.

McCALL, David, *Treasurer of Edinburgh, alias* MAKALL, MACKALD. ★88, ★23262; epistle ★18360.

MacCALL, Mungo, *Bailie of Edinburgh, alias* MACALA, MACAIL. ★5927 (5909), W. M., ★*Edinburghs alphabet*-E.

MacCARTY, Charles, *I Viscount Muskerry.* *See* 10667.

MacDONNELL, Randal, *I Marquis of Antrim.* 11159; *see* 10667 [perhaps intended for his father].

MACKGILL, James, *Clerk register* (*DNB*). Certifies 21875, 21879–82.

MAKGILL, James, *I Viscount Oxfuird.* *See* 10667.

MAKGILL, Robert, *Lord Foord, College of Justice.* Verse D. Primrose, *Apologie for advocates, 1628*-ROSEBERY.

MACHABAEUS. *See* MACALPINE.

MACHELL (Aungier), Elizabeth = John (*Vis. Surrey*). Epistle ★11763.

MACILMAINE (Makilmenaeus), Roland, *of St. Andrews.* Edits 15242 and *1574*-F.

MACHIN, Lewis, *Author* (*DNB*). Verse 1429.

MACKAY, Donald, *I Lord Reay.* 14929; see 10667.

MACKENZIE, Colin, *I Earl of Seaforth.* *¶22567, 25214 (25207), St. Andrews (Leonard) *Theses*, 1614-E.²; see 10667.

MACKENZIE, Patrick. Verse 14929.

MACLELLAN, Robert, *I Lord Kirkcudbright. See* 10667.

McNACHT, John, *Dean of gild, Edinburgh.* *88, *138 only, *13258, *23262, W. M., *Edinburghs alphabet*-E.

MACWILLIAM, Henry, *Gentleman pensioner* (*CSPD*). *884, 5797; prose *884, 5797.

MACY, Henry, *Somerset clergyman* (Foster 1606). Epistle *1941 as Masy.

MADD, I., '*Student at Douay*' [*untraced*]. *See* 657 = 24903.

MADEN, Richard, *B.D.* (Venn 1611). Prose 24142.

MADDESTON *or* MADESON, Edward, '*of St. Andrew Hubbard, London*'. *20678 (20668) by editor.

MADDISON, Henry, *Mayor of Newcastle upon Tyne.* 14488.

MADDISON, Lionel, *the elder, Mayor of New-castle.* *1335 (1336).

MADDISON, Sir Lionel, *Mayor of Newcastle* (Venn 1612). *12202.

MAERCKT, Joannes van der. *557 and *1629-HD.* [from foreign].

MAERS (5906). Misprint for Masters.

MAGENNIS, Hugh, *II Viscount Magennis. See* 10667.

MAGIRUS, A. Verse 2774, 20506.

MAGUIRE, Connor, *II Baron Maguire. See* 10667.

MAHAT, Philip, *M.A.* (Foster). Edits 15134.

MAHONIDES *alias* CHRISTOPHER, Edward [*pseudonym of* Francis Godwin]. Name or initials used in 11938, 11941, 11943, 11944.

MAIER, Michael, *Alchemist* (*NBG*). Epistle and verse 667.

MAINWARING, MAYNWARING, MANNERING, etc.

MAINWARING, Sir Arthur, *of Ightfield, d. 1590. See* 25438.

MAINWARING, Sir Arthur, *Carver to Prince Henry, son of next.* *605 by bookseller, 24063 by bookseller.

MAINWARING, Sir George, *of Ightfield, d. 1628.* *†605 by bookseller, 25440; see 25438.

MANWARING, George, *Bishop of St. David's. See* 10667.

MAINWARING, Sir Henry, *Sea captain* (Foster). Epistle 6343.

MAINWARING, John, *Son of next.* Verse 17201 as Egnirawniam.

MAINWARING, Matthew, *Romancist* (*DNB*). 18318.

MAINWARING, Matthew, *Son of preceding.* Verse 17201 as Egnirawniam.

MANWARING, Matthew, *Son-in-law of M. Hanmer* (*CSPI* 1628). Prose one issue 25067a.

MAINWARING, Ralph, *Son of Matthew-DNB.* Verse 17201 as Egnirawniam.

MAINWARING, Sir Randall *the younger* (*Vis. Ches.*). *¶23720.

MANWARING, Randolph, *City captain.* *21095; epistle *1507.

MANNERING, Thomas, *Anabaptist burnt at Norwich 1597. See* 19489 as T. M.

MAINWARING, Thomas, *Son of Matthew-DNB.* ¶13340; verse 17201 as Samoth Egnirawniam; see 13327 plate i.

MAITLAND (Metellanus), John, *I Lord Mait-land, Chancellor.* †5192 by printer, ¶6217; verse 4473, 14380 (14344, 14346).

MAITLAND, John, *I Earl of Lauderdale.* †12481, 14710, *¶22567, 26107, St. Andrews (Leonard) *Theses*, [*1610*]-o.⁶; see 10667.

MAKGILL, etc. *See* MACGILL, etc.

MALAVICUS, Hermes. Verse 667.

MALCOLM, M[aster] I. [presumably John, *Minister at Perth*]. Verse 14376, 14380.

MALENUS, Joannes. 6818.

MALIM, William, *Schoolmaster* (*DNB*). Edits 4938; verse 6577, 12188; see 25438; see also W. M.

MALONE, William, *S.J.* (*DNB*). *See* 24542 as W. B.

MALYNES, Gerard, *Economic writer* (*DNB*). Prose 5584.

MAN, Bartholomew, *of Bath Abbey parish.* Verse 14793.

MANN (Colfe), Elizabeth = Thomas *Draper (Vis. London).* *25790.

MAN, John, *Schoolmaster* (Venn 1589). Prose 13877.

MAN, Jonas, *Bookseller.* Prose 4177.

MAN, Richard. Verse 13480.

MAN, Thomas, *the elder, Bookseller.* Signed prose 11871, 22717; unsigned 3768, 5390, 25625 [revised and signed 25626 (25620)].

MANBY, William, *Treasurer of the Artillery Company.* *1505.

MANFIELD, Henry, *of Cliveden (Vis. Bucks.).* 4603.

MANFIELD, Thomas, *Bailiff of Yarmouth.* *26097.

MANNERING. *See* MAINWARING.

MANNERS, *Lady* Briget. *See* TYRWHITT.

MANNERS (Tufton), Cecily = Francis *VI Earl.* *3894, 17128.

MANNERS, Edward, *III Earl of Rutland.* 17790.

MANNERS (Sidney), Elizabeth = Roger *V Earl.* 17386, *18041 [see changes].

MANNERS (Montagu), Frances = John *VIII Earl.* *1888 = 1889.

MANNERS, Francis, 'Lord Roos', *d. 1620.* 18170.

MANNERS, Francis, *VI Earl of Rutland.* 1362, *17699, 22444; *see* 17331.

MANNERS, Sir George, *Father of John VIII Earl.* *†25254 by bookseller.

MANNERS, George, *VII Earl of Rutland.* 16945; *see* 10667.

MANNERS (Holcroft), Isabel = Edward *III Earl.* 18418 by bookseller; *see* Norden's map of Surrey, *1594*-L.

MANNERS, Sir John, *of Haddon Hall, son of I Earl.* *25254 by bookseller; epistle *1603-CHI. version of 24600.

MANNERS, Roger, *V Earl of Rutland.* *11908 [see changes]; epistle 6333; *see* 6789 as E. of R., 25695.

MANNING, Ralph, 'of London'. T. Wilcox, *Christian exposition, 1587*-F. (25620).

MAUNSELL, Andrew, *Bookseller (DNB).* Unsigned prose 4072 = 10672, 4858.

MANSELL, Sir Edward, *of Margam, grandfather of Sir Walter below.* Epistle *1095 (1077) as Manxell.

MANSELL (Sidney), Elizabeth Catherine = *Sir* Lewis *II Bt.* 11544; epistle 1598.

MANSELL, John, *President of Queens'* (Venn 1594). Prose 4477.

MAUNSELL, John [*perhaps* Foster 1600]. Edits 26077.

MANSELL, *Lady* Katherine. *See* ELIZABETH *above.*

MANSELL, Sir Robert, *Admiral (DNB).* *¶4497, *17388 (17390), *¶21869, engr. print *Councell of warr*-L.[5]

MAUNSELL, Thomas, *of Middle Temple.* Mock licence in 6308.

MANSELL, Sir Walter, *II Bt.* Verse 23352.

MANSFIELD, Ernst von, *Count (STC).* 20980.

MANTHORPE, Thomas, *Bailiff of Yarmouth.* *21093.

MANWOOD, Bowes *and* Frances, *Daughters of Sir Peter.* Epistle 3917 (25890).

MANWOOD, Dorothy *and* Elizabeth. *See* BARNES *and* WALSINGHAM.

MANWOOD, Sir Peter, *Antiquary (DNB).* 3193, *11127, 15485 = 19800, 17092, 18154, ¶23582a (23575, 21653), 24564; prose 25731; *see* 15051.

MANWOOD, Sir Roger, *Judge (DNB).* Epistle 21864.

MANXELL. *See* MANSELL.

MAPES, Richard, *Master of Barber Surgeons.* *24577; epistle *25962.

MAPLESDEN, John, *Archdeacon of Suffolk* (Venn 1562). Approbation in 737.

MARBECK, Rob. [*perhaps misprint for next*]. Verse 1892.

MARBECK (Marbeccus), Roger, *Provost of Oriel (DNB).* Prose 1924.

MARBURY or MERBURY, Francis, *Clergyman* (Venn). Prose 21215, 21286.

MARBURY, Thomas, *of Marbury (Vis. Ches.).* *7293.

MARCELLINE, George, *Writer (STC).* Edits 20980 as G. M.

MARCHAM. *See* MARKHAM.

MAREES, Joannes de. 557 and *1629*-HD. [from foreign].

MARENZIO, Luca, *Italian musician* (Grove). Verse 25119; prose 7091.

MARGARET, *Duchess of Burgundy, d. 1503* (*DNB*). 15375.

MARGARETE, *or allegorically*, Holy Church. ¶5068 (Usk, *Testament*).

MARIA, *Infanta, daughter of Philip III*. All jointly with Charles I: 42, 17956; epistle 7376.

MARINO, Giovanni Battista, *Italian poet* (*NBG*). Verse 345.

MARIUS (Marie), Nathaniel, *Pastor of French Church*. ★7358 by editor; *see* 23920 and 23923.

MARJORIBANKS, Joseph, *Dean of gild, Edinburgh*. ★13173, W. M., ★*Edinburghs alphabet-*E.; epistle ★18360.

MARKHAM, Gervase, *Author* (*DNB*). Edits 3314 as G. M., 13202; prose 15555.

MARKHAM, *Sir* John, *Lieutenant of the Tower*. 1499 as Marcham.

MARKHAM, Robert, *of Cottam, father of Gervase*. 17346.

MARKHAM, Valentine, *Merchant* (*Vis. London*). Prose 17224.

MARLOWE, Christopher, *Dramatist* (*DNB*). *See* C. M.

MARMION, Shackerley, *Dramatist* (*DNB*). Verse 11070, 13358, 13367, 25227.

MARPRELATE, Martin [*Pseudonym*], *including* Martin Junior, *etc*. ★12914, 17463, 19456, 26030; epistle 17452, 17457, 19457; *see* 681 = 15102.

MARQUIZIUS, Lazarus, 'Rei medicinae C.' Verse 21657.

MARRIOT, John, *Bookseller*. Verse 7045 [answered in 7046]; signed prose 11993, 16774, 25903 (25912); unsigned 17733.

MARSH *or* MERSH, John, *Governor of Merchant Adventurers*. ★19548.

MARSHE, Thomas, *Printer*. Prose 17114.

MARSH, Thomas, *Esq*. [*perhaps* Venn 1581]. 22142.

MARSHALL, Fulk, *of Clare College* (Venn). Verse 23278 as Martialis.

MARSHALL, Hamlet, *D.D.* (Venn). Minsheu List.

MARTIALL, John, *Divine* (*DNB*). 4368; prose 12759.

MARSHALL, Io. Verse 12748.

MARSHALL, Ralph, *of Carleton* (*Vis. Notts.*). †17206.

MARSHALL, William, *Printer* (*DNB*). Presumably edited 15986, etc.

MARSTON, John, *Dramatist* (*DNB*). 17486 by himself; verse 14782 only.

MARSTON (Powle), Mary. *See* CHENEY.

MARTIALIS *and* MARTIALL. *See* MARSHALL.

MARTIN, Anthony, *Bishop of Meath*. Verse 24551.

MARTIN (Ecclestone), Dorcas = *Sir* Richard. 20580 [earlier lost, ent. 4 Oct. 1585].

MARTIN, Edward, *Dean of Ely* (*DNB*). *See* 13518; book licenser *1630-1*.

MARTYN, Edward, *Son of William-DNB*. Verse 17526.

MARTYN (Castelyn), Elizabeth = *Sir* Roger. 6039.

MARTIN (Grey), Elizabeth = James *M.A. below*. *See* 23580.

MARTIN, Gregory, *Translator* (*DNB*), *unnamed sisters of*. ¶17507 whence 17504 [falsely dated].

MARTEN, *Sir* Henry, *Civilian* (*DNB*). 108, 3133, 6598, 17525, 17606 (17612), 17824, 18997, (21720), 20929; prose 23345.

MARTIN, Humfrey, *Mercer, son of Sir Roger*. 15191 [o. is earlier ed.].

MARTIN, Isaac, *Germanus* (Foster). Anagram 4746 (17509).

MARTIN, James, *Provost of Salvator's, St. Andrews*. Salvator *Theses*, ★*1603*-E. and [*1610*]-O.[6]

MARTIN, James, *M.A., preacher* (Foster 1604). 16803 = 16804; edits 23580, supposedly 19020.

MARTIN, James, 'S. Theol. candidatus'. Edits 25369.

MARTIN, John, *Vicar of New Windsor*. Minsheu List.

MARTYN, *Sir* Nicholas, *Son of William-DNB*. 17530; verse 17526.

MARTIN, *Sir* Richard, *Lord Mayor* (*DNB*). 4169 by bookseller, 4427 (4429), 4924, 5840, 11852, 17695, 18261, 26018.

MATTHEW, Tobie, *Archbishop of York.* 1012, *1364, 1467, 1814, 1815, *1829, 1941 [see changes], 1958, 4610 by editor, 5659, 7077, 10716, 11732, 11814, 12940, 13472 [paste-on slip in L., only copy found; see changes], ¶13799, 14088, 14267, 17470 (*Five sermons, 1627-*NY.[II], *17698 [*1614-*HD. a frag.], 19770, 23452, 23548 [see changes], 25195, *25394 (25389), *¶25682 (25685).
Epistle: 16696; *see* 17331, 25373.
Household of: R. Bernard, *Sinners safetie, 1609-*HD.

MATTHEW, William, *M.P. for Glamorgan* (PCC 1587). Epistle *1095 (1077).

MATHEW, William, *Esq.* Verse 19775; *see* W. M., *Esq.*

MATHEWE, William, '*Kinsman of author*'. Verse 23352.

MATTHIAS, *Emperor.* *17699.

MATTOCK, Anthony, *Rector of Westford* (Venn). 5680.

MAULDAEUS, John, *Germanus* (Foster). Verse further piece 21661-F. (21649).

MAULE, Patrick, *I Earl of Panmure.* *10530 only.

MAULEVERER, James, *the elder, of Arncliffe, Yks.* *14297a.

MAUNSELL. *See* MANSELL.

MAURICE, *Landgrave of Hesse-Cassel.* *3875; *see* 19511.

MAURICE, *Prince of Orange, d. 1625.* *12858 and *1613-*HD., *22103 (22064), sometimes 11810 accidentally from loss of title paste-over.

MAURITIUS (19302). *See* MORRIS.

MAURUS, Terentianus (825). Signature seemingly to preface actually applies to quoted line of verse that follows.

MAWDISLEY, Thomas, '*of Lincoln College, Sussex preacher*'. *See* 13923.

MAWE, Leonard, *Bishop of Bath and Wells.* N. Taylour, *Meditations, 1627-*ILL.; epistle some copies *4747-O.

MAXEY, Anthony, *Dean of Windsor* (DNB). Minsheu List.

MAXEY Henry, *of Lincoln's Inn* (Venn 1624). *See* 15466.

MAXWELL, David. Verse 18167 as Maxuellius.

MAXWELL, James, *Master of Maxwell, brother of Robert I Earl.* *17699.

MAXWELL, James, *Author* (DNB). *See* 7547.

MAXWELL, James, *Groom of Bedchamber and Black Rod.* *1203.

MAXWELL, John, *III Earl of Nithsdale.* *See* 10667.

MAXWELL, John, *Archbishop of Tuam.* *See* 10667.

MAXWELL, Robert, *I Earl of Nithsdale.* *See* 10667.

MAXWELL, Robert, *Bishop of Kilmore.* Verse 15498, 15499.

MAY, Edward, *Chaplain of Lincoln's Inn.* Minsheu List.

MAY, Edward, *Poet* (STC). Verse 14788.

MAY, Henry, *Separatist elder at Amsterdam* (Burrage). *18789.

MAY, Sir Humphrey, *Statesman* (DNB). 15193a.

MAY, Thomas, *Author* (DNB). Verse 351, 11877, 13554, 17642, 19925, 21470, 21624, 22460, 23447; *see* 1393.

MAYERNE, James, *Son of next.* Verse 7476.

MAYERNE, Sir Theodore, *Physician* (DNB). *¶14704; edits 17993; prose 19300, 19302; *see* 16777, 17709.

MAYNARD, Sir John, *Brother of next* (Venn 1612). R. Aylett, ¶*Brides ornaments, 1625-*F.

MAYNARD, William, *I Baron Maynard.* 1004, 3919, †21202, A. Darcie, *Way to immortality, 1635-*F.; epistle *25025, R. Aylett, *Brides ornaments, 1625-*F.; *see* 10667.

MAYNE, Jasper, *Dramatist* (DNB). Verse 7045, 21351.

MAYNSON, Oliver. Verse 24603.

MAYO, John, *Clergyman* (Foster 1583 and STC). Verse 5582.

MEEDE, Edward, '*Merchant adventurer at Hamburg*'. ¶16684.

MEDE, Sir John, *of Wendon Loft* (Venn 1608). 12083 (12071).

MEADE, Richard. Verse 22796.

MEAD, Robert, *Poet* (DNB). Verse 5906.

MEADE, Thomas, *Judge* (Foss). 12907, 13020.

MEADE, Sir Thomas, *Son of preceding* (Venn 1582). 12909.

MEARES. *See* MERES.

MEASE, Peter, *B.D.* (Venn). Verse 14269 as Measius.

MEAUTYS, *Sir* Thomas, *Clerk of Privy Council.* 20165 as Mewtys.

MEDE *and* MEEDE. *See* MEADE.

MEDICI, Cosimo II, *Grand duke of Tuscany.* 1153.

MEDOWE, *Sir* Thomas, *Mayor of Yarmouth.* ★21093.

MEETKERK, Edward, *M.A.* (Foster). Minsheu List.

MEG, *Long, of Westminster.* Ghost-written prose 23706.

MEIGHEN, Richard, *Bookseller.* Epistle 19333 unnamed; prose 5371, 11977, 11980.

MELANCHTHON, Philipp, *Reformer* (NBG). ★1304 [from foreign original]; verse 17174; *see* 5290, 10674.

MELHUISH, Helen, '*Mother of author*'. 24331.

MELISSUS, Paul, *Schedius, savant* (NBG). Verse 2032 = 2357, 3988 and 3990 [all from foreign eds.].

MELITITYRUS [*Pseudonym*]. Verse 12964.

MELLER. Listed with Miller.

MELLIS, John, *Southwark schoolmaster* (DNB). Edits 18794, 20802.

MELTON, Evan, *Father of next.* 17804.

MELTON, *Sir* John, *Politician* (DNB). Verse 10784.

MELTON, Richard, *Stepfather of John Foxe-DNB.* 20847.

MELVILLE (Melvinus), Andrew, *Presbyterian leader and scholar* (DNB). ¶13950, T. Mierbekius, ★*Theses*-E.²; epistle 7547; verse 3990, 3991, 4660, 6217, 13245, 14293, 14786, 14787, 21274 as A. M. [fewer in first issue-E.²], 22186, 25239, W. Welwood, *Aurei tituli,* 1605-L.¹³; *see also* A. M.

MAL-VILL, Elizabeth. *See* COLVILLE.

MELVILLE, James, *Reformer* (DNB). ★18171; verse 21271.

MELVILLE, Patrick, *Professor at St. Andrews.* T. Mierbekius, ★*Theses*-E.²

MELVINUS. *See* MELVILLE.

MEMPHITOS, Joannes [*untraced*]. Greek verse 12346.

MENDOZA, Bernardino de, *Spanish ambassador* (NBG). *See* 7570, 15412 and French and Italian versions-HD.

MENYMAN, William, '*Fellow of Whittington college*'. *See* 18846.

MENZIES, *Sir* Paul, *Provost of Aberdeen.* ★1494, ★1495, 21099, ★22472, ★25189, W. Mercer, ★*Bon-acords decorement, 1633*-E.

MERBURY. *See* MARBURY.

MERCATOR, Gerardus, *Geographer* (NBG). 6463 (15483).

MERCERUS (Mercier), Josias, *Scholar* (NBG). Verse 21673.

MERCURIE, Mihill, '*Pothecarie*' [*fiction*]. Verse 19975.

MEREDITH, William. 14595.

MERES, Francis, *Divine and author* (DNB). Verse 257.

MERES, Francis, *the younger, Son of preceding* (Venn 1625). Verse 20692.

MEARES, George, *Gent.* Verse 12299.

MERES, *Sir* John, *of Aubourn* (Vis. Lincs.). 17833.

MEERE, Will., '*Tavern keeper, Ship, Old Bailey*'. Epistle 3585.

MEIRICIUS *or* MERRICK. *See* MEYRICK.

MERIELL, MERRILLS, etc. *Listed with* MYRIELL.

MERY, Francis, '*London merchant*'. 20779.

MERRY-MATE, Martin [*fiction*]. Verse 22645.

MERSH. *See* MARSH.

MERVYN, James. Verse 22454.

MESLIER, Hugo, *Apparently a bookseller.* ¶16899 and perhaps editor.

METAXAS, Nicodemus. Edits 15083.

METCALFE, Robert, *Regius professor* (DNB). ★18206; licence ★13518.

METELLANUS. *See* MAITLAND.

METELLUS (Matal), Johannes, *Sequanus, scholar* (NBG). Verse 21657.

METFORD, John, *M.A.* (Foster). Verse 91.

METHAM, *Sir* Thomas, *of the Inner Temple* (Venn 1591). 20561, †¶21638; Minsheu List.

METHWIN, Anthony, *Clergyman* (Foster 1595). Epistle ★1941.

MEVERALL, Othowell, *Physician* (DNB). ★¶14704; verse 19300; prose 21426; Minsheu List.

MEWS, Peter, *Bishop of Winchester.* Verse 22888.

MEWTYS. *See* MEAUTYS.

MEYRICK, *Sir* Gelly. *Conspirator* (*DNB*). 24621 (24608) as Meiricius.

MEYRICK, *Sir* John, *Ambassador, d. 1638* (*DNB*). Early issue only *19566-F.

MEYRICK, Rowland, *Bishop of Bangor.* *1710.

MICHAEL, David (15369). *Presumably* Mitchell.

MICHAELL, Edward. Verse 11564 and re-issues.

MICHAELSON, John, *Controversialist* (*STC*). Verse 18360; *see* 4354.

MICHELBORNE, Edward, *Poet* (*DNB*). ¶10934; verse 1311, 1560, 4012, 10934, 23294.

MICHELBORNE, Lawrence, 'of Gloucester Hall' [*at Oxford but not in* Foster]. ¶10934; verse 21029 (21032).

MICHELBORNE, Thomas, *of Gray's Inn, brother of Edward.* ¶10934; verse 1468, 10944, 23294, 24610.

MITCHELL (Meldrum), Barbara = Thomas *Minister of Turriff.* Epistle 17857 as Michel.

MITCHELL, David, *Bishop of Aberdeen.* Presumably verse 15369 as Michael.

MICHELL, Humfrey, *Surveyor of Windsor, father of Sir Francis-DNB.* 17301.

MYCHELL, John, *Printer.* Prose 9968.

MICHELL, Roger, *Bookseller. See* 5569 as Muchill.

MICHELL, Thomas, 'Parson of Hurst' [*presumably* PCC 1615]. *See* 13923.

MICHELL, Th. Verse 12066.

MICKLEBOUND, Miles [*Pseudonym*]. *See* 1525.

MIDDLETON family, *of Wales.* 2744 = 17915 by printer.

MYDDELTON (Vanacker), Ann = *Sir* Thomas *Mayor.* 21620.

MIDDLETON, Gilbert, *M.A., King's College, Aberdeen.* Verse 16930.

MIDDLETON, Richard, *Divine* (*DNB*). Minsheu List.

MIDLETON, Theodorus [? *Franciscan*]. Verse B. Jackson, *Manuductions,* 1616-F.

MYDDELTON, *Sir* Thomas, *Lord Mayor* (*DNB*). *2744 = 17915, *5062, *12750, 14676, *17886, 17903, 17914, 18589, *18995, *19513, 20986, *¶25699.

MIDDLETON, Thomas, *Dramatist* (*DNB*). Edits 3001 [cf. 5560]; verse 25176 only.

MYDDELTON, William, *Poet* (*DNB*). Verse 19775.

MIDDLETON, William, *London merchant* [? *and alderman*]. *5533.

MILBOURNE, Richard, *Bishop of Carlisle. See* 12662 (12706, 12635).

MILBOURNE, Robert, *Bookseller.* Epistle 12963 with reply; perhaps unsigned prose 39, 5361, 13270, 24703.

MILBOURNE, William, *Parson of Brancepeth and mathematician* (Venn). Edits 17918.

MILDMAY (Gourdon), Amy = *Sir* Henry *of Graces.* *21187 and *1627*-HD.

MILDMAY, *Sir* Anthony, *Ambassador* (*DNB*). 21080.

MILDMAY, Anthony, *Brother of Sir Henry below.* Du Moulin, *Elegant combat,* 1634-F. [rival version of 7344].

MILDMAY (Ratcliffe), Frances = *Sir* Thomas *of Mulsham, Essex. Tarletons tragical treatises,* 1578-F. [frag.].

MILDMAY, *Sir* Henry, *Master of the jewel house* (*DNB*). *7307 by bookseller, ¶12657a (12635), 18497.

MILDMAY (Crofts), Jane = *Sir* Humphrey. Epistle 19909.

MILDMAY (Deane), Joan = Robert *of Tarling and alderman.* *¶1477.

MILDMAY, *Sir* Walter, *Chancellor of the Exchequer* (*DNB*). 5263, 5314, 6577, 7498, *11839, 12905, 13061, 17408, *19101, *25888, L. Rosius, *Echo*-L.; *see* 24020, C. Bill, *Genethliacon* [1586]-O.

MILICHIUS, Georgius, 'of Ratisbon'. Verse 10674.

MILL *and* MILLES. *See* MILLS.

MILLEN, ——, 'Lieutenant, Middlesex militia'. Epistle *5668.

MILLAR, Edward, *Music master, Edinburgh Chapel Royal.* Edits 2418 = 16599.

MILLER, George, *Printer.* Prose 1888 = 1889, 3243 (3224).

MELLER, Jasper, *of Dorset* (Foster). *14745.

MILLER, John, *Master of Leathersellers.* *1600-BO. of 21288 [see changes].

MILLER, John, *Captain. See* MILWARD.

MELLER, Laurence, *Brother of Jasper.* *14745.

MILLICENT, *Sir* John, *Sergeant-porter* (Venn). 23754 (23725).

MILLINGTON, Thomas, *Bookseller*. Prose 14433 = 17153.

MILLES, Francis, *M.A.* (Foster). Edits 15000 and possibly 15005.

MILLS, James, *Deputy clerk of Privy Seal* (*CSPD*). Minsheu List.

MILLES, Thomas, *Customer* (*DNB*). Edits 11922.

MILL, Thomas, *Brother of author* (Foster 1620). Verse 17921.

MILLS, William, *Esq.* 18344 (18337).

MILLOT, Thomas, *of Whitehill, Durham, d. 1620.* ¶5332 as My-lot [see changes].

MILNER, Thomas, *Mayor of King's Lynn.* T. Purchas, *Communicants duty, 1639*-PN.[2]

MILTON, John, *Poet* (*DNB*). Unsigned verse 22274 [initialed in 22344].

MILWARD (——), —— = *Sir Robert.* ¶4577.

MILWARD, John, *Master of Vintners and city captain.* *5533 by editor, *18901 as Miller.

MILWARD (Fleetwood), Katherine = William. 23398.

MILWARD, Matthias, *Divine* (*DNB*). *128 (107); edits 17942; verse 25224; see 12662 (12706, 12635).

MILWARD, William, *of Eaton Dovedale, Derby.* *†21437; epistle *1603-CHI. of 24600 [see changes].

MINGAY, John, *Mayor of Norwich.* 426 for 1618-L.[2]

MINGAY, John. Verse 15036.

MINSHULL, Richard, *of Nantwich* (*Vis. Ches.*). 17201; verse 17201.

MINUTELIUS, Philip, *Obscure assistant to Secretary of State.* Coranto licenser *1640; also see SR 9 se. *1640* [book untraced].

MIRA GUARDA [*Anagram or motto of an Oxford don*]. Verse 3683, 4759, 4762, 24042.

MIROCINIUS [*Pseudonym*]. Verse 7232 only.

MISSELDEN, Edward, *Merchant* (*DNB*). Minsheu List.

MITCHELL. *Listed with* MICHELL.

MNEMOSYNE, *Mother of the muses.* J. Patridophilus, *Preservative poem, 1636*-BO.[4]

MOCKET, Richard, *D.D.* (*DNB*). See 5811; licenses 12550.

MOERIS (7253). *See* DAVID MURRAY.

MOFFETT, Thomas, *Physician* (*DNB*). 19064.

MOFFET, William, *Vicar of Edmonton* (Venn). Verse 13554, 13555.

MOHUN, John, *I Baron Mohun.* 17636; see 10667.

MOHUN, Sir Reginald, *I Bt.* 10938.

MOHUN, Sir William, *of Boconnoc, father of preceding.* ¶18777, 25977 as Moune.

MOLIN, Domenico, *Venetian senator* (*CSPV*). 10704.

MOLINES, James, *Surgeon, d. 1639* (*DNB*). Epistle *11203.

MOLINUS, MOLINAEUS. *See* MOLIN, MOLINES, *and* MOULIN.

MOLLE, Henry, *Cambridge orator and composer* (Venn *and* Grove). Edits 4530; verse 12964; see 24099.

MOLLE, John, *Translator, inquisition prisoner, father of preceding.* Edits 18162; see 12662 (12706, 12635).

MOLYNEUX, Edmund, *of Thorpe* (*Vis. Notts.*). 11502.

MOLYNEUX (Gerard), Frances = *Sir Richard Bt.* 11055.

MOLYNEUX, Sir Richard, *I Bt.* 3921, ¶25224.

MOLYNEUX, Richard, *I Viscount Molyneux.* *1628*-L. of 7342 [see changes], ¶23720; see 10667.

MOLYNS or MULLINS, John, *Archdeacon of London* (*DNB*). *3048, *4403, ¶11760.

MOMFORD. *See* MOUNDFORD.

MOMPESSON, Sir Giles, *Politician* (*DNB*). Minsheu List as Mount-Person.

MOMUS. Numerous verses to Momus are not indexed; verses by, 18498.

MONACHUS. *See* LE MOYNE.

MO(U)NCASTER, MONDFORD, MONTFORT. *See* MULCASTER *and* MOUNDFORD.

MONIPENNY, David, *Dean, St. Andrews.* St. Andrews (Salvator) *Theses, 1603*-E.

MONRO, John, *Colonel, brother of the author.* See 18022.

MONRO, Robert, *Colonel, d. 1633* (*DNB*). See 18022.

MOUNSON, John, '*of Charterhouse*' [*probably the next*]. 11523.

MONSON, Sir John, *II Bt.* ¶4548, 23819.

Monson, *Sir* Thomas, *I Bt.* 378, ¶4548, 5329, 7100, ¶7193 (7189, 7216), 15267, 21332.

Monson, *Sir* William, *Admiral (DNB)*. *¶4497, 15240 (15241).

Monson, William, *Viscount Monson. See* 10667.

Montagu. *See* "Ορος-ὀξύ.

Montagu, *Sir* Charles, *Brother of Edward I Baron*. *19731 (19649, cf. 19648) by editor.

Montagu, Christopher, *Son of Edward I Baron*. *1888 = 1889, *11463.

Montagu, *Sir* Edward, *of Boughton, father of next*. 17580, *19101.

Montagu, Edward, *I Baron M. of Boughton*. 1887, 3250, 12888, *19731 (19649, cf. 19648) by editor, 22801 by editor; *see* 10667, 17332.

Montagu, Edward, *II Baron Montagu*. *1888 = 1889, *11463, *11464.

Montagu, Edward, *II Earl of Manchester*. 4127, 22476 by editor, †22491 by editor; epistle one issue *4747-O.; *see* 10667.

Montagu (Harington), Elizabeth = *Sir* Edward. *4884, 19732 (19649) by editor.

Montagu, George, *Son of next*. Verse 6044a.

Montagu, Henry, *I Earl of Manchester*. *104, 120, 125, ¶1227, 4017, 5106, †5698, some copies *6014-CHI., 6205, †7151 (7143), 10717 by printer, *11496, 12013, 12430 by editor [see changes], 13455, *18263, *19731 (19649, cf. 19648) by editor, *23331 [see changes], *24132 [see changes], 24394, 25648, D. Touteville, *Christian purposes*, 1622-HN.; presentation 17944; Minsheu List; *see* 10667, 17331, 23779 (23725).

Montagu, James, *Bishop of Winchester*. 1939 [see changes], 5944 (5909), 7113, ¶7125, 7145, 7469, 7474, *11496, 11965, 14314, *17698 [1614-HD. a frag.], 18323, *19731 (19649, cf. 19648) by editor, 19777 by editor, 22976, 23276, 24015 by printer [see changes], 24395, *Augustine his enchiridion*, 1607-HD.; epistle 6238; edits 14344, 14346; Minsheu List; *see* 5811, 12662 (12706, 12635); *see* "Ορος-ὀξύ.

Montagu (Crouch), Margaret = Henry *I Earl, previously* Hare. 7104 by editor.

Montagu, Richard, *Bishop of Norwich*. 14692, ¶18040; edits 12346; *see* 10300, 10667.

Montagu, *Sir* Sidney, *Master of requests* (Keeler). *19731 (19649, cf. 19648) by editor.

Montagu, *Sir* Walter, *Brother of preceding*. Like preceding.

Montagu, Walter, *Abbot (DNB)*. ¶21624.

Montagu, *Sir* William, *Judge (DNB)*. *1888 = 1889, *11463.

Montaigne or Mountain, George, *Archbishop of York*. 12178, 13260, 21708 (21705), R. Aylett, ¶*Brides ornaments*, 1625-F., possibly the unnamed bishop 17195; epistle 3926, 10689, 11189; pastoral letter sometimes 25375a; licenses 5816 [and earlier 5817], 22526; Minsheu List.

Montanus, Gulielmus [? Hill, *unidentified*]. Verse 4782.

Montchrétien, Antoine de, *Poet (NBG)*. Verse 10513.

Montcreif, Gilbert, *Physician to James I*. Epistle 13942.

Monteith, John, 'Officer under Col. Brog' [? *and son-in-law*]. Epistle 25939.

Montgomerie, Alexander, *Poet (DNB)*. Verse 14373 as A. M.

Montgomerie, Alexander, *VI Earl of Eglinton*. *¶22567; *see* 10667.

Montgomery, George, *Bishop of Meath and Clogher*. *1404 by editor.

Montgomery, Hugh, *I Viscount Montgomery*. *See* 10667 [possibly Hugh, II Viscount].

Montgomery, *Sir* James, *Son of preceding*. 17207.

Montgomery, Richard, 'of Shropshire'. Verse 24043.

Monyns, *Sir* William, *I Bt.* 3465 [title-page], *21175.

Moody, ——, 'of St. Antholin, London'. Epistle *12203.

Moody, *Sir* Henry, *II Bt.* Verse 17639.

Moore, ——, 'of St. Antholin, London'. Epistle *12203.

Moore, Mrs. ——, 'of Talmage hall, Briset'. 3087.

Moore, Adrian, *Haberdasher and merchant*, (PCC 1618). †3925 by editor, second issue-HD. †3922 by editor.

Moore, Charles, *II Viscount Drogheda. See* 10667.

MORE, Cresacre, *Biographer* (*DNB*). 18097 by printer, rewritten 18098.

MOORE, *Sir* Francis, *Lawyer* (*DNB*). *25263.

MORE, *Sir* George, *Lieutenant of the Tower* (*DNB*). ¶12917, ¶23806 only.

MORE, George, '*Captain, Southwark martial garden*'. *14922.

MORE, Jean. Verse 21735.

MOORE, John, '*Almoner, St. Bart's, Gloucester*'. *12171 only.

MOORE, John, *Serjeant-at-law, Lincoln's Inn.* *11670.

MORE, John, *Clerk of the Signet, Winwood's secretary.* Minsheu List.

MOORE (Morus), John [*Scottish*]. Verse 135, 24523.

MOORE (Borough?), Mary = Adrian, *Charity dispenser.* 6112 by editor, 6673, ¶12116.

MORE, Poynings, *of Loseley* (Keeler). 22389.

MOORE, Richard, *B.D.* (Foster 1593). Verse 18114.

MOORE, Richard, *Bookseller.* Prose 3192.

MORE, T. Verse 18496.

MORE, *Sir* Thomas, *Lord Chancellor and saint* (*DNB*). 24319; epistle Whittinton, *Epigrammata, 1519*-HN.; verse 13604 and earlier-ILL., 15635; *see* 11381 and 11387 (24436).

MOORE, Thomas, '*Parson of Wetheringsett, Suff.*' ¶1710.

MORAVIUS *and* MORAY. *See* MURRAY.

MORDAUNT (Howard), Elizabeth = John I Earl. *6270.

MORDAUNT, Henry, *IV Baron Mordaunt.* 21535.

MORDAUNT, Henry, *II Earl of Peterborough.* 12959.

MORDAUNT, John, *I Earl of Peterborough.* 11165, 19828; *see* 10667, 17332.

MORDAUNT, *Sir* Le Strange, *I Bt.* †12336 [earlier lost] (12327), †12337 (12327) [*see* changes], ¶21869.

MORDAUNT, *Sir* Robert, *II Bt.* H. Greenwood, †*Ioyfull tractate, 1616*-L. (12327).

MORE. *Listed with* MOORE.

MORGAN, Anthony, *D.D.* (Foster 1609). Minsheu List.

MORGAN, Cicilie, '*daughter of Marie*'. 20485 = 20106 [20486 anr. version].

MORGAN, *Sir* Edmund, *Veteran soldier* (*Vis. Soms.*). *23545.

MORGAN, John, *of the Inner Temple, 1610.* Verse 3914.

MORGAN (Golding), Margarite = *Sir* John *of Chilworth, Surrey.* 3216.

MORGAN, Philip, *of the Middle Temple, 1625.* *See* 15466.

MORGAN, William, *Bishop of St. Asaph.* *20148; verse 23895.

MORIN, Martin, *Rouen printer.* Verse 16233.

MORLEY, Henrietta Maria. *See* PRICE.

MORLEY, William, *of Glynde* (*Vis. Sussex*). *11367.

MORPHORIO [*fiction*]. Prose 3677; epistle 3679 as Morphorius.

MORRICE, MORRIS, etc.

MORRIS, Edward, '*Captain*'. Epistle and prose 3128.

MORRICE, Francis, *Clerk of the ordnance* (*CSPD*). 13263.

MORRIS, John, *Regius professor* (Foster 1609). *4259, *14457; prose 12612.

MORRICE, John, *Isleworth botanist.* Verse 19302, some as Mauritius.

MORRIS, John, *Esq. See* GREG 560(a).

MORICE, Nicholas, *of Corpus Christi* (Foster). Verse 4761, 4762.

MORRIS, Richard, *Gent.* 18864 by printer.

MORISIUS, Gulielmus. Verse 23229.

MORRISON, *Sir* Charles, *Father of next.* *†2051, *25622 (25620).

MORRISON, *Sir* Charles, *Bt.* ¶107, *23830.

MORRISON, Elizabeth (649). *See* CLINTON.

MORRISON, Henry, *Bailie of Edinburgh.* *13258.

MORISON, *Sir* Richard, *Ambassador* (*DNB*). Epistle *24673.

MORYSON, *Sir* Richard, *Lieutenant of ordnance* (*DNB*). *15325.

MORTIMER, John, *Bailie of Aberdeen.* *22471.

MORTON (Apsley), Elizabeth = *Sir* Albertus. *See* 19511.

MORTON, *Sir* George, *Father of George I Bt.* 4013, ¶20778.

MORTON *alias* MOURT, George, *Colonist* (*DAB*). Edits 20074 [cf. 18484].

MORTON, Hoby [? *fiction*]. Verse 13540.

MORTON, John, *Archbishop of Canterbury.* 13604, 17105 by printer; *see* 16173.

MORTON (Hopton), Katherine = *Sir* George. ¶20778.

MORTON, Thomas, *Bishop of Durham.* 579 = 4836, 4767, 17101 by editor, 20308, 24930; epistle 12709 (12636), 19412; prose 12709 (12636); *see* 559, 560, 10667.

MORTON, William, *Archdeacon of Durham* (Venn 1575). 19053.

MOSLEY, —— [? *of London*]. *5700.

MOSELEY, *Sir* Edward, *of Gray's Inn, attorney for Duchy.* 1157 only by bookseller, *6024, *22508.

MOSELEY, Humphrey, *Bookseller* (*DNB*). Prose 1157.

MOSSE, Miles, *Divine* (*DNB*). Epistle 21238.

MOSSE, Peter. Verse 23720.

MOSTYN, *Sir* Roger, *Grandfather of Roger I Bt.* ¶23720, *25716 (25718).

MOTLEY, John, *Sussex preacher* (Venn). *See* 13923.

MOTTERSHED, Thomas, *B.D.* (Foster). Verse 24926 and 24928 [where only initialed].

MOULIN (Molinus), Antoine (*NBG*). Verse 13482 = 17787 [? *from foreign ed.*].

MOULIN, Pierre du, *Divine, d. 1658* (*DNB*). Verse 21139; prose 7323, 14367; *see* 5857, 12662 (12706, 12635).

MOULIN, Peter, *the younger, Divine* (*DNB*). Verse 961 as Molinaeus.

MOULSON (Ratcliffe), Anne = *Sir* Thomas *Lord Mayor.* *18156.

MOUNDFORD, etc. *All spellings.*

MOUNDEFORD, *Sir* Edmund, *Brother of Thomas-DNB.* †¶21896.

MOUNTFORD, John, *Prebend of St. Paul's* (Venn 1594). 12086 (12071).

MOUNDEFORD (Hill), Mary = Thomas-*DNB.* 23057.

MOUNTFORT, Thomas, *D.D., d. 1632* (Foster 1584). 15569; *see* 1454, 25695.

MOUNDEFORD, Thomas, *Physician* (*DNB*). P. Bowne, *Pseudo-medicorum anatomia,*

1624-L.; verse 5808 and 5810 [cf. 23769] as Momford.

MOUNE *and* MOUNSON. *See* MOHUN *and* MONSON.

MOUNSLOW, Richard, *Last abbot of Winchcombe. See* KEDERMYSTER.

MOUNT, William, *Master of the Savoy* (*DNB*). Verse 16649.

MOUNTAIN. *See* MONTAIGNE *and* MONTANUS. Dydimus Mountain is Thomas Hill.

MOUNTSTEVEN, Edmund, *of Gray's Inn* (Venn). Presentation 6843.

MOURT. *See* MORTON.

MOYLE, Robert, *of Bake, father of John-DNB.* Epistle †16696.

MUCHILL, Roger (5569). *See* MICHELL.

MULCASTER (Moncasterus), Richard, *Schoolmaster* (*DNB*). Verse 1410 only, 1411, 6735, 12626, 18775a (18773), 23666; prose 23361.

MULLINS. *See* MOLYNS.

MUN, Thomas, *Writer on economics* (*DNB*). Epistle *25963.

MUNCK, Levinus, *Clerk of the signet* (Brown). 15194; presentation 5986; Minsheu List.

MUNK, Peter, *Danish admiral.* *¶6217.

MUNDA, *Lady* Prudentia [*fiction*]. 18257.

MUNDAY, Anthony, *Poet* (*DNB*). Edits 4461, 23344, etc.; verse 12625 [from lost earlier 18258], 20402 as A. M., 24062; *see* 4537.

MURGATROID, Michael, *Author* (*DNB*). S. Harward, ¶*Three sermons, 1599*-LINC.

MURIELL, MURRELL. *See* MYRIELL.

MURRAY *or* MORAY family, *Kinsmen of John, Courtier.* 23775 (23725).

MURRAY, Agnes. *See next.*

MURRAY (Murray), Anne = Mungo *II* Viscount Stormont. 18167 as Agnes.

MURRAY, *Sir* David of Gorthy, *Poet* (*DNB*). 143 by editor, ¶2773, 5929 (5909), 5933 (5937, 5909), 12068, *12178, *13158, 20303 = ¶20304; verse 7253 as Moeris; *see* 12662 (12706, 12635), 19511, 23779 only; Minsheu List.

MURRAY, David, *I Viscount Stormont.* 5926 (5909), 17856, 18166; *see* 10667 [error for Mungo, II Viscount].

MURRAY (Schaw), Elizabeth = John *I* Earl *of Annandale.* 15311, 20389.

N

N., M. Verse 13482 = 17787.

N., R[ev.] P[resbyter] N., *Anglo-Oxoniensis, S[oc]. J[es]. See* 21072 = 21072a [clarified in *1636* Douay edition].

N., N., '*of St. John's, Oxford*' [*untraced, presumably a mask*]. Verse 1311.

N., N., '*father of author*' [*fiction or mask*]. 10431 = 18330.

N., P., *Editor of Sibbes. See* PHILIP NYE.

N., R. (4701), *see* ROBERT NORMAN; (18611), *see* ROBERT NICHOLSON.

N., R. [*doubtless* Robert Nicholson]. Verse 21649.

N., R., '*of the Inner Temple*'. ★11928.

N., S., *Oxon.* Verse 19168, 21752.

N., S., *Cantab.* Verse 19168.

N., S. 15351 as M. S. N.; verse 13358, 23580.

N., T. (17206). *See* HENRY CHETTLE.

N., T., *Petit ardua virtus* [*perhaps* Thomas Newton]. Verse 6984, 18276.

N., T. Edits 3475 [? Norton], 5685, 13524; verse 189, 3053 [? Newton], 6726 (6676), 20163, 24157.

N., Tho. [? Nabbes]. Verse 17921.

N., Thomas [*supposedly* Norton]. Prose 12147 = 12146.

NABBES, Thomas, *Dramatist (DNB).* Verse 4945, 14788, 17444, 17921 *and see* THO. N., 23704, 25227.

NAEARCHUS (17805). *See* C. S.

NAHUM, Justus, '*Pastor, Acad. Nassau*'. ★14047.

NANSIUS, Franciscus, *Brugensis, Poet* (Schotel). Verse 21657.

NAOPHILUS, Theophilus [? *pseudonym; conceivably* Churchward]. Verse 12964.

NAPIER, Archibald, *I Lord Napier. See* 10667.

NAPPER, Gregory. *See* DORMITANUS.

NAPPER, John, '*Cheapside apothecary*'. 4940.

NAPIER, Robert, *Half-brother of Archibald.* Edits 18350.

NARSSIUS, Joannes, *Dort physician* (Jöcher). Verse 18022.

NASH, Gawen, *Divine (DNB).* Verse 12967 (12964), 12964.

NASH, Thomas, *Author (DNB).* Prose 12272, 22536 only.

NASH, Thomas, *of the Inner Temple (DNB).* Prose 14444.

NAUNTON, Sir Robert, *Politician (DNB).* 11205, 11705, 12029 (12030), 12756, ¶21096, 23824; epistle 24604; verse 21657; Minsheu List.

NEALE, NEELE, NEILE, etc.

NEALE, Sir Francis, *of Bourne, Hants.* 14089 = 14070.

NEALE (Uvedale), Honor = *Sir* Francis. Epistle 14089 = 14070.

NEILE, Richard, *Archbishop of York.* 13587 by editor, 14306, 16461, ★17698 [*1614*-HD. a frag.], ★18333 [unnamed], 18782, 24123, 24124, 25380 (25389); epistle ★20476; *see* 10667; Minsheu List.

NEALE, Walter, *Explorer (DNB).* Epistle ★1506.

NEASSMITH, Arthur, '*Servant to Duke of Richmond*'. J. Taylor, ★*True loving sorow, 1624*-L.[5] (23725).

NEEDHAM (Dutton), Eleanor = Robert. *See* GERARD.

NEEDHAM, Robert, *I Viscount Kilmorey.* 23076 by bookseller.

NEEDHAM, Robert, *II Viscount Kilmorey. See* 10667.

NEGUS, Jonathan, *Son of William*-DNB (Venn). Edits 18420.

NEILE. *See* NEALE.

NELSON, J. Verse 24137.

NELSON, Thomas, *Bookseller (DNB).* Prose 11727.

NETHERSOLE, Sir Francis, *Scholar (DNB).* Verse 11058.

NETLEY, Ja. Verse 12885.

NETTERVILLE, Nicholas, *I Viscount. See* 10667·

NEUB., W. (10428). *See* NEWBURGH.

NEUTER, Christian [*fiction*]. 151 by editor.

NEVILLE, Alexander, *Scholar (DNB).* Verse 12048.

NEVILL (Vaux), Catharine = Henry *IX Baron Bergavenny.* 10676, 11033, ★17699.

NEVIL, Cecilie. *See* CONINGSBY.

NEVILL, Charles, *Fellow of King's* (Venn 1627). Verse 13519.

NICHOLAS, *Sir Ambrose, Lord Mayor.* *24713 [thence 24706], by editors, J. Danyel trans., *Jehovah*, [1576]-L.²

NICHOLAS, *Sir Oliver, Cupbearer* (Foster). *¶19850.

NICHOLAS, Thomas, *of Prestbury* (*Vis. Gloucs.*). †13039, †23861.

NICHOLAS Y SACHARLES, Juan, *Spanish protestant* (*STC*). Verse 24703.

NICOLSON, George, *Provost of Aberdeen.* *22471.

NICOLSON, John, *of Lasswade, advocate.* 15057.

NICHOLSON, Otho, *Examiner in chancery, Gray's Inn.* Minsheu List.

NICHOLSON, Robert, *Merchant and patron* (*N & Q 1954*). 15216 (†21649 revised), ¶18618 and *1599-O.*, 23583 (21653), G. Dicher, *Discors concordia, 1595-U.*; epistle 21654; verse 18611 [with anagram], 18635; *see* Norden map of Surrey-L.; *see* R. N.

NISBET, George [? *Portioner of Inveresk*]. Verse 10696, 22567.

NISBET, *Sir William, Lord Provost of Edinburgh.* *10670, *¶15715, W. M., *Edinburghs alphabet*-E.

NIXON, Anthony (*DNB*), *Widow of his Maecenas* [untraced]. 18586.

NIXON, James, *Irish lawyer at Liège* (BM). *See* 21152.

NOARE, John [*presumably of Cambridge*]. Verse 11780 (11773).

NOEL, NOWELL, etc.

NOWELL, Alexander, *Dean of St. Paul's* (*DNB*). *3048, *4403, 5259, 5644, ¶11758, ¶11760, 13060, *14608, 16425 [anr. work from 16424], 24411, 24664 by editor, 24891, 25295; verse 5686, 19299; *see* 25438.

NOEL, Baptist, *III Viscount Campden.* Verse 11688, 11877.

NOEL, Edward, *II Viscount Campden.* ¶18987; *see* 10667, 17332; Minsheu List.

NOEL, Henry, *Courtier* (*DNB*). 23691, 24337, ¶24340 [see changes], 25116.

NOEL, Henry, *Brother of Baptist above.* Verse 11688.

NOEL (Hickes), Julian = Edward *II Viscount.* *11688.

NOKES, John a [*presumably fiction*]. Epistle R. Aylett, *Brides ornaments, 1625*-F.

NORDEN, John, *Poet-topographer* (*DNB*). Verse 16870 and *1597-HN.*; *see* 21654.

NORDEN, Samuel, *of Peterhouse* (Venn as Northen). See 13923.

NORMAN, Robert, *Instrument-maker* (*DNB*). Edits 4700 [signed, later initialed].

NORMAN, Thomas, '*Pimlico tippler*'. 19936.

NORRIS, NORICE, NORREYS, etc.

NORRIS (Vere), Bridget = Francis *Earl of Berkshire.* *6271-L., *18509.

NORICE, Edward, *Religious writer* (*STC*). See 3450.

NORRIS, Henry, *I Baron N. of Rycote.* 5247, 12589, 21315-PFOR.

NORRIS, *Sir John, Soldier* (*DNB*). *19537, 24570; epistle 16696, 23080; *see* 25438.

NORRIS (Williams), Margaret = Henry *I Baron.* 12422.

NORREIS, S. Verse 14275.

NORRIS, William, *Son of Henry above.* Epistle 21315-PFOR.

NORREYS, *Sir William, K.B., of Speke, Lancs.* 1586.

NORRIS, William, *Headmaster of Eton* (Venn 1623). Verse 11772, 13519.

NORTH, Dudley, *III Baron North.* 3649, *¶4497, *7336; *see* 10667, 17332.

NORTH, Dudley, *IV Baron North.* Epistle some copies *4747-O.

NORTH, Dudley, *Brother of Sir Henry I Bt.* *5657.

NORTH, Edward, *I Baron North.* 7674.

NORTH, *Sir Henry, of Mildenhall, d. 1620.* Epistle *5698.

NORTH, *Sir Henry, I Bt.* *†5657, ¶19850.

NORTH, John, '*Theologus*'. Verse 12184.

NORTH, *Sir John, Brother of Dudley III Baron.* Epistle *4747 [twice in some copies-O.].

NORTH, John, *Son of Dudley III Baron* (Venn 1629). See 15466.

NORTH, Mary (5657). *See* BLAGGE.

NORTH, Roger, *II Baron North.* Epistle 16696.

NORTH, *Sir Roger, of Mildenhall* (Keeler). *†5657.

NORTHEN. *See* NORDEN.

NORTON, Bonham, *Printer* (*DNB*). 17372 (17396 and *1625-N.*).

NORTON, George, *Bookseller*. Signed prose 25906 (25890); unsigned perhaps 1705.

NORTON, Gregory, *Son of Gregory I Bt.* (Venn). Verse 6044a.

NORTON, John, *the elder, Printer* (DNB). Epistle 23354 unnamed; prose 18855; *see* 5811.

NORTON, John, *the younger, Printer*. Prose 10658, 16917.

NORTON, Robert, *Divine* (DNB). Verse 23095.

NORTON, Robert, *Engineer* (DNB). Verse 22790; tables 20815 thence 20807.

NORTON, Thomas, *Lawyer and poet* (DNB). J. Danyel trans., ★*Jehovah*-L.²; supposedly edits 785; verse 24368; *see* THOMAS N.

NORTON, Sir Thomas, *of Northwood* (*Vis. Kent*). ¶10513.

NORWICH, William, *of Peterhouse* (Venn). Verse 22400.

NOWELL. *See* NOEL.

NOYE, William, *Attorney-general* (DNB). 6153; epistle one issue-HD. of ★5369, 20166; *see* 25327.

NUCE, Thomas, *Translator* (DNB). ★25680; verse 22222.

NEWCE, Thomas, *of Much Hadham, Herts.* 23116 and *1617*-O.

NEWCE, Thomas, *of Lincoln's Inn* (Venn 1635). ★3.

NUGENT, Richard, *I Earl of Westmeath*. *See* 10667.

NUMANNUS. *See* NEWMAN.

NUTHALL, John, *of the Inner Temple* (Venn 1597). 7304.

NUYTS, David, *Antwerp merchant* (Schotel). ★557 and *1629*-HD. from foreign ed.

NYE, Philip, *Divine* (DNB). *See* THOMAS GOODWIN.

NYS (Nijs), Joannes, *Franeker advocate* (Schotel). ★¶550 from foreign ed.

O

OLN., Ar. Verse 18635.

O., *Lady* G., *C.K.* (7240). *See* G. O. C. K.

O., G. Verse 20167.

O., M[r]. I., *Chir*[*urgico*] *Parisi* [? L'Oiseau]. Verse 16870.

O., I. Verse 17752; prose 21049 [? John Old], 23554.

O., N. [*probably a fiction*]. Prose 21427.

O., O. Perhaps sense of cipher (ω. ῶ.) in 11629.

O., R. Verse 1577, 18202 [Gent.], 19337.

O., S. [*Puritan editor, probably Stephen Of-wod*]. Edits 555, 4748, 11129, 14555.

O'BRIEN, Donough, *IV Earl of Thomond*. 6183.

O'BRIEN, Henry, *V Earl of Thomond*. *See* 10667.

O'BRIEN, Murrough, *I Earl of Inchiquin*. *See* 10667.

OCKOULD, Richard, *Bookseller*. Prose 12981.

O'DEMPSEY, Terence, *I Viscount Clanmalier*. *See* 10667.

OFFLEY, Hugh, *Alderman, father of next*. 979 [see changes], 12309.

OFFLEY, Robert, *Master of Haberdashers* (Brown). ★11653 (11652) by editor.

OFIELD. *See* OWEFIELD.

O'FIHELY (de Portu), Maurice, *Archbishop* (DNB). Edits 22580.

OFWOD *or* OFFWOOD, Stephen, *Puritan* (STC *and* Burrage), *family of*. Epistle 18789; *see also* S. O.

OGDEN (Fulke), Hester, *Daughter of William-* DNB. Prose 2947.

OGILVY, James, *I Earl of Findlater*. 12484; *see* 10667.

OGILVY, James, *I Earl of Airlie*. *See* 10667.

OGILVY, James, *V Laird of Boyne*. Epistle 1406.

OGILBY, John, *Author* (DNB). Verse 22454.

OGILBIE, William, *Benedictine abbot at Würz-burg*. 1202.

OGLE (Bryan), Anne = Thomas, *Sister-in-law of Dorothy*. H. Clapham, ★*Sinners sleepe, 1596*-L.²

OGLE, Cuthbert, *VII Baron Ogle*. ★¶4102.

OGLE (Ashfield), Dorothy = *Sir* Richard *of Pinchbeck*. H. Clapham, ★*Sinners sleepe, 1596*-L.²

OGLE, Sir John, *Commander* (DNB). 1803, ★17388 (17390), 19512, engr. print ★*Council of war*-L.⁵

OGLE, Thomas, *Esq.*, 'Philalethist'. ¶3571.

OVERBURY, *Sir* Thomas, *Anonymous editor of* [*probably* John Webster]. *See* 23250.

OVERTON, William, *Bishop of Lichfield.* 4077, 18926 by editor.

OWEFIELD *or* OFIELD, Roger, *Fishmonger and merchant, d. 1608.* ¶13478, *25624.

OWEFIELD (Moore), Thomasine = Roger, *Charitable puritan.* *6601, *20675 (20668) by editor.

OWEN, Francis, 'Philomedic'. Verse 13548.

OWEN, Israel, *of Cornhill* (*Vis. London*). †12986.

OWEN, Jane, *Learned Oxford woman* (STC). Epistle 18994 (12974); verse 18985 and *1606*-HD.

OWEN, John, *Epigrammatist* (*DNB*). Verse 3370, 5808 and 5810 [cf. 23769], 13799, 22218 only.

OWEN, John, *Bishop of St. Asaph.* 6639, 15008; verse some copies 6347; *see* 10667.

OWEN, Richard, *Rear admiral* (*CSPD*). 22451.

OWEN, Richard, *Divine* (*DNB*). Verse 21351.

OWEN, Robert, *of the Middle Temple* (Foster 1626). *See* 15466.

OWEN, *Sir* Roger, *Politician* (*DNB*). ¶18987, *18995, 20331.

OWEN, Thomas, *Judge* (*DNB*). 18498, 22555.

OWEN (Elkin), Ursula = *Sir* Roger. 20329.

OWEN *or* AWEN, William, *Bookseller.* Prose earlier ed. of 24798-PFOR.

OWEN, William, *Compiler* (*DNB*). Edits 9516.

OWEN, *Sir* William, *of Condover, d. 1662.* 7465.

OXENBRIDGE, John, *Bookseller.* Epistle 17323; prose 15340.

OXENBRIDGE, *Sir* Robert, *of Hurstbourne, Hants.* ¶7367.

OXENDEN, *Sir* James, *of Deane, Kent, father of 1 Bt.* *21175.

OXENSTJERNA, Axel Gustafsson, *Chancellor of Sweden.* D. Kraus or Denukrois, *Panegyricus G. Adolphi, 1629*-F.

P

P., *Lady* [Porditch *in some copies; presumably* Pordage (Gage), Mary = *Sir* William *of Rodmersham, Kent, later* Ashfield]. 6015.

P., *Mrs.* A. *See* 12662 (12706, 12635).

P., A. Prose 12995 [? mask of author]; *see* 25438 as D. A. P.

PR., Al. Verse 13309 [perhaps Alexander Preston].

P., C. (244). *See* CHRISTOPHER POTTER.

P., C. Verse 22796.

P., Charles. Verse 12907.

P., D. Edits 15751 [lawyer]; verse 15096.

P., D. H. S. W. (19060). *See* H. S., *W.P.*

P., D. P. [D. P., P(*ater*)?]. Verse St. Andrews (Leonard) *Theses, 1612*-O.[6]

P., E. (516), *see* EDWARD POND; (13579), *see* ELIAS PETLEY.

P., E. Edits 240; verse 7192, 21408.

P., Elizabeth (24168). *See* PALMEL.

P., G. (21072a). *See* GEORGE PERKINS.

P., G. [*if not fiction, brother of author,* Edward Daniel *alias* Pickford]. 19073.

P., G. Edits 17663 [? George Perrot]; verse 19734 [? Perkins the author], 21455 [chemistry student].

P., G. B. T. H. [*perhaps construable as verses for* G. B(uckley) *by the editor* T. H., *q.v.*]. Verse 4009 (22251 and *1570*-C.[7]).

P., H. *and* E. (4469). *See* H. PERROT.

P., H., '*of Britain's Burse*'. Edits 16917.

P., H., '*of London*'. P. G., *Most strange report,* [*1604*]- NLW.

P., H. Verse 1506 [? Petowe], 1547 [changed to P. H. in 1548], 4765, 13245, 19338 [Gent.].

P., I. (10733). *See* JOHN PORY.

P., I. [*presumably* John Penry]. *20881.

P., *Sir* I. 13001.

P., I., *of Sidney Sussex College.* Verse 23273.

P., I., *of Oxford.* Verse 73, T. Brasbridge, *Quaestiones, 1586*-O.[3] [*of* St. John's].

P., I., *Musophily.* Verse 23779 only.

P., I. 20074 [? John Pierce]; verse 1695, 5950, 11096 [? Pettie], 13207, 16684 [? Powell], 20167 [? Powell], 21501, 23791 (23725), Calvin, *Sermon of persecution, 1581*-L.[2]; *see* 12662 (12706, 12635) [papist].

P., Jo. [*Englishman in Paris*]. *See* 25403.

P., I. M. (4477). *See* JOHN MANSELL, *P[ro-cancellarius]*.

P., I. W. (3941, 11728). *See* JOHN WILSON, *P[riest]*.

PR., I. [*? of Oxford*]. Verse 24610.

P., L. Verse 2765 = 16696, 19242 [? Price]; prose 11171 [? Pyott].

P., L. M. *utcunque.* Verse 15555.

PH., Lewis, *Gent.* Verse *Tarletons treatises, 1578*-F.

P., *Lady* M. 20571.

P., *Signior* M., '*of France*'. 17215.

P., M. Verse 6033.

P., M. M. B. G. T. [*? the author*]. Verse M. Maier, *Arcana*-L.

P., N. Verse 778, 1695, 6364.

P., N. R. Verse 3108.

P., P. (12757). *See* PHILIP PAPILLON.

P., R., '*of West Ilsley, Berks.*' Edits 12026.

P., R. ¶Second ed. of 25779-w.; edits 3468, 5491 [soldier]; verse 1167 from 1177, 13247, 13620, 25967 [gent.]; *see* 25438.

PAR., Ric. Verse 18498.

PER., R., *B.D., C.C.C.* [*Cambridge*]. Verse 21069.

PR., R., *Cantabr.* Verse 164.

P., S., *S.T.D.* Verse 25745 and 25747.

P., S. *See* 680 [pastor], *Epitaph of Helen Branch, 1594*-HN.

P., St. [*perhaps misprint for* St. G(osson)]. Verse 6787.

P., T., *of Cambridge* [*probably* Pierson, *possibly* Pickering]. Edits W. Perkins, *Treatise of vocations, 1603*-C.² (19647).

P., T., *S.T.D.* Verse 13872.

P., T. Edits 21316, J. Smyth, *Retractions*-YK. [*? Pygott*]; verse 5444 [former patient], 11158, 17805, 18073.

P., Th. *or* Tho. Verse 19337; *see* 12354.

P., T. W. (17546). *See* T. WORTHINGTON, *P[riest]*.

P., V. Verse 13964.

P., W. Verse 3635, 21523.

P., W. I. (23505). *See* WILLIAM JONES, *P[rinter]*.

PACE, Richard, *Diplomatist* (*DNB*). 11719.

PACHETUS, Nicholas (18089). A fiction.

PADDY, *Sir* William, *Physician* (*DNB*). 17993 by editor; verse 4761, 12550, 12555, 20768; *see* 24033 [from foreign ed.]; approbation in 12550.

PAEDTS. *Listed with* PATES.

PAGE, Edmund, *Haberdasher and merchant* (*Vis. London*). *5533 by editor.

PAGE, Edward, *of Gray's Inn* (Foster 1623). *See* 15466.

PAGE, Samuel, *Poet* (*DNB*). Verse 5808 and 5810 [cf. 23769].

PAGE, *Sir* Thomas, *Fellow of King's* (Venn 1628). Verse 11769 and 11782, 13519.

PAGE, William, *Secretary to Sir Philip Hoby.* 18067.

PAGET (Masterson), Bridget = John-*DNB*. Prose 19099.

PAGIT, Ephraim, *Heresiographer* (*DNB*). Verse 7304.

PAGETT, James, *Baron of the Exchequer.* *14482; epistle *841.

PAGET, John, *Divine* (*DNB*). *See* 1974.

PAGET (Newton), Nazareth = Thomas IV Baron. ¶24373 [? earlier lost].

PAGET, Robert, *Minister at Dort, son of John.* Edits 19099.

PAGET, Thomas, *IV Baron Paget.* ¶24373.

PAGETT, Thomas, *Treasurer of the Middle Temple.* Epistle *841.

PAGET, William, *I Baron Paget.* 19479, 22429, 24372.

PAGET, William, *V Baron Paget.* 1872, 7184; *see* 17332.

PAGET, William, *VI Baron Paget. See* 10667.

PAYNTER, Richard, *M.A.* (Foster). Verse 22888.

PAINTER, William, *Author* (*DNB*). Verse 11419.

PAKENHAM, *Sir* Henry, *of Belton* (*Vis. Lincs.*). †1953 and *1609*-YK. [see changes].

PALAVICINO (Hoostman), Anne = *Sir* Horatio. *Italians dead bodie, 1600*-L.² by editor.

PALAVICINO, *Sir* Horatio, *Merchant* (*DNB*). 964, 5789, ¶11739, F. Betti, *Lettera, 1589*-L.

PALFREY, William, *of Lincoln's Inn*. Verse 7160.

PALFREYMAN, Thomas, *Author* (*DNB*). Edits 1257.

PALL., Cl. [*presumably* Claude Palliot]. Verse De Beau Chesne, *Clef de l'escriture*-N., headed 'Cl. Pall. de D. Beliquerco'.

PALLANT, Robert, *Actor*. Verse 13309.

PALLIOT, Claude, *French Poet* (BN). *See* PALL. *above*.

PALMEL (?Traheron), Elizabeth, '*Widow of a clergyman, sister of author*'. 24168 as Elizabeth P. [fuller in 24169].

PALMER, Sir Anthony, *of Putney* (Venn 1579). ¶14809; Minsheu List.

PALMER, Anthony, '*Married author's widow*'. Edits 22801.

PALMER, Catherine, *Abbess of Syon*. *19784.

PALMER, Eliah *or* Elias, *Editor of Wing* W-3526 (*Vis. London*). Verse 17921.

PALMER, Francis, *M.A.* (Foster). Verse 10829.

PALMER, Sir Henry, *Naval commander* (*DNB*). *11127, *¶25795.

PALMER, Sir Henry, *Son of preceding*. 3274.

PALMER, James, *Divine* (*DNB*). Minsheu List.

PALMER, John, *Divine, d. 1614* (*DNB*). *25680.

PALMER (Digges), Margaret = *Sir* Anthony. 5367.

PALMER, Thomas, *of Bristol* (Venn 1613). Verse 1986.

PALMER, Sir Thomas, *II Bt.* *21175.

PALMER, William, *Alderman and Haberdasher*. 1626-0.[2] of *13515.

PALTOCKE, Edward, '*Cursitor, Court of Chancery*'. *6582.

PAMENT, Robert. Verse 18981.

PANORMUS, Nicolas (18089-DUR.[5]). A fiction.

PANTON, Edward, *Captain of the Artillery Garden*. *127 only; epistle 18522 as Edmund.

PAPILLON, Philip, *Versifier* (*DNB*). Prose 12757 as P. P.

PARAMOR (Stone), Anne = Thomas *of Thanet*. *¶25795.

PARCEL, John [*presumably* Percell, Venn 1569]. Verse 3695.

PAREUS, David, *Controversialist* (*NBG*). 18800.

PARHAM, Sir Edward, *Soldier in Spanish service*. 22091 (22090, 22064) [22091 *not* by Scott].

PARKENS *and* PARKIN. *See* PERKINS.

PARKER, Anthony, *Deputy Clerk, Star Chamber*. Minsheu List.

PARKER (Tresham), Elizabeth = William XIII *Baron Morley*. 17197.

PARKER, Frances. *See* acrostic 26040 [source unknown].

PARKER, Henry, *XIV Baron Morley*. ¶7373 and 7375, 19260; *see* 10667.

PARKER (Drake), Joan = John *Haberdasher* (Waters). 11656.

PARKER, John [*probably* Foster 1583]. Verse 23278 only.

PARKER, John, '*Esq., courtier*'. *12178.

PARKER, John, *Alderman and Merchant Taylor*. ¶23725 [earlier lost].

PARKER, Matthew, *Archbishop of Canterbury*. *1710 and ¶1710, 4078, 11893 by editor, 11997, *13963, 18308, 18478 (18773) posthumously, *18701, *18708, *18711, *18712, *18726, *18730, *21692.
Edits (*mostly anonymously*): 863, 2099 [cf. 2105], 14591 only as M. C[ant.], 17653, 19209, 25004; prose 17409, perhaps 159 (160, 15705).
See 159, map in some copies 4345, 10026.

PARKER, Sir Nicholas, *Commander* (*DNB*). *11380.

PARKER, Richard, *Historian* (*DNB*). Verse 4508 (4509).

PARKER, Roger, *of Kirby, Marian exile*. †24170.

PARKER, Roger, *Dean of Lincoln* (Venn 1578). Minsheu List.

PARKER, W. Verse 22222.

PARKER, William, *Merchant Taylor*. W. Dorke, *Tipe of friendship*, 1589-HN.

PARKER, William, *XIII Baron Morley*. 6785, ¶7193 only; *see* 17332.

PARKHURST, ——, '*of London*' [*perhaps Sir* Robert]. *5700.

PARKHURST, Anthony, *Bristol merchant* (Hakluyt). Verse 19523.

PARKHURST, John, *Bishop of Norwich*. *1710, 1755 (1710) [*see* changes], *4063 (4058);

PEPWELL, Henry, *Printer* (DNB). Unsigned verse 7271.

PERCELL, John (Venn 1569). *See* PARCEL.

PERCIVALL, Sir Anthony, *of Dover* (*Vis. Kent*). 20787.

PERCEVAL, Richard, *Colonist* (DNB). J. Geere ed., *Troposchematologia, 1602*-o.[3]

PERCY, Algernon, *IV Earl of Northumberland*. 708, 1506, ¶6332 [6331 a ghost], 22786 by bookseller [see changes]; presentation 13222; *see* 9336, 10667.

PERCY (Cecil), Anne = Algernon, *IV Earl*. 1333.

PERCY (Devereux), Dorothy = Henry *III Earl*. *4226, *19793.

PERCY, *Lady* Dorothy (6332). *See* SIDNEY.

PERCY, Ed. Verse 12216 [earlier lost].

PERCY, Henry, *III Earl of Northumberland* (DNB *as* IX *Earl*). 5586, one issue *7326 [Darcie translation], 10833, 12784, 17757 [divulged in 17758], 19539, 20118 only by editor; epistle 1469-L., 6165, 6333, 16696, 23080; *see* 17331.

PERCY, Sir Josceline, *Brother of preceding* (Foster 1594). 23060.

PERCY, *Lady* Lucy, *Sister of preceding, subsequently* Wotton *and* Owen. 24097.

PERCY, Mary, *Benedictine abbess* (Gillow). 269 by editor, 4553, 20483.

PERCY, William, *Poet* (DNB). 1469-L.; verse 1468.

PERIER, Henry, B.D. (Foster). Minsheu List.

PERKINS, George, *Grammarian* (Wing). Edits 21072a = 21072 as G. P. [*clarified in 1647 ed.*].

PERKINS, Richard, *Actor*. Verse 13309.

PARKENS, Samuel, M.A. (Venn). Verse 6843.

PERKINS, Samuel, *Almanac-maker* (STC). Verse 16944.

PARKIN, Thomas, 'Surgeon'. Verse 5446.

PERKINS, William, *Theological writer* (DNB). *See 1609*-C.[2] of 20826.

PERKINS, William [*? of Lincoln School*]. Verse 5363 (5355).

PERNE, Andrew, *Dean of Ely* (DNB). 4347, *16827.

PERROT, H. *and* E., *Parents of George Perrot, O.F.M.* 4469 [initials only].

B 8564

PERROT, Sir James, *Politician* (DNB). Verse 24610.

PERROT, Sir John, *Lord-deputy of Ireland* (DNB). Arms in Irish *Statuta*-HD.

PERROT, Sir Thomas, *Son of preceding*. 21593.

PERRY, Hugh, *Alderman*. *13347, 16917 by editor; *see* 22531.

PERRY, Hugh, *Bookseller*. Prose 5125, 12051.

PIRRY, Thomas, B.D. (Foster 1548). Verse 4612 (21052).

PERSONS. *See* PARSONS.

PERT, ——, 'Captain, Middlesex militia' [*possibly* Richard]. Epistle *5668.

PEART, Paul, *of Lincoln's Inn, Exchequer officer*. Verse 11087; Minsheu List.

PERT, Ri. Verse 15036.

PERUGINO, M. A. *See* M. A.

PERYAM, *Lady* [*presumably the next but marriage date elusive*]. 18119.

PERYAM (Bacon), Elizabeth = Sir William. 17126; *see preceding*.

PERYAM, Sir William, *Judge* (DNB). 4172, *6282 by editor, *6439, 11754 [11753 a ghost], 19696 (19743, 19646), 24274, *25629, *¶25697 [see changes]; epistle 16696.

PETREUS, Henricus, *Marburg professor* (ADB). Verse 5591.

PETRE, John, *I Baron Petre*. 498, ¶4243 (4245), 12338, 18810.

PETER, John, *of Horton* (*Vis. Bucks.*). Minsheu List.

PETER, John, *of Boohay* (*Vis. Devon*). 21526.

PETRE (Waldegrave), Mary = John *I Baron*. *25764.

PETRE (Montagu), Mary = Robert *III Baron*. 18001 by editor.

PETRE, Robert, *III Baron Petre*. *See* 10667.

PETRE, William, *II Baron Petre*. 3125, 19044; *see* 4252 = 11827, 17332, 23088 (23084).

PETERHOUSE, John. Verse 24062.

PETERSON, William, *Dean of Exeter* (Venn). 21850.

PETLEY, Elias, *Translator* (Venn). Verse 13580 as El: Petl: (13579 as E. P.).

PETRE *and* PETREUS. *See* PETER.

PETT, Peter, *Navy official, d. 1670* (DNB). Licenses 13367.

U

PIERS, John, *Archbishop of York*. 11733, 20369, 23547 [see changes].

PEIRCE, John, *Plymouth colony patentee*. *See* I. P.

PIERCE, Robert, *B.D.* (Foster 1611). Verse 14793.

PIERS, Thomas [? *the elder*], *of the Chapel Royal*. Verse 20756.

PIERS, William, *Bishop of Bath and Wells*. *3419; edits 19025, 19027; verse 19028; *see* 10667; Minsheu List [erroneously duplicated].

PIERREPONT, Sir George, *Father of next* (*Vis. Notts.*). 1739 (1710).

PIERREPONT, Sir Henry, *Father of next*. 12210, 25061; presentation 13366.

PIERREPONT, Robert, *I Earl of Kingston*. *See* 10667.

PIERS. *See* PIERCE.

PIERSON (——), Helen = Thomas, *previously* Harvey, *Mother of C. Harvey-DNB*. C. Harvey, *Conditions of christianity, 1636*-L.4 by son-editor.

PEIRSON, Henry, *Son of Richard, Merchant Taylor* (*Vis. London*). Minsheu List.

PEERSON, Martin, *Composer* (*DNB*). Verse 20756.

PIERSON, Thomas, *of Emmanuel* (Venn 1590 and STC). Edits 19678, 19722, 19732, 19748, 19751—all (19649); *also see* T. P.

PIGAFETTA, Marco Antonio, *Italian traveller* (*STC*). Verse 12625.

PIGEON, ——, '*Citizen and Grocer*'. Minsheu List.

PIGOT, Bartholomew, *of Gray's Inn*. Verse 17921.

PYGOT, Thomas, *Esq.* [? *of Bucks.*]. *Rameae rhetoricae libri, 1597*-L.

PIKELING (3043). Misprint for Pickering.

PILE, Sir Francis, *I Bt.* 19346.

PILE, Sir Francis, *II Bt.* 19351.

PILKINGTON, Henry, *the elder, of Gaddesby, Leics.* 21686.

PILKINGTON, James, *Bishop of Durham*. *1710.

PINCIER, Joannes, *Marburg teacher of medicine* (BM). *14047.

PINCK, John, *M.A.* (Foster). Verse 4196.

PINCK, Robert, *Warden of New College* (*DNB*). Edits 5021 = 19036; *see* 25327; Minsheu List.

PINDAR, Sir Paul, *Diplomatist* (*DNB*). *6267, 12072 (*Sermons, 1639*-O.), 12983 [see changes], 15048, 19505 [*date is 1639*], *23625, *24660 [24659 a ghost], W. Painter, *Chaucer new painted*-HN.

PYNDER, R. Verse 23704.

PINE, Io. Verse 13595.

PIPE, Sir Richard, *Lord Mayor*. 4067, 1579-HN. of *23325 [see changes]; epistle *12097.

PIPER, John, *Bookseller*. Prose 24525; Minsheu List.

PIRRY. *See* PERRY.

PISCATOR (Fischer), Johannes, *Theologian* (*ADB*). *14047, 23873, ¶23874.

PITCAIRN, Andrew, *Master of hawks, Groom of the Bedchamber*. *1203, *10530; epistle some copies *4747-O. [Archibald in uncorrected state-HN.].

PYTTS, Sir Edward, *of Kyre* (*Vis. Worcs.*). *21608 by editor.

PITT, Edward, *of the Middle Temple* (Foster 1608). Verse 13018 as Ewart.

PIT, Ewart. *See preceding*.

PITT, George, *of Harrow* (Brown). †12877 [see changes].

PYTTS, Sir James, *Son of Sir Edward*. *21608 by editor.

PIUS V, *Pope*. 19549; epistle 12598.

PIZZAMANUS, Antonius, *Bishop of Feltre*. 22580 by editor.

PLAMER, Sir Henry (25795). *See* PALMER.

PLAYFER, John, *Pastor of Debden* (Venn). Epistle, *18805.

PLUMME, Edm. Verse 25025.

PLUMBE, William, *of Fulham, d. 1593*. 21672 (21649).

PLUNKETT, Luke, *I Earl of Fingall*. *See* 10667.

PLUNKETT, Oliver, *VI Baron Louth*. *See* 10667.

PLUNKETT, Patrick, *VII Baron Dunsany*. 24806.

PLUNKETT, Patrick, *IX Baron Dunsany*. *See* 10667.

POETON, Edward, '*Petworth physician*'. Edits 3279.

POTTER, Barnaby, *Bishop of Carlisle.* 20134; see 10667, ★24702 only, Minsheu List.

POTTER, Christopher, *Provost of Queen's* (*DNB*). 20667; edits 245; prose 244 as C. P.; see 25327.

POTTER, Gilbert, *Tapster who lost ears for Mary I.* 20188.

POTTICARY, Thomas, *Master of Salisbury School* (Foster). Verse 19813.

POULET *and* POWLETT. *Listed with* PAULET.

POULTER *and* POULTON. *See* POLTER *and* PULTON.

POULTNEY, John, *the younger, of Langley* (*Vis. Bucks.*). ★†25371.

POULTNEY, Mary, *Sister of preceding.* ★25371.

POVEY, William. Verse 10694.

POWELL, Christopher, *of Gray's Inn.* Index-*1583*-HD. for 15164.

POWEL, Daniel, *Gent.* (?*DWB*). Verse 24607.

POWELL, David, *Historian* (*DNB*). Edits 20109.

POWELL, Sir Edward, Bt., *Master of requests.* 13219; epistle 20166.

POWELL, Edward, 'de Sanford, esq.' *See* 25327.

POWELL (ferch Cynwrig), Elizabeth = David-*DNB*. G. Powell, *Mystery of redemption, 1607*-F.

POWELL, Gabriel, *Divine* (*DNB*). Verse 7304, 12315, 24607, 24610, 24620; prose 23592.

POWELL, Griffith, *Principal of Jesus College* (*DNB*). Edits 756; verse 4759, 24610; Minsheu List.

POWELL, John, *Clerk of market, royal household.* Edits 870, again 871.

POWELL, John, *of Oriel* (Foster 1610). Verse 11544.

POWELL, John, *Merchant adventurer* (*Vis. London*). ¶16684.

POWELL, Samuel, M.A. (Foster 1592). Verse 24607, 24610.

POWLE, Sir Stephen, *One of six clerks* (Brown). †3641 as Poll.

POWLE, Thomas, *One of six clerks, father of preceding.* 12419, 18862 by printer, W. Panke, *Receite for writing*-HN.

POWELL, Thomas, *Attorney* (*DNB*). Supposedly edits 194.

POWER, Henry, *Viscount Valentia. See* 10667.

POWER, John, *V Baron Power. See* 10667.

POYNTELL, Dannet, *Master of Drapers.* ★22150.

POYNTZ, Sir Anthony, *Diplomatist* (*DNB*). *See* 4891.

POINTZ, Sir Gabriel, *of North Wokenden, Essex.* 25765.

POYNTZ, Sir John, *Father of Sir Robert-DNB.* 13424 (13378).

POYNTZ, Sir Nicholas, *of Iron Acton.* 6081.

PRANNELL, Henry, *Alderman.* 257, 17143.

PRATT, Sir Henry, I Bt., *Alderman.* ★13351.

PRAT, Th., *Gent.* Verse 936 [diff. book from 935].

PRATT, William, *Mercer and merchant adventurer. See* 15394; consider 21429.

PRATT, William, *Mathematician* (Taylor and STC). *See* 465 for *1621*.

PRAUDE, ——, 'Captain, Dutch service' [? Sir John Proud]. Epistle 25939.

PRESCOTT, Alexander, *Alderman.* ★11829, ★17886.

PRESTON, Elizabeth, *Abbess of Syon* (at Lisbon). ★10928 [the earliest ed.].

PRESTON, James, *of Airdrie. See next.*

PRESTON, Sir John, II Bt. R. Williamson, *Elementa, 1624*-E.; epistle with two brothers Williamson, *Paedagogia, 1635*-E. and (for John and Walter) earlier at C.³ (impf.).

PRESTON, John, *Devon clergyman* (Foster 1621). *See* 13037.

PRESTON (Gilbert), Lilias = Sir John-*DNB.* 21276.

PRESTON, Nicholas, *VI Viscount Gormanston. See* 10667.

PRESTON, Richard, I Earl of Desmond. ★1203, ¶18296; see 19511.

PRESTON, Walter, *of Airdrie. See* SIR JOHN.

PRICE, PRYCE, PRYS, etc.

PRICE, Arthur, *Rector of Calbourne* (Foster). *See* 14747.

PRICE, Da. Verse 19260.

PRYS, Edmund, *Translator* (*DNB*). Epistle 6346; verse 6346.

PRICE, Henrietta Maria, *Daughter of Sir Herbert, later Morley.* ★14739 [? after *1640*].

PSEUDONYMS. Cross-referenced for the curious are: (*a*) Unsolved or dubiously solved pseudonyms; (*b*) unsolved signature mottoes, some perhaps anagrams, and (*c*) names clearly fictitious or suspect. Initials used as pseudonyms or fictions are excluded, while the names and supposed identities of poetic mistresses like Delia and Stella are ignored throughout this book.

Pseudonyms

PURFOOT, Thomas, *the younger, Printer.* Unsigned prose 21300, 24573.

PURSET, Christopher, *Bookseller.* Edits 20514.

PURSLOWE (——), Elizabeth = George. Unsigned prose 14784.

PURSLOWE, George, *Printer.* Apparently edits 15332.

PUTTENHAM (Elyot), Margery = Robert. 20057.

PYE (Ireland), Hester = Sir Walter. *23717.

PYE (Croker), Mary = Sir Robert. *¶25971.

PYE, *Sir* Robert, *Remembrancer of Exchequer, brother of Sir Walter.* ¶25971.

PYE, Thomas, *Divine (DNB).* Epistle 13887.

PYE, *Sir* Walter, *Lawyer (DNB).* †3569, 20752 by editor.

PYE, *Sir* Walter, *Son of preceding.* 24158.

PYM, John, *Statesman (DNB).* 10940, *20278 by editor; *see* 25327.

PYNCHON, *Sir* Edward, *of Essex* (Foster). *22842 [earlier lost].

PYNSON, Richard, *Printer (DNB).* Signed prose (some adapted from Caxton) 5084, 15726, 17105; unsigned prose 18389; unsigned verse 5088; *see* 22408 (material modified in some later eds.).

PYTTS. *See* PITT.

PYX, William, *M.A.* (Foster). Verse 23278.

Q

Q., F. *See* FRANCIS QUARLES.

Q., T. M. [*supposedly* Tam Marte quam Mercurio, *for* George Gascoigne]. Verse 24328.

Q., W. [*presumably* Walter Quin]. Verse 23352.

QUAERENGUS, Antonius, *Italian poet (NBG).* Verse 1390 [from Paris *1621*].

QUARLES, Francis, *Poet (DNB).* Verse 3129 borrowed from 20529, 11082 (one from 20529), 22509, *1635-*F. of 25097. Verse 17824 variantly unsigned, as by M. S[parke], and F. Q.; edits T. Wetherel, *Five sermons, 1635-*PLUME.

QUARLES (Parvis), Mary = Sir Robert. 20551.

QUARLES, *Sir* Robert, *Brother of Francis* (Venn 1598). *20337 by editor.

QUARLES, William, *Alderman and Mercer.* *20756.

QUARME, Robert, *of Wood House, Devon.* 25093.

QUESTER, Mathew de, *Postman* (Brown). *20678 (20668) by editor.

QUIET, Margery, *of Tame* [*fiction*]. Verse 23766; *see* 23747.

QUIN, Walter, *Poet (DNB).* Verse 349 (343), 5808 and 5810, 10828, 23576, presumably 13191 as Walt. O. Quin, Armig.; *see also* W. Q.

R

R. (7031). *See* RICHARD REDMER.

R., E[arl] of (6789). *See* ROGER MANNERS.

R., M[rs]. 19434 and *1588-*HD.

R., A. (15688). Misprint for R. A[llot].

R., A. Verse 545, 3422, 12312, 12420, 15520 [? Cambridge].

R., B. (12259). *See* BARNABE RICH.

R., B. Verse 4366, 6611 [R. R. in later eds.], 24908, 25090 [? Beke].

R., C. (18904). *See* G. R.

R., C., *Gent.* Verse 19615.

R., C. A., *alias* Coricaeus. Verse 21137.

R., C. R. [*presumably* C. R. R(egin.), *Queen's College, Oxford*]. Verse 17245.

R., D. 23614.

ROB., Da. Verse 19775.

R., E., *of Magdalene College, Cambridge.* Verse 24928.

R., E., *Oxon.* Edits 16814.

R., E., *Familist.* Prose and reply 21182.

R., Ed. Verse 12205.

R., F. (10943). *See* FRANCIS ROUS.

R., *Ladies* F. *and* H. 17135.

R., F. Verse 1695, 12210; prose 15599.

R., G. Verse 18904, etc. [but C. R. in earlier *1614-*C.²].

R., *Lady* H. *See* LADY F. R.

R., H. Verse 501 for *1609*, 548, 11921.

R., H. R. [*Student of occult*]. Does presentation 13218.

R., I. (4628), *see* JOHN RHODES; (4849), *see* JOHN RAE; (17101), *pseudonym of* John Floyd.

R., I., *of Inner Temple.* Verse 6014.

R., I., *M.A., Cambridge.* Verse 14920.

R., I. 4279, C. Thimmelthorpe, *Short inventory, 1581*-HN.; edits *Manual of meditation,* [*c. 1580*]-O. [prior-C. impf.]; verse 1445, 3635, 7388, 12935, 24157; prose 20397.

RE., I. Verse 6364.

R., L. Edits 21428.

R., M. Presentation 19447; verse first issue 4946, 6485, 17824.

R., N. (4703), *misprint for* R. N[orman]; (13313), mystification of author Heywood.

R., N. Verse 11645 (11638), 16642 [anon. in original ed.-L.²], 19808; *see also* R. A. (370).

R., O., *Clergyman: his parish.* O. R., *Entraunce into religion*-L.²

R., P., *of the Middle Temple.* 23529.

R., P., *Scotus.* Verse 3978.

RE., Pere. Edits 5343.

R., R. (10943). *See* RICHARD ROUS.

R., R., *Malum patienti lucrum.* Verse 21649.

R., R. Verse 5811 [sailor], 6364, 6612 and earlier-HD. [but B. R. in 6611], 17201.

R., Rob. Verse 11223 [and see ii, 1938].

R., S. (13582). *See* SIMEON RUYTINCK.

R., S. Edits 12243 [? Rowlands]; verse 18856.

R., T. (4943). *See* THOMAS RAWLINS.

R., T. Verse 1304 [gent.], 6333, 25738; prose 19057 [cf. 19081], 26037a [clergyman].

R., Th. [*perhaps* Sir Thomas Roe]. Verse 14782 only, 14783 only as T. R.

R., Thom. [*Secret printer*]. Prose 24247.

R., Thomas. *See* 25566 *and* O. ed. of 25558.

R., W. (1158, 21069), *see* WILLIAM RAWLEY; (16884, 23080), *see* SIR WALTER RALEIGH.

R., W., *M.D.* Verse 111.

R., W. Verse 5673 [? Rowley], 15715, 19338 [gent.], 21510 [? reversed initials of translator]; *see* 12662 (12706, 12635).

R., W[illiam]. Verse 22222 catchworded William.

RO., W. *See* 25438.

RABAN, Edward, *Printer (DNB).* Verse 11151; prose 17857, 20113; unsigned prose 3905, *1623*-HN. of 6780 [? from foreign ed.]; prose 10442 is retained from London *1621*-O.

RABBARDS, Ralph, '*Alchemist and intelligencer*'. Edits 21057.

RABILAE. Anagram of Barlaeus.

RABLET, Richard [*Pseudonym*]. Edits 5452.

RADCLIFFE (Sussex) family. *See* 6270.

RADCLIFFE, *Sir* Alexander, *of Ordsall, d. 1654,* 3591, 20691.

RATCLIFFE, Anthony, *Alderman.* *11478.

RADCLIFFE (Morrison), Bridget = Robert *V Earl.* 1433, 11622, 12296, 14973 [earlier lost].

RADCLIFFE, Edward, *VI Earl of Sussex.* †20086; *see* 10667.

RADCLIFFE (Howard), Elizabeth = Henry *II Earl.* *See* 22610 (22608).

RADCLIFFE, Elizabeth, *Poor Clare at Aire.* *6185.

RADCLIFFE (Sidney), Frances = Thomas *III Earl.* 11858 by editor, 13059, ¶13975.

RADCLIFFE, Henry, *IV Earl of Sussex.* 25344; epistle 21029 (21032).

RATCLIFFE (Brerewood), Jane = John *Mayor of Chester.* 4236.

RADCLIFFE, *Sir* John, *of Ordsall, father of Sir Alexander.* Presentation 13218.

RATCLIFFE, John, *Mayor of Chester.* *¶23720.

RATCLIFFE, John, '*Secretary to Juxon*' [*untraced*]. 631.

RADCLIFFE, Margaret, *Maid of honour, d. 1599.* Epistle 11831.

RADCLIFFE, Margaret, *Poor Clare at Aire.* *6185 [cf. Elizabeth].

RADCLYF, Rafe [*untraced Catholic exile*]. Verse 21361 [Badclyf in 21363].

RADCLIFFE, Robert, *V Earl of Sussex.* 10922, ¶11171, 16656 by editor, W. Comley, *New copy-booke, 1622*-CU., J. Trendle, *Trendles arke*-PN.²; epistle †13633 (13624), 16696, 17385; *see* 17331.

RADCLIFFE, Samuel, *Principal of Brasenose* (Foster 1597). *See* 25327; Minsheu List.

RADCLIFFE, Thomas, *III Earl of Sussex.* 718, 1304, *¶10674, 11849, 14104, 17296, †17406, *18270, 19138; *see* 2108 (Chronicles).

REGIUS *and* REID. *See* KING *and* READE.

REIGESBERGIUS, Jonas, *Dutch theologian* (Schotel). *See* 12662 (12706, 12635).

REINHART, Chr. [*presumably the alchemist* Johann C.—Jöcher]. Verse M. Maier, *Arcana*, [1614]-LC.

RENATUS, Misonices [*Pseudonym*]. Verse 21141.

RENSIE, Mathias de, *of Venice* [*fiction*]. 24585.

REPINGTON, Sir John, *of Amington* (*Vis. Warw.*). *4746 = ¶17509.

REUSNER, Nicholas, *German poet* (*NBG*). Epistle 3988.

REVELL, Thomas, *of Gray's Inn.* Verse 3074, 3075.

REYNARDSON, Sir Abraham, *Lord Mayor* (*DNB*). Epistle *25963.

REYNELL, Sir Carew, *Gentleman pensioner, d. 1624.* *20267.

REYNELL, Carew, *of the Inner Temple* (Foster 1618). Verse 13988.

REYNELL, Sir George, *Brother of Sir Carew* (Foster 1587). *20267; Minsheu List.

REYNELL (Periam), Mary = Richard *of Creedy.* 19522.

REYNELL, Richard, *Brother of Sir Carew.* *20267.

REYNELL, Sir Richard, *of the Middle Temple* (Foster 1602). *20248.

REYNELL, Sir Thomas, *the elder, of Ogwell.* *20267.

REYNELL, Sir Thomas, *the younger* (Foster 1602). *20248.

REYNELL, Walter, *Brother of Sir Richard* (? Foster). *20248.

REYNOLDS, RAINOLDS, RAYNOLDS, etc.

RAYNOLDS, ——, '*London schoolmaster*'. Minsheu List.

REYNOLDS (Wythipool), Elizabeth = Henry [*the next*]. ¶26079.

REYNOLDS, Henry, *the elder, Father of Henry-DNB.* ¶26079.

RAINOLDS, John, *Bible translator* (*DNB*). Prose 13887.

REYNOLDS, John, *Master gunner of England.* 18676.

REYNOLDS, John, *Author and merchant* (*DNB*). Verse 7190, 7229.

RAINALDS, Paul, '*Scottish controversialist*'. 4285.

RAYNALDE, Thomas, *Physician* (*DNB*). Edits 21154 [alteration 21156].

RAINOLDS, William, *Divine* (*DNB*). Epistle 20613 and 1613-C.; verse 23229.

RODES, Edward, *Master of Barber Surgeons.* *5326.

RHODES, Godfrey, *of Denham, West Suff.* *20337 by editor.

RHODES, John, *Bookseller.* Initialed prose 4628 [*see* GREG].

RHODES, Matthew, *Bookseller.* Verse 189, 21094; prose 17401 only.

RICCOMONTANUS. *See* RICHMOND.

RICE, John [*probably* Foster 1590]. Verse 18114.

RICE, John [? *the actor*]. Verse 13508.

RICE, William, *Esq.* 3180.

RICH (Cavendish), Anne = Robert *III Earl.* Epistle *15465.

RICH, Barnabe, *Author* (*DNB*). Edits [? or writes] 12259 as B. R.; verse 16653.

RICH, Elizabeth. *See* ISABEL.

RICH (Wray), Frances = Robert *I Earl,* *previously* St. Paul. 1962, *¶4497, 19041, *21013.

RICH (Hatton), Frances = Robert *II Earl.* Parallel with husband ¶12116, 21199.

RICH, Henry, *I Earl of Holland.* *¶5769, 7365, *¶10553, 13264, 13265, ¶14743, 17494, *¶17699, 20526, *21639, †¶21869 misprinted Richel, 22446, 23302 –4 –6 –8 by editors, *24926a [*see* changes], *24928, *25900, rare issue ¶26068 by editor [*see* changes]; epistle *4747, 23070, 24604; *see* 10667, 17331; Minsheu List.

RICH (Cope), Isabel *alias* Elizabeth = Henry *I Earl.* 5722, *¶5769.

RICH, Sir Nathaniel, *Merchant* (*DNB*). 12040, ¶12116, *20278 by editor; *see* 25327; Minsheu List.

RICH (Devereux), Penelope, *Lady Rich* (*DNB*), *subsequently* Blount. 1480, 5679 [vaguely], 11158, *18041 [*see* changes], 18044, *19793, 23918; epistle 6333, 16696; prose Devereux, *Apologie*-HN.

RICH, Richard, *I Baron Rich.* 21613.

RICH, Robert, *I Earl of Warwick.* 357, 5536, 6640 by editor, 13399 and *1607*-F. (13378), 17741, 19569, 19677 (19649), 19680 (19649) by editor, 20306, 23316, 23825; Minsheu List.

RICH, Robert, *II Earl of Warwick.* *362, †1003, *¶5769, 7161, 7239, *¶10553, †¶12116, 12125, 13536, 13988, *15554 and *1624*-L., ¶16887 cancelled, *¶17699, 17743, 18156a, 18691, 20208 by editor, †21199, †¶21869, †22498 by editor, 22515 by editor, 22839, 23303 (23311) by widow, *23314, 23584, *24928; epistle *25025; presentation 10779; *see* 10667, 10738, 17331; Minsheu List.

RICH, Robert, *III Earl of Warwick.* 13804, *23314; *see* 10667.

RICH, Sir Robert, *Master in Chancery.* Minsheu List.

RICH (Rowe), Susanna = Robert *II Earl.* 21167 (21173).

RICH, William, *of the Middle Temple.* Verse 5807.

RICHARD I, *King.* ¶13569.

RICHARD II, *King.* 12143.

RICHARD III, *King.* 3326.

RICHARD, *Abbot* (16790). *See* KEDERMYSTER.

RICHARDS, John, *M.A.* (Foster 1608). Verse 13018.

RICHARDS (Topsfield), Mary = Henry. *15334 spelt Richars.

RICHARDS, Nathaniel, *Dramatist (DNB).* Verse 20770.

RICHARDSON, David, *Bailie of Edinburgh.* *138 only.

RICHARDSON, Ferdinand. *See* HEYBOURNE.

RICHARDSON, John, *Biblical scholar (DNB).* Epistle *636; verse 6206; prose 635; Minsheu List.

RICHARDSON, John, *M.A.* [*numerous*]. Verse 6044a.

RICHARDSON, Sir Thomas, *Judge (DNB).* 1541, 1792, 4911 (291), *11202, *11670, *12495, 23796 (23725).

RICHARDSON, Sir Thomas, *the younger* (Venn 1614). Epistle 15037.

RICHARDSON, Thomas, *Curate of St. Benet Fink* (Venn 1580). Minsheu List.

RICHARDSON, William, *of Queen's College* (Foster 1599). Prose 5976.

RICHARS *and* RICHEL. Misprints for Richards and Riche.

RICHER FOR BOOKES. Anagram of Christopher Brooke.

RICHMOND (Riccomontanus), Robert. Verse 5808 and 5810 [cf. 23769].

RICKARD, Thomas, *of Hatfield* (*Vis. Yks.*). 11491.

RIDDAEUS, Da., 'Fermiloduni ludimag.' [*probably error for* Ja(mes) Reddie]. Prose 25737.

RIDDELL, Sir Peter, *Mayor of Newcastle.* *12202, *14491.

RIDDELL, Sir Thomas, *the elder, Father of Sir Thomas-DNB.* *12202, *14491.

RIDER, John, *Bishop of Killaloe.* Epistle 11025.

RYDER, Sir William, *Lord Mayor (DNB).* 14343, 20053 by bookseller, 23607 by bookseller [*see changes*], *23864, J. Bentley, *Harmonie of scriptures, 1600*-L., N. Breton, *Soules heavenly exercise, 1601*-F.

RIDGELEY, Thomas, *Physician* (Venn 1594). See 14791.

RIDGEWAY (Macwilliam), Cicely = Thomas *I Earl.* 20981; *see* 23779 only.

RIDGEWAY (Weston), Elizabeth = Robert *II Earl.* See 23779 only.

RIDGEWAY, George, *Esq.* 24908.

RIDGEWAY, Robert, *II Earl of Londonderry.* See 10667, 23779 only.

RIDGEWAY, Thomas, *I Earl of Londonderry.* †17682, 20985, some copies 20994, *21003; epistle 25891 (25911); *see* 19511, 23779 (23725); Minsheu List.

RIDLEY, Nicholas, *Bishop of London.* Epiphanie [variant of 10878-L.].

RIDLEY, Robert, *Uncle of preceding* (Venn 1515). Edits 11892.

RIDLEY, Sir Thomas, *Chancellor of Winchester (DNB).* Verse 11224.

RIDLEY, William, 'Sussex preacher' (?Foster 1544). See 13923.

RIES, Hans de, *Dutch sectary* (Schotel). *13053.

RIGBY, Alexander, *Baron of the Exchequer (DNB).* 3590; epistle 3585.

RIGHTWISE (Rituissus), John, *Grammarian (DNB).* Edits 15607, perhaps 15118; verse prior-HN. of 10478, 13811 as Rightwichus, Treveris ed.-CU. of 15610 (5542, 25944), 15118.

RINDEUS. *See* RYND.

RISLEY, James [*cf.* Wriothesley]. 1964.

RITUIS(s)US. *See* RIGHTWISE.

RIVERS, *Sir* George, *of Chafford, father of next.* 17363 by bookseller but by author 17364 (17396).

RIVERS, *Sir* John, *I Bt.* 895 = ¶900.

RIVET, Timothy, *Archdeacon of Bath* (Venn 1595). Epistle ★1941.

ROBARTES. *Listed with* ROBERTS.

ROBERT, *Duke of Normandy* (DNB). Supposedly 21596 and 21605 as 'English king'.

ROBERT, *Earl of Gloucester, d. 1147* (DNB). ¶21783.

ROBERT, *Bishop of Hereford* [*either* de Bethune *or* de Melun, *both DNB*]. 11121.

ROBERTES, Anne. 23624 = 25118.

ROBERTS, Benedict, 'Son of Nicholas, Esq.' Some copies 18343.

ROBARTES, Foulk, *Divine* (DNB). Verse 18493.

ROBERTS, Gabriel, *Son of Lewes-DNB.* Verse 21094.

ROBARTES, Gylbert. H. Roberts, *True relation*-HN.

ROBERTS, Griffith, *Welsh grammarian* (DNB). Edits M. Clynog, *Athravaeth Gristnogaul, 1568*-N.

ROBERTS, James, *Printer* (DNB). Prose 11004; perhaps unsigned 5638.

ROBARTES, John, *I Earl of Radnor.* ¶971, 11548, 21341, †22475 by editor; *see* 10667.

ROBERTS, Lewes, *Merchant and city captain* (DNB). Epistle ★1507; verse 11082.

ROBERTS, Nicholas, *Examiner in Chancery* (? Inner Temple). Minsheu List.

ROBERTS, Robert, 'of Llanfair, Anglesey, cousin'. Verse 21094.

ROBERTS, *Sir* Thomas, *I Bt.* †¶59, ★1646 by editor.

ROBERTS, *Sir* Walter, *II Bt.* †¶59, ★1646 by editor, †11080.

ROBERTSON *alias* ROBINSON, Bartholomew, *Author* (STC). Edits 10442 and *1621*-o. as B. R. M.

ROBERTSON, Eleazar. Verse 15713.

ROBINS, John, *Bailiff of Yarmouth.* ★21093.

ROBINSON, Anthony, *Mayor of Gloucester.* ★12171.

ROBINSON, Clement, *Song-writer* (DNB). *See* 5236, 22644.

ROBINSON, Ed., 'Soldier under Smith'. Verse 22788 (22790).

ROBINSON, Henry, *Bishop of Carlisle.* 6388, 6389, ★25786.

ROBINSON, *Sir* Henry, *of London* (Brown). Minsheu List.

ROBINSON, Henry, *Haberdasher.* 1626-o.² of ★13515.

ROBINSON, Hugh, *Divine* (DNB). Verse 13018; Minsheu List.

ROBINSON, John, *of Pilgrim Fathers* (DNB). *See* 556 = 3520, 12662 (12706, 12635).

ROBINSON, John, *of Denston Hall, Suff.* 17216 by printer.

ROBINSON, John, *Actor.* Verse 21011.

ROBINSON, Richard, *Author and Leatherseller* (DNB). Edits 5644, 21288.

ROBINSON, Richard. Verse 18673.

ROBINSON, Richard, *Actor.* ★6314.

ROBINSON, Thomas, 'of St. Margaret, Fish st.' ★¶21202.

ROBINSON, William, 'Secretary to L. Treasurer'. Minsheu List.

ROBSART, *Sir* John, *Father of Amy.* 1721 (1710).

ROBSON, Charles, *M.A.* (Foster 1615). Verse 24702.

ROCHE, David, *VII Viscount Roche. See* 10667.

ROCHEID, James, *Bailie of Edinburgh.* ★139.

RODES. *See* RHODES.

RODNEY (Southwell), Frances = *Sir* Edward *of Somerset.* ★23492 [see changes].

ROE, ROWE, etc.

ROWE, Bryan, *Scholar* (Venn). Prose 15790-90a.

ROWE, *Sir* Henry, *the elder, Lord Mayor.* ★1092 by editor, ★23330 [see changes].

ROWE, *Sir* Henry, *the younger, Alderman.* ★7307 by bookseller.

Row, John, *Principal of King's College, Aberdeen.* Verse 10692 (10696).

ROWE (Gresham), Mary = *Sir* Thomas *Lord Mayor.* 1063.

ROWE, Simon, *Master of Leathersellers.* ★21118.

ROE, *Sir* Thomas, *Ambassador (DNB).* 1071, 3669, 12807, ¶15055 [and see 15054], 21152; verse 23273; *see also* TH. R.

ROE, Thomas, *Fellow of King's* (Venn 1611). Verse 12964, 13519.

ROWE, *Sir* William, *Lord Mayor.* 16890, 19817.

ROGERS (Digges), Anne = Richard *Bishop.* 21174.

ROGERS, Daniel, *Diplomatist (DNB).* 7570; verse 13963, 21315, Agas map of Oxford-0.

ROGERS, Edward, '*Sussex preacher'. See* 13923.

ROGERS, Edward, *Lawyer* (? Foster 1597). *See* 25327.

ROGERS, Francis, *Gentleman pensioner, brother of Richard.* 10499.

ROGERS, *Sir* Francis, *of Cannington* (*Vis. Soms.*). ★24642.

ROGERS, G. Verse 23248.

ROGERS, George. Verse 25295.

ROGERS, *Sir* George, *of Cannington, d. 1582.* ★3099.

ROGERS, George. Welsh epistle 2744 = 17915.

ROGERS, Hugh, *Son of Sir Francis* (Keeler). †21179.

ROGERS, John, *of New College* (Foster 1603). Verse 13018.

ROGERS, John, *Puritan divine, d. 1636 (DNB).* Prose 3733.

ROGERS, John, *of Queens' College* (Venn 1624). Verse 12936.

ROGERS, Lewis, *Warden of Barber Surgeons.* Epistle ★25962.

ROGERS (Cressy), Mary = Hugh *of Everton, Notts.* ¶12270.

ROGERS, Nehemiah, *Divine (DNB).* Edits 21244.

ROGERS, Richard, *Bishop of Dover.* 5551.

ROGERS, Thomas, *of Bryanston* (Foster 1584). Verse 24042, probably 23135.

ROGERS, William. Verse 21094.

ROKEBY, Ralph, *Master of requests (DNB).* 12744 as Rukeby.

ROLAND, ROLLAND. *Listed with* ROWLANDS.

ROLLE, Denys, *of Bicton, Devon, d. 1638.* ¶23573.

ROLLE, Robert, *Schoolmaster* (Foster). Verse 12188, 21029 (21032), 22241.

ROLLES, Robert, *of Lincoln's Inn.* Verse 9529.

ROLLOCUS, A. Verse 21463.

ROLLOCK, Hercules, *Schoolmaster (DNB).* Verse 14293, 14373, 21101.

ROLLOCK, Peter, *Scottish divine (DNB).* Verse 5971, 22624.

ROLLOCK, Robert, *Divine (DNB).* Verse 3991, 14293.

ROLT (Jacob), Ellen = Henry *of St. Margaret's, Kent.* ★15333.

ROMANUS, Adrian, *Flemish mathematician* (Schotel). ¶18809.

ROMBOUTIUS, Joannes. Verse 21361.

ROMNEY (Taylor), Rebecca = *Sir* William. 1642 by editor, ★5700, 23590.

ROMNEY, *Sir* William, *Alderman and merchant* (*DNB*). ★5062, ★12750, 19001, ★22061.

RONTAL, Thomas, '*Royal secretary'.* 12413.

ROPER, Anne. *See* CONSTABLE.

ROPER, Christopher, *II Baron Teynham. See* 17332.

ROPER, Christopher, *IV Baron Teynham. See* 10667.

ROPER, John, *I Baron Teynham.* 5412.

ROPER (Petre), Mary = John *III Baron Teynham.* 12957.

ROPER, Thomas, *I Viscount Baltinglass. See* 10667.

ROSCARROCK, Nicholas, *Poet (DNB).* Verse 3393; consider N. R. (16642).

ROSE (Rosa), John, *Scottish poet* (BM). Verse 6580.

ROSENDALE, Agnes, '*Fleming with English Carmelites at Antwerp'.* 10677.

ROSEWELL, *Sir* Henry, *of Ford* (Foster 1607). †1954 [see changes]; Minsheu List.

ROSS, James, *VI* [? *or VII*] *Lord Rosse. See* 10667 misnamed Robert.

ROSSE, Jo. Verse 25436.

ROSSE, John, *of the Inner Temple.* Verse 10824 as Rose, 18985 [cf. 18994].

ROTA, Michael. Verse 11739.

ROTHERAM, Edward, *Alderman.* *11829.

ROTHERAM, George, *of Luton, d. 1599.* T. Barne, *Sermon, 1591-*U.

ROTHERHAM, John, *One of six clerks* [? *of Great Marlow, d. 1601*]. 1804.

ROTHERHAM, Sir John, *of Luton.* *†5692.

ROTHERHAM (Good), Katherine = *Sir* John. *5696.

ROTHERUPPE, Richard, '*Soldier*'. Verse 22855.

ROTHWELL, John, *Bookseller.* Perhaps prose 5217.

ROTTE. *See* WROTE.

ROURKE, O. *See* O'ROURKE.

ROUS. *See also* ROSS.

ROUS, Ambrose, *of Halton, brother of Francis.* ¶13378.

ROUS, Sir Anthony, *of Halton, father of next.* ¶13378, 21338.

ROUS, Francis, *Puritan* (*DNB*). Verse 10943 as F. R. [signed 10944], 18114; *see* 25327.

ROUS, Francis, *Physician* (Foster 1634). Verse 91.

ROUS, Sir John, *of Waltham* (*Vis. Essex*). *1476.

ROUSE, John, *Librarian* (*DNB*). ¶5097; edits 14451; *see* 25327.

ROUS, Richard, *Brother of Francis-DNB* (Foster 1593). Verse 10943 as R. R. [signed in 10944], 18114; *see* 25327.

ROUS, Robert, *Brother of preceding* (Foster). Verse 18114.

ROUS, William, *of Halton* (Foster 1612). 10942.

ROVERE, Gerolamo della, *Cardinal, Archbishop of Turin.* 17524 [earlier abroad].

Row *and* ROWE. *Listed with* ROE.

ROWBOTHAM, James, *Bookseller.* Prose 724 only, 6214, 15487, 15542.

ROBOTHAM, John [*possibly the DNB John*]. Edits 14474.

ROWBOTHOM, William. 21632 and *1580-*HN.

ROLLAND, John, *Poet* (*DNB*): his '*aunt called Cait*'. *See* 21254.

ROWLANDS *alias* VERSTEGAN, Richard, *Antiquary* (*DNB*). All as R. V., edits 16094; prose 17507; verse O. Vaenius, *Emblemata,*

*1608-*F., probably B. Jackson, *Manuductions, 1616-*F.

ROWLANDS, Samuel, *Writer* (*DNB*). Verse 584, 5567, 23791 (23725).

ROLANDUS, Thomas. 22218.

ROWLANDS, William, *M.A.* (Foster 1632). Verse 24157.

ROWLEY, Edward, '*Son of Mary and John Esq.*' 23100a.

ROWLEY, William, *Dramatist* (*DNB*). Verse some copies 23760, 23779, 25176.

ROYDON, Humfrey (? Venn 1594). Edits 172.

ROWDON, John, *Exchequer clerk. See* 23779 only.

RAWDON, Marmaduke, *City captain.* *21095; epistle *1507.

ROYDON, Matthew, *Poet* (*DNB*). 4985, 4990; verse later state 19523-L., 25118a.

ROYDON, Owen [*untraced*]. Verse, perhaps part-edits 20402.

ROYDON, Thomas, *of Peckham* (*Vis. Kent*). 1738 (1710).

ROYSTON, Richard, *Bookseller.* Prose 1369.

RUBEN, Abraham, '*Archisynagoge in Constantinople*'. H. Broughton, *Familia Davidis, 1605-*NY.

RUCKSHAW, William, *D.D.* (Venn). Epistle 22608.

RUD, Richard, *Warden of Haberdashers.* *13514 [13513 impf.].

RUDD, Robert, *Archdeacon* (Venn 1582). *See* 12527.

RUDOLPH II, *Emperor.* *14401 and *14405 (14344 and 14346), *15507; *see* 3538.

RUDSTONE, Sir John, *Lord Mayor. See* 864.

RUDSTONE, John, *Mathematician and almanac-maker* (*STC*). Verse 5374, 18673.

RUDYARD, Sir Benjamin, *Politician* (*DNB*). *15325, 21340, ¶25327 [and see text].

RUDYERD, Thomas, *of Rudyard* (*Vis. Staffs.*). *†21437.

RUGELEY, Nicholas, *of the Inner Temple.* Verse 10824.

RUGG, Robert, *of Farne* (*CSPD*). 23785 (23725).

RUKEBY. *See* ROKEBY.

RULMANUS, Annaeus, *French writer* (BN). Verse 21649.

RUPERT, *Prince* (DNB). ¶6304.

RUPEUS. *See* CRAIG.

RUSSELL, Anne. *See* SOMERSET.

RUSSELL (Hussey), Bridget = Francis *II Earl.* 649 [see changes], *2051, *15319, *23024, 25979, O. Pigge, *Sermons, 1591*-F.

RUSSELL, Edward, *III Earl of Bedford.* †4110, †4216, †4883 [see changes], ¶7193 (7189, 7216), †14294, 15696, 18245, 19700 (19712, 19646), 19703 (19646), †20084 by editor and *1595*-U. by translator, †20889, by editor 22776 and *1592*-F. (22761, 22781), 25342, by editor †25620 misnamed Francis, *†25621, O. Pigge, *Sermons, 1591*-F.; *see* 17331, 25695; Minsheu List.

RUSSELL (Cooke), Elizabeth = John 'Lord Russell' (*DNB as* Hoby). 85a, 10790, 10797, 16660, 19153, 23135.

RUSSELL, Elizabeth, *Maid of honour, daughter of preceding.* Epistle *16696.

RUSSELL, Francis, *II Earl of Bedford.* 293 (312), 309, 374, *1005, ¶1710 [? earlier lost], 1754 [see changes], 2728 = 22134, ¶2962, 3371, 4434, †4457, 5274, 6776 by author, *¶10674, 11641, 11697 and *1582*-F., *11839, 15218 [see changes], 16947, *18270, 19783, 19848, 19849, 21090, 22224, 23675, 24503 (24491), 24631, 24683 by author, 25013. *See* 6155; arms 2107 (Jeremie), 2108 (Esai), 6797.

RUSSELL, Francis, *Earl of Bedford* (25620). Error for Edward.

RUSSELL, Francis, *IV Earl of Bedford.* 539, 4109, 4975-E.², ¶12657a (12635), *Fens map in 17827, 18692, ¶20944; *see* 10667, 17332; Minsheu List.

RUSSELL, John, 'Lord Russell', *d. 1584.* 12448 by editor.

RUSSELL, Sir John, *of Strensham, Worcs., d. 1593.* ¶5220.

RUSSELL, John, *Advocate* (STC). Verse 22626.

RUSSELL, John. Verse 23720.

RUSSELL (Harington), Lucy = Edward *III Earl of Bedford. See also* †*entries under Edward.* 4220 and *1619*-HD., 4234 (4212), *4466, *5849 [see changes], 6265 (6238), *6338, 6735, 7095, 7187, ¶7193 (7189, 7216), 7192 (epistle reprinted 7195, 7216 in text), 7205, 7207, *7232, 7398 by editor, 7410 (7394) by

editor, *11098 [see changes], *11765 [see changes], 11780 by bookseller [see changes], ¶12748, *14296, 16884, *18041 [see changes], 19624, 19742 (19646), 20789, 21772 [and 21773 by editor], *23273, R. Bruen, *Summary of Bible, 1623*-HD.; presentation 14773. *Epistle:* 3926, *5695 [see changes], 6258 (6263, 6238), 13633 (13624), 15227, *23581 (23575, 21653); *see* 7045; Minsheu List.

RUSSELL, Richard, 'Merchant, cousin'. 11377.

RUSSELL, William, *I Baron R. of Thornhaugh.* 19724 (19649, cf. 19648) by editor, †19748 (19649, cf. 19648) by editor, 25339 (25340), ¶25697 [see changes]; epistle 16696; *see* 25438.

RUSSELL, William, *I Duke of Bedford. See* 10667.

RUSSELL, Sir William, *I Bt.* *Fens map in 17827.

RUTHVEN, Alexander, *Brother of John below.* Verse 21101.

RUTHVEN, Beatrix. *See* HOME.

RUTHVEN, John, *III Earl of Gowrie.* *21267.

RUTHVEN, Thomas, *I Lord R. of Freeland.* St. Andrews (Salvator) *Theses, 1628*-E.²

RUTINGIUS. *See* RUYTINCK.

RUTTEN, Mathias, *Brewer near Tower of London.* 11747 by printer.

RUYTINCK, Symeon, *Pastor of Dutch Church* (STC). Verse 13582 as S. R.; *see* 17944; Minsheu List.

RYDER. *Listed with* RIDER.

RYLEY, Thomas, *Fellow of Trinity* (Venn 1626). Epistle 20692 with reply; verse 7365, 21460.

RYND (Rindeus), A., 'Schoolmaster of Linlithgow'. Prose 25737.

RYND, John, *Bailie of Edinburgh.* W. M., *Edinburghs alphabet*-E.

RYTHER, Augustine, *Engraver* (DNB). Edits 24481.

RYVES, Charles, *of New College* (Foster 1585). Verse 24042 [date *1592*].

RYVES, George, *Warden of New College* (Foster 1579). *6420, *20914, *¶23913; *see* 17944.

RYVES, Sir Thomas, *Civilian* (DNB). 16858.

S

S., M[rs]. *See* MRS. M. S.

S., A. (143). *See* ARCHIBALD SIMSON.

S., A., F[ilius] C. *See* A. S. F. C.

S., A., T[rinity] C., [*Cambridge*]. Verse 1880 [1879 a ghost].

S., A. ¶22877; verse 633, 19513; prose 7538 as shorthand reporter.

St., Mrs. A. ¶13586.

Ste., Alex. Verse 11596.

Str., Arth. ¶25890.

S., A. H. Verse 16696, perhaps A. H., S[cutifer].

S., B. Prose 25786.

S., C., *alias* NAEARCHUS. 17805.

S., C. Verse 17997 [cousin], 21640.

S., D. ¶22965 as M. D. S., Gent.; verse 7498.

S., E., *Esq.* (12772). *See* EDWARD SHELDON.

S., Mrs. E. Allison 366.

S., E. Verse 14783 [? Scory], 19511, T. Tuke, *Treasure of true-love, 1608*-F.; *see* 23106.

Sc., E. (7193). *See* EDMUND SCORY.

S., S[ir] F. (7325 and 22879). *See* SIR FRANCIS STAFFORD.

S., Mrs. F. 22630.

S., F. Verse 3894.

S., Frances, '*Akin to translator*' [? Staverton]. 10477 by editor.

Sa., Fr. (23067). *See* FRANCIS SANDERS.

S., G. Epistle 21057 [gent.]; verse 889, 1404, 6151, 13799; prose T. R., *Catechisme in meter, 1583*-C.¹⁹; *see* 25327 [? of Oxford].

S., H. (22540). *See* HUGH SANFORD.

S., D[om]. H., *W. P.* [*presumably Sir* Henry Sidney, *president of Wales*]. 19060.

S., *Sir* H. [*perhaps* Spelman]. 21752.

S., H., *Esq.* 1039.

S., H. '*Communem viduarum procum.*' *See* 25438.

S., H.—'Concussus, surgo. C. A.—H. S.' Prose 12476.

S., H. 1062; verse 18532; *see* 1525 [? misprint for H. B.].

Sal., H. (19775). *See* HENRY SALISBURY.

S., H. L. Dutch verse 17224 (tp., pt. ii).

S., J. (4712), *see* JOHN STROUD; (12421), *see* JOHN SPENCER, bookseller; (13713), *see* JOHN SPENSER, President; (19513), *see* JOHN SELDEN; (21413), *see* JOHN STRANGE.

S., I. [*probably* John Stow]. Edits 17028, 21499, 22608.

S., J. [*Editor 1631–40, possibly* J. Spencer]. Edits 3227 (3224), 3235 and *1630*-FLEMING (3224), 12363, 22808.

S., I., *of Lincoln's Inn* [? Stephens]. Verse 18904.

S., I., *M.A.* Verse 6190.

S., I. Edits 23069; verse 3905, 6983, 15555, 17805 [gent.], 17997, 18114 [? of Broadgates Hall], 19260, 20050, 21510, 23380; prose 17913 with reply, 25786; errata 23294 [? Sprint or misprint for T. S.].

St., I. (14377). *See* JOHN STOCKWOOD.

St., I. Verse 14793 [? Stoughton].

St. G., I: O: (18511). *See* JOHN ST. GEORGE.

Sw., Io. Verse 14926.

S., I. A., *SS.Th.S.R.* Verse 19074.

S., I. M. Verse 22274 [many conjectures].

S., J. T. J. [*perhaps* J. T. *and* J. Stroud]. Prose 10850.

S., *Lady* L. Epistle 7196 (7216, etc.).

S., L. Edits 5216; verse 1892.

S., M. (17824). Explained under FRANCIS QUARLES.

S., M[rs]. *or Mrs.* M. S. Epistle 778.

S., M. Verse 1079 [? Smith], *1622*-C.⁶ of 11122 [dubious], 15036; *see* 3249.

Sp., M. I., *S.E.Min. See* JAMES SPENSE.

S., M. L. (18157). *See* LE SAUX.

S., M. M. Verse 11224.

S., Marie P. [*Recusant*]. *1620*-F. of 24627a by editor.

S., N., *Oxoniae.* Verse 17824.

Sc., No. Verse 6818.

S., P. Verse 12748 [but P. T. in 12747].

S., R. [*presumably* Ralph Sidley]. Verse 12253-L. only.

S., R., *Esq.* [? Salisbury]. Verse 19338.

S., R., *of the Inner Temple.* Edits 21516.

S., R. [*Merchant in Barbary*]. *See* 1377.

SALTER, Guilielmus, *Templ.* [*untraced*]. Verse 22375.

SALTER, *Sir* William, *of Iver, Bucks., royal carver.* 14469 by editor [see changes].

SALTERNE, George, *of the Middle Temple* (Foster). Verse 10536.

SALTMARSH, John, *Mystical writer* (*DNB*). Verse 7294, 21460.

SALTONSTALL, Charles, *Writer* (*DNB*). 21645 as brother C. S.

SALTONSTALL, *Sir* Peter, *Royal esquire, son of next.* *¶25677 [see changes].

SALTONSTALL, *Sir* Richard, *Lord Mayor* (*DNB*). *23328 [see changes], *23363, †24208 and *1590*-U., Norden engr. of London Bridge-F.

SALTONSTALL, *Sir* Richard, *Colonist* (*DNB*). 12875, *†14320.

SALTONSTALL (Pointz), Susan = *Sir* Richard *Lord Mayor.* 20180-HD. (Horblit).

SALTONSTALL, Wye, *Translator* (*DNB*). Verse 21640.

SALTWOOD, Robert, *Monk* (*DNB*). See 3186.

SALUSBURY. *See* SALISBURY.

SALUSTE du Bartas, Guillaume de, *Poet* (*NBG*). Verse 14379.

SALUSTE, Voy Sire. Anagram of Josuah Sylvester.

SAMMES, *Sir* John, *of Much Totham* (Venn 1606). 16920.

SAMMES, William, *of the Middle Temple.* 16902; consider WILLIAM SA.

SAMMES, William, *LL.D.* (Venn 1582) [? *same as preceding*]. *Fens map in 17827; Minsheu List.

SAMPSON, Thomas, *Divine* (*DNB*). *6810 = 11888 (10400); prose 3500.

SANDERS, Francis, *of Congham, Norf.* Epistle 23067.

SANDERS, Henry, *City captain.* *21095; epistle *1506, more *1507.

SAUNDERS, John, *Recorder of Reading* (Foster 1601). *23840.

SAUNDERS, *Sir* Matthew, *of Leic.* (PCC 1623). 22949 by editor.

SANDERS, Nicholas, *Controversialist* (*DNB*). *See* 99, 5407, 11433.

SAUNDERS, Nicholas, *of Ewell, Surrey.* 11097, 11100 = ¶11097, 12261 by bookseller.

SAUNDERS, Thomas, *Mayor of Coventry.* *15450.

SANDERSON, John. Verse 23041 and 23044.

SAUNDERSON (Elltoft), Mildred = Nicholas *I Viscount.* 21016, ¶21705.

SAUNDERSON, Nicholas, *I Viscount Castleton.* ¶21705; *see* 10667.

SANDERSON, Robert, *Bishop of Lincoln.* Minsheu List.

SANFORD, Hugh, *Tutor to III Earl of Pembroke.* Edits 22540 as H. S.; verse 13790a.

SANDFORD, James, *Author* (*DNB*). Verse 1582, 7169, 17244.

SANDFORD, John, *Poet* (*DNB*). *22398; edits 7322; verse 6333, 11956, 21659, 21660, 23024, 24042 [date is *1592*].

SANDILANDS, *Lady* Alison. *See* COCKBURN.

SANDYLANDS, Andrew, *of Christ's College* (Venn). Verse 12964.

SANDILANDS, James, *Rector of Aberdeen university.* Aberdeen *Theses, 1629*-L. (frag., Harl. 5938).

SANDILANDS, John, *Gentleman to Prince Charles* [? *later Bt.*]. Epistle some copies *4747-O.

SANDILANDS, John, *IV Lord Torphichen.* *See* 10667.

SANDS. *Listed with* SANDYS.

SANDSBURY, John, *Poet* (*DNB*). Verse 12551, 12555.

SANDYS, SANDS, SONDS, etc.

SANDYS, Edwin, *Archbishop of York.* *1710, *13963, *14608, *18708, *18711, *18712, *18726, *18730, *19355; prose 16965.

SANDYS, *Sir* Edwin, *Statesman* (*DNB*). *17362; Minsheu List [Edward in some states].

SANDYS, Henry [*presumably father of* William *VI Baron*]. *21731.

SANDYS (Hanbury), Mary = *Sir* Miles *of Gloucs.* *11769 [cf. 11782].

SONDS or SANDS, *Sir* Michael, *of Throwley, Kent.* *11127, 19615.

SANDYS, *Sir* Miles, *I Bt.* *Fens map in 17827, ¶19879.

SCOT, John [? *Surgeon*]. Epistle *11203.

SCOTT, *Sir* John, *Scottish lawyer* (*DNB*). ¶1496, 14714, ¶15366, 15372, 17616, St. Andrews (Leonard) *Theses, 1629*-E.; epistle R. Williamson, *Elementa, 1624*-E.

SCOTT (Smith), Katherine = *Sir* John *of Nettlestead, previously* Hayward. *¶6499, *21013, 22666 only by printer.

SCOTT, Reginald, *Author* (*DNB*). 12561.

SCOTT, Richard, *Father of preceding.* 1731 (1710).

SCOTT, *Sir* Thomas, *of Kent, d. 1594* (*DNB*). Epistle 21864.

SCOTT, Thomas, *Political writer, d. 1626* (*DNB*). Verse 1106.

SCOTT, Walter, *I Earl of Buccleuch. See* 10667.

SCOTT, *Sir* William, *of Ardross and Elie, director of chancery.* ¶3448, St. Andrews (Leonard) *Theses, 1635*-E.
Mostly by editors: 21269, 21270, 21272, 21274, 21277, ¶21279, 21281, 21282, 21283, 21286.

SCOTT, William, *Minister of Cupar.* *18171-A.

SCRIVEN, *Sir* Reginald, *M.A.* (Foster). *¶6230 as Skreven.

SCROOBY (Scrubaeus), James, *of Peterhouse* (Venn). Verse 1492.

SCROPE, Emanuel, *XI Baron Scrope.* 18783 and *1619*-L.

SCROPE, Emanuel, *I Earl of Sunderland. See* 17332.

SCROPE, Henry, *IX Baron Scrope: family of. See* 6270.

SCROPE, Jane. *See* BREWS.

SCROPE (Carey), Philadelphia = Thomas *X Baron.* ¶4577-LINC. [F. impf.], *5538; epistle 16696.

SCROPE, Thomas, *X Baron Scrope.* ¶19649 by editor [? earlier lost].

SCROW, Thomas, '*Friend of Bishop J. Yonge*' (? Foster). Epistle 21800.

SCRUBAEUS. *See* SCROOBY.

SCRYMGEOUR, John, *I Viscount Dudhope.* 15656.

SCRYMSHAW, ——, '*Schoolmaster at New Windsor*'. Minsheu List.

SCUDAMORE, *Sir* James, *Father of John I Viscount.* 15193.

SCUDAMORE, *Sir* John, *Gentleman usher, father of preceding.* 356, ¶5220.

SCUDAMORE, John, *I Viscount Scudamore.* 10701, 11947, 24984; *see* 10667.

SCUDAMORE, John, *of Kentchurch, Heref., d. 1669.* †11659 = ¶11680 (11652).

SCUDAMORE (Shelton), Mary = *Sir* John, *Lady of Bedchamber.* 566.

SCUDAMORE (Hampden), Ruth = *Sir* Philip, *later* Leigh. 4237 and *1619*-F. (4220), 15411.

SCUDAMORE, Williambrose, *Gent.* Verse Penkethman, *Purchasers pinnace, 1629*-L. (frag. Harl. 5949).

SCUDDER, Henry, *Divine* (*DNB*). Edits 25317.

SCULTETUS, Abrahamus, *Theologian* (*ADB*). Verse 19021, 24551.

SEABRID. *See* SEBRIGHT.

SEAMAN, John, *Chancellor of Gloucester* (Venn 1579). *25150, R. Web, *†*Key of knowledge, 1622*-PN.[2]

SEAMAN, Lazarus, *Divine* (*DNB*). Edits 22497.

SEBASTIAN, *King of Portugal.* 12593 (12594) by editor.

SEBRIGHT, *Sir* Edward, *I Bt.* †22835 as Seabrid.

SECKFORD, Thomas, *Lawyer* (*DNB*). ¶13568; prose Saxton's atlas, *1583*-L.; *see* 23095.

SEDGWICK, John, *Divine* (*DNB*). Edits 22475, 22491, 22498, 23829.

SEDGWICK, William, *Fellow of Caius* (Venn 1631). Verse 7366.

SEDLEY *or* SIDLEY, sometimes erroneously Sidney.

SIDLEY, *Sir* Isaac, *I Bt.* 14301.

SEDLEY, *Sir* John *of Aylesford, II Bt.* 13046 by bookseller [*see* changes].

SIDLEY, Ralph [*perhaps Sir Ralph of Norfolk*]. Verse 12253 [Sidney in later eds.]; *see* R. S.

SEDLEY, *Sir* William, *I Bt.* ¶18987, *1607*-O. of 23278 [misprinted Syley in 23279; *see* changes]; verse 4508 (4509); Minsheu List as Sidney.

SEGAR, Francis, *Translator* (*DNB*). Edits 5058.

SEGAR, *Sir* William, *Herald* (*DNB*). Verse 12500, 19511, 24756; prose 3219 = 16749, 3220; Minsheu List.

SEGGETT (Seghetus), Thomas, *Scottish poet* (BM). Verse 21657 as Sigaetus.

SEGRAVE, ——. 18787.

SEILE, Henry, *Bookseller.* Prose 957 = 13268; unsigned prose 1396.

SEINTCLER or SEINTLER, Giles, *Puritan preacher* (Venn *as* Synkler). See 4709.

SELBY, *Sir* George, *Mayor of Newcastle.* *4100, *14491.

SELDEN, John, *Jurist* (DNB). 18427; epistle 18037, 22634; edits 823, 7438, 11197; apparatus 7226; verse 3914, 7219 [7220 earlier?], 13778, 14751, 16883, 19513 as I. S., 20505; prose 24756; *see* 25327.

SELDIUS, Georg Sigmund, *Imperial vicechancellor. See* 10674.

SEMPILL, Hugh, *V Lord Sempill. See* 10667 misnamed James.

SEMPILL, Robert, *IV Lord Sempill.* ¶1597-HN. of 16870 [see changes].

SENHOUSE, Richard, *Bishop of Carlisle.* Minsheu List as Sinewes.

SENOVELLANUS, Antonius, *Navarrenus* [*pseudonym or fiction*]. Prose 23872.

SENTLIGER. *See* ST. LEGER.

SERAE, Henr., *Gen.* Verse 18498.

SERES, William, *Printer* (DNB). Unsigned prose 4778, 12897, 20378; unsigned verse by compositor 12890.

SERGIER, Richard, *senior, Bookseller.* Prose 22996 [probably not translator].

SERLO, Io. [*? misprint for* John Searle, *surgeon*]. Verse 11564.

SERRURIER, Philippe, *Elder of the French Church.* Verse 21139.

SETON family. ¶22567.

SETON, Alexander, *I Earl of Dunfermline.* 1405, 3990 by editor, 13946, 15058, ¶15366, 18357, 20104, Edinburgh *Theses*, 1600-O., St. Andrews (Leonard) *Theses*, 1611-E.[2], (Salvator), 1615-O.[6], W. Welwood, *Aurei tituli*, 1605-L.[13]
Epistle: *15715; verse 4473; *see* 22567.

SETON, Charles, *II Earl of Dunfermline.* *¶22567, St. Andrews (Salvator) *Theses*, 1632-E.; *see* 10667.

SETON, George, *III Earl of Winton. See* 10667.

SETON, Gregory, *Bookseller.* Prose 16987.

SETON (Stewart), Grizel = John *of Meldrum.* Epistle 12067.

SETON, John, *Divine and dialectician* (DNB). Verse G. Petrus, *Opus sane*, 1524-O.[9]

SETON (Hay), Margaret = Alexander *I Earl.* 22566.

SETON, Robert, *II Earl of Winton.* *¶22567 [? error for George, III Earl].

SEWALL, William, *Coventry draper* (PCC 1624). Epistle *4023.

SEWARD, John, '*Yeovil preacher*' (? Foster 1604). Epistle 5808; *see* 5809.

SEYLIARD. *Listed with* Sulyard.

SEYMOUR (Stanhope), Anne = Edward *Duke of Somerset,* later Newdigate. 920, *1561*-F. of 1720 (1710) [1720 impf.], ¶2854, 3015 = 17117 by bookseller, 3195, 14576 by bookseller, 15178, *15319, 17119, W. Samuel, *Abridgemente of statutes,* 1551-HN.

SEYMOUR (Sackville), Anne = Edward '*Lord Beauchamp*'. *¶4497, *22971 (22965) by editor; epistle R. Bruen, *Pilgrimes practice,* 1621-O.

SEYMOUR (Portman), Anne = *Sir* Edward *III Bt.* 23570 (23572).

SEYMOUR, Arabella. *See* ARABELLA.

SEYMOUR, Edward, *I Duke of Somerset.* 4059, 4407, 11220, 12857, 13745, 15205, 15217 [see changes], *17115, 17317, 17792, 18765, 24359, 24365 [see changes], 24666, 26142; prose 25255.

SEYMOUR, Edward, *I Earl of Hertford.* 1253 rewritten 1256, 1539, 4399, 5478, few copies ¶6259-HN., 7312, *11496, 15487 by bookseller, 17846, 18637, 18675, †19567, 19914, 21225, ¶21328, 24351 (24366) [see changes], G. Ledoyen, *Playne treatise,* 1576-HN.; presentation 22791; Minsheu List.

SEYMOUR, *Sir* Edward, *I Bt.* ¶25941.

SEYMOUR, *Sir* Edward, *III Bt.* ¶23573.

SEYMOUR (Howard of Effingham), Frances = Edward *I Earl.* 1599 by printer, 21320.

SEYMOUR (Howard of Bindon), Frances = Edward *I Earl. See* STUART.

SEYMOUR, *Sir* Henry, *of Marwell, brother of Edward I Duke.* 13491 [see changes].

SEYMOUR, *Lord* Henry, *Son of Edward I Duke.* 5234.

SEYMOUR, *Lady* Jane, *Sister of preceding.* 1726 (1710) [1725 a frag.].

SEYMOUR, Robert, '*Lord Beauchamp*', *d. 1646.* See 10667.

SEYMOUR, William, *of Gray's Inn.* Verse 14927.

SEYMOUR, William, *II Duke of Somerset.* †887, 3818, *†¶4497, one issue *7326-F. [Darcie trans.], 25377; *see* 10667, 17331.

SHACKLOCK, Richard, *Divine (DNB).* Epistle 12598.

SHAMLER, William, *of Broadgates Hall* (Foster). See 25327.

SHARPE, Andrew, *M.A.* (Venn). Verse 22375.

SHARPE, Edward, *B.D.* (Venn 1576). Verse 22375.

SHARP, Joan [*presumably a fiction*]. See 22974.

SCHARP, Sir John, *of Houston, d. 1608.* 22368.

SHARP, Patrick, *Theologian (DNB).* Verse 14293.

SHARPE, Peter, *of Chester* (Foster). Prose 1853.

SHARPE, William, *B.D.* (Venn 1581). Verse 22375.

SHARPHELL, Edward, '*Student of author*'. Verse 6332 [6331 a ghost]; *see* Ὅρος-ὀξύ.

SHAW, James, *Bookseller.* Prose 5795, 13848, 18856 [18857 anr. version].

SHAW, Tobias, *Son of author* (Foster). Hebrew epistle 22389.

SHAXTON, Nicholas, *Bishop of Salisbury.* 6083; prayer in 2064 and variant 2063-C.

SHEAFE, Edmund, *the younger* (Venn 1614). Verse 11780 (11773).

SHEERE, John, *Mayor of Exeter.* 5614.

SHEARES, William, *Bookseller.* Prose 17471.

SHEFFARD, William, *Bookseller.* Perhaps prose 23009.

SHEFFIELD family. 1233; *see* 6270.

SHEFFIELD (Howard), Douglas = John *II Baron.* *1233, 3695, 13065, 18277.

SHEFFIELD, Edmund, *I Earl of Mulgrave.* *†1233 rewritten 1234, *†1934, ¶2772 [first ed. of pt. iii], 10824, 14427, 15202, ¶15715, ¶16887 cancelled [blunder as Edward, Earl Mowbray], 17839, *19699 (19649) by editor, 21630 [cf. 21517], 22802; *see* 10667, 17332; Minsheu List.

SHEFFIELD, Edmund, *Son of preceding.* Epistle *12494 as Edward.

SHEFFIELD, Edward: (12494), *see preceding*; (16887), *see* EDMUND, *I Earl.*

SHEFFIELD (Anderson), Grizel = Sir John. ¶2773, H. Clapham, *Tract of prayer, 1602-L.*

SHEFFIELD, Sir John, *Son of Edmund I Earl.* *19678 (19649) by editor; epistle *12494.

SHEFFIELD, Sir William, *Brother of preceding.* Epistle *12494.

SHELDON, Edward, *of Beoley, Worcs., d. 1643.* 1802 by editor, 12772 as E. S., 12779 and prose as Philostilpnos.

SHELLEY, Sir John, *I Bt.* Minsheu List.

SHELLEY, Richard [*of Sussex; several of name*]. *11367.

SHELTON, Henry, '*Captain, Norwich militia*' [? *of Barningham, d. 1634*]. Epistle 15037.

SHELTON, Thomas, *Translator, Dublin recusant in exile (DNB).* Verse 18745, 21361.

SHELTON, Thomas, *Stenographer (DNB).* Edits J. Lewis, *Right use, 1631-PN.²*

SHEPHERD [? Robert], *of Kirby Bedon, Norf.* Epistle 15037.

SHEPHERD, Thomas, *London merchant.* Epistle *25847 only.

SHERARD, William, *I Baron Sherard.* See 10667.

SHERBURNE, Sir Edward, *Translator (DNB).* Verse 353, 18947.

SHERBORNE (Walmisley), Elizabeth = Richard *of Stonyhurst.* Epistle *23580.

SHERLEY. *See* SHIRLEY.

SHERMAN, Abraham, *M.A.* (Foster). Edits 4937.

SHERMAN, John, *of Trinity College* (Venn 1626). Verse 7365.

SHERMAN, Thomas, *Rector of Hintlesham* (Foster 1596). *3926.

SHERMAN, William. Epistle 23791 (23725).

SHILLITO, George, *of Gray's Inn, receiver for Yorkshire.* 25409 by bookseller.

SHIPTON, Thomas, '*of London*'. *25624.

SHIRLEY, SHERLEY, SHURLEY.

SHIRLEY (*adventurers*) Family and friends. Late issue 6417-L.

SHIRLEY, Sir Charles, *III Bt.* ¶1354.

20544, *21132, 23527, *†¶23578 (23581, 23575, 21653), 23649, 25915 (25897, 25911), T. Powell, *Loves leprosie, 1598*-SILVER. *Epistle:* 6333, 13633 (13624), 25891 (25911). *See* 6789, 10667, 17331; Minsheu List.

SIDNEY, Robert, *II Earl of Leicester.* 587, *¶13162, *¶23578 (23581, 23575, 21653), 24810.

SIDNEY (Blount), Sarah = Robert *I Earl.* 24691.

SIGAETUS, SEGHETUS. *See* SEGGETT.

SIGISMUND II, *King of Poland.* 16571.

SIGNARD, I., '*Huguenot minister*'. Verse 21139.

SILVESTER. *See* SYLVESTER.

SIM the butler [*fiction*]. Verse 13540.

SIMAND, Jo. [?John Symondes *of Middle Temple*]. *3.

SYME, John, '*Preacher at Leigh, Essex*' (STC). Prose 18420.

SYMKINS, Christopher, *Schismatic separatist at Amsterdam.* *5345.

SIMLER, Josias, *Swiss scholar* (NBG). Prose 4074; *see* 24668 and 24669.

SIMS, John, '*of Charde, Soms.*' [?*the next*]. 19945.

SYMES, John, *of Poundsford* (*Vis. Soms.*). *21838 as Simmes.

SIMMES, Valentine, *Bookseller.* Prose 1053, 5653; perhaps 749, 3068, 15379, 17844, 24097.

SYMONDS, William, *Divine* (DNB). Edits ¶22791 as W. S.

SIMONIDES. *See* SIMSON.

SIMSON, Adam, *Minister of New Abbey.* Verse 22567.

SIMSON, Andrew, *Scottish divine, d. 1590* (DNB). ¶13950.

SIMPSON, Andrew, *Bailie of Edinburgh.* W. M., *Edinburghs alphabet*-E.

SIMSON, Andrew, *Clergyman* (STC, *father of Andrew*-DNB *d.* 1712). Prose 6112.

SIMSON, Archibald, *Divine* (DNB). Edits 143 as A. S., 23598–23600 inc.

SIMSON, Gabriel, *Printer.* Perhaps prose 3869.

SYMPSON, George, '*Vicar of Syndon* [*sic*], *Sussex*' [cf. Foster]. *See* 13923.

SIMSON, John, '*London preacher*' [*presumably* Venn 1576]. Minsheu List.

SIMPSON, Nicholas, *D.D.* (Foster 1565). 165.

SIMSON, Samuel, *of Notts.* (Venn 1606). Verse 11468.

SIMSON, William, *Divine, d. 1620?* (DNB). Verse 4660, 22624, 25210.

SINCLAIR, George, *V Earl of Caithness.* *See* 10667 [blunder as St. Calre, Carceynes].

SINCLAIR, Henry, *III Lord Sinclair.* 24797 [sig. B2].

SINCLAIR, John, *Soldier, son of George above.* *See* 18022.

SINCLAIR, Sir John, *Dean of gild, Edinburgh.* *88, *139, *23262.

SINCLAIR, John, '*Master of Berriedale*', *grandson of George.* *20697.

SINCLAIR, John, *IX Lord Sinclair.* *See* 10667 [blunder as Henry St. Char].

SINGLETON, Hugh, *Printer.* Signed prose 20848, undated-F. of 25258; unsigned prose Lemnius, *Sanctuarie of salvation*-HD.

SINGLETON, Thomas [*probably the next*]. Verse 24776.

SINGLETON, Thomas, *Principal of Brasenose* (Foster 1573). *6420 as Shingleton, 20172, *25150; edits 19021, 19022; verse 3194, 4756.

SINGLETON, William, *of the Middle Temple* (Foster 1621). Verse 11163, 17636.

SIXESMITH, Thomas, *Fellow of Brasenose* (Foster). Edits 3625 (3629), 3627, 3628.

SKELTON (Crisp), Anne = [?Samuel], *daughter of Nicholas.* *11672 (11679, 11652).

SKELTON, John, *Poet* (DNB). Epistle 24796, Whittinton, *Epigrammata, 1519*-HN.; Skelton's Ghost [i.e. editor], verse 22614.

SKENE, Alexander, *Advocate, brother of Sir John.* Prose 24623a.

SKENE, Sir James, *I Bt. and Judge.* *17207, *17208, Edinburgh *Theses, 1630*-O.

SKENE, Sir John, *Lord Curriehill* (DNB). Edits 21877 with privilege; certifies 21892 [date *1611*-HD.], 21893, s. sh. *Act . . . seasings*-F.

SKENE, Robert. Edits 5957.

SKEVINGTON, Thomas, *of Skeffington* (Venn 1565). 23277.

SKIDMORE. *See* SCUDAMORE.

SKINNER, John, *Douay scholar and priest.* *See* JOHN WARREN (*alias*).

SKINNER, Robert, *Bishop of Worcester*. *See* 10667 misnamed John.

SKINNER, Thomas, *Lord Mayor*. 23606 by bookseller [see changes].

SKINNER, Sir Vincent, *of Thornton College* (Venn). *1816.

SKIP, John, *Bishop of Hereford*. *2983 = 21617.

SKIPPON, Philip, *Soldier* (DNB). ¶7366.

SKIPWITH, Sir Henry, *I Bt*. ¶25992.

SKIPWITH, Sir William, *Father of preceding*. 11068 only, 25057.

SKREVEN. *See* SCRIVEN.

SLADE, James, '*Captain*'. *16942.

SLANY, —— [*London*]. *5700.

SLANY (Phesant), Margaret = *Sir* Stephen. *21165.

SLANY, Sir Stephen, *Lord Mayor*. *19799, *21296; epistle *18282.

SLATER, SCLATER, etc.

SLATYER, John, *Brother of author* (Venn 1598). Verse 22634.

SCLATER, William, *Divine* (DNB). Epistle *1941.

SCLATER, William, *the younger, Divine* (DNB). Edits 21844, 21846, 21848; verse 13519.

SLEEP, Anthony, *of Trinity College* (Venn). *18206.

SLEIGH, Edmund, *of Derby, uncle of Hall*. *21523; see 12662 (12706, 12635).

SLYGH, R., '*of Egginton*'. *20207.

SLINGSBY, Sir William, *Carver to Queen* (Vis. *Yks.*). Minsheu List.

SLOPER, John, *Fellow of King's* (Venn). Verse 13519.

SMALMAN, Stephen, *of Wildertop, Shrops*. †26014 by bookseller.

SMALLWOOD, Alan, *M.A.* (Venn). Verse 3.

SMARLET, Joshua, '*Physician and surgeon*'. Verse 5446.

SMART, Humfrey, *M.A.* (Foster). Verse 13595.

SMART, Ithiel, *M.A.* (Venn). Edits 20683.

SMETHWICK, John, *Bookseller*. As Stationers' warden registering copyright, name accidentally put in imprimatur of 21544.

SMITH, SMYTHE, etc.

SMITH, Adam. Verse 5375 and *1618*-private hands [cf. 5373, etc.].

SMITH [Cleophas?], '*of St. Antholin, London*'. Epistle *12203.

SMITH, Edward, *B.D.* (Venn 1597). Verse 24309.

SMITH, Edward, *of Lincoln's Inn*. Minsheu List.

SMITH, Edward, *Brother of Miles below*. 23508 by editor.

SMITH, Frances (2024). *See* CECIL.

SMITH, George, '*of London*'. *25624.

SMITH, Sir George, *City captain*. Epistle *1507.

SMITH, Gervase. Verse 19299.

SMITH, Henry, *Master of Magdalene* (Venn 1591). ¶21638; edits 4479.

SMITH, Sir Hugh, *of Long Ashton* (Vis. Soms.). †¶21869.

SMITH, Humphrey, *Alderman*. *5676.

SMITH, Ja. Verse 633.

SMITH, John, '*Student of author*'. 6759 [see changes].

SMITH, Sir John, *Brother of Sir Thomas the merchant*. Epistle 1598 [N3ᵛ].

SMITH, John, *the Se-Baptist* (DNB). Epistle *12567; see 235, 5450, 12662 (12706, 12635).

SMITH, John, *Alderman* [= *mayor*] *of Kendal*. *24475.

SMITH, John, '*of Norfolk*'. Verse 24043 [cf. Thomas].

SMITH, John, *Soldier and colonist, d. 1631* (DNB). Verse 18673, 23726.

SMITH, John, *Genealogist, d. 1640* (DNB). 24821.

SMITH, Sir John, *Son of Sir Thomas the merchant*. 25902.

SMITH, Sir John, *Bailie of Edinburgh*. *139, *13173, W. M., *Edinburghs alphabet-E.

SMITH, Jude, *Religious writer* (STC). Verse 21485.

SMITH (Langton), Margaret = *Sir* Richard. 18623; epistle 18521.

SMITH, Miles, *Bishop of Gloucester*. 1869; prose 1086 (1077).

SMITH, N., '*Cousin of author*'. Verse 22788 (22790).

SMITH, *Sir* Nicholas, *of Exeter and Lincoln's Inn* (Foster 1590). Verse 5461, 5808 and 5810 [cf. 23769].

SMITH, *Sir* Owen, *of Stiffkey* (Venn). *7373 [cf. 7375].

SMITH, Peter, *D.D.* (Venn 1602). Edits 25688, 25700a.

SMITH, Richard, *Chancellor at Douay* (DNB). See 5991.

SMITH, Richard, '*Clerk*' (*supposedly* Venn 1560). Verse 21120.

SMITH, Richard, *Surgeon* [*two in Royal college indistinguishable*]. Verse 1360 only.

SMITH, Richard, *Bookseller.* Edits *1577*-E. of 185, 5638, 12403; anon. verse 11636 but signed in 11638 [cf. also R. S.]; prose 7, perhaps 629.

SMITH, Richard, *Mayor of Gloucester.* *12171.

SMITH, *Sir* Richard, *Surveyor-general, brother of Thomas the merchant.* One issue 18641 [see changes].

SMITH, Richard, *Bishop of Chalcedon* (DNB). 1019, *S. Austins rule, 1636*-DE.; see 10740.

SMITH (Blount), Sarah = *Sir* Thomas *Merchant.* *¶6499.

SMITH, Simon, '*Notable swimmer*'. 6840.

SMITH, Solomon, *Marshal of Admiralty Court.* T. Fettiplace, *Celestiall lampe, 1637*-PN.[2]

SMITH, Thomas, *unidentified:* 10601 [cousin]; verse 7100 [gent.], 23752 only [neighbour], 25295 [student].

SMITH, Thomas, *Clerk of Council to Queen, jailed 1541.* See W. GRAY, *Brefe apologye*-L.

SMITH, Thomas, '*Pastor of Henfield, Sussex*'. See 13923.

SMITH, *Sir* Thomas, *Presumably the Master of Requests, d. 1609* (DNB). *21787.

SMITH, Thomas, *Customer, d. 1591, father of next.* *800, *15441.

SMITH, *Sir* Thomas, *Merchant, d. 1625* (DNB). 810, 1649, by editor, ¶6499, 6845, *†7133, 11655 (11652), 12736, 12796, 14699, 14700, 14817 by editor [see changes], 15493, 16657, *18417, 18420 by editor, 18532, *¶19091, *¶19088 = ¶*1616*-HD. of 19093, *19967 [see changes], 21085, ¶21649, 21828, 22577, *23350, 23677, 24628, 25354, *25952, 25962, J. Bentley, *Harmonie of scriptures, 1600*-L.,

T. Cooper, *Mysterie of government*-F.; epistle *13697.

SMITH, Thomas, '*of Clerkenwell, gentleman to Lord Lisle*'. 17155.

SMITH, Thomas, '*of Norfolk*' [*cf. John*]. Verse 24043.

SMITH, *Sir* Thomas, *of Hough, Ches., d. 1614.* *7293, 19923.

SMITH, *Sir* Thomas, *Mayor of Chester* (Keeler). *†21437, *¶23720.

SMYTHE, Thomas, *I Viscount Strangford.* See 10667.

SMITH, Thomas, *Bishop of Carlisle.* Verse 1441a.

SMITH, W. Verse 22454.

SMITH, William, '*Parson of Ford, Sussex*'. See 13923.

SMITH, William, *Master of Clare* (Venn 1573). 25797; edits 4493.

SMITH, William, *Warden of Wadham* (Foster 1599). See 25327.

SNAPE, Nathaniel, *of Gray's Inn.* Edits 19089, 19092.

SNELLING, Henry, *Gent.* Verse 19808.

SNELLING, Thomas, *M.A.* (Foster 1634). Verse 91.

SNODHAM, Thomas, *Printer.* Perhaps unsigned prose 19454, 24912; consider 21520.

SNOW (Cavendish), Elizabeth = Richard, *Gentlewoman of the chamber.* J. Marbeck, *Youth and age*-L.[43]

SOBER, *Sir* Seldom. See JOHN TAYLOR.

SOLOMEAUX, Paul, '*Gallus Vandomiensis*'. Verse 6044a.

SOME, Robert, *Master of Peterhouse* (DNB). 19604.

SOAME, *Sir* Stephen, *the elder, Lord Mayor.* *12307, *18131, *20756, *23864, †24216 by A. Munday.

SOME, Thomas, *Divine* (DNB). Edits 15271 and earlier-HD. (15276); verse 24368; perhaps prose 15274.

SOME, Thomas, *Vicar of Staines* (Foster). Minsheu List.

SOAME, *Sir* Thomas, *Alderman* (Keeler). *1505, *3536.

SOMERS, *Sir* George, *Discoverer* (DNB). Epistle 21660.

SOMERSET (Russell), Anne = Henry *I Marquis.* 21456; epistle 11831, *16696.

SOMERSET, Charles, *I Earl of Worcester. See* 1967, 12140 = 14999a = 17017.

SOMERSET, Sir Charles, *Son of next.* Minsheu List.

SOMERSET, Edward, *IV Earl of Worcester.* 3398, 4165a, 4247, 5374, ¶10926, *11496, 13309, 13323 (24151), 13324, 13326, 13366, ¶17334; epistle *3832, 6333, 18105; *see* 17331.

SOMERSET, Edward, *II Marquis of Worcester.* 3562.

SOMERSET, Henry, *I Marquis of Worcester.* 22553; *see* 10667, 17332.

SOMERSET, Thomas, *Viscount Somerset.* *17699, 21625; *see* 10667.

SOMERVILLE, Peter, *Bailie of Edinburgh.* *13258.

SONDS. *See* SANDYS.

SOPPETH, Edward, *Augustinian* (Foster). Edits 19816.

SOROCOLD, Thomas, *Divine* (*DNB*). Verse 10513 as S. D. [signed in 10514].

SORRELL, John, *of Waltham* (*Vis. Essex*). *1476.

SOTHEBY, John, *of Gray's Inn.* Verse 3.

SOTHEBY, Samuel, *Chaplain on 1604 embassy to Russia* (? Venn). *See* 12662 (12706, 12635).

SOTHERTON, Nowell, *Baron of the Exchequer.* 5485.

SOTO, Andreas à, *O.F.M., Spanish writer.* Epistle and approbation B. Jackson, *Manuductions, 1616*-F.

SOUCH. *Listed with* ZOUCHE.

SOUTH, John, *Regius professor* (Foster 1608). Verse 13018.

SOUTH, Thomas, *Esq.* 18073 by editor.

SOUTH, Warner, *Canon of Wells* (Foster). Verse 4192, 24703; Minsheu List.

SOUTHCOT, Thomas, *of Mohun's Ottery* (*Vis. Devon*). 21841.

SOUTHWELL family, *of Woodrising. See* 6270-L.

SOUTHWELL (Howard), Elizabeth = *Sir Robert, Lady of the Privy Chamber.* 23474 (23488), 23484; epistle 16696.

SOUTHWELL, Elizabeth, *Daughter of preceding, maid of honour eloping with Sir Robert Dudley.* 23491 [see changes].

SOUTHWELL, Frances *and* Katherine (23492). *See* RODNEY *and* VERNEY.

SOUTHWELL, Richard, *Father of Robert.* ¶22969 and earlier-USH.

SOUTHWELL, Robert, *S.J., poet* (*DNB*): Cousin of. 22956 identified as W. S. in 22963.

SOUTHWELL, Sir Thomas, *of Wood Rising* (*Vis. Norf.*). ¶21869; epistle 15037.

S[OUTHWELL?], W. *See* ROBERT *above.*

SPALDING, Samuel, *Great Level adventurer.* *Fens map in 17827.

SPARKE, Geo. Verse 23704.

SPARKE, Michael, *the elder, Bookseller.* Prose 10416, 12391, 13449, 18010, 23016; *also see* FRANCIS QUARLES (17824).

SPARKE, Michael, *the younger, Bookseller.* Prose 1432.

SPARKE, Thomas, *Divine* (*DNB*). 21019.

SPEED, John, *Historian* (*DNB*). Verse 12500; *see* 25327.

SPEED, John *the younger, Scholar* (*DNB*). Verse 23047; prose 19302.

SPEED, Oswald, *of Pembroke College* (Venn). Verse L. Staveley, *Breef discourse*-HN.

SPEGHT, Thomas, *Schoolmaster* (*DNB*). Edits 5077, more 5080; verse 1411, 11049 as Th. Sp. Ebor., 20768.

SPEIDELL, John, *Mathematician* (Taylor). Prose 5584.

SPEIR, Sara [? *of Edinburgh*]. 12319 by printer.

SPEKE, Sir George, *of White Lackington, d. 1584.* 19894.

SPEKE, Sir George, *the younger, of the Middle Temple.* 12358.

SPEKE, George, *III, of the Middle Temple* (Foster 1607). *See* 5811.

SPEKE, Sir Thomas, *of the Privy Chamber, father of Sir George I.* 2760 by printer.

SPELMAN, Sir Henry, *Historian* (*DNB*). *11572, ¶14443; verse 1853, 23041 and 23044; Minsheu List; *consider* SIR H. S.

SPELMAN, Sir John, *Author* (*DNB*). Edits 2369.

SPENCAEUS. *See* SPENS.

SPENCER (Sidney), Dorothy = Henry *I Earl of Sunderland.* 21063; epistle *15465.

SPENSER, Edmund, *Poet* (*DNB*). 21499 by

editor; verse 5642 as Edw., 12900, 15318, 18428.

As Colin Clout: 22872; epistle presumably 16658.

SPENCER, *Sir* Edward, *Son of Robert below* (Foster 1609). Epistle 23071; Minsheu List.

SPENCER, *Sir* John, *Lord Mayor* (*DNB*). *19875.

SPENSER, John, *President of Corpus Christi* (*DNB*). *6420; edits 13713 as I. S.; *see* 17944.

SPENCER, *Sir* John, *of Offley, Bt.* †351 [see changes]; Minsheu List.

SPENCER, John, *Bookseller and librarian*. Signed prose 12417, 12421, 17889, 24331, 25670; probably 24397 as Anonym. Musophil.; perhaps 1675.

SPENCER, Richard, *Son of next*. Epistle 23071.

SPENCER, Robert, *I Baron Spencer*. 3418, 10763, 14311, 25103; *see* 17332.

SPENCER, Thomas, *of Lincoln's Inn, d. 1629*. *11670; epistle *6205; Minsheu List.

SPENCER, Thomas, *of Claverdon, uncle of next*. 11200.

SPENCER, *Sir* Thomas, *I Bt*. Minsheu List.

SPENCER, William, *II Baron Spencer*. 19323, 23071, 24294, †25102; *see* 10667.

SPENCAEUS, Georgius, *M.D*. Verse 23070.

SPENCE, *Sir* James, *of the royal household*. Minsheu List.

SPENSE, James, *Minister of Alva*. Verse 10696, 23070, R. Williamson, *Paedagogia*-c.³ [impf.]. and partly *1635*-E. as M. I. Sp.

SPENS, Josephus, 'SS. Theol. Dr.' Verse 23070.

SPENCE, Robert, *Scotobritannus* (*STC*). Verse 15078.

SPENSER. *See* SPENCER.

SPICER, Richard, *Physician* (Foster 1611). Verse 12974; prose 21426.

SPICER, Thomas (? Venn). Verse 5461.

SPIGURNELL, Andrew. Edits 21740 [postdating 21741].

SPIGURNEL, Thomas. Verse 18276.

SPILJARDUS, Johannes, *Dutch preacher* (Schotel). Verse 1106.

SPINOLA, Ambrose, *Marquis, soldier* (*NBG*). 1529 = 13926a.

SPOTTISWOOD, John, *Archbishop of St. Andrews*. 698a, ¶1496, 11138, ¶11144, *12480, 15368,

¶16870 [see changes], St. Andrews (Leonard) *Theses, 1616*-c.²; *see* 10667.

SPRATT, Thomas, *Somerset clergyman* (Foster 1606). Epistle *1941.

SPRATT *or* SPROT, William, *of St. Antholin, London*. Epistle *12203.

SPRING, *Sir* William, *I Bt*. Presentation 18981; verse 18981.

SPRINGHAM, —— *[of London]*. *5700.

SPRINT, John, *Theologian, d. 1623* (*DNB*). Verse 23294 [cf. I. S. at errata].

SPROT. *See* SPRATT.

SPURSTOW, William, *East India committee-man* (Keeler). Epistle *25963; Minsheu List.

SQUIRE, Adam, *of Balliol* (Foster). Verse 14725.

SQUIRE, John, *Vicar of St. Leonard, Shoreditch* (Venn 1600). *See* 23920 and 23923; Minsheu List.

SQUIRE, William (Foster 1620). *See* W. SQ.

STADELL, *Baron* Gottfried, *Styrian noble*. A. Sözinger, *Disputatio, 1610*-O.⁵

STAFFORD, Anthony, *Writer* (*DNB*). Epistle 20692.

STAFFORD (Stafford), Dorothy = *Sir* William, *Lady of Bedchamber*. 6134 by printer.

STAFFORD, Edward, *III Duke of Buckingham*. 7571-LC (Rosenwald), 13256.

STAFFORD, Edward, *IV Baron Stafford*. *See* 17332.

STAFFORD, *Sir* Edward, *Usher of Privy Chamber, d. 1623*. 7355.

STAFFORD, *Sir* Francis, *of Dublin*. 7325 (22879) as S. F. S. [7326 anr. trans.].

STAFFORD, Henry, *I Baron Stafford*. 24595; see first state only of 14652a-O. [earliest ed.].

STAFFORD, Henry, *V Baron Stafford*. *See* 10667.

STAFFORD, John, *of Blatherwick, Northants., d. 1595*. ¶11872.

STAFFORD, John, 'ar., *Leicestrensis*' [? *of Huncote*]. Verse 24043.

STAFFORD, John, *Bookseller*. Prose 20224 [only initialed in 20225].

STAFFORD, Simon, *Printer*. Prose 6134.

STALLENGE, William, *Searcher, port of London* (Brown *and STC*). *See* 19511.

STAMPE, John, *London merchant adventurer*. ¶16684, N. Cannon, †*Casket of iewels, 1625*-O.

STORY, John, *Roman Catholic martyr (DNB)*. 5772, ¶5999.

STORIE, Io. (? Foster 1590). Verse 19777.

STORY, Richard, *Surgeon at Bart's*. Edits 24713 thence 24706.

STOUGHTON, I. [*presumably* John (Foster 1564)]. Verse 4738.

STOUGHTON (Browne), Jane = John-*STC*. Prose 23302, 23304 (both 23306), 23303 (23311).

STOUGHTON, John, *M.A.* (Foster 1564). *See* I. STOUGHTON.

STOUGHTON, Nicholas, *of Stoughton* (Foster 1610). Verse 14793, 26130.

STOUGHTON, Robert, *Printer*. Perhaps prose 4080.

STOUGHTON, Thomas, *Clergyman* (STC): children of, ¶23314; parishioners, epistle 23315.

STOURTON, Charles, *VIII Baron Stourton*. 5409 [see changes].

STOURTON, Edward, *X Baron Stourton*. *See* 10667, 17332.

STOURTON, John, *IX Baron Stourton*. 12174.

STOW, John, *Chronicler (DNB)*. Edits 5075; *see* 5077; *also see* I. S.

STRACHIN, William, *'of Tibbertie, kinsman'*. 11146 = ¶11150.

STRACHEY, William, *Colonist (DNB)*. Edits 23350; verse 14782 only.

STRADLING, *Sir* Edward, *Scholar, d.1609 (DNB)*. 15695 and *1594-PN.²*, 20966; epistle *1095 (1077).

STRADLING, *Sir* John, *I. Bt. and poet*. Verse 4508 (4509), 20966.

STRANG (Strangius), John, *Principal, Glasgow university (DNB)*. Verse 74, 3447.

STRANGE, STRONGE, etc. *See also* LE STRANGE.

STRANGE, Joh. Verse 21409 (21413 as I. S.).

STRAUNGE, *Lady* Margaret. *See* STANLEY.

STRONGE, S. Verse 20978.

STRANGWAGE, John [*perhaps the next*]. Verse 24603.

STRANGWAYS, *Sir* John, *of Melbury* (Keeler). 288 as Estrangwayes, *†11126, 11994; verse 5808 and 5810 [cf. 23769].

STRANGWAYS, Nicholas [*probably brother of preceding*]. 3397.

STRANGWAYS (Edwards), Susanna = Giles *of Melbury*-Keeler. 4914.

STRETTON, Richard, *'of St. Andrew Hubbard'*. *20678 (20668) by editor.

STRICKLAND, *Sir* Thomas, *K.B., of Sizergh*. *15342 spelt Stikeland.

STRINGER, Henry, *Regius professor* (Foster). *14457.

STRODE, *Sir* George, *Author (DNB)*. *1959.

STROUD, John, *Puritan preacher-printer*. Prose 4712 as J. S. [? and unsigned 4711]; *see also* J. T. J. S.

STRODE (Southcote), Mary = *Sir* William. 13407 and *1608*-O. (13378).

STRODE, Ralph, *Schoolman (DNB)*. *5094 (5068).

STRODE (Crisp), Rebecca = *Sir* George. *1942, *11672 (11679, 11652).

STRODE, *Sir* William, *of Newnham, Devon*. *1440 (1435), *13396 (13379), 13426 (13378).

STRODE, William, *Poet (DNB)*. *4259; verse 5097, 21351.

STRODE, William, *of London, brother of Sir George*. *1959.

STRONG, Richard, *'Minister of Climping, Sussex'* [*cf.* PCC 1598]. *See* 13923.

STRONGE *and* STROUD. *See* STRANGE *and* STRODE.

STRUTHER, William, *Minister at Edinburgh* (STC). Verse 7486, 7487.

STUART, STEWART, etc.

STEWART, Alexander, *I Earl of Galloway*. *See* 10667.

STEWART, Andrew, *II Lord Castle Stuart*. *See* 10667.

STUART, Arabella. *See* ARABELLA.

STUART, Bernard, *III Seigneur of Aubigny* (DNB). *See* 7347.

STUART, Bernard, *Titular Earl of Lichfield*. *24809.

STUART (Clifton), Catherine = Esmé *III Duke of Lennox*. J. Andrewes, *Caveat*, 1627-O.⁶

STEWART (Houghton), Catherine = James *II Earl of Galloway*. Epistle *23580.

STEWART (Howard), Elizabeth = John *Earl of Carrick*. *17699.

STUART, Esmé, *I Duke of Lennox.* Epistle 14373.

STUART, Esmé, *III Duke of Lennox.* 5396, *†6272, ¶14751, 20940, *†23657.

STUART (Howard), Frances = Ludovick *II Duke of Lennox, previously* Pranell *and* Seymour. 3075, *¶4497, 6269, *6270, *6272, 10860 [see changes], ¶12748, *1609-c.² of 20826 by editor, 22790, 23127, *23657, *25900; epistle *23581 (23575, 21653).

STEWART, Francis, *Earl of Bothwell.* 25239.

STUART, Sir Francis, *Admiral* (Foster). *¶5393, 13615, 14763 [? earlier lost] (14751), 16883; epistle some copies *4747; Minsheu List.

STEWART, George, *Son of James III Earl of Moray.* St. Andrews (Leonard) *Theses, 1630-*E.²

STUART, George, *IX Seigneur, son of Esmé III Duke of Lennox.* *24809.

STUART, Griseel (12067). *See* SETON.

STEWART, James, *I Earl of Moray, d. 1570.* 12968, *22194.

STEWART, James, *III Earl of Moray.* Allison 458; *see* 10667.

STUART, James, *IV Duke of Lennox.* *10667, 17160, 17168, 17357 [see changes], 18003 [cf. 18002], ¶19781, 23516, 23600 by editor [see changes], *25900; *see* 17331.

STEWART, James, *IV Lord Ochiltree. See* 10667.

STEWART, John. Verse 5933.

STUART, John, *Son of Ludovick II Duke.* *¶5393.

STUART, John, *Son of Esmé III Duke.* *24809.

STEWART, John, *I Earl of Traquair.* ¶19781; *see* 10667.

STEWART, John, *Earl of Carrick. See* 10667 misnamed James.

STUART, Ludovick, *II Duke of Lennox.* 3075 by author, 3658 [? earlier lost], 4105, ¶4578, *7336, ¶11160, *11496, ¶15715, 16925, ¶17334, *17699, 17710, 23598 by editor [see changes], 24038, 25090 [see changes], *25237, *¶25682 (25685).
Epistle: 1402, *3832, 6333, 7547, 13633 (13624), 20567; *see* 19511, 25939; Minsheu List.
Household and friends: J. Taylor, *True loving sorow, 1624-*L.⁵ (23725).

STUART (Douglas), Margaret = Matthew

IV Earl of Lennox. 21288 by editor [earlier lost; see changes].

STEWART (Stewart), Margaret = Andrew *Master of Ochiltree.* 76.

STEWART (Home), Margaret = James *IV Earl of Moray.* 12747 (12748).

STUART (Villiers), Mary = James *IV Duke of Lennox, otherwise* Herbert *and* Howard. 11057 by bookseller; epistle *15465.

STUART, Matthew, *IV Earl of Lennox.* 21356.

STUART, Robert, *Earl of Lennox and March, d. 1586.* 7552.

STEWARD (Lewkenor), Sara = Thomas *of Barton Mills, Suff.* Epistle *4693.

STEWART, Sir Thomas, *of Grandtully, d. c. 1608.* †5917 (5909).

STEWARD, Thomas, *of Denham, West Suff.* *20337 by editor.

STEWART, Sir William, *Lyon King of Arms.* Verse 16577, intermittently later.

STEWART, William, *II Lord Blantyre. See* 10667 misnamed James.

STUBBE, Richard, *of Sedgeford, Norf.* 12527.

STUBBS, Justinian, *M.A.* (Venn). Edits 1636.

STUBBS, Philip, *Pamphleteer* (DNB). Verse 11225; prose 6168.

STUBENBERG, Georgius *Senior* à, 'in Wurmberg'. A. Sözinger, *Disputatio, 1610-*O.⁵

STUCLEY, Thomas, *Adventurer* (DNB). 18662.

STUDLEY, John, *Translator* (DNB). Verse 23278 [? earlier lost].

STURMAN. *See* STERMYN.

STURTEVANT, Simon, *Preacher* (Venn). Verse 15434.

STUTVILLE, George, *Actor.* Verse 13316 as Estoutevile.

STUTVILE, Tho., *Esq. See* 25438.

STUTEVILL, Tho., *Philomathes* (? Venn 1615). Verse 1099.

STYLES, Matthias, *D.D.* (Foster). Prose 12980.

STYLES, Thomas, *East India committee-man* (Brown). Epistle *25963.

SUB FOED. SP. Verse 24523.

SUCKLING, Sir John, *the elder, Father of next.* †11574; verse 5808 and 5810 [cf. 23769] as Sutclin.

SUCKLING, *Sir* John, *Poet* (*DNB*). 18339 (18337); verse 6304, 17220, 18938.

SUERDERUS, Guil. Verse 15607.

SUGAR. *See* SHUGER.

SUGDEN, —— [*of Cambridge; undistinguishable*]. Epistle 21638.

SUIS CUIQUE MOS. Verse 14973.

SUITE, Timothy, '*Pastor of St. Andrew Hubbard*' [*untraced unless* Shute (Venn)]. *See* 23920 and 23923.

SEYLIARD (Jacob), Barbara = Robert *of Gabriel, Kent.* *15333.

SULYARD, *Sir* Edward, *of Flemyngs, Essex, d. 1610.* 25172.

SULIARD, Edward, *Esq.,* '*of Essex*'. Minsheu List.

SULYARD, *Sir* Edward, *of Haughley, Suff., d. 1673.* *5129.

SULZER, Simon, *Reformer* (*ADB*). *1304 by author.

SUMMASTER, George, *Principal of Broadgates Hall* (Foster). 6167, *6420, 13723 (13716) by editor, ¶20614 by editor; Minsheu List.

SURIGONUS, Stephanus, *Milan humanist* (*TLS 1937,* p. 28). Verse 3199 (5068).

SUTCLIFFE, John, *Groom of Privy Chamber, nephew of next.* Epistle 23447.

SUTCLIFFE, Matthew, *Dean of Exeter* (*DNB*). ¶3463; *see* 4706, 14909, 19391.

SUTCLIN (5808). *See* SUCKLING.

SUTTON, *including* SUTTON *alias* DUDLEY.

SUTTON, Edward, *V Baron Dudley. See* 10667, 17332.

SUTTON, *Sir* Ferdinando, *Son of preceding.* †22837 as Dudley.

SUTTON (Howard), Mary = Edward *IV Baron Dudley.* 2762.

SUTTON, *Sir* Richard, *Co-founder of Brasenose* (*DNB*). *See* 4815.

SUTTON (Harington), Theodocia = Edward *V Baron Dudley.* *3788, *4884, *5775 partly by editor, 6603.

SUTTON, Thomas, *Founder of Charterhouse* (*DNB*). *See* 12662 (12706, 12635).

SWAINE, Robert, *Bookseller. See* 10635.

SWAYNE, William. Edits 6220, 6221.

SWAN, John, *Preacher* (Venn 1569). Edits 14299.

SWAN, William, *of Wye* (*Vis. Kent*). *†4404.

SWETNAM, Joseph, *the woman-hater* (*DNB*). Epistle 18257, 23058.

SWIFT, Barnham, *Viscount Carlingford. See* 10667.

SWIFT (Sheffield), Elizabeth = *Sir* Edward. *1934.

SWIFT, William, *Master of Bristol Grammar School.* Posthumous verse 13260.

SWINNERTON, Henry, *Son of next.* Epistle 19165.

SWINNERTON, *Sir* John, *Lord Mayor.* *5105, 6530, ¶7216, †11262, *11829, 12467-0., 12673 (12706, 12635), *13589 [see changes], 16757 = 18248, ¶16911 by editor [see changes], †18163, 18322, 18588, †19165, *19513, *20756, 22871, *25470 [25739 a ghost]; epistle *6165; *see* 23779 only.

SIDNAM, ——, '*Lover of religion*'. Presentation J. Taylor, *Court of guard, 1626.*

SYDENHAM, Edward, *Equerry and captain of Portland Castle* (*CSPD*). *23574 (23572).

SYDENHAM, George, *of Brimpton* (Foster 1606). Verses 5808 and 5810 [cf. 23769].

SYDENHAM, John, *Brother of preceding* (Foster 1606). 23569 (23563).

SYDENHAM, *Sir* Ralph, *Uncle of John I Bt.* *23574 (23572).

SYDSERFF, Thomas, *Bishop of Galloway. See* 10667.

SYLEY (23279). Misprint for Sidley.

SYLBURG, Frederick, *German scholar* (*NBG*). Verse 3988 [earlier abroad].

SILVESTER, *Butler* [? *at Geneva*]. 1544.

SYLVESTER, Josuah, *Poet* (*DNB*). Verse 3129 extracted from 16829 = ¶23582, 7492 [earlier than 7491], 13247; prose 13475 (21653); *see* 23779 only; Minsheu List.

SYME, SYMONDS, etc. *See* SIME, etc., *also* SIMAND.

SYRINGIUS, Ioh., *Turingis,* '*linked to Queen Anne*'. Verse 21657.

T

T., A., *of Royal Exchange, charitable puritan.* *19489.

T., A. 3869.

T., B. Verse 11128, 14608 [? of Cambridge].

T., B. E. [*supposedly* Anthony Batt]. Edits 12350.

T., C., *I.C., F.A.* Verse 6014.

T., Cl. D. D. Verse 7376.

T., D. Verse *1614*-C.² only of 18904, others 18909 [? Tuvil].

T., Ed. Prose 21786.

T., F., *M.A., Oxon.* [*presumably* Francis Tucker]. Verse 3819, more as F. T.

T., F., *'Protestant gentleman'. 1600*-OS. of 23618 and again *1600*-L.²; epistle 1449.

T., F. Verse 1360.

T., G. (12583). *See* GEORGE TALBOT.

T., G., *'Scholae Radclivensis rector, [Stepney]'. See* 25695.

T., G. 741 = 14833; verse 3695, 12100; prose 11635 only.

T., H. (1167), *see* HERBERT THORNDIKE; (1383), *see* THOMAS HEYWOOD [reversed].

T., H., *Author of* 23618. *See* THOMAS WRIGHT.

T., H. Edits *1635*-F. of 5845 [? foreign printing]; verse 3648 and 3649, 3894, 19337 [? Townshend].

T., Hen. C. Verse 25559.

T., I., *Esq. See* 25438.

T., I., *Mousophilos.* Verse 12210.

T., I., *A.M.* [*Oxford*; ? Terrent]. Verse 20694.

T., I. Edits 3225, 9277; verse 3506, 3647, 24296 [apparently not author], 25227 [? Taylor]; prose 12630 [apparently the author]; *see* motto 21542; *also see* J. T. J. S.

T., Katharine, *Recusant. See* 23558.

T., L. 18654; prose 15040.

T., M. [*Sister of John Heigham*]. ¶3369 [see changes].

T., N. ¶13600; verse 5807, 24308.

T., P. Verse 12747 (12748 as P. S.).

T., R., *Esq. See* 25438.

T., R., *Cantabrigiensis, 'of Islington'.* Prose 12188.

T., R., Q.L. [*supposedly* James Martin]. Prose 19020.

T., R. *¶13579; edits 4655, 22519; verse 3894, 4749.

T., Ri. Verse 11096.

T., Ro., *'of Lincoln's Inn'.* Verse 17921.

T., R. G. P. Verse 3108.

T., S. B. Jackson, *Manuductions, 1616*-F. as M. S. T.; verse 6436; unsigned prose 6617, signed 6618 [but cf. T. S. in 6617].

TH., M[r]. S. (17495). *See* SIMON THELWALL.

T., T., *Phil. Cand.* Verse 6190.

T., T. Verse 1483, 1578, 22790, 24296, 24316 [? the author].

T., W. (20036). *See* WILLIAM TYNDALE.

T., W. [*presumably* William Tod]. Verse 11596.

T., W. [*presumably* Walter Travers]. *20881.

T., W. Epistle 17981; verse 6983, 12210, 18014.

TAAFFE, John, *I Viscount Taaffe. See* 10667.

TAB *or* DABBE, Henry, *Bookseller. See* 12468.

TADLOWE, George, *Haberdasher* (PCC 1557). *See* 18094 only.

TAILOR. *See* TAYLOR.

TALBOT, Alathea. *See* HOWARD.

TALBOT (Herbert), Anne = Francis *'Lord Talbot' d. 1582.* 13874.

TALBOT, Clere, LL.D. (Venn). 26089.

TALBOT (Hardwick), Elizabeth = George VI Earl of Shrewsbury, *'Bess of Hardwick'.* 12787.

TALBOT, Elizabeth. *See* GREY.

TALBOT, Francis, *V Earl of Shrewsbury.* *3480, *24361.

TALBOT, George, *VI Earl of Shrewsbury.* 724 only by printer, *¶10674, 14725 pts. i–iii.

TALBOT, George, *IX Earl of Shrewsbury. See* 17331.

TALBOT, George, *Brother of John X Earl.* Verse 12583 as G. T. [signed 12584].

TALBOT, Gilbert, *VII Earl of Shrewsbury.* 5457, 5865, 11053, 12922, 21119 by bookseller, 21120, 23867, 26094, N. Bownd, ¶*St. Pauls trumpet, 1615*-LINC.; epistle 6165, 16696.

THURSBY, Thomas, *Esq.* ¶21869.

THYNNE, Francis, *Lancaster herald* (*DNB*). Verse 5080.

THYNNE (Hayward), Joan = Sir John *of Longleat d. 1623.* 17749.

THYNNE, *Sir* John, *the younger, of Longleat, d. 1623.* 5211.

THYNNE (Touchet), Mary = *Sir* Thomas. ¶3544.

THYNNE, *Sir* Thomas, *Son of John above, father of Henry I Bt.* †1946; *see* 6270-L.

THYNNE, William, *Editor of Chaucer* (*DNB*). Edits 5068.

TICHBORNE, *Sir* Richard, *II Bt.* ¶11166, 11980 by bookseller [variant setting-HD.]; Minsheu List.

TICHBORNE, *Sir* Walter, *Brother of preceding.* 11977 by bookseller, 11988 and 11989.

TICKRIDGE, Edward, 'Minister at Newtimber, Sussex'. *See* 13923.

TILDESLEY. *See* TYLDESLEY.

TILMAN, Edward, *B.D.* (Venn). Verse 24316.

TILNEY (Brews), Margaret = *Sir* Philip. *See* 22610 (22608).

TIMPERLEY, M., *Esq.* Verse 6190.

TINDALL, &c. *See* TYNDALL.

TINKLER, Isaac, *of Caius College* (Venn). Verse 18948.

TINLEY, Robert, *Canon of Ely* (Foster). *25680.

TIRILL *and* TIRWHITT. *See* TYRRELL *and* TYRWHITT.

TISDALE, Roger *the younger, Son of the author.* Epistle 24090.

TITYRUS. Verse 12964.

TOD, Archibald, *Dean of gild, Edinburgh.* *88, *23262.

TOD, William. Verse 12067; *see* W. T. (11596).

TOLLEMACHE, *Sir* Lionel, *II Bt.* 21543.

TOLNEIUS, ——, *'Hungaro-Transylvanus'* [? John, *schoolmaster*]. *See* 23305.

TOLSON, John, *Provost of Oriel* (Foster). *20461 (20458), 24404.

TOMANNUS. *See* THOMANNUS.

TOMBES, John, *Baptist divine* (*DNB*). Prose 19576a (19570) [19576 a ghost but a *1627*-L. tp. survives].

TOMKINS, Giles *and* John, *Musicians* (*DNB*). *See* 24099 with verse by John.

TOMKINS, N. [*probably* Nicholas, *but possibly next*]. Verse 10827.

TOMKINS, Nathaniel, *M.A.* (Foster 1598). Verse 6333, 21660, 22218.

TOMKINS, Nathanael, Nicholas, Peregrine, Robert, *and* Thomas, *Son, brothers, and father of author. See* 24099.

TOMLINS, Thomas, *Gent.* Minsheu List.

TOMLINSON, Robert. Verse 24368 as Thomlynson.

TONSTALL. *See* TUNSTALL.

TOOKE, John, *Auditor of Court of Wards, of Herts.* 21520.

TOOMES, William, *of St. James, Clerkenwell, d. 1655. See* 13327 (plate ii).

TOPCLIFFE, Richard, *Priest-catcher* (*DNB*). ¶5332 [see changes], 18260.

TOPHAM, Anthony, *Dean of Lincoln* (Venn). *¶5359, 23513.

TOPSELL, Edward, *Divine* (*DNB*). Edits 13587; prose 21016; *see* 17944; Minsheu List.

TOPSFIELD (Palmer), Elizabeth = William, *previously* Fawcit. *15334.

TOPSFIELD, Henry, *Grocer* (PCC 1599). 18125 as Tapsfield.

TORQUATUS, Henricus. Verse 13941.

TORY, Geoffroy, *Paris printer* (*NBG*). Epistle 19166 as Troy.

TOTHILL, William, *of Shardelos, one of six clerks, d. 1626.* 11040 by printer [see changes], *†12891.

TOTTEL, Richard, *Printer* (*DNB*). Signed prose 9278, 23213; unsigned 9280, 9345, 13860; his shop did index 19633.

TOUCHET (Stanley), Anne = Mervyn *Earl. See* BRYDGES.

TOUCHET *or* TUCHET, James, *III Earl of Castlehaven. See* 10667.

TOUCHET (Mervyn), Lucy = George *I Earl of Castlehaven.* 3544.

TOUCHET, Mervyn, *II Earl of Castlehaven. See* 17332.

TOURNEY, John, *Fellow of Pembroke* (Venn 1620). Epistle 6009.

TOURVAL. *See* L'OISEAU DE TOURVAL.

TOWERS, Robert, *Canon of Paul's* (Venn 1560). *4403.

TOWERS, William, *Divine* (DNB). Verse 10829.

TOWNLEY, Zouch, *M.A.* (Foster). Verse 13798, 14771.

TOWNSEND (9770). *See* SIR ROGER, *Judge*.

TOWNSEND, Aurelian, *Poet* (DNB). Verse 17220.

TOWNSHEND, Sir Henry, *Justice of Chester, d. 1617.* 19337.

TOWNSHEND (Vere), Mary = *Sir* Roger. *See* FANE.

TOWNSHEND, Sir Robert, *Son of Sir Roger–DNB d. 1590.* *11068 only.

TOWNSON, Robert, *Bishop of Salisbury*. Minsheu List.

TOWNSHEND, *Sir* Roger, *Judge, d. 1493* (DNB). *See* 9770, 9779 as Townsend.

TOWNSHEND, Sir Roger, *I Bt.* 11062, ¶11081, 21129, *†26087; epistle 15037; presentation 12530.

TOWSE, William, *Serjeant-at-law, of Inner Temple.* †1475.

TOY, Humphrey, *Bookseller* (DNB). Epistle 21615.

TRACY (Lyttelton), Bridget = Robert *II* Viscount. N. Byfield, *Signes of wicked, 1619*–F., really ¶1619 of 4220 (4220).

TRACY, Sir John, *of Tuddington, Gloucs., d. 1591.* Verse 5415.

TRACY, Richard, *Reformer* (DNB). 24720; prose 11393 [11392 impf.].

TRACY, Sir Richard, *II Bt.* 21234.

TRAFFORD, Sir Edmund, *of Trafford, d. 1590.* 17631.

TRAFFORD, Sir Edmund, *d. 1620, son of preceding.* 1437 (1435) as Tryfoord, 24344.

TRAHERON, Bartholomew, *Reformer* (DNB). Verse 19299.

TRAPPES, Robert, *of Bermondsey, nephew of next.* 17867 by bookseller.

TRAPPES, Rowland, *of Bermondsey, d. 1616.* 7612.

TRAVERS, Walter, *Divine* (DNB). *See* W. T.

TREDWAY, Letice Mary, *Abbess* (DNB). *23992 by editor [see changes].

TREFFREY, John, *of Cornwall* (Foster). 6266, *19066.

TREFUSIS, John, *of Lincoln's Inn* (Foster 1605). *19066.

TREGIAN, Francis, *Recusant exile, son of Francis–DNB.* Verse 21361.

TRENCHARD, *Sir* George, *the elder, of Wolveton, Dorset.* 5212, 17752.

TRESHAM, Francis, *of the Gunpowder plot* (DNB). 21536.

TRESHAM, Sir Lewis, *I Bt.* Minsheu List.

TRESHAM, William, *Esq.* [?Foster 1622; *or the II Bt.*]. 22456.

TRESWELL, Robert, *Somerset herald* (STC). Minsheu List.

TREVERIS, Peter, *Printer* (DNB). *See* 25508.

TREVILIAN, John, *of Nettlecombe* (*Vis. Soms.*). 4681.

TREVOR, Sir John, *Secretary of State* (DNB). Verse 60444a.

TREVOR, Sir Thomas, *Judge* (DNB). Presentation 24954; *see* 10667.

TRIPP, Simon, *M.A.* (Foster 1559). Verse 23229.

TROTMAN, Edward, *the elder, of the Inner Temple, d. 1638.* Edits 5527; Minsheu List.

TROY, Geoffrey (19166). Misprint for Tory.

TRUMBULL, William, *Diplomatist* (DNB). *17333 as Trumball, †20790 as Thrumball; Minsheu List.

TRUNDLE, John, *Bookseller*. Prose 14899-0. [undated; *1619*-L. is tp. only].

TRUSSELL, John, *Poet* (STC) [*identity with historian–DNB uncertain*]. Edits 22971 (22965 but signed S. W.).

TRYE, Elizabeth. Minsheu List.

TRYFOORD, Sir Edmund. *See* TRAFFORD.

TRYON, Moses, *of Harringworth, brother of Sir Samuel.* 10722 [10721 ghost].

TRYON, Peter, *of Lincoln's Inn, son of preceding* (Foster). Epistle 10722; verse 11877.

TRYON, *Sir* Samuel, *I Bt.* †3417.

TUCKE, ——, 'Ensign in Dutch service'. Epistle 25939.

TUCKER, Francis, *M.A., Oxford* (N & Q 1956, p. 235). Verse 17444; *see* F. T.

TUCKER, Thomas, *B.D.* (Foster 1601). Verse 13018.

TUDOR, Jasper, *Duke of Bedford.* See 14477 = 22605.

TUFTON, Nicholas, *I Earl of Thanet.* Verse 24042 [*date* 1592]; *see* 10667.

TUKE, *Sir* Brian, *Treasurer of household* (*DNB*). Supposedly ghost-wrote prose 5068.

TUKE, George, *of Corpus Christi* (Venn 1601). Verse 14665.

TUKE, Nathaniel, *B.D.* (Venn). Verse 24316.

TULIDOFF, Samuel, *Schoolmaster of Culross* (*Reg. Gt. Seal*). See 25737.

TULLY, Thomas, *Divine* (*DNB*). Verse 1441a.

TULSE, William, *the elder, of Christchurch, Hants.* One issue *13507.

TONSTALL, Anthony, '*Militis amanuensis*' [?*Gray's Inn*, PCC 1627]. Verse 13540; also appendix [not in early state HN.].

TUNSTALL, Cuthbert, *Bishop of Durham.* 11892 by editor; oversees 2072.

TUNSTALL, *Sir* John, *of Croydon, usher to Queen Anne.* ¶6069, †24323 by bookseller.

TURBERVILLE, George, *Poet* (*DNB*). Verse 10791, 15336.

TURBERVILLE, Nicholas, *Brother of preceding, murdered 1580.* 24330.

TURING, John, *London schoolmaster* (Venn). See 25737.

TURNBULL, George, *S.J.* (*DNB*). Epistle 1493.

TURNEBUS, Adrianus, *French savant* (*NBG*). Prose 3990 and 3988 [from foreign ed.].

TURNER, Christopher, *Mayor of Reading.* *23840.

TURNER, Humfrey. Verse 25348.

TURNER, John. Verse 24590.

TURNER, John, *Oxon.* (? Foster 1588). Verse 23278.

TURNER, John [*Merchant in Holland*]. *11131.

TURNER, Patrick, *Minister at Dalkeith.* See TURNETUS.

TURNER, Peter, *Physician* (*DNB*). Verse 19916.

TURNER, Richard, *Divine* (*DNB*). Epistle 4036-L. [earlier O. impf.].

TURNERUS, Thomas. Verse 13482 = 17787.

TURNER, Thomas, *Master of Peterhouse* (Venn 1592). Epistle *18805; Minsheu List.

TURNER, Thomas, *Esq.* 23249 rewritten 23250.

TURNER, William, *Dean of Wells* (*DNB*). *6810 = 11888 (10400); prose 23004.

TURNER, William, *Oxford printer.* Epistle unnamed 10635, 23754 (23725); verse 19034, 19035; signed prose 241; unsigned prose 4190, 4194, 11102, 17950.

TURNETUS, Patricius [*Edinburgh M.A., physician, usually identified with* Turner *above*]. Verse 22567; author of untraced broadside.

TURPIN (Fiennes), Elizabeth = *Sir* William. ¶18057.

TURPIN, *Sir* William, *of Knaptoft, Leics.* 18058.

TURSWELL, Thomas, *Canon of Paul's* (*DNB*). Verse 5447.

TURVILE (Anderton), Margaret = Henry *of Leics.* Epistle *23580 by editor.

TWISSE, Thomas, *of Gloucester Hall* (Foster). Verse 1311.

TWISTLETON (Stapylton), Catherine = *Sir* George *Bt.* 24812.

TWYNE, Brian, *Antiquary* (*DNB*). Minsheu List.

TWYNE, John, *Author* (*DNB*). Prose 3186.

TWYNE, John, *the younger, and* Lawrence (*DNB*). Verse 16636.

TWYNE, Thomas, *Physician* (*DNB*). Addressee and editor 24407; verse 6748, 23229.

TWYNE, William, *Clerk of kitchen to Queen Anne.* Minsheu List.

TWYSDEN (Finch), Anne = *Sir* William *I Bt.* 13532.

TWYSDEN, Charles, *Chancellor of Lichfield* (Foster). *14482; Minsheu List.

TWYSDEN, *Sir* William, *I Bt.* Minsheu List.

TYLDESLEY, Elizabeth, *Abbess at Gravelines, Clara Mariana in religion.* 3902, 11315 by editor, *13034 by printer [? earlier lost].

TILDESLEY, *Sir* Thomas, *of Gray's Inn and Council in North.* *6024, 15423.

TYMME, Thomas, *Translator* (*DNB*). Edits 12448.

TINDALL, *Lady* [*perhaps* (Egerton), Anne = *Sir* John]. *21165.

TINDALE, Drugo [*pupil of John Gower M.A.*]. Verse 12141.

TYNDALE, Gristine [? *Christian*]. 22992.

TYNDALL, Humphrey, *Dean of Ely* (Venn 1555). ¶3437 [see changes], 3439 by editor, *17913, *25680.

TYNDALE, William, *Bible translator* (*DNB*). Edits 20036-o. as W. T. [L. edition unsigned].

TYRIE, David, *Brother of next. See* 24476.

TYRIE, James, *S.J.* (*DNB*). *See* 15062.

TYRINGHAM, *Sir* Thomas, *of Tyringham* (Foster). *Fens map in 17827 [miscalled Bt.].

TYRLING, Robert [*presumably* Foster]. Verse 11464.

TYRRELL (Ussher), *Lady* Elizabeth. *See* USSHER.

TIRILL, Jonas, '*of Burstow,* [*Surrey*]'. 15340 by bookseller.

TYRWHITT (Manners), Briget = John *of Kettleby, Lincs.* Epistle 1469-L.

TYRWHITT (Oxenbridge), Elizabeth = *Sir* Robert *of Kettleby.* 15512 as Terwhitte.

TIRWHITT, Robert, *Equerry to Charles I* (*CSPD*). Epistle some copies *4747-o. as Terwit.

U

U. Initials alphabetized with v.

UVEDALE *alias* UDALE, Edmund, '*of Sherborne, Dorset*'. 21121 [see changes and Henry below].

UDALL, Ephraim, *Divine* (*DNB*). Prose 12980.

UVEDALE, Henry, *of More Crichel* (*Vis. Dorset*). †1591-Y. of 21121 [see changes].

UDALL, Nicholas, *Dramatist* (*DNB*). Verse 25799; pupils of: 23899.

UVEDALE (Cary), Victoria = *Sir* William *of Wickham.* Epistle *15465.

UDWARD, Nathanael, *Edinburgh M.A., 1590.* Verse 21101.

UDWARD, Nicol, *Bailie of Edinburgh.* W. M., *Edinburghs alphabet-E.

UEMIUS. *See* WEMYSS.

UNDERHILL, John, *Bishop of Oxford.* Verse 4759, 4761, 4762, 21029 (21032).

UNTON (Wroughton), Dorothy = *Sir* Henry. *See* SHIRLEY.

UNTON, *Sir* Henry, *Diplomatist* (*DNB*). 4016, *4755, 15556, 21673; prose 17823.

UPCHER, Henry, *of St. John's* (Venn). Verse 12272.

UPTON, John, *of Lupton.* †20268.

UPTON, John *and* Nicholas [*of Kent*]. *11127.

URANIA. 14931.

URBAN VIII, *Pope.* 12812; epistle 12808; *see* 12641 (12636).

URBANE, '*Friend*'. ¶13910.

URQUHART, John, *Tutor of Cromartie, d. 1631.* †12482.

URSINUS (Orsino?), Hannibal, *Neapolitanus.* Verse 19511.

URREY, John. Verse 12066, 12067 spelt Wrrey.

USSHER, Elizabeth, *later* Tyrrell, *Daughter of next.* 20543.

USSHER, James, *Archbishop of Armagh.* 4669; prose 3767, 12612.

UT NOS UNDA [? *anagram of* W. Standon]. Verse 23294.

UTENHOVE, Charles, *Writer* (Schotel). ¶3990; verse 3990 and 3988 [all from earlier foreign].

UTIE, Emanuel, *of Chigwell* (Venn and *STC*). Edits 10805.

UVEDALE. *See* UDALL.

V

All U and V initials listed here.

V., A. 24569.

V., C. D. (19741). *See* CIPRIANO DE VALERA.

V., D. [*Preacher* ?]. Prose 5842.

VUH., Diag. (18114). *See* DEGORY WHEARE.

V., G., *Armiger* [Gualterus Vavasour?]. 3575.

V., H. Verse 16887 only.

V., I. Verse 1022, 17824 [Vicars?].

V., J. vanden. Dutch verse 17224.

VASS., Mrs. I. (14720). *See* VASSALL.

V., M. (24928). *See* MAPTID VIOLET.

V., M. [*altered in pen to* M. W.]. Edits 23863 [epistle cancelled].

V., M. D., *N.G.* (7376). *See* M. D. V. N. G.

V., N. Prose 2795 and 2798 [? from foreign ed.].

V., R. [*possibly* Robert Vaughan]. Verse 19775.

V., R. (17507, *etc.*). *See* RICHARD VERSTEGAN, indexed as ROWLANDS.

V., S. Verse 21361.

V., T., *Englishman.* Verse 15507.

VIC., T. (Cipher in 4642). *See* THOMAS VICARS.

VADES-FORTE. *See* WADSWORTH.

VADIANUS, Glareanus [*Pseudonym*]. Verse [five languages] 5808 and 5810 [cf. 23769].

VADISLAVUS *and* VALENS. *See* WLADISLAUS *and* VALLANS.

VALENTINE, Henry, *D.D.* (Venn). Verse 7045.

VALERA, Cipriano de, *Schoolmaster* (Foster, STC). Prose 19741 as C. D. V.

VALESIUS. *See* WALLACE.

VALLANS, John, *Father of the author.* Epistle 24590.

VALENS, Robert, *'Friend'.* 24588.

VALENS, Thomas, *of Lincoln's Inn.* Verse 5686.

VALLANS, William, *Poet* (*DNB*). Verse 25295.

VAN DE PUT, Giles, *Dutch merchant in London.* Minsheu List.

VANE. *Listed with* FANE.

VANEGAS, Michael, *'Hispanus'.* Verse 25671.

VAN HAESDONCK, John, *Denizened fen drainer* (*CSPD*). *Fens map in 17827.

VAN VREDENDAEL, Justus. Edits 151.

VARNAM *and* VARNEY. *See* VERNAM *and* VERNEY.

VASSALL (Aborough), Judith = John-*DNB.* *14720 as I. Vass.

VATUM CHORUS. Verse 5119.

VAUGHAN, Edward, *Deputy clerk of pipe* (PCC 1612). 12607; epistle *1603-CHI. of 24600.

VAUGHAN, Edward, *M.A.* (Foster 1615). Verse 11877.

VAUGHAN, John, *I Earl of Carbery.* 24610, 24619; epistle some copies *4747-F. [also alternate epistle some copies-O.].

VAUGHAN, Jo., *M.A.* (*probably* Foster 1604 *Jesus*). Verse 11544 as Vauhan.

VAUGHAN, Sir John, *Judge* (*DNB*). Verse 7190, 16887.

VAUGHAN (Meyrick), Margaret = John *I Earl.* 24612 [see changes].

VAUGHAN, Richard, *Bishop of London.* *1352a, 5344, 20145 (20146), 23591, 25260, *¶25682 (25685); epistle 23592; verse 20309 partly as Ri. Va.; *see* 25695; licenses 737.

VAUGHAN, Richard, *II Earl of Carbery.* 24606; epistle 24604; *see* 10667.

VAUGHAN, Sir William, *Poet* (*DNB*). Verse 12974 [and see text].

VAUTROLLIER (du Thuit), Jaklin = Thomas, later Field. *See* next entry.

VAUTROLLIER, Thomas, *Printer* (*DNB*). Signed prose 1340, 6446 [earlier lost except impf. 1570-CU.], 15266, 15511a, 17279 and 1579-L. [earlier untraced]; unsigned prose 4414 only, 24668; patents to, 15/4-F. of 15242, 17409. *His widow or shop:* Unsigned prose 15412 and French, Italian versions-HD. [more prose in latter].

VAUX, Anne, *Recusant* (*DNB*). ¶15524, 20967; for her sisters (15524) *see* ELEANOR BROOKSBY *and* ELIZABETH VAUX.

VAUX, Edward, *IV Baron Vaux. See* 10667, 17332; Minsheu List.

VAUX (Roper), Elizabeth = George, *Mother of preceding.* *¶15524 unnamed, 23987 [see changes].

VAVASOUR, Nicholas, *Bookseller.* Prose 21416.

VAVYSOR (Vavisorus), Thomas, *of Cambridge* (Venn 1535). Verse 22250.

VAVASOUR, Sir Thomas, *Knight marshal, father of Charles I Bt.* †1614-FLEMING of 11768 [see changes].

VAVASOUR, Sir Walter, *II Bt.* †¶3586; *observe* G. V.

VEALE, Abraham, *Printer.* Unsigned prose 18095.

VIELL, Abraham [? *Mercer in Vis. London*]. Verse 23725.

VECHNERUS, Georgius, *German preacher* (BM). Verse 15082 [? from foreign ed.].

VELSERUS (Welser), Marcus, *Augsburg scholar* (*NBG*). H. Wotton, *Epistola*, [1612]-M., LINC.

W

W. Prose T. Field, *Earths encrease, 1624*-C.²

W., *Lady* A., *Recusant.* 7234 under monogram [often cancelled], S. Binet, *Life of Aldegond, 1632*-O.

W., A., *Oxoniensis.* Verse 13941.

W., A. Verse 5869, 11636, 14927 [gent.], La Ramée, *Art of arithmeticke, 1592*-L.

W., B., *Esquire.* Verse 25349.

W., B. Verse 12885; *see* 22235 colophon.

W., D. (3809). *See* DAVID WEDDERBURN.

W., D., *Arch[deacon]. See* 20974 [reprinted from 24901].

W., D., *M.A., Trinity College, Cambridge.* Verse 7294.

W., D. Epistle 7628 as M. D. W.; verse 3901, 6124, 15356.

WED., D. (12065). *See* DAVID WEDDERBURN.

W., E. (21549). *See* EDWARD WRIGHT.

W., E. [*supposedly Sir* Edward Waterhouse]. Edits 6364.

W., E., *of Hadleigh, Suff.* Prose 12963.

W., *Lady* E. *See* 19511.

W., E. Verse 5663, 5665, 17386.

W., Fr. *See* 25438.

W., G., *Sr.*, and G., *Jr.* [? Whitney]. Verse 23076 (23084).

W., G., *Joan.* [*Oxford*]. Verse 20694.

W., G., *Neaberdeanus.* Verse 1404.

W., G. Edits 1634, 23607; verse 5869, 11636, 17824, 23132.

W., Gilb. Verse 352.

W., H. Edits 24048; prose 11635.

WHIT., Hen. [*presumably* Whitehead (Venn 1575)]. Verse 14926.

W., I. (*all St. Omers books*), *see* JOHN WILSON; (19029), *see* JOHN WILKINSON; (19431), *see* JOHN WRIGHT, *Sr.*

W., I., *T.C.* Verse 10688.

W., I., *I.C.* Verse 13580 (13579).

W., I., *Theol.* Verse 20505.

W., I. Verse 1429, 4503 (4509), 4507 (4509) [*Gen.*], 18133; *see* 12662 (12706, 12635), 19204.

W., Io., *Gent.* Verse 21773 [date is *1618*].

WAL., Io. Verse 6364.

WA., Iz. *See* IZAAK WALTON.

W., L. [*presumably Scottish*]. Verse 15710, 15716.

W., M. Verse 14269 [? Wiseman], 14373 [possibly misprint for M. W. F(owler)]; *see also* M. V. (23863).

W., N. Prose 7395 (7394) [earlier lost], 11900 [from Oxford].

W., *Lady* P. (3571). *See* WHARTON.

W., P. Verse 11636, rarely 17824-F.

W., R. (1852), *see* RICHARD WROTH; (19822), *see* RICHARD WATKINS; (20595 = 25752) *see* RICHARD WILLIS.

W., R. [*presumably* Robert Woodford]. Verse 407 for *1629*.

W., R. [*friend of dramatists*]. Verse 3820, 18346 (18337), 20770.

W., R., *'Brother'* [*presumably Willet, unverified but cf.* PCC 1597]. *See* 25695.

W., R. ¶3532; verse 345, 4271 = 4271a, 18282, 18763, 19162 [19161 impf.], 20097, 21408, Faureau, *Briefe direction, 1618*-O.⁵; *see* 13522 [? Wyer the printer].

W., Ra. *See* 25438.

W., Ro. *19806.

WR., R. Verse 6364.

WYM., Ra. Verse 14008.

W., S. (22950, etc.). Presumably S[outh] W[ell]; for 22965 *also see* TRUSSELL.

W., S., *S.T.D.* Verse 11597.

W., S., *Medicus.* Verse 21455.

W., S. [*presumably of Oxford*]. Verse 4190, 4194, 4195.

W., T. (4442), *see* THOMAS WOODCOCK; (13980), misprint for W. H[unnis]; (17546), *see* THOMAS WORTHINGTON.

W., T., *Esquire.* Verse 25337.

W., T., *Stationer* [? Thomas Walkley]. Epistle 12026.

W., T. Edits 21434; verse 15078, 15516, 16884, 18525-HD. [normally unsigned], 21029 only; *see* 244.

W., W., *Oxoniensis.* Verse 3.

W., W. 11460 by editor; edits 12159, 25124; verse 6968, 12210, 19778, 24908.

W., Guil. Verse 21356.

C C

WATERSON, John, *Bookseller*. Prose 12416.

WATERSON, Simon, *Bookseller*. Prose 12415; *see* 5811.

WATESON. *Listed with* WATSON.

WATIES, Edward, *of Ludlow and Inner Temple*. 13825.

WATKINS, Richard, *Printer*. Unsigned prose 19819 [initialed in 19822].

WATKINS, Thomas, *Fellow of New College* (Foster 1598). Verse 13018.

WATSON (Wentworth), Anne = Edward II Baron Rockingham. 1396.

WATESON, Henry, *Warden of Barber Surgeons*. Epistle *25963.

WATSON, John, *Bishop of Winchester*. 13252 and *1580*-Y. [cf. 19182].

WATSON, Lewis, *I Baron Rockingham*. 10724.

WATSON, Richard, *Warden of Barber Surgeons*. Epistle *11203, *25963.

WATSON, Richard, *Royalist writer* (*DNB*). Verse 7366, 22400.

WATSON, Thomas, *Bishop of Lincoln*. Epistle 6093; verse 22250.

WATSON, Thomas, *Poet* (*DNB*). Verse 12224, 18775a (18773).

WATSON, Sir Thomas, *Exchequer teller, of Kent* (Brown). Presentation 22791.

WATTS, —— [*Soms. preacher*]. Epistle *1941.

WATTS, Sir John, *Merchant* (*DNB*). 24649.

WATTS, Mary, '*Widow*'. *15319.

WATTS, Richard [*probably the son of Sir John*]. Minsheu List.

WATTS, William, *Royalist chaplain* (*DNB*). Edits 19210; prose 14444 [variant issue signed X. Z.].

WATTS, William, *of Gray's Inn*. *3.

WAWKER *and* WAWLLAR. *See* WALKER *and* WALLER.

WAYLAND, John, *Printer*. Unsigned prose variant-L.6 of 3178, 25414; royal privilege 1256, rare copies 3178-HD., 4564, 7552.

WEALSH *and* WEAVER. *Listed as* WALSH *and* WEEVER.

WEBBE, ——, '*of Breckles* [*Norf.*]'. Epistle 15037.

WEBBE, Benedict, *Clothier, of Kingswood, Wilts*. 6902.

WEBBE, Edward, '*Roffensis*'. Verse 4938.

WEBB, George, *Bishop of Limerick*. Epistle *1941.

WEBBE, William, *Mayor of Salisbury, d. 1553*. 17319.

WEBBE, Sir William, *Lord Mayor*. *5840, 14686, 16659, *16767 [16766 a ghost], *¶17648 [see changes], 19054.

WEBBE, William, *Author* (*DNB*). Prose 25764.

WEBB, William, *Composer* (Grove). Verse 19924.

WEBB, William, *Oxford bookseller*. Prose 4736 as G. W., perhaps 24884.

WEBBER *or* WEBSTER, Richard, *Printer*. Unsigned prose 3131.

WEBBER, Thomas, '*Servant to the King*' [*see* CSPD]. Verse 11087.

WEBSTER, John, *Dramatist* (*DNB*). Verse 5461, 12863, 13309, 19165; *see* 23250 [attacked although unnamed].

WEBSTER, Richard. *See* WEBBER.

WEBSTER, Thomas. Verse 4035.

WEBSTER, Thomas, '*of Middlesex militia*'. Epistle *5668.

WECKHERLIN, Georg R., *Under-secretary of State* (*DNB*). Book licenser *1637–40*.

WEDDELL, John, *Sea captain* (*DNB*). 23753 (23725).

WEDDERBURN, David, *Poet* (*DNB*). Verse 3809 as D. W., 12065 as D. Wed., 16694, G. Gray, *Oratio funebris, 1614*-A.

WEDDERBURN, William, *Divine* (*DNB*). Verse 22471.

WEEKES. *See* WYKES.

WEERT, Davidus de. *557 and *1629*-HD. from earlier foreign.

WEEVER, John, *Poet* (*DNB*). Verse 4207, 17868.

WEAVER, Thomas, *Fellow of Eton* (Venn). *25129.

WEICKARDUS, ab Au[e]rsperg. ¶11730.

WELBY, Sir William, *of Gedney* (*Vis. Lincs.*). 17924.

WELBY, William, *Bookseller*. Epistle 6029 unnamed.

WELD, Sir Humphrey, *Lord Mayor*. *14303 spelt Wylde.

WELD (Slany), Mary = *Sir* Humphrey. *1629 by editor, 20669 (20668) by editor, *21165, 22838.

WELDON, Robert, *M.A.* (Foster). Verse 19778.

WELLS, John, *Bookseller.* Prose 18975.

WELLES (Manfield), Mary = Gilbert *of Brambridge, recusant.* Part I, *1634*-w. of 13469.

WELLES, Thomas, *Secretary to Bishop James Montagu.* Minsheu List.

WELSER, Marc. *See* VELSERUS.

WELTON, John. Verse 2497.

WEMYSS (Wemius), John, *Divine (DNB).* Verse St. Andrews (Leonard) *Theses, 1612*-O.⁶

WEMYSS, John, *Minister of Rothes.* Verse 15368 as Vemius.

WEMYSS, John, *I Earl of Wemyss. See* 10667.

WENDY, Thomas, *of Camb.* (Venn 1555). *15516.

WENMAN, Richard, *I Viscount Wenman.* 1546; *see* 10667.

WENMAN, Thomas, *II Viscount Wenman.* Verse 3914.

WENTWORTH (Hopton), Anne = Henry *III Baron,* later Pope. By editor 6938 and *1610*-O. (also in *Sermons, 1610*-BO.).

WENTWORTH (Crofts), Anne = Thomas *I Earl of Cleveland.* 10832, 11176.

WENTWORTH, *Lady* Anne (1396). *See* WATSON.

WENTWORTH (Holles), Arabella = Thomas *I Earl of Strafford.* 3565.

WENTWORTH (Finch), Catharine = *Sir* John Bt. 7422.

WENTWORTH, Henry, *III Baron Wentworth.* †4170 (4165a).

WENTWORTH (——), Jane = Thomas *II Baron, remarried Wm. Borough-DNB.* 14014.

WENTWORTH, John, *Esq.* [*various; perhaps* PCC 1588]. 25012.

WENTWORTH, Sir John, Bt. 23128, 26055.

WENTWORTH, Sir John, *of Somerleyton, Suff.* *3789, 3790.

WENTWORTHE, Margery. *See* 22610 (22608).

WENTWORTH, Thomas, *I Baron Wentworth.* 3603, 16992.

WENTWORTH, Thomas, *II Baron Wentworth.* ¶1881, 4061, 4656 [see changes], 24366 [see changes].

WENTWORTH, Thomas, *I Earl of Cleveland.* *362, *11496, ¶12109 [see changes], 23254 by his tenants; epistle †19909; *see* 10667, 17332.

WENTWORTH, Thomas, *V Baron Wentworth, son of preceding.* 11914; *see* 10667.

WENTWORTH, Thomas, *I Earl of Strafford.* 1530, 3223, 3563, 5753, *†14320, 15498, 15499, 20520, 23226, 24553, 25066, ¶¶25067 by editor [and variant-LC.]; epistle 23597; arms 14137 and *1635*-HD.; *see* 10667.

WENTWORTH, William [*presumably of Gray's Inn* (Venn 1576)]. Presentation 6843.

WEST (Knollys), Anne = Thomas *II Baron De La Warr.* 19946.

WEST, Charles, *V Baron De La Warr. See* 10667.

WEST, Henry, *IV Baron De La Warr.* *¶4497; *see* 17332.

WEST, John, *Groom of Privy Chamber, son of Thomas II Baron.* Minsheu List.

WEST, Nicolas, *Bishop of Ely.* 1242 by printer, 16896; epistle A. Barclay, *Life of St. George, 1515*-C.²

WEST, Richard, *D.D.* (Foster 1633). Verse 10829, 20694.

WEST, Thomas, *II Baron De La Warr.* 5254, †7304.

WEST, Thomas, *III Baron De La Warr.* 6038 [date *1607*], some copies *23350.

WEST, William, *I Baron De La Warr.* 17051.

WEST, William, *Legal author (DNB).* Edits 15745; table 10978.

WESTALL, John, *Oxford bookseller.* Prose 20515.

WESTBURY, Robert, *Esq.* [*of Christchurch, Hants*]. One issue *13507.

WESTERMAN, William, *D.D.* (Foster). Verse 11750 only.

WESTFIELD, Thomas, *Bishop of Bristol.* H. Robrough, *Balme from Gilead, 1626*-F.

WESTLEY, Thomas, *Canon of Canterbury* (Foster 1600). *5410 by editor.

WESTON (Waldegrave), Frances = Richard *I Earl of Portland.* ¶4874 and *1633*-F.

WESTON (Stuart), Frances = Jerome *II Earl.* Epistle *15465.

WESTON, *Sir* James, *Judge* (Foster). Verse 11516.

WESTON, Jerome, *II Earl of Portland*. 11911; *see* 10667.

WESTON (Lloyd), Mary = *Sir* Simon. *See* 23779 only.

WESTON, Richard, *I Earl of Portland*. 1399, 1977, *¶4497, 6302, ¶11166, *14741, *22842 [earlier lost]; Minsheu List.

WESTON, *Sir* Richard, *Judge, d. 1652* (*DNB*). *See* 10667.

WESTON, *Sir* Simon, *of Lichfield*. *See* 23779 only.

WHALLEY. *Listed with* WALLEY.

WHARTON, Humphrey, *of Gillingwood, Yks., d. 1635.* 3082.

WHARTON, John, *Writer* (*DNB*). Prose 22805.

WHARTON, John, '*Pastor of Ticehurst*'. *See* 13923.

WHARTON (Carey), Philadelphia = *Sir* Thomas. ¶3571 as Lady P. W. [named-PFOR.].

WHARTON, Philip, *III Baron Wharton*. 1852; *see* 17332.

WHARTON, Philip, *IV Baron Wharton*. Samuel Wales, *Totum hominis*, 1627-C.²; *see* 10667.

WHARTUN, Richard, *Esq.* [? *the Suffolk J.P.*]. 17469.

WARTON, Robert, *Bishop of Hereford*. *2983 = 21617.

WHARTON, *Sir* Thomas, *Son of Philip III Baron*. ¶13799, *†14320.

WHATMAN, Thomas, *of the Inner Temple*. Minsheu List.

WHEALAKAR, Richard, '*Minister of Auberly* [? *Amberley, Sussex*]'. *See* 13923.

WHEARE, Degory, *Historian* (*DNB*). Verse 10943 as D. W. [Diag. Vvh. in 10944], 18114 as Diag. Vuh., 22218; prose 12612, more 12613.

WHEATLEY, Andrew, *of Gray's Inn*. Verse 1506.

WHETELEY, Thomas. *See* 25438.

WHITLEY, Thomas, '*Lieutenant*'. Verse 1507 [cf. Andrew].

WHEELER (Hanbury), Elizabeth = *Sir* Edmund (*Vis. Bucks.*). *20537.

WHEELER, William, *of Datchet Manor, son of preceding*. *20537.

WHEELOCKE, Abraham, *Linguist* (*DNB*). Verse 7365.

WHETENHALL, George, *of Kent, Marian exile*. 1742 (1710).

WHETELEY. *Listed with* WHEATLEY.

WHETSTONE, George, *Author* (*DNB*). Verse 14927.

WHICKS. *Listed with* WYKES.

WHISTON, Henry, *Fellow of King's* (Venn). Verse 11769 and 11782, 13519.

WHITAKER (Crisp), Hester = Henry *of Amsterdam*. *11672 (11679, 11652).

WHITAKER, Laurence, *Poet and Clerk of Council* (Keeler). ¶5811; verse 5807, 5808 and 5810 [cf. 23769], 22218; Minsheu List.

WHITAKER, Richard, *Bookseller*. Prose 2798, 21806.

WHITAKER, William, *Master of St. John's, Cambridge* (*DNB*). Epistle 20613 and *1613-C.*; *see* 4709, 20632, 25695.

WHITAKER, William, *Lawyer* (Keeler). *See* 25327.

WHITBY, Edward, *Recorder of Chester* (Foster). *¶23720.

WHITBY, Robert *and* Thomas, *Mayor and alderman of Chester*. *¶23720.

WHITCHURCH, Edward, *Printer*. (*DNB*). *See* 4417.

WHITE, M[r]. D[r]. ——. 5706.

WHITE, Anthony, *M.A.* (Foster). Verse 19778.

WHITE, Charles, *Canon of Canterbury* (Venn 1620). Edits 5410.

WHITE, Edward, *the elder, Bookseller*. Prose 21634, perhaps 12003.

WHITE, Francis, *Bishop of Ely*. *3789, 19110 (19112), *22398; approves 18030; *see* 10667.

WHITE, Francis, *Son of preceding* (Venn 1607). Verse 25380 (25389).

WHITE, Harry [*London character, or perhaps fiction like* John Jarret]. 19242.

WHITE, Henry, *Rector of Rougham* (Venn 1611). Verse 18981.

WHITE, John, *Virginian pioneer* (*DNB*). *See* 12786.

WIFFING, Richard, *Virginia colonist.* Verse 22788 (22790).

WIGHT. *Listed with* WHITE.

WIGHTHAND, Matthew (? PCC 1589). Verse 18276.

WIGHTMAN, William [? *of Harrow,* PCC 1580]. Edits 24800 only.

WIGMORE, *Sir* Richard, *of the Privy Chamber* (PCC 1621). 25618.

WILBORE. *See* WILDBORE.

WILBRAHAM, *Sir* Richard, *I Bt.* *7293.

WILBRAHAM, Thomas, *Father of the preceding.* *7293; see 25438.

WILBRAHAM, Thomas, *of Lincoln's Inn* [*more than one; perhaps* Foster]. Epistle 23500 only.

WILBRAHAM, Thomas, *Esq.* [*perhaps the preceding*]. Presentation 17944; Minsheu List.

WILCOX (Greenbury), Catherine Frances, *Abbess at Brussels.* 19167 by editor.

WILCOX, Thomas, *Divine* (*DNB*). Edits 18151, 20084 [revised from *1595*-U. of Elijahu Wilcocks (Foster), ? his son].

WILD or WILDE. *See* WYLDE.

WILDBORE, Augustine, *M.A.* (Venn). Verse 14948 as Wilbore [date is *1616*-Y.].

WILDGOSE, *Sir* John, *of Sussex* (Foster). *11380 as Wilgose.

WILFORD, *Sir* Thomas, *the younger, son of Sir Thomas-DNB.* *21175.

WILKES, William, *D.D., Royal chaplain* (Foster 1572). 17755.

WILKIE (Willichius), James, *Principal of St. Leonard's, St. Andrews.* Verse 4660.

WILKIE, Robert, *Principal of St. Leonard's.* Leonard *Theses, 1603-*ST. A.; verse 7351 as R. W.

WILKINSON, Henry, *Schoolmaster* (Venn 1565). Verse 14608.

WILKINSON, John, *Principal of Magdalen Hall* (Foster 1580). *6420, *19589 (19570) by editor; leads off 19029.

WILKINSON, John, *Rector of Babcary, Soms.* Epistle *1941.

WILKINSON, Matthew, *M.A.* (Foster). Verse 1441a.

WILKINSON, Richard, *Chaplain* (Venn 1564). Edits 1092.

WILKINSON, Richard [? *the preceding*]. Verse 10698.

WILLAEUS, Da., '*Stirling schoolmaster*'. See 25737.

WILLAN, Ro. [*presumably* Venn 1596]. Verse 6316.

WILLET, Andrew, *Divine* (*DNB*). Prose 3437.

WILLET, Thomas, *Father of preceding.* See 25695 as M. T. W.

WILLIAMOT. *Listed with* WILMOT.

WILLIAMS, GUILLIAMS, GUILLIM, etc.

GUILLAM, ——, '*Clerk to Cofferer of Household*'. Minsheu List.

WILLIAMS. Verse 1167 from 1177 [sometimes supposed Archbishop John; possibly William (Venn 1625)].

WILLIAMS, *Sir* Abraham, *Agent for the Palatine.* Minsheu List.

WILLIAMS, *Sir* Henry, *I Bt.* 22123.

WILLIAMS, John, *Archdeacon of Gloucester.* *13756.

WILLIAMS, John, *Dean of Bangor* (Foster 1569). *6420; epistle *20147; edits 1181; verse 4759, 6787, 21029 only, 24610, 24621 = ¶24608; see 17944.

GUILLIAMS, Jo., *Gent.* [? *Guillim the herald; also see head of this series*]. Verse 11087.

WILLIAMS, John, *of Cheapside, King's goldsmith* (*DWB*). See 5811.

WILLIAMS, John, *of Tyneham, Dorset, d. 1627.* †18012.

WILLIAMS, John, *Archbishop of York.* Chronologically, all as Bishop of Lincoln and Lord Keeper:
1621: 4528 by editor, 13227.
1622: 1002, 13914, 21326 (21324), *25241, 25669, 25716 (25718).
1623: 1000, 1001, 3416, 6212, 7438 by editor, 19862, *20163.
1624: 6594 only, 7320, 7466, 14458, 18039, 23496, 23919 = 23922.
1625: 1657, 14460, 15083 by editor, 17945 [see changes], ¶20509, 24991, 25996; epistle 24604; see 17331.
1627: 21020, 24985.
1630–2: 4327, ¶5359, 6192, 11326, vol. ii of 17730, *25688 by editor.
Later: 4329a [see changes], ¶5906, 6194, 11199; see 10667, 13270 [unnamed].

WILLIAMS, R. (19699). Error for Williamson.

WILLIAMS, Richard, *Fellow of King's* (Venn 1624). Verse 7235, 13519.

WILLIAMS, Thomas. Verse 374.

WILLIAMS, Thomas, *of the Inner Temple* (Foster 1590). Verse 4985.

GUILLIM, Thomas, 'Cousin of the author'. Verse 12500.

WILLIAMSON, Caesar, *Fellow of Trinity* (Venn). Verse 21460.

WILLIAMSON, David, 'of Edinburgh university'. Edinburgh *Theses, 1604–0.*

WILLIAMSON, Dove, *Fellow of King's* (Venn). Verse 11769 and 11782, 13519.

WILLIAMSON, Hugh, *Mayor of Chester.* ★¶23720.

WILLIAMSON (Anderson), Mary = *Sir* Richard. ★¶2773.

WILLIAMSON, *Sir* Richard, *of Gainsborough and Council in North.* ★19699 (19649) by editor, misprinted Williams.

WILLIAMSON, Thomas, 'Brasenose graduate, Sussex preacher' [?Williams-*DNB*]. *See* 13923.

WILLICHIUS. *See* WILKIE.

WILLIS, Francis, *Dean of Worcester* (Foster). Verse 4759, 4761, 4762.

WILLIS, Richard, *Secretary to Lord Coventry* (*CSPD* and text); wife and children of. 20595 = 25752.

WILLIS, Thomas, *Schoolmaster* (*DNB*). Minsheu List.

WILLIS, Timothy, *Alchemist* (*DNB*). Verse 667, 4762.

WILLOUGHBY, Anne (21688). *See* ASTON.

WILLOUGHBY (Ridgeway), Cassandra = *Sir* Francis *of Wollaton. See* 23779 only.

WILLOUGHBY (Thornborough), Elizabeth = *Sir* Robert (*Vis. Staffs.*). ¶4187, 18902.

WILLOUGHBY, *Sir* Francis, *Grandfather of next.* 1359 only.

WILLOUGHBY, *Sir* Francis, *of Wollaton* (Foster 1607). *See* 23779 only.

WILLOUGHBY, Francis, *V Baron Willoughby. See* 17332.

WILLOUGHBY, *Sir* Henry, *I Bt.* 7462, †11085.

WILLOUGHBY, John, *of Broadgates Hall* (Foster 1585; cf. Wood). Verse 18114; Kinsmen of, 14641.

WILLOUGHBY, Thomas, *Brother of Henry-DNB.* Verse 25756.

WILLOUGHBY, *Sir* William, *of Aston Rowant, d. 1615.* 6596.

WILLOUGHBY, William, *of Gray's Inn* (Foster 1581). 18869.

WILLOUGHBY, William, *VI Baron Willoughby. See* 10667.

WILLWELL. *See* WOULWELL.

WILMER (Jacob), Elizabeth = Thomas (*Vis. London*). ★15333.

WILMER, George, *of Mdsx.* (Brown). †¶11680.

WILMOT, Charles, *I Viscount Wilmot. See* 10667.

WILLIAMOT *or* WILMOT, Samuel, *of London* (Foster). Verse 21094.

WILSHIRE, Lawrence, *Mayor of Gloucester.* ★12171.

WILSON, Aaron, *Divine* (*DNB*). Verse 1789.

WILSON, Arthur, *Dramatist* (*DNB*). Verse 7045.

WILSON, John, *Priest and supervisor of St. Omers press* (*STC*). As I. W., I. W. P., or W.I., edits or does prose 269, 3941, 11315, 11728, 14628, 16877, 17533, 18000, 18001, *1622-w.* of 19937, 19938, 20487, 21148, 23530 as W. I., F. La Croix, *Little garden, 1626-*M.; *see* Allison 269, 366, 432.

WILSON, John, *Headmaster of Westminster School.* Minsheu List.

WILSON, Jo., 'Interioris Templi' [*untraced*]. Verse 17921.

WILSON, Matthew. *See* EDWARD KNOTT, *pseudonym.*

WILSON, Michael, *Scotus.* Verse 23278.

WILSON, Nicholas, *Divine* (*DNB*). Prose 10898.

WILSON, R. [*probably* Richard, *clerk of Christ's Hospital*]. Verse 11096.

WILSON, Rowland, *City captain* (*DNB*). ★21095; epistle ★1507, ★25963.

VOLUSENUS, Sylvester, 'Glascuensis'. Edits 1404.

WILSON, Thomas, *Secretary of state, d. 1581* (*DNB*). 944, 4686 by editor, 5251, ¶20613 and *1613*-C., 26123, J. Rivius, *Notable discourse, 1578*-F.; epistle 6577; verse 826, 6577, 19299; prose 12595, 12596.

WILSON, Thomas, *Divine* (*DNB*). Epistle 24702.

WILSON (Volusenus), Thomas, *Advocate, son-in-law of Adamson.* Edits 146, 148.

WILSON, William, *Alderman* [*i.e. Mayor*] *of Kendal.* *24475.

WIMPEW, John *and* William, *both M.A.* (Foster). Verse 13555.

WINCH, *Sir* Humphrey, *Judge* (*DNB*). *11670.

WINCH, Onslow, *of Lincoln's Inn, son of preceding.* J. Wedhouse *1619*-L.² Irish almanac [distinct from 531].

WINDEBANK, *Sir* Francis, *Secretary of State* (*DNB*). *548; *see* 10667; Minsheu List; licenses books in *1640*.

WINDET, John, *Printer.* Epistle 25185 (1357) unnamed.

WINDHAM. *See* WYNDHAM.

WINDSOR, Henry, *V Baron Windsor.* ¶25206.

WINDSOR, Thomas, *VI Baron Windsor.* ¶686, 1020 = ¶12350, 3913, 4187, 11370, *11496, 13798 by bookseller, 14771 by bookseller, 20124, 20781, four Cambridge and Oxford foundation broadsides, *1622*-L.⁵ by printseller [see changes in 4485, 21868]; verse 11087; *see* 10667, 17332; Minsheu List.

WINGATE, Edmund, *Mathematician* (*DNB*). Edits 3804.

WINGFIELD (Deane), Anne = *Sir* Anthony *I Bt.* 276.

WINGFIELD, *Sir* Anthony, *I Bt.* 11078.

WINGFIELD, *Sir* Edward, *Soldier, of Carnew, Wicklow, d. 1638.* 1659 [see changes], 5262; epistle 6333, 17385.

WINGFIELD (Harington), Mary = *Sir* Edward. *3788, *4884, *5775 partly by bookseller, ¶6886.

WINGFIELD, *Sir* Robert, *of Letheringham, son of Sir Anthony*-DNB. 4035, 24417, L. Staveley, *Breef discourse*-HN.

WINGIUS, Gottfridus, *Minister of Dutch Church, London.* Prose 2740, 15262.

WINIFFE, George, *of Brettenham, Suff., father-in-law of author.* *See* 12662 (12706, 12635).

WINNIFFE, Thomas, *Bishop of Lincoln.* 4673 by editor, *13584; *see* 25327; Minsheu List.

WININGTONUS, Hugo. Verse 3944.

WINRAM, John, *Reformer* (*DNB*). *See* 10820.

WINSSEN, Adriaen van, *Heer van Hoencoop, of Utrecht, d. 1639.* Epistle 25939; also his wife.

WINSTON, John, *Shorthand reporter* (? Foster 1600). Edits 6945 and *1609*-U., 6950 (*Ten sermons, 1610*-BO.; cf. 6944, 6938); prose 6951 only.

WINSTON, Thomas, *Physician* (*DNB*). Minsheu List.

WINTER, *Sir* Edward, *of Gloucs.* (Foster). Minsheu List.

WINTER, *Sir* John, *Secretary to Queen* (*DNB*). 23704.

WINTER, *Sir* William, *Admiral* (*DNB*). 3432, 23659.

WINTERTON, Francis, 'of Claybrooke, gentleman to Countess of Denbigh' [? father of Ralph]. ¶19850.

WINTERTON, Francis, *Brother of next.* Verse 11772, 11780 (11773).

WINTERTON, Ralph, *Regius professor* (*DNB*). Edits 6900, 12211, 13518, 13519, Terence, Comoediae, *1633*-F.; verse 18954, 22257. *As press corrector:* verse 4477 as R. W. [name in 4478], 4480, 4484.

WINWOOD (Ball), Elizabeth = *Sir* Ralph-DNB. 7319 by bookseller.

WISE (Chichester), Mary = *Sir* Thomas *of Devon.* ¶1789, Bedford, *Ready way, 1638*-F.

WISEMAN, Agatha. *See* WINIFRED *below*.

WISEMAN, Anne, *Nun at Lisbon, d. 1650.* *10928 [earliest ed.].

WISEMAN, Barbara, *Abbess of Syon at Lisbon.* *10928 [earliest ed.], *19938 by editor.

WISEMAN, Bridget, *Canoness at Louvain, d. 1627.* *10928 [earliest ed.].

WISEMAN, Henry, 'Curate of Bosham'. *See* 13923.

WISEMAN, Jane [Mary in religion], *Prioress of St. Monica's, Louvain.* *10928 [earliest ed.], *18000 by editor.

WISEMAN, John, *of the Privy Chamber, brother of Sir Robert.* *23788 (23725).

WISEMAN, Mary. *See* JANE.

WISEMAN, *Sir* Richard, *Brother of next.* Verse 14269.

WISEMAN, *Sir* Robert, *of Torrell's Hall, Essex.* 17637, *23788 (23725); verse 14269.

WISEMAN, Winifred [Agatha *in religion*], *Benedictine at Brussels.* *10928 [earliest ed.].

WISHART, *Sir* John, *Judge (DNB).* 6321.

WISLAKE, Abraham. Verse 14926.

WISTOW *or* WYSTO, Richard, *Master of Barber Surgeons.* 19426 and 1573-HN.

WITHER, George, *Father of the next.* Epistle 25891 (25911).

WITHER, George, *Poet (DNB).* By himself 25891 (25911); epistle 11509; verse 3129 [extracted from 25899], 3830, 3914, 4193, 7229, 12974, 22788 (22790), 23447, 25097-F. [*recte* third ed.], 25103 and 25102.
Friends visiting him in prison: 25920 (25890, 25911).

WITHER (Hunt), Mary = George *the elder.* Epistle 25891 (25911).

WITHERS, Nathaniel. *See* 5584.

WITHER, William, *Cousin of George.* Epistle 25891 (25911).

WITHINGTON, Oliver, *M.D.* (Foster 1555). Verse 4759.

WITHY, Humfrey, *Verger of Worcester cathedral. See* 24099.

WITHYMAN, John, '*Theological student and press corrector*'. *See* 7537.

WITHYPOLL, Edmund, *of Ipswich, d. 1580.* 16936 (16932); *see* 23095.

WITHYPOLL, Peter, *LL.B., son of preceding* (Venn). *See* 23095, 25438.

WITT, John, *of St. James, Clerkenwell. See* 13327 (plate iv).

WITT, Richard, *Mathematician* (STC). *See* 5584.

WLADISLAUS IV, *King of Poland.* Epistle 3370.

WODEHOUSE. *See* WOODHOUSE.

WOLFIUS (Wolf), Hieronymus, *Scholar* (NBG). Verse 24230 (23970) [? from foreign ed.]; prose 15483.

WOLPHIUS, Johannes, *Zürich minister, d. 1572.* Epistle 93.

WOLFE, John, *Printer (DNB).* 12902; signed prose 1599, 11747, 15691; unsigned prose 1034, 3470, 4202, 11735 [and one signed J. de la Croy], 12003, 12903, 13817, 21508.
Presumably the mystification epistles in the following with false imprints [*not otherwise indexed*]: 10511, 12004, 17158, 17159, 17161, 19911, 19912, 19913, B. Felippe, *Tractado, 1589*-L., F. Perrot, *Aviso piacevole, 1586*-HD.

WOLFE, Reyner, *Printer (DNB).* Unsigned prose 4415 [and cf. 4417], 6186, 6464.

WOLFERSTONE [*cf.* WOLVERTON]. Verse 12205.

WOOLEY, *Lady* Elizabeth. *See* EGERTON.

WOLLEY, *Sir* John, *Latin secretary (DNB).* 4557, 5220, 5253, †18061.

WOOLLEY, Randolph, *Master of Merchant Taylors.* ¶13841.

WOLSEY, Thomas, *Cardinal, Archbishop of York.* 6279, 11534, 21427 with mock arms [see changes], ¶¶22608, 22609, Whittinton, ¶*Epigrammata, 1519*-HN.; *see* 4082; arms unaccountably in 10477.

WOLSTENHOLME, *Sir* John, *Merchant (DNB).* *6267, *19967 [see changes], *23625, *24660 [24659 a ghost].

WOLSTENHOLME, *Sir* John, *Son of preceding.* 20539 = ¶20552.

WOLSTENHOLME, John, *of Gray's Inn* (Foster). *3.

WOOLTON, John, *Bishop of Exeter.* *24885.

WOOLTON (——), Mary = John *Bishop.* 4665.

WOLVERTON, R[oger; see SR 23 June 1640], '*Phil. & medicus*'. Verse 6190 [cf. WOLFERSTONE].

WOOD, Ambrose [*Shorthand reporter*]. Prose 25039 (25031 and 1623-F.).

WOOD, *Sir* David, *Servant to Richmond, Overbury witness.* Minsheu List.

WOOD, Gerard, *Archdeacon of Wells* (Venn 1595). *1943; epistle *1941.

WOOD, John, *Nephew of Sir T. Smith* (one of Venn's). Epistle 12905.

WOOD, Nicholas, *of Harrietsham, the Great Eater.* 23761 only.

WOOD, Richard, *Master of Barber Surgeons.* Epistle *25962.

WOOD, Richard (Foster 1598). *See* AIWOOD.

WOOD, Robert, '*of St. Andrew Hubbard, London*'. *20678 (20668) by editor.

WOOD, Thomas, *Rector of St. Margaret, Fish St.* *¶1477, *21201-HN. shifted in 21202; *see* 23923 and 23920.

WRAY, Edward, *Groom of Bedchamber* (Venn). ★¶4497, 11823, ★19516, ★20603, ★23890 unnamed.

WRAY (Norris), *Lady* Elizabeth = Edward *above.* ★¶4497, 7318.

WRAY (Drury), Frances = *Sir* William *I Bt.* ★21013.

WRAY, *Sir* John, *II Bt.* †1959, ★19516, ★20603, ★23890 unnamed.

WRAY, Nathaniel *and* William, *Sons of next* (Venn). ★23890 unnamed.

WRAY, *Sir* William, *I Bt.* 6036, 22874.

WREITTOUN, John, *Edinburgh printer.* Unsigned prose 5967.

WREN, Matthew, *Bishop of Ely.* Epistle some copies ★4747-O.; censure 13518; *see* 10667.

WRIGHT, Edward, *Mathematician* (*DNB*). Edits 21549 as E. W.; prose 11883; *see* 3160.

WRIGHT, Elizabeth, *Dominican at Dartford, half-sister of J. Fisher.* ¶10899.

WRIGHT, Henry, *Spy, metallurgist, Sovereign of Tallow* (*CSPD*, *CSPI*). ★14509, ★14511; verse 20768.

WRIGHT, John, *the elder, Bookseller.* Initialed prose 19431 and variant-L.[16] [usurped from R. Jones].

WRIGHT, Laurence, *Physician* (*DNB*). ★¶14704.

WRIGHT, Richard [? *Scottish*]. Verse 18360.

WRIGHT, Robert, *Scholar, d. 1596?* (*DNB*). Verse 1492.

WRIGHT, Robert, *Bishop of Lichfield.* ★6420, ★¶7471, 20830, R. Lougher, *Sermon at Cern, 1624*-F.; edits 24520; verse 1653 [identity conjectural]; *see* 10667.

WRIGHT, Thomas, *Author and divine* (*DNB* as two men). ★21152; *see* 26002 as H. T.

WRIGHT, William, '*of Chepping Wycombe*'. Prose 4854 and 1545-PML.

WRIGHT, William, *the elder, Bookseller.* Initialed prose 12245, 22689 but unsigned in collections.

WRIOTHESLEY (Southampton) Family. ★17361.

WRIOTHESLEY (Vernon), Elizabeth = Henry *III Earl.* 3583a, 11831 by editor, ¶14747.

WRIOTHESLEY, Henry, *II Earl of Southampton.* See 19867 spelt Wrisley.

WRIOTHESLEY, Henry, *III Earl of Southampton.* 90-C., 998, 3218 by editor, 3583, 5349, 5624, one issue ★7326-F., ★7336, 10828, ★11098 [see changes], ★11496, 12740, 13510, 18380, 20170, ★20339, 22345, 22354, ¶23582 (23575, 21653), 26040 rewritten 26041 by editor.

Epistle: 1469-L., 6165, 6258 (6263, 6238), 6333, 13633 (13624), 16696, 17385, 25891 (25911).

Presentation: 17944; *see* 19511; Minsheu List.

WRIOTHESLEY, James, '*Lord Wriothesley*', son of preceding. ★17699.

WRIOTHESLEY (de Massue), Rachel = Thomas *IV Earl.* Epistle ★15465.

WRIOTHESLEY, Thomas, *IV Earl of Southampton.* ¶14747 by editor, 19322; *see* 10667, 17331.

WRISLEY. *See* WRIOTHESLEY *and cf.* RISLEY.

WROTE, Samuel, *of the Council for Virginia* (Brown). ★17362 as Rotte.

WROTH, John, *of Christ's College* (Venn 1567). Verse 1852 and 1853.

WROTH (Rich), Margaret = *Sir* Thomas [*d. 1672*]. Epistle 18521; *see* 26053.

WROTH (Rich), Mary = *Sir* Thomas-*DNB* [*d. 1573*]. 11755.

WROTH (Sidney), Mary = *Sir* Robert, *Author* (*DNB*). 14736, 14755 (14751), ★¶23578 (23581, 23575, 21653); epistle 1598, 13634 (13624) [rarely in 13633], 25891 (25911); *see* 5112.

WROTH, Richard, *of Christ's College* (Venn 1570). Verse 1852 as R. W., signed 1853.

WROTH, *Sir* Robert, *the younger, husband of Lady Mary.* 22977.

WROTH, *Sir* Thomas, *Parliamentarian, d. 1672* (*DNB*). 18517.

WROTHE, William, *Warden of Mercers.* 978 as Wrathe [see changes].

WROTH, William, *of Christ's College* (Venn). Verse 1852 and 1853.

WROUGHTON (Paulet), Katherine = *Sir* Giles. 19172.

WRREY, John. *See* URREY.

WYATT, *Sir* Francis, *Governor of Virginia* (*DNB*). Verse 21725.

WYATT, *Sir* Thomas, *Poet* (*DNB*). 1735 and 1775 (1710).

YETSWEIRT, James, *of St. John's* (Venn) [? *kin of preceding*]. Verse 19150 as Itzuertus.

YOMANS *and* YONGE. *See* YEOMANS *and* YOUNG.

YORK, Sir John, *Master of the mint* (DNB). 24682.

YOUNG (Junius), Andrew, *Professor at Edinburgh.* Verse 18349, 18357 and thence 6267, 22567.

YONGE, Edmond, *'Student of the law'* [*untraced*]. 4685 (22805).

YOUNG, Francis *and wife* Susan, *'of Brent Pelham, Herts.'* Pt. ii of 19158 [earlier lost; see changes], Pt. ii of 19161 [earlier lost], Pt. i of 19162 [19161 impf. and earlier lost], 20366a–L. [see changes].

YONGE, John, *Master of the Rolls* (DNB). 20060 and 20061.

YONGE, John, *Bishop of Callipoli* (DNB). *21800.

YOUNG, Sir John, *of Bristol.* 1244 [and 1245–F.], 18670.

YOUNG, John, *Bishop of Rochester. See* 25665.

YOUNG, John, *Dean of Winchester* (Venn 1606). 5973, 11959 [see changes], ¶12485, 15134 by editor, 22398.

YOUNG, John, *Fellow of King's* (Venn 1625). Verse 13519.

YOUNG (Junius), Patrick, *Biblical writer* (DNB). 823, ¶5097; edits 5398, 11121, 18527; Minsheu List.

YOUNG, Sir Peter, *Tutor to James VI* (DNB). ¶21649.

YOUNG, Sir Peter, *Gentleman usher, son of preceding.* Epistle some copies *4747–O.

YOUNG, Richard, *Collector of customs* (CSPD). 21801 by editor [and lost work noted therein].

YONG, Richard [*presumably* Foster 1610]. Verse 26130.

YOUNG, Richard, *'of Woolley-farm, Berks., Esq.'* 12051 by bookseller.

YOUNG, Sir Richard, *I Bt.* *23307 (23313) by editor, *23850.

YOUNG, Robert, *Printer.* Prose 21654 usurped from Lownes; *see also* M. FLESHER.

YOUNG, Thomas, *Archbishop of York.* *1710.

Z

Z., M. C. [*perhaps* Zoilus]. Epistle 23060.

Z., Q., *'of Lyon's Inn'* [*presumably a fiction*]. Prose 24050.

Z., X. (14444). *See* WILLIAM WATTS.

Z., X. Verse 18904 and prior 1614–C.[2]

ZEPPER, Wilhelm, *Theologian* (ADB). *14047.

ZEROTIN, Carl, *Bohemian politician, d. 1636.* Epistle 19813.

ZOILUS. Innumerable verses and epistles to Zoilus have not been indexed. Variants include Authorimastix, Critics; *see also* M. C. Z.

ZOUCH (——), Dorothy = Sir Edward *of Woking.* 22391.

ZOUCHE, Edward, *XI Baron Zouche.* 3750, ¶3914, 3917 (25890), 6737, 6742 [see changes], *11496, 16650, 20792, 26130; epistle 16696, 17332.

SOUCH, Francis, *of New College* (Foster). Verse 13018.

ZOUCH, Sir John, *of Codnor* (Venn 1549). 21352 and earlier–F.

ZOUCH *or* SOUCH, John, *Esq.* [*perhaps Sir John of Codnor* (Venn 1578)]. *4268, 7096.

ZOUCH (Berkeley), Mary = Sir John [*preceding*]. *15469 [15468 a ghost].

ZOUCHE, Richard, *Civilian* (DNB). *14457; verse 13018; *see* 25327.

ZOUCHE (Harington), Sarah = Edward *XI Baron, previously* Hastings. 3699, *3788, *4884, *5775 partly by bookseller, ¶6890, 20788; epistle 1598, *23581 (23575, 21635).

ZOUCHE (Hart), Sarah = Richard–*DNB.* *19553.

UNCERTAIN READINGS

The names indexed as JOHN CANON and JOHN FARRER are illegible.

STC 13595: Of two known copies, the binder has trimmed off the top half of the name in L., while the leaf is missing from NLW. Possibilities are: CANON, GANON, GASSON, GALLON.

STC 5829: In the unique copy the dedication is not only damaged but over-stamped with the Bodleian cachet. Possibilities are FARRER and FATTER.

II. INSTITUTIONAL AND GEOGRAPHICAL

SINCE this index serves a different type of research from the Personal Index, and since much of its material involves or supplements personal dedications, the sigla ★ † ¶ are usually omitted. As a result, it approximates to a subject index of book preliminaries. The organization is as follows:

A. EUROPE

CHRISTIAN PRINCES (sovereigns collectively, including republics and the Emperor). 1897, 4002, 10512, 11351, 12860, 13080 and 13081, 13968, 14401 and 14405 (14344 and 14346), also 14408, 15314, 15507, 21751, broadside *Ad potentissimos reges, 1583*-L.

CHURCH UNIVERSAL. 972, 7005, 12703, ¶14344 and 14346; Christians, 21492.

EPISCOPAL CHURCHES. Bishops, ¶6994.

REFORMED CHURCHES. 16573, 18529 and 18530, 19969, E. D., *Memento for Christians, 1623*-F.; clergy, ¶21751; universities, 18434 = ¶7298; elect wheresoever dispersed, 5343 by editor; protestants in Catholic countries, 2741.

CALVINIST COUNTRIES. 22016; Calvinists, 16561 (16578) and 16565.

ROMAN CATHOLIC CHURCH [all hostile]. 7313, 18354 [as Beast]; pope and clergy, 20113 by printer; theologians, 18197; *see also below under* ROME.

CONTINENTAL PRINTERS OF RECUSANT BOOKS. 20625.

AIRE (Pas de Calais). English Poor Clares, *see* 24924.

AMSTERDAM. English congregation, 227, 21107 = ¶227, *see* 238; Clapham group, 5345; Se-baptists, 12567; unnamed friend, ¶4264.

ANTWERP. Merchant adventurers, 18535; English Carmelites, Pinelli, *Meditations, 1622*-W. by editor.

BARBARY. Jews, 12858 and *1613*-F.; Christian captives, 24582.

BRESLAU. ¶15082 [? from foreign ed.].

BRUSSELS. Houses of Englishwomen: Benedictines, 10928 [the earlier ed.]; Franciscan tertiaries (St. Elizabeth's), *Rule of third Order, 1624*-L.

CALAIS. 19078.

COLOGNE. 16778.

DELFT. Merchant adventurers, 13262, 25843.

DENMARK. Gentlemen learning English, 22430 and *1625*-O.[2]

DORT. Synod of Dort, *see* 2344.

DOUAY. Irish College, 11026; unnamed son at, 18212.

EMDEN. Merchant adventurers, 18535.

FLANDERS. 19063; English nuns, 10928 [the earlier ed.]; gentlemen learning English, 22430 and *1625*-O.[2]

FRANCE. 17310 and 17309; preservers of, 10512; Reformed Church, 3754; Universities, 18434 = ¶7298; French and neighbours, 1464; gentlemen learning English, 22430 and *1625*-O;[2] subjects, 6377 and French *1589*-L.

FRANEKER. Frisian university, ¶550 [from foreign ed.].

FRIESLAND. Magistrates, ¶550 [from earlier foreign].

GENEVA. University, 18434 = ¶7298; Genevans, 3875; English congregation, *see* 2093, 2384 [also 2394, 2396].

GERMANY. Reformed church, 3754; universities, 18434 = ¶7298; Germans, 23581 (23575, 21653); gentlemen learning English, 22430 and *1625*-O.[2]

GRAVELINES. English Poor Clares, 13034 [? earlier lost], 14628 only by editor, Silva, *Chronicle of order, 1618*-L.

GRISONS. Church, 16576 [foreign printing].

HAMBURG. English congregation, ¶16684; Merchant adventurers, 25846.

HEIDELBERG. University, 18434 = ¶7298, 19022.

HOORN. 25340.

INGOLSTADT. University, 12064.

ITALY. Poets, 23700 and 23701; Italians learning English, 11096.

LEPANTO. Battle heroes, 14386 = 18298.

LEYDEN. University, 18434 = ¶7298.

LIÈGE. Jesuit novitiate, 16877 by editor [16878 shows removal to Watten].

LISBON. English Brigittines (Syon abbey), 10928 [the earlier ed.], 19938 by editor.

LOUVAIN. English Augustinians (St. Monica's), 10928 [the earlier ed.], 18000 by editor; Sodality of Immaculate Conception, 23531; English at, 7167 = 22271.

MIDDELBURG. English congregation, 11136; Merchant Adventurers, 11134.

MONTPELLIER. University, 19595 (16650).

NETHERLANDS. States General, ¶550 from foreign ed., 553 from foreign ed., 12858 and *1613*-F., 20489, 21657, 25939; officials at all levels, 17450; inhabitants, 12001, 13053, 16571a and 16575; Dutch reader, 22069 (22102, 22064); universities, 18434 = ¶7298; constant Reformed congregations, 553 from earlier foreign; pastors, 21746 (21749, 21751); Mennonites, 13053; splinter Freewillers, 13053.
English in: H. P[eters], *Milk for babes, 1630*-HD.; English soldiers, 1106; British nonconformists, N. E., *Information for ignorant, 1640*-U.

PARIS. Sorbonne, 7026 and 7027; College of Surgeons, *1597*-HN. of 16870 naming 14 ignored in this index; English Augustinian nuns, 23992 by editor [see changes], *S. Austins rule, 1636*-DE.

PERUGIA. *See* 25671.

POLAND. Rulers, 1463 = 10577 (1464).

RHEIMS. English seminarians, 21493.

ROME. Papal consistory, 7026 and 7027; Congregation of Holy Office, 3106; English seminarians, 21493; *see also* ROMAN CATHOLIC CHURCH *at head of series*.

ROTTERDAM. English congregation, H. P[eters], *Milk for babes, 1630*-HD.

ROUEN. English Brigittines (Syon abbey), 10541.

ST. OMERS. Mary Ward's community, 3941 by editor.

SAXONY. 'Duces', 13083.

SPAIN. Potential protestants, 4426.

WATTEN (near St. Omers). *See* LIÈGE.

ZÜRICH. Pastors and teachers, 4406 = ¶15259.

B. BRITISH ISLES

In such categories as occupations, *undifferentiated entries have been listed under* ENGLAND, *even though some may have been intended generally for the* BRITISH ISLES.

BRITISH ISLES. 25915 (25897, 25911). *Inhabitants*: 1796, 20103.

GREAT BRITAIN. 4291, 12726; Diva Britannia, 13222; lovers of Britain's glory, 23045. *Nobility, clergy, gentry*: 6498.

impf.], 21002, 23813 (23725), N. Breton,
Historie of Frederigo, 1590-0.[5]
Young gentlemen: 3146, 12234, 12279, 12281,
23130, 24356, 25348; *see* UNIVERSITY
STUDENTS.
Gentlemen readers: 1469-L., 4579, 15589,
16660, 17068; Gentle Reader, not indexed.
Gentry and yeomanry: 837.

YEOMANRY [*see also under* NOBILITY *and*
GENTRY]. 12281.

COMMONALTY [*see also under* NOBILITY]. 638
and 639, 7471.

SUBJECTS *or* INHABITANTS (often faithful, loyal,
etc.).
Official statements: 5168, 9177, 9262, 13086.

Epistles: 369, 780, 784 = 24916, 1845, 3129,
3658, 4536, 4668, 5682, 5883, 7582, 7751,
augmented issue-L.[2] of 12605, 13597, 16980,
16998 and *1570*-F., 17518, 18110, 18432,
18983, 19505 [date *1639*], 20562, 20576,
21919 and 21922, 22234, 23465, 23581
(23575, 21653), 24637 [cf. 24639], 24754,
25372.

English reader: 2207, 6734, 10765, 24484,
24485, 26000; loyal reader, 24269; wishing
to amend disorders, 6480.

CHILDREN. 5400, 13503, 25971, Plutarch,
President for parentes, 1571-HN.; *see* STUDENTS.
Babes: 13207.

YOUTH. 4843, 10445, 10555, 16116, etc.,
19195, 22136, 24677, 24702, 25939; *see*
STUDENTS, CAMBRIDGE, etc.
Giddy or wanton: 12306, 23533.

HOUSEHOLDERS (heads of families). 1642,
6064 and *1619*-0., 18540, 20586.
Families: 6173.
Parents: 5180, 6064 and *1619*-0., 11503, 13503,
17861 = 17141a [earlier lost], 22136, 23277,
24007, Plutarch, *President for parentes,*
1571-HN.
Prospective parents: 19599.

MARRIED PEOPLE. 4091, 20397; those intend-
ing matrimony, 19286.
Husbands: Good, 20596; jealous, 24593.
Wives: See below.

LOVERS. True, 1855; unhappy, 3570 (3588).
Bachelors and virgins: 13312.

MALES. Masculine reader, 6908, 23123.
The mal-gender: 23706.
Fathers and sons: 715.
Bachelors: 6479.

WOMEN (by social class). On literary patronage, *see* 11276, 15334.
Ladies (sometimes inexactly): 91, 778, 3899,
3937, 12270, 12293, 12496, 15227, 19162
[19161 impf.], 19864, 20388, 21378, N.
Breton, *Historie of Frederigo, 1590-0.*[5];
recusants, 13541; unnamed ladies [perhaps
nuns of Syon], 21473 [the earlier ed.].
Ladies and gentlewomen: 3632, 3705 [earlier
lost], 11831, 12174, 17068, 18302 [see
changes], 19883 and *1639*-F., 21359, 25755.
Ladies . . . women: 22974, 25329 [religious].
Gentlewomen: 1, 313, 644, 3565, 19819 only,
20996, 25095.
Women: 3555, 3678, 11930 [satirical], 21154,
21544, 21634, 23123, 23381, 23747, 24517,
25180; *also see under* 3 (*c*), UNNAMED
PATRONS.

WOMEN (by categories). *See also* HOUSEHOLDS
OF INDIVIDUAL SOVEREIGNS, RELIGIOUS ORDERS,
and LONDON.
Beauties: 18994 = ¶12974.
Maids: 12047, 13312, S. Rowlands, *The*
bride, 1617-HD.
Housewives: ¶23703; aspirants to house-
wifery, 19426, 19978.
Wives: See preceding and next. Consider all
† entries in main index.
Miscellaneous: Gossips, 19331; dainty doxies,
3555; archwives and widows, 5734;
brawling wives and malapert mistresses,
23620; common sort, 23533; looser sort,
24393; non-weathercock, 10854; an unnamed widow, 20397.

3. *Occupational and Miscellaneous*

(*a*) *Occupations and avocations*

The clergy appear in 4. RELIGIOUS; office-holders in
I. POLITICAL. *See also the place-name file, especially*
LONDON (City companies).

MISCELLANEOUS. Noble spirits, 18342
(18337); judicious, 1667 only; lovers of
worth, ¶21872 and *1616* often with 21870.

ACCOUNTANTS. 13548 = 13549 [both *1634*
in MS.].

ACTORS. *See under* LONDON.

ADULTERERS. 11235.

ADVENTURERS (capital investors). *See* LONDON
(*Merchant companies*), BRITISH COLONIES, *and*
below, SEAMEN.

ALCHEMISTS. 21057.

ALEHOUSE KEEPERS. *See* TAVERN KEEPERS.

ANTIQUARIANS. 15444, 22633.

APPRENTICES. 12234, 12243, 12279, 12281, 14295; *see* LONDON (*City companies*).

ARTS AND LETTERS. Lovers of, 15026, 15444; philologus, 13206; learned, 23045.

ASTRONOMERS. 6871, 11185, J. B[ainbridge], *Astronomiae studiosis, 1622*-O.; reprovers of [astrology], 6860.

BALLAD-MAKERS. 14923.

BAWDS. 4295.

BOOK BUYERS. Of this book, 17366; of almanacs, 1547.

BOTANISTS. 11748.

BROKERS. 3588.

CIVILIANS (professors of civil law). 638 and 639, 5977; students, 5406, 26131 = 26131a rewritten 26132.

CLERGY and DIVINITY STUDENTS. *See under* 4. RELIGIOUS.

CLOTHIERS. 21484; hard-hearted cloth-masters, 25970.

CLOTHWORKERS. 6559 [earlier lost].

CORN-MASTERS. 25970.

COTTONEERS (cotton-spinners). 3566.

COUNTRYMEN. *See* HUSBANDMEN.

COURTIERS. *See below* FAVOURITES, *but chiefly* COURT *and* HOUSEHOLD *under individual sovereigns.*

DEBT NEGOTIATORS. 21779.

DRUNKARDS. *See* TIPPLERS.

DUELLERS. 10637.

EXPLORERS. 11185, 18244.

FALCONERS. 3314.

FARMERS. 12234, 12243, 12279, 12281.

FARRIERS. 17334.

FAVOURITES. A. Pérez, *Pedaços de historia*-HD.

FENCING MASTERS. 23543.

FLOOD SUFFERERS OF *1570.* 15032.

FREEHOLDERS. 22079 (22102, 22064).

GALLANTS. 6519.

GAMBLERS (cheating). 17916.

GENTLE CRAFT. *See* SHOEMAKERS.

GEOGRAPHERS. 11185, 15692, 18638.

GLASIERS. 11695.

GOOD FELLOWS. 20766.

GOWNSMEN. 13968.

GULLS. 6500, 6519.

HACKNEY-MEN. 23816 (23725).

HORSEMEN. 17334.

HOUSEKEEPERS (liberal). 23745.

HOUSEWIVES. *See under* 2. CLASS, AGE, SEX, ETC.

HUNTSMEN. 3314, 17334.

HUSBANDMEN *or* COUNTRYMEN. 12243, 12279, 17580.

ILL *or* SICK. *Grouped under* PHYSICIANS.

INNHOLDERS. 20766, 22614; *see* TAVERN KEEPERS.

JAILERS. 7160.

LANDLORDS. 18639; land owners and capitalists, 5375, etc. and *1618*-Private library [5372 a ghost].

LANGUAGE STUDENTS. Dutch, 25340; English, 11096, 22430 and *1625*-O.[2], 25340; foreigners knowing English, 16998 and *1570*-F.; French, 6736, 6737, 6748, only *1596*-Y. of 6749 [specifying journeymen and apprentices], 6761, 6762, 7574 [teachers as well], 19166, 21736, R. Faureau, *Briefe direction, 1618*-O.[5] Greek, 638 and 639 [patrons], 15409 [biblical], 21072a [21072 a ghost, *1636* was Douay]; Italian, 11096; Latin, *see* STUDENTS (*Grammar school*).

LAWYERS. Civil law, *see* CIVILIANS; Common law, *see* LONDON (*Inns of Court*).

MAGNETISM. Students, 1443 (1444).

MATHEMATICIANS. 6462, 10678, 12784, 15692, ¶17669, 18350, 25234; philomatheus, *Letter of myraculous starre, 1573*-L.[2]

MERCHANTS. 4699, 12234, 12243, 12279, 12281, 15692, 21094; *see* LONDON (*Merchant companies*), etc.

MIDWIVES. 21442.

MISERS. Pinching pennyfathers, 25970; Mammonists, 23745.

MUSICIANS. 4252 = 11827 [see changes], 4649; students or lovers of music, 2575 [sacred music], 4244 [earlier lost], 6040, 10698, 24715-C.; cithern scholar, 13562; 'musical murmurers', 14734; 'cunning catcher', 20757.

NATURAL PHILOSOPHERS (scientists). 199; *see also* ALCHEMISTS, BOTANISTS, GEOGRAPHERS, MAGNETISM, MATHEMATICIANS.

NAVIGATORS. *See* SEAMEN.

NEEDLEWORKERS. 23776 [earlier lost].

NOVEL *and* FANTASTIC ENTRIES. *See next series*, 3 (*b*).

ORTHOGRAPHERS. 12889.

PAINTERS. W. Painter, *Chaucer new painted*-HN.

PEACE-MAKERS. 14542 [author Traske; cf. *1616*-HD.], 21138, 22264; peace-lovers, 21747 (21751), 15442.

PHYSICIANS (*see also* SURGEONS *below*, LONDON (*College of Physicians*), *and* YORK). 638 and 639, 1359, 3374 and *1547*-WIS., 5832, 10665, 15204, ¶17669, 21442 [youthful], 21455, 21543; attending Henrietta Maria, 12509.
Students of physic, 19831, 25953 only, Latin version-O.¹⁴ of 18204.
Patients of author, 3723.
Sick and wounded, 3374 and *1547*-WIS.; gout, 12539; stone, 4733 (4731).
Those careful of health, 4304 and *1578*-F., J. Ghesel, *Rule of health*, *1631*-O.³

PILOTS. *See* SEAMEN.

PLANTERS *and* GRAFTERS. 17574 and earlier-F.

PLAYGOERS. 22384.

PLAYWRIGHTS. 12245.

POETS. 778, 1058, 6151, 12247 by editor, 21393, 22872 [shepherds], 25172, 25436 [with dew of Helicon], 26124 [sons of Muses].
Profane [erotic] poets, 21408; Welsh poets, 17914; Italian poets, 23700; 'Vatum Chorus', *see* 5119; *also see* BALLAD-MAKERS, PLAYWRIGHTS.
Muses, 15715; Calliope, 1666 = 18972 (1665); Urania, 14931.
Cherishers of poetry, 3672, 6820, 7190, 7205, 21537; sacred poems, 21010-F. [often cancelled]; rhyme, 6259 (6263); hexameters, 13076.

PRINTERS. *See* LONDON (*Stationers' Company*).

PRODIGALS. 23745.

PROMOTERS. 3588.

READERS. *Formal dedications to the Reader are listed below in* 3 (*c*). *Normal epistles to the Reader, or Gentle Reader, are ignored; others are classified, e.g., to Ladies (*2. CLASS, AGE, SEX, ETC.*).*
Ignorant and honest, 22592-C.⁶; long-eared, 23130; unlatined, 19894; 'preiudicate' 4964.

Readers of comedies, 14780, 17908, 22384; Dramatophilus, 1672.

RICH. 17319; and charitable, 25316.

RUFFIANS. 13815.

SAILORS. *See* SEAMEN.

SAINTS. *See* 4. RELIGIOUS.

SCHOOLMASTERS ('Painful' and otherwise). Royal injunctions to: prescribing catechism, 4807, 4812, 4813; prescribing Lily, 15605 [? and earlier] by Henry, 15611 by Edward, *1567*-F. by Elizabeth, 15625 by James.
Dedication (as 'laureat Lillies'), Lily, *Fairest fairing*-L.
Epistles, 188 and *1617*-HN., 3767, 3772 and *1628*-HD., *1622*-HD. of 3774, 4861, 5301 by editor T. Cogan, *1619*-O. of 6064, 12417 [reipublicae literariae toparchis], 13260, 15605 and *1540*-L.², 15612, 15635, 19599, 21641 (15080), 22136, 23410 and two other Sturtevant books-Y., 23597, 24818, only *1568*-F. of 25878 by editor, 25884 by editor.

SEAMEN. Mariners, sailors, 3389 (18647), 3427 [cf. 13696], 5803 [see changes], 21088, 21545, 22592-C.⁶, 23265.
Navigators, 15692, 25952 [especially East India]; well-willers to, 22784, 22794; pilots, 4699; Trinity House, *see* DEPTFORD.
Adventurers at sea, 22784, 22794.

SERGEANTS *and* CATCHPOLES. 3588.

SERVANTS *or* SERVING-MEN. 1555, 6274, 14295.

SHOEMAKERS. Gentle craft, 6523, 6555 and *1627*-SHEFF., 21422 by printer; *also see* LONDON (*Cordwainers' Company*).

SMITHS. *See* FARRIERS.

SOLDIERS of all ranks. *See also military organizations under* LONDON, *etc.* 1500, 1506, 1542, 1926, 1955, 6531, 6536, 10598, 13926, 13968 [men of sword], 17403, 20978, 20995, 20996, 21088, ¶21872 and *1616* often with 21870, 22855, 24675, 25339 (25340), 26062, R.B., *Mirrour to warres*, *1589*-L.
Artillery companies and trained bands, 4933, 5667, 7366; gentlemen active in training, 5376, 22855, 22885 and more briefly *1594*-HN., 23520.
English serving abroad, 25025; Netherlands, 1106.

SORCERERS. 21405.

STUDENTS (grammar school and undifferentiated). 4861, 5059, 6188, 7176, late issue

14860, 15635, 22406, 23597, 24825; Latin, 21029 (21032), 23895, 24017; tyros, punies, petits, 12421, 23280.

STUDENTS. *See* CAMBRIDGE, LONDON (*Inns of Court*), OXFORD. *In this sequence, apart from* LANGUAGES, *students appear under professions like* CIVILIANS, PHYSICIANS, *etc. See also* CLERGY *and* YOUTH.
Unclassified, at university or divinity level, 3701, 3705 [earlier lost], 5332, 11239, 22638, H. Clapham, *Sommons to doomes daie*, 1595-P.

SURGEONS. *See also* PHYSICIANS *above, and* LONDON (*Barber Surgeons*). 3374 and 1547-WIS., 5442, 5444, 5448 (5442) [see changes], 11716, 12499 (1362), 15192, 16870, ¶17669, 24367, 24713 thence 24706, 25964.
Apprentices at sea, 19191; students, 11529 (24723), 11531 and 1567-AML. (24723 some copies), 15192, Latin version-o.[14] of 18204, 19191.

SURVEYORS. 18640.

TAPSTERS. 22614; *see next.*

TAVERN FREQUENTERS. 23764; *see* TIPPLERS.

TAVERN KEEPERS. 20766; *see* INNHOLDERS, TAPSTERS.
Taverns: See under BRENTFORD, CASTLE HEDINGHAM, LONDON; *see also* ANDREW HILTON.

TEACHERS. *See* SCHOOLMASTERS.

TENANTS. 18639.

TIMBER DEALERS. 15553.

TINKERS. 4581.

TIPPLERS. 20766, 22614; drunkards, 20766; *see* 19936 *and* TAVERN FREQUENTERS.

TRAVELLERS. 3389, 3654, 12007, 15692, 16689, 19936.

USURERS. 3129, 3588.

VINTNERS. 20766; *see* TAVERN KEEPERS.

WISE. 11162.

WITCHES. 21405.

WITS. 12247.

WOUNDED *and* SICK. *See under* PHYSICIANS.

WRITERS. 22633; *see* BALLAD-MAKERS, PLAYWRIGHTS, POETS.

WRITING-MASTERS. 3905, 4861.

(b) Novel and facetious dedications
This list generally ignores the fictitious names consolidated in the main index under PSEUDONYMS, *which should be* consulted. *Facetious and satirical dedications also occur elsewhere, as under sex and occupations, as well as under individuals, e.g.* GREGORY COLE, RICHARD LICHFIELD, *and* WILLIAM PRYNNE.

ANYBODY. 25924; 'No matter who', 23742 (23725), C. T., *Laugh and lie down*, 1605-HN. *See also below:* EVERYBODY, MAN, PATRON, QUISQUIS, WORLD.

AUTHORIMASTIX. Epistle 13203 [variant on unindexed Zoilus].

BAW-WAW, M[aster]. *Pil to purge melancholie*, [1599]-PFOR.

BOOKS, 'Those who importune authors to give'. Epistle 25900.

BRITANNIA, Diva. 13222.

CLUTCH-FIST, *Sir* Christopher. 17881 [earliest ed.].

COUNTER, prospective tenants. 10781.

DEATH. ¶11600.

DETRACTION. 17485. Incidental verses to Detraction are ignored.

ENVY. Verses to Envy (as in 12716) are generally ignored.

EVERYBODY. 23731 (23725) [earlier lost], 23800 (23725); 'Omnibus et singulis', 21858.

FOLLY, *Dame*. Prose 11634.

FOOL, Tom. 21381.

FORTUNE, *Madam*. Epistle 11634.

FUSTIS, *Knave of Clubs*. 21387.

GEORGE, British of that name: 25409.

GHOSTS, shades or spirits. *See in main index:* ARISTOTLE, W. ELPHINSTONE, HANNIBAL, JAMES KENNEDY, RALEIGH, SCIPIO, SKELTON.

GOOD ACCEPTANCE, '*patroness of the world*'. 24559.

GOOD FELLOWS. 23764; 'the pleasant conceited', 5123.

GOOD OPINION. 17482 (4276).

HAND, The. Presentation 22791 [cryptic].

LUST, *Lady*. 25196.

MAN. Epistle 21338; Children of men, 19084.

MEMORY OF: *See in main index:* R. DEVEREUX, ERRA PATER, HENRY FREDERICK, GUSTAVUS ADOLPHUS, SIR E. LEWKENOR, MARY OF SCOTLAND, O'TOOLE, T. RANDOLPH, SIR P. SIDNEY.

MNEMOSYNE. Patridophilus, *Preservative poem*, 1636-BO.[4]

MONEY, *All that lack.* Epistle 21424. *See below,* PECUNIA, SHILLING.

MORPHEUS, '*brother to Oberon*'. Epistle 21314-HN.

MULTITUDE, *Monsieur, purblind, or giddy.* 23792 (23725) [see changes], 24636, 25967.

MUSES. 15715. *See also in main index:* CALLIOPE, URANIA, *etc.*

MYSELF. *See dedications to author,* 3 (*c*) *below.*

NEMO, *Sir* Nicholas, *alias* NOBODY. 12199.

NOBODY. 6411, 12199, 17473; epistle 23795 (23725).

PATRON, Unchosen. 12935; unknown, 194.

PEACE. *See under* OCCUPATIONS *and* RELIGIONS.

PECUNIA, *Lady.* 1486; subjects of Pecunia, 15439.

PIPE. *See* WHIFFE.

PLEASURE. Epistle 157.

POSTERITY. 1650, 4496 (4497, 4502), *25899; epistle 3833.

QUISQUIS, *Emperor.* 21853.

RASH JUDGMENT. 21381.

ROUNDROBIN DEDICATION. 3.

SENSELESS, Trim Tram, '*Hedgborough of Gotham*'. 23795 (23725).

SHILLING, *All masters of a.* 23793 (23725).

SNIPSNAP. Prose in *Pil to purge melancholie*, [*1599*]-PFOR.

SNUFFE. Prose in *Pil to purge melancholie*-PFOR.; *see also* WHIFFE.

SWASH, *Sir* Richard. 11208.

THRIFT, *Professors of.* 1650.

TRUNCHEON, *Sir* Timothy, *alias* BASTINADO. 22573.

TRUTH, *Lady.* 25169; lovers of truth, 1056, 22875. *See also under* RELIGION.

VIRTUE, *Lovers of.* 12562a [see changes].

WHIFFE, PIPE, *and* SNUFFE, *Captains.* ¶3585.

WORLD. 6521, 12027; epistle 10828, 23725, 25915 (25897, 25911).

ZOILUS. No dedications; epistles not indexed.

(*c*) *Unnamed patrons, factotum epistles, etc.*

The category of unnamed patrons does not repeat all the instances indexed elsewhere. In this group one suspects that fictions outnumber true masked identities.

READER, Formal dedications to: 1841, 3715, 4530 by editor, 13419 (13378), ¶14684,

14780 [vs. playgoer], 19995, 20600 [with God & Church], 23524, 23525, 23759-E., 25612, J. G. E., *Englands hope, 1600*-L.[2], W. Smith, *Qui non credit, 1625*-C.[19]

AUTHOR
Facetiously, by himself, 17486, 25891.
Sincerely, by editor, 11728, 12113 [anonymous], 14591 only, 17320, 18926, 19167; borderline case, 3191; Memory of author, 20694.

FRIENDS and other vague groups
Author's friends, 537, 14721.
Parishioners or sermon auditors, 6114 and prior-U., 19601, 23315, H. P[eters], *Milk for babes, 1630*-HD., H. Paynter, *St. Pauls rule, 1632*-F.
Pupils, 23899.
Medical patients, 3723, 5833.
Backers of the book, 2734, 14446, 24007a.

UNNAMED INDIVIDUAL PATRONS
Earl, 5057; Lord, 6182, 17757 [disclosed in 17758], J. Durie, ¶*Motives, 1639*-F.; Knight, 3847; Honourable, *Vertues reward, 1639*-C., W. Wright, *An epistle, 1622*-HD.; Gentleman, 1573, 1574, 1575.
Lady, ¶3305, 5625, 11027 [*see* PRESENTATION EPISTLES], 15296, 17093, 22697, 24055, 24779; Gentlewoman, W. Thomas, *An argument, 1551*-HD.
Pre-Reformation nun, 14042; monk, 6904.
Anglican bishop, 17195; Protestant friend, Palatinate, *The copy of a letter, 1622*-O.[8]
Catholic prelate, 661; two Jesuits in England, 25289; recusant, S. N., *The copie of a letter, 1601*-USHAW; recusant in Flanders, 19836a.
Father, 156; brother, 1047; brother-in-law, 11504; cousin, 22956; late kinsman, 14641.
Unnamed friend, 1000, 2792 = 14499, 3131, 11113, 13576, 14574 = 24249, 18443, 19000, I. P., *A treatise of Masse, 1614*-PARIS. Verses and prose by unnamed friends are in Anonymous section.
Widow of his Maecenas, 18586; unknown patron [mystification], 194; unchosen patron [facetious], 12935, ¶19338, C.T., *Laugh and lie downe, 1605*-HN.
Unidentified writers, 12113, 23632.
Occasioner of this book, 15348.
Some patrons are unknown simply because no complete copy survives, e.g., 20366, and *1580*-L. abridgment of Habermann, *Enemie.*

CRYPTIC DEDICATIONS
To the Hand, 22791 by editor.

CRYPTIC DEDICATIONS, *cont.*

Theophilus, 4664, 24597.

To Digbies noble worth [? fustian epistle], 11125.

Fascinating evasion, 18198.

FACTOTUM DEDICATIONS (blank space for individual MS. completion): 1191, 1193, 1199, 5987-F. P. WILSON, 11682.

For completion in print or MS.: M. Maier, *Arcana*-L. [*see* PRESENTATION EPISTLES].

Anomalous blank dedications, 6271-L.[2] [freak pre-publication state].

FACTOTUM PRESENTATION LEAF (to be completed in MS.; normally missing). 18382 [special bindings], F., O.; 24637, F.; perhaps 5670, F.

4. *Religious*

The classification is intended to facilitate use rather than argue issues: (*a*) Church of England (by chronological phases); (*b*) Dissatisfied and dissenting groups; (*c*) Roman Catholics after 1558; *and* (*d*) Miscellaneous.

ATHEISTS. 5336.

ADHERENTS OF DEVIL. 6794 and earlier-L.[2]

JEWS. 10873, 11149, 12858 and *1613*-F.

CHRISTIANS. 904, 3900, 4410 rewritten 4411 [4413 earliest?], 12726, 14950, 21905.

'Wandering Christian', 11512; imitators of Christ, 23973.

'Christian Reader', not indexed.

ENGLISH SAINTS. Canonical, 4602, ¶19416; general, 21344; *see also* ELECT *in section* (*d*).

PROTESTANTS. Distributed below, chiefly under Church of England.

(*a*) *Church of England*

For provinces, dioceses, and parishes, see geographical file. Identifiable prelates are in the personal index. For saints, see above.

Pre-Schism, to 1534

Holy Church: ¶5068 [acrostic in Usk's *Testament*, as 'Margarete'].

Clergy: 4115, 6813 and earlier-O., 15790, 15818, 17107 [all epistles, not dedications].

Religious: 278 [especially Carthusians]; unspecified communities of nuns, 6833, 25417= 13925 [Augustinian]; Augustinian novices, 19816; unnamed nuns, 5065, 13608, 16939 (16932), 24766.

Houses: See COVENTRY, DENNY, ROMSEY, SYON, WHERWELL, WINCHESTER, WINTNEY.

1534–53

Church of England: 3963, 15188: hierarchy and clergy, 11233, prose 5163; bishops, 21428 [see changes].

Faithful (*Protestant*): 359 and earlier-LINC., 10430, 18576, 21428 = 20582.

Papists: 20582 = 21428.

1553–8

Hierarchy: 11593, 17518.

Papists: 20175.

Marian exiles: 21854, 25111, 26140.

Protestants: 1307, 1716 (1710), 10016, 12020, 17821, 17822, 18798; imprisoned, 21854; of Calvinist tinge, 15059, 15073, 16561 (16578) and 16565.

Church of England from 1558

Deo et Ecclesiae: See main file, GOD.

Church of England: 60, 3754, 4157, 4711, 4714, 5332, 5346, 5843 [see changes], 6060, 6286, 6288, 6440, 6876, 11223, 11878, 11896, 12649 (12706, 12635), ¶12706 (12635), 14455, 14896, 15207, 18485 = 25858, 18538, 18541, ¶19969, 21692, 22039, 22526, 24178, 25427, 26085, 26115, 26121a [from foreign ed.].

Archbishops (*exclusively*): 18333.

Bishops: 3473 [earlier lost], 3879, 6873 = 3518, 7061, 9247, 10392, *10667, 14555 [earlier lost], 17497, 18305, 18701 (and 18708, 18711, 18712, 18726, 18730), 19829, 20457, 20476, 26084.

Endorsement by, 159: recommendation to, 18773 only.

Prelates: 10850, 14453, 20475, 20484, 24499; 'clergy masters', 17453; prelates and supporting clergy, Marprelate reprint-L. of 19903a.

Bishops and clergy: 21748 (21751), 24637 [cf. 24639].

Convocation: 7585, 17453; Synod of *1611*, 21751; Synod of *1621*, 18529 and 18530.

Clergy: 364, 638 and 639, **1658**, 1736, 1939, 2771, 3436, 4056, 4650, 5370, 6235, 10589, 10688, 11026, 12648c (12635), 13065, 13503, 13663, 14333 = 14334, 14338, 14555, 14933, 15049, 17456, 17732, 18040, 19059, 19611, second *1592*-C. of 19735 thence English version *1607*-HD. (19649), 20555, 20766, 22079 (22102, 22064), 22374 and 22372, 22398, 24923, 25923, 25970, H. Burton, *Conflicts* of conscience, 1628-L., W. Jones, *Exposition of catechisme*, 1633-U.

Subscribing clergy, 24273; cold or careless, 21090, 24357; unnamed preacher, censure in *Myraculous discourse*, 1588-HN.

Divines: 6014, 6093, 11636, ¶17669, 23459, 25210 (25207), R. Aylett, *Brides ornaments*, 1625-F.

Divinity students: 14458, 21621, 23459, 24668, 25212 (25207).

Pastors and teachers: 3882, 6284, 15078; cate-chizers, T. Downing, *Catechisers encourage-ment*, 1623-U.

Patrons: 6890, 21752, 23514.

Laity: 18797; public defenders, 19171; 'true Christians', 24281; 'true Catholics', 14445.

Foreign congregations (conforming): *See* AMSTER-DAM, HAMBURG, MIDDELBURG.

Protestants (addressed by Protestants): 2093 [later titled 'To reader'], 3533 [non-Brownist], 3788, 6173, 6574, 7085 [7084 a ghost], 11225, 13054, 13247, 13743, 18185a, 18604, 24127, J. Walker, *Glasse for papists*, 1623-O., A. Ross, *Gods house*, 1640-U.

Conforming, 25593; kneeling, 6877; un-settled, 23115.

Protestants (addressed by Catholics): 577 [learned], 580, 3606, 3801, 4007, 10414 [especially persecutors], 11112, 13454, 14571 = 24249, 17981 and earlier-HN., 18335 [including Catholic-like], vol. ii of 19416, 20486 [20485 diff. trans.], 23232, 23938, *Epigrammes*-HN.

Nobility, 580; writers, B. C., *Adelphomaxia*, 1637-W.; unnamed individual, 5475.

(b) Dissatisfied and dissenting groups

From 1558. Some entries in (a) perhaps belong here by intention.

Puritan clergy: 11335.

Puritans (variously designated): 1040, 4264, 10389, 10390, 10770 (10400), 11575, 11888 = 6810 (10400), 13712, 14574 = 24249, 19612, 19613, 21068, 24357, 24962, 25594; those favouring, those slandered by, 18851.

Nonconforming clergy: 20145 and 20146.

Nonconformists: 6588, 6876, 14333 = 14334, N. E., *Information for ignorant*, 1640-U. [in-cluding New England and Netherlands].

Separatists: 227, 5336, 6286, 7186a, 19068, 22876, 22877.

Brownists: 12861.

Anabaptists: *See* 10682.

Sabbatarians: 13274.

Foreign congregations: *See* AMSTERDAM, GENEVA, NETHERLANDS, ROTTERDAM.

(c) Roman Catholics after 1558

For the international Church, see EUROPE *and* ROME.

Bishops: 20147; unnamed prelate, 661.

Clergy (undifferentiated): 5557, 6929, 18186, 18335, 21090, 24305; unnamed priest, 5662.

Seminary priests and Jesuits: 5742, 7048, 18182, 18189.

English Jesuits: 1817, 4535, 11149, 12746, 14569, 14921, 16642 and earlier-L.[2]; 18999; novitiate, *see* LIÈGE.

Seminary priests: 1817, 1829, 12746, 19449; younger sort, 576.

United under Archpriest, 4321, 7628; sub-scribe to item in 19392.

Imprisoned, 22946; at Wisbech, 1829.

Seminary students: 576, 18193, 20625, 20626 and 20630; *see* RHEIMS, ROME.

Religious : 11539 [*1612* unlocated], S. Austins rule, 1636-DE.; nuns, 1923 as 'virgin reader'; Franciscan Third Order, 23212; communi-ties abroad, *see* AIRE, ANTWERP, BRUSSELS, DOUAY, FLANDERS, GRAVELINES, LISBON, LOU-VAIN, PARIS, ROUEN, ST. OMERS.

Parthenian Sodality: 12958.

Catholics (addressed by Catholics): 983, 1032, 1702 by author, 3272, 4955, 5557, 7238, 14049, 14909, 14910, 14914, 15348, 17533, vol. i of 19416, 21505, 24992, 25076, 25125, 25771, S. Stock, Pt. iii of *Practise*, 1623-W.

Catholic reader, 1188, 4008, 4554, 6929, 12761, 13032, 14907 and prior-C.[5], 17263, 17275 by editor, 1630-C.[2] by another edi-tor 18335, 19411, 24264 = ¶5189, *Manual of meditation*-O., *Mistical crowne of Marie*, 1638-L.

Imprisoned recusants, 22946; persecuted, 3107, ¶3369 [signed by editor in 1611-HD.], 4833, 13376, 14527, 19392 = 4832.

Ladies, 13452.

Who are: propertied, 18984; loyal [anti-Jesuit], 19449; believers in deposition, 25598; devout, 17278; seeking perfection, 11539 [*1612* not found].

Catholics (addressed by Protestants): 1071, 1571, 1794, 1830, 3077, 3081, 3788, 3793, 4097,

Roman Catholics—cont.

4137, 4321, 4879, 5156 = 15526, 5336, 5658, 6014, 6059, more 6060, 6075, 6084, 6091, 6168, 6204, 6325, 6377, 6883, 7048, 7085 [7084 a ghost], 11149, 11216, 11222, more 11223, 11242, 11249, 11597, 11629, 12030, 12704 and English version-LC., 12746, 12866, 12870 [Lancashire], 12880, 13453, 13457, 14497, 14896, 15034, 15311, 15595, 18063, 18147, 18174, 18184, 18185, 18311, 19171, 19174, 19421, 19736 and *1597*-F. (19646) and 19741, 20832, 21024, 21510, 22094 (22064), 23030, 23113, 23592, 24305, 24912, T. Bedell, *Lively antithesis, 1604*-M.

Jesuited, 1817: anti-Jesuit, 780; moderate, 17095 [17094 a ghost], 23115, 23453; disapproving Powder plot, 12814 and 12815; malcontent, 23130, 24269.

Ladies (Romish collapsed), 11262, 13541.

Learned, 4101, 6574.

Unnamed individuals: Mother, 155; kinsman, 15562; perverted, 17149.

(d) Miscellaneous

Afflicted consciences: 11080 [poor in spirit], 11234, 11242 [and 11247 as to Reader], 12891, 12985, 15460 [mourners in Zion], 16965, 18629 [earlier lost], 23831, 25314 [wearied sinners], *Key of David, 1610*-U.

Bible-readers: 4056, 5842 [see changes], 15409 [Greek Testament], 24468a; Gospel lovers, 10512; promoters of Welsh Bible, 24007a.

Compassionate: 10937.

Doubting or weak: 5330, 24421.

Elect: 588, 590, 592, 595; saints-to-be, 6175; citizens of Heavenly Jerusalem, 12567.

God, Those loving, fearing, promoting: 1662, 19591 (19570), 19926, 21432, 25653 [later To reader]; Jesus Christ, 4238, 14573, 15598.

Guardian angel: 7234.

Hard-hearted: 25236.

Haters of Antichrist or Babylon: 13054, 24025.

Militant Christians: 10636 and *1633*-DUL., 14485, T. Bedell, *Lively antithesis, 1604*-M.; Hierusalem's artillery, 11251 [11250 a ghost]; lovers of Christian chivalry, 25409.

Neuter, Christian: 151.

Peace-seekers: 12980.

Persecuted: 25721.

Saints-to-be: See ELECT.

Soul: 21343 and *1631*-F.

Traducers of final perseverance: 20471.

Truth, Seekers or lovers of: 3998, 4575, 5341, 13855, 17729, 19709 (19646), 22876, 22877, [T. Helwys], *Declaration of faith, 1611*-C.[2]; lovers of true religion, 1596.

Types of virtuous or well disposed: See in main file ABGAR and THEOPHILUS.

Well living, students of: 26088.

BRITISH AND IRISH PLACE-NAMES

Alphabetically, including Home Counties, the North, and Wales, but ignoring almanacs 'rectified' for individual towns. Colonies are grouped at the end.

COUNTRY (*as opposed to London*). 6457, 10688, 18698.

TOWN READER. 11032.

ABERDEEN. Corporation: 1494, 1495, 12494, 25187, 25189, 25191, G. Gray, *Oratio funebris, 1614*-A., W. Mercer, *Bon-accords decorement, 1633*-E.

   University, 575, 18790; Grammar School, 24623a; clergy, 64, etc., 68 (70); professors of gospel, 5962; papists, 145 (148).

ABERGAVENNY. 24600.

ABINGDON. School, 11956.

APPLETON (Berks.). 6822.

ARRETON (Wight). W. Jones, *Exposition of catechisme, 1633*-U.

AUDLEM (Ches.). School, 25438.

BANBURY. Corporation, 25308, 25317; charitable, 25316; neighbours, 25322.

BARLEY (Herts.). 25677.

BARNSTAPLE. Corporation, 4682 (*Three sermons, 1617*-LINC.), 6057; adventurers for New England, 22788.

BATH AND WELLS. Clergy of diocese, 6069.

BATH. 14725, 24351 (24366).

BELLAPORT HALL (Shrops.). 5870.

BERKELEY. *1632*-L.[4] of 5127.

BERMONDSEY. St. Mary Magdalen, 7619.

BERWICK-UPON-TWEED. 15059, 15064, 15073.

B[OVINGTON] (Herts.). T. Wilcox, *Forme of preparation*-HD.

BRENTFORD. Honest Ralph, tavern-keeper, 3585.

BRISTOL. Corporation, 20513, 24027; Military Garden, 19155; trained bands, 5667; Merchants, 1049 and *1589*-O.[8]; adventurers for New England, 22788; general, 14725, 21091, 24351 (24366); the pious, 4167 (4165a), 4170 (4165a), 5127, 24028.

BURY ST. EDMUNDS. 11819.

CAMBRIDGE. St. Peter, 23820; saints-to-be, 6175.

CAMBRIDGE *and* OXFORD UNIVERSITIES (jointly). 637, 638 and 639, 1167, 4093, 5351, 5883, ¶13582, 14783 (14751), 18172, 18189, 19412, 22143, 22551, 23458.

Heads, 18333; doctors, 636; divines and lawyers, 19417; theologians, 6093; 'learned artists', 14315; learned, rarely 22213–HN.

Students, academic reader, etc., 80, 737, 775, 4535, 4759, 11515, 12095, 12241, 12252 [12251 impf.], 12272, 13962, 15516, 16788, 18657, 20158, 20601, 21698 = 21699 [earlier abroad], 24621 (24608).

Students of logic, 15575 [and Oxford editions]; schoolmen, 10637; philosophy, 4106; philosophy beginners, 4758.

CAMBRIDGE UNIVERSITY. 1127 (1109), 6296, 11020, 19171, 19655, 24926a, 25026 (7068), 26001, 26085; epistle 3189, 4473, 22400, 22609, 23354.

Heads, 6193, 24139 [see changes]; prose 19011.

Students or youth, 4108, 17801; divinity, 14444; mathematics, 10678; medicine [with teachers], 21455; philosophy, 18809; alumni studying French, 7294.

Textbook edited for, 15576 and *1497-C.*⁵, 25674.

Book licensers, 14955.

Musae Cantabridae, 5870, 12964, 12966; unrecorded anthology, 1460.

College arms, 19292.

Cambridge friend, 12342.

University Library: Minsheu List.

Caius College, 13877, Minsheu List.

Christ's College, 19749 (19649), 25679 [see changes], 25695; Minsheu List.

Clare Hall, 3467; Minsheu List.

Corpus Christi (Benet): Minsheu List.

Emmanuel College, 2772 [earliest ed. of pt. ii]; Minsheu List.

Jesus College: Minsheu List.

King's College, 11054; Minsheu List.

Magdalene College, Pembroke Hall: Minsheu List.

Peterhouse, 16827; Minsheu List.

Queens' College, 1788, 17913; Minsheu List.

St. Catharine's, St. John's: Minsheu List.

Sidney Sussex College, 21203; Minsheu List.

Trinity College, 636, 1167, 18206, 24180 by editor; Minsheu List.

Trinity Hall, 5899; Minsheu List.

CANTERBURY PROVINCE, Clergy. 12648c (12635).

CANTERBURY ARCHDEACONRY, Clergy. 5336.

CANTERBURY. Cathedral clergy, 14305; St. Andrew, 23546; St. George, 24966; friends, 24966.

CARDIFF. 14729 only.

CASTLE HEDINGHAM (Essex). Falcon tavern, 12141.

CHARD (Soms.). 24351 (24366).

CHARING DEANERY, Clergy. 57.

CHARLWOOD (Surrey). 3798.

CHESHIRE. Justices, 5701 [see changes]; friends, 13928.

CHESTER. 5701 [see changes], 23580, 23720, J. Barlow, *Seasonable discourse,* 1627-F. (1435).

CHICHESTER DIOCESE, Clergy. 13923.

CINQUE PORTS. 20791, 23287.

CORNWALL. Clergy, 11754 [11753 a ghost]; non-subscribing clergy, 14035 = 16449, 14036 = 16449a; rebels, *see Copye of a letter, 1549-L.*²

COVENTRY. Corporation, 4022, 5704, 11841, 13770, 15450, 17311; Drapers, 7185; Military garden, 4023; Thomas, prior of Charterhouse, 278.

CRANBROOK (Kent). 58, 59, 60; young men, R. Abbot, *Warning-peece,* 1639-F.

CRANHAM (Essex). 12876 [see changes].

CUCKFIELD. 24701.

DARTMOUTH. Adventurers for New England, 22788.

DEDHAM. ¶4962-L. (3406.a.12), 21191.

DENHAM (West Suff.). 20337.

DENNEY ABBEY. Unnamed nun, 3276.

DEPTFORD STRAND. Trinity House: 11221, 19090 = ¶19091, 19968 [see changes], 22784, 23265, 24574; *see also* KINGSTON-UPON-HULL.

DEVONSHIRE. Rebels, 7506; clergy, 11754 [11753 a ghost]; non-subscribing clergy, 14035 = 16449, 14036 = 16449a.

DIGBY (Lincs.). Conceivably intended in 11125.

DITCHEAT (Soms.). 358.

DOVER. Corporation, 20791.

DOVERCOURT (Essex). 7173.

DROWFEILD [*unidentified*]. *See* STANTON.

DUMBARTON PRESBYTERY. Clergy, 5753.

DUNDEE. Provost, 7351.

DURHAM. Prebends, 15538 and *1609*-L.

ECKINGTON (Derby). 14933.

EDGEFIELD (Norf.). 12527.

EDINBURGH. General, 12726, 21271, 23705;
Corporation and civic, 88, 138, 3923, 5927
(5909), 6032, 6217, 10670, 13173, 13258,
13945, 14995, 17700, 18360, 18572, 20696,
23262, 25860, 26106.
Kirk, 4358, 21271; clergy, 25737; dispersed
brethren, 15075; householders, 11183.
University, 138, 575; schoolmasters, 25737.
Surgeons, 16870.

ELY DIOCESE. Clergy, 277.

EPPING. 7423.

EPWORTH. R. Bernard, *Large catechisme*,
1602-C.[19]

ESSEX. Military, 25025; friends in, 23316.

ETON COLLEGE. 11054.

EXETER DIOCESE. 12690 (12636); clergy, 7152,
12645; people, 12648b.

EXETER. 12710; Corporation, 13989, 24887–
24889 inclusive; dean and chapter, 24885;
trained bands, 5667; adventurers for New
England, 22788.

FAVERSHAM. Corporation, 10639 and *1596*-F.,
19683 only, 19878, J. Phillips, *Christians
A.B.C.*, *1629*-HD.

GAINSBOROUGH. R. Bernard, *Large catechisme*,
1602-C.[19]

GLAMORGANSHIRE. Gentry, 1095 (1077).

GLASGOW. University, 575; 'indwellers',
3449.

GLOUCESTER DIOCESE. Clergy, 13756, 13759.

GLOUCESTER. Corporation, 21653; Chapter,
21653; Cathedral clergy, 13756; St. Bartholomew's hospital, 12171.

GOTHAM. Corporation, 23795 [facetious].

GR[ANTHAM]. Unnamed vicar, 13270.

GUERNSEY. 3767.

H. (Herts.). T. W[ilcox], *Forme of preparation*-
HD.

HAMPSHIRE. Housewives, 23703; gentlemen
with Romish hearts, 6091.

HANWELL (Oxfs.). Justices, 12827 (12816).

HARWICH. Corporation, 7173

HAWARDEN. 23720.

HAYES (Mdsx.). 20830.

HEMPSTEAD. H. Greenwood, *Joyfull tractate*,
1616-L. (12328) [? 12327 impf.].

HENHAM (Essex). 19601.

HEREFORD. 6333; cathedral, 24046.

HERTFORDSHIRE. Brethren in, 12804.

HILGAY (Norf.). 11085.

HOLLINGBOURNE. Neighbours, 3463 only.

HOME COUNTIES. Tavern frequenters, 23764.

HUNTINGDON. Corporation, 1661.

IPSWICH. Corporation, 25044 (25031 and
1623-F.); School, 25944.

ISIS. *See* THAMES.

JERSEY. 3767.

KENDAL 'Barony'. Gentry, R. Brathwait,
Querela clientis-HN.

KENDAL. Corporation, 24475.

KENT. Justices and gentry, 58; trained bands,
5667; friends, 3753, 23316.
East Kent: Militia chiefs, 21175; friends,
24966.

KILRENNY (Fife). 17816.

KING'S LYNN. Corporation, 11492, 11816,
21123, T. Purchas, *Communicants duty*, *1639*-
PN.[2]

KINGSTON-ON-THAMES. 24501; children, R.
Byfield, *Candle lighted*, *1627*-BO.

KINGSTON-UPON-HULL. Trinity House, 11221.

LANCASHIRE. Friends and kin, 14299; countrymen, 25394; papists, 12870.

LEICESTER. Corporation, 19788.

LEICESTERSHIRE. Banished preacher, prose
15069.

LEIGHS (Essex). 23584, 23585.

LEITH. 15436.

LEWES. 11367, 25304.

LINCOLN DIOCESE. Clergy, 13267.

LINCOLNSHIRE. Gentlemen, 1412, 26103;
friends, 6033.

LONDON DIOCESE. Clergy, 3282; clergy and
wardens, Abbot directive, [*1610?*]-HN. and
L.[5]; [Protestant] faithful, 1289.

LONDON. *Organized as* (1) General and
civic; (2) City companies; (3) Merchant

LONDON—*cont.*

companies; (4) Ecclesiastical; (5) Inns of Court; and (6) Miscellaneous. *See also* BERMONDSEY, SOUTHWARK, WESTMINSTER.

1. *General and civic*

London: 4684, 4853, 4971 [4970 impf.], 7537, 10688, 11935 [plague-afflicted], 14968, 15439, 19884 as Troynovant, 21091, 23705.

Inhabitants [*see also under* CITY *and* MERCHANT COMPANIES]: 13587; young men, 14676.

Gentlewomen: 21409; dames, 19551; matrons, *Letter sent by maydens, 1567-*L.²; maids, 21413; unnamed widow, 23916.

Friends: 56, 14068, 14328, 23316, T. Wilcox, *Christian exposition, 1587-*F. (25620), 25624, J. SEDGWICK, *Eye of faith, 1640-*PN.²

City reader: 18698; all who love London, 3536.

Mayor and Corporation. Chronologically. See also mayors by name:
1520: 5017.
1567: 23321 and later 16° eds. [no ded. in 23320 (3 16° copies seen)].
1570-9: 6092, 10673, 12097, 20117, 20850, J. Danyel trans., *Jehovah-*L.²
1580-9: 6736, 7577, 10607, 10845, 15595, 20852 revised 20854, 25341.
1590-9: 5840, 13465, 15250, 16767 [16766 a ghost], ¶17648 [see changes], 18131, 19799, 21296, 23327 and later 8° eds. [see changes], 23341 [later modified], 23363, T. Nelson, *Blessed state, 1591-*F.
1600-9: 6070, 11936, 12863, 14303, 14362, 14671, 14690, 16676, 18417, 23864, 23929, 24637 including 24639.
1610-19: 5105, 5693, 11829, 13159, 15517, 17700, 18522, 21015, 25163, ¶25699, 25740 [25739 a ghost], 26024.
1620-9: 3219 = 16749, 3837, 4324, 5708, 6017, 14669, 15325, 16750 but related book-BO.⁴ dates *1636*, 17744 [see changes], 17886, 18321, 20766, 22150, 23074, H. Goodcole, *Prodigals teares, 1620-*O. [cf. 18488], H. Robrough, *Balme from Gilead, 1626-*F.
1630-40: 11346, 11347, 13069, 13467, 14489, 14722 by bookseller, 17649 by editor, 19598, 19600, 22531, 22532 [diff. work from 22531], 22533, 23505 by printer, 23509.

2. *City companies*

City companies: 10929; see 26018.

Citizens: 12307, 17938, 21805, 22615; gentlewomen citizens, 12097.

Masters of apprentices: 3219 = 16749.

Apprentices: 3219 = 16749, 13321, 18327, 19057 [cf. 19081], 22974.

Apothecaries: ¶1592 by editor, ¶11751, 14702, ¶14704.

Barber Surgeons: 1359, 1360 only, 3279 by editor, 5326, 5447 [see changes], 6062, 7511, 10658 by printer, 11529 (24723) [young men], 13215, 15192, 16870, 18204 by editor, 18510, *1634-*L.¹⁷ of 20784 [see changes], 20816, ¶24367, 25962 modified 25963; surgeons, 24577.

Blacksmiths: 13566.

Bowyers: 17333, 21512.

Butchers: 23765 (23725).

Carpenters: 1068, 1337, 18075.

Clothworkers: 14321, 19875.

Cordwainers: 6556 [earlier lost], 23816 (23725).

Distillers: 16777.

Drapers: 5850 [see changes], 5867-F. [there are 2 eds.], ¶11346, 18280, 25643; W. Freake, *Priviledges of upright-*F.

Fishmongers: 5699, 18266, 23765 (23725); presentation 22792.

Fletchers: 17333, 21512.

Goldsmiths: 4698, 12201, 17649 [see changes], 18263, 23055.

Grocers: 5710, 10802, 18321; see 16767 [16766 a ghost].

Haberdashers: 7109, 7146, 11653 (11652) by editor, 13515, ¶19303, 24142 by editor, 24143, Pin-makers' broadside, *1619-*HN.

Innholders: 20766.

Ironmongers: ¶4102, 18278.

Leathersellers: 5131, 21118, *1600-*BO. of 21288 [see changes].

Mercers: 1092, 11878, 12554, 12871 [F. has general tp. missing-L.], 18249, 22466; unnamed mercer [? W. Pratt], 21429.

Merchant Taylors: 1505, 3491 by editor [see changes], 5304, 11476 rewritten 11478, 18263, 23326 through 23329 and 16° *1575-*HN. [see changes].

Saddlers: 23816 (23725).

Salters: 25183 [*1625-*Y. has no ded.]; see *Library, 1937-8*, p. 51.

Shoemakers: See CORDWAINERS.

LONDON—*cont.*

Skinners: One issue-F. of 4531, 5699, 23284.

Stationers: 12167, 17669, 19489, 22563, 23345; do dedication to 23550; printers, 1058, 2771, 20963; *see also* BIBLIOGRAPHICA.

Surgeons: See BARBER SURGEONS.

Vintners: 18901, 20766.

Watermen: ¶23779 (23725), 23816 (23725).

3. *Merchant companies*

See also BRITISH COLONIES *below, and* ENGLAND (*Official agencies*)

Merchant community: 6437, 16784, 20296.

Africa (Guinea and Binny): 14623.

Barbary: 25639.

East India: 150, 861, 1504, 4661, 5534, 5707 [see changes], 6188, 7448, 16825, 17224, 18351, 18417, 19088 = ¶1616-HD. of 19093, 19091, 22061, 25663 by editor, 25952, T. Cooper, *Mysterie of affections*-F.; sea surgeons, 25962.

Eastland: 17224.

Guinea and Binny: see AFRICA.

Levant (Turkey): 17224, 24137.

Merchant Adventurers: 1210 and 1562-L.[38] revised 1210a [Flanders specified], 2769, 3882, 16687, 16688, 17224, 19547, 19548, 23620.
  Specific communities: Antwerp, 18535; Delft, 13262, 25843; Emden, 18535; Hamburgh, 16684, 25846; Middelburg, 11134.

Merchants Adventurers for the discovery . . .: see MUSCOVY.

Muscovy (Russia): 5798 [see changes], 11255, 17224, 19566, 20820.

Somers Islands (Bermuda): 12391, 23272.

Trade upon the coasts of America: ★¶17224.

Turkey: see LEVANT.

Virginia: 1042, 3767, 5727, 7051 (7057, 7042-F., 7041), 12391 by bookseller, 14378, 17362, 22938, 23350, 25104, C. B[rooke], *Poem on the massacre, 1622*-GILCREASE; *also see* SOMERS ISLANDS.
  Adventurers: 12204, 12785, 22788, presentation 22792, 22793, 23594.

4. *Ecclesiastical*
General, Parishes, Other communities

London clergy: 23074, 25971 [with teachers], H. Burton, *Conflicts of conscience, 1628*-L.

Faithful (Puritans): 13752, 15059, 15073; Bible-readers, 5842; saints-to-be, 6175; donors to Wolverhampton preaching, 15354; societies of citizens [? parishes], 25386.

All Hallows, Bread Street: 21683, 23275 and *1608*-PN.[2]

Blackfriars: See ST. ANNE.

Christ Church: 20334, J. Trendle, *Arke, 1608*-PN.[2]

St. Andrew Hubbard: 10, 20678 (20668) by editor.

St. Andrew Undershaft: 17610.

St. Anne, Blackfriars: 7537, 12116, 12117 (supposedly *1639 Works* but no complete copy found), 12119 (12109), 12122 rewritten 12123 (12109 and *1639*-N.), 12125, 21221 by editor.

St. Antholin: 12203.

St. Benet, Paul's Wharf: 104.

St. Bride: 14514 [earlier lost].

St. Christopher, Royal Exchange: 3419.

St. Clement Danes: 22658 (22718).

St. Giles, Cripplegate: 128 = ¶107.

St. Gregory: 120.

St. Katherine Coleman: 26037.

St. Katherine Cree: 6599 [earlier lost], 6601.

St. Katherine, Tower Hill: 21014.

St. Lawrence Jewry: T. Sanderson, *Briefe summe, 1640*-U. [earlier lost].

St. Leonard, Eastcheap: H. Robrough, *Balme from Gilead, 1626*-F.

St. Margaret, Fish street: 1477, 21194, 21201-HN. (21202).

St. Martin-in-the-Fields: 13472, 22182.

St. Mary Abchurch: 21201-HN.

St. Mary Aldermanbury: 23307 (23313), 23823 by editor, 23850, T. Downing, *Catechisers encouragement, 1623*-U.

St. Mary, Whitechapel: 6021 [see changes].

St. Matthew, Friday street: 4143.

St. Mildred, Bread street: 22151.

St. Nicholas Acon: 14720.

St. Nicholas, Cole Abbey: 5133, 5134.

St. Paul's Cathedral: Dean and chapter, 106 (115).

St. Sepulchre: 25386, H. P[eters], *Milk for babes, 1630*-HD.

LONDON—*cont.*

St. Stephen, Coleman street: 12031.

St. Swithin: 5676.

Whitechapel: See ST. MARY.

Dutch Church: 6582, 17864 by author, 21471, 24761, Dutch Church *Theses*-L.[13]; Minsheu List; Dutch community, 15260.

French Church: 6582, 6775, 15449 [? earlier lost] (15550), 19783, 21139 and *1627*-C.[5]; Minsheu List.

Francis Johnson's Separatists: 19608.

5. Inns of Court

Inns of Court and Chancery: 4861, 15388, 17801 and *1582*-C.[2]

Inns of Court: 775, 1955, 5883, 6204, 10824, 11111, 11410, 12367, 13539, ¶14751, 15466, 16653, 16903, 16907 and later Catholic eds., 17824, 18338 (18337), 20464, 20561, 22459, 25341 and 25335, unidentified epistle by W. Broughton bound in 5301-0.

Inns of Chancery: 15017 (14886).

Serjeants at law: 5369.

Lawyers: 1955, 5369, 7435, 11343, 13778, 18660, ¶21872 and *1616* often with 21870; patrons of law and equity, 4861.

Students of common law: 1848, 7388 by editor, 9278, 9587 only, 14901 by editor, 17518, 18394, 20040, B. C., *Buccina, 1599*-HN.

Gray's Inn: 1663, 4094, 6024, 10799, 11163, 11343, 12665 (12635), 18319, 19622 [see changes], 22508; Prince of Purpoole in *1618*, Minsheu List.

The Temples jointly: 5784 (5786), 6014, 6204, 6204a.

Inner Temple: 1663, 5527, 10824, 13964, 17640, 25764.

Middle Temple: 6050, 7388, 10978 revised 10980, 20040, 23364, 25764.

Lincoln's Inn: 1848, 6205, 7039 (7057, 7042-F., 7041), 11670, 20464, 20934 and 20933.

Strand Inn: Undated-HN. of 23879.

6. Miscellaneous

Actors: 13309; Queen's Men, 6507.

Artillery Garden or Company: 127 (104), 162, 1506, 6313, 11828, 12111 (12116), 13913, 14127, 15364, 19803, 22152, 23504 by editor, 26064; surviving founders, 5668; *see also* TRAINED BANDS.

Belgian merchants: 20912; *see also* DUTCH CHURCH.

Belsavage Inn: 6225.

Charterhouse: 4126.

Christ's Hospital: 421 for *1618*-L.[2], 7164, 17649 [see changes], 24698, G. Browne, *Introduction to pietie, 1613*-C.; the children, 5208, 21521.

College of Physicians: ¶1592 by editor, 6786, 7498, 14790, 16650, 20385, 21455, P. Bowne, *Pseudo-medicorum anatomia, 1624*-L.; physicians of London, 23074.

Counters: 10781 [especially Wood Street]; *also see* MARSHALSEA.

Finsbury Archers: See under SOCIETY.

Gaming houses, as Bedlam, Moorfields, etc.: 17916.

Gresham College: 20756.

Key in Thames Street: 22611 (22608).

Marshalsea: Friends visiting him there, 25920 (25890, 25911).

Mathematical Lecture (City-sponsored): 13070, 13697, 13698, 15250.

Mermaid Tavern: Literary society, *see* 5811.

Milford Lane: 20171.

Military Yard or Garden: 10598, 14127; surviving founders, 5668; *see also* TRAINED BANDS.

Museum Minervae: 15099 = 16780.

Physicians: See under COLLEGE OF PHYSICIANS.

Pin-sellers: Pin-makers' broadside, *1619*-HN.

Queen's Men: 6507; *cf*. Actors.

Ram Alley: 20171.

Royal Exchange: 19489.

St. Bartholomew's Hospital: *1636*-C.[2] of 14538 [see changes], 24713 thence 24706, W. Freake, *Ezras pulpit, 1639*-F.

St. Paul's School: 23897.

Ship in the Old Bayly: 3585.

Society of Archers: 800, 15441; Finsbury archers, 19419 and *1601*-C.[6] [earlier lost].

Taverns: See BELSAVAGE, KEY, MERMAID, SHIP.

Trained Bands or City Companies [*see also* ARTILLERY, MILITARY, *and* SOCIETY OF ARCHERS]:
City captains, 1505, 1507, 4933, 21095, 22152.

OXFORDSHIRE. Justices, 14459.

PERTH. Corporation, 135.

PLYMOUTH. 23543; Corporation, 1434 (1435), 10937, 12393, 14926; auditors at, 1789; adventurers for New England, 22788.

PLYMPTON ST. MARY. 12395.

PRESTON. Corporation, I. Ambrose, *Prima & ultima*, 1640-F.

PRESTONPANS. J. Davidson, *Some helpes, 1602*-G. as Salt Preston.

PRITTLEWELL. 22850.

READING. Corporation, 23840; auditors, 23828.

REDBURN (Herts.). 11692 [earlier lost].

ROCHESTER. 6610.

RODBOROUGH. R. Webb, *Key of knowledge, 1622*-PN.²

ROMSEY ABBEY. Abbess, 1859.

RYE. Broadside welcome to Elizabeth-HD.

ST. ANDREWS DIOCESE. Clergy, 12731 = 22056.

ST. ANDREWS. University, 575, 18434 = ¶7298; Castle congregation, 1340.

ST. DAVIDS DIOCESE. 2960.

SALISBURY DIOCESE. *See* 643 *and* 642 (641).

SALISBURY. 23778 (23725); Corporation, 19169; Dean and chapter, 1425.

SALT PRESTON. *See* PRESTONPANS.

SANDWICH. Corporation, 1718 (1710), 23317, 25844.

SEMINGTON (Wilts.). 25158.

SHAFTESBURY. Corporation, 17755.

SHREWSBURY. Corporation, 20328; parents, 24109; friends, 11571 *and 1599*-HN.

SOMERSET. Justices, etc., 1947.

SOUTHAMPTON. Corporation, 24348.

SOUTHWARK. St. Olave, 1338; St. Saviour, 20746 [? earlier lost]; Martial garden, 14922.

STAFFORDSHIRE. Countrymen, 5127.

STAMFORD. 11125.

STANDISH (Lancs.). 15424.

STANTON (Gloucs., near Stanway). 1363 with unidentified 'Drowfeild' [? Dronfield, Derby].

STEEPLE ASHTON (Wilts.). 25158.

SUFFOLK. Justices, 5698; clergy, ¶1710; gentry, 15038, 15041; friends, 3753, 23316.

SUSSEX. Papist gentry, 6091; liberal housekeepers, 24125. East Sussex: Clergy and laity, 11380.

SYON Monastery. Nuns, 4815, probably 21473 [the earlier ed.]; confessor, 17542; abbess, *see* Agnes Jordan; unnamed brother, *Pomander of prayer, 1530*-F. and *1528*-Private library.

TALLOW (Waterford). Corporation, 14509, 14511 as Tallaugh.

TEY, MUCH (Essex). 21242 and *1627*-PN.²

THAMES, RIVER. 4015 = 19308; Isis, 15444.

TOTHAM, MUCH (Essex). 23315.

TOTNES. Adventurers for New England, 22788.

TOTTENHAM. 19925.

TROYNOVANT. *See* LONDON.

WADDESDON. 25644 [earlier lost].

WALES. *See also* COUNCIL FOR WALES *in* political section.
Wales, Welsh, Welsh reader, 2960, 6639, 7226, 19605, 20966, 21616, 24599, 24600.
Gentry, 19775; clergy, 19775; churchmen, 24007a.
Poets, 17914, 19775, 20966; preservers of Welsh language, 2743; promoters of *1630* Welsh Bible, 24007a.

WALSINGHAM. 21518.

WALTHAM, MUCH (Essex). 1476.

WAPPING. New chapel, R. Sedgwick, *Short summe, 1624*-F.

WARWICK. Two unnamed women, 18553.

WELLS DIOCESE. *See* BATH AND WELLS.

WELLS. Neighbours, 14725, 24351 (24366).

WESTMINSTER. Trained bands, 4933; gaming houses, 17916.

WEYMOUTH *and* MELCOMBE REGIS. Corporation, 17180, 18822 and later editions of this undifferentiated long version [? earlier lost].

WHERWELL ABBEY (Hants). 1859 spelt Wharwel.

WIGHT. Baronets, knights, captains, 14741.

WILTSHIRE. Nobility, etc., 23778 (23725), 25165.

WINCHESTER DIOCESE. Benedictine nuns, 1859.

WINCHESTER. College, 25671, Minsheu List; unnamed abbess of St. Mary, 1859; Ch[apter] Library, Minsheu List.

WINDSOR. College and chapel, Minsheu List.

WINSHAM (Soms.). 24351 (24366) as Wynsam.

WINTNEY PRIORY (Hants). Prioress, 1859.

WISBECH. Seminary priests in Castle, 1829.

WOLVERHAMPTON. Benefactors of preaching at, 15354.

WORCESTER DIOCESE. Clergy, 13759.

WORCESTER. 23271.

WORKSOP. R. Bernard, *Large catechisme,* 1602-C.[19]

WRINGTON (Soms.). 6066.

WYE (Kent). 4404.

YARMOUTH, GREAT. Corporation, 586, 20832a; Artillery company, 21093.

YORK. 23705; Corporation, 20493; physicians, 6441.

YORKSHIRE. Friends, 6033.

BRITISH COLONIES

See also LONDON (*Merchant companies*) *and* ENGLAND (*Council for New England*).

BERMUDA. *See* SOMERS ISLANDS.

CAPE BRETON. *See* NOVA SCOTIA.

GUIANA. Adventurers and well-willers, 12754; favourers of *1595* voyage, 14947.

NEW ENGLAND: *General, including Virginia.* Adventurers, 22788, presentation 22792.

NEW ENGLAND: *Proper.* Adventurers or well-willers, 6149, 18169, 25855; Non-conformists, N. E., *Information for ignorant,* 1640-U.

NOVA SCOTIA. Undertakers for New Scotland, particularly 'Cape Briton, now New Galloway', 12069.

SOMERS ISLANDS *or* BERMUDA. 13918, 23272.

VIRGINIA. *See* NEW ENGLAND.

III. ANONYMOUS AND BIBLIOGRAPHICAL

ANALYSIS

A. ANONYMOUS AND BIBLIOGRAPHICAL

1. ANONYMOUS COMMENDATORY VERSES

The purpose of this index is to indicate the unsigned verses of which authorship is known and to facilitate comparison of the others with manuscript or printed texts. Doubtful cases are included; some were probably written by the author, translator, or editor, others by contributors of adjacent signed verses.

Unsigned and pseudonymous verses (including lines on frontispieces) are indexed by first line, occasionally curtailed to save space. Spelling and punctuation are retained, but excess capitalization is ignored. Openings are alphabetized as though spelling were normal. At the right is given any actual signature, or, with bracket, identification from outside evidence. A queried identification is a conjecture from internal evidence.

11992 (11993) A Leuite in his iourney goes
[? author

22634 A stately nymph of Nereus traine,
[? author

18743 and *1609*-FLEMING. A sword against swearing God send vs, God send vs,

18022 Accipe, posteritas, Scotici miranda tribuni [? J. Narssius

Earlier-L.[2] of 16642 Achilles neuer durst at once [N. R.

1404 Admonuit si fortè tuum deponere plectrum

12142 Eneidos Bucolis que georgica metra perhennis Quidam philosophus

4897 Against good counsell who will shut his eare, [? Editor

14414 Agnosco hîc, cryptaee, tuae vestigia dextrae;

254 [253 impf.] Alanum breuis hora breui tumulo sepeliuit

5811 All our choise wits, all, see, thou hast engrost:

18911 All right, all wrong befalls me through a wife,

19598 All services that to the bakers trade [? author

22186 All sinne seemes sweete; all sacrilege is sinne, ? S. S.

6735 Although my floure be waxt a wethered weede: The Daysie

22790 Amongst so many that by learned skill, Ἀνώνυμος

18805 Amongst the mournfull multitude which stand [? author

6085 Anglia quid meres? quid solicitare beata [? J. Heron

1295 Angligenis mores qui sint, artesque, decorę Eruditus quidam

6738 Anglois, tu as esté separé du françoys Pax in bello

7203 Ankor tryumph, vpon whose blessed shore, Gorbo il fidele

25227 Arabia yeilds a phenix, and but one.

13309 Fallor? en haec solis non solùm grata theatris? Anonymus . . . .

Scotland, *Actis, 1540-E.* Fama secunda ferat, Iacobum ad sydera quintum

19048 Favete linguis, carmen affero novum.

18964 Fire, aire, earth, water, all the opposites [? Sandys

Rivius, *Discourse, 1578-F.* Fond fansies pend in rowling verse,

11223 Friuola quum multi deliramenta, meramq́;

20637 From death and darke obliuion (neere the same) [B. Jonson

19028 Gens patrem sequitur: pater hic Insignia nato [? W. Piers

21605 Go booke, and (like a marchant) new ariu'd, [? Harington

19781 Goe ventrous booke, thy selfe expose

17843 Gods ship, Gods church, with many a tempest tost, [? translator

5119 Good fate, faire Thespian deities, Vatum chorus

P. Anderson, *Grana, 1635-F.* Grammothetam duro cruciabit ventre saburra,

23762 (23725) Great mogul, landlord, and both Indies king, [? Taylor

Engr. port.-F. of IV Duke Norfolk Great statist, greatest peere, most high in bloud

12345-HD. Gregorius sanctus pulchri preceptor honesti

19619 Hactenus Hispanis, Hispanica lingua refulsit,

14269 Had I a veine for verse, then know, I would [? J. Foy

18911 Hadst thou like other sirs and knights of worth

24827 Haec est Vergilij quam cernis buccina, nuper

Gaultier, *Miles, 1630-L.* He doth run farre, that neuer turnes,

22553 Hee that in words explaines a frontispiece, [? Brathwait

14627 Hence Venus idle ympes, hence, hence in haste,

23132 Hir scepter sweet, hir sword was seldome sharp. [? G. W.

2123 (21494, etc.) Here is the spring where waters flowe, [? Gresshope

7045 Here lies Deane Donne; enough, those words alone [? R. B.

4497 Here read the dayes, when Britanne ground, [? Darcie

10758 Heere, th'Vniuerse in natures frame, [? author

20490 Here, undisguis'd, is seene in this true mirrour

24812 Here wounded by her owne hand Dido lyes. [? Stapylton

17574 and earlier-F. Hesperidum campi quicquid Romanaq́; tellus,

10461 Heus puer, ingenuis mentem virtutibus orna. [? foreign

12731 = 22056 Hic liber est sacer, diuini dogmata verbi

Engr. port., *1600-L.* Hic tuus ille comes generosa Essexia nostris

12776 His body's here by figure represented,

12964 Hoc te caballo, Tityre laurifer,

14973 How dares the author passe vnto the presse,

25226 How ioyfully the authors poem goes,

24436 and *1572-HN.* How light is chaffe of popish toyes, if thou . . . [? Foxe

23123 I doe not tremble, when I write

6023 I, liber, Europae per singula regna, per vrbes: [? G. F.

11596 I seeme like Cynthia while thou shines I sweare, Anonimos

11977 I will not praise this worke, 'twere labor lost, [MS. copyist

6385 I would commend your labours and I finde Akokakos

19149 If Chaucer nowe shoulde liue,

23058 If he that for his countrie doth expose Philomathes

18904 If I were to chuse a woman, [? author

23058 If little Dauid that for Israels sake, Philalethes

14422 If men may credit auncient writs,

5569 If the grand rabbies of our moderne times, T. Veridicus

15192 If they whiche haue illustrated,
[? T. Gale

15520 If thy good work work good upon this nation,

14269 If with distinctive eye . . .
[E. Rainbowe

13910 Jf ye lyst to lerne wyllyngly to dye
[? author

13624 Ille simul Musas, et Homerum scripserit ipsum,

1404 Illic imperium fore jactavere quirites,

25755 In Lauine land though Liuie bost,
V. Dormitanus

5080 In reading of the learn'd praise-worthie peine,

3202 In thee (Boetius) that rule appeares,

7046 In thy impression of Donnes poems rare,

13018 In tua diffundens epigramma epigrammata, guttam [? R. Zouch

686 Incipe, sis primus sophiae, qui mystica iura

11082 Ingeniose tuo ne libro supprime nomen;

13150 [earlier impf.] Inuidia mors tristi Gulielmum funere Wallam,

24001 Is arte obtaind by reasons rudiments.

14973 It is no tale, the hermite is beli'd,

11995 (11993) It was when industry did sleepe [? author

24667 Italiae, Heluetijs, Germanis, Galliae et Anglis

4414 Ie pensoy' que la mort auoit trop tost fermé [? foreign

13018 Iocos, delitias, sales, lepores,
[? J. Rogers

14783 Ionson, to tell the world what I to thee
[? T. R.

17201 Iust in the cloud doth louely Cupid stand, [? author

11099 Kinde friend, the strictnesse of these few-few lines ✲✲ [? J. Mab

25588 Kyng Edward the .iii. did Wicklife defend [? Crowley

14973 King neuer prou'd more King in any thing,

25223 Lanchashire gaue him breath,

14973 Lately the Muses from their forked hill Suis cuique mos

17824 Learning, the Atlas of the world . . .
[Quarles

23294 Legerat Aoniam nuper Wolseida Momus, [? Fitzgeffrey

23123 Lend me Elias chariot to inspire
[? author

14269 Let hoary Time's vast bowels . . .
[R. Crashaw

24368 Lyke as in tyme of Goddes reuengyng wrath: [? Grimald

736 Lilia miretur vulgus: tua Primula veris V. Φιλάρετος

20490 Loe, Death invested in a roabe of ermine, [? translator

3168 Lo here the braunches fresh and greene.
[? translator

6735 Loe here the path, that leades to vnderstand, The Daysie

23338 Londinum templis, & turre, & ponte superbum, [? Quoted

21524 London esteemed is for choise of ware,
[? author

3107 Londres peut bien à Rome en beaucoup ressembler,

Earlier-LINC. of ¶5937 Lord intimate thy loue into mine heart,

5808, 5810 Lordings, full well I hope you know Ἀποδημουντόφιλος

1572-F. of 770 Lordes and maisters, wise and honourable,

7222, 7190 Lux Hareshulla tibi Warwici villa, tenebris,

7376 Lysses y purpurea rosa.

74 Mans onely one, and chiefest one, thou art

15600 Many doe seeke, but few there be who finde, [? editor

3107 Martyrs de Iesus Christ, d'inuincible courage

3107 Massacrer ses subiets qui font profession

13553 Materiâ peccat, non peccat imago, figurâ,

18805 Me list not search the hidden mysterie
[? author

7232 Michaell which dost great Roberts fame compile, Mirocinius

5325 Princeps virorum Mercurialium

13964 Prometheus theft cloasd in Deucaleons babe   [? A. B.

4193 Quae natura apibus, quae membra, scientia, sensus   [? Wither

18357 (6267) Quae terrere solent ab amore matheseos, illa

18349 Quae tibi cunque sinus, tangentes atque secantes

 736 Qualia iam moriens modulatur carmina cygnus,   Il Candido

12142 Quam cinxere freta Gower tua carmina leta   Quidam philosophus

5021 = 19036 Quam stabilis quadrata, capaxq; rotunda corona est,

5613 Que vix antiqui potuerunt scribere libris

3108 Quelle Muse epandra mes vers

11205 Quem Charis asseruit sibi, quem sibi Musa, suumq;

1404 Quem Galli, Hispani, Germana ac Itala tellus

15134 Quem pietas, quem prisca fides, doctrinaq; fecit   [? editor

P. Anderson, *Grana, 1635*-F. Qui cupit haud durum, sed molle aut . . . Anonymus

12560 Qui cupit haeretici, nunc scire sophismata Frythi,

15608 Qui natos generant, laudandi quiq; parentes,   [? Rightwise

19292 Qui non defendit alio culpante, solutos   [? author

19783 Qui sumptum metuis librorum, nec satis amplum

24368 Qui uoudra bien du tressainct lauement   [? T. Norton

11688 Quicquid sub Arcto, quicquid in gremio latet   [? H. Noel

 135 Quid fles? Quid tristi rumpis praecordia luctu?

5582 Quid quaerit titulos, quid . . .   [Indexed to S. D.

11082 Quid tuas retegis nimis tegendo

24820 Quis non Virgilij ingenium admiratur acutum?   [? translator

16248 Quis satis enumeret q̃ptam pressoria nobis

1378 Quis varios casus, quis dura pericula Brussi,

16642 Quo tibi iam de te parias certamine palmam,

4108 Quod vetus est, juvenes, in relligione sequamur:

15676 Reade and regarde, then gratifull gaine   [? printer

22634 Reader, abide, marke, buy: diuisa Britannia mundo

15600 Reader, this booke was pen'd with single heart,   [? editor

15520 Reader, what here thou'lt finde is so good sense,

18525 Receiue my show'r of teares into thy flood,   [T. W.

7570 Rex longum latéque potens, quem occasus & ortus   Anonymus

19775 Rhetoricen Perraee tuam doctissime versans,   [? H. Salisbury

4200 'Ρητορικὴ τεχνῶν φύτο . . .   [R. C.

12299 Ride Epicure deum, gere nescia pectori fati,

16694 Saepius externis pugnans Logiaeus in oris   [? Cargill

11323 Sales an Sal-es Francisce vocandus? Vtrumque,

22608 Salue plus decies *quam* sunt momenta dierum,   [? editor

1497 Sancta salutiferi lector si dogmata *quaeris*   [? author

 74 Sanior I sanè, vt non pecces, sed benè viuas,   [? Dantiscanus

 74 Sanior, vt mens sit, sanè mysteria pandis: [? Dantiscanus

3194 Scripsimus indocti, doctiq;, vt . . .   [adapted fr. Horace

6994 Scriptura, patres, concilia nolunt tegi.

 91 See for the sceane a troubled sea, whereon   [? Hodges

609 etc. See heer a shadow from that setting sunne,   [R. Crashaw

11057 Se here that stately Muse, that erst could raise,   [? Walkley

15601 Selecti Lilij duo lilia legimus: horto   [? I. H.

15658 Sen that it is maist worthie for to be
[? Charteris

13624 Seuen kingdoms stroue, which theyrs, should Homer call,
Scotiae nobilis

4647 Shew me that man who can, one amongst ten, Gilpin kinsman

25317 Siccine disposuit fatum, sic fecit vt huius [? editor

Engr. of C. Howard, *1596*-L. Si domitos bello Hispanos, Gadiumq; ruinam,

4505 (4509) Si iactare licet magnorum munera diuûm,

14901 Si tibi cura magis multum, quam multa legendi; [? J. Croke

555 Sic fuit (ah, fuit!) Amesius. Quid funere tanto [? S. O.

3988 Σίγησον Ὀρφεῦ, ῥίψον ἑρμῆ τὴν λύραν.
Incerti auctoris [foreign

24193 Siluer & golde, & al metalles eke:
'Printer'

18042 Since honor from the honorer proceeds.

21482 Sleepe not, passe on, ring in the eares of all,

19048 Solvere iusta tibi cupimus, Bodleie: sed ista,

12964 Some clothe fair tales in sluttish eloquence:

3683 Some scoffe at all that write, write not at all,

961 Sparserat audaces, diviso idiomate, gentes Anonymus

22274 Spectator, this lifes shaddow is; to see

24523 Springs nigh their source into a brook extended Sub. foed. sp.

12964 Suauia nonnulli lutulento carmine narrant:

11205 Sum cinis, hic qua sum; sed & hic cinis emptio Christi est.

1001 Susanna was of all thy poems best
[? R. C.

11691 Suspiciens solis radios aquila, aspicit escam: [? author

7253 Swanne which so sweetly sings,
Clorus

11097 Sweete friend whose name agrees with thy increase, Phaëton

15520 Take so much rubarb, learned Galen sayes;

23132 Talis erat vultu, sed lingua, mente, manuq; [? author

Ellesmere print-L. (rarely 22213-HN.) Talis is est pictum quem cernis corpore . . .

4161 Ten distinct squares heere seene apart,
[? author

12496 Tergeminam merito laudem sibi ven-dicet author

4044 Terrifico nuper crepitantem fulmine bullam

14973 That I haue lou'd, and most respected thee,

22435 That this play's old, 'tis true; but now if any [? J. Kirke

Elizabeth print-L. Th'admired empresse through the worlde applauded,

16636 The British soyle, with all therin that lies,

12123 (12109) The constant compleat souldier doth oppose [? author

6542 The Aegyptian sages, who were wont to sing

23950 The farthest scope of heauen and earth also, [? Hacket

1557 The goddesse (like her selfe so plac't on high, [? Basset

21605 The gods vpon a time in counsel sitting,

74 The honey sweet from grace vnto thee came:

15600 The lilies pure, delight in waters pure,
[? editor

T. Riley, *Triall*, *1639*-F. The night once come, which lampe implyes, [? author

12500 The noble Pindare doth compare somewhere,

4497 The pillers deckt with arms, palms, laurell bows, [? Darcie

13964 The prouydence eterne that all doth guyde, [? V. P.

11691 The sacrificed lambe of old,
[? author

18855 The sway, by sea & land, great Iames doth beare,

21130 The witnesse of the eye doth farre excell,

23273 This ample coate speaks auntient vertues praise,   [? author

18945 This author needs not owe any friend

23123 This blessed Virgin had the grace
deuine,   [? author

12184 This book's a garden where doth grow
a tree,   [? I. I.

16887 This dying figure that rare Lucan
showes,   [? May

13223 This Heav'n-aspiring tree's th'imperiall
state,

12964 This horse doth here afresh that fountain move,   Tityrus

21094 This is th'effigies, yet his real worth

18909 and *1614*-C.² This perfect creature, to
the easterne vse

22344 This shadowe is renowned Shake-
spear's? Soule of th'age
    [botched fr. Jonson

25870 = 13189 This spreading vine, like
these choyce leaves invites

24593 Thou that beleeu'st no female virtue,
thou   Incognito

19781 Though in the former leaves you may
descry

14008 Though loue & worth before me
brightly shines,   Philomus:

1506 Though this effigies here does represent

6543 Thrise noble Nepier by his learned
straine,

7226 Through a triumphant arch, see
Albion plas't,   [? Selden

7205 Thy learned poeme (friend) I will not
prayse,   Anonimos

5810 Thy mother towne that bred thee in
her wombe,   [? editor

24624 Thy pleasant notes with sweet concents
ygilt,   Calophysus

14782 Thy poeme (pardon me) is meere
deceat.   Φιλοε [*sic*]

17922 Time censures all things, darknes
envies time;   [? author

11163 Tis not the language, nor the fore-
plac't rimes   'Ο Φιλος

22614 To all tapsters and tiplers,   [editor

7238 To find Nicetas vertues in his name,
    [? translator

14973 To grace the man whom all the graces
fauour,   Vincor, non vinco

7031 To haue liu'd eminent in a degree
    [H. King

23080 To looke vpon a worke of rare deuise
    Ignoto

19904 (19908) To read strange newes, desires
manye,   [? editor

12205 To see the glorious Edgar on the
mayne,   [? author

12731 = 22056 Totius legis (fateor) volumen,

148 Tristia sic vates cecinit sua tempora,
nostri

1404 Tunè sacros audes infensâ voce poëtas

23918 Tu n'es pas seulement des François
louange

18006 Tu solus sacras extollis Apollinis artes
    [? foreign

7023 (7045) Two soules moue here, and mine
(a third) must moue   [? J. Hall

18911 Vpon a marble fram'd by th'cunning'st hand,

22580 Vt reliquos flores placido rosa vincit
odore

1404 Vt sublime volans tenuem secat aëra
falco;

12417 Vtilis est ignis nebulas, & frigora
pellens,   Anonymus

24884 Vade liber manibus passim volvende
bonorum,   Philalethes

21270 Vendibili (vetus est verbum) suspen-
dere vino,   [? J. Ray

21657 Vera docent versus, ne palpum obtru-
dere dicas.

Engr. Essex port.-L. Vertues honor, wis-
domes valure, graces . . .

18478 (18773) Virbium ne putabis abs auara

23273 Virtutem antiquam haec spirant insignia multam: [? author

3282 Viue, uale, & si quid nouisti rectius
istis.

4761 Viuere cui vires & robora sana dedisti
    [? author

23544 Vouchsafe to reade, I dare presume to
say,

P. Anderson, *Grana, 1635*-F. Vulgata & vetus
est multis contentio . . . Anonymus

11688 Vultu, canitie, senio venerandus, &
       annis,   [? author

  151 Waert dat sot sweghe / men souw him
       wijs achten   [? editor

21510 Wee thought the Tuscans are more
       strange then true,   [? translator

18909 Weep on kinde soule; and though thou
       commest in view,

25227 Welby, hadst thou, like others, given
       the reines

 7022 (7045) Wel dy'de the world, that we
       might liue to see   [? J. Hall

12796 Well hath thy labors thriu'd since first
       I saw   [? I. C.

11468 What means this mourning on mount
       Libanon?

22274 What neede my Shakespeare for his . . .
                                 [J. Milton

 3706 What thing is Will . . .   [C. A.

18043 When first this portlike frontispeece
       was wrought,

13190 When first thou traueldst I disswaded,
       then   [? C. H.

24096 When I by chance do reade thy dulcet
       verse,   Ignoto

14782 When I respect thy argument, I see
                             Cygnus [q.v.]

11323 Whence this burning globe, lou's
       simbole? Loue . . .

 4525 Whilst this ile of Great Brittaine,
       keepes ye name,

 1378 Who can the hazards hard, the chances
       strange

18244 Who hath not of sowrenes felte the
       bitter tast,   [? Eden

19501 Who is it (under thirty) that beleeves
                                Anonymos

 4061 Who list to moue his lippes,
                              [? translator

14627 Who so in quiet calme of conscience
       cleare,   [? translator

 3202 Who tasts those ioyes which fading
       pleasure yeelds,

12001 Wilt ghy doorsien / seer Godvruch-
       tighe Christen /   De Drucker

25382 Wisdome and grace, see, in that
       modest looke

21605 Wit, learning, order, elegance of
       phrase,   Anonimus

13480 With passing paines & labor great, the
       ants . . .

 6543 Within a little circle, or a round

 6479 You batchelers that with vs meane to
       feast,

 3217 You friendly readers heare,
                              [? translator

12890 You may be incouraged by mee,
                               Compositor

18498 You shew what fathers ought and how,
                        Momus [? author

2. UNSIGNED PROSE AND BIBLIOGRAPHICA

*The unsigned epistles reviewed below were written with-
out thought of the problem of indexing. Since the term
Printer was used with masterly imprecision, an unsigned
epistle of 'The Printer to the Reader' is about as valuable
and negotiable as an unsigned cheque. At the outset the
editor attempted assignments from internal evidence, and
transferred various items to the main index; as the project
advanced, he became increasingly cautious, but did not
reverse his previous decisions. At least five senses can
be distinguished for* Printer:

(1) *The actual printer, as proved by many signed
     epistles and by some unsigned ones* (24756).
(2) *Very often the bookseller, as proved by signed
     epistles* (288, 16874, 17401, 18073, 18868,
     21416, 25626, *etc.*) *and some unsigned ones*
     (17050, 23078).
(3) *The editor, as is sometimes clear* (13183, 18076,
     20616) *and more often may be suspected.*
(4) *The provider of the manuscript.*
(5) *The author, sometimes innocently* (22575 [965 *is
     a false case*]), *but more often in mystifications*
     (5898, 7026) *or as a voluntary ghost-writer*
     (3114, 6787).

The term Publisher *is almost as vague, but most often
means* Editor, *as can be seen in signed examples* (4023,
7527, 14335, 23580, 25663).
   *The opening series, however, treats a 'printer' problem
of an entirely different nature. The section concludes
with miscellaneous material of bibliographical interest.*

PRINTER TO READER, in books without, or
with false, imprint. *This material is not cross-
indexed.*

Recusant books (following Allison & Rogers):
English secret presses: 4573 [the earlier ed.],
21022, V. Bruno, *Meditations*-F.

St. Omers College press: 1650, 11021,
11022, 15519-ST. *Also see* JOHN WILSON *in
main file.*

Douay, Pierre Auroi: 14910.

PRINTER TO READER—Recusant—*cont.*

Antwerp, J. Trognesius: 6989 = 9492 [ineligible for *STC*].

Rome, V. Accolti: 19767 [ineligible for *STC*].

Calvinist or Puritan:

Probably Wandsworth, J. Stroud: 4711.

Perhaps Geneva [false Edinburgh imprints]: 1463 = 10577, 1464.

Unstudied: Second issue of 7540-HD., 21139.

For further mystifications *see* JOHN WOLFE.

PRINTER TO READER, Authorship dubious: 711 [secret press], 1469-L., 1700, 1707, 2130, 3530, 4270, 5117, 6981, 7026 and 7027 [? author], 7137, 8448, 13020, 14084, 15612, 15627, 20616 [editor], 20827, 21094, 21116 [editors], 22575 [? author], 23591 [on choice of title], 24062 [also verse], verse in 24193, 24627 and earlier-E.³, 24930, 25332, J. Floyd, *God and the king, 1620*-F., W. Thomas, *Apparaile of women, 1551*-HD.

Typographus: 1167, 5898 [mystification], 24884.

'De Drucker': Verse in 12001.

Bibliop[ola]: Verse in 1547.

PUBLISHER TO READER, Mostly editors: 1705 [? translator], 6164, 15113, 15135, 15332, 16450, more in 16451, 20468 [? author], 20652, 21718.

Setter-forth: 4572 [abridged from 'Printer' in earlier 4573].

ANONYMOUS EDITOR. *Of these epistles, some may be by printer, bookseller, or even author. Rare instances solved in variants or other editions are here ignored (like 6125 and 6789). Little effort has been made to identify editors from external evidence; a few examples appear in the main file.* 135, 151, 159 (15705), 226, 256, 555 [? S. O.], 629, 679, 806, 863 [? Parker], 943, 1344, 1408 [? J. Barclay], 1448, 1455, 1462, 1519, later-BO. of 1524, 1537, 1647, 1983, 2055 [? foreign], 2741, 2754, 2775, 2877, 2992, 3068, 3092, 3276, 3309 [? Worde], 3480 [? T. E.], 3484, etc., 3533, 3867, 4009 (22251 and 1570-C.⁷; *see* T. H.), 4063, 4080, 4407, 4537, 4876, 5112 [? Holland], 5217 [? Ro. Lo.], 5413, 5540, 5691 [MS. procurer], 5810, 5893 = 4073, 5945 (5909), 5992, 5999, 6155, 6282, 6315, 6475, 6619, 6790, pirated *1634*-F. of 6939, 6967 [unauthorized reporter], 7526, 7689, French version-HN. of 9183 = 5041, 10431 = 18330, 10454, 10545, 10715, 10768 (10769), 10774,

11183, 11228, 11267 [? foreign], 11289, 11395, 11425, 11618, 11792 (3758), 11968 [11967 impf.], 12021, 12115, 12399, 12789, 12950, 12998, 13084, 13127, 13149, 13152, 13155, 13385, 13499 and 14808, 13955, 14448 [? J. Verneuil], 14563 (17263), 14627, 14632, more 14632a, 14656, 14905, 15003, 15143 only, 15195, 15598, 15676, 16096, 16130, 16505, 16605, 16610, 16820, 16909 [the adapter], 17029, 17518, 17706 [? mystification], 17810, 18164, 19128, 19194, 19294, 19409, 19571 (19570), 19574 (19570) [? Capell], 19587 (19571a, 19570), 19607, 20131, 20435, 20867, 20917, 20923, 21046, 21048, 21177 [? W. C(rashaw?)], 21271, 21433, 21468 [? translator], 21697, 21815 [? foreign], 21821, 22236 [adapter], 22393, 22424, 22569 [kinsman], 22614, 22643, 22693, 22857, 22969 and earlier-USHAW, 23095, 23421, 23966, 24020 [? Berthelet], 24045, 24167 (24436 and 1572-HN.), 24180, 24334, 24397 [? J. Spencer], 24531, 24630 [24629 impf.], 24749, 24872, 24957, 25004 [? Parker], 25245, 25404, 25432, 25590, more 25591 [? M. C.], 25647, 25824, 25862, 26127, Allison 551.

Arias, *Treatise of benignity, 1630*-F., R. Brasier, *Godly wil*-F., *New defense of tabacco, 1602*-HN., T. Field, *Earths encrease, 1624*-C.², *Safe returne of king of Bohemia, 1622*-O., Perkins, *Reformation of covetousness, 1603*-F., [T. White], *Catechisme, 1637*-O.

Law-book editors and indexers: 3803, 9314, 9555, 9558, 9587 (partly 9582), 9610, 9616, 9798, 11193 and 11194, 14873.

Bible editors: *Bible editors have been treated as translators. Except for a few entries above, anonymous prefaces have been ignored.*

Sternhold & Hopkins (earliest appearance of editorial material):

'Short introduction to music': 2429.

Athanasius treatise: 2430.

'Note on music': *1569*-L.¹³ quarto [usual in BL quartos].

ANONYMOUS PROSE PUFFS (some perhaps by editor):

560, 5215, 6459, 7395 (7394) [earlier lost], *1637*-CHI. of 10635, 11535, 15069 [exiled preacher], 21713 [clergyman; *see* 21714], 23916, 24761.

COMPOSITOR: For verses supposedly by, *see* 12890 *and* C. THIMMELTHORPE, *Short inventory, 1581*-HN. [signed R. S.].

CORRECTOR OF THE PRESS:
Prose: 5789, 11017, 19401, 24568, *1612*-CU. of 3771.
Variants: Overseer, some copies 22539; Curator, 21806; Inspector, 24703, verse 22389.
Also see 7537 *and, in main index,* P. C., JOHN MARTIALL, *and* RALPH WINTERTON; *likewise* ERRATA *below.*

Oxford corrector: '*Si monumentum requiris, circumspice.*'

ERRATA LISTS: *Lists and unsigned apologies are not indexed, but these unusual types may interest.*
Parody errata, 17454.
Errata for *other* books: 6424, 18078, 21197.
Initialed errata: 20241, 23294.
Fastidious reference system: 1867.
Sandwiched in table of contents: 14307.
Differentiating errors of printer & author: 1073.
Grouped as in all, some, or few copies: 606.
Assurance errata have been corrected: 20030.
Sample verse apologies: 10755, 13776, 20748 [also 5454, 24331], 20799, 21141, 25914.

REPORTER (shorthand or memorial): *The following are among books containing epistles by reporters or relevant materials:* 5491, 6939 *on unauthorized 1634*-F., 6967, 7578, 7626, 11858, 12115, 12124, 22660, 22664.
In main index, see A. S., JOHN WINSTON, AMBROSE WOOD, H. YELVERTON.

BINDER: *Routine instructions to the binder are ignored.*
Epistle to binder: R. Armin, *Foole vpon foole, 1600*-F.

BOOK SUBSCRIBERS (defaulting): *See* 23767.

PROMOTERS OF A BOOK: Dedications to, 2734, 14446, 24007a.

ADVERTISEMENTS: *Advertisements in books before 1641 are uncommon, brief, and inconspicuous. This selection illustrates the types.*
Books and prints [up to four items]: *1640* of 419, *1633* of 490, 11106 [for related newsbook], 15330 [prepublication puff], 17733 [for lost original of 17739], 19528 [four items], 20875 [plague broadside puffs *Crums of comfort!*], Dahl 282, Dahl 393 [for print extant at L.⁵]. *Some authors list their own works at length* (5220, 23730).
Mathematical instruments: 1797, 6542, 6544, 12520, 17123.

Scriveners [only in almanacs]: *1631* of 407, *1640* of 442, *1636* of 490, *1627* of 522.
Language and mathematics teachers: 23060.
Nostrums: 25960.
Cooking moulds: 18301.
Book lists and other inserts are rarely found in, or bound with, S.T.C. items, but none has been observed demonstrably earlier than 1641. Example: Wakeley insert in 14444-L. *[accepted as early by* Taylor].

3. LICENCE AND PRIVILEGE

This survey of the preliminaries of early British books may be rounded out with facts on the formal evidence in the books of censorship and privilege. The classification is: (a) English licences and imprimaturs, (b) English privilege and prescription, (c) Scottish privilege and control, and (d) Foreign control in English books. No attention is given to copyright because the books do not record entry at Stationers' Hall (with the unique exception of 21544, where the imprimatur accidentally names the Warden authorizing entry, John Smethwick). The material is extracted from notes that are substantially complete but not exhaustive.

(a) English Licences and Imprimaturs

In contrast with the Stationers' Register, formal evidence of censorship in the books is slight except for the Laudian period (terminating beyond our cut-off date). The true imprimatur appears in 1630 and becomes common in 1633. All legally published books were in theory approved, but no pattern can be seen in the distribution of imprimaturs, which appear fitfully in new books and reprints, without regard to subject, author, or printer. One may appear in a trivial advertising pamphlet (25075), yet be missing from a major folio, whether literary (14753), historical (17529), or even religious (13720). A survey of the licit output of the London trade in 1640, when control was rigorous, shows that even after exclusion of almanacs, broadsides, bibles and service-books, etc., fully 65 per cent. of the books are without imprimatur. Furthermore, there is uncertainty, overlapping, and even duplication in authority. For fuller discussion, see 'The Laudian Imprimatur', The Library, 5th ser., xv (1960), 96–104.

After listing sporadic early licences, this section gives a census of licensers, grouped by issuing authority. Two books are cited for each censor—his earliest and latest dated imprimatur. An appendix illustrates aspects of press control.

EARLY LICENCES: *Apart from a few noted below under special authorities, these examples have been observed before 1630. Not included are informal commendations obviously by the licenser. There are, too, some dubious or borderline approbations, as in 5844, 5983, 14624, 19813, 25026.*

1536 A dedication to the book licensers, 3943.
1586 Leicester, licensing as Governor of Netherlands, 25340.
1605 Textbook licence, 737.

EARLY LICENCES—*cont.*

1611 By R. Mocket after College of Physicians approval, 12550.

1620 Joint Irish–English licence for schoolbook, 3767.

1625 Controversial book licensed by F. White, 18030.

1625 Formal imprimatur, 18806 [misprint for *1635*].

1627 Episcopal licence of G. Montaigne, 22526 and 5816 [& 5817 probably earlier, a controversial book].

ECCLESIASTICAL AUTHORITY: *Most imprimaturs were issued by the Bishop of London or the Archbishop of Canterbury, at the hands of a chaplain. The chief licensers were Baker, Bray, Clay, Haywood, and Wykes, especially the last (names identified in the main file).*

John Alsop, *1639*: 25955, 12648b.

Robert Austin, *1633–4*: 20249, 12334.

Samuel Baker, *1634–40*: 25182, 17921.

William Bray, *1632–40*: 24633, 11530.

Thomas Browne, *1639–40*: 7038, 12978.

Matthew Clay, *1638–40*: 6304, 4620.

John Hansley, *1639–40*: 12397, 12363.

William Haywood, *1631–7*: 957 = 13268, 24075 (perhaps relieved after trouble over 11321).

Edward Martin, *1630–1*: 11326, 14269.

John Oliver, *1637–9*: 21178, 12980.

Thomas Wykes *or* Weekes, *1634–40*: 25355, 14922.

Exceptional: Personal episcopal licence of John Williams, *1637*: 25724 [his own anonymous book!].

SECRETARY OF STATE: *This office handled news pamphlets and a few politically sensitive books, though the former were sometimes approved by the chaplains* (18165).

Sir John Coke, Secretary, *1635–7*: 17719, 18022.

Sir Francis Windebank, Secretary, *1640*: Some copies of 21915.

G. R. Weckherlin, Under-secretary, *1637–40*: 17668, Dahl 369.

Robert Reade, corantos, *1639–40*: Dahl 303, Dahl 348.

Philip Minutelius, corantos, *1640*: Dahl 349, Dahl 364; A. S., *Terrible Sea-fight*, *1640*-F.

MASTER OF THE REVELS: *Besides licensing stage performances, the Revels sometimes authorized printing. But plays might also be licensed by the chaplains* (22442, 17643). *For a conspectus, see* Greg, iii. 1480–7.

Sir Henry Herbert, *1632–40*: 249, 21542; jointly with chaplains, 5770; imprimatur in a non-dramatic work, 7043.

Mock-imprimatur (Master of Revels, Middle Temple): 6308 [actually countenanced in SR].

EARL MARSHAL: *For an early reference to his sporadic approval of works on chivalry and heraldry, see* 22164.

Earl of Arundel, *1622–40*: Four Oxford and Cambridge broadsides, *1622*-L.[5] [cf. 4485, 21868], 7366 [jointly with Cambridge], 13264 [warrant for import], 19846.

NAVY MASTER BUILDER: *Exceptional concurrence in a normal licence.*

Peter Pett, *1637*: 13367.

COLLEGE OF PHYSICIANS: *Approbation by the College is not a substitute for ecclesiastical licence, nor even a mandatory supplement. Sometimes it takes the form of a prose endorsement, recognizable only from the writer; these are noted in the main index.*

Early instances: *1602*, vague reference to a licence, 5446; *1611*, approbation by President (Paddy) and chaplain's licence, 12550; *1605*, none, but privilege of Whitgift at hands of H. Saravia, 16650.

True licences or censures, supplementing imprimatur except in instances noted:

Licence by president and fellows: Argent, Clement, Gulston, 12888 [no imprimatur]; Argent, Gifford, Baskerville, Ridgeley, 14791 [no imprimatur]; Argent, Meverell, Spicer, 21426.

Licence by president: S. Fox, 20384.

Censure: Reid, 3723, 7511, 25355 [with Clement]; Fryer, 3931.

Epistles by A. Reid, supplementing imprimatur except as noted: 1592, 10658 [no imprimatur], 21543, 21544, 25356, 25955.

Medical books with chaplain's imprimatur only: 10666, 20383, *1634*-L.[17] of 20784 and 20786 [who censors the censor?], 21442.

CAMBRIDGE UNIVERSITY: *The licence is normal in Cambridge books 1633–40. Unlike other English imprimaturs, the licence sometimes specifies the printer (e.g. Thomas Buck in* 12531).

Earlier licence data: *1618*, author's epistle to licensers, 14955; *1619*, professorial approbation, 636; *1631* licence without names, 18206.

Vice-chancellor alone: 4338, 10779; embodied in commendatory verses, 20540.

Vice-chancellor and panel: 6295, 6298, 7365, 7366 jointly with Earl Marshal, 11464, 12531, 13518, 13554, 13555, 18948, 22571.

OXFORD UNIVERSITY: *The Oxford press did not use the imprimatur except for a flurry in 1638.*
Vice-chancellor: 4259 with professorial approbation, 5138 with similar approbations, 16789; *1640* sharing in a London imprimatur, 25641.
Quasi-approbation by a Head: 24571.

DUBLIN: *Archbishop and press conformed tardily in 1639.*
Edward Parry: 5753, 13600, 25066.

Appendix: Aspects of Control

Editions with imprimatur variants (both states at library cited):
With and without imprimatur, 21915-M.
With one and two imprimaturs, 7043-F.; *see also* Greg 507a.

Imprimatur contingent on prompt printing:
Within two months, 12334; three months, T. Riley, *Triall of conscience,* 1639-F.; four months, 25955; six months, 6874.

For new editions of old books: 6492 (eighth), 6669 (about twenty-ninth), 7037, 18919 (sixteenth), 25168.
'Fiat altera editio': 17759, 24434 (eighteenth).
Actual MS. licence in copy for reprint: 6118-F., 20782-A.
First edition with, second without, third with fresh one: 19110–12.

'Imprimatur, lingua vernacula': 20490.

Double licence by rival authorities: Church and Secretary of State, 24761; other instances are noted above.

Parody imprimatur: 6308.

Chronology: Legally, licence must precede entry at Stationers' Hall.
Entered same day as licensed: 4627, 17718, 23420.
Entered day after licence: 24633.
Anomalous entry *before* licence: 4620, 22442.

Samples of thoroughness: Multiple for parts of a volume, 12710; multiple yet ignoring one part, 20944; specifying exact length of copy, 13180.

Scrupulosity: Extra imprimatur for dedication, 12397, 13264; for one added commendatory poem, 17220; for preface, 25700a [25700 a ghost]; for appendix, 14269; for index, 13730.

(b) English Privileges and Prescription

Monopoly-privileges are surveyed in so far as they appear in the books in full or abstract, for some holders did not print them (e.g. 17944). First granted to printers, later more commonly to authors, patents might cover single titles or whole classes of books. Routine notices 'Cum privilegio ad imprimendum solum' are here ignored.

CHANCELLOR OF OXFORD: To Scolar, 6458.

HENRY VIII: To Bankes, 2967; Berthelet, 7659; Gough, 3033, 15453; Grafton and Whitchurch, 15835, 16034, etc.; Palsgrave, 19166; Rastell, 20836; Salesbury and Waley, 2983 = 21617.

EDWARD VI: To Day, 4812; Jugge, 2869, sometimes 2867-O.; Nicolls, 24056; Oswen, 12564; Seres, 20373; Whitchurch, 2376.

MARY I: All to Wayland, 1246 [sometimes found in 3178], 1256, 4564, 7552, 16060.

ELIZABETH I: To Day, 2436, 6119; Morley, 2497; Tallis and Byrd, 23666; Vautrollier, *1574-F.* of 15242, 17409, Ovid, *De tristibus, 1574-*FSF.

JAMES I, all for authors: 6248, 16650, 18205, 23200, fancier 23201, 23204.

CHARLES I: To Cotton, *1630-F.* of 7126; Delamain, 6542; Farnaby, 10704, 14892, 17493, 22220; Marriott, 16776; Young, 5398.

Copyright holders also profited from official prescription of certain books. This list, showing date and nature of the act and earliest edition in which it appears, incorporates some border-line material.

HENRY VIII: *1542,* prescription of Lily, 15605; renewed by Edward, 15611; Elizabeth, quarto *1567-*F.; and James, 15625.
1545: Injunction authorizing primer, 16034.

EDWARD VI: *1548,* 'proclamation', 16456 and 16459.
1550: Authorization of foreign congregations, 16571, –71a, –74, –75.
1552: Act of Uniformity, 16279.
1552: Privy Council authorization, 2868.
1553: Prescription of catechism, 4807 (4812, 4813).

ELIZABETH I: *1559,* Act of Uniformity, 16291, etc. [often omitted in small formats].
1560: Authorization of Latin liturgy in colleges, 16424.
1566: Act for Welsh translations, 16437.
1582: Letters of Council and Commissioners, 18773.

JAMES I: *1604,* Proclamation [8344], 16327, etc.
1604: Proclamation [8355], 25633.

JAMES I—*cont.*

1609: Royal warning against unrevised copies, 14402.

1618: Abstract of proclamation [8565], 16773.

1622: Royal and Privy Council endorsements, 25373, 25375a [plus episcopal letter].

CHARLES I: *1629*, Council order for reprint, *1629*-C.² of 9245.

OFFICIAL PRICE CONTROL: 5168, etc., 16267, etc.; publisher's self-control, 10954.

'PRINTED BY ORDER': *This vague rubric is not indexed. The authority may be royal, parliamentary, ecclesiastical, or unspecified.*

Sample: Royal, 1237, 16431, 22628; House of Lords, 25727; 'request of friends', 21240; 'by command', 17734; 'suche whose aucthority could not wel be withstand', 3838; 'request of diuers well disposed', J. Hayward, *Sermon of stewards danger*, *1602*-FLEMING.

AUTHOR'S ENDORSEMENT OF TRANSLATOR: 7323; *also see* 11805.

(c) Scottish Privilege and Control

While Scottish privileges are comparable to the English ones, the imprimatur is practically unknown.

ARCHIEPISCOPAL ALLOWANCE: St. Andrews, 12066 [printed abroad!].

EXTRAORDINARY ROYAL LICENCE: Hamilton, 22058.

PRIVILEGES:

James V: To printer Davidson, *New actis*, *1540*-E.

Mary: To editor Henryson, 21875.

James VI: To Browne, 3905; Huntar, 13993; Skene, 22624 and 22626; Skene and Waldegrave, 21877; Waldegrave, 22023.

Charles I: To Lightbody, 15592; Wedderburn, 25192 [mentioned, not printed].

ROYAL AUTHORIZATIONS:

1566: Commission to publish, 21875.

1579: Proclamation to publish, 21884.

1635: Letters patents promulgating, 22055.

1636: Proclamation promulgating, 16606.

CERTIFICATES OF AUTHENTICITY: *See names in main file.*

Civil: J. Balfour, J. Foulis, A. Hay, J. Hay, J. Mackgill, J. Skene.

Ecclesiastical: Archibald Johnston.

(d) Foreign Control in English Books

English books printed legally abroad were subject to civil and ecclesiastical control in bewildering variety. Both types are conveniently illustrated in recusant books

printed in the Spanish Netherlands (such as 1528, 1778, 7062, 12758, 16098, 16906, 20082, *but not* 21361, *which was for London sale). The proliferation justifies Milton's quip that 'Sometimes 5 Imprimaturs are seen dialoguewise in the Piatza of one Title page'.*

Extreme example: *1630*-w. of 25779.

Bilingual apparatus: 4469, 10927.

Franciscan faculty dated from London: 19794.

United Provinces under Leicester: 25340.

*Occasionally English translations or reprints of foreign books reproduce the original licences. Presumably this was not oversight, but a means of affirming veracity or authority, as in medical works (*15520*) or news pamphlets (*17854*). Examples include: Belgian,* 24653; *Dutch,* 18799; *French,* 3841, 20490; *and Spanish,* 19844. *It is not unusual to find a Polish Catholic imprimatur in the recusant-printed Glory of S. Ignatius, 1632*-F., *but indeed odd to see a similar one retained in an Oxford textbook,* 22652.

B. VARIANT DEDICATIONS

This section attempts a bibliographical survey of variant dedications, both within single editions and between successive editions. The first four groups in the following classification apply to trade publications, the fifth group to unique presentation copies: (1) Cancelled dedications, (2) Split editions, (3) Anomalous dedications, (4) Change of patron, and (5) Presentation epistles. With further study it may be necessary to reassign some individual examples; certainly the student of one class should as a matter of routine scan the other groups. For Factotum dedications, *see* ENGLAND, 3 (*c*).

That this is the most vulnerable section of the book can be confidently predicted. More variant dedications are likely to turn up, including hearsay examples omitted here for lack of confirmation. Existing in unique copies, Presentation epistles are almost impossible to enumerate.

1. CANCELLED DEDICATIONS

Dedications cancelled before or just after publication sometimes escape destruction. In the following books the normal form is undedicated unless otherwise noted.

4613 CAREW, Elizabeth. The tragedie of Mariam, *1613*.

HD., HN. Mrs. Elizabeth Carye [*see* Greg 308].

4946 CHAMBERLAIN, Robert. The swaggering damsell, *1640*.

L. Thomas Kendall [Greg 589 but *not* YALE EC.].

13446 NICCOLS, R. A winters nights vision, *1610, in* Mirror for magistrates.

HN. Prince Henry.

Normally replaced by: Earl of Nottingham.

16887 LUCAN. Pharsalia, *1627.*
At publication Thomas May retained only
the preliminary epistle to the Earl of
Devonshire. *Cancel-slashed part dedications occasionally survive,* L. *and* HD.
showing all:
ii. Pembroke; iii. 'Mowbray'; iv.
Essex; v. Lindsey; vi. Devonshire;
vii. Vere of Tilbury; viii. Lincoln;
ix. Warwick.
*The blunder of 'Mowbray' for Mulgrave
may have prompted the cancellation.*

17834 MERES, Francis. Palladis tamia, *1598.*
ROS. Thomas Eliot [loose leaves].
*Cancelled by the printer while excising
unrelated offensive epistle.*

18089 [MORE, Thomas]. Opus quo refellit
calumnias, *1523.*
DUR.⁵ *has a pre-publication state prior to
extensive substitutions in the mystification, including a dedication to Franciscus
Lucellus.*

19850 PHILIPPSON, J. The key of historie,
1627.
*A typical Darcie array of part-dedications
contains press variants not affecting the
patrons,* Sir R. Aytoun, *etc.*
O., L.³ All cancelled, *apparently anticipating the later editions.*

21010 RICHARDS, Nathaniel. The celestiall
publican, *1630.*
F. Lover of divine poems [retained in
disguised reissue, *1631*-HD.].

23863 TEIXEIRA, José. The Spanish pilgrime,
1625.
HD. Earl of Pembroke, by M. V.
[*altered by pen to* W].

2. SPLIT EDITIONS

(*a*) FREAK OMISSIONS: *Absence of the dedication in these
instances seems due to error either in perfecting the sheets
or in press-work before the dedication was in type.*

13355 HEYWOOD, Thomas. A marriage
triumph, *1613.*
Normally sig. [A2] has epistle to
Frederick on recto, Princess Elizabeth
on verso.
L. Sig. A2ʳ blank.

13805 HORACE. A medicinable morall, *1566.*
Title-page verso inscribed to Ladies
Bacon and Cecil (L., F., PN.).
PN. Blank.

23080 SPENSER, Edmund. The Faerie Queene,
1590.

Normally the title-page verso has inscription to Elizabeth (23081).
F. Title verso blank.

(*b*) DEDICATION ADDED: *Usually without dedication,
each of these editions has an issue with dedication, as
indicated.*

4531 CAMERON, John. An examination of
the Romish church, *1626.*
F., HD. Company of Skinners, by
W. P[inke].

4570 CANISIUS, Petrus. Opus catechisticum,
1611.
L., L.² James, Cardinal Perron, by R.
Smith.

7020 DONE, John. Polydoron, *1631.*
L., F. Earl of Dover.

11643 GASCOIGNE, George. The glasse of
governement, *1575.*
C.⁶ Sir Owen Hopton [Greg 68].

14632 JOHN, Chrysostom. An exposition
vpon Ephesians, *1581.*
C., F. (14632a): Countess of Oxford.

25870 WIT. Wits recreations, *1640.*
L., F. Francis Newport, by Blunden.

(*c*) DIFFERENT PATRONS: *The following split editions
are not listed under dedication changes because there is
no evidence of chronological sequence.*

1199 BAILEY, Walter. A short discourse,
1588.
1199 Factotum dedication.
1200 Address to reader.

7326 DUMOULIN. Heraclitus, *1624* (Darcie
version, distinct from 7325, with
variant titles).
L., O. *Heraclitus:* Earl of Bridgewater,
Lord St. John, etc.
F. *The teares:* Earls of Oxford,
Northumberland, etc.
7327 is a reissue without dedication.

13507 HILLIARD, John. Fire from heaven,
1613.
L., F. (trade edition): Nicholas Hilliard.
O. (local consumption): W. Lea, R.
Westbury, etc. [epistle incongruous].

17401 MARKHAM AND SAMPSON. Herod and
Antipater, *1622* [Greg 382].
Usually (17401): Printer to reader, by
Rhodes.
O., BO. (17402; *not* CH.): Sir T. Finch
and family, by Sampson.

18343 NABBES, Thomas. The springs glorie,
　　1638 [Greg 543].
　　L., etc.: Benedict Roberts.
　　F., etc.: William Ball.
　　Sometimes without dedication. Similar
　　variants in 18343a.
— NOOT, J. van der. Het bosken, [*1568*].
　　F. Marquis of Northampton.
　　HAARLEM (for Netherlands sale):
　　Added title inscription to Karl Fried-
　　rich of Gulick.

19824 PEYTON, Thomas. The glasse of time,
　　1620.
　　All forms have verse dedications to
　　Prince Charles and Bacon.
　　F., HD. [? early state]: Added epistle
　　to James I.

20118 PORTA, G. B. della. De furtiuis litera-
　　rum notis, *1591.*
　　L., etc. (20118): Earl of Northumber-
　　land, by Castelvetro.
　　L., F. (20118a): Joannes Sotus [retained
　　from *1563* Naples ed.].
　　Latter perhaps for Continental sale.

20994 RICH, Barnaby. Opinion diefied,
　　1613.
　　L., O., etc.: Sir Thomas Ridgeway.
　　L. [rare]: Prince Charles.

(*d*) VARIANT LISTS: *In these books minor substitutions*
appear in elaborate lists of patrons (changes in press).
　4497 CAMDEN, William. Annales, *1625* (*a*
　　Darcie catch-all).
　　The confusing variants in the part dedica-
　　tions may be reduced to the formula that
　　the following appear in some but not
　　all copies:
　　Bk. i: Spencer, Lord Compton.
　　Bk. ii: Lord Howard de Walden,
　　Viscountess Wallingford, Lord
　　Brooke / Viscount Andover,
　　Countess of Salisbury, Sir P.
　　Harte / Earl and Countess of
　　Kent, Katherine St. John /
　　Lord Berkeley and mother,
　　Lord Mountjoy.
　　Bk. iii: Merely a type shift!

　4747 CASAUBON apocrypha. The originall of
　　idolatries, *1624* (*a Darcie atrocity*).
　　The secondary dedication to the Courtiers
　　with Prince Charles in Spain is in two
　　states (both at O.). *One includes* Lord
　　Vaughan, Sir Francis Stuart, *and*
　　Edward Montagu; *the other substitutes*

Lord Digby, Sir Dudley North, *and*
Sir William Croft.
The rare added epistle to the Prince's
Household *is likewise in two states,*
that at HN. *showing* Archibald Pit-
carne. *The* O. *state corrects to* Andrew
Pitcarne *and adds:* C. Gleamon, R.
Clare, T. Coke, *and* T. Hen.

6014 CRASHAW, William. Falsificationum
　　tom. i, *1606.*
　　Names in margin to dedication to the
　　Two Temples.
　　L., F., U.: J. Hare, H. Hall.
　　CHI.: In addition, Sir H. Montagu, Sir
　　J. Jackson.

19566 PELLHAM, Edward. Gods power, *1631.*
　　The dedication to the Muscovy Company
　　is in two states (both at F.). *One begins*
　　with, the other omits, Sir John Merick
　　[Meyrick].

3. ANOMALOUS DEDICATIONS

The following examples resist classification, usually
because of the rarity of copies and lack of evidence. The
section ignores anomalies of a factual variety—errors in
name, posthumous dedications, and similar discrepancies.

　6259 DANIEL, Samuel. A panegyricke,
　　[*1603*].
　　Besides the normal dedications, a rare extra
　　leaf of text is inscribed to the Earl of
　　Hertford. HN. *has both forms.* L. *has*
　　the leaf loose in the Bagford collection,
　　Harl. 5927 (187).

　6271 DARCIE, Abraham. The honour of
　　ladies, *1622* (*two copies known*).
　　L.[2] Pre-publication state with six blank
　　epistles (patronesses not yet chosen).
　　L. (*a*) Fresh epistle to Countesses of
　　Derby, Montgomery, and Berkshire.
　　(*b*) One of the original six epistles to
　　Lady Anne Herbert.

10863 FIELD, Theophilus. A watch-word,
　　1628 (*dedicated to Charles I*).
　　In the O. *copy the conjugate final leaf is*
　　the end (? for transfer by binder) of a lost
　　epistle by Field to 'your Grace', *appa-*
　　rently either Buckingham *or* Arch-
　　bishop Abbot.
　　The leaf is missing from the only other
　　known copy, F.

13957 HUME, T. Captaine Humes poeticall
　　musicke, *1607.*
　　Pt. i [missing from F.]: L., M.[3], Queen
　　Anne.

Pt. ii: L., None; M.³, Sir C. Hatton, K.B.; F., Philip, Earl of Arundel [apparently error for Thomas].

19157 PALMERIN, de Oliva. Palmerin d'Oliua, *1588.*
    19157 i. Earl of Oxford.
    19158 i. Unique copy impf.; ii. †Francis Young.
    19159 Order of dedications reversed, epistles revised.

20606 RAINOLDS, John. De idololatria [*sic*], *1596.*
    The epistle to the Earl of Essex *is reprinted in the* text *of 20613 as a* letter *to* Elizabeth!

20937 REYNOLDS, Edward. The vanitie of the creature, *1637.*
    Ostensibly 1637 without dedication, all known copies were in fact issued in 1654 with additional material inscribed in MS. to George Thomason *and usually with engraved verses acrostic to his name.* So: L., F., HD., HN.

4. CHANGE OF PATRON

This census lists only overt substitution of patrons. It normally takes no notice of (a) simple omission *of dedication in a late edition, (b) the prefixing of an* additional *dedication, (c) the augmentation of a list of patrons, or (d) textual alteration in the dedicatory epistle (sometimes mentioned in the main index). When the reason for the change can be deduced, it is noted at the margin with the following code, in which the factors sometimes combine:*

D Death of the previous patron.
S   Succession in office.
F   Fall from favour or public disgrace.
R Removal from scene or retirement.
P   More powerful patron preferred.
E   Editor, reviser, or stationer's substitution.
N New book, essentially, from extensive revision.
U Uncertain or Unclassified (including supposed quarrels).

Dedications are by the author (or translator) unless otherwise noted. A dedication applies to succeeding issues and editions until a change is listed. Later editions may be disguised in title, revised, or expanded. Examples are included (notably Drayton and Saluste) in which revision is so extensive that identity is lost (see code N). Certain secondary epistles found in the main index are, for simplicity, here ignored (as in 25847).

ADAMSON, John. Stoicheiosis.
  138   *1627* D. Aikenhead, D. Richardson, etc.
  139   *1637* Aikenhead, J. Cochran, etc. [6 changes]   S

ALEYN, Charles. The battailes of Crescey.
  351   *1631* †Sir John Spencer, Bt.
  352   *1633* Lord Coleraine.   D

ALLEN, William. The copie of a letter.
  370   *1587-0.*¹⁷ R. A.
  0.⁵   *1587* N. R. [? fiction].

AMADIS, de Gaule. The second booke.
  542   *1595* Gualter Borough, by Pyott.
  544   *1619* Earl of Montgomery, by Munday.   E

ANDREWES, John. Andrewes resolution.
  590   *1621* Bacon.
  L.   *1630* King of Kings.   D

ANGLERIUS, Petrus. The decades (*with title changes*).
  645   *1555* Philip and Mary.
  649   *1577* Countess of Bedford, by Willis.   RD
  650   *1612* Sir Julius Caesar, by Lok. D
               Omitted from later issues.

AUGUSTINE. The citie of God.
  916   *1610* Earl of Pembroke, by bookseller.
  917   *1620* Pembroke, Arundel, and Montgomery, by editor. E

AVERELL, William. A dyall for darlings (*with title change*).
  978   *1584* William Wrathe.
  979   *1590* Hugh Ofley.   U

BACON, Francis. Essayes (*with text expansions*).
  1137 *1597* Anthony Bacon.
  1141 *1612* Sir John Constable.   D
  1147 *1625* Duke of Buckingham.   P

BAKER, Humphrey. The well sprynge.
  L.³⁸ *1562* John Fitzwilliams and Merchants to Flanders.
  1210a *1574* Merchants, *rewritten.* ? D

BALBANI, Niccolo. Newes from Italy.
  1233 *1608* Lord Sheffield and family.
               Thus later editions and unrecorded issues.
Out of series, with title change:
  1234 *1612* Pembroke, etc.; Sheffield, etc.

BALDWIN, William. A treatise (*merging rival versions*).
  1253 *1547* Earl of Hertford.
  WIS. ['*55*?] Lord Henry Hastings, by Palfreyman.   E
  1256 n.d. Hertford, rewritten by Baldwin.

BALDWIN, William, *cont.*
- 1257 *1557* Hastings.
- 1258 *1564* Both, in two parts.
- 1259 *1567* Hastings only. ? F

BARCKLEY, Richard. A discourse of felicitie.
- 1381 *1598* Elizabeth.
- 1383 *1631* Earl of Somerset, by editor. D

BEARD, Thomas. The theatre of judgements.
- 1659 *1597* Sir Edward Wingfield.
- 1661 *1631* Mayor, etc., of Huntingdon. R

BECON, Thomas. The relikes of Rome.
- 1754 n.d. Earl of Bedford.
- 1755 *1563* John Parkhurst; also ¶1710. U

BEDA. The history of the Church.
- 1778 *1565* Elizabeth.
- 1779 *1622* Name of James substituted. D
- 1780 *1626* Elizabeth restored. D

BELLOT, Jacques. The French grammar (*with title change*).
- 1852 *1578* Philip Wharton.
- 1853 *1588* Thomas Egerton. ? N

BERNARD, Richard. The faithfull shepheard.
- 1939 *1607* James Montagu.
- 1941 *1621* Tobie Matthew. D

BERNARD, Richard. Josuahs godly resolution (*title modified*).
- YK. *1609* †Sir Henry Pakenham.
- 1954 *1629* †Sir H. Rosewell and †Sir J. Drake. D

BIBLE. *English patrons of variant New Testaments in London reprints of foreign bibles. Cf. 2802 below.*
- 2057 *1581* Earl of Huntingdon, by Loiseleur.
- 2059 *1585* Elizabeth, by Tremellius.
- 2061 *1593* Walsingham, by Junius.

BIBLE. *Coverdale version (scattered among others).*
- 2063 *1535* Henry VIII.
- 2080 *1550* Edward VI. D

BIBLE. *London reprints of Beza's Testament.*
- 2802 *1574* Earl of Huntingdon, by Loiseleur.
  Later 8° editions thus.
- 2805 *1577* Elizabeth, by Beza.
  Thus later 16° and 12° editions, including several not in *STC*.

Out of series: 2807 = ¶2056, 2808 = ¶2057, 2810a = ¶2061, 2811 = 3735.

BIBLE. *Coverdale's diglot Testament.*
- 2816 *1538* Henry VIII, 'by Coverdale'; also 2818.
- 2817 *1538* Cromwell, by Coverdale, repudiating 2816.

BODENHAM, John. Englands Helicon.
- 3191 *1600* Bodenham, by editor.
- 3192 *1614* Lady E. Carie, by bookseller. D

BONAVENTURA. The life of S. Francis.
- 3271 *1610* A. B., by editor E. H.
- 3272 *1635* Lady Englefield, by F. C. E

BOOKS. Six spiritual bookes (*part iii*).
- 3369 n.d. His sister, M. T., by [J. Heigham].
- HD. *1611* L. A. B. V. M[ontagu]. U

BOURNE, William. A regiment for the sea.
- 3422 n.d. Earl of Lincoln.
- 3427 *1592* Earl of Cumberland, by editor. ED

BOWND, Nicholas. The doctrine of sabbath (*with title change*).
- 3436 *1595* Earl of Essex.
- 3437 *1606* i. John Jegon; ii. H. Tyndall. FD

BRADFORD, John. Holy meditations (*previously undedicated*).
- 3491 *1614* Merchant Taylors, by editor. E
- 3492 *1622* Lord Bergavenny, by printer. E

BRASBRIDGE, Thomas. The poore mans iewell.
- 3549 *1578* Sir Thomas Ramsey.
- 3552 *1592* †Anthony Cope. D

BRATHWAIT, Richard. Essaies (*part i*).
- 3566 *1620* Sir Henry Yelverton.
- 3567 *1635* Thomas, Lord Coventry. D

BURTON, William. Certaine questions.
- 4167 *1591* Richard Fletcher.
- ¶4165a *1602* Earl of Worcester. D

BURTON, William. An exposition . . . Lords prayer.
- 4174 *1594* Earl of Essex.
- ¶4165a *1602* Sir William Knollys. D

CADE, Anthony. A sermon of conscience.
- 4329 *1621* Sir H. Hobart and Sir E. Bromley.
- 4329a *1636* John Williams, bishop. D

CAMBRIDGE. The foundation of the Universitie.
- L.⁵ *1622* Lord Windsor, by print-seller.
- 4485 *1634* Earl of Arundel, by same. P

CAMDEN, William. Britannia.
4503 1586 Lord Burghley.
4507 1600 Elizabeth. D
4508 1607 James (likewise 4509). D

CAMDEN, William. Remaines.
4521 1605 Sir Robert Cotton.
4525 1636 Prince Charles Lewis, by editor. DE

CARLETON, George. Tithes examined.
4644 1606 Archbishop Bancroft.
4645 1611 Archbishop Abbot. DS

CARLILE, Christopher. A discourse . . . Peter.
4655 1572 Sir Henry Sidney, by editor.
4656 n.d. Lord Wentworth, by author.

CAWDREY, Robert. A shorte treatise.
4882 1580 Lady Golding, by editor.
4883 1604 †Earl of Bedford, by author.

CHARRON, Pierre. Of wisdome.
5051 n.d. Prince Henry.
5052 n.d. Samson Lennard (dropped after 5053). D

CLAPHAM, Henoch. A briefe of the Bible.
5332 1596 i. T. Mylot; ii. R. Topcliffe.
5333 1603 Prince Henry.
5334 1608 i. Henry; ii. Archbishop Bancroft.

CLERKE, John. Opusculum de resurrectione.
5408 1545 Earl of Surrey.
5409 1547 Charles Stourton. FD

CLOWES, William. A short treatise.
5447 1579 Company of Barber Surgeons.
5448 1585 Surgeons (young surgeons in 5442).

CONWAY, John. Meditations and praiers (*with title change*).
5651 n.d. Elizabeth I.
5653 1611 Princess Elizabeth, by printer. D

COOPER, Thomas. The christians sacrifice.
5694 1608 Princess Elizabeth (also 1609-F.).
5695 1615 Nobility and gentry. R

COOPER, Thomas. The mystery of witch-craft (*with title camouflage*).
5701 1617 Mayor, etc., of Chester.
5707 1622 East India Company. U

COOPER, Thomas. The worldlings adventure (*with title camouflage*).
5710 1619 Company of Grocers.
5708 1621 Sir F. Jones and aldermen. U

CORRO, Antonio de. Dialogus theologicus (*with title change*).
5784 1574 Gentlemen of both Temples.
5785 1581 Oxford University. U

CORTES, Martin. The arte of navigation.
5798 1561 Garrarde, Lodge and Muscovy company.
5803 1596 Mariners of England, by editor. E
5804 1609 Sir William Waad, by editor.

COTTON, Clement. The christians concordance.
5842 1622 Students of scripture.
5843 1627 Church of England.
5844 1631 Thomas, Lord Coventry. Inscription to clergy added in 5846 only.

COTTON, Clement. The mirror of martyrs.
5848 1613 Princess Elizabeth.
5849 1615 Countess of Bedford and Lady Harington. R
5850 1631 Company of Drapers. D

CRAIG, Alexander. The poetical recreations.
5959 1609 Earl of Dunbar.
5960 1623 Earl of Enzie. D

CRASHAW, William. Milke for babes (*for varied audiences*).
6020 1618 Sir H. Griffith and W. St. Quintin.
6021 1622 E. and B. Thelwall and Whitechapel.
6022 1633 None. Many editions are lost.

DANIEL, Samuel. The works.
6236 1601 Elizabeth [*see also presentation epistles*].
6238 1623 Prince Charles, by editor. DE

DANIEL, Samuel. The . . . historie (*part and whole*).
6246 1612 Viscount Rochester.
6248 1618 Queen Anne. FP

DAVIES, John. Orchestra.
6360 1596 Richard Martin.
¶6359 1622 Prince [Charles?] D

DESAINLIENS, Claude. The Frenche Littelton.
6738 1576 Robert Sackville.
6742 1593 Lord Zouche. U
6743 1597 Sir W. Herbert of Swansea. U

DESAINLIENS, Claude. The French schoolemaister.
6748 1573 Robert Sackville.

DESAINLIENS, Claude, *cont.*
   Y. *1596* Journeymen studying French.
                                         U
  ILL. *1602* and later eds. None.

DESAINLIENS, Claude. Arnalt & Lucenda (*with title change*).
  6758 *1575* Sir Jerome Bowes.
  6759 *1597* John Smith.   U

DRAXE, Thomas. Calliepeia.
  7176 *1607* Sir J. Harington, [II Baron].
  7178 *1613* Thomas, [I Baron] Leigh. U
                  Followed by 7177, etc.

DRAYTON, Michael. Englands epistles (*Katherine–O. Tudor*).
  7193 *1597* Lord Henry Howard; this ed. only.
  7216 *1605* Sir John Swinnerton; also 7218, etc.   U

DRAYTON, Michael. Mortimeriados (*completely rewritten*).
  7207 *1596* Countess of Bedford.
  7189 *1603* Sir Walter Aston.   N

DUMOULIN, Pierre. The christian combate (*by translator*).
  7316 *1623* Archbishop Abbot.
  7317 *1636* Elizabeth of Bohemia and Charles Lewis.   D

DUMOULIN, Pierre. Theophilus (*by translator*).
  7339 *1610* George Hakewill.
    L. *1628* Sir Ri. Molyneux (and perhaps lost prior ed.).   U

EDMONDES, Clement. Observations (*sequence tangled*).
  7488 *1600* i. Sir F. Vere; ii. Sir R. Drury.
  7489 *1604* Prince Henry.   P
  7492 [*1606*] Newly to Henry (followed by 7491).

ELYOT, Thomas. The dictionary (*and its sequel*).
  7659 *1538* Henry VIII.
  7662 *1552* Edward VI, by Cooper. D
  5686 *1565* Earl of Leicester, by Cooper. D

EPICTETUS. Manuall.
  10424 *1610* John Florio, by bookseller.
  10426 *1616* Earl of Pembroke, by same. P

EUSEBIUS. The auncient histories.
  10572 *1577* i. Countess of Lincoln; ii. C. Kenne.
  10573 *1585* Earl of Leicester.   P

FEATLEY, Daniel. Ancilla pietatis.
  10725 *1626* i. Duchess of Buckingham; ii. Countess of Denbigh.

10729 *1639* Countess of Denbigh alone.
                                      U

FIELD, Theophilus. A christians preparation.
  10860 *1622* Duchess of Lennox.
  10861 *1624* Duke of Buckingham. P

FLEMING, Abraham. The footepath of faith.
  11039 *1581* †Sir Rowland Hayward.
  11040 *1619* Wm. Tothyll, by printer. DE

FLORIO, Giovanni. A worlde of wordes (*with title change*).
  11098 *1598* Rutland, Southampton, and Countess of Bedford.
  11099 *1611* Queen Anne.   P

FOXE, John. Christ Jesus triumphant (*by translator*).
  11231 *1579* William Killigrew.
  11232 *1607* William, Lord Howard. U

FREAKE, William. The doctrines of Jesuites (*with title change*).
  11346 *1630* J. Cambell and aldermen.
  14538 *1632* None (a reissue).
   C.² *1636* Governors of St. Bart's Hosp.

GATES. The two gates of salvation (*title camouflaged*).
  11682 *1609* Curious blank dedication.
  3001 *1620* R. Fishborne and J. Browne, by T. Middleton.
  5560 *1627* None [but intrusive one in L. copy].

GEMINI, Thomas. Compendiosa delineatio (*and translation*).
  11714 *1545* Henry VIII.
  11716 *1553* Edward VI, by author. D
  11718 *1559* Elizabeth, by author. D

GERARD, John. Catalogus arborum.
  11748 *1596* Lord Burghley.
  11749 *1599* Sir Walter Raleigh. D

GERARDUS, Andreas. A speciall treatise.
  11760 n.d. Alexander Nowell.
  11761 *1602* Lancelot Andrewes. D

GERARDUS. The true tryall of selfe (*tr. T. Newton*).
    L. *1586* Countess of Leicester (also *1587*-HD.).
    F. *1602* Francis Heyton.   U

GERHARD, Johann. A christian mans worke (*with title change*).
  11764 *1611* Ladies D. Hobart and D. Crane.
  11765 *1615* Countess of Bedford and Lady Harington. U

11766 *1621* Countess of Bedford alone.
D

GERHARD, J. The conquest of temptations.
FLEMING *1614* †Sir Thomas Vavasour.
11768 *1623* Sir Edward Conway. D

GERHARD, J. Gerards prayers (*bookseller vs. author*).
11780 *1623* Countess of Bedford, by bookseller.
¶11773 *1631* Anne Henshaw, E. Dilke,
H. Proby, by author.
Discarded in the Scottish reprints.

GESNER, Conrad. The newe iewell (*with title change*).
11798 *1576* Countess of Oxford.
11799 *1599* Earl of Oxford (widower). D

GIBBONS, O. [or W. Byrd]. Parthenia.
HN. n.d. Frederick and Elizabeth, by
engraver.
11827 n.d. Masters and lovers of music;
= 4252. U

GODWIN, Francis. A catalogue of bishops.
11937 *1601* Lord Buckhurst.
11938 *1615* James I. D

GODWIN, F. Romanae historiae anthologia
(*with revision*).
11956 *1614* Francis James.
11959 *1623* John Young. D

GOUGE, William. Panoplia.
12122 *1616* Sir J. Jolles and aldermen.
12123 *1619* Sir S. Harvey and aldermen.
S
¶12109 *1627* Earl of Cleveland. D
N. *1639* None.

GRAILE, Edmund. Little Timothe.
To officers of St. Bart's, Gloucester, including
12171 *1611* . . . J. Thorne, W. Locksmith,
J. Moore . . .
12172 *1632* . . . C. Capell . . . S
Intermediate edition lost,
probably thus.

GREENWOOD, Henry. A treatise of judgement
(*successive wives*).
12337 *1606* M. Lestrange and wife Margaret.
L. *1614* Sir Mordaunt and Lady
Frances. DS

GRIMESTONE, Edward. A generall historie
(*fathers and sons*).

12374 *1608* I Earls of Salisbury and
Suffolk.
12376 *1627* II Earls of Salisbury and
Suffolk. DS

GUARINI, Battista. Il pastor fido (*by stationers*).
12415 *1602* Sir Edward Dymock, by
S. Waterson.
12416 *1633* His son Charles, by J. Waterson D

GUEVARA, Antonio de. The diall of princes.
12427 *1557* Mary I.
12430 *1619* Sir H. Montagu, by editor.
DE

GUICCIARDINI, L. The garden of pleasure
(*with title disguise*).
12464 *1573* Earl of Leicester.
12465 *1576* Sir Christopher Hatton. U

GUILLIM, John. A display of heraldrie.
12500 *1610* James I.
12502 *1632* Earl of Arundel, by bookseller. DE

H., B. The glasse of mans folly.
12562 *1595* Sir Owen Hopton.
12562a *1615* Lovers of virtue. D

HAKLUYT, Richard. Diuers voyages (*and sequels*).
12624 *1582* Sir Philip Sidney.
12625 *1589* Sir Francis Walsingham D
12626 *1598* i. Nottingham; ii–iii. Cecil. D

HARINGTON, John. Epigrams.
12775 *1615* Earl of Pembroke, by J. Budge.
12776 *1618* Buckingham, by Budge; also
¶748. P

HARSNET, Adam. A touchstone of grace.
12876 *1630* People of [Cranham, Essex].
12877 *1632* †George Pitt. P

HAYNE, Thomas. The times of scripture
(*with title change*).
12981 *1607* Sir J. Brograve, by bookseller.
12982 *1614* None (piracy, out of series =
12975).
12983 *1640* Sir Paul Pindar, by author. D

HELIODORUS. An Aethiopian historie.
13041 n.d. Earl of Oxford.
13046 *1622* Sir J. Sedley, by bookseller.
DE

HERESBACH, Conrad. Foure bookes of hus-
bandrie.
13196 *1577* Sir William FitzWilliams.
13202 *1631* Earl of Exeter, by editor. DE

HERRING, Francis. Pietas pontifica (*with expansion*).
13244 *1606* James I.
13245 *1609* i. Henry; ii. Harington; iii. James and Henry.

HIERON, Samuel. The sermons (*the general dedication*).
13379 *1620* †Sir H. Yelverton, by bookseller.
13384 *1635* Sir John Bankes, by same. D

HIERON. The spirituall fishing.
13423 *1618* Lady M. Yelverton, by bookseller.
¶13384 *1635* †Bart. Beale, by same. ? D

HILL, Robert. Christs prayer expounded.
13472 *1606* St. Martin-in-the-fields and [paste-on slip] Bishop of Durham [unique L. copy].
F. *1607* Lord Ellesmere. U
St. Martin's reduced to epistle.

HILL, Thomas. A most briefe treatise (*with title change*).
G. [? '*63*] Thomas Counstable.
13491 *1568* Sir Henry Seymour. U

HOLLAND, Abraham. Naumachia (*ded. by H. Holland*).
13580 *1622* George, Lord Gordon; also ¶13579.
¶26068 *1632* Earl of Holland [rare issue]. U

HOLLAND, Henry. Spirituall preseruatives.
13588 *1593* Mayor and aldermen and T. Aldersey.
13589 *1603* Sir R. Lee and aldermen. S & D?

HOLYOKE, F. Dictionarium. *Involved with Rider, q.v.*

HOMER. Iliades (*7 and 12 books*).
13632 *1598* Earl of Essex; cf. 13635.
13633 *n.d.* Prince Henry; also later eds. D

HULOET, Richard. Abcedarium (*with title change*).
13940 *1552* Thomas Goodrich.
13941 *1572* Sir G. Peckham, by editor. DE

HUMPHREYS, R. The conflict of Job (*with title change*).
13967 *1607* Earl of Salisbury.
13968 *1624* William, II Earl. D

IVE, Paul. The practise [*name Ivie in 14290*].

14289 *1589* Lord Cobham and Walsingham; = ¶7264.
14290 *1597* Elizabeth. DP

JAMES, Thomas. Catalogus librorum.
14449 *1605* Prince Henry.
14450 *1620* James, Charles, and Bodleian benefactors. D

JANUA. Janua linguarum (*becomes confused with 15078, etc.*).
14466 *1615* Sir C. Edmondes, by Welde; and *1616*-O., *1623*-HD.
14469 *1626* W. Salter, by Harmar. DE
14472 *1634* None; including *1636*-F.
Out of series:
14467 *1617* Prince Charles, by J. Barbier.

JOURDAIN, Silvester. A discovery of the Barmudas (*with title change*).
14816 *1610* John FitzJames.
14817 *1613* Sir T. Smith, by editor. EP

JUAN, de S. Maria. Christian policie (*with title change*).
L. *1632* Earl of Carlisle, by Blount.
14832a *1637* Viscount Dorchester, by Blount. D

LANQUET, Thomas. An epitome of cronicles (*ded. by Cooper*).
15217 *1549* Duke of Somerset; inc. unauthorized 15221.
15218 *1560* Earl of Bedford. FD

LENTON, Francis. Characterismi (*with title disguises*).
15463 *1631* Oliver, Lord St. John; and *1632*-NY.
15464 *1636* Henrietta Maria; and *1640*-N. P

LITHGOW, William. A . . . peregrination.
15710 *1614* 1st issue: Earl of Somerset. 2nd issue: Gentlemen, heroic spirits. F
15713 *1632* Charles I. P

L'OBEL, M. de. Balsami explanatio.
16649 *1598* Lord Hunsdon.
¶16650 *1605* Carolus Clusius. D

LOWE, Peter. The whole course (*with title modified*).
HN. *1597* i. James VI; ii. Lord Sempill.
16870 *1612* i. Earl of Abercorn; ii. Spottiswood. UD

LUIS, de Granada. Of prayer (*with Protestant version*).
16907 *1582* Inns of Court; so *all* Catholic eds.

16909 *1592* i. †Ferdinando, Lord Strange, by editor; ii. J. Banester, by ed. (through *1602*). E

HD. *1596* i. Sir Julius Caesar, by editor. D

16910 *1599* i. Wm. Dethick, by ed. (and *1601*-L.²⁶). U

16911 *1602* i. Sir J. Swinnerton, by editor. U

16913 *1623* i. Sir C. Cottrell; ii. Lady C., by printer. D

MARKHAM, Gervase. Cavelarice (*books i and ii*).
17334 *1607* Prince Henry.
17335 *1617* Prince Charles. D

MARKHAM, G. The English husbandman.
17355 *1613* Lord Clifton.
17357 *1635* Duke of Lennox. D

MARKHAM, G. The inrichment (*change in dedicator*).
17363 *1625* Sir G. Rivers, by bookseller.
17364 *1631* Same, by author.

MARKHAM, G. Markhams maister-peece.
17376 *1610* Lord Clifton.
17378 *1631* Earl of Carnarvon. D

MASTERSON, Thomas. Arithmeticke.
17648 *1592* i. Essex; ii. Webbe and aldermen; iii. Puckering.
17649 *1634* Sir M. Lumley and Christ's Hosp., by ed. DE

MAYER, John. A treasury (*with general revision*).
17744 *1622* Sir E. Barkham, P. Proby, and aldermen.
17730 *1631* Maurice Barrow. U

MEXIA, Pedro. The historie (*with expansion*).
17851 *1604* Sir Horace Vere.
17852 *1623* Earl of Middlesex, by editor. E

MINSHEU, John. Ductor in linguas (*with title change*).
17944 *1617* James I.
17945 *1625* John Williams. D

MONTAIGNE, M. de. The essayes.
18041 *1603* In 3 bks. to Countesses of Bedford, Rutland, 4 more.
18042 *1611* Queen Anne. P

MORE, Thomas. Utopia (*supplemental dedication*).
18094 *1551* William Cecil; this ed. only.

18097 *1624* Cresacre More, by printer. E
18098 *1639* Same, by different printer.

MORNAY, Philippe de. A woorke of religion.
18149 *1587* Earl of Leicester.
18151 *1604* Prince Henry, by editor. DE

MORNAY. A treatise of the Church (*with revision*).
18158 *1579* Earl of Leicester.
18162 *1606* James I, by J. Molle. DE

MURRELL, John. A new booke (*and related titles*).
18299 *1615* Frances Herbert.
18301 *1617* Elizabeth Bingham.
18302 *1621* Ladies and gentlemen.
NY. *1631* i. Martha Hayes; ii. Lady Browne.

MUSCULUS, Wolfgang. Commonplaces.
18308 *1563* Matthew Parker.
18309 *1578* Sir C. Hatton, by printer. DE

NORDEN, John. A pensive soules delight.
18627 *1603* Anne, Countess of Warwick.
18628 *1615* Sir John Daccombe. D

NORDEN, John. The surveyors dialogue.
18639 *1607* Earl of Salisbury.
18641 *1618* Normally: Salisbury.
One issue-L.: Sir R. Smith. D

NOWELL, Alexander. *Whitaker's Greek version* (*temporary shift*).
18726 *1575* Parker, Grindal, Sandys, etc.
18728 *1578* Grindal, Sandys, Aylmer, etc. S
Original form in later eds.

OXFORD. The foundation of the Universitie.
21868 *1634* Exactly as in 4485 above, q.v.

PALINGENIUS, M. The zodyake of lyfe (*3 and 6 bks.*).
19148 *1560* Lady Hales.
19149 *1561* Sir W. Cecil; and later editions. P

PALMERIN, de Oliva. *See under* ANOMALOUS DEDICATIONS, p. 243.

PARSONS, Robert. Christian exercise (*rival versions*).
There is no change, dedications being confined to the Protestant recensions (19355, etc., and 19380, etc.).

PEACHAM, Henry. The garden of eloquence.
19497 *1577* John Aylmer.
19498 *1593* Sir John Puckering. U

PEACHAM, Henry. The art of drawing (*and expansion*).

19500 *1606* Sir Robert Cotton; and *1607*-HN.

19507 *1612* Sir Edmund Ashfield.   ? N

PERCYVALL, Richard. Bibliotheca Hispanica (*with title change, revision*).

19619 *1591* Earl of Essex.

19620 *1599* i. Sir J. Scot, H. Bromley, etc., by Minsheu.   E
            ii. Students of Gray's Inn, = 19622.   E

PERKINS, William. A golden chaine (*interspersed Hill recension*).

19659 *1592* Sir Julius Caesar; so 19662, 19663, ¶19648, etc.

19664 *1612* Sir J. Egerton; and *1621*-HD. U

PITISCUS, Bartholomew. Trigonometry.

19967 *1614* Sir T. Smith and J. Wolstenholme.

19968 *1630* Trinity House.   DU

POLANUS, Amandus. The substance of religion (*tr. E. Wilcocks*).

    U. *1595* †Earl of Bedford, by trans.; also *1597*-L.

20084 *1600* Same, by reviser T. Wilcocks.

20085 *1608* Sir Edward Coke, by T. Wilcocks.   U

PRIMALEON, of Greece. The first booke (*etc.*).

20366 *1595* i. Unique copy imperfect.

20366a *1596*-L. ii. †Francis Young.

20367 *1619* i, ii, iii. Henry, Earl of Oxford.   U

RAINOLDS, John. Sex theses (*expanded*).

20624 *1580* Oxford University.

20625 *1602* Whitgift; fresh epistle to Oxford.   P

RATRAMNUS. A booke of Bertram (*previously undedicated*).

20751 *1582* Sir W. Pelham, by bookseller.   E

20752 *1623* Sir Walter Pye, by editor; and 4th ed.-F.   DE

READ, Alexander. A manuall of anatomy (*expanded*).

    L.[17] *1634* Company of [Barber] Surgeons.

20784 *1638* Charles I.   P

RECORDE, Robert. The ground of artes (*many unrecorded eds.*).

20798 *1542* Richard Whalley.

    CU. *1558* Edward VI [from lost earlier ed.].   P

So all later eds. except 20800 and *1566*-F. [without ded.]

20802 *1582* Added: Robert Forth, by Mellis.

20815 *1615* Sir H. Fanshaw, by bookseller.   DE

20807 *1618* Edward VI only.   D

REDMAN, John. A compendious treatise (*? again from MS.*).

20826 n.d. Mary I.

    c.[2] *1609* Countess of Hertford, by editor.   DE

REGIUS, Urbanus. An instruccyon.

20847 n.d. Richard Melton.

20848 *1579* Sir F. Knollys, by printer.   ED?

REGIUS. The solace of Sion.

20852 *1587* Sir G. Barne and aldermen.

20854 *1594* Sir C. Buckle and aldermen.   SD

RICH, Barnaby. Faultes faults (*and revision*).

20983 *1606* Prince Henry.

20984 *1616* Lady St. John.   D

RIDER, John. *In the mingled Rider–Holyoke series of dictionaries, changes appear in the Holyoke section.*

21029 *1589* Walsingham, by Rider; remains unchanged.

21032 *1606* Prince Henry, by Holyoke.

21036 *1627* Lady [Alice] Dudley [sometimes missing; ? cancelled].

13620 *1633* Laud and Lord Craven, by Holyoke.

13621 *1640* Craven dropped; Laud shifted [and *1639*-HD. variant].   U
            Added: Prince Charles and Lord Dunsmore, by T. Holyoke.

ROBERTS, Henry. Pheander.

21086 *1595* Capt. Thomas Lea.

21087 *1617* Raleigh Gilbert.   U

ROBINSON, Richard. The vineyarde of vertue.

21121 n.d. Edmund Uvedale.

    Y. *1591* †Henry Uvedale.   ? D

RODRIGUEZ, Alonso. A treatise of prayer (*title modified*).

21148 *1627* Abbess at Ghent, by editor.

21149 *1627* Same (now named), by translator.

ROMANS. Gesta Romanorum (*Robinson version*).

21288   *1595*   Margaret, Countess of Lennox. So 4 lost eds. from before *1578*.

   BO.   *1600*   J. Miller and Leathersellers. D [Lost *1602* to Ant. Watson, bishop].
Later eds. have no dedication.

ROY, William. Rede me (*with 2nd ded. in text*).

21427   n.d.   i. Mr. P. G.; ii. Wolsey.
21428   *1546*   i. Lovers of Word, by L. R. U
ii. Bishops of England.   D

SALERNO. Regimen sanitatis.

21596   *1528*   John, Earl of Oxford.
21600   *1557*   Marquis of Winchester.   D
21603   *1617*   Joseph Fenton, by editor. DE
21604   *1634*   None.

SALLUSTIUS. The famous cronycle.

21626   n.d.   J. Vesey and Duke of Norfolk.
¶10752   *1557*   Viscount Montagu, by Paynell.   D

SALUSTE DU BARTAS. A canticle (*completely rewritten*).

21669   *1590*   J. Parkinson and J. Caplin.
¶23582   *1615*   Earl of Dorset; and later collections.   N

SARAVIA, Hadrianus. De diuersis gradibus.

21746   *1590*   Whitgift, Hatton, Burghley; so 21749.
¶21751   *1611*   Clergy, Church of England.   D

SCOTT, Thomas. Foure paradoxes.

22107   *1602*   Marchioness of Northampton.
  E.[2]   *1611*   Sir T. Gorges (her husband).

SENECA, L. A. The workes.

22213   *1614*   Lord Ellesmere.
22214   *1620*   Earl of Suffolk.   D

SETON, John. Dialectica (*incorporating annotations*).

22250   *1545*   Stephen Gardiner.
  DUL.   *1568*   Earl of Derby, by Carter [from *Annotationes*, *1563*-L. frag.].
  C.[7]   *1570*   Both; and so all later editions.
Many editions not in *STC*, as *1560*-YK., etc.

SIMSON, Archibald. A godly exposition (*with title change*).

  F.   *1622*   Countess of Mar.
22568   *1623*   †Earl of Morton.   U
22569   *1638*   Same, by anon. editor.

SMITH, John. An accidence.

22784   *1626*   Privy Council and Council of War.
22786   *1636*   Earl of Northumberland, by bookseller.   E

SMITH, John. New Englands trials.

22792   *1620*   Various: *see* PRESENTATION EPISTLES.
22793   *1622*   Prince Charles.

SOROCOLD, Thomas. Supplications (*many editions lost*).

22932   *1612*   Princess Elizabeth.
22933   *1616*   Prince Charles.   R

SPELMAN, Henry. De non temerandis ecclesijs.

23067   *1613*   Deo et Ecclesiae; and 23068 *following* next.
23069   *1616*   Clergy, Church of Scotland, by editor.   E

STOCKWOOD, John. Disputatiunculae (*an edition lost*).

23278   *1598*   William Lambarde.
  O.   *1607*   Sir William Sedley; also *1634*-HN.   D

STOW, John. A summarie of chronicles (*in 2 series*).

Early octavo editions:

23319   *1565*   Earl of Leicester; until his death, including *1566*-O. and *1573*-F.

The 16° (and later 8°) editions:

23320   *1566*   None.
23321   *1567*   Roger Martin and aldermen.
23323   *1573*   Lionel Ducket and aldermen.   S
  HN.   *1579*   Sir R. Pipe and aldermen. S
23326   *1587*   Sir G. Barne and aldermen. S
23327   *1590*   Sir J. Hart and aldermen.   S
23328   *1598*   Sir R. Saltonstall and aldermen.   S
23329   *1604*   Sir T. Bennett and aldermen. S
23330   *1607*   Sir H. Rowe and aldermen, by Howes.   S
23331   *1611*   Same, adding: Sir W. Craven and aldermen.   S
23332   *1618*   Sir G. Bowes and aldermen, by Howes.   S

STOW, John. The chronicles, *alias* Annales.

23333   *1580*   Earl of Leicester.
23334   *1592*   John Whitgift.   D
23338   *1615*   Prince Charles, by Howes. DE

STOW, John. A suruay of London.

23341   *1598*   Lord Mayor, etc.

STOW, John, Survey, *cont.*
23343 *1603* Robert Lee, etc.   S
23344 *1618* G. Bolles, etc., by Munday. S
23345 *1633* R. Freeman, etc., by [Dyson?].
                                                   S

STUBBES, Philip. The anatomie of abuses.
23376 *1583* Earl of Arundel.
23379 *1594* Magistrates.   F

SUTTON, Christopher. Godly meditations.
23491 *1601* Elizabeth Southwell.
23492 *1613* Frances and Katherine South-
                well.   F

SWINBURNE, Henry. A briefe treatise.
23547 *1590* John Piers.
23548 *1611* Tobie Matthew [23549 a
                ghost].   DS
23550 *1635* William Laud, by Stationers'
                Co.   D

SYMSON, Patrick. A short compend (*and
sequels*).
23601 *1613* i, ii, iii. Countess of Mar.
23598 *1624* Anew to Countess, and so later.
                Added: Duke of Richmond,
                by editor, but
23600 *1634* Duke of Lennox, by editor. D

T., A. A rich storehouse (*some editions lost*).
23606 *1596* Thomas Skinner, by Blower.
23607 *1607* Sir Wm. Rider, by Blower. S
23608 *1612* Sir James Pemberton, by
                Blower.   S

TAYLOR, John. The nipping or snipping (*one
section*).
23779 *1614* R. Warner and Watermen.
¶23725 *1630* N. [Warner], R. Clarke and
                Watermen.   S

TAYLOR, John. The sculler (*with title change*).
23791 *1612* Sir William Waad.
23792 *1614* Monsieur Multitude; also
                ¶23725.   U

TAYLOR, John. Verbum sempiternae (*part i*).
23810 *1614* Queen Anne.
   L. *1627* Henrietta Maria; also *1631*-F.
                                                    D
                But shifted to pt. ii in 23725.

TAYLOR, John. The world on wheels.
23816 *1623* Cordwainers, Watermen, etc.;
                also 23725.
23817 *1635* Masters of Barges and Water-
                men.   U

THAYRE, Thomas. A treatise of pestilence.
23929 *1603* Sir Robert Lee, etc.
23930 *1625* John Gore, etc.   S

THOMAS, à Kempis. The following of Christ.
23987 *1613* Elizabeth Vaux (omitted *1616*-
                DE. and 23990).
23992 *1636* Mary Tredway, by editor.
                                                    DE

THOMAS, Thomas. Dictionarium (*9th ed. lost*).
24008 n.d.   Lord Burghley; inc. *1589*-ILL.
24012 *1600* None.   D
24013 *1606* Earl of Salisbury (his son), by
                Legate.
24015 *1615* James Montagu, bishop, by
                Legate.   D
24016 *1619* Bacon, by Legate.   D
   E. *1631* Thomas, Lord Coventry, by
                Legate.   DS

TOPSELL, Edward. Times lamentation.
24131 *1599* Lord Mountjoy.
24132 *1613* Sir H. Montagu, T. Fanshaw,
                G. Alington.   D

TORRIANO, Giovanni. New directions (*two
audiences*).
24138 *1639* Countess of Kent.
24139 n.d.   Cambridge University.

TURNBULL, Richard. An exposition (*pt. iii*).
24339 *1591* Sir Christopher Wray.
24340 *1592* Henry Noel.   D

TURNER, William. A new herball.
24365 *1551* i. Duke of Somerset.
24366 *1562* ii. Lord Wentworth.
24367 *1568* All: Queen Elizabeth.   DP

TYMME, Thomas. A silver watch-bell (*key
eds. lost*).
24421 *1605* Only epistle to weak Chris-
                tians.
24422 *1606* Sir John Popham (*see below*).
24424 *1610* Sir Edward Coke.   D
Depending on the reprint *copy*, 24425 and
  24432 revert to Popham. Aberdeen editions
  omit the dedication.

VAUGHAN, Edward. A method (*and later
versions*).
24597 *1590* 'Theophilus & Lydia'.
24598 *1591* Tobie Wood.
  CHI. *1603* Huntingdon, Popham, etc.
24600 *1617* Bishop of Lichfield.

VAUGHAN, William. Natural directions (*title
changes*).
24612 *1600* Lady Margaret Vaughan.
  NY. *1611* Lady L. Chichester.   U
24616 *1617* Added: Sir F. Bacon.   P
24617 *1626* Earl of Pembroke.   D

VENNAR, Richard. The right way (*revised and title changed*).

24637	*1601*	Elizabeth.	
24638	*1602*	None in unique copy (? impf.).	
24639	n.d.	James I; = 24640.	D

VENNER, Tobias. Via recta.

| 24643 | *1620* | Bacon. | |
| 24644 | *1622* | Prince Charles. | F |

VILLEGAS, A. de. Flos sanctorum (*otherwise undedicated*).

| 24730 | n.d. | Aloysia [Carvajal]. | |
| 24732 | *1623* | Sir William Stanley. | |

VIRGILIUS. Eneidos (*expanding version*).

24799	*1558*	Queen Mary, by Phaer.	
24800	*1562*	Sir N. Bacon, by editor.	D
24801	*1573*	Same, by Twyne.	
24802	*1584*	Robert Sackville, by Twyne.	D

VIRGILIUS. The bucolikes.

| 24816 | *1575* | Peter Osborne. | |
| 24817 | *1589* | John Whitgift. | P |

VIRGILIUS. Virgilius evangelisans (*revised*).

| 24826 | *1634* | Charles I; also anr. *1634*-F. | |
| 24827 | *1638* | Prince Charles. | |

WADSWORTH, James. The English Spanish pilgrime.

| 24926 | *1629* | Earl of Pembroke. | |
| 24926a | *1630* | Earl of Holland and Cambridge University. | D |

WARRE, James. The touch-stone of truth.

| 25090 | *1621* | Duke of Lennox. | |
| 25090a | *1624* | Prince Charles. | D |

WASTELL, Simon. A true . . . delight (*revised, title changed*).

| 25103 | *1623* | Robert, Lord Spencer. | |
| 25102 | *1629* | William, II Baron. | D |

WEEVER, John. An agnus Dei.

| 25220 | *1601* | Elizabeth. | |
| 25222 | *1606* | Prince Henry. | D |

WHEARE, Degory. De ratione legendi historias.

| 25325 | *1623* | William Camden. | |
| 25326 | *1625* | Earl of Pembroke. | D |

WHETSTONE, George. A mirour (*with title camouflage*).

| 25341 | *1584* | Sir Edward Osborne, etc. | |
| 25335 | *1586* | Wolstan Dixie, Osborne, etc. | S |

WILLET, Andrew. A catholicon.

| 25673 | *1602* | Martin Heton. | |
| ¶25677 | *1614* | Sir Arthur Capell, etc. | D |

WILLET, Andrew. An harmonie upon Samuel.

| 25678 | *1607* | Prince Henry. | |
| 25679 | *1614* | Christ's College, Camb. | D |

WILLET, Andrew. Synopsis papismi.

Besides unrecorded variant issues, this series is complicated by a ghost (25700) and a special Presentation Copy (q.v.). The general dedication varied thus: *1594*, Elizabeth; *1603*, James; *1613*, James and Elizabeth, with prayer to Jesus. The part patrons follow:

25696	*1592*	i. Elizabeth; ii. Essex; iii. Cecil.	
25697	*1594*	i. Sir W. Russell; ii. Essex; iii. None; iv. Popham and Peryam.	
25698	*1600*	i. Whitgift and Bancroft, ii. Essex; iii. Egerton; iv. Popham and Peryam; v. Cecil.	
o.	*1603*	Reissue for James: part dedications unchanged.	
25699	*1613*	i. Abbot and King; ii. Charles; iii. None; iv. Coke; v. Exeter and Caesar; appendix, Sir T. Middleton and City.	

WILLET, Andrew. Tetrastylon papisticum.

| 25701 | *1593* | Sir John Puckering. | |
| 25703 | *1599* | Sir T. Egerton; also ¶25699. | D |

WITHALS, John. A shorte dictionarie (*with revisions*).

25874	CU.	Sir T. Chaloner; through 25878.	
	F.	*1568*	Grindal, by L. Evans.	D
25879	*1574*	Leicester, by Evans; omitted 25883.	P
25884	*1602*	Schoolmasters, by Clerk.	DE

WOODALL, John. The surgions mate (*plural epistles*).

25962	*1617*	a. Sir Thomas Smith.	
		b. Barber Surgeons: C. Frederick, etc.	
25963	*1639*	Added: Charles I.	
		a. East India Co.: Sir C. Clitherow, etc.	D
		b. Barber Surgeons: W. Clowes, etc.	S

WRIGHT, Edward. Certaine errors in nauigation.

| 26019 | *1599* | Earl of Cumberland. | |
| 26020 | *1610* | Prince Henry. | D |

ZOUCH, Richard. Elementa iurisprudentiae.
26131 *1629* Earl of Pembroke; = 26131a.
26132 *1636* William Laud. D

Appendix: Patrons discarded on Disgrace

Substitution of a new patron when the previous one suffered downfall or disgrace is illustrated above. In other instances the dedication was suppressed without replacement.

AGRIPPA, H. C. Of the vanitie of artes.
204 *1569* Duke of Norfolk; omitted from 205.

DRAYTON, Michael. Idea.
7202 *1593* Sir Robert Dudley; omitted in 7217, etc.

JOHN XXI. The treasury of healthe (*earliest ed.*).
14652a n.d. First issue-o. Duchess of Northumberland.
[*'53*] Second issue (normal form): None.

A similar device:

2068 GREAT BIBLE. The byble, *1539*.
Title woodblock includes arms of Cromwell.
Arms excised in 2072–6 [the last now thought earliest].

5. PRESENTATION EPISTLES

Each of the following books contains a specially printed epistle prepared for presentation to someone other than the normal dedicatee. They are not commercial issues; theoretically, each is unique, but in fact more than one copy may have been prepared (as 17944–a), or even a small issue (22792). The census ignores (a) presentation copies to normal dedicatees, and (b) gift copies inscribed to libraries by independent donors. The editor is unaware whether other cases exist of belated, post-1640, epistles like 22918. For fuller discussion, see The Library, 1952, pp. 15–20.
Unless specified, each presentation epistle is by the author or translator. Entries indicate location of the copies and the fate of the normal dedication. The few bracketed hearsay examples are not noticed in the main index.

379 ALLOTT, Robert. Englands Parnassus, *1600*.
Normal dedication to Sir T. Mounson (378, etc.) is cancelled.
(*a*) HD. John Gybson.

583 ANDREWE, George. A quaternion, *1625*.
Normal dedication to Viscount Falkland is cancelled.
(*a*) L.² George Abbot.

716 AP-ROBERT, J. The younger brother, *1634*.

Normal epistle to Fathers and Sons is retained.
(*a*) MIN. William Burton, by 'Publisher' [editor].
(*b*) HD. (1) Brian Duppa and Christ Church; (2) Sir W. Dorington; both by Philadelphus [editor, noted in MS. as I. H.].

3573 BRATHWAIT, Richard. The shepherds tales, *1626* [*unique reissue of part of 3572, normal dedication to Richard Hutton cancelled*].
(*a*) HN. Richard Louther.

4963 CHAPMAN, George. Al fooles, *1605* [*normally undedicated*].
(*a*) TEX. Sir Thomas Walsingham, unsigned.
Leaf authentic but perhaps intruded from another (unknown) book.

5669 COOKE, Edward. The prospective glasse, *1628* [*and var. issues*].
Normal dedication to Sir John Coke is retained.
(*a*) F. Verses to W. Gualter and J. Foster.

— COURT. A court of guard for the heart, *1626* [normal form unknown].
(*a*) F. Sir George Hastings, by Joseph Taylor.
(*b*) PN.² Master Sidnam, by Joseph Taylor.

5986 CRANE, Ralph. The workes of mercy, *1621* [all copies differ].
(*a*) HN. Earl of Bridgewater.
(*b*) Y. Levynus Munck.
(*c*) O. Mrs. Dorothie Osborne.

6236 DANIEL, Samuel. The works, *1601*.
Normal dedication to Queen Elizabeth is cancelled.
(*a*) O. Bodleian Library.

6498 DEKKER, Thomas. The double PP., *1606*.
Normal dedication to the Nobility, etc., is retained.
(*a*) PFOR. Sir Henry Cock.

6514 DEKKER, Thomas. Newes from Hell, *1606*.
Normal dedication to Sir John Hamden is cancelled.
(*a*) L. John Sturman.

6843 DIGBY, Everard. Theoria analytica, *1579*.

Normal dedication to Hatton is retained. Recipient's name is inserted on title-page above the imprint.

(*a*) C. Kellamus Dygbeius.
(*b*) F. Gulielmus Wentworth.
(*c*) U. Robertus Boothe.
(*d*) L.[38] Edmundus Mounsteuing.

7031 DONNE, John. Deaths duell, *1632* [normally undedicated].
(*a*) F. Mrs. Elizabeth Francis, by Redmer.

7575 ELIOT, John. The suruay of France, *1592* [normally undedicated].
(*a*) C. Sir John Puckering [on title verso].

10779 FENNER, William. The souls lookingglasse, *1640* [normally undedicated].
(*a*) Y. Earl of Warwick, by author's widow.
Epistle and patron slavishly copied from 23303.

11027 FLAMEL, Nicolas. Exposition of figures, *1624.*
Name space in the dedication to a lady is normally blank.
(*a*) L. C. D. of E. [presumably Countess Dowager of Exeter].

11319 FRANCIS, of Sales. An introduction, *1616* [normally undedicated].
(*a*) F. Sara Jones and Alice Gamwell, by Burre.
But perhaps one of many cancellations to appease authority [cf. 11321].

11496 G., H. The mirrour of maiestie, *1618* [and imprint variants].
Normal dedication to Court group is cancelled.
(*a*) HD. James I.

11516 GAGER, William. Vlysses redux, *1592* [Greg L4].
The normal (O., F.) dedication to Lord Buckhurst is absent.
(*a*) HN. Countess of Pembroke.

12030 GOODWIN, George. Babel's balm, *1624.*
Normal dedication to Earl of Pembroke is cancelled.
(*a*) HN. Earl of Bridgewater.

12530 GURNAY, Edmund. The Romish chaine, *1624.*
The normal (L., L.[4]) dedication to Parliament is retained.

(*a*) HN. Sir Roger Townshend.
Mentioned in MS. letter, Gurnay to Townshend 13 Dec. [1624?] at F.*; possibly a case of cancellation.*

12551 GWINNE, Matthew. Nero, *1603.*
Normal dedication to J. Egerton and F. Leigh is cancelled.
(*a*) L. James I.

13218 HERMES. Opuscula, *1611* [a fabricated book].
(*a*) O. Sir John Radcliffe, by R. H. R.
On this curiosity, see The Library, *1957, p. 19, and Jonson's epigram liii.*

13222 HERODIAN. Herodian his history, *1629.*
Normal dedication to Diva Britannia is retained.
(*a*) F. Earl of Salisbury and Algernon Lord Percy.

13366 HEYWOOD, Thomas. Troia Britanica, *1609.*
Normal dedication to the Earl of Worcester is retained.
(*a*) F. Sir Henry Perpoint.

14773 JONSON, Ben. The fountaine of selfeloue, *1601* [normally undedicated].
(*a*) HN. William Camden.
(*b*) CLARK. Countess of Bedford.

15083 KORUDALEUS, T. Περὶ ἐπιστολικῶν τύπων, *1625.*
All copies seen are dedicated to John Williams, by N. Metaxas.
[At second hand Émile LeGrand reports copies for presentation abroad.]

15433 LEIGHTON, Sir W. The teares of a sorrowfull soule, *1613.*
Normal dedication to Prince Charles is retained.
(*a*) HN. Lord Ellesmere.

16696 LOK, Henry. Ecclesiastes, *1597.*
Dedication to Elizabeth is retained, other complimentary sonnets cancelled.
(*a*) L.[2] John Whitgift [sonnet facing title].

— MAIER, Michael. Arcana arcanissima, [*1614*].
Engraved leaf for dedication overprint is normally blank (L., C., LC., HD.).
(*a*) L.[3] [Lancelot] Andrew[es], rather garbled by Maier.
[*Untraced copies are dedicated to* Sir G. Carew *and* Sir W. Paddy.]

17944 MINSHEU, John. Ductor in linguas, *1617*.
Normal dedication to James I is retained.
(*a*) HD., PN., L.[38] Sir George Carew.
(*b*) L.[38] Sir Henry Montagu.
(*c*) L.[38] Thomas Wilbraham.
(*d*) L.[38] Earl of Southampton.

18633 NORDEN, John. A progresse of pietie, *1596* [or later edition].
Normal dedication to Elizabeth is retained.
(*a*) F. R. M. to his Wife [loose proof for leaf to insert in this book].

18662 NORTH, George. The description of Swedland, *1561*.
Normal dedication to Thomas Steuckley is cancelled.
(*a*) STOCKHOLM. Nicholas Guildenstern.

18981 OVID. De tristibus, *1639* [normally undedicated].
(*a*) HN. William Springe.

19447 PASQUALIGO, L. Fedele and Fortunio, *1585* [Greg 86].
Third known copy (F.) lacks preliminaries.
(*a*) F. Maister M. R., by M. A.
(*b*) HN. (impf.) John Heardson, by A. M[unday?].

21393 ROWLANDS, Samuel. The letting of humours blood, *1600* [normally undedicated].
(*a*) O. Hugh Lee, Esq.

21725 SANDYS, George. A paraphrase upon divine poems, *1638*.
Normal dedication to Charles I and other verses are retained.
(*a*) F. Extra verses to the Queen of Bohemia.

22784 SMITH, John. An accidence for seamen, *1626*.
Normal dedication to the Privy Council, etc., is cancelled.
(*a*) CB. Sir Robert Heath.

22788 SMITH, John. A description of New England, *1616*.
Normal dedication to Prince Charles is retained. Inscription printed at head of title-page.
(*a*) HN. Lord Ellesmere [*printed* Elesmore].

(*b*) ? Sir Edward Coke [Sotheby sale 28 Feb. 1956].

22791 SMITH, John. A map of Virginia, *1612*.
The cryptic dedication 'To the Hand' is retained.
(*a*) NY. Earl of Hertford.
(*b*) PN. Thomas Watson and John Bingley, by Philip Fote.

22792 SMITH, John. New Englands trials, *1620* [all copies different].
(*a*) N. Sir Edward Coke.
(*b*) HN. Earl of Bridgewater.
(*c*) L. Company of Fishmongers.
(*d*) O. Advent[ur]ers to plantations [tp. & ded. in dup.].

22918 SOMNER, William. The antiquities of Canterbury, *1640*.
The normal dedication to Laud is retained.
(*a*) HN. Charles II [in *1660*].

23350 STRACHEY, William. For the colony in Virginea, *1612*.
Normal presentation material is retained [varying, 3 or 4 leaves].
(*a*) PN. Sir William Wade.
(*b*) L. Sir Anthonie Anger [corrected to Auger and expanded in MS.].

— SWEDISH. The Swedish intelligencer compleat, *1634* [rare cumulative reissue of 23521 series, normally (L.) without dedication].
(*a*) STOCKHOLM. Queen Christina, by Watts.

24954 WALBANCKE, Matthew. Annalia Dubrensia, *1636*.
Normal dedication to Robert Dover is retained.
(*a*) L. Sr. Thomas Trevor [completed in MS.].
[Unlocated copies are for Sir Simon Rolston and Sir Peter Kiligree.]

25698 WILLET, Andrew. Synopsis Papismi, *1600*.
Dedication to Elizabeth and all part dedications are cancelled.
(*a*) L. James I.
Presentation copy anticipating *1603* trade reissue at O.

25971 WOODWARD, Ezekias. A childes patrimony, *1640* [bibliography tangled].
Normal material is retained; epistle added in pt. ii.
(*a*) HN. Lady Margaret Garraway.